AF262792

GREAT ART EXPLAINED

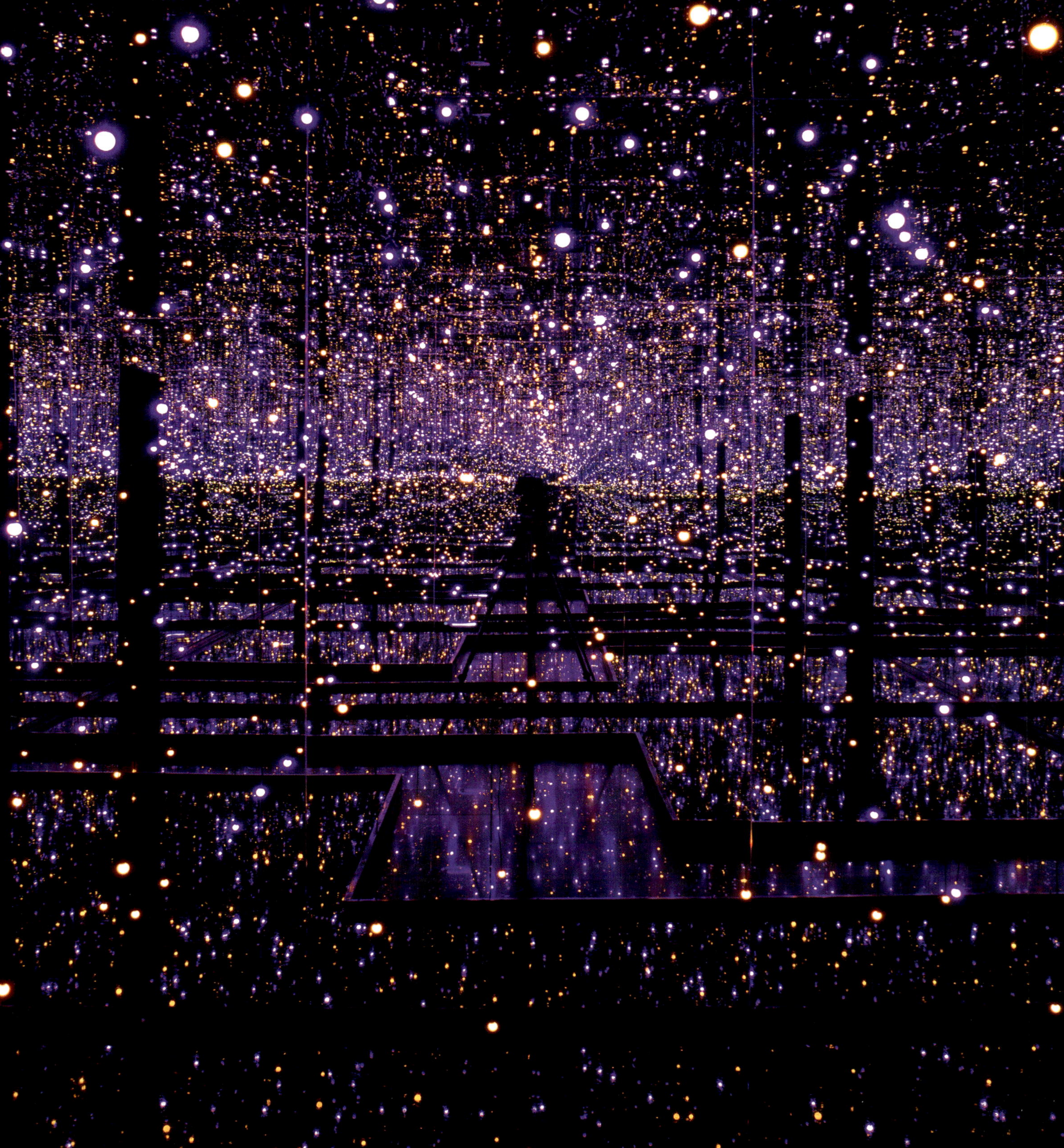

JAMES PAYNE

GREAT ART EXPLAINED

THE STORIES BEHIND THE WORLD'S GREATEST MASTERPIECES

WITH 223 ILLUSTRATIONS

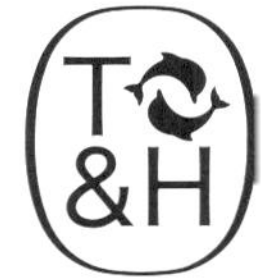

CONTENTS

INTRODUCTION

Knowing what we know about Van Gogh's life
doesn't make *Starry Night* a better painting,
but it does make it more interesting.

Art doesn't exist in a vacuum. Monet's *Water Lilies* can be seen on a purely aesthetic level, but we can also go beyond their surface beauty to consider whether these works, created during the First World War, can also be viewed as profound meditations on the power of art in the face of human conflict. We can appreciate Michelangelo's *Pietà* for its Christian symbolism and its mastery of marble, but we can also view it in more universal terms as an exploration of motherhood and grief. Frida Kahlo's self-portraits are not just personal expressions, they are lenses into Mexican culture, identity and the artist's own complex relationships.

Every great work of art carries within it the echoes of its time: the politics, the religion, the economy, the social norms and the individual struggles that shaped its creation.

This book looks at those contexts. My hope is that by understanding the worlds in which these works were born, you'll not only appreciate them on an aesthetic level but also through their wider significance. Art is a dialogue across time, and each chapter in this book invites the reader to join the conversation.

When I launched my *Great Art Explained* channel on YouTube in May 2020, I had no idea how successful it would become. The goal was simple: to create an approachable yet deeply informative platform where people could discover art without fear of 'not knowing enough', to make videos that are as appealing to those who know a great deal about art as those who don't.

It was an approach which seemed to resonate with viewers, and the project quickly grew into a community of millions of curious minds eager to explore the history of artworks and the contexts behind them, from the monumental to the understated, the ancient to the avant-garde.

I started the *Great Art Explained* project because, like many of you, I was once overwhelmed by the sheer scope of art history, and the endless procession of names, dates and movements. As a lifelong art enthusiast but not an art historian by training, I often felt I needed a guide – a voice that could explain why certain works resonated across centuries, why some artists became household names while others faded into obscurity, and how art could transform the way we see ourselves and the world.

For this book, I have expanded on the ideas, the artists, the mediums and the contexts I explore in my channel. I see it as the natural continuation of my YouTube journey: a curated exploration of art's most compelling moments, aimed at both newcomers and experienced art lovers.

The term 'art history' is widely contested and debated, due to differing perspectives on its scope, canon and relevance in contemporary history, with scholars and critics often disagreeing on how to define it. And that's how it *should* be. The evolving nature of art itself, as well as its expanding boundaries in the 20th and 21st centuries, has contributed to ongoing controversies about the validity and function of art history.

The name *Great Art Explained* can be seen as equally contentious because it inherently raises questions about what qualifies as 'great' art, and who gets to define it. Art, by its very nature, is subjective, and what one culture, generation or individual deems 'great', another might dismiss as irrelevant or inaccessible. Ultimately, while the title may invite debate, I see this contention as a strength: it sparks discussion.

This is not intended to be a definitive history but rather a series of 'essays' designed to encourage readers to bring their own experiences, interpretations and questions to the table and to engage critically with the art and the narratives that surround it. Art is most powerful when it creates dialogue, and this book, like my channel, is meant to be the start of a conversation – not the final word.

I have structured the book in a similar way to how I curate my channel. Each chapter takes a specific work of art as the starting point to look at the artist's 'story', the broader context of the times and the techniques employed in creating that work.

I look at works across disciplines and borders, including contemporary creators working in nontraditional media. I include art that, I think, helps to broaden out the discussion about what is 'great'.

Art should not be seen as a relic of the past, frozen in museums, but as a living, breathing conversation between generations. While the contemporary Ghanaian artist El Anatsui and the Chinese artist Zhang Zeduan are separated by continents – and a millennium – their works connect as intricate cultural records that celebrate human activity and the passage of time, albeit through distinct materials and contexts.

Monet was just as revolutionary (and just as reviled by some critics) as Picasso and Kahlo, and we can connect them through their shared exploration of emotional intensity, and their ability to communicate the inexpressible.

We live in an era defined by images. Social media platforms, streaming services and advertising inundate us with visual content, demanding our attention at every turn. Yet, in this cacophony, the profound visual narratives that art offers are at risk of being drowned out. We need to stop and consider the impact of one image, one work of art. Art is not just something to *look at*, it's something to *engage with*. It challenges us to pause, to question and to connect with ideas that transcend time and place.

One of the guiding principles of *Great Art Explained* has always been accessibility: art history should not be the exclusive domain of scholars and critics. I've written this book for those who have ever stood before a painting or sculpture and felt a deep emotional connection, an inexplicable pull. I've written it for the curious, the sceptics and the dreamers. I've written it for anyone who has ever wanted to see beyond the surface and understand the layers of meaning that art can offer.

ZHANG ZEDUAN (ATTRIB.)

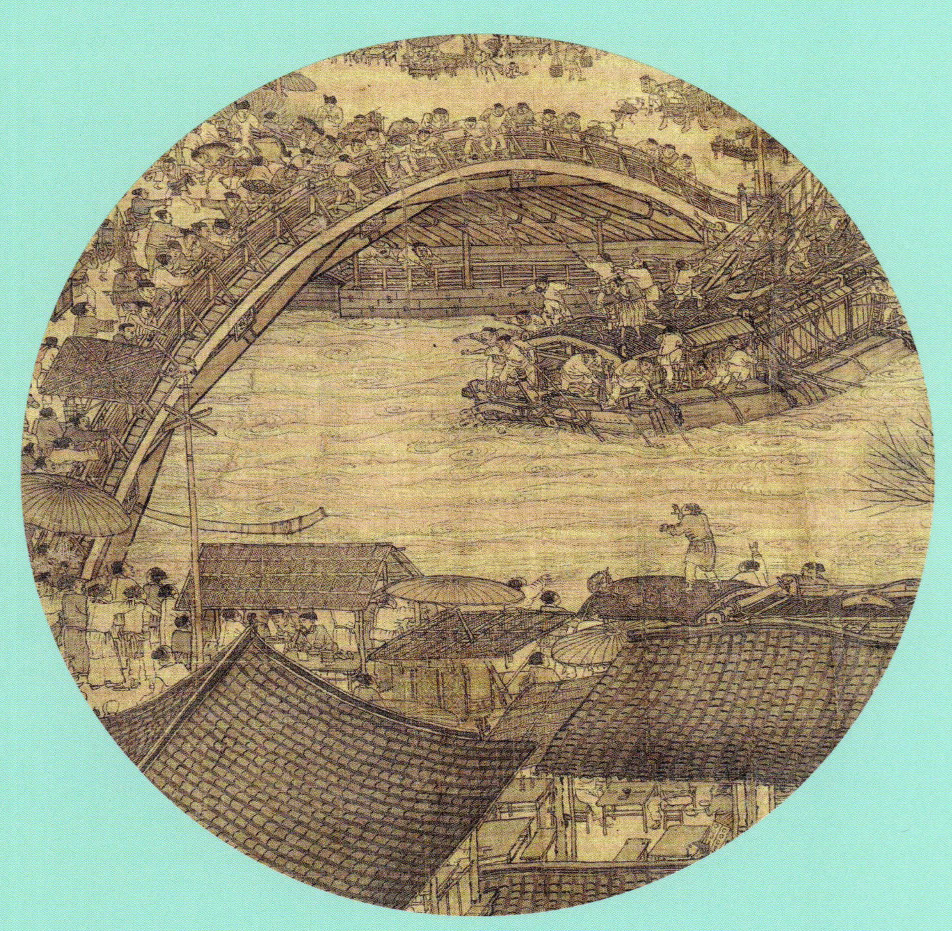

ALONG THE RIVER DURING THE QINGMING FESTIVAL

1085–1145

AN IDEAL CITY

When thinking about the differences between Eastern and Western painting, a major one to consider is format. *Along the River during the Qingming Festival* is a handscroll, and these works were not meant to be permanently on display, unlike the paintings on walls or the sculptures on plinths that we are used to in the West.[1] It was designed to be read section by section as it is unrolled (bringing the viewer into physical contact with the artwork).

We should look at it not only as a work of art but also as a form of documentation. It has long been suggested that it is a depiction of the busy Qingming Spring Festival (also known as Tomb Sweeping Day).

The scroll is designed to take us on a journey through time and space as it follows the Bian River in Kaifeng, the Northern Song dynasty capital. Starting on a quiet early morning in the rural suburbs, as people wake and commercial activity begins with people travelling towards the city, the work continues through an urban river scene focused on and around the iconic rainbow bridge, to a bustling and diverse urban sprawl in the mid-afternoon. On the way, we experience human stories: eating, sleeping, romancing, arguing, socializing and above all shopping. The immense diversity of human connections is pulled together by the river that brings life into the city, and all classes, professions and characters are depicted with unbelievable precision.

A TURNING POINT

After the fall of the Tang dynasty (618–907), China descended into political chaos, fragmenting into independent kingdoms as rebellions swept through the land. It took more than fifty years for the Song dynasty (960–1279) to reunify the country, which led to a long era of political and economic stability. During this time, urban centres blossomed into bustling hubs of trade and culture, leading in turn to an artistic renaissance. The Qingming scroll is a celebration of that stability.

By the 10th century, landscape painting in China had evolved into an independent genre,[2] but the technique had been used as a form of creative practice since the Han dynasty (1046–256 BCE). It used the same tools as Chinese calligraphy – ink on silk and paper – and would grace scrolls, album leaves and fan paintings.[3] As well as exquisite draughtsmanship, the scroll has a scattered perspective from a bird's-eye view, allowing for multiple viewpoints in the picture rather than the single, fixed viewpoint that we see typically in Western art.

It is painted on an enormous piece of silk, more than 5 metres long but only 25.5 centimetres wide (17 ft × 10 in.) and has an extraordinary level of detail, with approximately 814 humans (only 2–3 cm high).

THE SONG DYNASTY

The scroll is a rich source of information regarding the socio-cultural life of the Song dynasty. However, its depiction of a prosperous and harmonious society can also be interpreted as a sophisticated piece of Song dynasty propaganda, a way of legitimizing and reinforcing the ruling order, a metaphor for a well-regulated state.

Song China was one of the richest countries in the world, and rivers were the transportation highways of the period, vital in sustaining the thriving economy and linking up to the canal system to transport grain, the mainstay of the economy.

If, as many scholars believe, the Qingming scroll *does* represent a version of present-day Kaifeng, then the river, the core of the painting, would be part of the Bian canal system, the main route for trade between north and central China.[4]

A PERFECT CITY?

The scroll would have been kept at the court and brought out when scholars, officials and other court attendees required it as a visual reminder of the emperor's efficient governance.

Yet, anyone who has lived in a city knows that this depiction is too 'perfect'. While the markets, bridges, hotels and restaurants are vibrant and practically overflowing with people, there is a total absence of beggars, there is no illness (the one clinic is empty), no food waste outside the restaurants, no litter, poverty, crime or any other common urban realities.

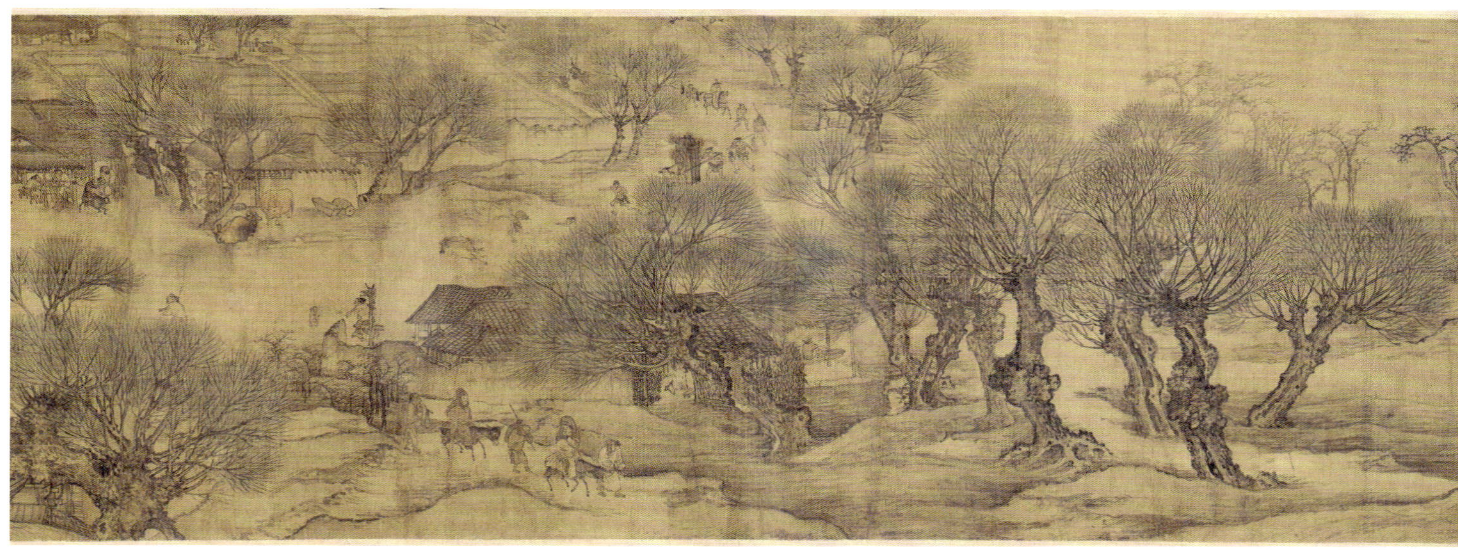

ZHANG ZEDUAN (ATTRIB.)

So, despite the detailed and historically accurate depictions of clothing, architecture and other cultural elements, things that provide valuable insights into how people lived 1,000 years ago, the work remains fundamentally a fictionalized, or maybe 'enhanced', narrative.

THE HANDSCROLL

The handscroll has three major sections, which are read right to left. It is a continuous and immersive viewing experience, with each section seamlessly transitioning into the next. The story begins with the suburbs on the right, progressing to the central section, which shows the commercial and social activity just outside the city, and ends on the inner city to the left.

The first imagery on the scroll is an idyllic agricultural scene, set on a misty morning. A procession of five donkeys moves along a narrow dirt path as they prepare to cross a small bridge on their way to the big city. They are heavily laden with bundles of charcoal for the city's charcoal shops. This was an essential industry, crucial for heating homes, cooking and fuelling various industries such as metalwork, ceramics and printing.

As the morning unfolds along the scroll, small shops start to open, hinting at the commerce that will dominate the imagery and reflecting its critical role during the Song dynasty, when economic liberalization created a vast network of trade routes across China.

The narrative transitions to a busy port filled with warehouses and wharves, where dockworkers unload goods from ships onto the shores.

Further along the scroll, we come to our first dramatic action, a scene with a group carrying a sedan chair overflowing with willow brooms. During the Qingming festival, Chinese families traditionally visit the gravesites of their ancestors to clean them, offer prayers and make ritualistic offerings. The presence of the brooms suggests that this group has recently completed the grave cleaning. A man leading the procession of the sedan chair is shouting out as a donkey breaks loose and begins to flee. As we look further across the scroll, the

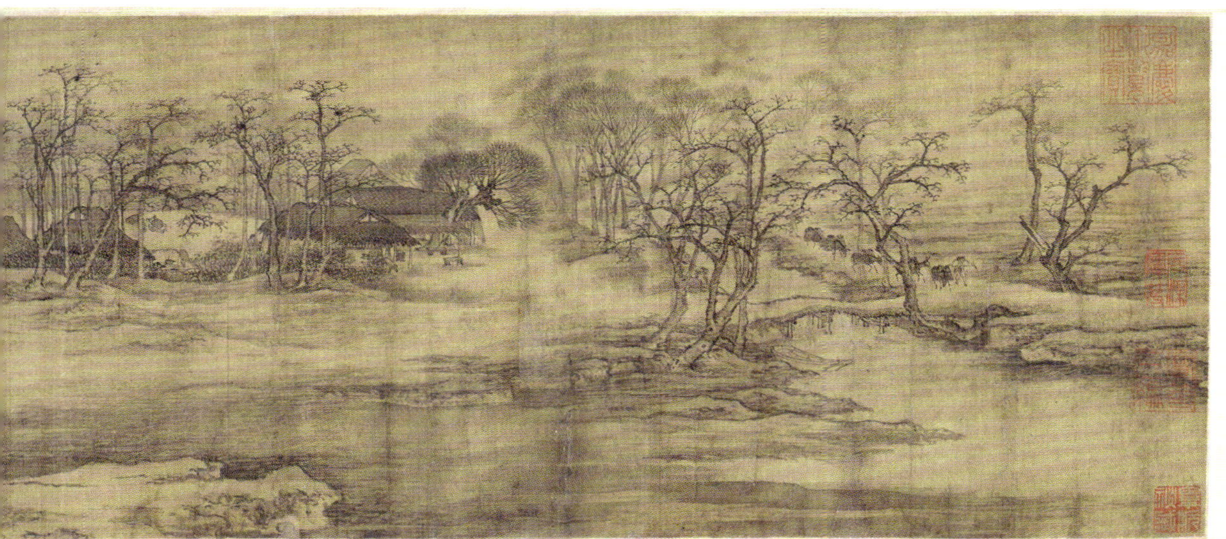

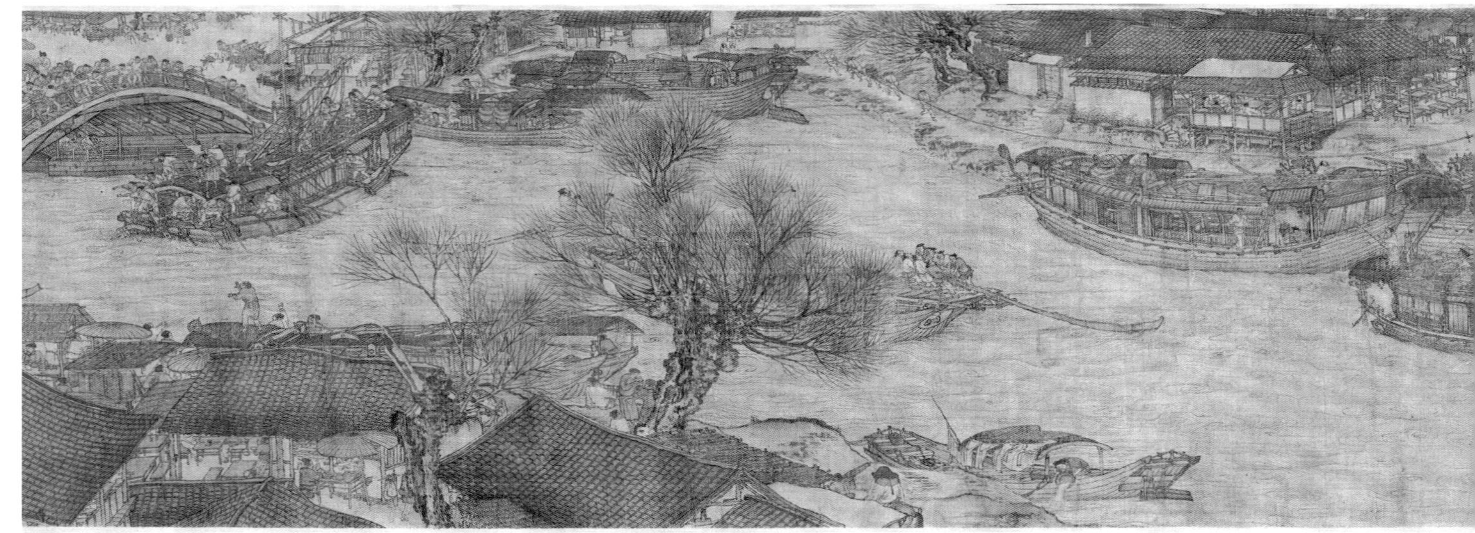

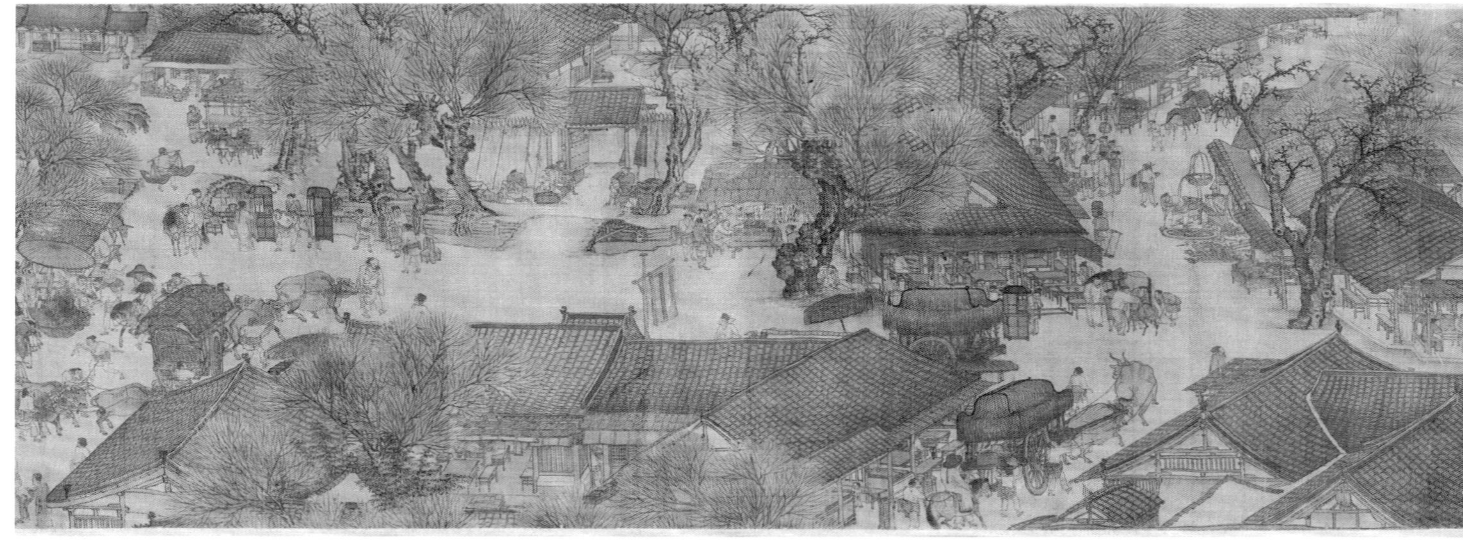

As the morning unfolds along the scroll, small shops start to open, hinting at the commerce that will dominate the imagery

situation escalates when a small child ends up in the path of the runaway donkey. Fortunately, a woman intervenes at the critical moment, rescuing the child from harm. Disaster averted.

At the scroll's midpoint, we arrive at its central feature: the 'Rainbow Bridge', an extraordinary piece of medieval engineering constructed from straight timbers using the sophisticated 'beam-weaving' technique

top
Along the River during the Qingming Festival (middle section detail).

ZHANG ZEDUAN (ATTRIB.)

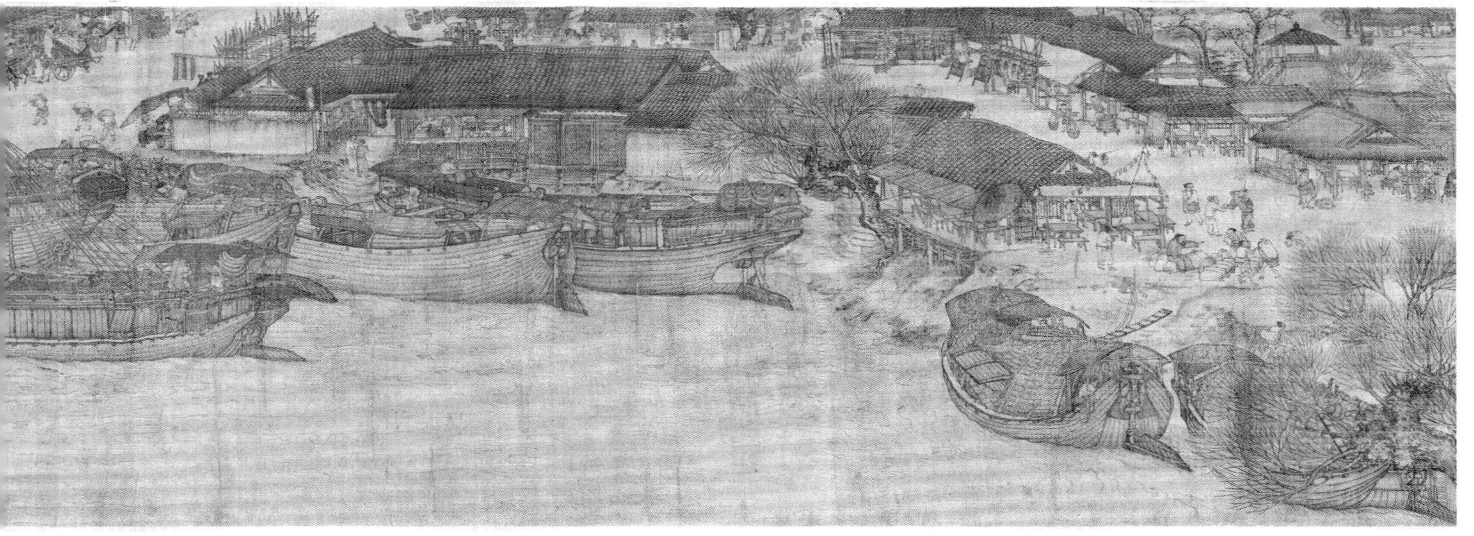

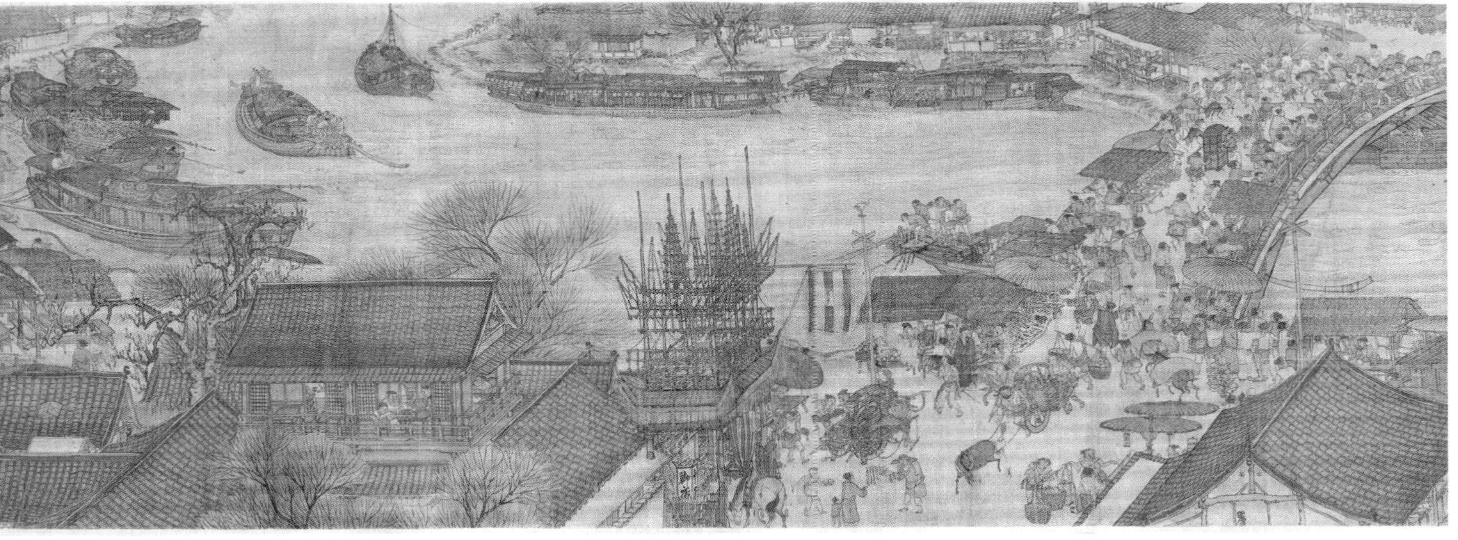

that distributes weight efficiently across the span of the bridge, allowing for its expansive arched design.[5]

The bridge is bustling with activity, as people crowd the area, purchasing snacks from numerous eateries and shopping at stalls offering a variety of goods, including wine, grain, cookware, musical instruments and fabrics. The open market depicted here reflects the more liberal economic policies of the Song dynasty, which allowed markets to operate freely at any time.[6]

It is midday at this point in the scroll, and the clothes of the people on the bridge indicate a shift in both time and weather, with lighter clothing suggesting a warmer climate than the early morning chill we saw before. Such subtle details would have given viewers a real sense of the passing of time depicted within the scroll.

As the scroll continues to unfold, a second drama emerges: a goods boat approaches the bridge at an awkward angle, its tow rope having snapped, threatening a collision with the bridge or a drift downstream. The tension of this scene, still palpable after more than a millennium, builds suspense that can only be resolved by unravelling the scroll further.

On the bridge, spectators shout and gesture towards the dangerously drifting boat until a passer-by at the top of the bridge comes to the rescue, lowering a rope to the crew below and averting yet another disaster.

Further along, we come to the area adjacent to the city walls, where a variety of shops, food stands and other businesses such as barbers and fortune tellers are shown. Notably, the gaol is shown empty, reflecting a crime-free, perfect city. And despite the Song dynasty's constant vigilance against external threats in the real world, in this artwork there are no guards at the city walls.

The scroll concludes within the city walls, where it shows all the advantages of China's

expanding market economy, without any of its associated challenges. Within the city are elegant residences for city officials, while hotels and enormous restaurants accommodate various social classes, providing insight into the social stratification of Song dynasty society. Dining out was a by-product of financial stability, and here we have high-end establishments for the elite, mid-tier restaurants serving the upper-middle class and street vendors meeting the needs of the general populace. Some are licensed to serve wine, others specialize in mutton; some feature hostesses, and most offer takeaway services, all catering to diverse tastes.

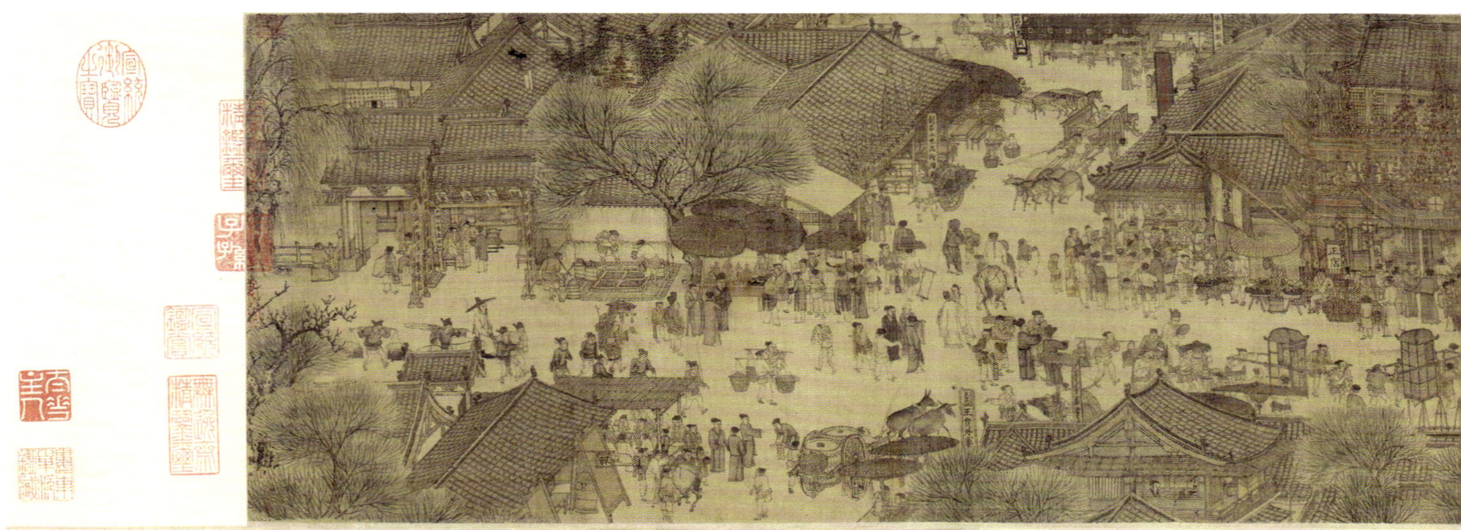

ZHANG ZEDUAN (ATTRIB.)

A curious motif in the scroll is that of men using handheld fans to obscure their faces. These 'face blockers' served as a means of anonymity for respectable gentlemen navigating through areas rife with businesses known for vice, such as brothels or gambling dens – though such establishments are conspicuously absent here.

The scroll begins with a caravan of donkeys transporting coal into the city, and in a nice narrative throughline, we can now see shops within the city walls selling that very same coal.

A lovely touch is the depiction of signs telling us what is sold inside the businesses. These signs were a common sight in China: crafted from delicate paper, they emitted a soft glow when illuminated from within by large candles, reminiscent of early neon signage.

SHROUDED IN MYSTERY

The entire scroll can be seen online in great detail,[7] but the real thing is rarely shown, owing to its delicate nature, and those fortunate enough to see it form their own opinions. The scroll could symbolize a bustling medieval city and its inhabitants, or perhaps it is a form of nostalgia for a 'perfect' city. Some see it as a tribute to harmony and peace, while others see it as homage to capitalism. Ultimately, its true significance remains shrouded in mystery.

As does its creator, who in a chapter about storytelling gets very little story time. While Zhang Zeduan is traditionally credited with the work, this too is highly disputed. The scroll's style and technique are consistent with the known works of Zeduan, suggesting his authorship, but some theories propose that the scroll may have been created by a team of artists, or that it evolved over time with contributions from different individuals.

The discussions about both the scroll and its author reflect broader questions about historical attribution, the language of propaganda and the complexities of artistic production in imperial China. But one thing is certain: the incredible artistry of the scroll, the insane amount of detail, its sheer scope and supreme storytelling make it one of the most remarkable artistic achievements in art history.

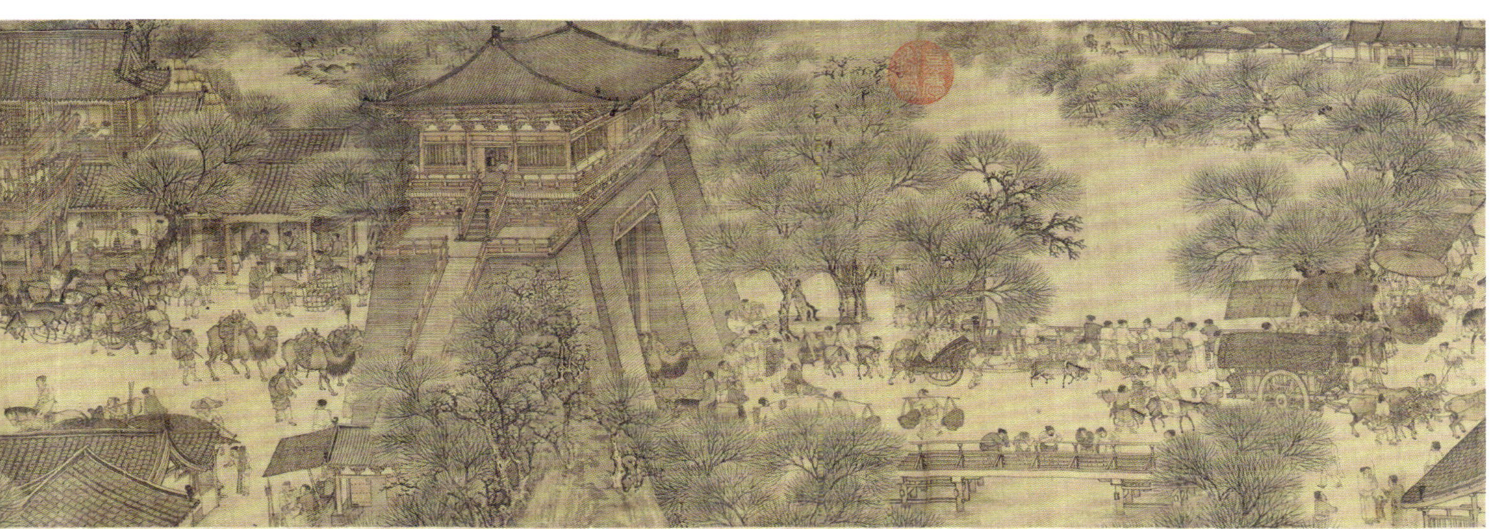

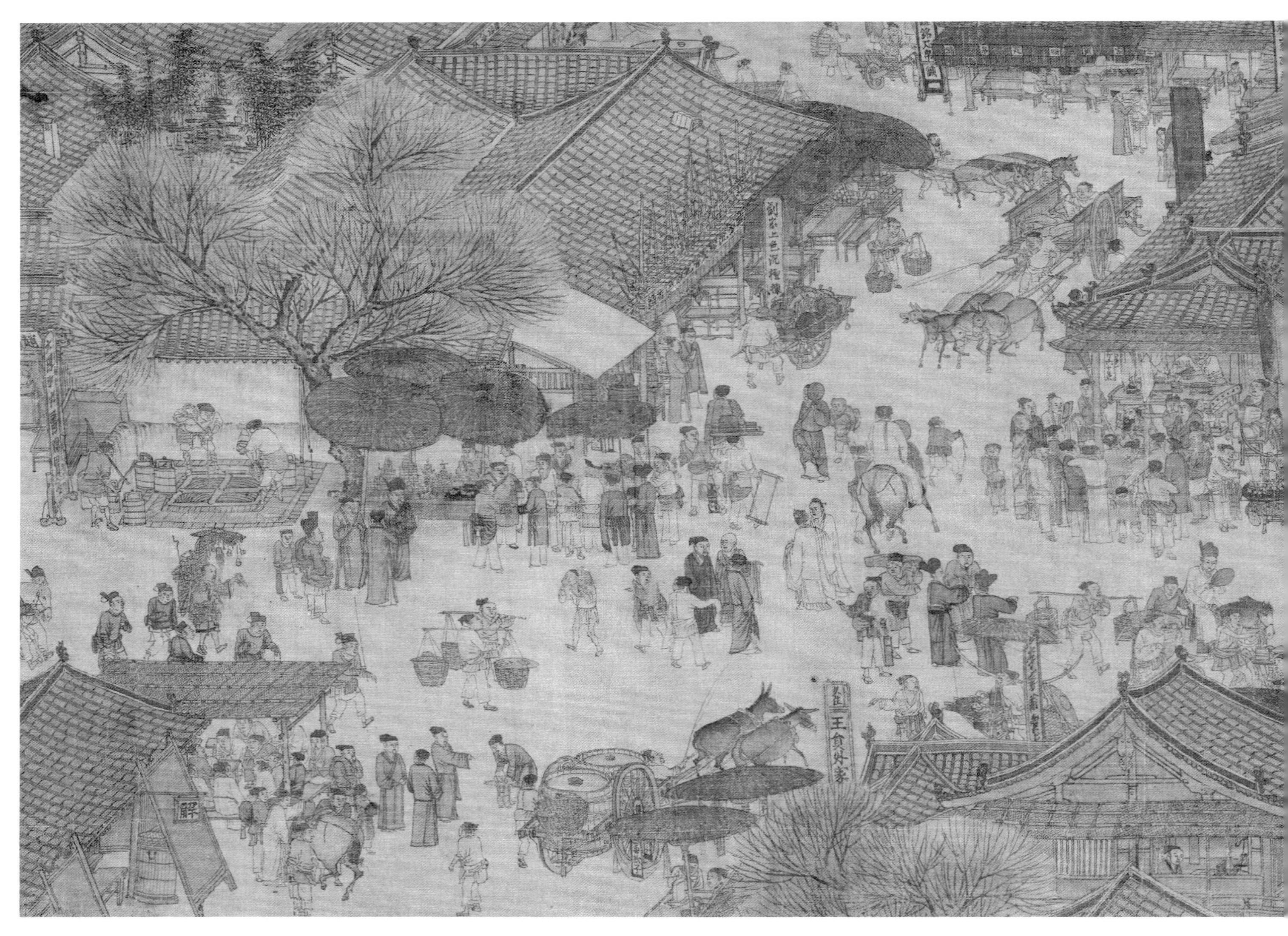

Zhang Zeduan (attrib.),
*Along the River during
the Qingming Festival*
(detail), 1085-1145.

ZHANG ZEDUAN (ATTRIB.)

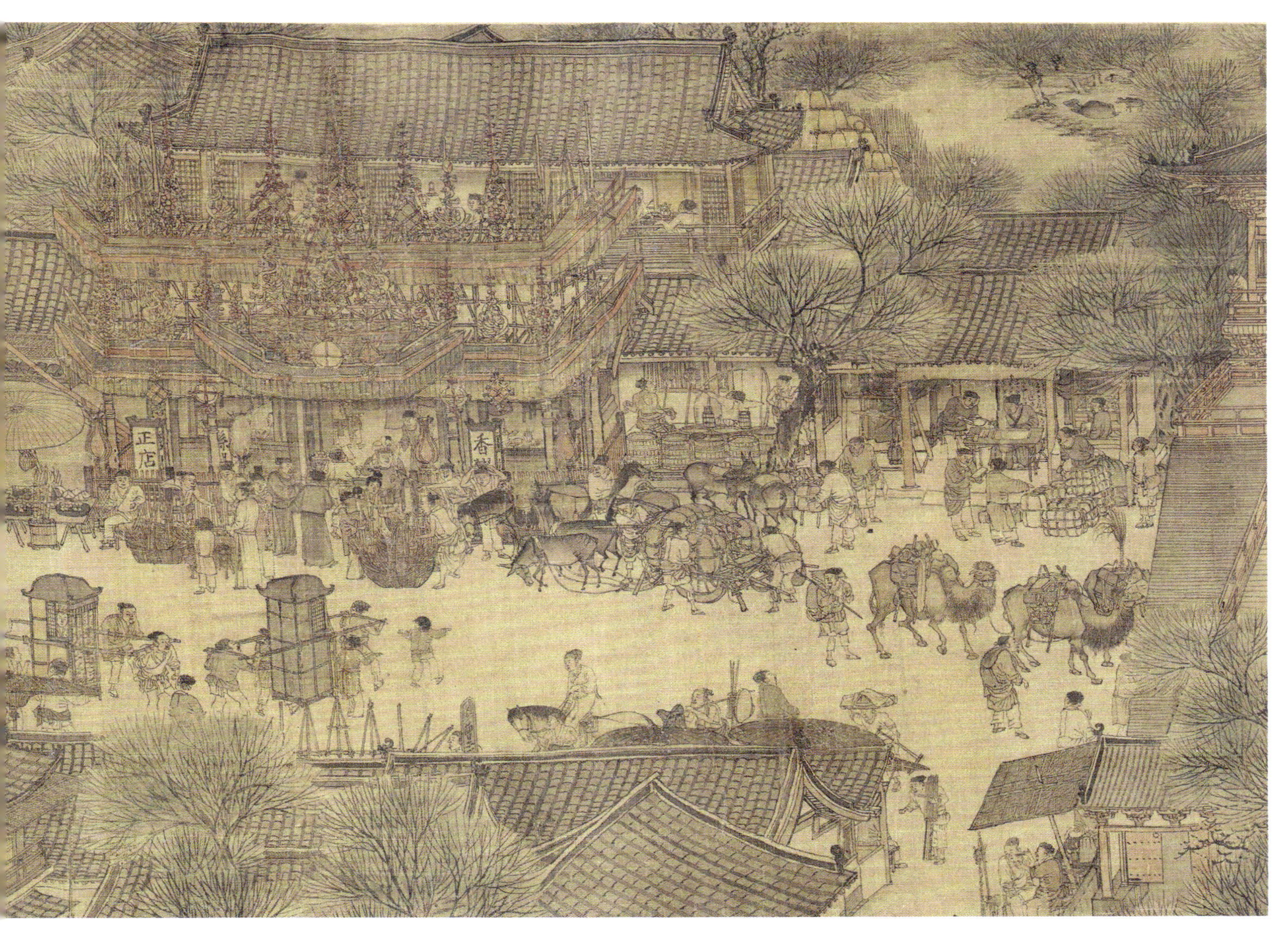

正店
香

2

JAN VAN EYCK

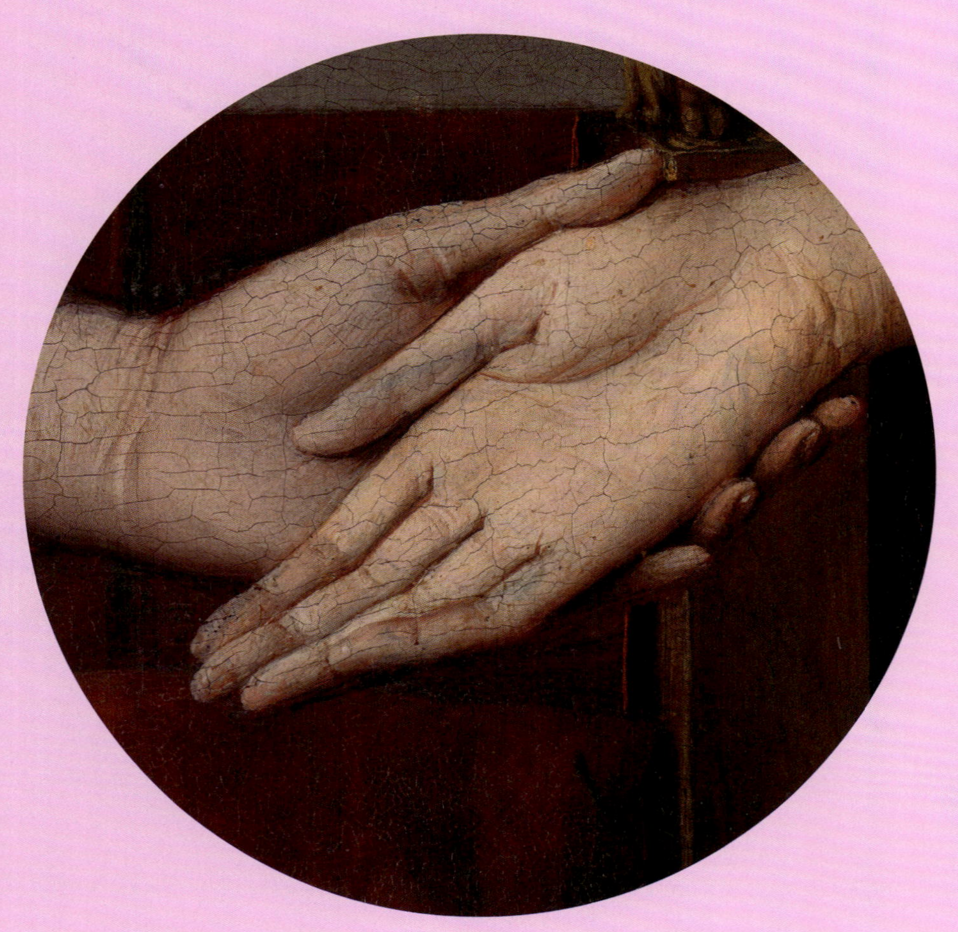

THE ARNOLFINI PORTRAIT

1434

A LOVE THAT TRANSCENDS DEATH

The Arnolfini Portrait, painted in 1434 by Jan van Eyck, has baffled art historians for centuries. For its small size, the work packs in a lot of information, but despite repeated dissection and analysis, it remains a mystery.

During the early Renaissance period, a rapid expansion in trade and commerce led to the rise of a new social tier: the wealthy and powerful merchant class. This was especially evident in Bruges in 15th-century Flanders (now northern Belgium), an important hub for international trade. People came there from all over the world seeking to make a fortune, including the Arnolfini family from Lucca in Tuscany, northern Italy.

Van Eyck was a pioneer of Northern Renaissance art, a successful artist who became court painter to Philip the Good, Duke of Burgundy, in 1425, but also worked on private commissions. Settling in Bruges in 1431, he was known for iconic works like the *Ghent Altarpiece* (completed in 1432), but portraits were an integral part of his career.[1]

As merchants became richer, their appetite for an increased social status grew. Consumerism was rampant, and the ultimate way to show off your wealth was to commission a portrait. And in the 1430s, a portrait by Jan van Eyck was *the* most exclusive status symbol.

THE ARNOLFINIS

The most likely candidates for the couple (linked by an inventory entry[2]) are the merchant Giovanni di Nicolao Arnolfini and his first wife, Costanza Trenta, whom he married in 1426. Arnolfini became wealthy trading in silks and other luxury fabrics, as well as tapestries and precious objects. The couple had no recorded children, and Costanza died in 1433, the year before this portrait was painted.

The Arnolfini Portrait is one of the earliest secular portrayals of a couple who are neither royal nor aristocratic, in a domestic setting rather than at court or in a church.[3] For many years it was assumed that this was a marriage portrait, but with no evidence of a second wife, it is more likely a memorial painting for Costanza.[4]

The dog at her feet points to this theory also. Traditionally, dogs in art symbolize loyalty and faithfulness, but this might instead reference the common practice of placing dogs at the feet of women on late medieval tomb effigies, in the belief that they would accompany their owners into the afterlife. Posthumous portraits were not unusual, and artists such as Titian, Hans Holbein and Bronzino all produced them during their careers, using death masks, sketches, written descriptions or earlier portraits to recreate an accurate likeness of the deceased.

Jan van Eyck,
The Arnolfini Portrait
(detail), 1434.

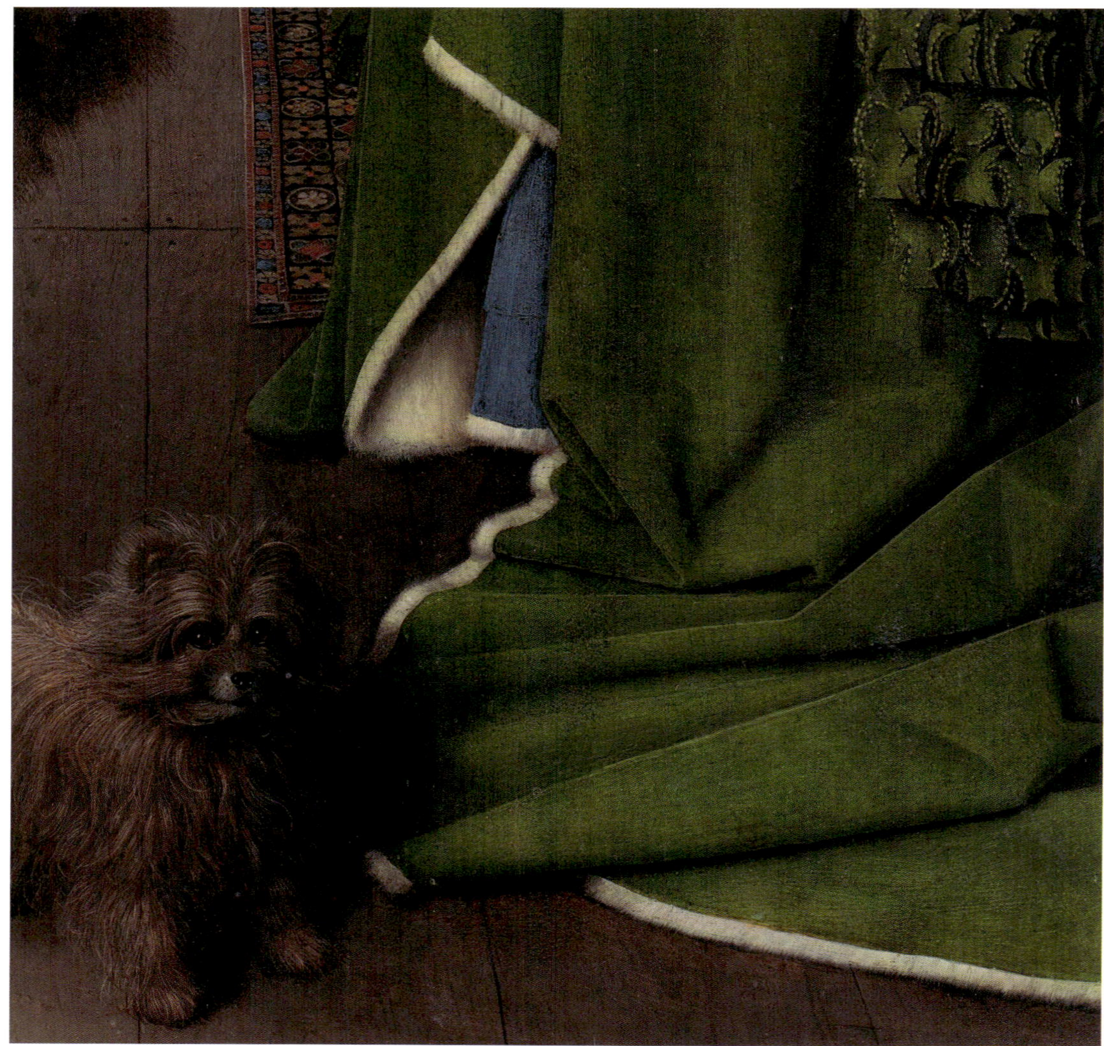

What is certain is that this double portrait was meant to cement the couple, part of the new, affluent middle class, in their position in society.

THE ARNOLFINI 'BRAND'

Fashion shapes identity in a multitude of ways; it can reflect one's culture, moral standards, economic status and social power, then and now. The couple are wearing products that not only made Bruges famous, but also serve as a showcase for the luxury materials Giovanni traded in. They are a walking advert for the Arnolfini 'brand'.

The first thing you notice about Costanza is her high-waisted green dress, which she holds bunched up at the front. The effect gave rise to the idea that she is pregnant here, but this is not so; it was a typical pose that artists used to symbolize a woman's much-prized fertility.

The intense green of the fabric shows just how expensive the dress was. Dyeing the

The Arnolfini Portrait (dog and dress detail).

opposite
The Arnolfini Portrait (pattens detail).

JAN VAN EYCK

wool to achieve such a rich, uniform shade
was an arduous task, requiring weeks of work
by a team of dyers and numerous chemical
processes using plants, herbs and exotic spices.
Fur was the ultimate luxury, however, and
Bruges was the centre of the world's fur trade.
Costanza's gown is fully lined with the white
belly fur (or 'miniver') of squirrels; if the lining
for a woman's gown usually required 600 such
pieces, a gown this size might have used as
many as 2,000.[5]

Costanza carefully avoids an excessive
use of blue, which was particularly associated
with the Virgin Mary (due to its extremely
high cost), but by subtly revealing glimpses
of her fur-lined skirt and the expensive blue
underdress beneath, she cleverly signals her
wealth without flaunting it.

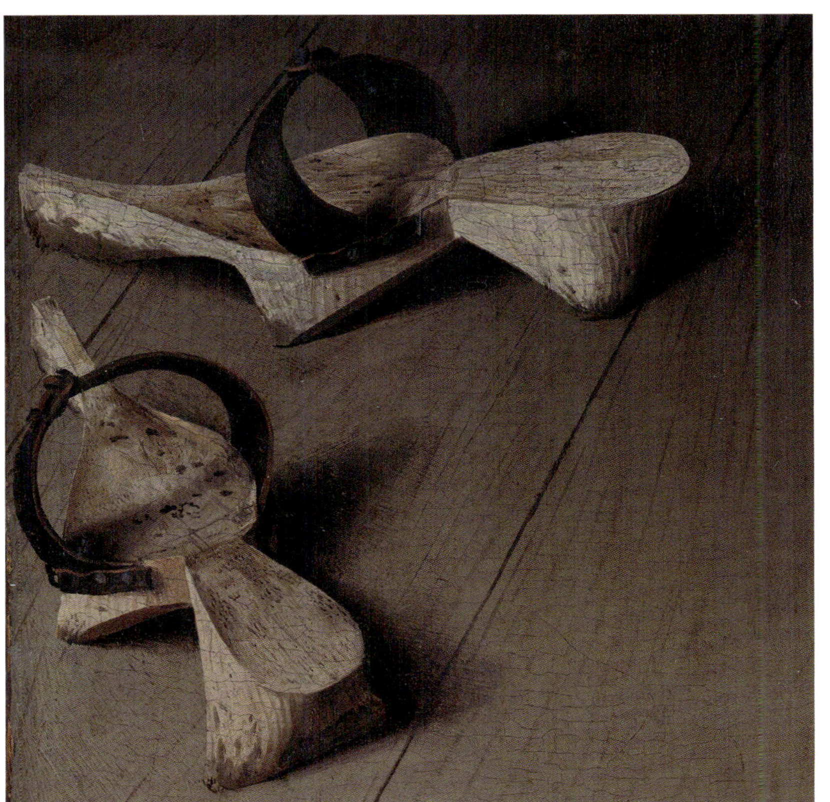

Giovanni is wearing equally exclusive
and fashionable fabrics dyed in rich plum and
black tones, which would have required an even
more expensive dyeing process than the green
dress. His lightweight hat, also dyed to match,
is made of straw (a closer view reveals it is
woven into tiny plaits) and is the latest fashion
imported from Italy.[6]

His tabard is made from silk velvet
(another promotion of imports from Lucca,
the Arnolfinis' home city[7]) and is lined with
the fur of an estimated one hundred pine
martens from Russia, making it comparable
in cost to sable, which was exclusively reserved
for the aristocracy. His boots are very soft
leather (we can see the contours of his feet),
dyed to match his outfit. In the left corner,
his pointed overshoes, or 'pattens', are still
muddy from a recent walk. Discarded shoes
are frequently seen as a symbol of the sanctity
of marriage.

THE ROOM SETS THE SCENE

The composition of this room may strike
us as bizarre, and that's because it is. Every
aspect was carefully decided on to symbolize
the couple's wealth and social status, without
appearing too 'aristocratic'.[8]

During the Renaissance, furniture was
a luxury beyond the means of most households,
yet the Arnolfini residence is full to the brim
with opulent furnishings. The bed, draped in
elaborate and expensive fabrics, positioned
behind the couple, suggests a bedroom.

Van Eyck often featured rugs in his works, showcasing his expertise in painting textures and textiles

But bedrooms were 'sacred' spaces, and if we look at the reflection in the mirror, we know the Arnolfinis are receiving two guests (acknowledged by Giovanni's raised right hand) – so, *not* a bedroom! This is a reception room, and, as strange as it seems to us now, it was common practice for affluent households to have a very expensive bed on display – but never used – as a status symbol.

In the background is a 'settle', a bench embellished with intricately carved gargoyles and sporting a sumptuous red velvet cushion. In an era with little comfort, cushions symbolized affluence. Gargoyles, believed to ward off malevolent spirits, perch directly above the couple's joined hands. Next to the bench is a high-backed chair reserved for the head of the house or esteemed guests, crowned with a carved depiction of a haloed woman atop a dragon – possibly St Martha, also known as 'St Martha the Dragonslayer', patron saint of housewives, as indicated by the nearby hanging brush, her emblem.

Van Eyck often featured rugs in his works, showcasing his expertise in painting textures and textiles, and here is a beautifully rendered oriental carpet in the reception room, a motif often found in paintings portraying the Virgin Mary, possibly as an indication of Costanza's piety.

Jan van Eyck,
Virgin and Child with Canon van der Paele, 1434.
A similar rug appears in this work by Van Eyck.

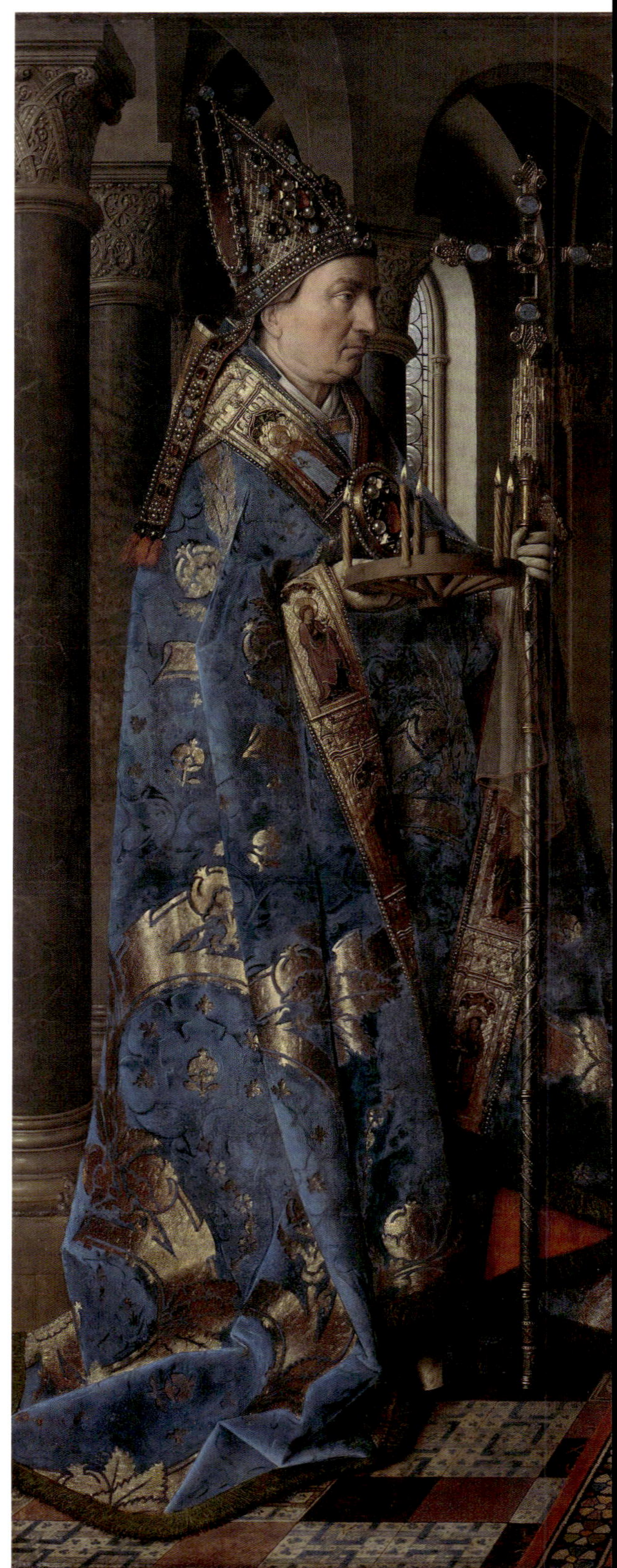

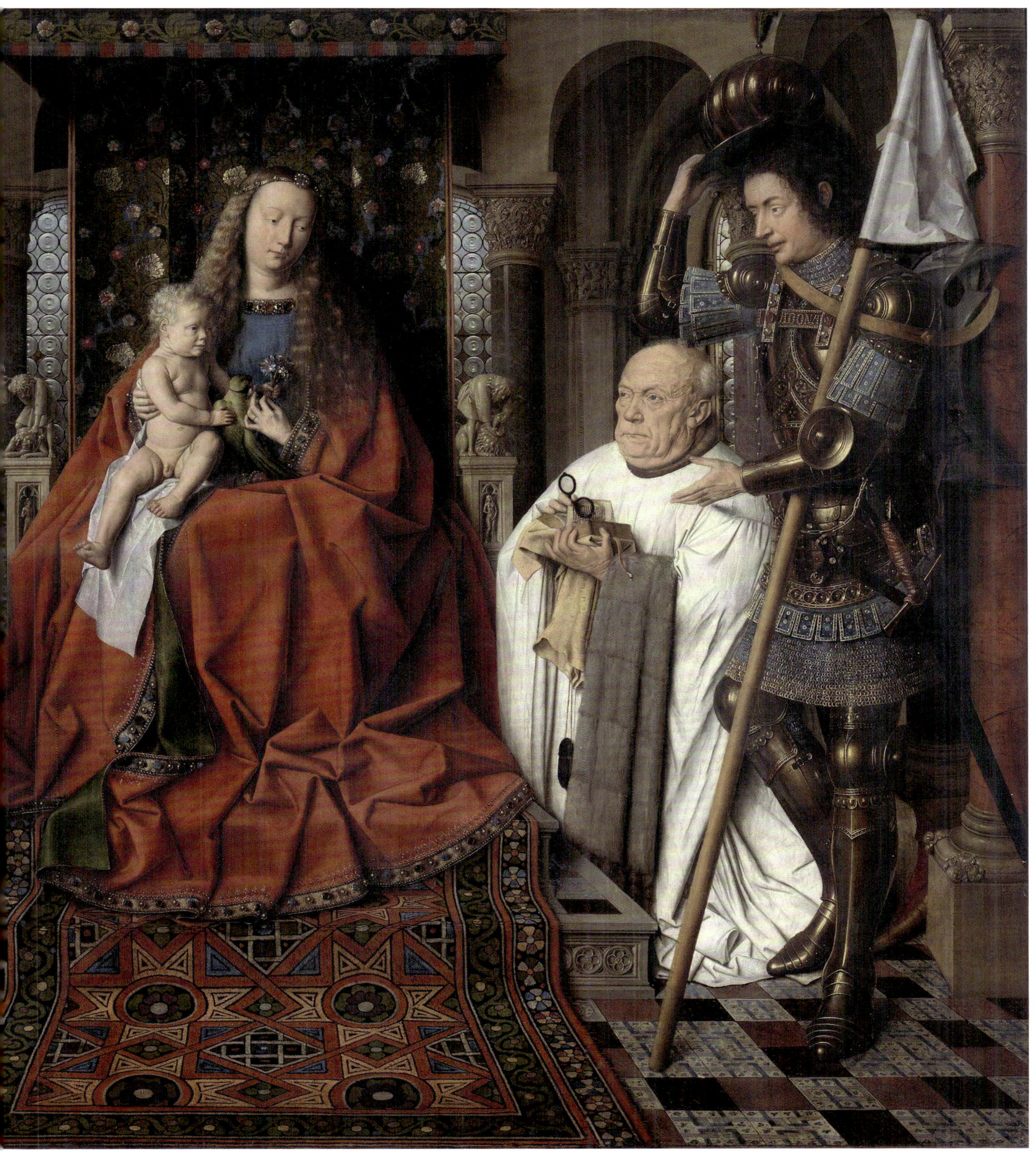

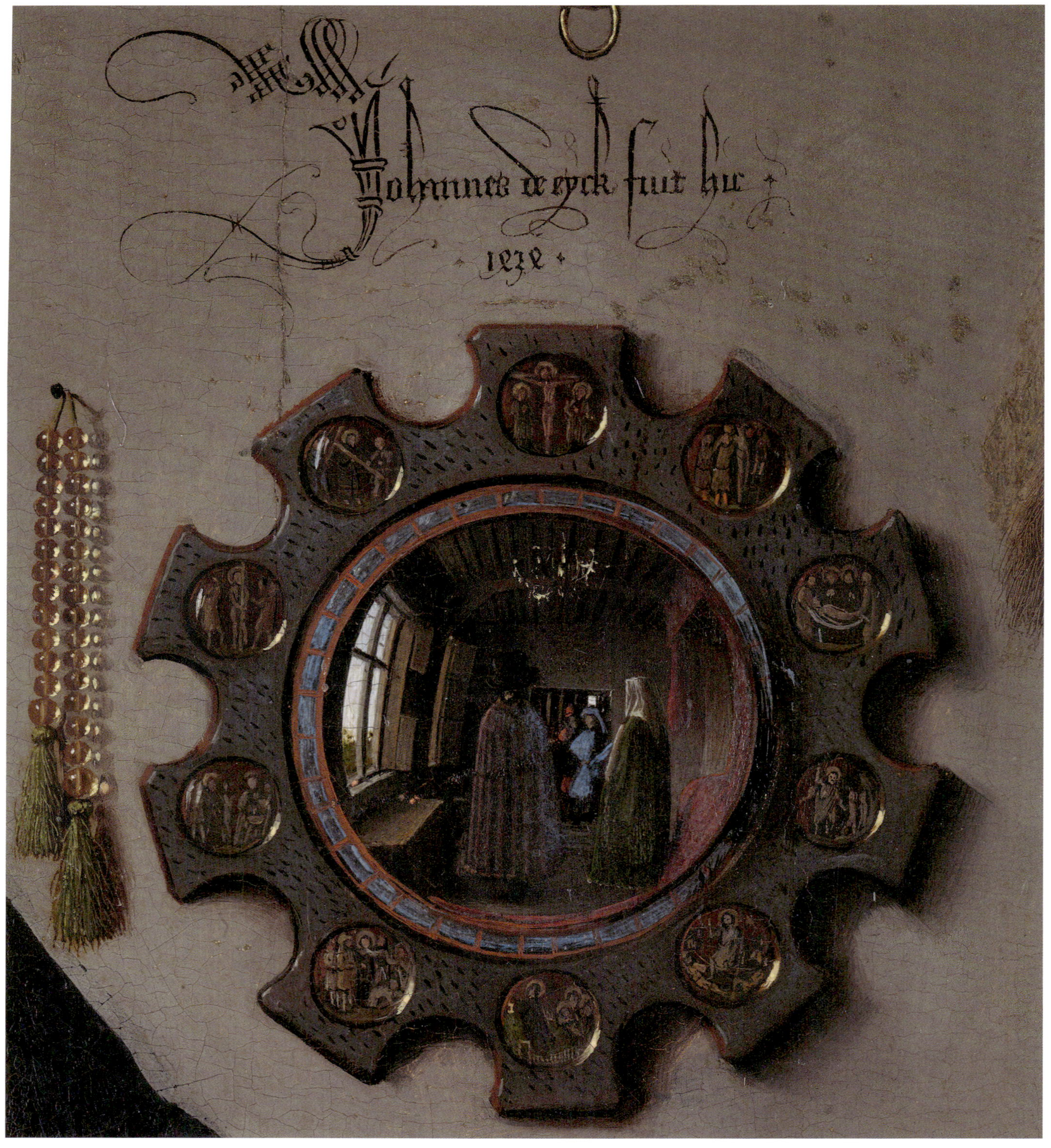

JAN VAN EYCK

Reflective surfaces are often used in art to evoke the idea of purity

Next to the mirror hang rosary beads, a common gift from a groom to his bride, which also reference her piety. But they serve a double purpose, at the same time subtly advertising more goods traded by Giovanni, since Bruges was a hub for the lucrative amber trade from the Baltic region. Here, the meticulous brushwork shows Van Eyck at his best, with each bead reflecting the light in the room and a delicate green silk thread running through the rosary, probably painted with a single-hair brush.

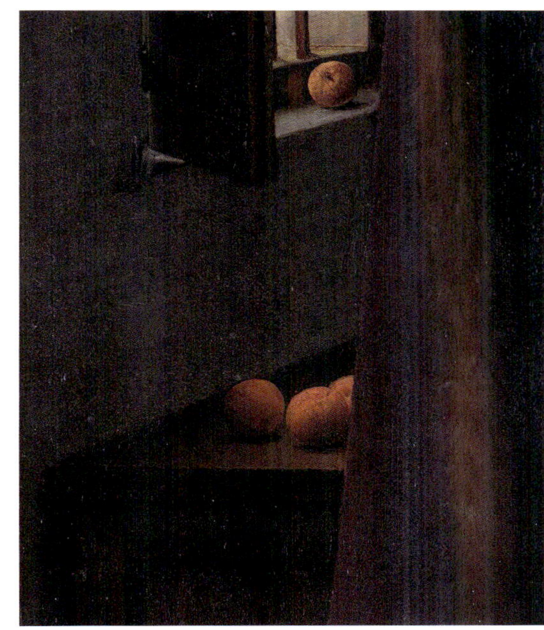

At a time when glass windows were a luxury, those in the portrait feature semi-glazing, known as 'crown glass', a common element in paintings by Van Eyck. The oranges by the window would have been imported, and only the wealthiest could afford them. Again, Van Eyck's detailing is extraordinary, and if we focus on the single orange on the windowsill, we can see not only that it casts a shadow, but it is also reflected in the glass behind it. A perfect still life, before such a thing was considered a genre in its own right.

THE MIRROR

The mirror is one of the most intriguing symbolic elements of the painting, showing Van Eyck's groundbreaking mastery of optical effects. It acts as a focal point in the composition, creating a sense of depth and adding dynamism to the static scene. Glass mirrors represented cutting-edge technology in this period, and were typically convex. The large size of the mirror depicted in this

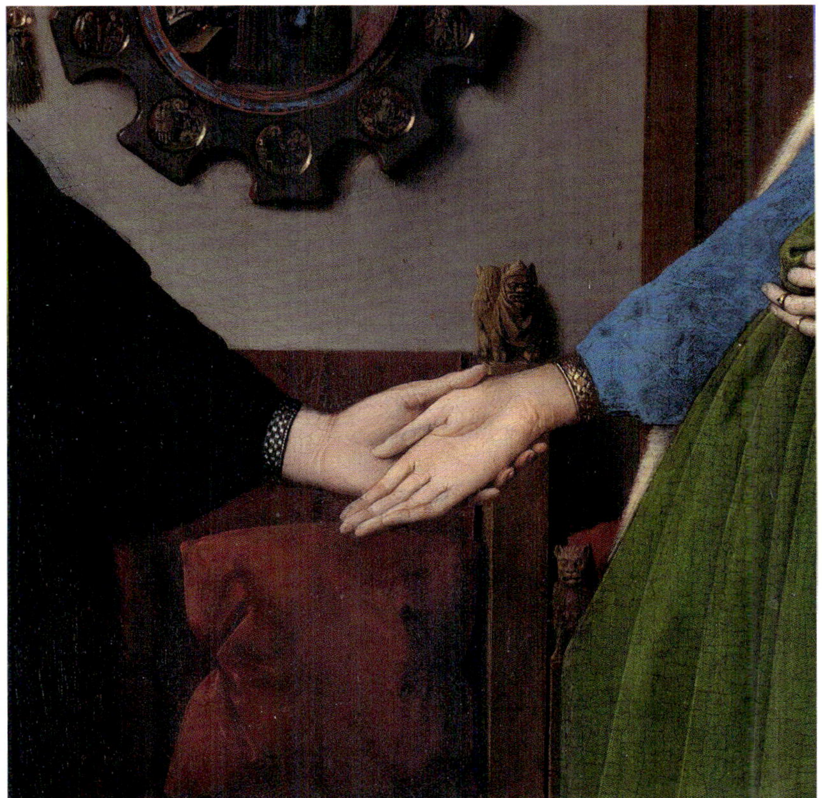

painting was technically impossible at the time, however, so the scaling up was a compositional choice by the artist.

In the reflection we see the Arnolfini couple from behind, and two other figures, implying that the staging is taking place in front of a wider audience. The figures are entering the room from outside the picture frame, and so the mirror bridges the gap between the painted world and our own. One of the figures (in blue) is said to be Van Eyck himself, while the other potentially represents the viewer.

Reflective surfaces are often used in art to evoke the idea of purity – an unblemished surface reflects truth clearly. Its inclusion in the portrait may be meant to emphasize the sanctity of the marriage and the couple's moral standing.

The only direct biblical references in the painting are the ten roundels encircling the mirror, illustrating the Passion and Resurrection of Christ. Despite their tiny size they are remarkably detailed. The scenes include *The Agony in the Garden*, showing Jesus and three of his disciples, Peter, James, and John; *The Flagellation*; and *The Crucifixion*.

By framing the mirror, which reflects the couple, with these religious scenes, Van Eyck could be suggesting that the couple's lives are intertwined with the earthly and divine realms, and where those scenes are placed in relation to the couple is important. Notably, all the depictions following Christ's death – *The Descent from the Cross*, *The Entombment*, *The Resurrection* and *The Harrowing of Hell* – are situated on Costanza's side.

THE ALCHEMIST

To claim that any painting holds a singular meaning would be presumptuous. However, several clues support the 'memorial' interpretation: the roundels on Costanza's

side portraying Christ's death, the presence of the dog at her feet and the possibility that Giovanni is dressed in mourning attire. Yet perhaps the most compelling evidence is the tentative way in which he holds her hand, as if she is on the brink of slipping away from his grasp. Ultimately, the painting can be seen to embody the essence of a love that transcends even death itself.

The true mystery of this painting lies in its unparalleled use of space, depth, colour and texture, creating the illusion that we could walk through the flat wooden panel of the painting into a mirrored universe. Jan van Eyck's contemporaries dubbed him an alchemist, but while he may not have invented oil painting, as early historians suggested, he undeniably refined the medium.[9] Understanding that some pigments become almost transparent when mixed with oil, he applied numerous thin layers – almost a wash – which gave the work a luminous quality and a finish so smooth that it suggests *The Arnolfini Portrait* has been untouched by human hands.

Van Eyck brought an unmatched realism to Northern Renaissance art, and his influence extended beyond the Low Countries. His work was sought after in England, France and Portugal, and he inspired artists who came after him, from Albrecht Dürer (*Self-Portrait*, 1500) to Diego Velázquez (*Las Meninas*, 1656) to the Pre-Raphaelite Brotherhood.

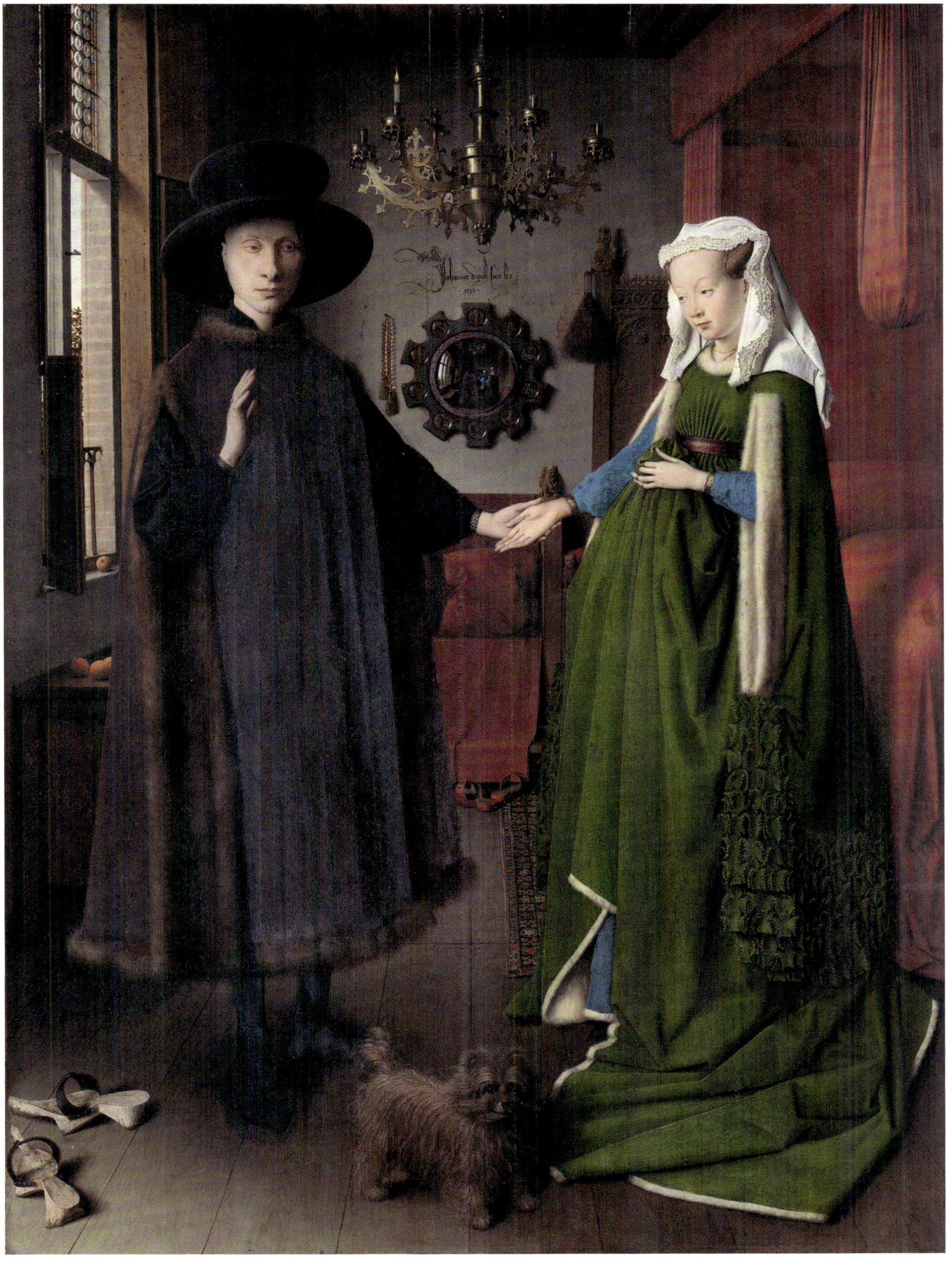

3

SANDRO BOTTICELLI

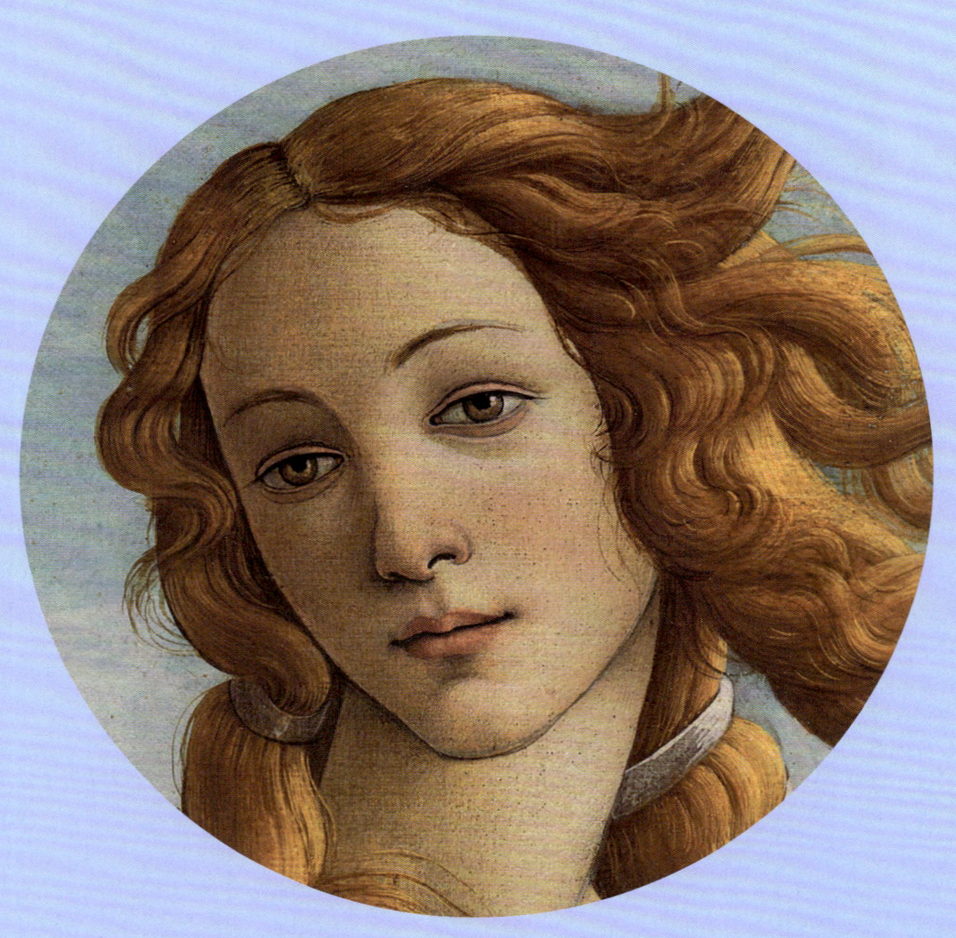

THE BIRTH OF VENUS

1485

WHEN CHRISTIANITY AND PAGANISM MEET

Sandro Botticelli's poetic sense of beauty captivated the Florentine court, but it was his subject matter that distinguished him from other artists: he was one of the first Western artists since classical times to depict nudes in non-religious scenes.

The Birth of Venus (1485) was art for pleasure, not to serve God, and Botticelli's depiction of an almost life-sized nude was radical.[1] It wasn't Eve being expelled from the garden of Eden, shamed by her nudity. It wasn't the naked hordes sent to Hell in Dante's *Inferno*. In fact, it wasn't nudity as symbol of shame at all, or even sin, or wickedness; this was a celebration of the naked human form.

But it was also a celebration of the act of procreation.

HUMANISM

In Florence, around the 14th century, a renewed interest in ancient Greco-Roman culture led to an intellectual and artistic 'rebirth' (in Italian, 'Renaissance'), a rise in humanist philosophy and radical changes in ideas about religion, politics and science that would turn art on its head.

Humanism was a philosophical and intellectual movement that emerged during the Renaissance; it is a broad term that encompasses various perspectives and interpretations, but at its core places a strong emphasis on the value and potential of human beings.

We can see how these new ideas affected art in two paintings of the Virgin Mary and Child, which are only approximately fifteen years apart. The first, by Gentile da Fabriano, is late Gothic, the period that preceded the Renaissance. It is heavily stylized and flat: flesh tones are pallid, expressions are vacant and it is unemotional. But by the time of Masaccio's painting of 1424, a work that inspired the young Botticelli, there is more emphasis on Mary as an individual; she is more three-dimensional, more lifelike and fleshier.

Botticelli was at the forefront of this momentous shift in Western art. He would bridge the gap between medieval Gothic art and emerging humanism, with the help of his patron, Lorenzo de' Medici, a cultured, intelligent man who dominated Florence's political and cultural life, and who was also a humanist.

'VENUS PUDICA'

The influence of sculpture on Renaissance paintings cannot be stressed enough. For *The Birth of Venus*, Botticelli was almost certainly inspired by an ancient marble statue in the Medici's collection, now known as the *Venus de' Medici*, whose modest pose is known as 'Venus Pudica', a stance where a nude female uses her right hand to cover her breast while her left hand tries to hide her pubic area. *Pudica* is a Latin term that translates to

By the time of Masaccio's painting of 1424, a work that inspired the young Botticelli, there is more emphasis on Mary as an individual

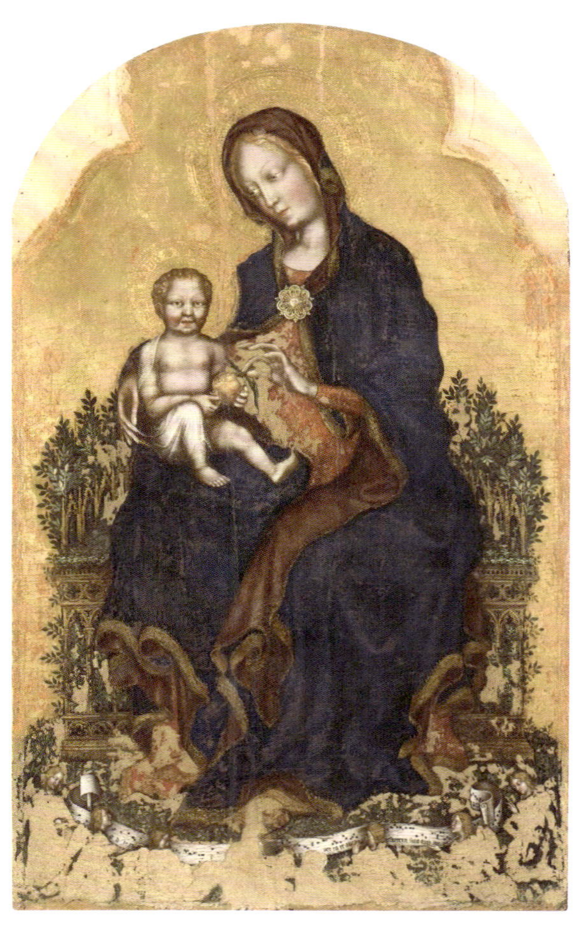

Gentile da Fabriano,
Madonna and Child,
c. 1405–10.

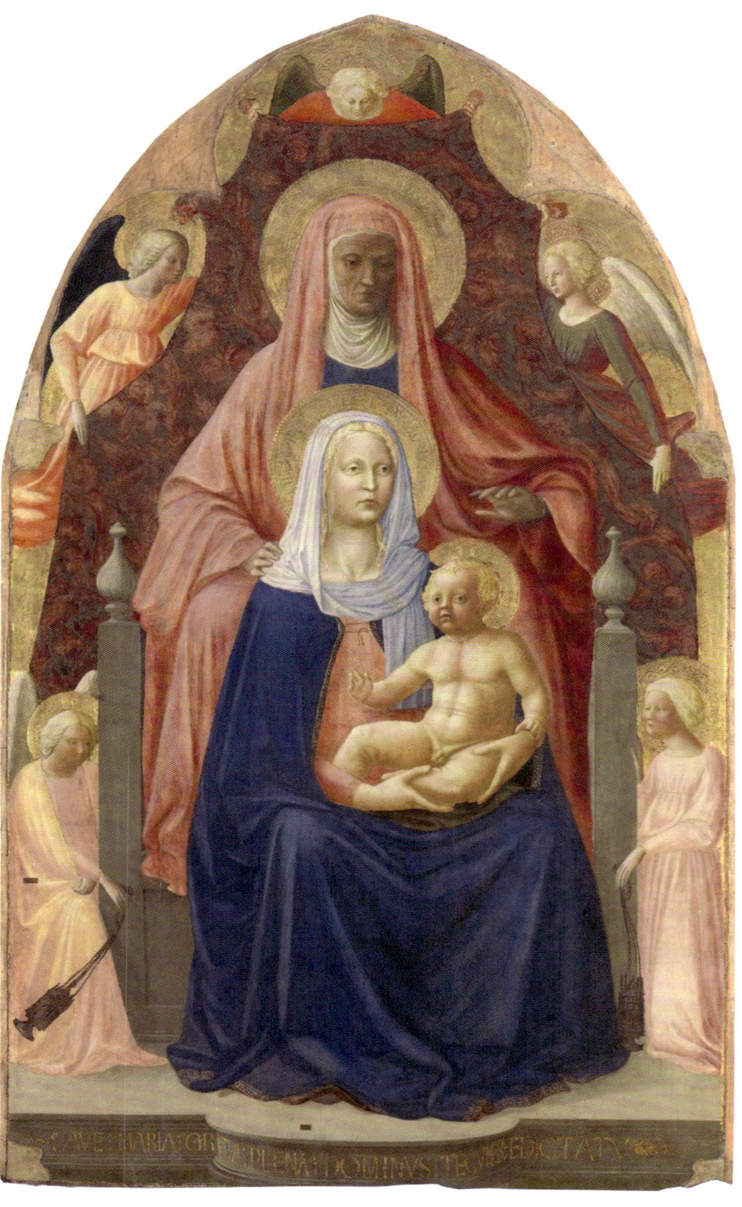

Masaccio, *Virgin
and Child with St Anne*,
c. 1424–25.

opposite
Unknown artist,
Venus de' Medici,
1st century BCE.

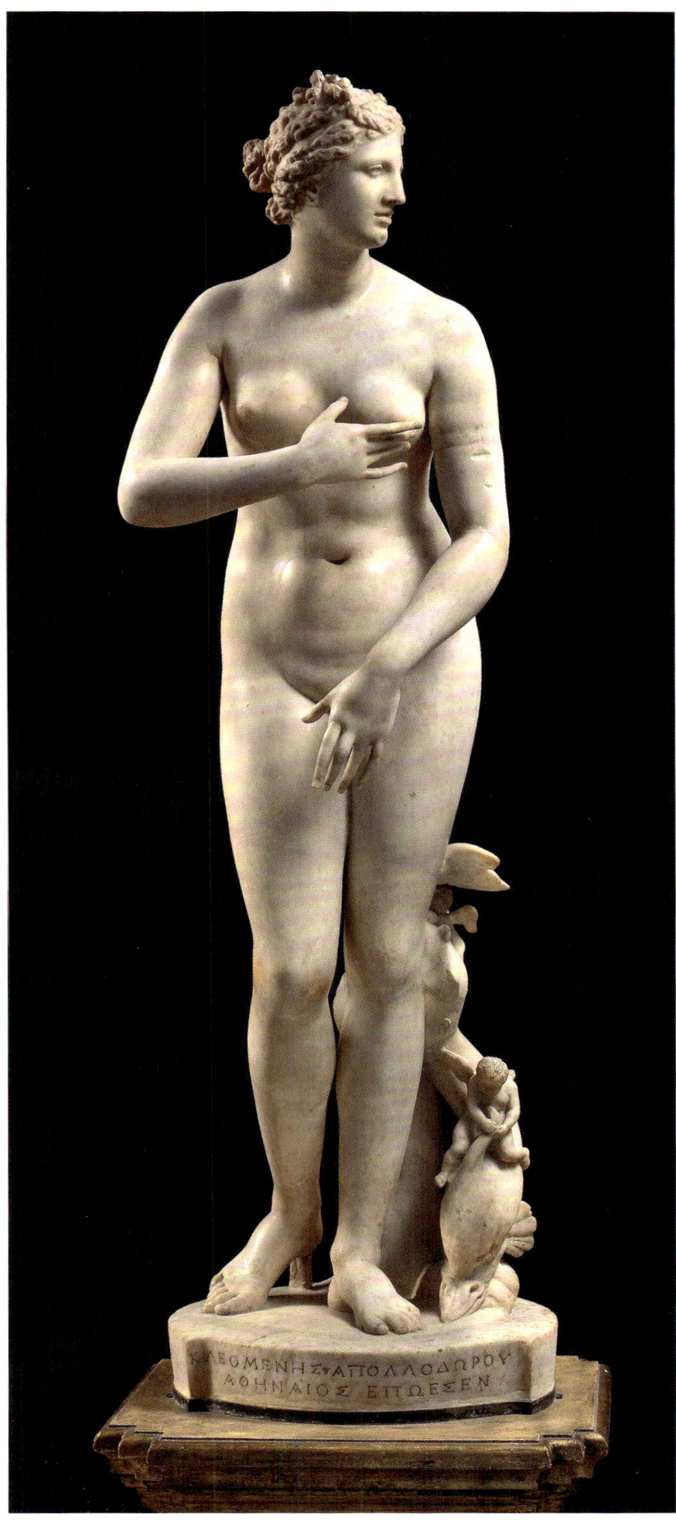

'modest', and 'pudenda', the feminine participle, can mean either external genitalia or 'shame'.

We don't see this coy pose with male statues either in antiquity or during the Renaissance. Naked men were associated with active heroism and triumph, and fully flaunted their nudity, but women were seen as passive sexual objects who often hid their nudity, shamed by the male gaze.

It is not only Venus's classical Greek and Roman pose that makes her statue-like; Botticelli also gave her pale alabaster skin, outlined with a dark, graphic line, emphasizing her contours, and giving the impression of a 'crafted' figure. The lack of heavy shading or texture reinforces the sense of her body as a polished, flawless surface, as if made from marble.

Her figure is elongated in the Gothic style. She appears graceful but she is not quite central, and her weight isn't evenly distributed – if it were, in this position, the shell would tip over. She has what is called the Gothic sway, a pre-Renaissance variation on the *contrapposto* pose – also known as an S-curve – which places the weight of the body on the forward stationary leg, creating an elegant pose often seen in Madonna figures.

A CLEVER SYMBOLIC LANGUAGE

The story of the goddess of love and beauty in Greek mythology starts with the castration of the god Uranus by his son, Cronus, who then tosses his genitals into the sea. Out of the sea foam created by Uranus's semen, an unbelievable beauty emerges fully formed: Aphrodite (or Venus in Roman mythology). At that very same moment, a rose bush blooms, and so becomes the symbol of Aphrodite. Botticelli nods to this with dozens of roses tossed in the wind.

Despite its title, the painting does not represent Venus's actual birth, but rather the

Botticelli was not aiming for realism, but a clever symbolic language

next part of the story, when she arrives on the island of Cyprus on a shell. We should stress that Botticelli was not aiming for realism, but a clever symbolic language that only a sophisticated audience would get.[2]

As far as the devoutly Christian Botticelli was concerned, his religious paintings were reality – history, even – and he painted them realistically to reflect that. His mythological works, however, are in a completely different artistic style, which signals that we are looking at a product of his imagination.

THE PAINTING

Venus is welcomed by a woman who is primed to cover her nakedness with a cloak and to welcome the goddess to the earthly realm. She is likely to be one of the Horae, the goddesses of the 'hours', or seasons (spring in this case, as her dress is decorated with cornflowers and primroses, and at her feet are anemones – all spring flowers). Horae are often linked with Venus in art and literature, as the forces of nature that align with love and beauty.

The male figure on the far left is probably Zephyr, the warm spring winds. He is puffing his cheeks out to blow Venus ashore, while locked in an embrace with his wife Chloris, who is also blowing gentle breaths as the roses fall around them, each with a golden heart. The wind deities are in an impossible convoluted embrace, and like all the characters, appear weightless and lacking in depth. They are all on the same pictorial plane, in the foreground, which creates an intense theatricality as none of the figures cast shadows.

The waves are mere gestures, a flick of Botticelli's wrist, and the backdrop shows a barren coastline, but once Venus steps ashore, the land will instantaneously blossom, like the lush greenery portrayed in Botticelli's *Primavera* (*c.* 1480).

There is a peculiar detail in the bottom left of the painting: bullrushes, out of place here as they don't grow in saltwater. A mistake? No. It is almost certainly a subtle phallic reference, an homage to the discarded member of Uranus that created Venus and an 'in joke' for those clever Florentines.[3]

VENUS AS A CHRISTIAN SYMBOL

When Botticelli painted *The Birth of Venus*, only a tiny percentage of Western paintings were non-religious, and most of those were portraits. Mythology paintings were a whole new art form, so it makes sense that Botticelli would incorporate familiar Christian references. Not to say that it is a disguised allegory, but there are elements worth examining.

If we look at a painting of the Virgin Mary that Botticelli painted a couple of years later for the Church of St Barnaba in Florence (p. 34), it has a comparable composition to *The Birth of Venus*. The two women are also strikingly similar, so Botticelli probably used the same model. In this image, Mary, like Venus, is dominated by the scallop shell; in Christian symbolism, such a shell represents baptism and resurrection, but in pagan symbolism it is a representation of fertility or female sexual organs.

It is entirely possible that Botticelli was depicting Venus as an emblem of sacred or divine love, a familiar Renaissance trope, to take a story rooted in mythology, and a nude female, and make them acceptable to contemporary Christian thinking, aligning artistic expression with religious ideals.

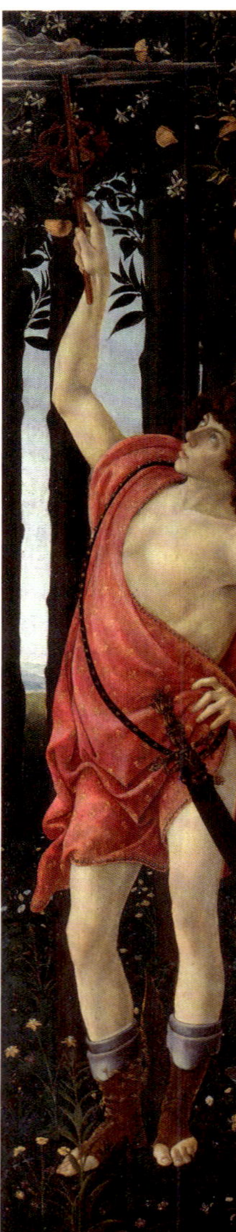

  SANDRO BOTTICELLI

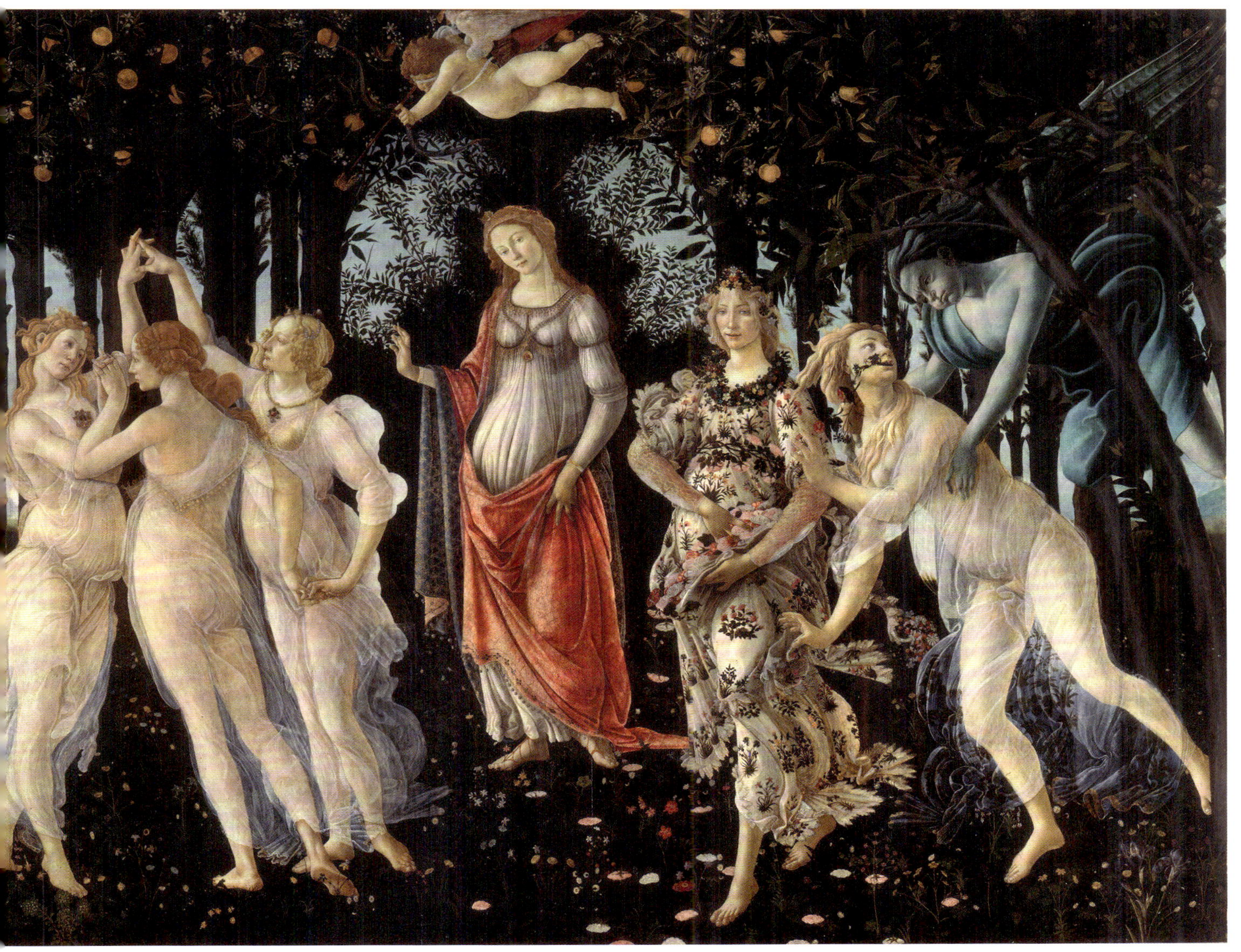

COMMISSION

Botticelli's other mythological work, *Primavera*, was possibly commissioned by Lorenzo as a wedding gift for his cousin.[4] In 1550, around seventy years after they were painted, the art historian Giorgio Vasari saw both paintings at the Villa di Castello, the Medici country residence. So, there is a strong possibility that *The Birth of Venus* was commissioned to be a companion piece to *Primavera*, perhaps also as a wedding gift.[5]

The Medicis' desire to continue the family lineage is the key to this painting. Noble families didn't marry for love, they married for power, which would be accelerated by important arranged unions. The function of women was their ability to reproduce, and the new bride's arrival into the Medici bedchamber for the

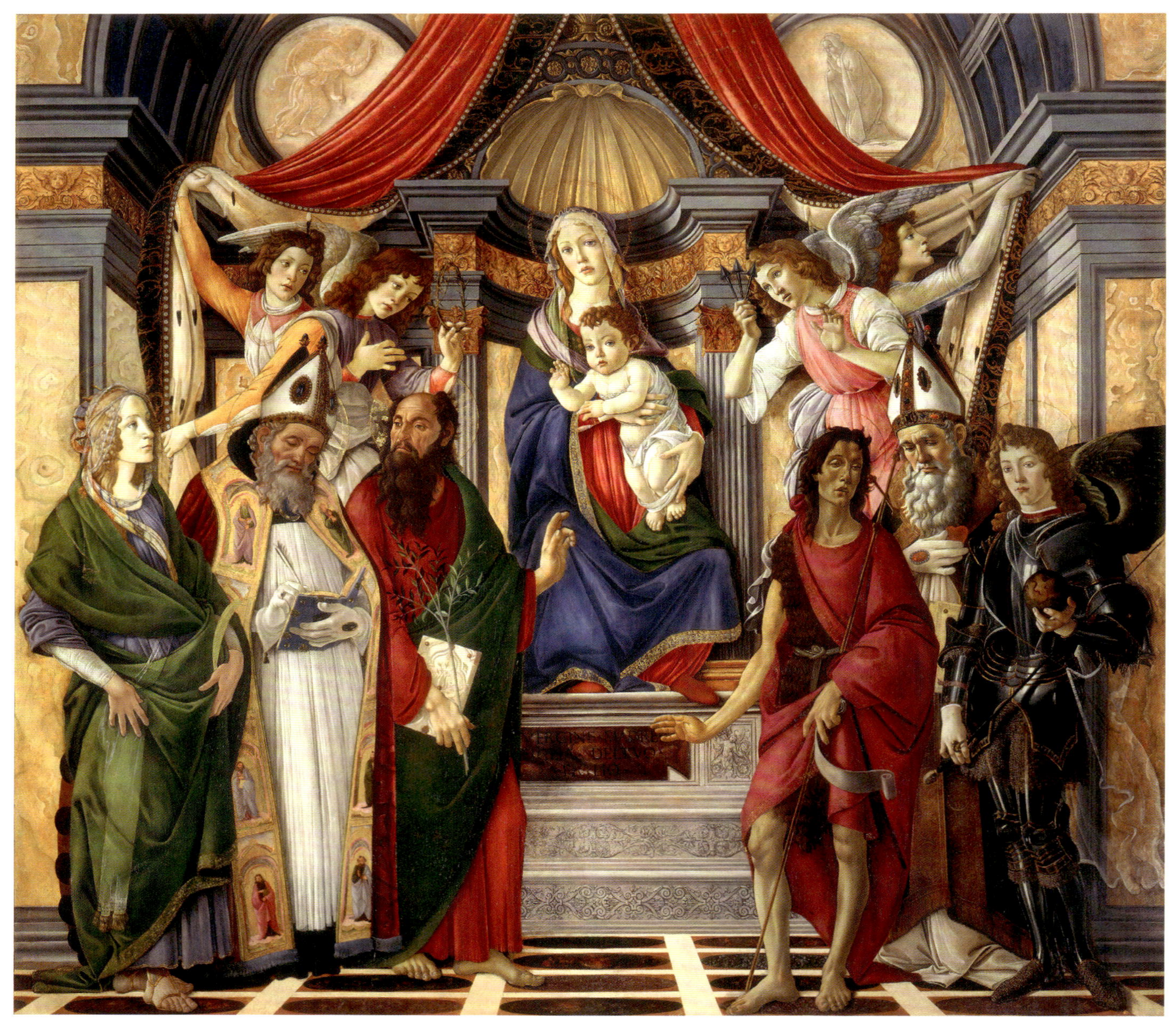

*In this image, Mary,
like Venus, is framed
by the scallop shell*

 SANDRO BOTTICELLI

purpose of creating life, the ultimate goal in a dynastic marriage, is paralleled by the arrival of Venus on Cyprus, literally about to step over the threshold and bring life to a barren island.

It can also be seen as an allegory of its Medici sponsor, ushering in a new Golden Age.[5]

BONFIRE OF THE VANITIES

On 7 February 1497, a huge bonfire that would come to be known as the Bonfire of the Vanities was lit in the centre of Florence. Books on poetry and classical texts were burned along with paintings, sculptures, mirrors, make-up and musical instruments. In fact, anything considered profane by the Dominican Order of the Catholic Church was burned.

The fire was started by the charismatic Dominican preacher Girolamo Savonarola, a popular figure who had a huge following in Florence and who succeeded in not only driving out the Medici family but also – albeit briefly – setting up a new democratic republic in Florence, with 'Jesus Christ as its only king'.[7]

At the time, mythological paintings attracted criticism, and one of the most vociferous critics was Savonarola.[8] Botticelli, already a committed Christian, had fallen under the spell of the preacher, who wanted to destroy everything the artist's former patron, Lorenzo, represented.[9] We know that some artists burnt their own works,[10] but it is likely a myth that Botticelli willingly threw some of his own paintings into the bonfires.

We are fortunate that his greatest mythological works *did* survive, but this is only because they were held at the Medici villa, outside the reach of Savonarola's followers.

THE RETURN OF THE MEDICI

In 1498 Savonarola was tried as a heretic by Pope Alexander VI and burned at the stake in Piazza della Signoria,[11] the very spot where he had once consigned books, jewellery and

fine art to the flames.[12] Botticelli's artistic output significantly declined after the Medicis were restored. He was still a firm believer in the apocalyptic visions of Savonarola,[13] and his style of religious art was less in demand. At any rate, the Medicis had moved on to other artists: by 1501, Michelangelo had started *David*; by 1503, Leonardo had begun painting the *Mona Lisa*; and in 1504 the young Raphael would arrive in the city.

It is a myth that Botticelli died poor and forgotten,[14] but by the time of his passing in 1510, it could be said that he had begun to fade into relative obscurity.[15]

With *The Birth of Venus*, Botticelli really did produce a work of art that shifted the course of art history, and one that still looks intensely modern to 21st-century eyes. In fact, *The Birth of Venus* is as influential now as it was five centuries ago and is one of the most recognizable images in the world.

The ancient gods may have given birth to Venus, but Botticelli gave her life.

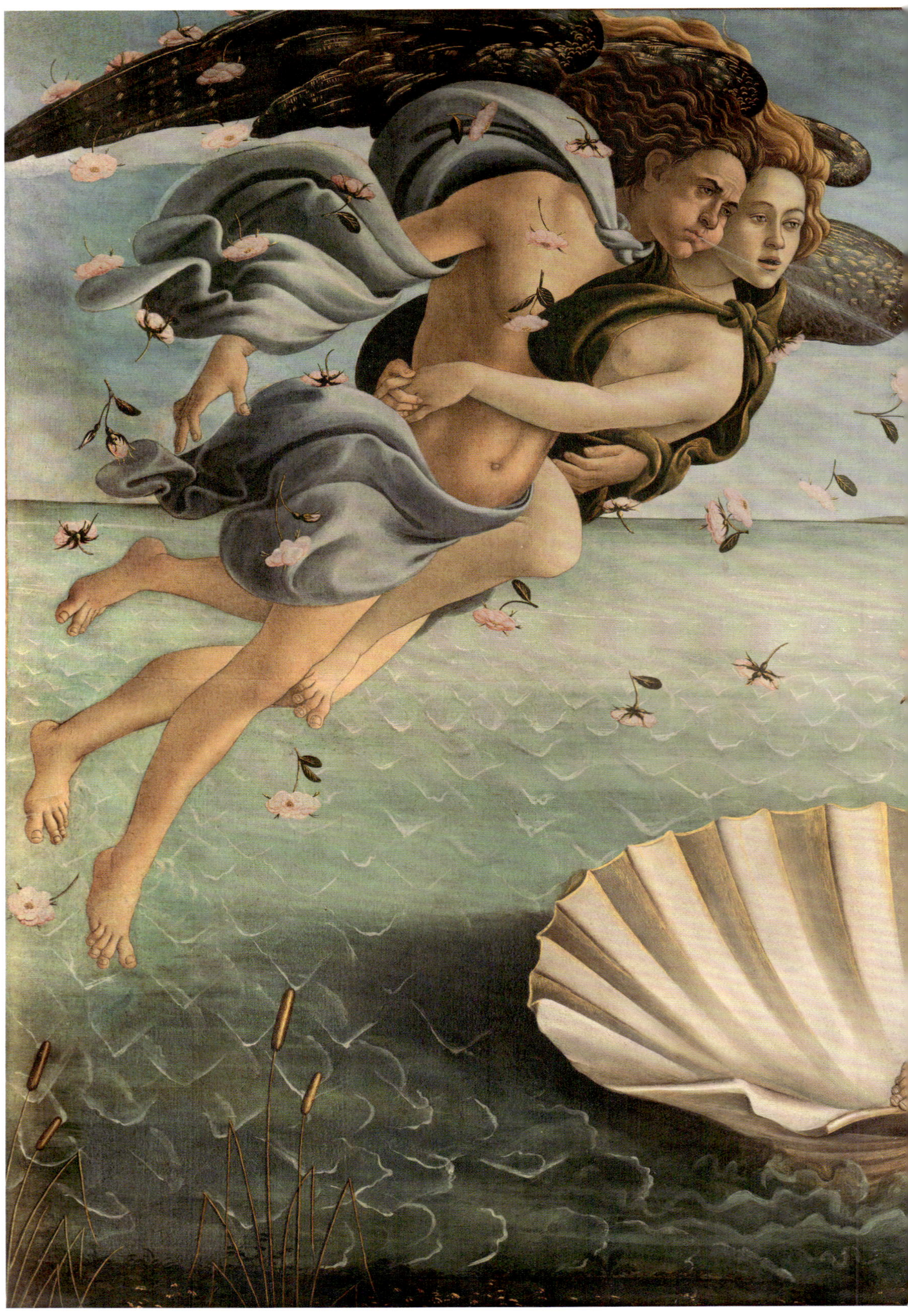

Sandro Botticelli,
The Birth of Venus, 1485.

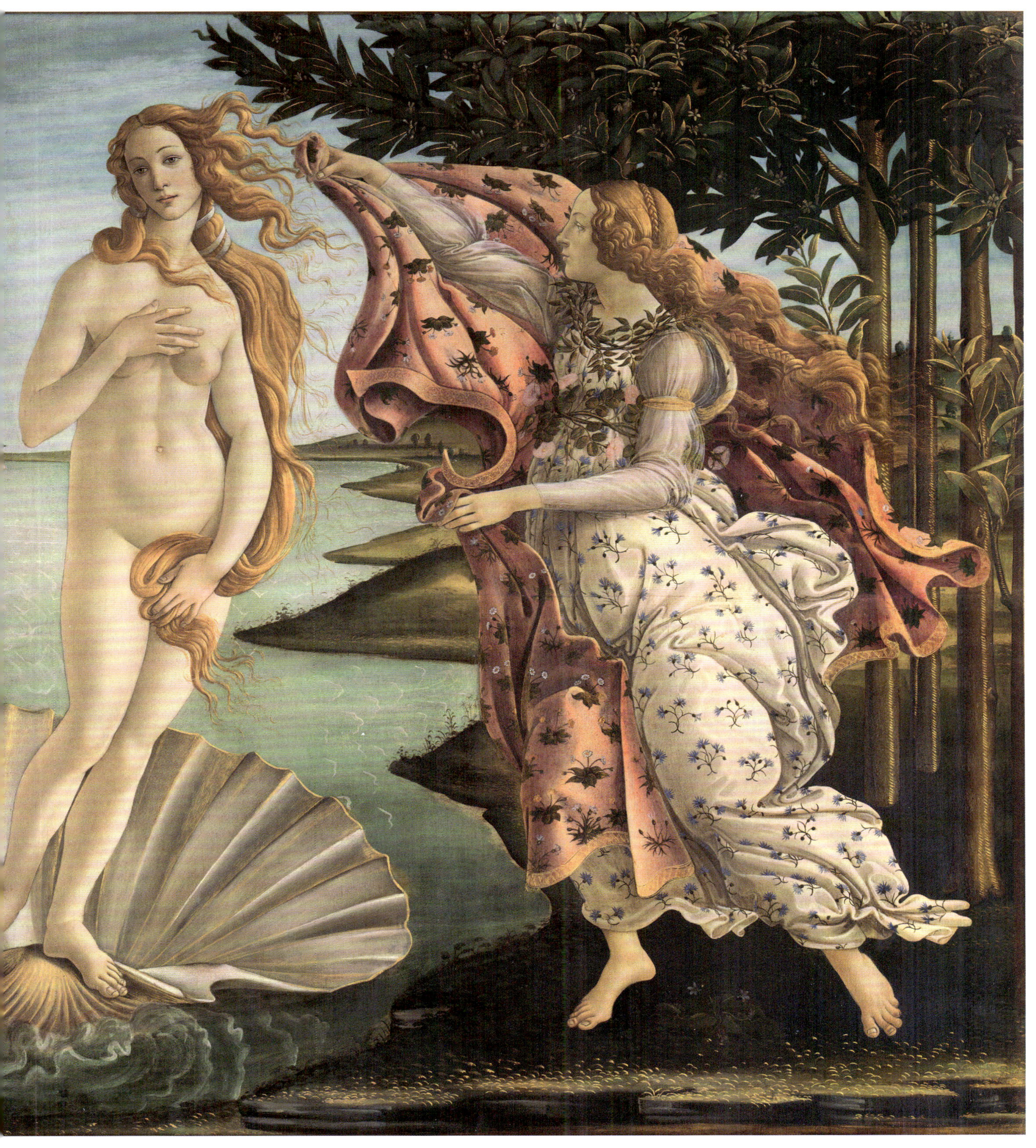

HIERONYMUS BOSCH

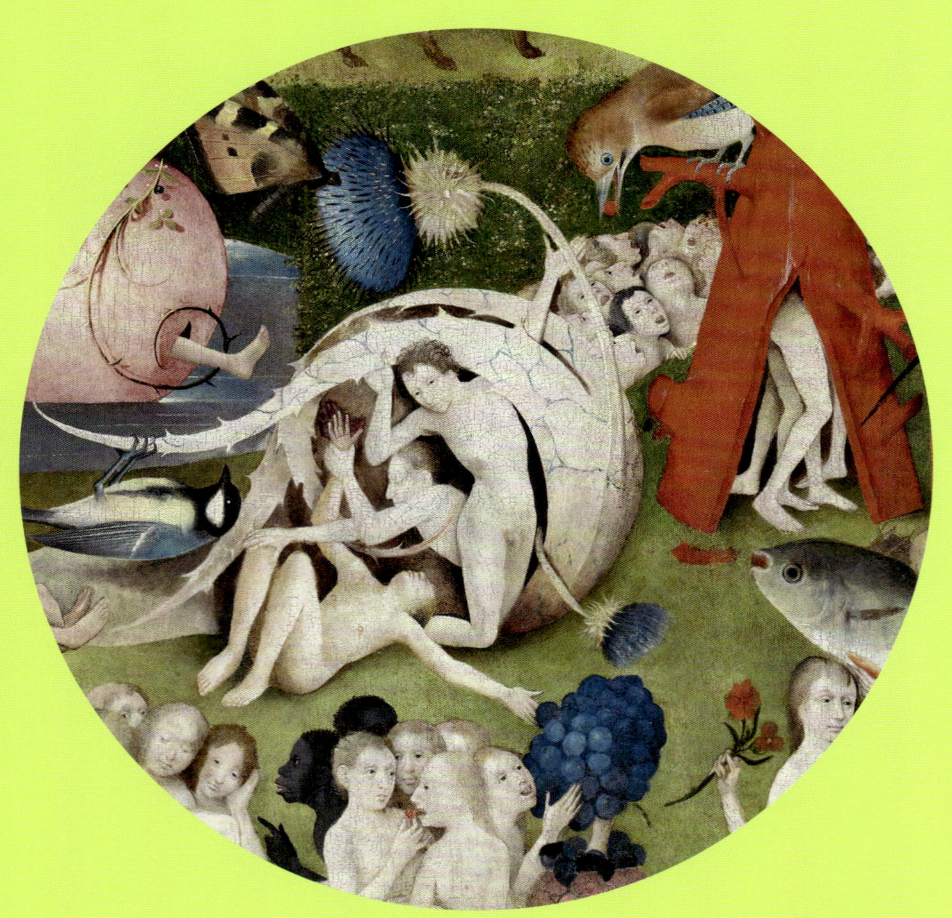

THE GARDEN OF EARTHLY DELIGHTS

1490–1500

THE FIGHT BETWEEN GOOD AND EVIL

We cannot look at Hieronymus Bosch's *Garden of Earthly Delights* with modern sensibilities. It is not a painting about sexual freedom, or a medieval acid trip; it is not Bosch's erotic fantasy or even a heretical attack on the Church; and it is not a painting by a member of an obscure free-love cult. This is a painting about human nature and the consequences of our actions.

In the Late Middle Ages, European artists, writers and theologians were shaping a new, terrifying vision of Hell and the punishments awaiting sinners, and Bosch's imagery (no matter how bizarre) is nothing more than a reflection of the world in which he lived. It is an intensely moralistic work that should be approached as what it is: a specific view of Christian doctrine in a period of growing religious turmoil.

A LITTLE-DOCUMENTED LIFE

Bosch was part of the Northern Renaissance, living and working in S'Hertogenbosch, commonly known as Den Bosch, in what is now the Netherlands.

We know that Bosch was a successful and prolific artist, born around 1450 and baptized Jeroen van Aken. Later he would change his surname to reflect Den Bosch, the town in which he lived, and take Hieronymus for his first name, the Latin for Jeroen.

In 1463, when the artist was a child, a major fire in Den Bosch burned the medieval city to the ground. He must have been affected as people panicked and screamed for their lives, and it's not too much of a leap to think that this event inspired his vivid depictions of hellfire, which we see in many of his works.

A CONVERSATION PIECE

Triptychs were typically altarpieces, but the inclusion of such highly provocative subject matter and abundant nudity suggests that this piece was commissioned by a lay patron, probably for the Brussels Palace of Hendrik III of the Nassau-Breda dynasty,[1] rather than for the Church. Paintings with nudes like this were often collected by elite families, and *The Garden of Earthly Delights* epitomizes the Renaissance taste for elaborate allegories rich in symbolism and decipherable only by a select and cultured audience. We know that in 1516, Hendrik showed Cardinal Luigi of Aragon and his entourage 'this curious painting' in his extensive art collection.[2]

All of this points to the idea that this work was a conversation piece rather than a religious one, and many of the characters within the painting are immersed in deep conversation, too, whispering secrets to each other – reflecting us.[3]

FOR HE SPOKE AND IT WAS DONE

When deciphering the meaning in Bosch's complex painting, it is crucial to acknowledge that this is a topic still debated among scholars.

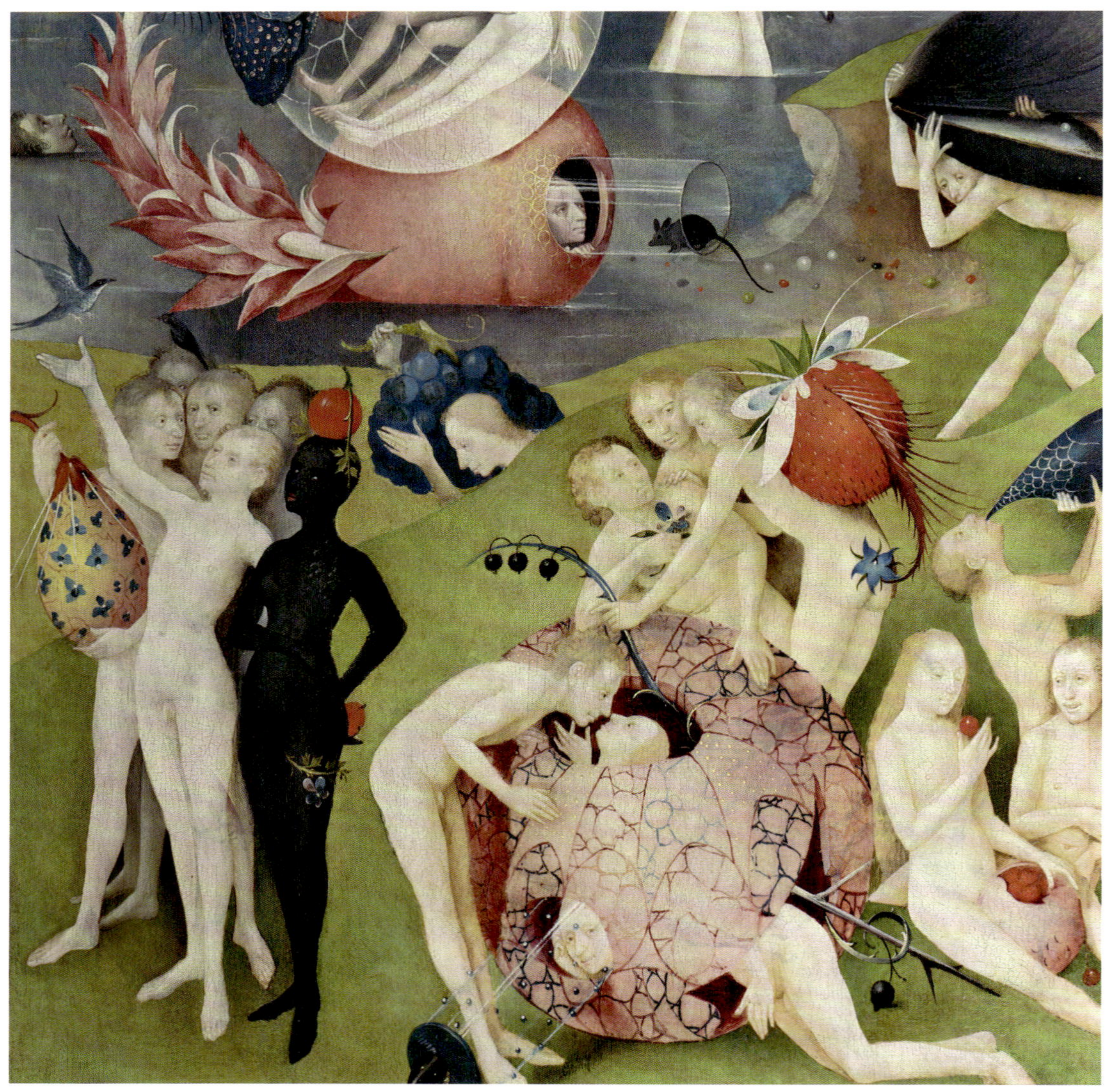

All of this points to the idea that this work was a conversation piece rather than a religious one

But it is interesting to look at that which often gets forgotten: the outer panels, or shutters, which are designed to protect the artwork.

When they are closed, they form an image in green/grey grisaille, showing the creation of the world as a flat disc enclosed in a transparent sphere, likely representing the Third Day of creation, when the separation of waters and land occurred, giving rise to the terrestrial Paradise or Eden.

God appears in the top left-hand corner, a tiny yet radiant figure in the darkness. His hands are raised, which is medieval code to tell us he is speaking, and he is reciting verse 9 of Psalm 33: 'For he spoke and it was done, for he commanded and it stood fast.'

The flat Earth and dome are peculiar to modern eyes, but can be explained by a translated passage in the Vulgate Bible which states that God created the sky 'under a dome'.[4] Bosch would have been aware of this idea, as it was a standard artistic convention.

BE FRUITFUL AND MULTIPLY

Following the outer panels' depiction of the creation of the Earth from Genesis, the left interior panel shows the second chapter of Genesis, the creation of man, 'before which

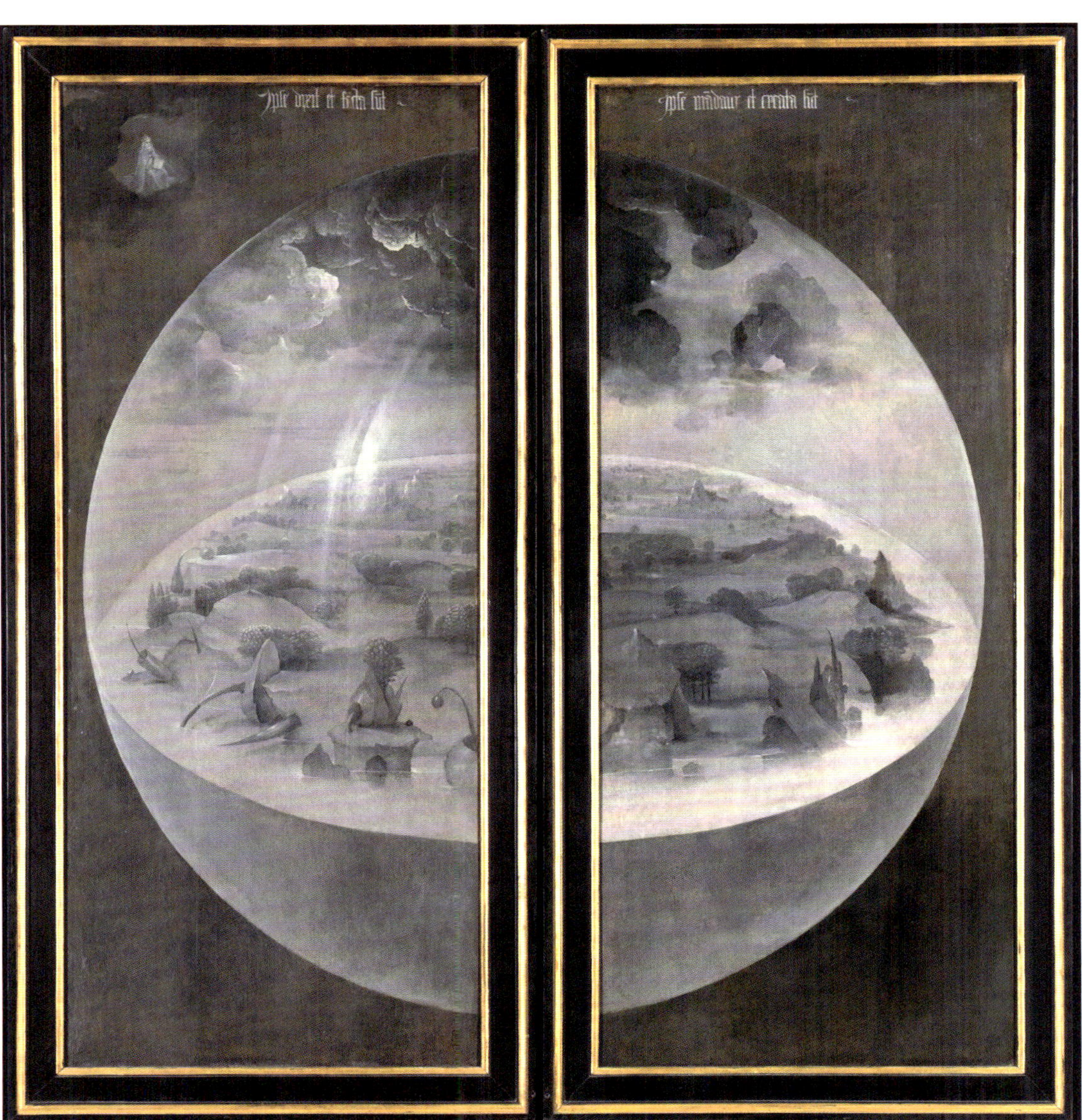

The Garden of Earthly Delights (outer panels).

THE GARDEN OF EARTHLY DELIGHTS

a fountain waters the earth'.[5] On it, God is presenting Eve to an astounded Adam in the Garden of Eden.[6] He is Christ-like, an illustration of the belief that Jesus is God in human form, or God incarnate.

We know from infrared scans that Bosch's original plan was a more classic image of God creating Eve from Adam's rib. By shifting the focus of this panel to highlighting their union, he primed the audience for the central panel's carnal depiction of 'Be fruitful and multiply.' To Renaissance audiences, the link would have been obvious: the Fall of Adam and Eve will inevitably lead to the crucifixion of Christ. This is underscored by the positioning of Adam's feet, mirroring Christ's while on the Cross.

Behind Christ is the Tree of Life, a dragon blood tree known for its dark red juice when cut. Its flat leaves represent Eucharistic wafers, while the grapes reference wine, establishing a direct association with the body and blood of Christ.

Though the Earthly Paradise appears peaceful at first glance, there is already the looming spectre of human sinfulness. The pool is populated with monstrous creatures who have already started to attack each other, foreshadowing the impending descent into chaos. One bird-like monster consumes a toad, a classic symbol representing the Devil's minions, associated with pestilence, which shows that the presence of evil exists even within the confines of Eden.

In the peculiar central fountain sits an owl – another recurring motif for Bosch, found in eighteen of his works. This painting features six owls: two in the left panel, three in the central panel and one in the right panel as 'the prince of Hell' (technically a nightjar). Contrary to its contemporary association with wisdom, in the Middle Ages the owl, a creature of the night hunting for prey, symbolized the Devil himself lying in wait for an opportunity to strike.[7]

The left panel also features an unusual rock formation in the form of a weeping face. This is Golgotha, the site of the Crucifixion, according to the Gospels, where we see the serpent coiled around a palm tree. Four hundred years later Bosch's painting would inspire the Surrealist movement, and Salvador Dalí in particular.

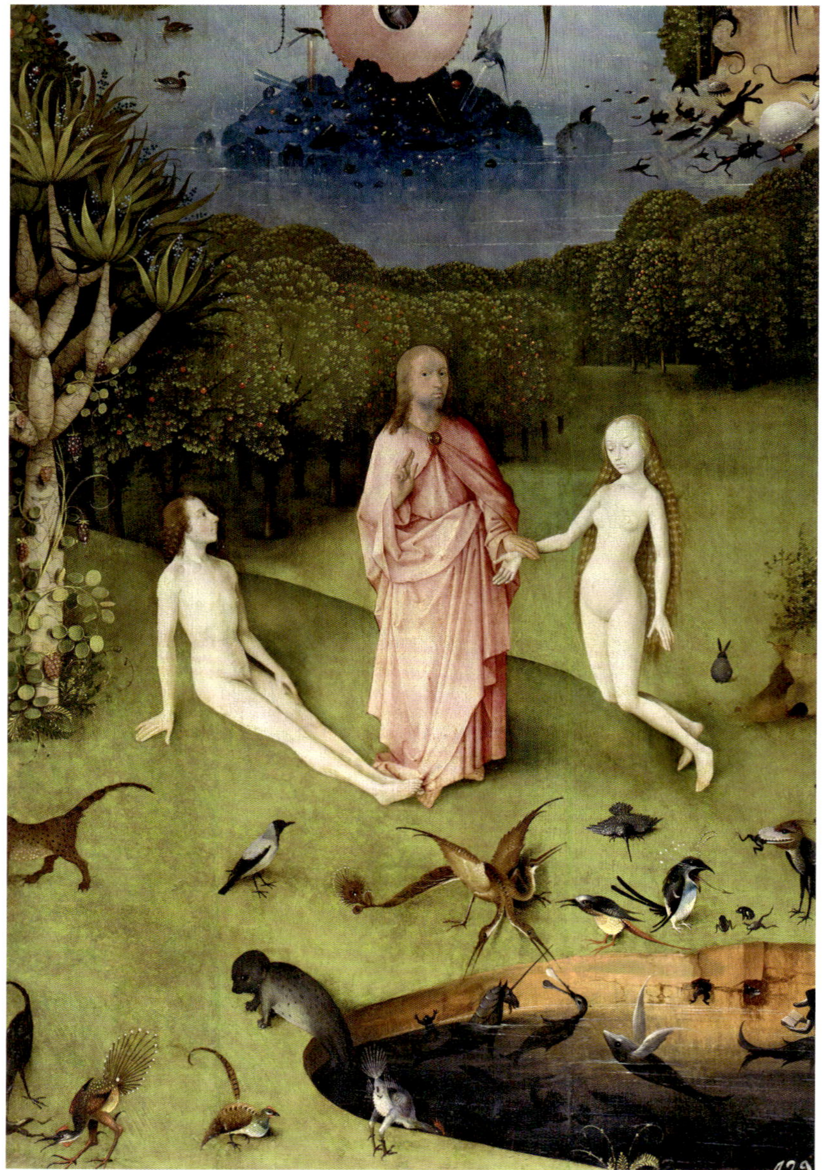

HIERONYMUS BOSCH

The central panel shows humanity indulging in earthly pleasures and desires, with imagery of excess and sensuality. Bosch shows us moral decay and the fleeting, hedonistic nature of a life detached from spiritual values.

If we go to the bottom right-hand corner, we find a possible depiction of Adam. He is looking directly at us, as if he is the only one to understand what's going on, and pointing at Eve as if to say, 'This is how it started.' Eve is holding the fruit she has just picked, and she is gagged by what looks like a communion wafer. Adam and Eve are also the only ones wearing clothes in the entire panel: animal skins, which ties into the biblical story.[8]

Everything in this paradise has some kind of sexual connotation; there is a voyeuristic edge to its supposed moral teachings.

The Earth's fertility is represented by enormous and abundant soft fruits that are consumed with gusto, representing the fleeting nature of pleasure (easy to rot/decay). Hollowed-out fruit was a symbol of female genitalia – two cherries together, male genitalia. In the Middle Ages to 'pluck fruit' was a euphemism for sex in Dutch, and blackberries, known for their multiple seeds, symbolized promiscuity. The empty mussel shells, peeled fruit, broken eggs and carcasses should be read, as with all the 'empty' metaphors that Bosch employs, as emblematic of a lack of spirituality.

Every figure is engaged in their own activities; whether eating, chatting, dancing, groping or swimming, they are all individuals. There is heterosexual and homosexual activity, and even interspecies, in groups and in couples.

Bosch also shows a keen interest in the natural world, along with a powerful imagination when it came to improvising species he could only find in illuminated manuscripts and early printed matter. This was a time of great

The Garden of Earthly Delights (Adam and Eve detail).

discoveries in the 'Indies' and the 'New World' of species of plants and animals.

APOCALYPSE

In the year 1500 (around the time Bosch was painting), it was widely thought by Christian Europeans that the end of the world was coming,[9] and the right-hand panel is a perfect illustration of this thinking. It depicts either the torments and tortures inflicted upon sinful souls in Hell or the Earth's destruction, but either way it is an apocalyptic vision, portraying the consequences of the central panel's indulgence.

What Hell is like, or whether it exists in the Bible at all, is widely disputed even within modern Christianity, but at the time Bosch painted this image, people firmly believed in Heaven and Hell. The Devil/Satan/Lucifer was also a major figure, but he became more so as reports of encounters with demons increased, heretics and witches were burned, and vivid descriptions of what was thought of as Hell were derived from paintings by Giotto, Fra Angelico and Jan van Eyck.

The right panel works as a frightening parallel to the previous lush and verdant panels; here, we see a wasteland where pools are now cess-pits and frozen rivers, the central fountain is a dead, hollowed-out Tree Man and the surrealistic towers and fountains are a raging inferno. Several motifs and figures are cross-referenced from Eden, not only reminding us how connected they are but also creating a sense of dread towards the incoming

This is a Hell that the medieval mind would have understood on many levels

apocalypse. We can compare Adam's positioning in the left panel to the unfortunate woman in the right panel (below); the severed hand holding a dice (the vice of gambling) to the word of God in the first panel. The frogs and toads that we saw crawling out of the pond of Eden become vicious thugs, doing the Devil's work.

Bosch's Hell is action-packed with heinous images, but two iconic details really stand out.

The first is the Prince of Hell, with a pot on its head and jugs for shoes. He sits on a giant potty chair, consuming human bodies and excreting them, simultaneously, straight into the sewer, where others are drowning. The prince's cauldron is like a crown, and in its reflection we can see a window, a cruel tease of a better world outside.

The second is the Tree Man, a gargantuan figure whose torso is a broken egg (again the emptiness metaphor), which doubles as a tavern.

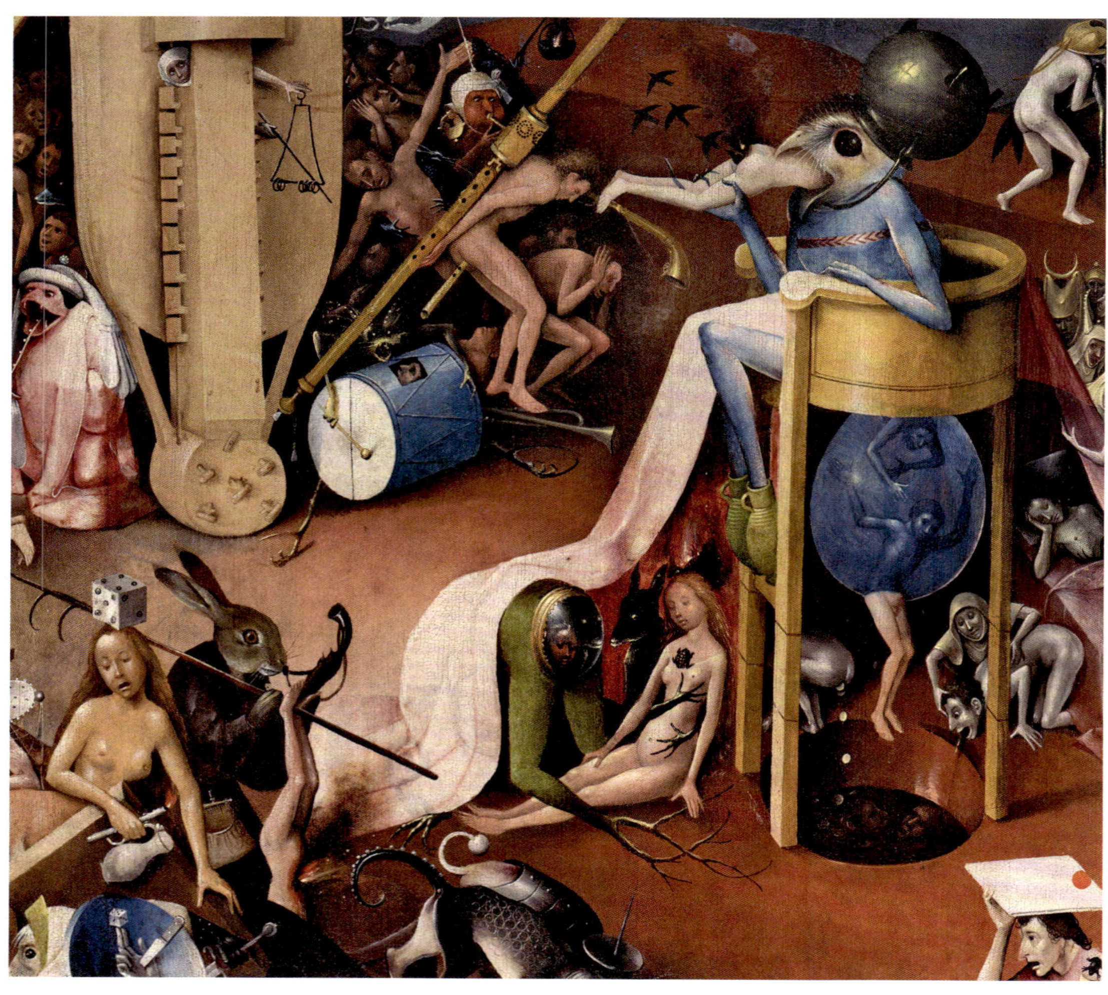

The Garden of Earthly Delights (Prince of Hell detail).

His head is topped with bagpipes, a common symbol of sloth and idleness at this time.

His face could be a self-portrait of Bosch,[10] as he is strangely self-conscious – not demonic, as with others – and stylistically out of keeping with the other depictions of human faces. He is looking back, possibly towards Adam in the first panel, and is balanced on two small boats with legs of dead branches. On one leg, a slipped bandage reveals a leper sore, and Hell below him is literally frozen over. Today, we associate Hell with fire and heat, but in the Late Middle Ages, there were several descriptions of Hell in which ice played a key role.[11]

DEATH WAS ALL AROUND

The climax of the painting is in the top right, a realistic portrayal of a city on fire that may

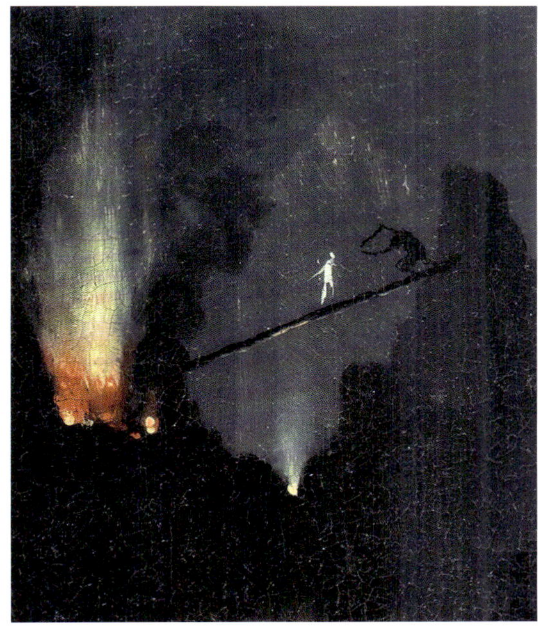

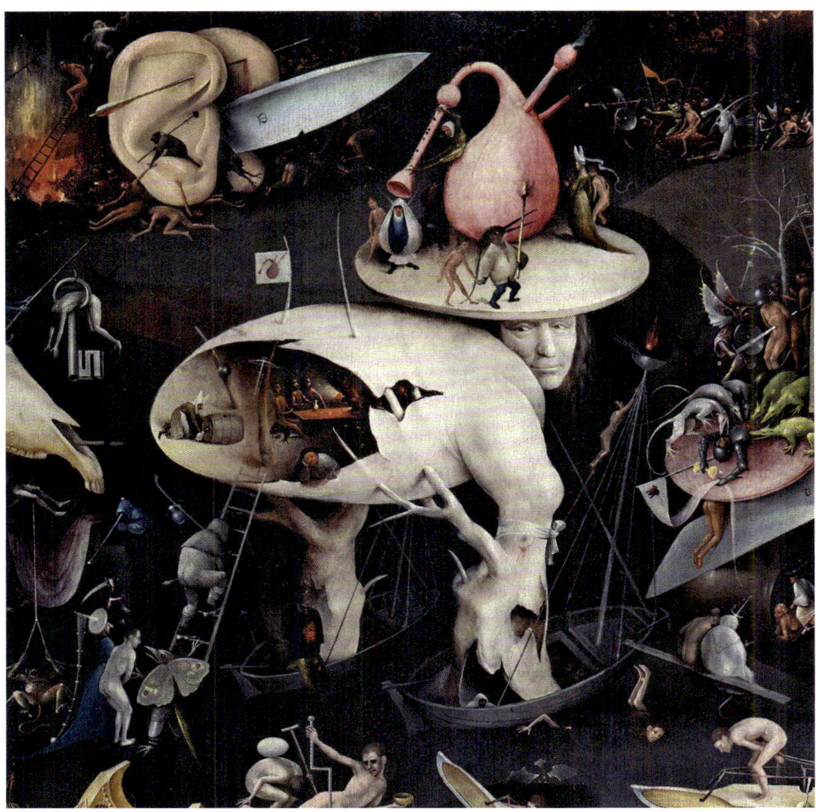

well speak to Bosch's childhood memories. A hostile army is seizing the city, and its gates are left wide open. Black silhouettes on horseback are galloping across a bridge while underneath, hundreds of wretches are drowning. This is a Hell that the medieval mind would have understood on many levels.[12] After all, death *was* all around them.

Finally, in a painting with thousands of details and hundreds of complicated metaphors, there is a further tiny feature at the apex of the volcano, where we can just make out two figures fighting, one a demon in black and one a human in white. This is the fight that Bosch's contemporaries would have seen as a lifelong battle: the fight between good and evil.

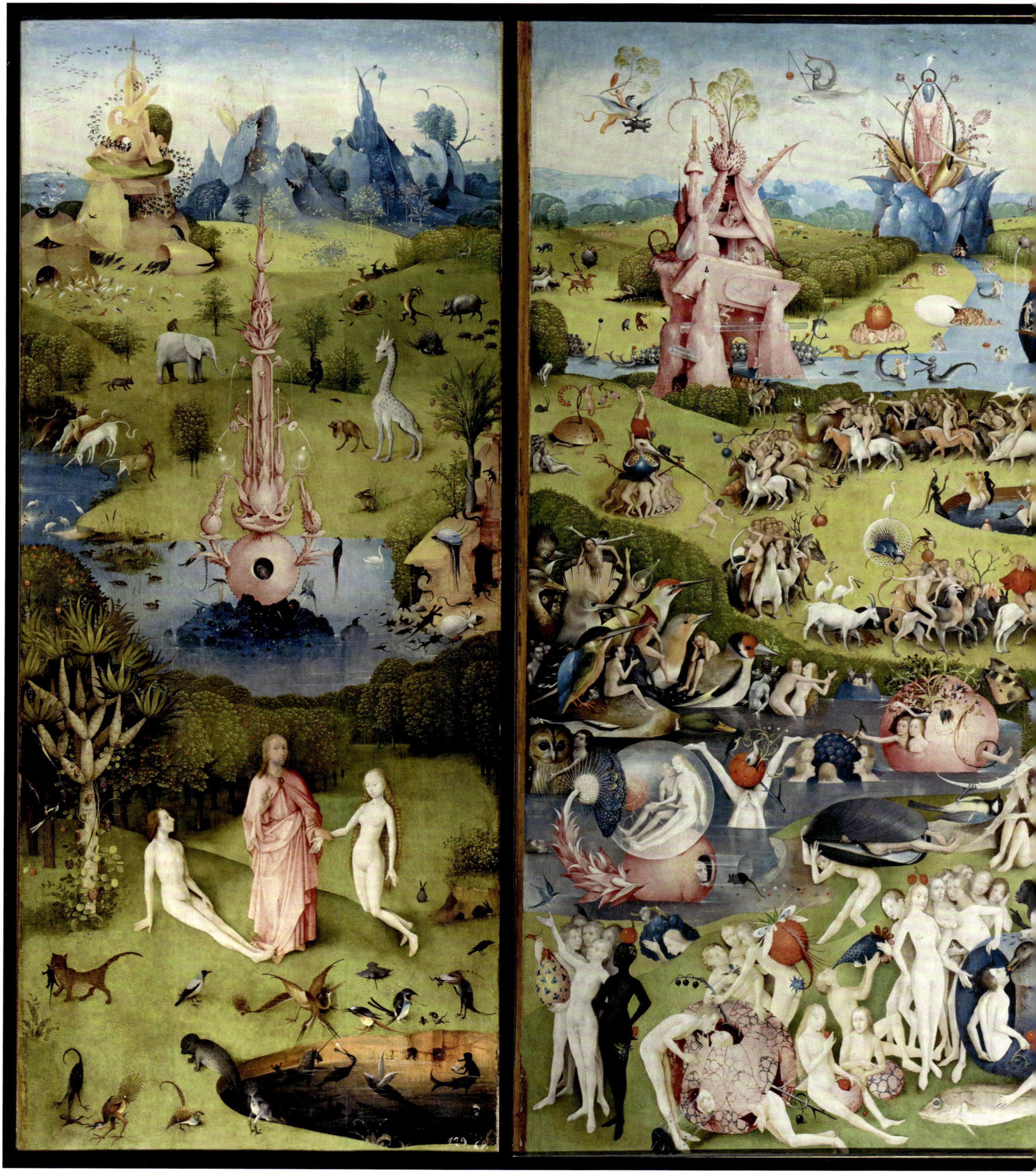

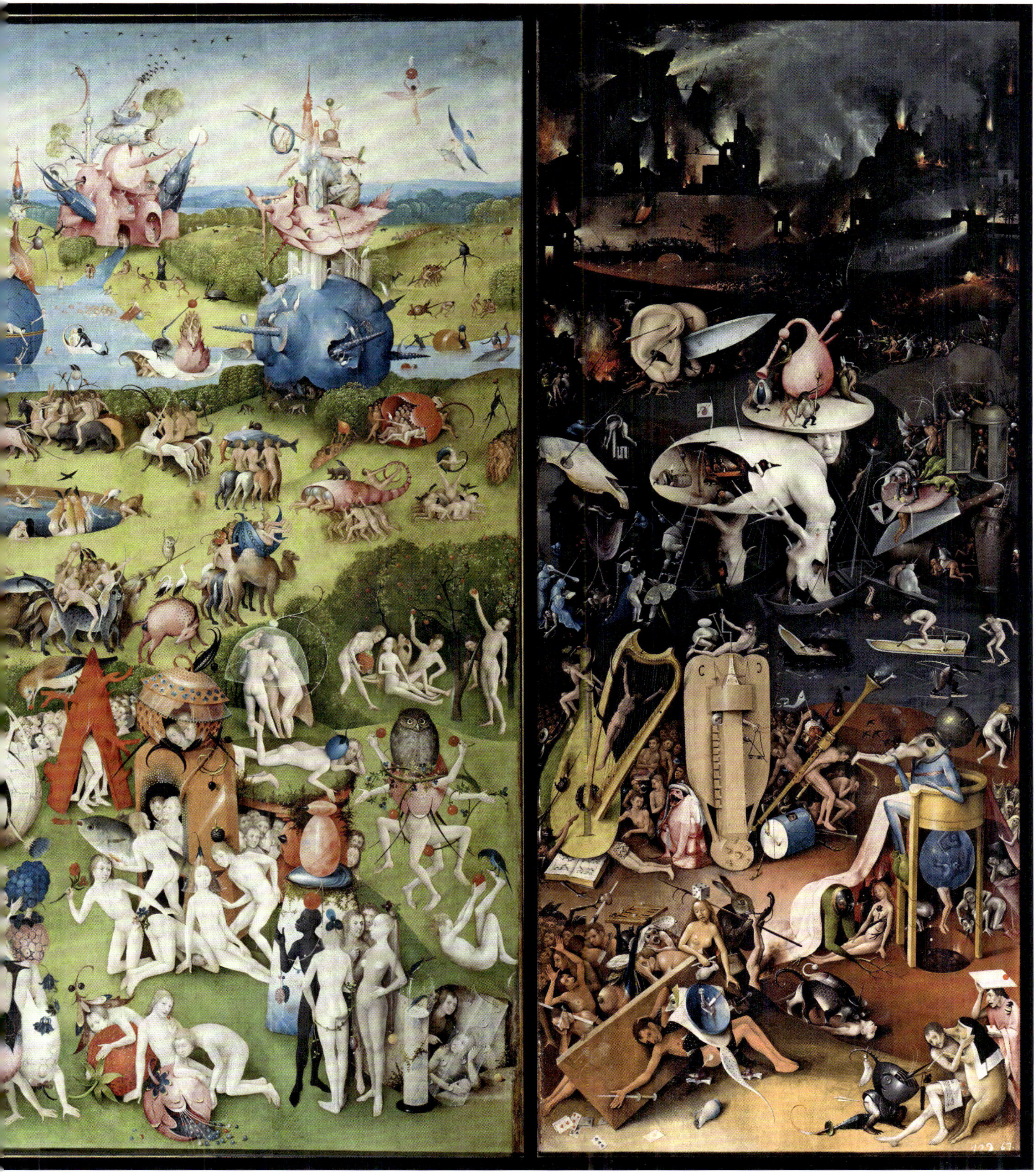

MICHELANGELO

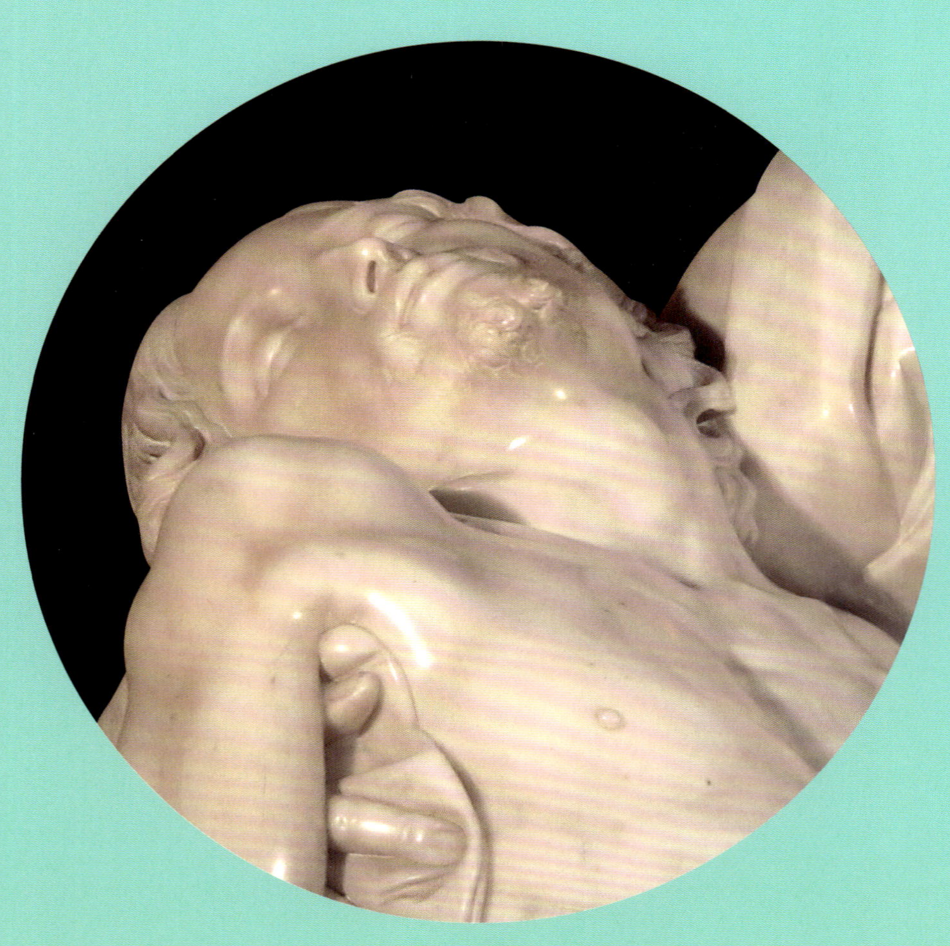

LA PIETÀ

1499

THE DIVINE ONE

Michelangelo Buonarroti created his first masterpiece at the age of twenty-four, *La Madonna della Pietà*, or *La Pietà* for short. It's a work that exemplifies the aesthetics of High Renaissance art and the technical expertise of Greek sculpture, while extolling the doctrine of the Catholic Church and revealing the emotional intensity of the death of a child.

Michelangelo was the first Western artist to have two biographies published in his lifetime – even then, his peers called him 'Il Divino' (the Divine One)[1] – and as well as being a sculptor, he was a painter, an architect, a poet and an engineer, an all-round embodiment of what we nowadays call a Renaissance man.

He was also difficult, competitive, anti-social and an extreme perfectionist. These qualities, combined with his spiritual devotion and intellectual brilliance, helped create one of the most emotionally sensitive and technically accomplished sculptures in art history.

THE COMMISSION

Michelangelo was born in Caprese in 1475 but grew up in Florence, where he became an apprentice to the painter Domenico Ghirlandaio at the age of thirteen. He was not particularly happy in this post, however, because even as a young man he considered himself first and foremost a sculptor. Then, in 1490, he was taken under the wing of Lorenzo de' Medici, the ruler of Florence,

who had his own workshops and saw the potential in Michelangelo. He was given bed and board and a wage of 5 ducats a month, alongside, most importantly, access to one of the greatest collections of ancient Roman statuary in existence at the time. Lorenzo's patronage would change his life, and possibly the course of Western art.

By the time the Medici family was overthrown in 1494, Michelangelo had already left Florence, and by 1496 he was living in Rome, an affluent and artistic city to which many artists were headed at the end of the 15th century.

In 1498 the wealthy French cardinal Jean de Bilhères de Lagraulas commissioned the then-twenty-two-year-old Michelangelo to create a sculpture for the cardinal's future tomb in the old Basilica of St Peter's. It was an audacious commission for a practically unknown sculptor, and one that would make him the most in-demand artist in Christendom for over six decades.

RELEASING THE FIGURE

Michelangelo's *Pietà* is the first in a long line of sculptural masterpieces that had their own unique take on a familiar story. Michelangelo was deeply religious and saw himself as a tool of God. He believed that rather than creating a sculpture from marble, he was simply releasing the figures imprisoned within the stone, and he just had to chip away the excess.

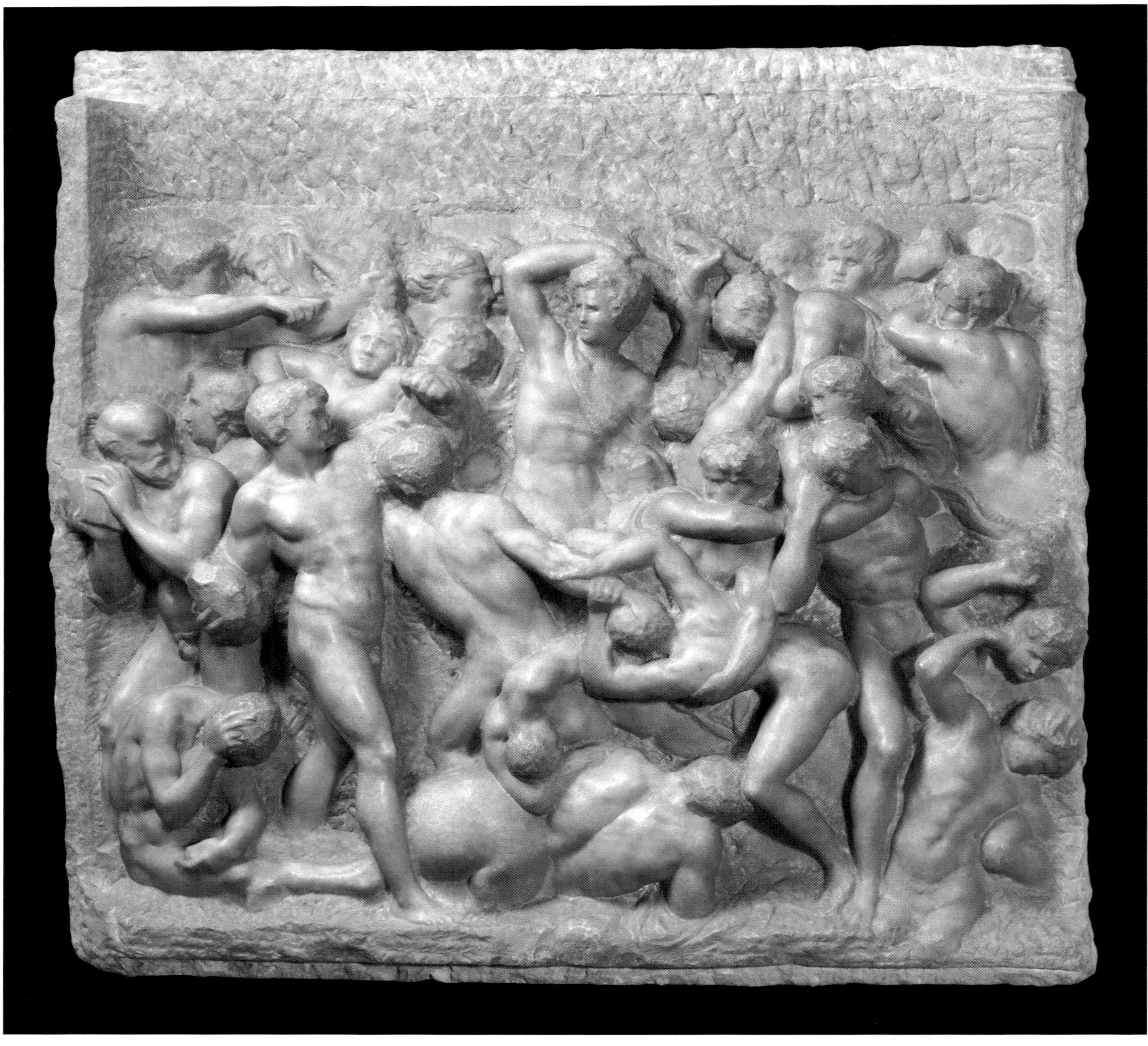

He was a painter, an architect, a poet and an engineer, an all-round embodiment of what we nowadays call a Renaissance man

Michelangelo, *Battle of the Centaurs*, 1492. This piece was the last work Michelangelo created under the patronage of Lorenzo de' Medici, at the age of sixteen.

To sculpt in marble requires incredible strength and dexterity, and any slip-up can destroy months of work. Michelangelo's work started with choosing the marble from the stone quarries; he had an uncanny empathy with both the stone and the quarry it came from, choosing the purest white marble, known as *statuario*, from Carrara, near Pisa. It was said he knew what he wanted and where on the rockface it could be found before it had even been extracted.[2]

We know that he worked morning, noon and night, rarely eating and hardly ever washing – he even designed a hat that supported candles so he could work in the dark.[3]

He would begin carving with a large chisel and hammer, followed by progressively smaller ones, such as claw chisels, a series of drills to make deeper holes, like in deep folds of cloth or eye sockets,[4] and then finally he would use a pumice stone to smooth and polish. Unfinished work by him gives us many insights into his techniques, and we can clearly see the marks of claw chisels, which give the effect of cross hatching.

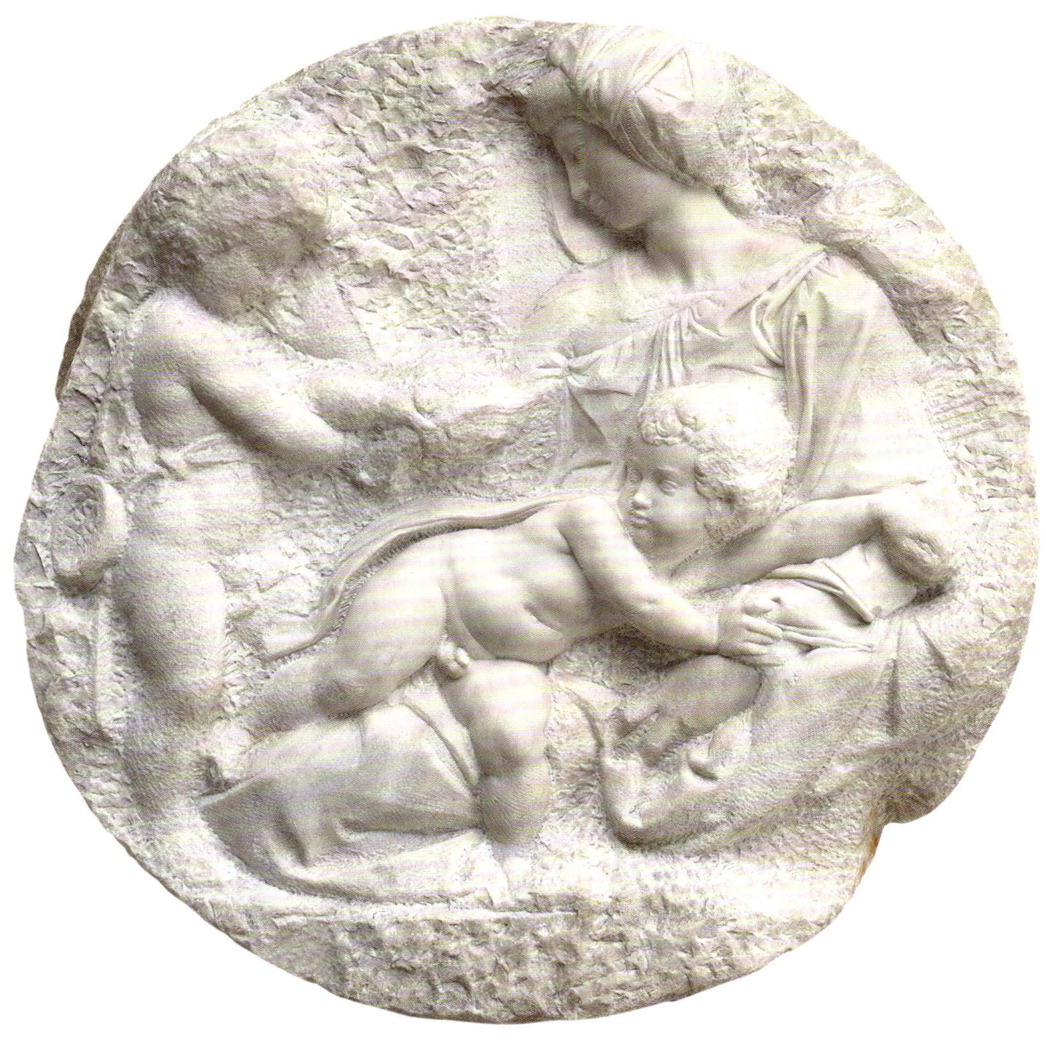

It is thought that he worked mostly free hand, starting at the front and working his way backwards,[5] and that he used no preparatory sketches or models for his sculptures, but this is unlikely and can probably be traced back to his secretiveness over his working processes. He actually created an estimated 28,000 drawings in his lifetime, but only about 600 survive as he burned many of them.[6]

LA PIETÀ

The word 'Pietà' has its roots in the Italian word for 'pity'. Technically it is *a* Pietà, not *the* Pietà, but the fame of Michelangelo's version has surpassed all the others. It would be the first of four that he would create in his lifetime, and the only one he completely finished.[7]

The first thing to note is that the Pietà scene, which depicts the Virgin Mary holding her dying son, is not in the scriptures – an unusual thing for such a prominent work in the most important Basilica. There is a brief mention of Christ being taken down from the cross in one of the gospels (John 19:38–42), but nothing else about what happened in the time between his death and his burial.

The Pietà first developed in Germany (where it is known as a 'Vesperbild') around the 1300s and reached Italy about a century later. Many Pietàs are stiff and unnatural; those by Lorenzetti or Perugino show the body still horizontal, with the arms and legs of Jesus extending beyond the lap, rigid, and

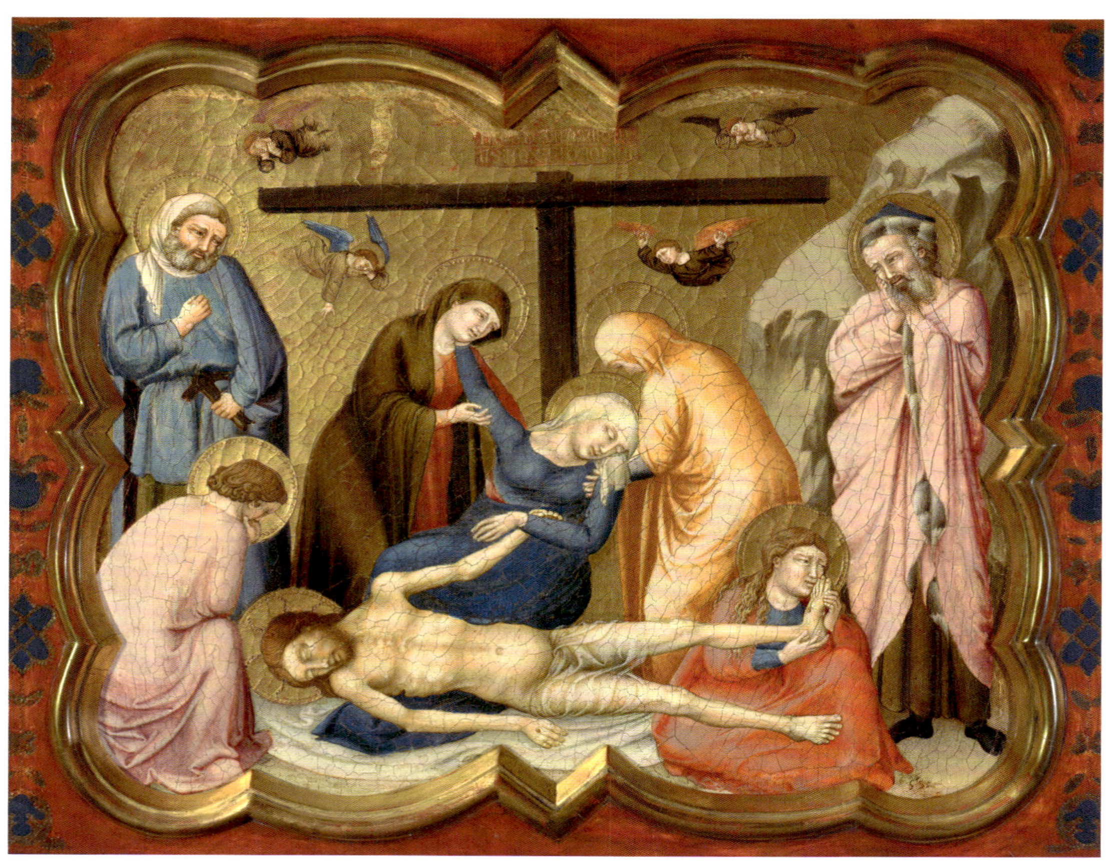

Master of the Fogg Pietà, *The Lamentation over the Dead Christ*, c. 1303.

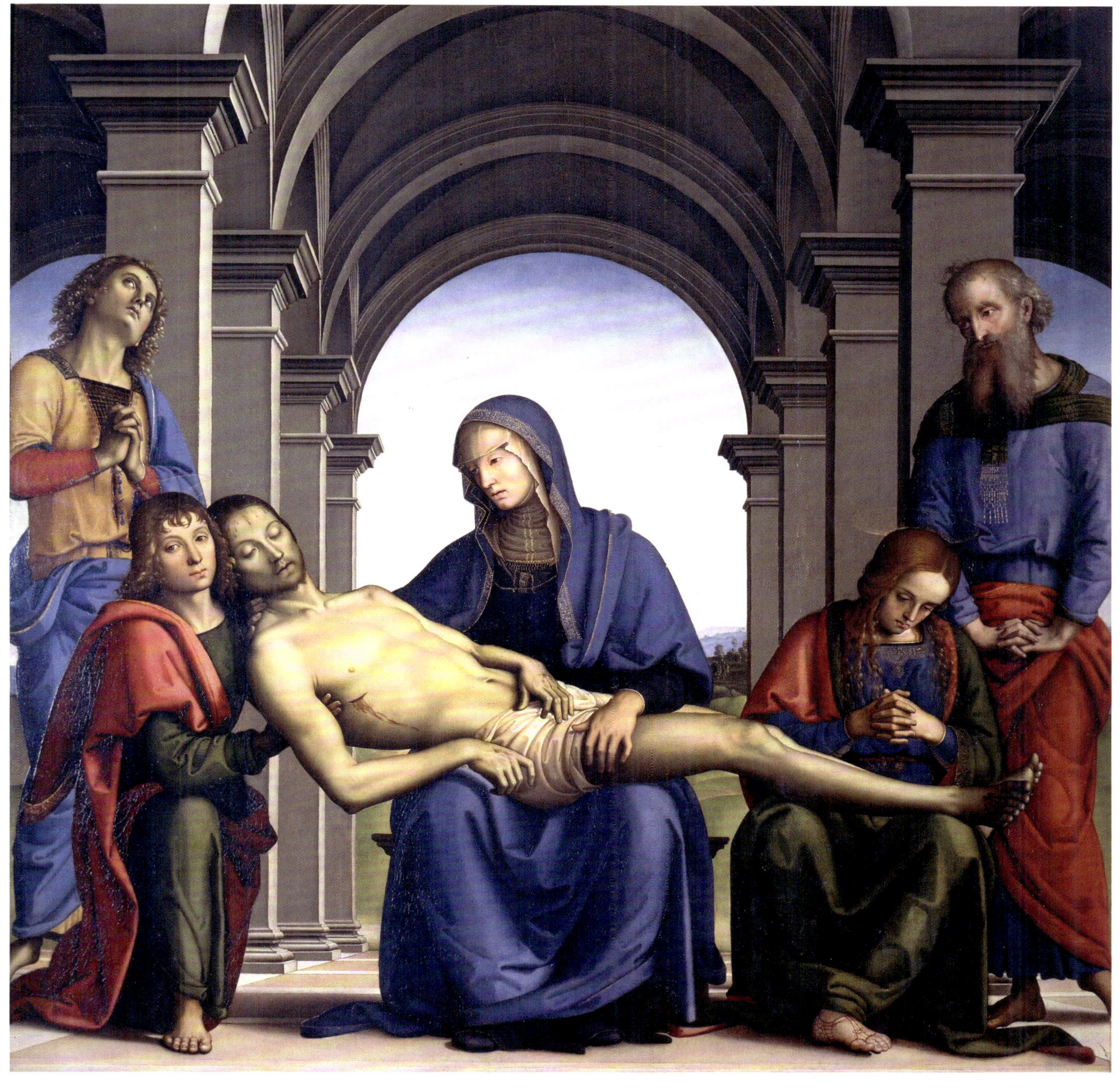

Pietro Perugino, *Pietà*,
c. 1483–93.

     LA PIETÀ

often held by John the Evangelist on the left
and Mary Magdalene on the right.

The Renaissance saw a move away from
images emphasizing Christ's divinity and
immunity from pain, instead focusing on
images of Christ's suffering and Mary's
anguish, designed to encourage believers to
think of themselves and their salvation in
relation to Christ's suffering. As the earlier
Pietàs show, the complexity of the scene –
a delicate woman holding the heavy dead body
of her son – is difficult to balance or make into
a coherent, naturalistic composition, but
through deception, the young Michelangelo
would succeed where those before had failed.

To demonstrate just how harmonious
and poignant this scene could appear,
he would have to create an anatomically
impossible sculpture.

MARY THE MOTHER

Michelangelo's portrayal of the Virgin Mary,
in line with Church doctrine, is not overtly
emotional, yet perfectly captures her humanity
and her maternal instincts. She has a calm
and introspective demeanour, as if she is
contemplating the deep significance of what
has happened – and what will happen. On the
one hand she is aware of her role as the mother
of the Messiah, but on the other she struggles
with the reality of her son's death. The young
artist has captured the nature of the Virgin's
duality perfectly.

In Michelangelo's hands, she is a mother
tenderly holding on to her son and continuing

to care for him, displaying the calm composure
characteristic of mothers comforting their
children in times of distress. The poignant
detail of Christ's right hand delicately gripping
Mary's robe is heartbreaking, and further
underscores the deep bond between mother
and child.

By isolating Mary and Christ alone,
Michelangelo, whose own mother passed away
when he was six, created a sculpture that gives
prominence to Mary holding her son for the last
time, but also unites mother and son for eternity.

A LITURGICAL MASTERPIECE

The first thing we notice is Mary's age. She is
shown as a teenage girl, rather than the mother
of a man in his thirties – an unusual choice, but
not unheard of. Michelangelo was criticized
for this at the time,[8] but as he told his second

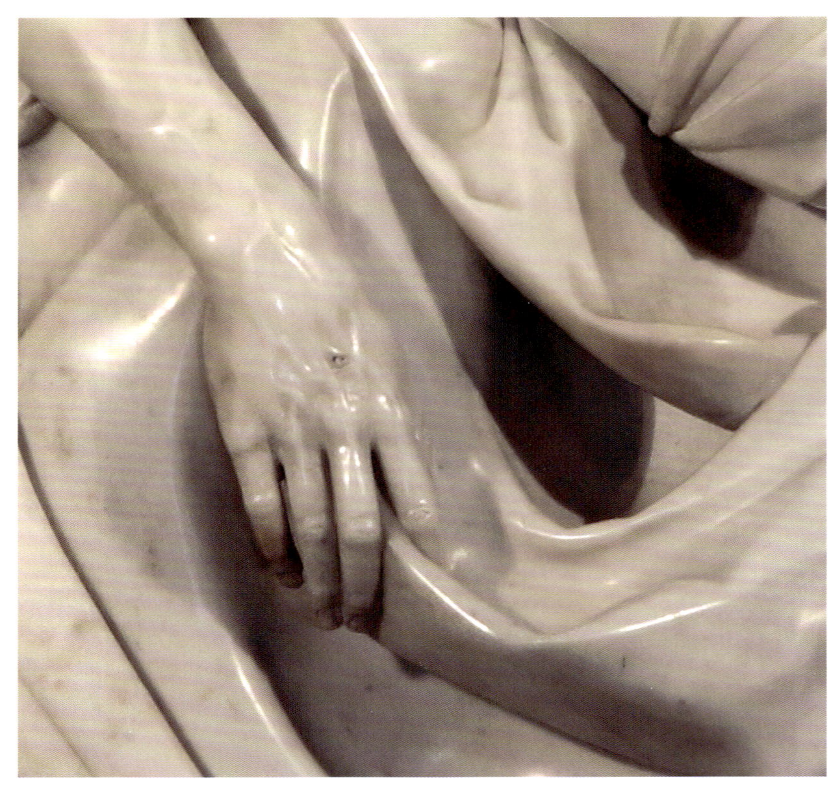

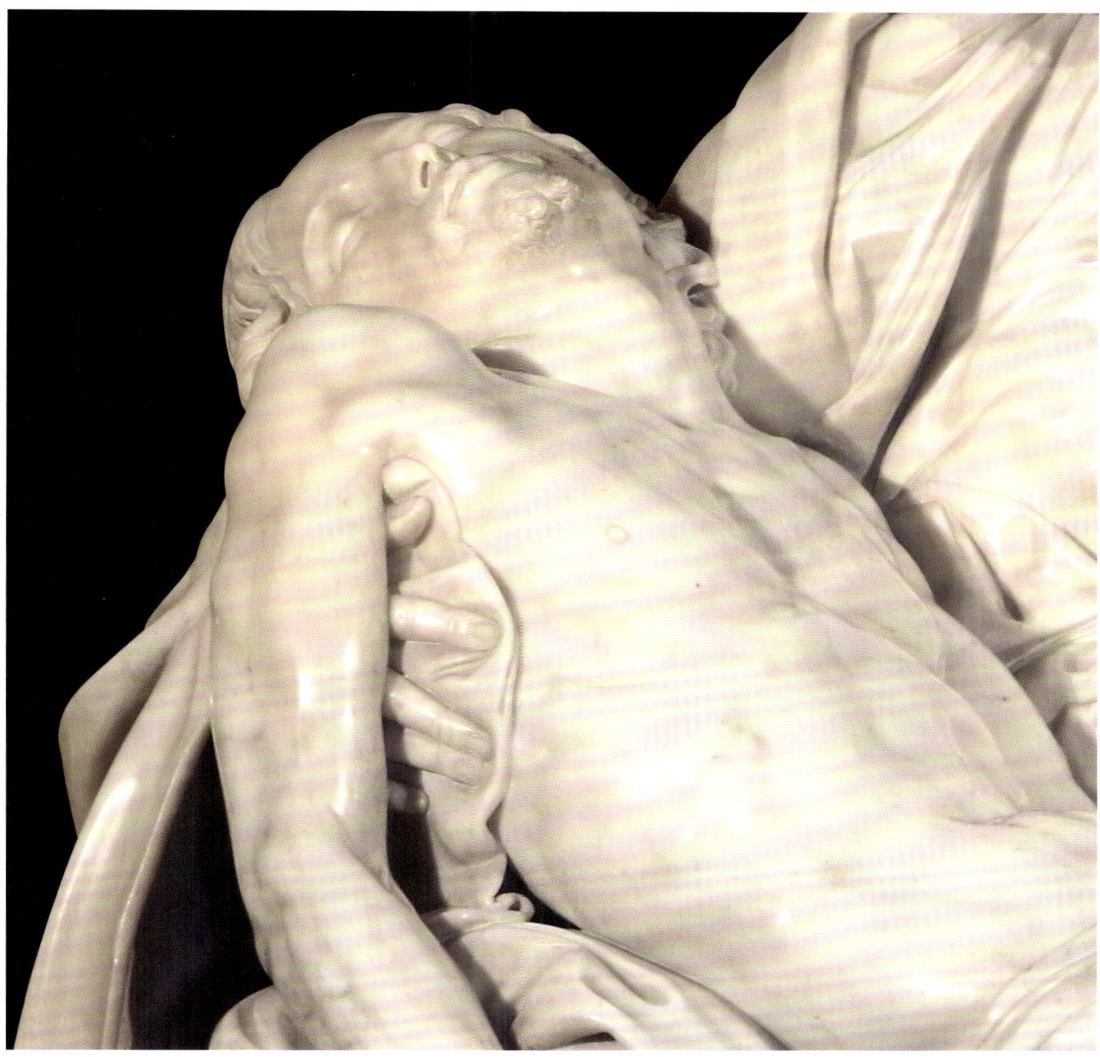

biographer, Ascanio Condivi, her youth was a sign of her uncorrupted purity.[9]

This sculpture should be understood as a liturgical creation, crafted by a profoundly religious artist for a precise location within the chapel. After the cardinal's death, daily masses were held in front of *La Pietà*, during which the priest would distribute the Eucharist to the congregation. In this context, Michelangelo's Virgin Mary takes on greater meaning, appearing as if she is presenting her dead son to the faithful, creating a profound link between worshippers and the divine, bridging the physical and the metaphysical.

Historical evidence indicates it would likely have been illuminated from above through a window, and in dim lighting the white marble would have glowed.[10]

Michelangelo shows the Virgin Mary holding the body of Jesus with ease, yet her pose is far from natural, as she supports the weight of an adult man with a single hand.

The Renaissance saw a move away from works that emphasize Christ's divinity and immunity from pain

There is no direct flesh-on-flesh contact between Mary and Jesus, which aligns with the symbolic and liturgical themes of the sculpture, reinforcing the spiritual separation between the human and the divine.

The proportions are incorrect – an obvious detail, once you notice it. If Mary stood up she would tower over her son; her body is significantly larger, especially her lap, but her billowing clothes hide her anatomy behind folds and crevices. Likewise, her cascading robes hide the fact that she has her legs spread wide to support his body, something that would have been seen as not only ungainly but unsaintly.

The mass of cloth gives the work an intense realism, expertly sculpted, but from the hood of her cloak to the voluminous layers of drapery pooling around her feet, it is designed simply to cover the necessary inconsistencies of her proportions.

The triangular composition is a hallmark of Renaissance art. At the apex of *La Pietà* is the crown of the Virgin Mary's head, and then her robes cascade down to envelop Christ's body like a shroud, forming the triangle. The diagonal lines of the hem of her robes mirror the angle of his lifeless arm, drawing the viewer's eye through the sculpture in a natural, contemplative flow. This creates an overall sense of heaviness, both metaphorically – representing the weight of humanity's sins – and physically, through the palpable mass of Christ's body.

For Christ himself, we can see Michelangelo's expertise in anatomy at work: the lifeless but serene face, the lack of tension in the leg muscles, the loose flesh of the right arm, drained of life. It is a peaceful acceptance of his sacrifice. He is seemingly untouched by the Crucifixion, and his passion wounds, while visible, are not graphic, avoiding the dramatic bloodshed often seen in Gothic or later Baroque depictions. This restraint shifts the focus from physical suffering to spiritual transcendence.

A MOMENT OF HUMAN EXPERIENCE

The Pietà was a subject that Michelangelo would look to throughout his long career. He would make three further versions (although one, the *Palestrina Pietà* is disputed), and he was working on the *Rondanini Pietà* (1552–64) just days before he died, at the age of eighty-eight.

It was his first, however, that catapulted him to the forefront of the great Renaissance artists, a work that masterfully combines technical brilliance with deep emotional and spiritual resonance. A work that seems almost uncanny for a twenty-four-year-old.

The young Michelangelo turned a religious subject into a moment of human experience: the sorrow of a mother mourning her son. The intimate portrayal of Mary cradling the body of Christ conveys a deeply personal moment of loss, which transcends religious context to resonate with anyone who has experienced grief or love.

It is this universal emotional pull that makes the sculpture timeless.

Michelangelo,
La Pietà, 1499.

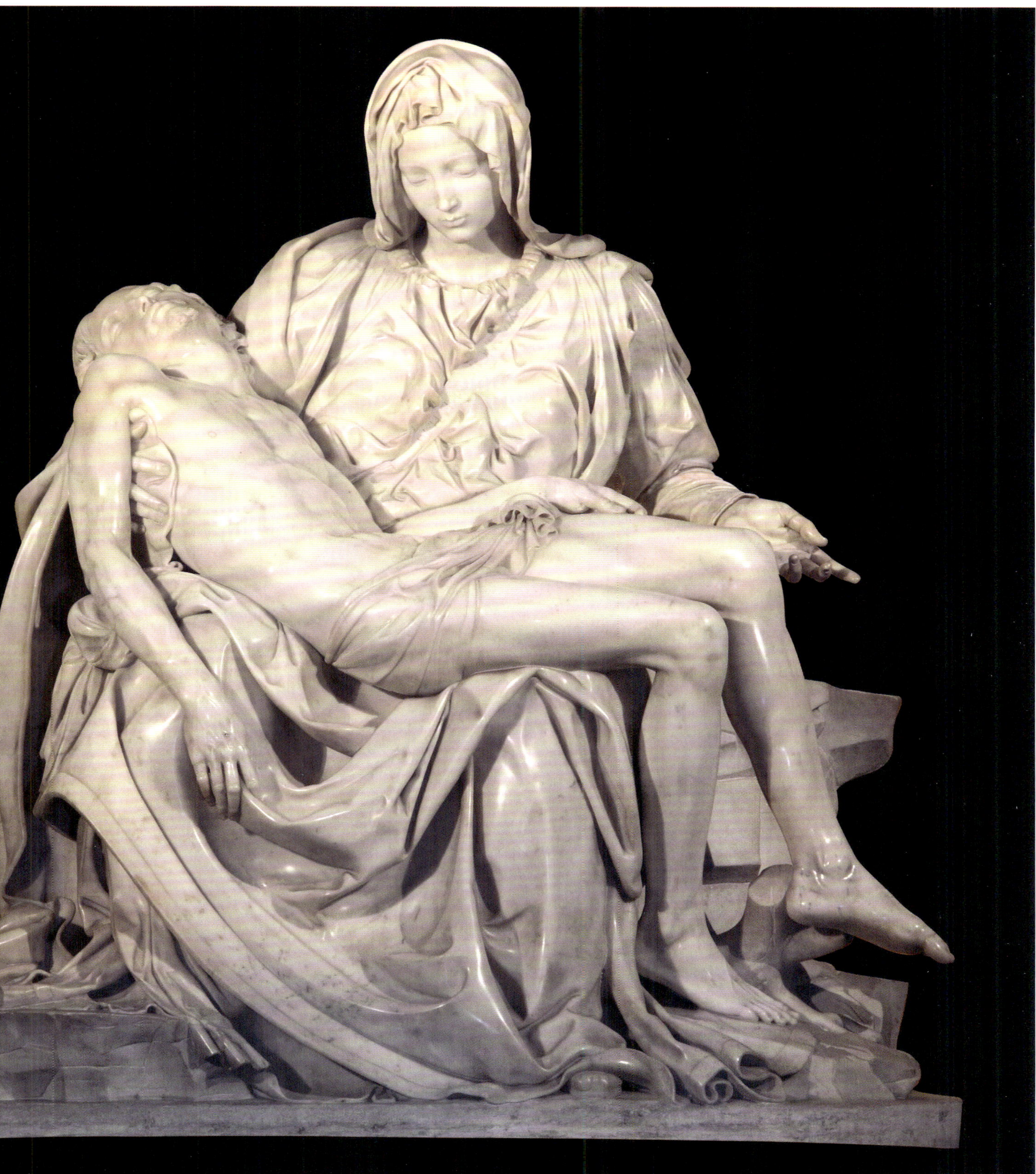

LEONARDO DA VINCI

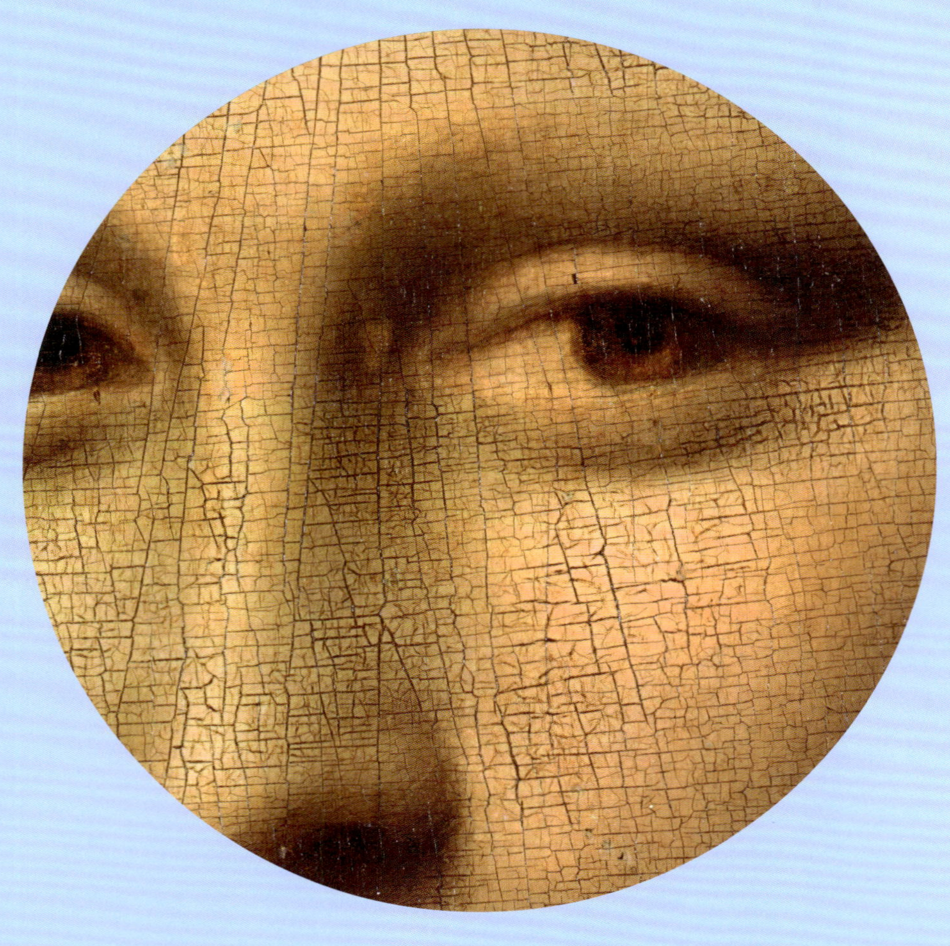

MONA LISA

1503

LOOKING AGAIN

The biggest problem facing the *Mona Lisa* is that she is so familiar. She has been stripped of meaning; her fame and her 'celebrity' status distract from what a masterpiece of science, philosophy, geology, chemistry and art she really is. Let's look again at why a painting created over 500 years ago was so ahead of its time that we are still trying to figure it out.

LISA DEL GIOCONDO

Agostino Vespucci visited Leonardo da Vinci in 1503 and wrote a note in the margin of a book, stating that the artist was 'working on a portrait of Lisa del Giocondo'. Five hundred years later, that note was discovered in the Heidelberg University Library.[1]

A year before the portrait was made, Leonardo was appointed engineer to the military commander Cesare Borgia,[2] and two years later he was invited to Rome to work for Pope Julius II. He was an artist at the height of his powers, and this small commission was unlikely to be the top of his priorities. But his father, Ser Piero da Vinci, was lawyer to Lisa's husband, Francesco del Giocondo, so perhaps it was pressure from Ser Piero that convinced Leonardo to take on the commission.[3] But it is also possible that he agreed to paint her because he wanted to try out new ideas, without fear of interference from popes or nobles.

We can't be sure how much of a good likeness it is, but in the 1500s, owning a

painting – or better yet, commissioning a painting – was a status symbol that only the very wealthy could afford. As we saw with *The Arnolfini Portrait* (see Chapter Two), having a painting on your wall by the most celebrated and in-demand artist of the day was an easy way to flaunt your wealth, expensive clothing and jewellery. And yet, Mona Lisa is stripped of all the usual high-status symbols (we know that Lisa owned a large amount of jewellery, for example, which is not shown in the painting[4]). Her clothes are nothing special; instead of the usual flamboyant, expensive outfits we see in commissioned portraits, her dark dress and robe are unusually simple for a wealthy woman. Her hair, too, is plain and unadorned, so it's quite possible that Leonardo was looking to avoid any 'anchors' that would interrupt the flow of our view as we scan the image.

Yet despite being such a 'simple' painting, it was endlessly copied.

COPIES

The word 'copy' has a negative connotation in art, but it's how Leonardo, Raphael, Michelangelo and other great artists learnt: they copied masters and then developed their own styles.

Leonardo had a team of about six assistants and apprentices, and copies of the *Mona Lisa* produced by his own studio are a

Leonardo da Vinci,
Mona Lisa (detail),
1503.

Digitally overlaid
image of the *Mona Lisa*
at Le Louvre and the
'Prado' *Mona Lisa*,
1507–16.

good source of information on how the original portrait looked in 1503.

There are several copies worldwide, such as the Vernon *Mona Lisa* and the Isleworth *Mona Lisa*, but perhaps the most important is the 'Prado' *Mona Lisa*, now in the Museo Nacionale del Prado. It was first mentioned in 1666, catalogued as an 'anonymous copy' in the Spanish Royal Collection and considered unimportant. In recent years, however, its importance has grown for *Mona Lisa* scholars, as it is now thought to have been created by an apprentice of Leonardo's at the same time as he painted the *Mona Lisa*.[5] Scans show that as Leonardo made changes to his painting, the pupil made the same changes to this copy, so the logical conclusion is that the 'Prado' *Mona Lisa* was painted by an apprentice working side by side with Leonardo, using the same pigments and making the same adjustments.

The excellent state of conservation of the copy gives us unique insights into how the original painting was structured. If we take the copy and overlay it with Leonardo's original, we get some idea of what the *Mona Lisa* might have looked like in its early iterations. Now we see the rosy lips described by Vasari in 1550, and the thin eyebrows and eyelashes.

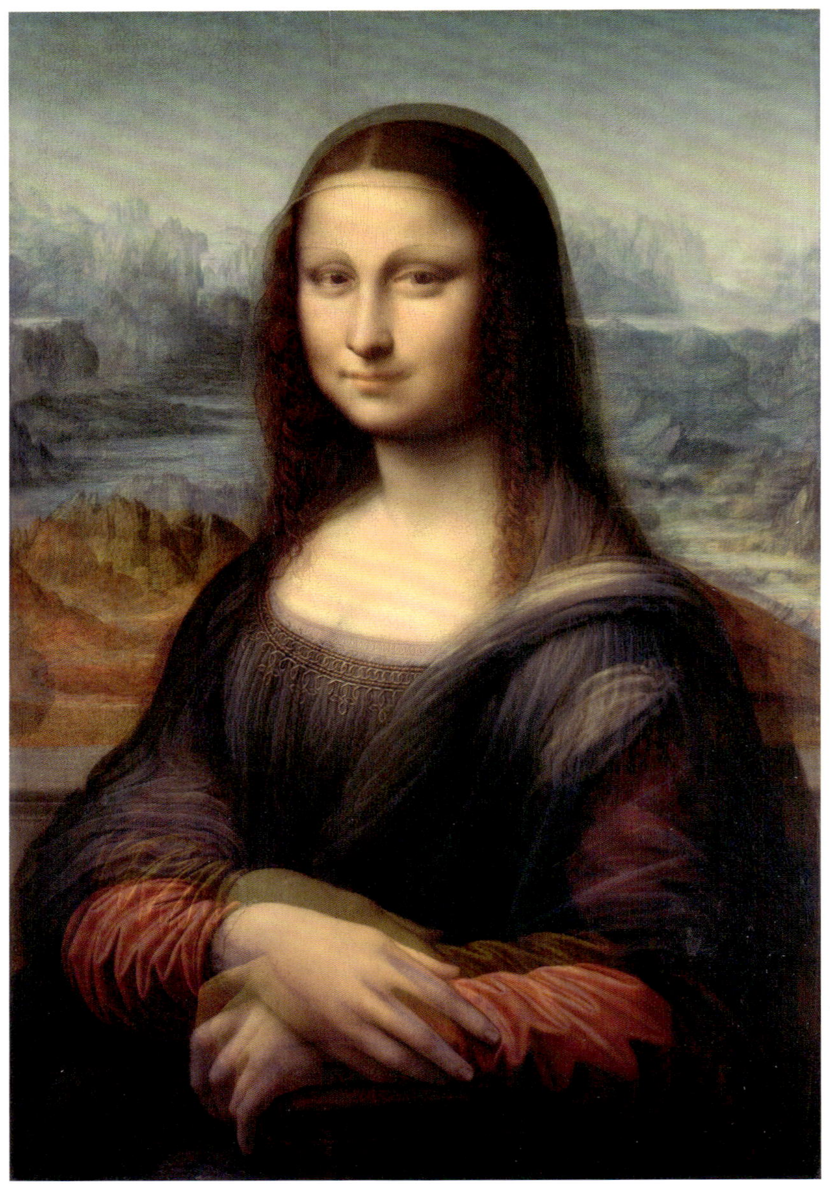

LEONARDO DA VINCI

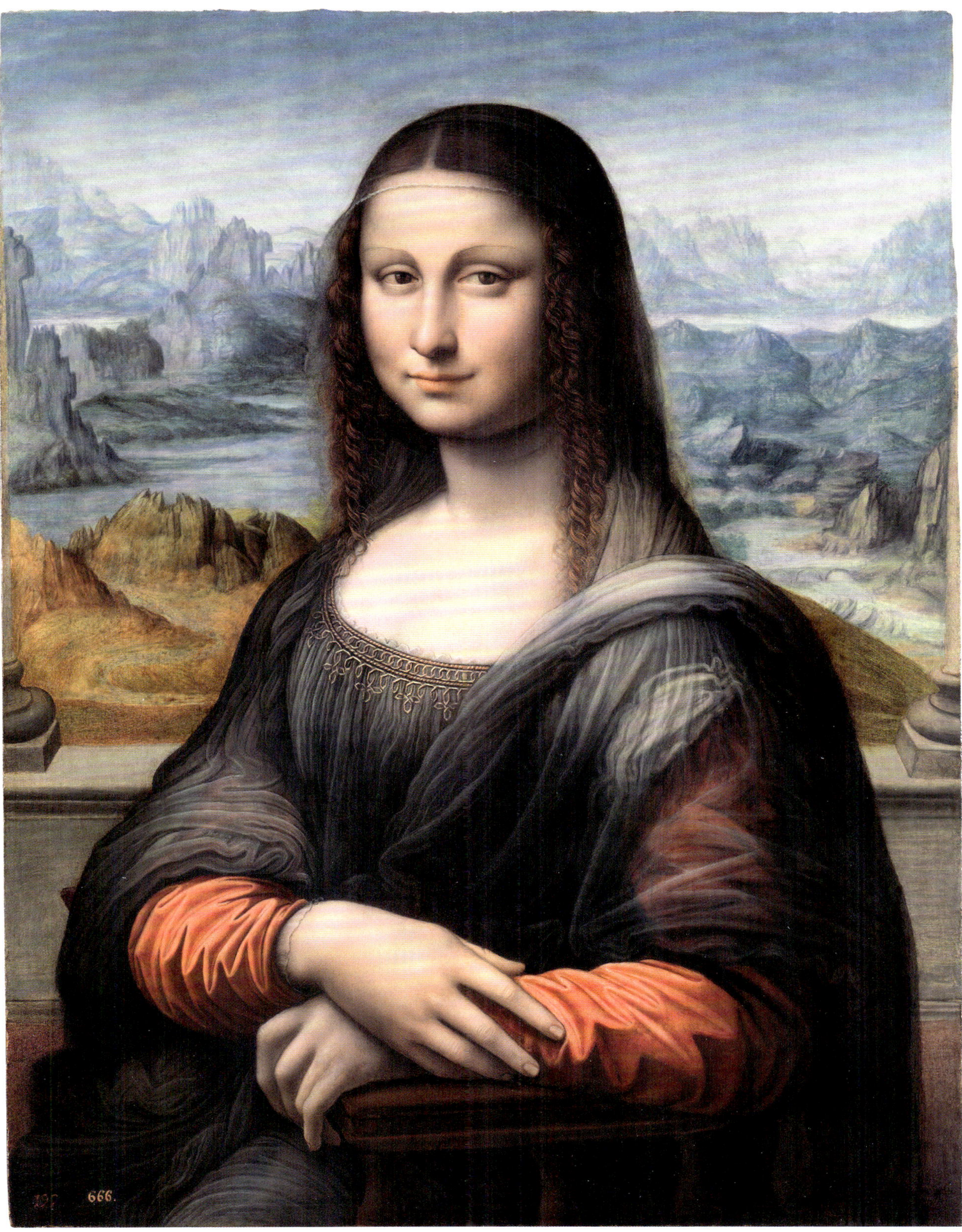

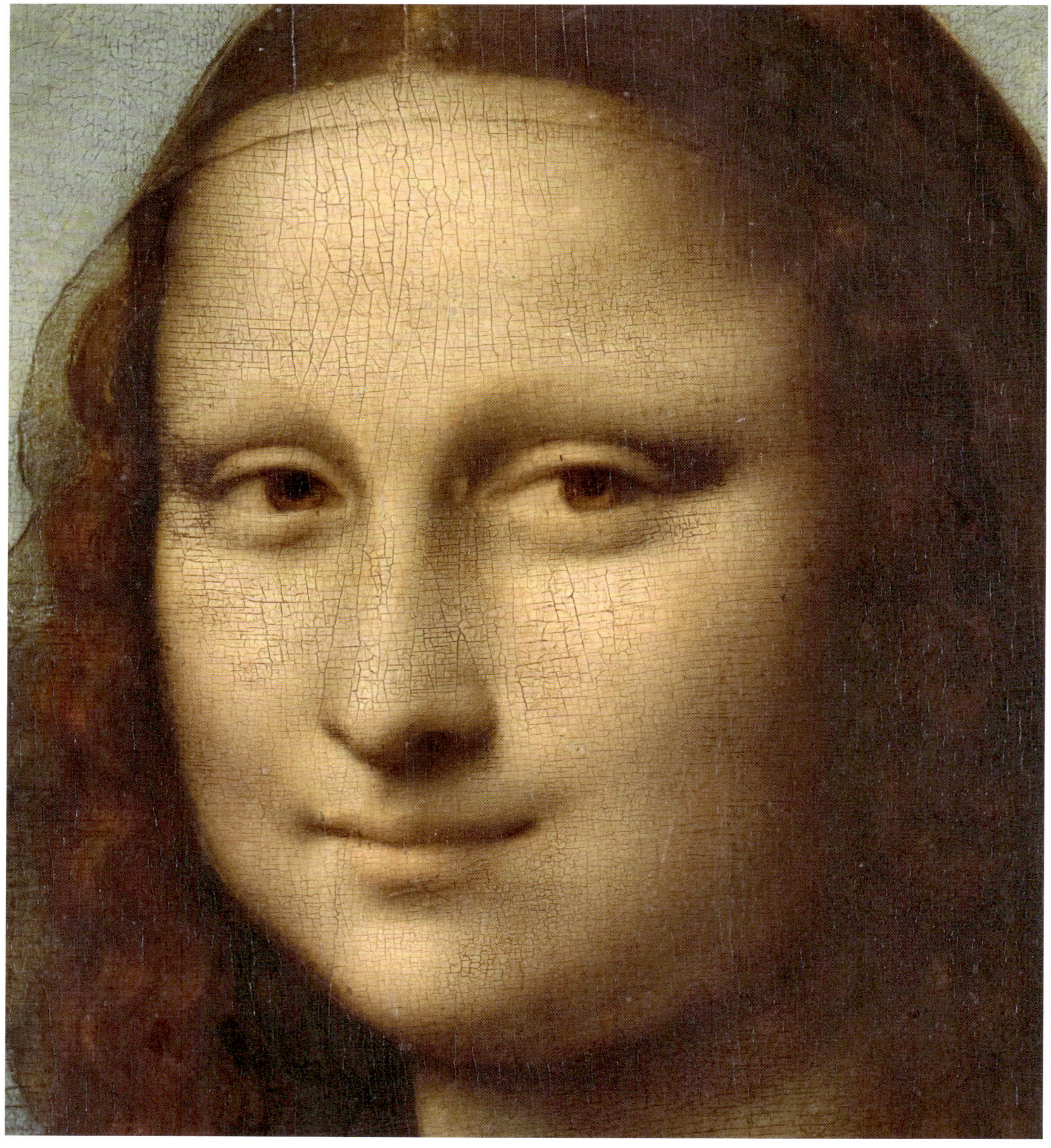

LEONARDO DA VINCI

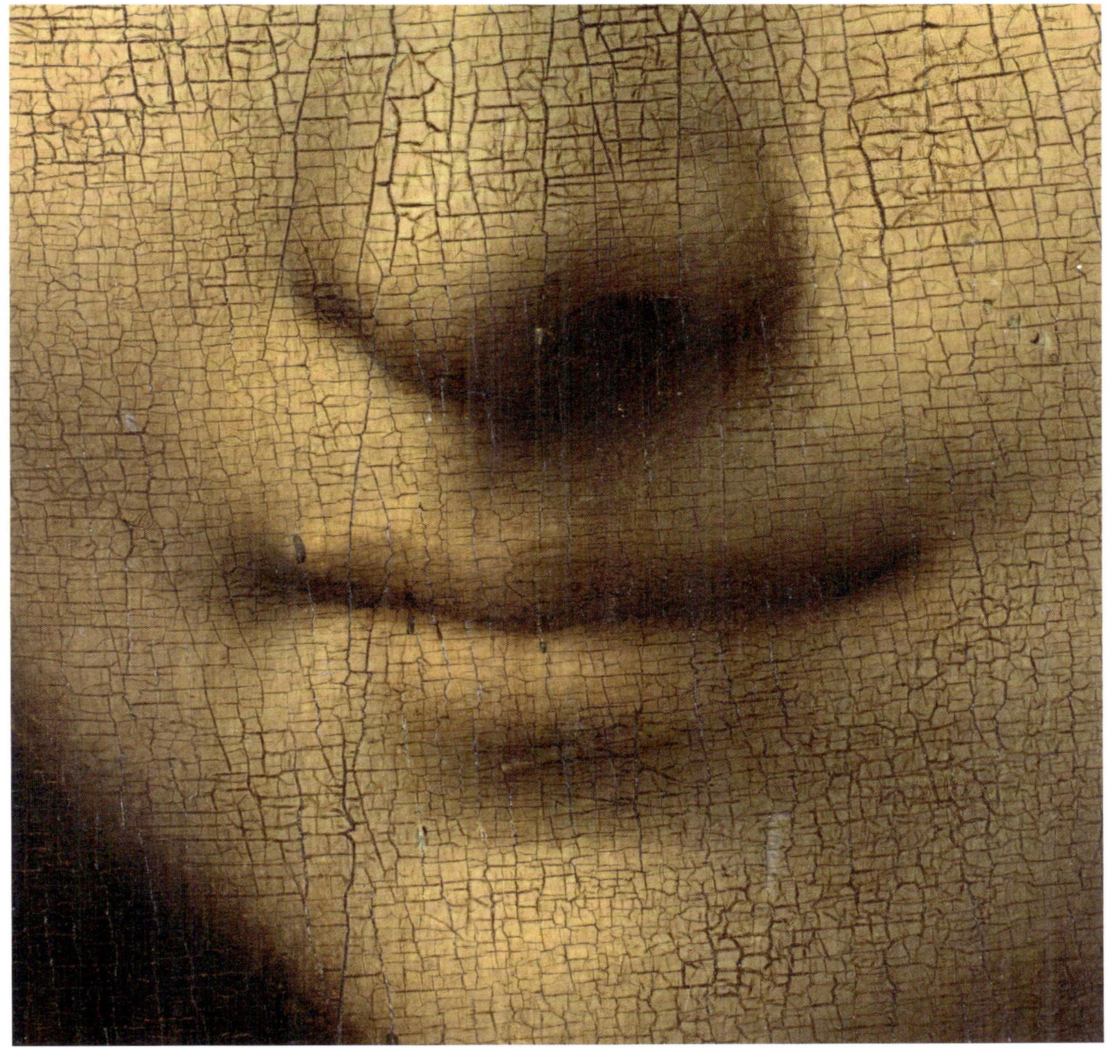

TECHNIQUES

Leonardo created a sense of depth by using semi-transparent glazes: a small amount of pigment mixed with oil, possibly linseed (which accounts for the yellowing). It would have been more like a wash, applied layer by layer, possibly as many as thirty different layers, applied so thinly that they total only 40 micrometres,[6] about the width of a human hair.

He used an undercoat of lead white rather than chalk and pigment. Lead white was used extensively by Renaissance artists as it had an exceptional opacity, it mixed well with oil, and it gave a very particular luminosity, reflecting light back through his thin washes of paint.

He also used tiny, uneven and almost invisible brushstrokes, applied over months (or in the *Mona Lisa*'s case, years) with varying amounts of pigments – a technique which ensures that, on a microscopic level, the marks refract the light in unique ways, in essence lighting Mona Lisa from within.

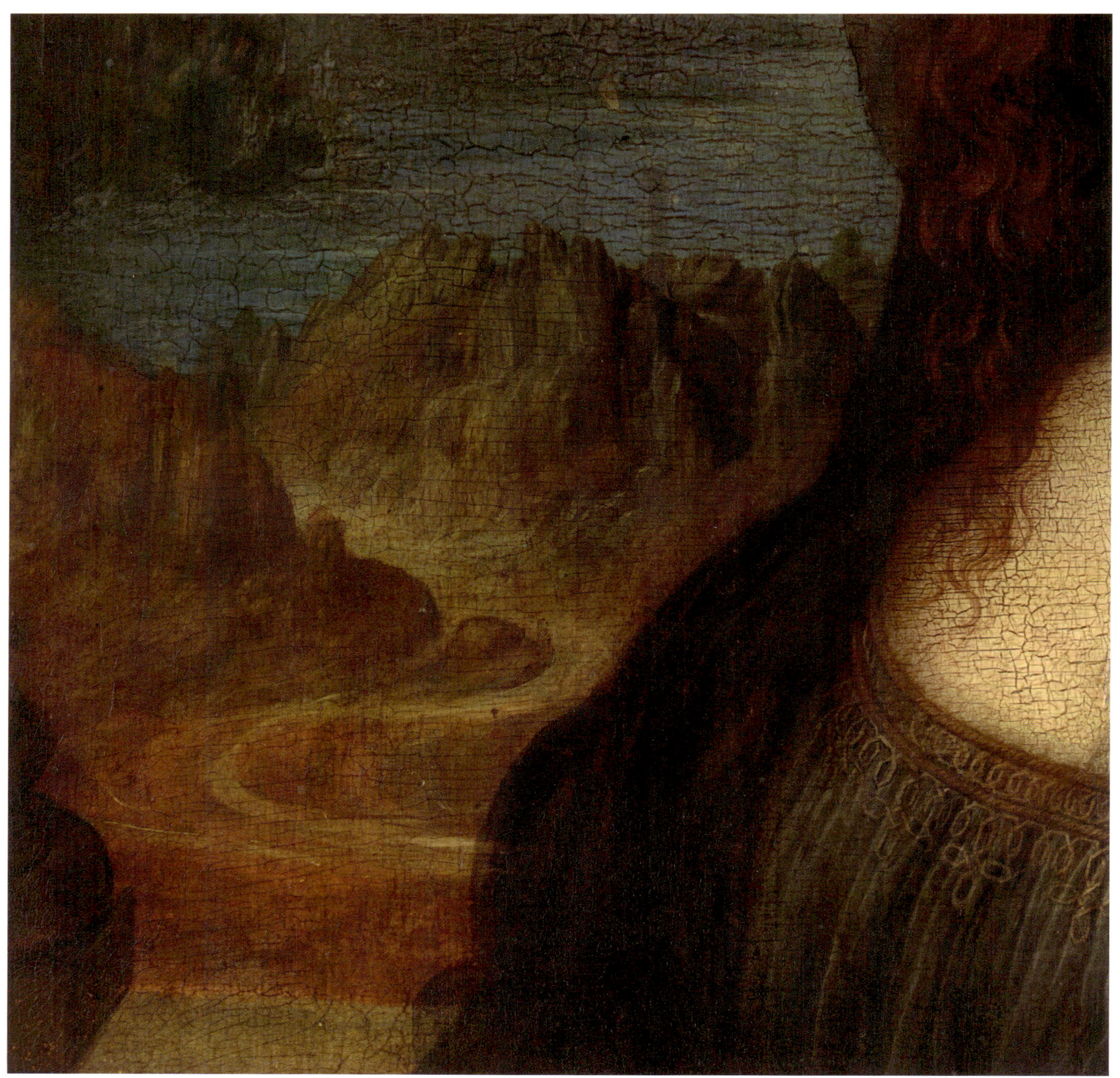

LEONARDO DA VINCI

For her flesh tones, he mixed a green-grey hue as a base, known as the *verdaccio* technique, common in the Renaissance and particularly effective when looking to produce lifelike portraits. (If you look at the hands of a pale person, there is a surprising amount of green showing through the skin!)

Another technique Leonardo used throughout his works was *chiaroscuro*, a balance of deep, contrasting shades of light and dark to create the illusion of three-dimensional forms. He was one of the first artists to use a mix of iron and manganese to create burnt umber for the shadows.[7]

Along with this, Leonardo used *sfumato*, a method he is credited with inventing. Translating as 'smoky', it is a blending technique for softening the transition between colours to make sure there are no sharp unnatural lines, made possible by his use of translucent layers. There are no hard edges anywhere on the *Mona Lisa*, unlike the works of Raphael, Botticelli and others at the time, who used strong, delineated outlines.

LOVE OF SCIENCE

Leonardo's scientific knowledge of light refraction and science, combined with his blending techniques, means that Mona Lisa shifts in an optical illusion. Through his craft, we are able to take in the painting in the same way our eyes reproduce reality. On different planes, with different lighting and different focuses.

Leonardo used a pyramid composition, introduced during the Renaissance to organize pictorial elements and create an illusion of space – an important change from paintings of the 15th century. The geometric structure provides stability, but more importantly, it provides a clear central focus and directs your gaze. In Mona Lisa's case, it is pulling us into her face.

Through his craft, we are able to take in the painting in the same way our eyes reproduce reality

He had already pioneered the use of the three-quarter-length pose in earlier paintings, but it is particularly effective in the *Mona Lisa*. Today we look at Mona Lisa's pose and it seems normal, but in its day it was considered ground-breaking. Previously subjects of portraiture tended to look stiff and aristocratic, but Mona Lisa is relaxed; her hands rest gently on the arm of her chair as she turns towards us, almost as if captured in a snapshot. She also seems rather content and self-assured, which was more typical of portrayals of men.

Standard Renaissance portraits of women were in profile, but Mona Lisa's pose means we are looking directly into her eyes, and she is looking back. Women in paintings just didn't do that; they didn't look boldly and directly at the viewer, and they certainly didn't smile.

She sits in front of a complicated background that scholars have now realized (after centuries of searching) existed only in Leonardo's imagination. Portraits painted in this period usually had both the subject and the background in sharp focus, but the background of the *Mona Lisa* was created using the illusion of depth, or recession. Its hyper-realism is thanks to his radical use of aerial perspective – another technique that he is credited with inventing. Leonardo subtly reduced the amount of pigment on his brush and used less detailed outlines on scenery receding into the distance, creating a 'hazy' – or to modern eyes, photographic – effect.

Everything in the painting is informed by Leonardo's interest in, and love of, science:

his studies of the sky and the elements; the light and how it refracts; even the background features sedimentary layers that he studied and sketched in the Apennines, and his pioneering studies of hydrodynamics inform the weight volume and direction of the curls of Mona Lisa's hair.

Leonardo was fixated on the mechanisms behind how a smile formed. By the time of Leonardo, human dissection was no longer completely forbidden by the Church, and as the Renaissance progressed, the practice became more common.[8] He spent many nights in the morgue dissecting cadavers and sketching muscles, sinews and nerves. He traced the origins of every nerve controlling each facial muscle – a particularly difficult feat, even for surgeons today.

Leonardo studied the pioneering 11th-century Islamic physicist Ibn al-Haytham, who wrote theories on the psychology of visual perception.[9] He knew from al-Haytham's optical analysis that light rays do not come to a single point in the eye but instead hit the whole area of the retina, and he used this information to experiment, creating works that shift as light moves across their surfaces.

When we look at a person's face, we spend most of our time focused on the other person's eyes, using detail-focused central vision, while our less detail-orientated peripheral vision focuses on the mouth, and Leonardo applied this to the *Mona Lisa*. Our gaze goes first to her eyes, before scanning back and forth between her eyes and her lips. As our peripheral vision picks up on the soft edges and the dynamics of light and dark, created with *sfumato* and *chiaroscuro*, her expression changes.[10] This is not your imagination; it is to do with how we see, not how we think. By looking into the eyes of Mona Lisa, we each develop our own unique relationship with her.

Some people are disappointed when they see the *Mona Lisa* for the first time, and there's a good reason for that. The one thing we need when it comes to a painting with so much weight, so much beauty and so much complexity is time. And time is exactly what we don't have. *Mona Lisa* is not only the most famous painting in the world, she is also the busiest.

But if we *could* stop for a while, and ignore the crowds, if we could forget she is 'famous', if we could linger just a tad longer on her enigmatic smile, we would realize that in an age when we are bombarded with images, it is more important than ever to stop… and look again.

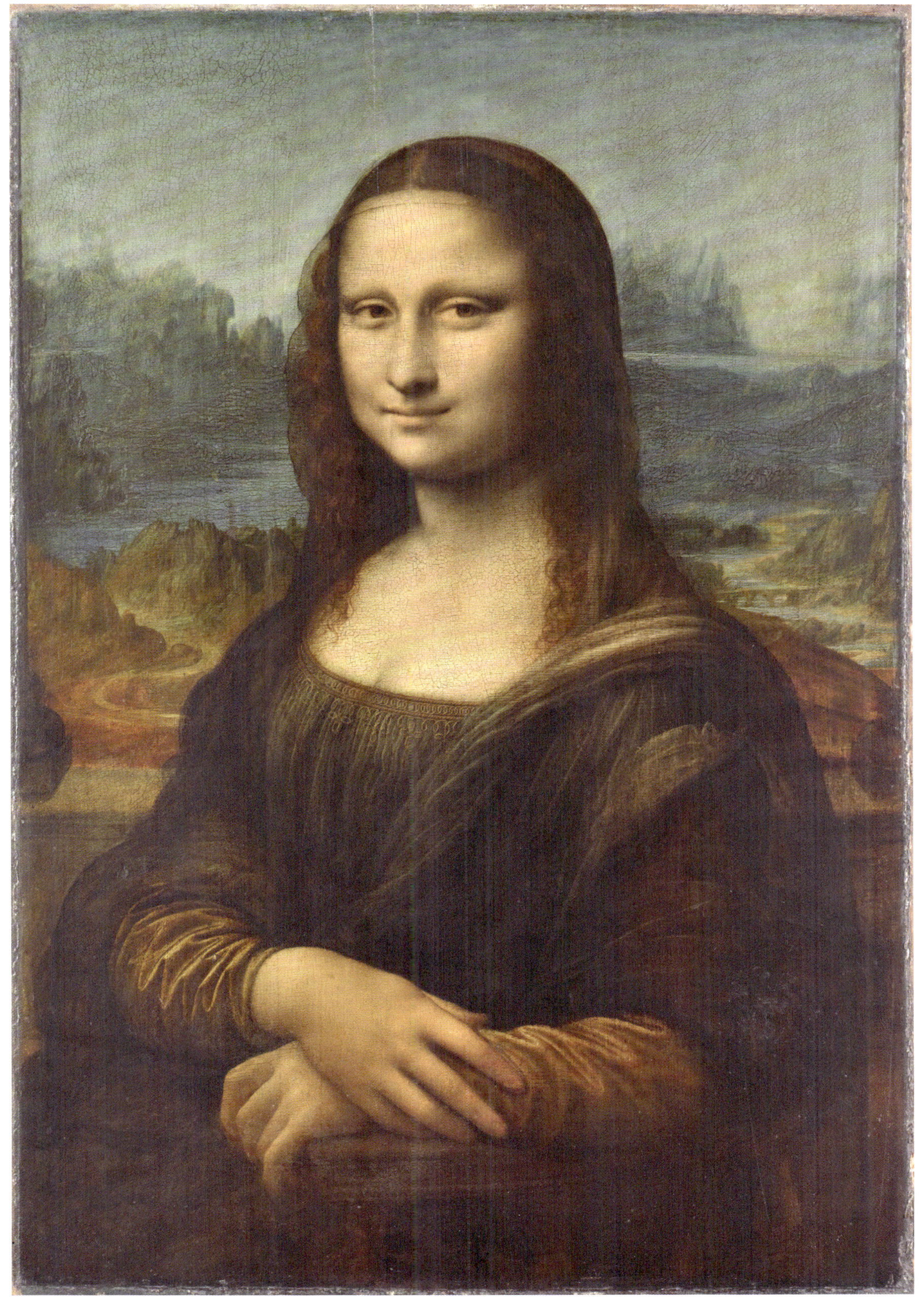

ARTEMISIA GENTILESCHI

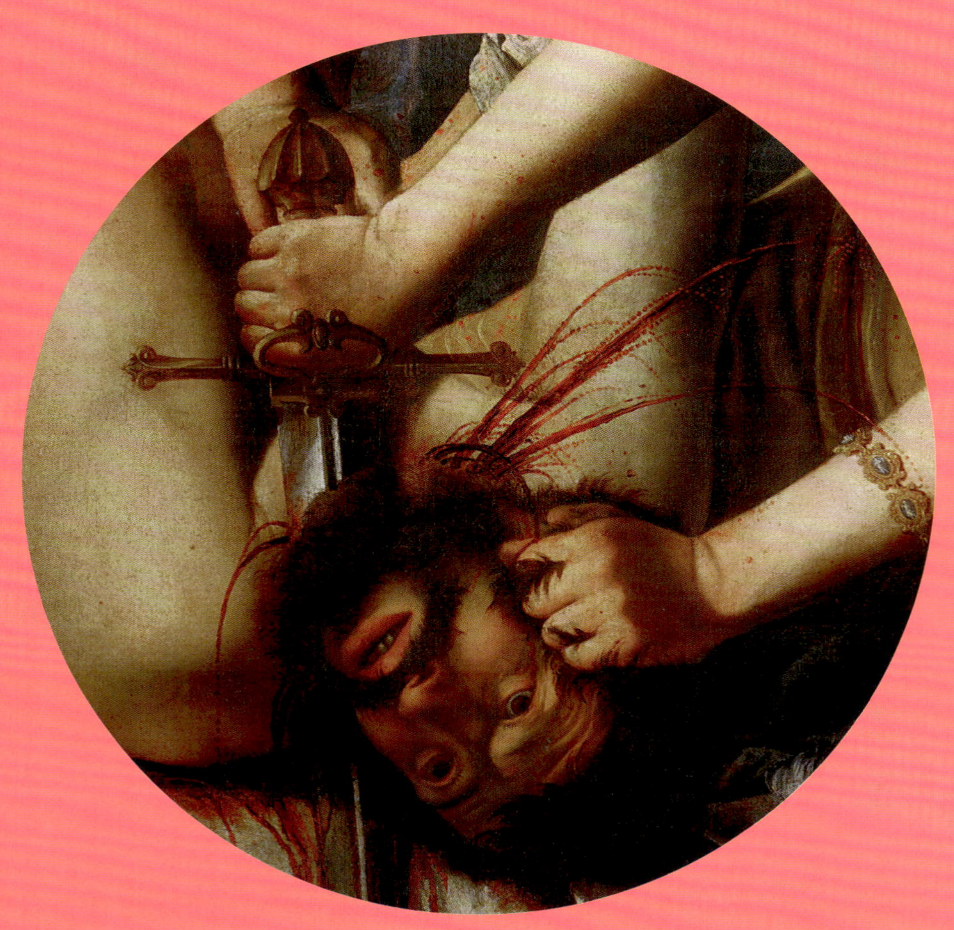

JUDITH BEHEADING HOLOFERNES

1620

BREAKING BARRIERS IN THE BAROQUE AGE

Two well-built women are using their combined strength to hold down a muscular, struggling man. Pushing his face into the bed, one of them hacks into his throat as blood cascades from the wound, soaking the sheets. The victim is still conscious; he knows exactly what is going on, but he is helpless. Despite his screams, the women continue their vicious slaughter.

For 17th-century Florence, this painting was unusually gruesome, but even more unusual was that such a scene was painted by a woman: Artemisia Gentileschi.

FEMALE ARTISTS IN THE 17TH CENTURY

Women were excluded from most cultural and social resources in Italy at this time, and visual artists were almost exclusively male before the 19th century. There were of course exceptions, like Lavinia Fontana (1552–1614), but these were rare.

There were little to no apprenticeships for women, life drawing classes were men only, and women were excluded from membership in the academies. They could generally only access the training expected of an artist through relatives, or if they belonged to a convent.

Artemisia's father, Orazio Gentileschi, was a well-known painter, and he took his daughter on as an apprentice around 1607, when she was fifteen. He had three sons already working with him, but his daughter was extraordinarily talented and soon eclipsed her brothers in skill. While they ground pigments and swept the floor, she began to take on her own commissions.[1]

RAPE AND TRIAL

When she was seventeen, a series of events occurred that often dominates conversations about the painter, skewing how we perceive her work.

Her father employed a friend of his, Agostino Tassi, to teach Artemisia and, during one of his visits to the Gentileschi family home, he raped her. Tassi, an odious man, then promised Artemisia that he would marry her, which she and her father would have seen as a way to 'restore' her honour, a common practice in cases of sexual violence in the 17th century.[2] Tassi was in fact already married, and around nine months after the attack, Artemisia's father publicly accused Tassi of rape and sued him for 'devaluation of his property'.

Next came a very public trial, meticulously recorded, in which she was forced to describe the gruesome attack in detail and was tortured with implements much like thumbscrews to prove she was telling the truth. After seven months a ruling was made in Gentileschi's favour, a verdict which meant that her reputation – and thus her future as an artist – was secure.

Artemisia Gentileschi, *Judith Beheading Holofernes* (detail), 1620.

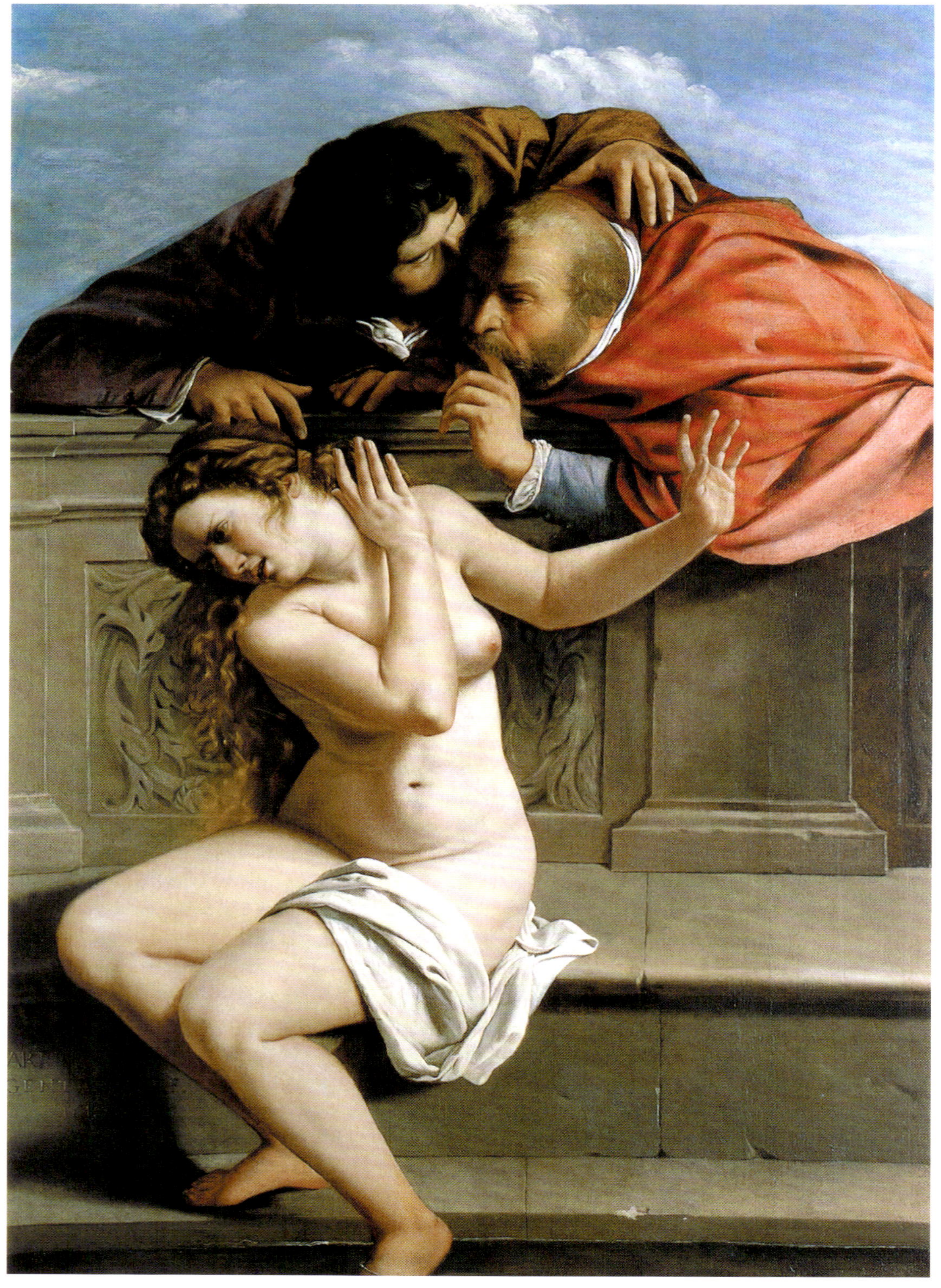

ARTEMISIA GENTILESCHI

The public nature of the trial did however lead to a widely held belief that her *Judith Beheading Holofernes*, which dates to this period, was influenced by her desire for revenge on Tassi.[3]

GIVE ME STRENGTH NOW

The Book of Judith is part of the Old Testament in Catholic Bibles and the Apocrypha in Protestant Bibles. The story is detailed and drawn out, but for the purposes of looking at the painting, we can distil it down to the part where, inspired by God, Judith, a beautiful Jewish widow, bravely seduces and then murders the Assyrian general Holofernes to save her city from invasion.

It is a story that takes many forms, but it is often seen as a symbol of the triumph of virtue over tyranny, a sort of David and Goliath story. It was a popular subject in Renaissance and Baroque art and was seen in Florence to parallel the small city-state – like David – coming up against its larger enemies. It had been painted by many earlier Italian artists, including Gentileschi's female precedent Lavinia Fontana, Andrea Mantegna, Botticelli, and her father (a work on which she almost certainly assisted[4]).

Such artists chose to show a more serene and idealized Judith, however, a heroine blessed by God, focusing less on violence and more on divine intervention and moral righteousness. They also portrayed the scene *after* the beheading of Holofernes, with Judith either in triumph or discreetly stuffing the severed head into a sack.

But by the end of the 16th century, with the arrival of the Baroque, the portrayal of the story had become much more dramatic and violent. Artists like Caravaggio had a different (and more visceral) take, often depicting Holofernes mid-beheading, while still alive.

JUDITH AND HOLOFERNES

Gentileschi created her first version of *Judith Beheading Holofernes* around 1612, producing an almost identical copy in 1620 (copies of well-known paintings were often ordered by collectors), although both dates are disputed. In around 1615 she painted *Judith and her Maidservant*, which depicts the moment after Judith has killed Holofernes and her servant Abra has placed his head in her basket. Holofernes' sword (which she used to kill him) rests heavily on her shoulder. Then in around 1623 she painted another version, also called *Judith and her Maidservant* and also post-beheading. Her periodic return to this subject suggests she felt a deep affinity with the biblical heroine.

As she was a follower of Caravaggio, it is useful to compare his depiction of the story (p. 73) with her 1620 version.

They are both classic Baroque paintings in their use of dramatic movements, stark contrasts of light and shadow, exaggerated expressions and intense, theatrical gestures, as well as in their violence.

However, Gentileschi's painting is notably more dynamic. She brings the figures closer together and pushes the action right into the foreground, creating a sense that the figures are tumbling out of the canvas, and the head of the very much awake Holofernes is about to flop into our lap, making us not only witnesses to the murder, but also accomplices. The tight composition of Gentileschi's work amplifies the intensity, making it feel both confrontational and suffocating.

In Caravaggio's version, Judith is an unconvincing assassin, a squeamish, youthful

Artemisia Gentileschi, *Susanna and the Elders*, 1610.

It is a story that takes many forms, but it is often seen as a symbol of the triumph of virtue over tyranny

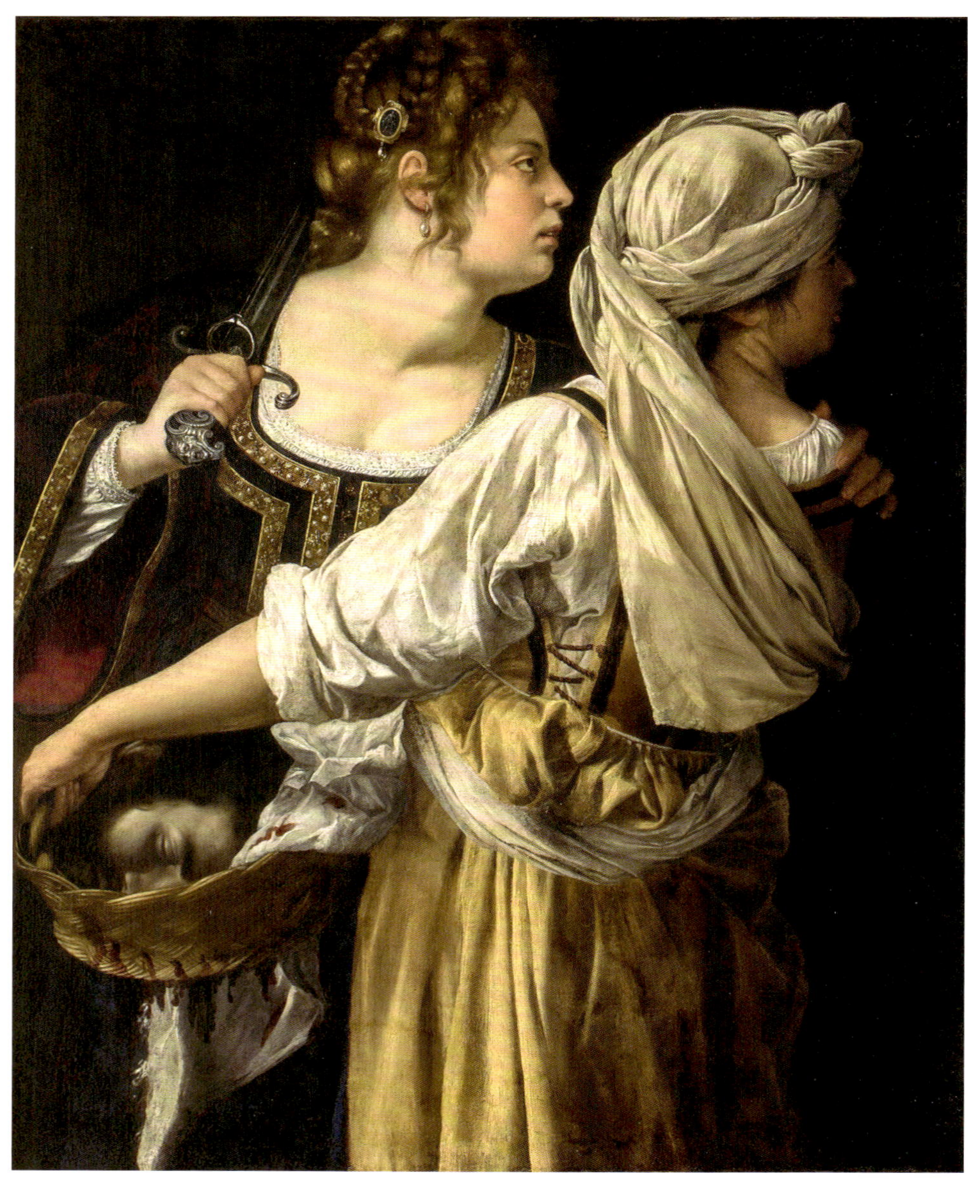

ARTEMISIA GENTILESCHI

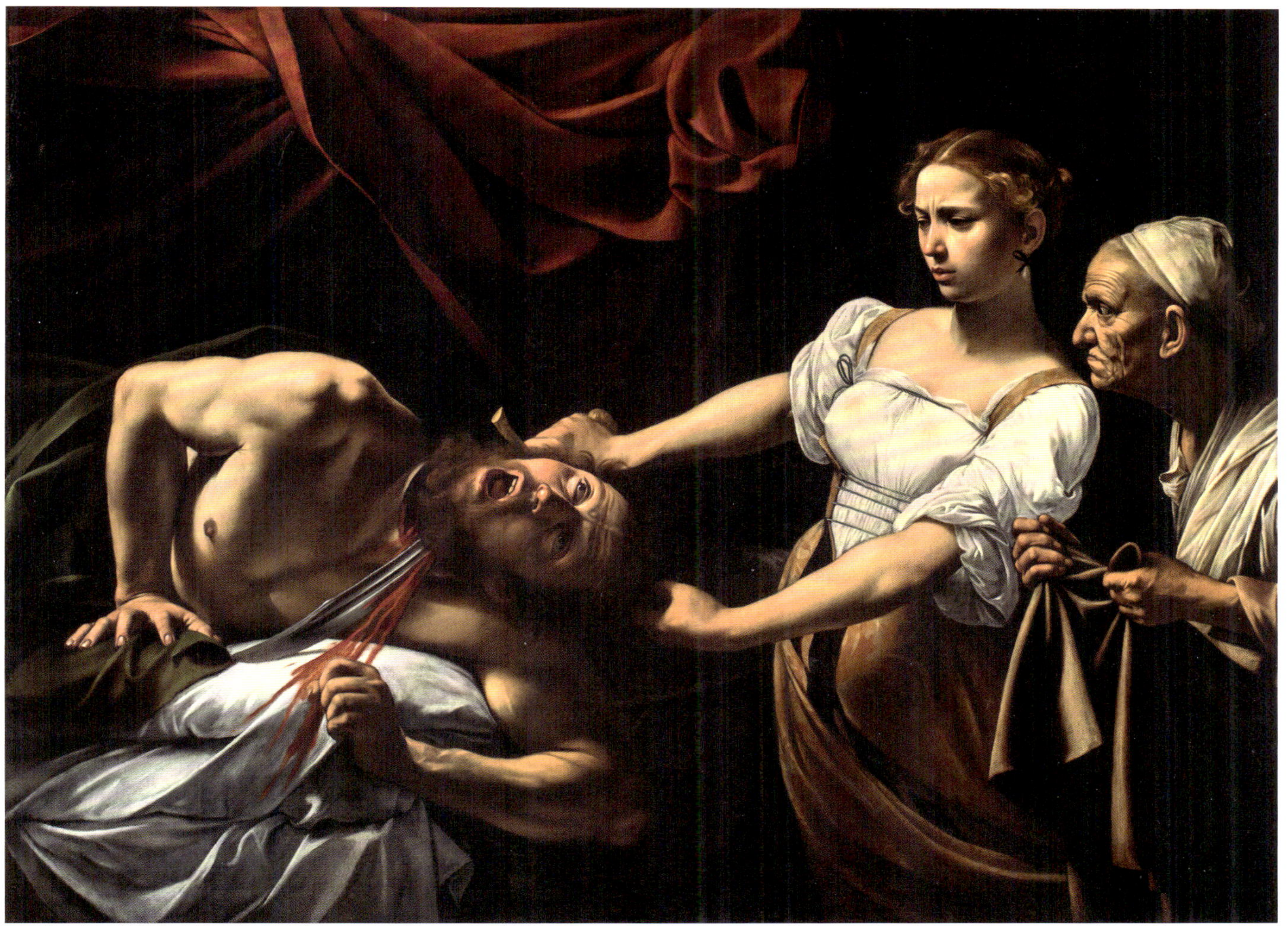

blonde who appears to be almost disgusted by the act of beheading Holofernes. In contrast, Gentileschi portrays Judith as strong and resolute; she is muscular (as she often portrayed her women) and fully engaged in the gruesome task. Gentileschi really understood that it would have been tough work for a woman to decapitate someone of Holofernes' size, even with God's help.

Gentileschi also highlights an aspect of the biblical narrative that male artists before her had not fully explored. In the apocryphal account the maidservant, Abra, keeps watch outside the tent while Judith completes the task; Gentileschi and Caravaggio, however, place her in the room alongside Judith.

But while Caravaggio's Abra is an old crone, as in the Bible, passively waiting nearby with a sack for the severed head, in Gentileschi's interpretation, the maid, now of a similar age to Judith, becomes an active participant in the execution. The two women are portrayed as equals, working together with determination and precision. Both are

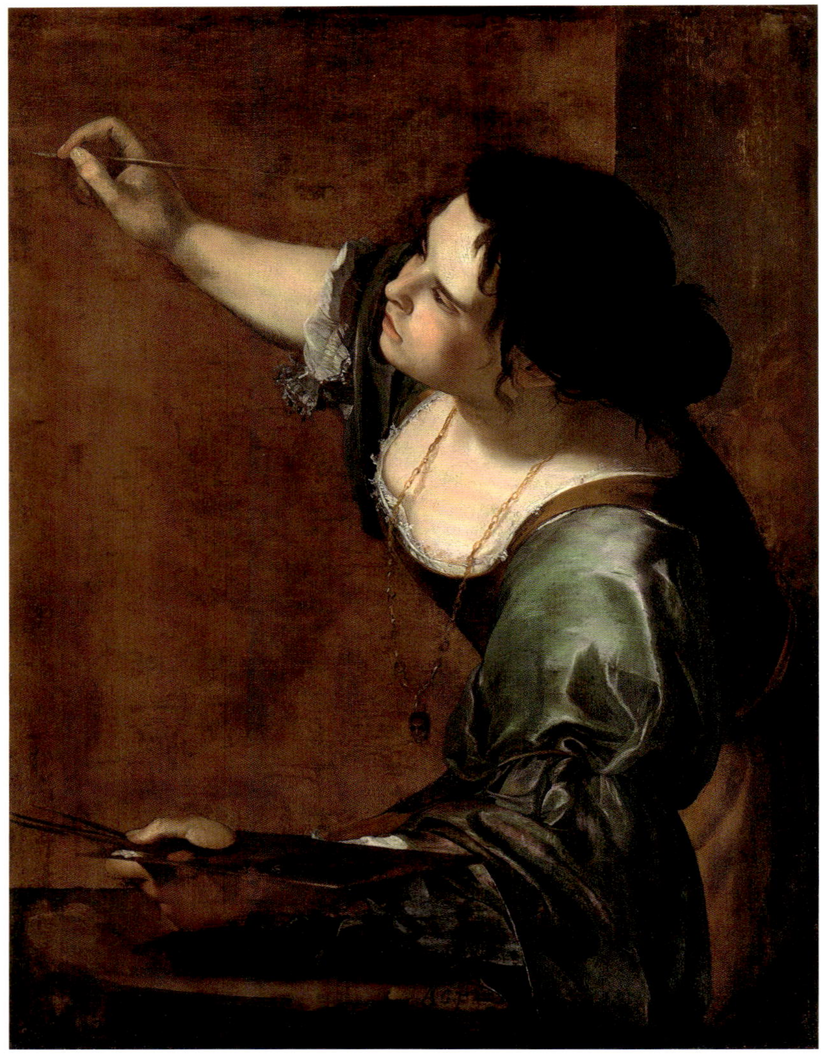

shown with their sleeves rolled up, ready for business, revealing their muscular arms and emphasizing their strength and capability.

The figure of Judith is generally accepted to be a self-portrait of Artemisia, who (like many artists) often used herself as a model – mainly because it was convenient, but also perhaps to articulate her identity as an artist. Over half of her known paintings are either self-portraits or portraits she modelled for.[5]

In one example from circa 1638–39, Gentileschi represents herself as the allegory of painting, a concept traditionally personified as a woman. But rather than the separate, idealized and rather fey female figure typically depicted by male artists, Gentileschi represents herself at work, fully engaged with the canvas in front of her.

In an era when women were often relegated to passive roles in art and society, she defied conventions by depicting herself – and the other women she painted – as active, courageous and self-possessed. This was not just an artistic choice but a bold statement about female identity, experiences and resilience.

Likewise, Judith and Abra's poses suggest immense physical effort. Look at the triangle of gold material between Holofernes' head and Judith's right arm: it tells us she has one leg up on the bed for extra leverage.[6] Holofernes' huge fist is aimed at Abra, but she holds steady, while Judith thrusts the sword with one hand as the other presses Holofernes' head down, gripping his hair as she cuts through his carotid artery.

The blood is not just a detail; it becomes a key element of the painting's dramatic tension. The crimson fluid spurts and flows from Holofernes' severed neck in an almost unnatural cascade, staining the white sheets beneath him.

All these elements give the painting a stark realism: it takes two women, and an

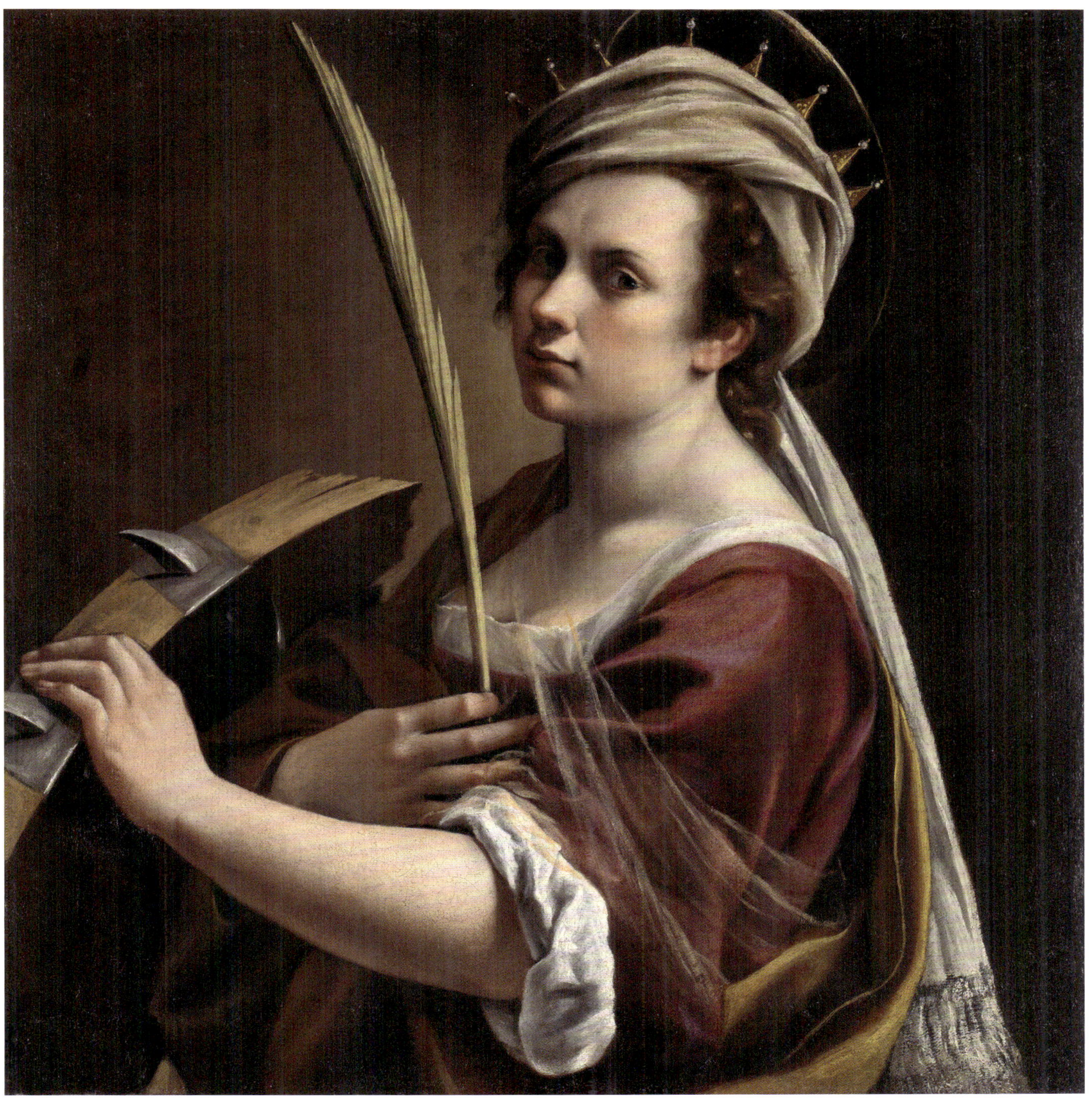

JUDITH BEHEADING HOLOFERNES

immense effort, to kill this brute. At the same time, Gentileschi introduces an early feminist perspective. Departing from the biblical account and many earlier artistic interpretations, she portrays the women as united in their struggle against male domination. By making the maid an active accomplice rather than a passive observer, Gentileschi underscores themes of female solidarity and mutual empowerment.

One last detail: in the 1620 version the sword has shifted slightly to the central axis of the painting, which makes it, I believe, a more cohesive work. Our gaze is directed down the centre of the painting through the right forearm of the maidservant, then the sword, and then finally the blood gushing down over the edge of the bed. The sword in this depiction can be considered symbolic in its resemblance to a crucifix, a further reminder that Judith's tightly clenched fist is in fact guided by the hand of God.

A FORGOTTEN ARTIST

Gentileschi was not the first female artist to achieve recognition in the male-dominated world of art, but it is her subject matter that makes her stand out. Because women were traditionally denied access to life drawing and art academies,[7] their practice tended towards portraits and still lifes.[8] But Artemisia tackled historical painting, which placed her in direct competition with her male contemporaries.

Through her talent and determination, Gentileschi had a successful forty-year career and was collected by the likes of Charles I of England and Philip IV of Spain. She was famous and wealthy in her own time, yet she would be almost forgotten for over 300 years, and like so many other female artists, her paintings would be wrongly attributed to her male contemporaries – in her case, to her father and Caravaggio.

Art criticism as a genre became popular in the 18th century, but its authors were of course all men, writing mostly about male artists. By the 1970s, however, feminist art criticism had risen to prominence as part of the broader feminist movement, bringing Gentileschi and so many other female artists out of obscurity.

The art world is now taking strides to correct gender and racial equality,[9] and Gentileschi is rightly seen as one of the great artists of the Baroque period.

LIFE AFTER JUDITH

In her paintings, Gentileschi celebrated the role of heroic women, and in her hands those characters never appeared as victims.

The crime committed against her and the subsequent trial were certainly significant,[10] but we should not let it define her work, any more than she let it define her life.

Gentileschi was an accomplished painter long before Tassi came along, and her upward trajectory continued. She was strong, successful and determined, a woman in a male profession who not only survived in that world but triumphed, surpassing most of her male contemporaries in both earning power and commissions.

Artemisia Gentileschi was a feminist artist ahead of her time, whose work is as powerful today as it was 400 years ago.

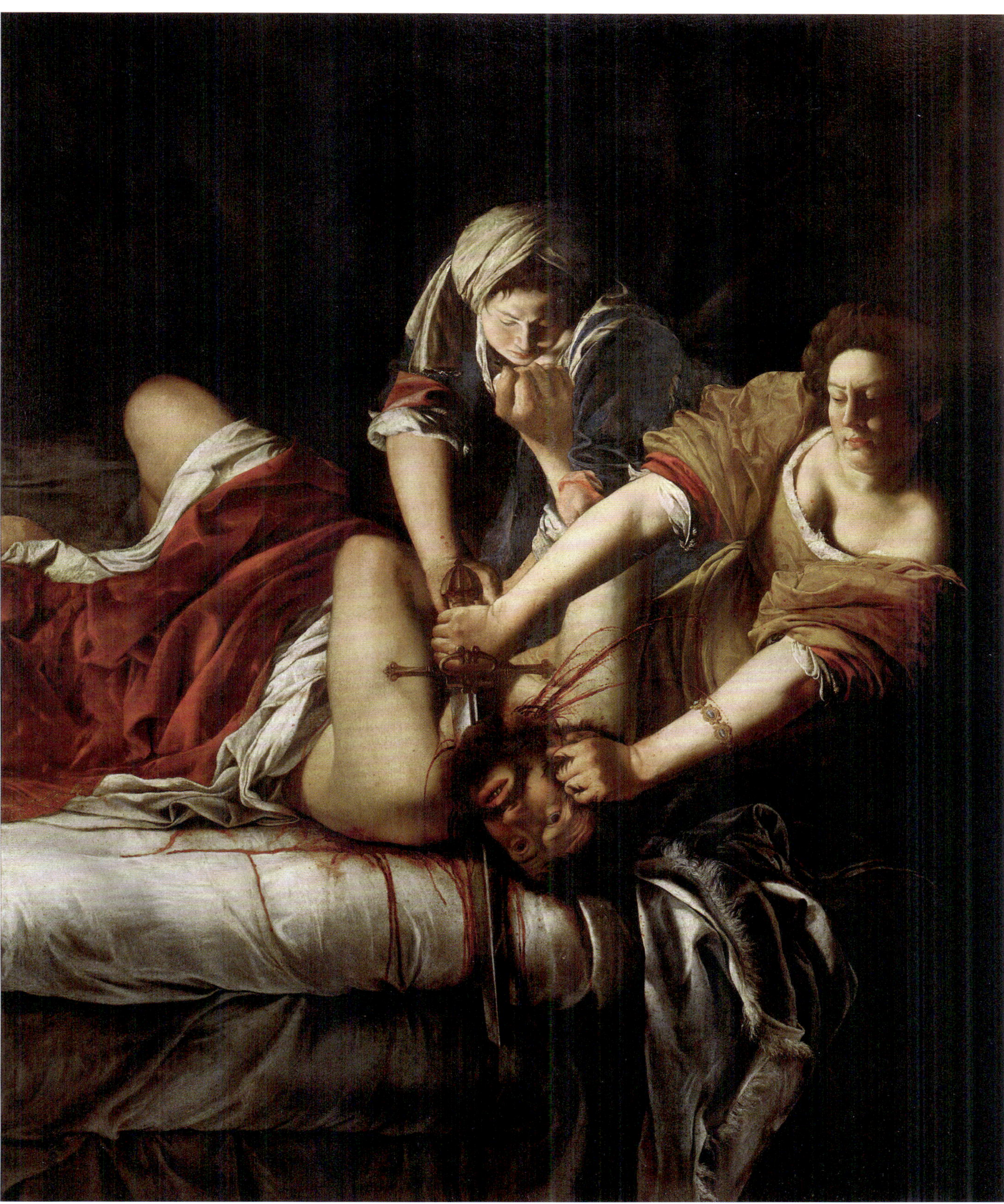

JOHANNES VERMEER

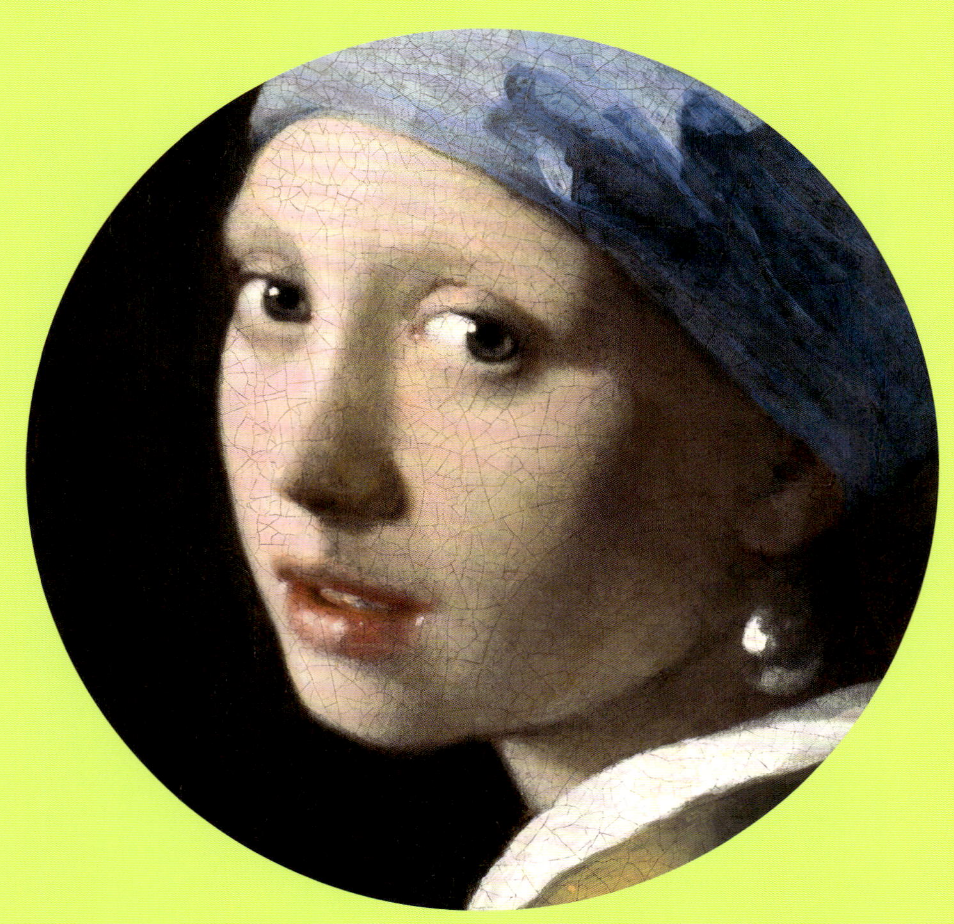

GIRL WITH A PEARL EARRING

c. 1665

THE ART OF CONTEMPLATION

By the mid-17th century, the age of flamboyant Baroque was in full swing, an art movement that, among other factors, arose from intense religious conflict. Europe had experienced the Reformation and Counter-Reformation, the wars of religion and inquisitions. The art being produced in Catholic countries had become a powerful tool of propaganda against the Protestant threat, characterized by a heightened sense of drama, movement and theatricality that had never been seen before.

But in the Netherlands, a new wave of realism was sweeping across the country. Johannes Vermeer was producing simple domestic interiors of middle-class life, quiet, private and unassuming secular works that contained stories of real human relationships.

REINVENTING ART

In 1482 the Austrian branch of the Habsburgs had taken over the Low Countries, known today as the Netherlands, Belgium and Luxembourg. The Eighty Years' War ended in independence for the northern Netherlands in 1648, and the official recognition and establishment of the Dutch Republic.

While the southern Netherlands remained Catholic under Spanish rule, in the northern Netherlands (then the Dutch Republic), the strict Protestant sect of Calvinism became the official religion, and an emphasis was placed on simplicity in both worship and decorative style.

However, it meant that artists in the north lost their main source of commissions – the Church and the aristocracy – and Dutch art had to reinvent itself almost entirely.

JOHANNES VERMEER

We know Vermeer was born in Delft in 1632, but next to nothing is known about him from that point until his marriage to Catharina Bolnes in 1653. She was Catholic, and Vermeer almost certainly converted to Catholicism secretly before they married. Although Catholic mass was banned in public spaces in the Dutch Republic, religious tolerance was mandated, and converting to Catholicism wouldn't have brought Vermeer any personal or professional disadvantages.

The couple moved in with Catharina's mother, Maria Thins, and Vermeer spent the rest of his life in the same town, even the same house, slowly producing paintings in the same room on the second floor. It is thought that Vermeer produced between forty-five and fifty paintings over his career, of which only about thirty-seven paintings exist today.[1] He couldn't afford to raise a family on that income alone, however, so we can be fairly certain that Vermeer also worked as an art dealer.[2]

Vermeer and Catharina had fifteen children, of which eleven survived. We know that at least five other adults lived in the same house as well as Vermeer's own family, yet he never shows us any suggestion of family life, or the chaos that naturally comes with a household that big. It is safe to say that the peace and quiet Vermeer depicts in his paintings was not what he experienced day-to-day.

TRONIES

In the 17th century the Dutch Republic dominated global trade. It was the wealthiest country in the world, but the Dutch Calvinists were a frugal and austere group, naturally inhibited and embarrassed by wealth. Smaller, secular paintings, often with domestic settings, became hugely popular, and could be found in shops, taverns and even the houses of the middle classes. It was a boom time for artists.

While Dutch Calvinists denounced devotional artwork in churches, they explicitly encouraged devotees to turn their attention to the visible world around them. Most of Vermeer's artworks portray women and conform to the prevailing theme in Dutch genre painting: domestic interiors depicting middle-class life, and often critiquing vices such as extravagance and untidiness; *Girl with a Pearl Earring*, however, is what is known as a tronie. It is a term that originated in Dutch art during the 16th century, meaning 'face' or 'expression'; they were not portraits in the conventional sense, but they were almost certainly based on live models.[5]

In contrast to traditional portraits, tronies were more like character studies. They were very popular in the Low Countries and often showcased exaggerated expressions, unusual costumes and dramatic lighting that highlighted the subject's features and emotions.

Vermeer made a small set of tronies between 1664 and 1667 that were close-up images of girls looking at the viewer.[4] Three of the four known tronies by Vermeer – *Girl with a Flute*, *Girl with a Red Hat* and *Girl with a Pearl Earring* – depict a seated young woman in an exotic costume. All of the tronie subjects wear pearl earrings, and all share similar facial expressions: slightly open mouth, glistening lips and an unusually direct stare.

WHAT LIES BENEATH

There is almost no information available about Vermeer's life, his working practices or most of his paintings, including *Girl with a Pearl Earring*. But in 2018 a research project initiated at the Mauritshuis Museum in the Hague, 'Girl in the Spotlight', went further than any other, using macroscopic imaging methods in conjunction with the analysis of microscopic

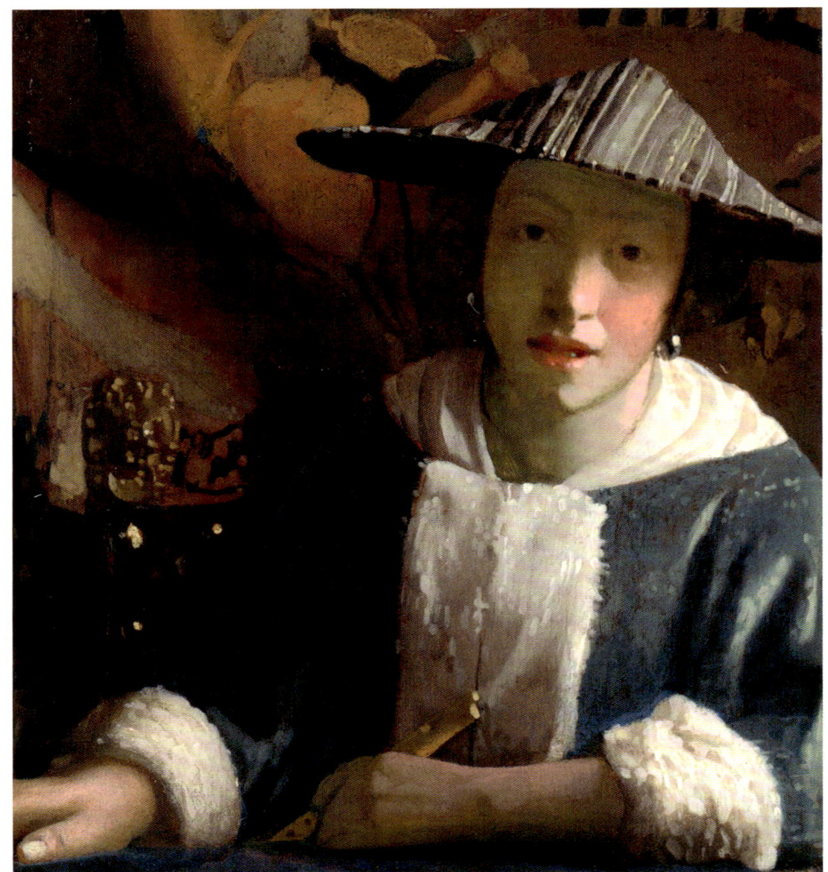

JOHANNES VERMEER

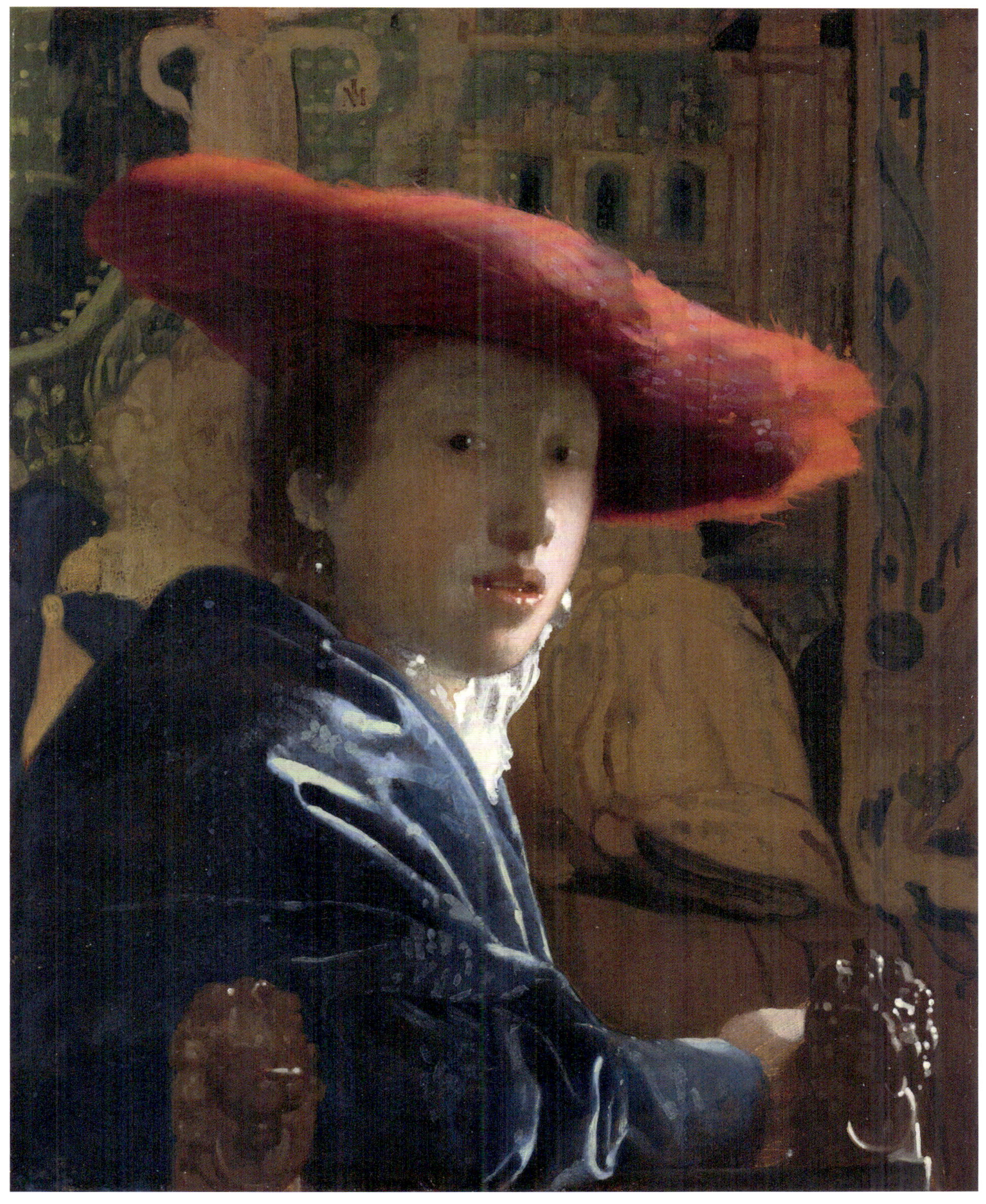

GIRL WITH A PEARL EARRING

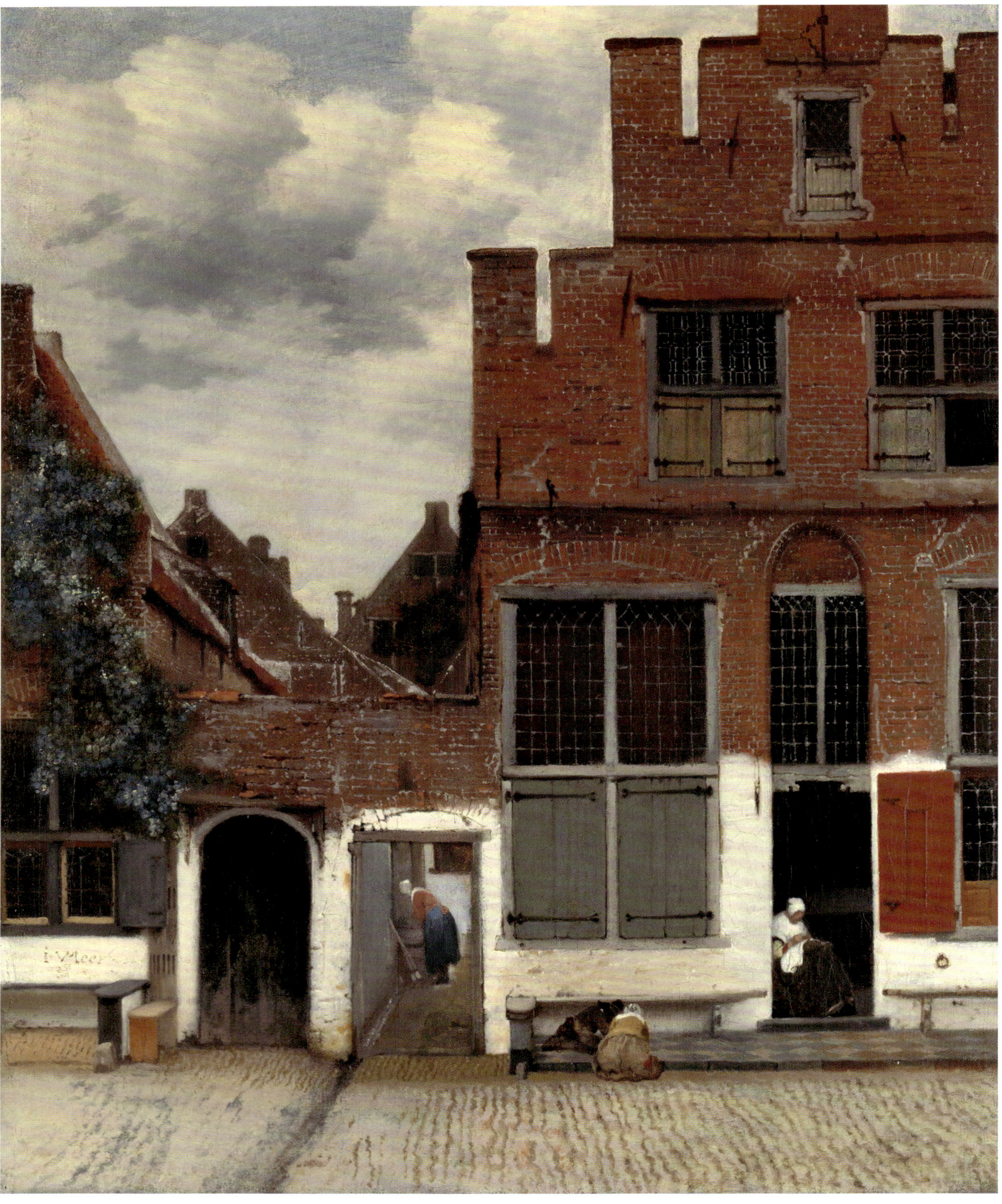

The peace and quiet Vermeer depicts in his paintings was not what he experienced day-to-day

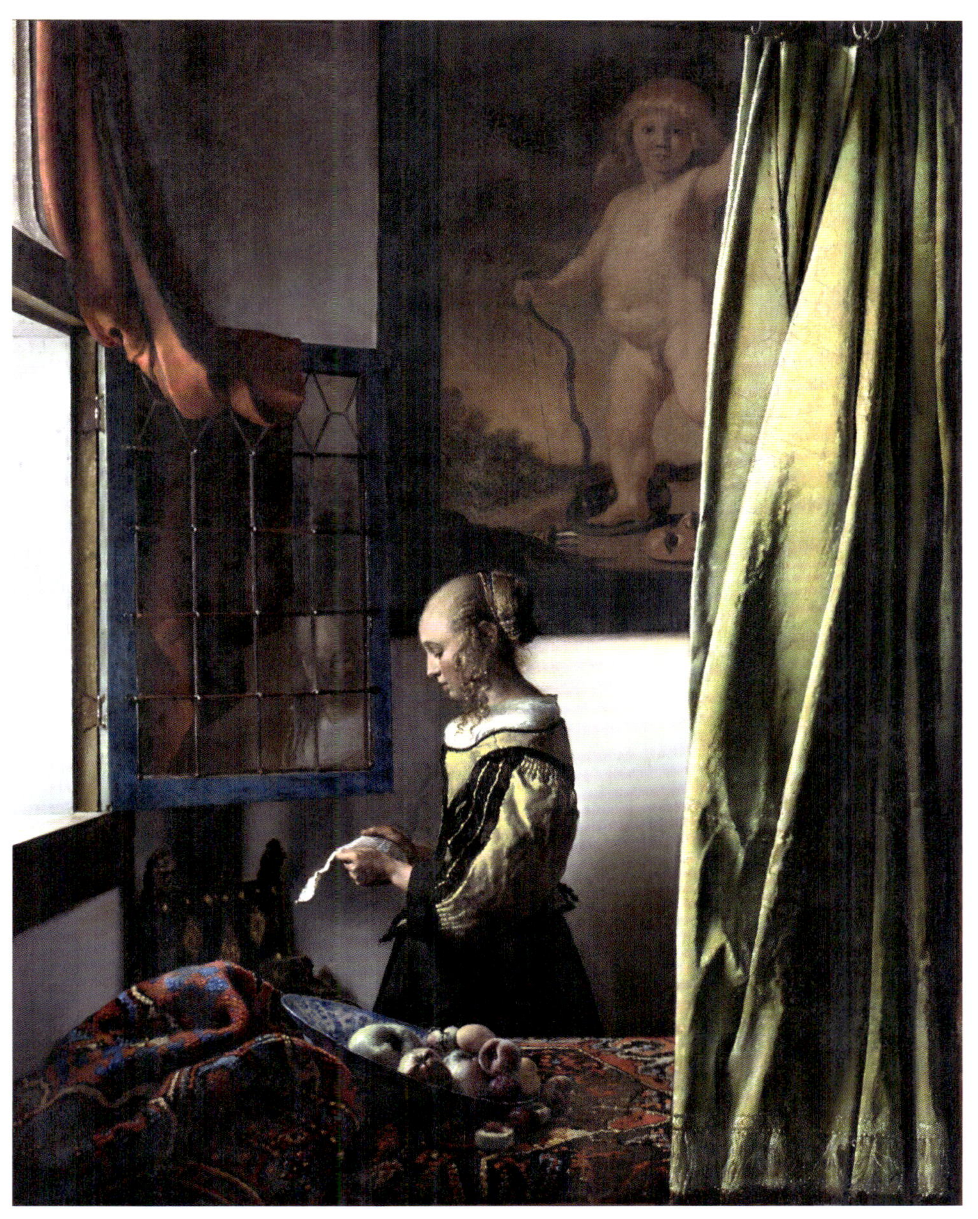

Vermeer uses what has been described as a sort of 'pointillist' technique

samples to go underneath the painting's layers to reveal previously unknown secrets about the mysterious girl.

The researchers were amazed to discover delicate eyelashes on the girl's face, which suggests he was painting a real person rather than just an idealized character, as was thought before.[5] But the main revelation was that the mottled dark backdrop was originally a dark green curtain, painted in a thin translucent layer of paint – a glaze, really – over the black background seen today. The curtain would have gradually disappeared over the centuries due to physical and chemical alterations in the plant-based paints he used, indigo (blue) and weld (yellow).

This means that the dark, neutral background of the painting with which we are familiar would have looked quite different three hundred years ago. As we see the work today, the subject is isolated, the illumination of her face our sole focus, but the curtain would have likely added a different dimension – a sense of place.

TECHNIQUE

We know he painted slowly and deliberately, waiting for each layer to thoroughly dry before applying another. He painted the background first (the curtain), then skin tones, clothing and headscarf, before the final touch: some lead white paint for the pearl earring, which sits on the very top surface of the work.[6]

The pearl is a masterclass in itself, showcasing his ability to evoke realism through little more than two brushstrokes,[7] one at the bottom of the earring to softly reflect her collar, and the thick dab of white used as a highlight on the upper left.

To demonstrate just how complex this painting is, we can take a good look at some of the pigments. We not only know exactly what palette he used, but now we also know that the ore used to make the lead white pigment for her collar, eyes and pearl earring came from England – the Peak District, to be precise. The red he used for her clothing was cochineal, a Mexican pigment made from crushed insects, but he used a different red for her skin, vermilion, which was derived from cinnabar from Spain or Italy.

The colour Vermeer is associated with more than any other was also the most expensive: ultramarine, a blue pigment more costly than even gold leaf. It is made from crushed lapis lazuli, a semi-precious stone imported from the mountains of present-day Afghanistan. It is a colour that was used by the Catholic Church to denote status, such as depictions of the Virgin Mary, who is rarely seen without blue clothing.

Different grades of ultramarine were available to Vermeer, but the 'Girl in the Spotlight' analysis revealed that he used the best (and most expensive) grade. It is known that Vermeer struggled financially most of his life,[8] and it is possible that his biggest collector, the wealthy Pieter van Ruijven, supplied the artist with such costly pigment.

'POINTILLISM'

Vermeer uses what has been described as a sort of 'pointillist' technique in the painting: small round dots that can be clearly seen in microscopic images.[9] They evoke the light that flickers off the textured surface of her clothing, and the technique appears in about half of Vermeer's works.

Microscopic investigation shows that some of those dots overlap, contributing to

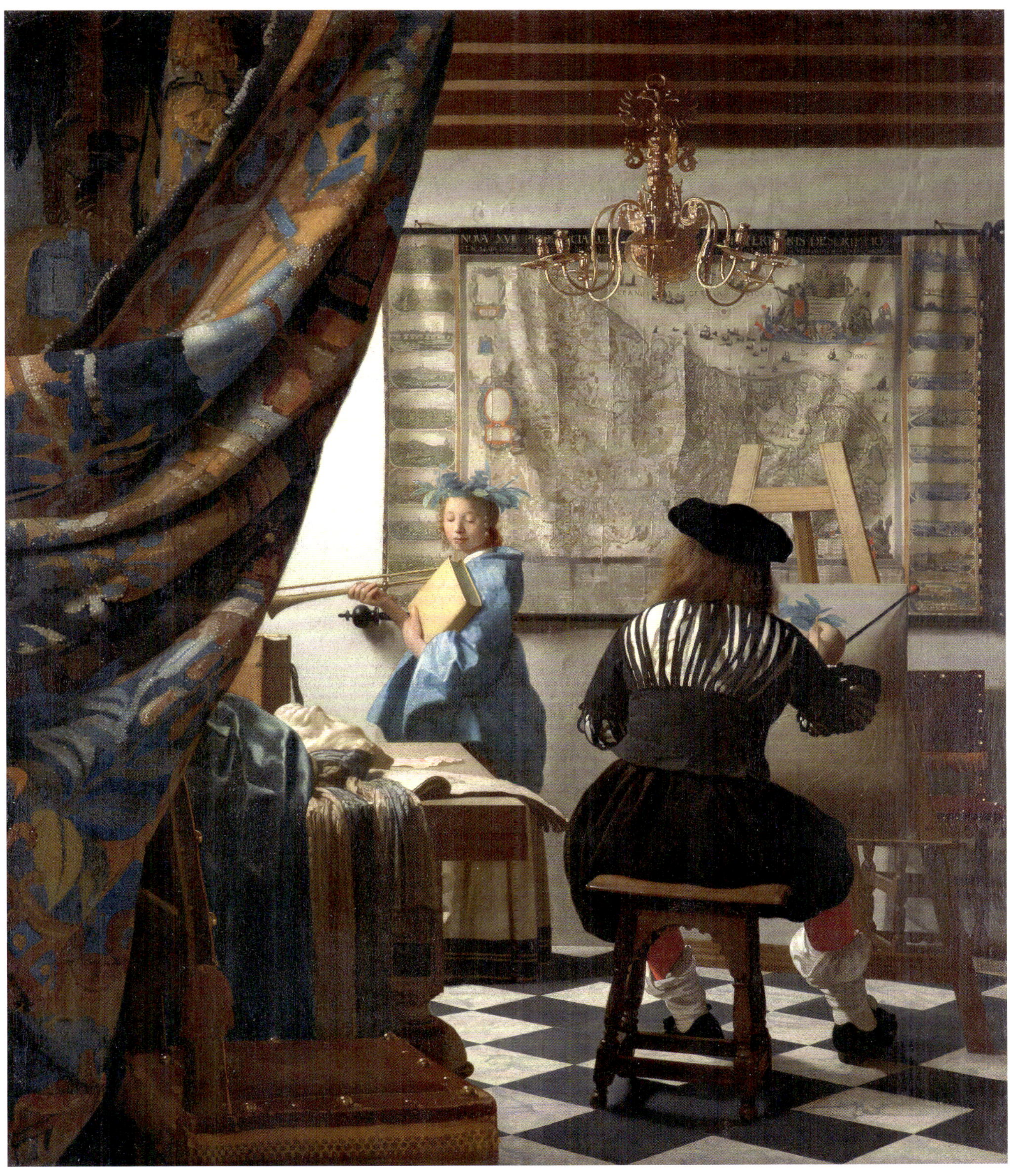

GIRL WITH A PEARL EARRING

the subtly blurred visual effect commonly associated with Vermeer's masterful portrayal of light, but they also intensify the three-dimensional impact by giving us depth of field; in other words, painting an image as our eyes see it. He creates a similar effect on the lips and eyes, using tiny overlapping brushstrokes to convey the illusion of moisture.

WHO IS THE GIRL?

Thanks to the Mauritshuis project, we now know much more about Vermeer's techniques and materials, but one mystery remains: the identity of the young girl in *Girl with a Pearl Earring*.

None of the sitters in Vermeer's existing paintings have ever been identified, but it is presumed that Vermeer used his family members or servants as models – for example, the figure in *Girl with a Pearl Earring* does somewhat resemble the girl in *The Art of Painting* (1668).

Identifying her, however, is made more difficult by the lack of narrative, something that we usually see in Vermeer's works, even if just by way of a letter being read or an instrument being played. Her clothes likewise tell us little. The artist dressed his young model in a contemporary ochre-green jacket featuring a pleated sleeve insert, a fashion characteristic of the Dutch Republic during the early 1660s.[10]

While the women in Vermeer's paintings do not wear *much* jewellery, eleven of them wear pearl earrings and/or necklaces. Pearls were a status symbol in the Dutch Republic, but Vermeer almost certainly couldn't afford the real thing. Additionally, the pearl in *Girl with a Pearl Earring* is an impossible size, so it is almost certainly an imitation.[11]

Unlike the jacket, the girl's turban was not a Dutch fashion. The Netherlands had strong commercial ties around the world, and Orientalist themes are commonplace in European art of the period. But girls in Delft would not have worn turbans, so this came straight out of Vermeer's dressing-up box, created with two pieces of material, one yellow and one blue.[12] In many of his paintings, we see the same props and outfits, jewellery, mirrors, carpets, tables and drinking glasses, which suggests he kept them in his Delft studio to be reused when required.

SOMETHING UNIQUE

Like Vermeer's other paintings, *Girl with a Pearl Earring* is modest, elegant and restrained, but it has something unique about it that makes it connect with so many people. It could be the girl's ambiguous expression and her parted lips, which suggest she is on the verge of speaking. Each of us can project our feelings and thoughts onto her, making the experience personal.

Or it could be that, unlike formal portraits of the time, it is a snapshot of a fleeting moment. Combined with the simplicity of the composition and the lack of clutter or detailed background, this ephemerality allows her to transcend time and place.

Despite being created over 300 years ago, *Girl with a Pearl Earring* may be exactly what we need in the 21st century, a painting that makes us realize that the quiet moments are often the most profound.

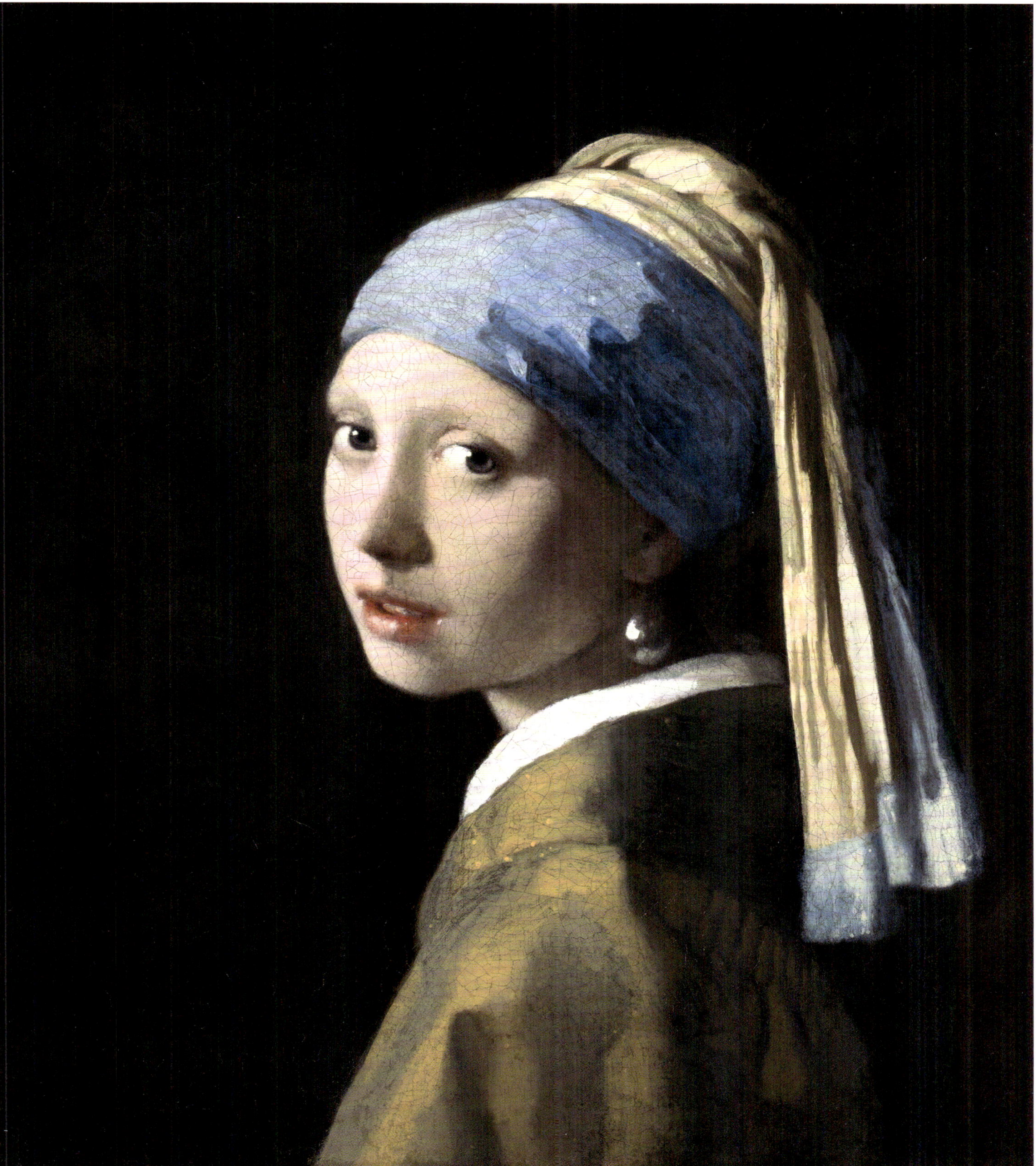

9

ÉLISABETH VIGÉE LE BRUN

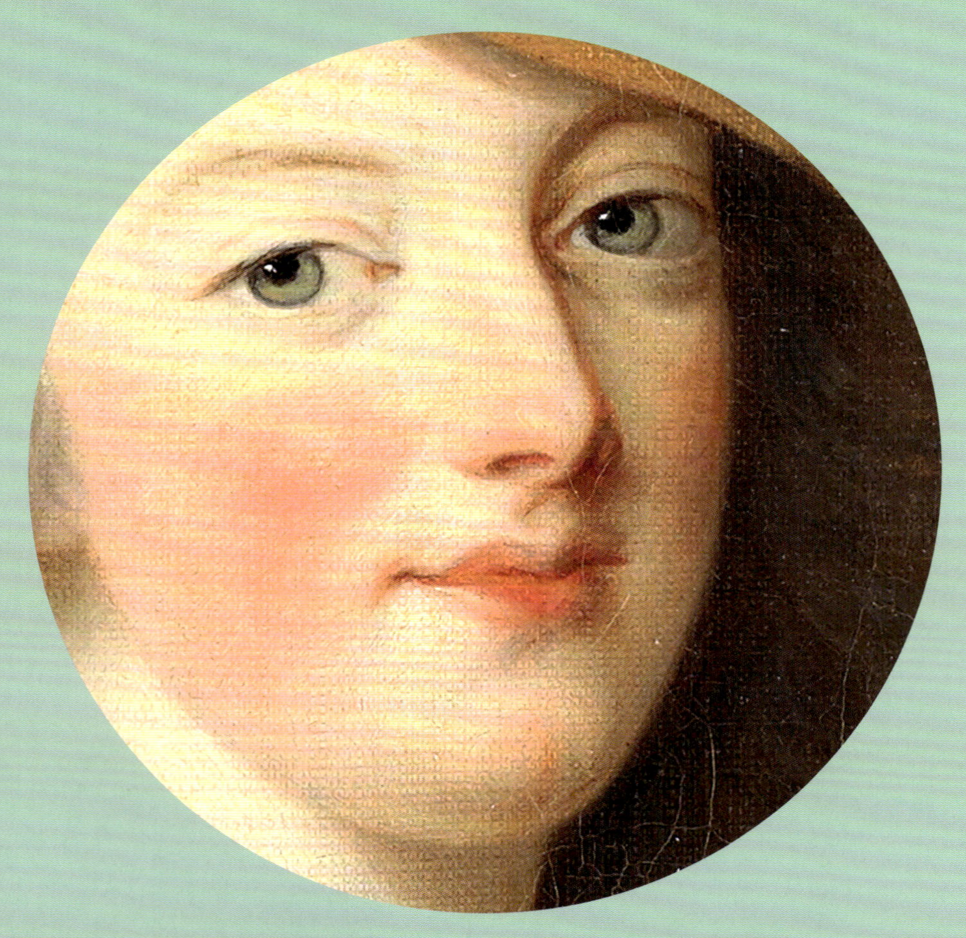

MARIE ANTOINETTE IN A CHEMISE DRESS

1783

A QUEEN IN HER UNDERWEAR

Marie Antoinette became dauphine of France at the age of fourteen, upon her marriage to Louis-Auguste, duc de Berry, the heir apparent to the French throne. Initially the public perception of her was favourable, but her unfortunate choice of advisors, embroilment (quite innocently) in financial scandals and disregard for French etiquette meant that by the time *Marie Antoinette in a Chemise Dress* was painted, she was intensely disliked. She was also an Austrian, a 'foreigner', and that made her a target.

She had hoped that the 1783 portrait by Élisabeth Vigée Le Brun would restore some of her popularity, but it turned into propaganda for the mob instead.

RISING THROUGH THE RANKS

Vigée Le Brun's father was a pastel artist and her mother was a hairdresser from a peasant background, making her eventual rise to the upper echelons of society even more remarkable.

She received some training from her father, who died when she was twelve, but otherwise she was virtually self-taught.[1] By the age of fourteen she had already started to paint professionally to help support her family and was admitted to the Académie de St Luc in 1774, a time when very few women were admitted.

Fiercely ambitious and hugely talented, Vigée Le Brun would gain access to the highest levels of power by becoming a portraitist to the French nobility. Whether for royalty, aristocrats or the ever-growing bourgeoisie, who could usually only afford pastel portraits, painted portraits were very important in the 18th century as historical records and status symbols, and Vigée Le Brun already had an impressive range of clients before she was twenty.

She achieved such remarkable success that she was able to command prices for her portraits higher than any other artist of her time and would produce more than 660 portraits over the course of her career.

In 1776 she married a wealthy art dealer, which gave her access to the Parisian elite, for whom she would eventually work. She travelled extensively with her husband and got to see the works of Flemish masters such as Peter Paul Rubens, whose painting *Portrait of Susanna Lunden* (1622–25) inspired her own painting (and masterpiece) *Self-Portrait in a Straw Hat* of 1782, which in turn would inspire *Marie Antoinette in a Chemise*.

Vigée Le Brun was known to be beautiful, funny, confident and deeply intelligent, and we can see that in the 1782 *Self-Portrait in a Straw Hat*. Here, a self-assured artist, holding the tools of her trade, looks straight at us. But Vigée Le Brun breaks away from tradition, showing a more informal and natural self-portrait than those in French

Élisabeth Vigée Le Brun, *Marie Antoinette in a Chemise Dress* (detail), 1783.

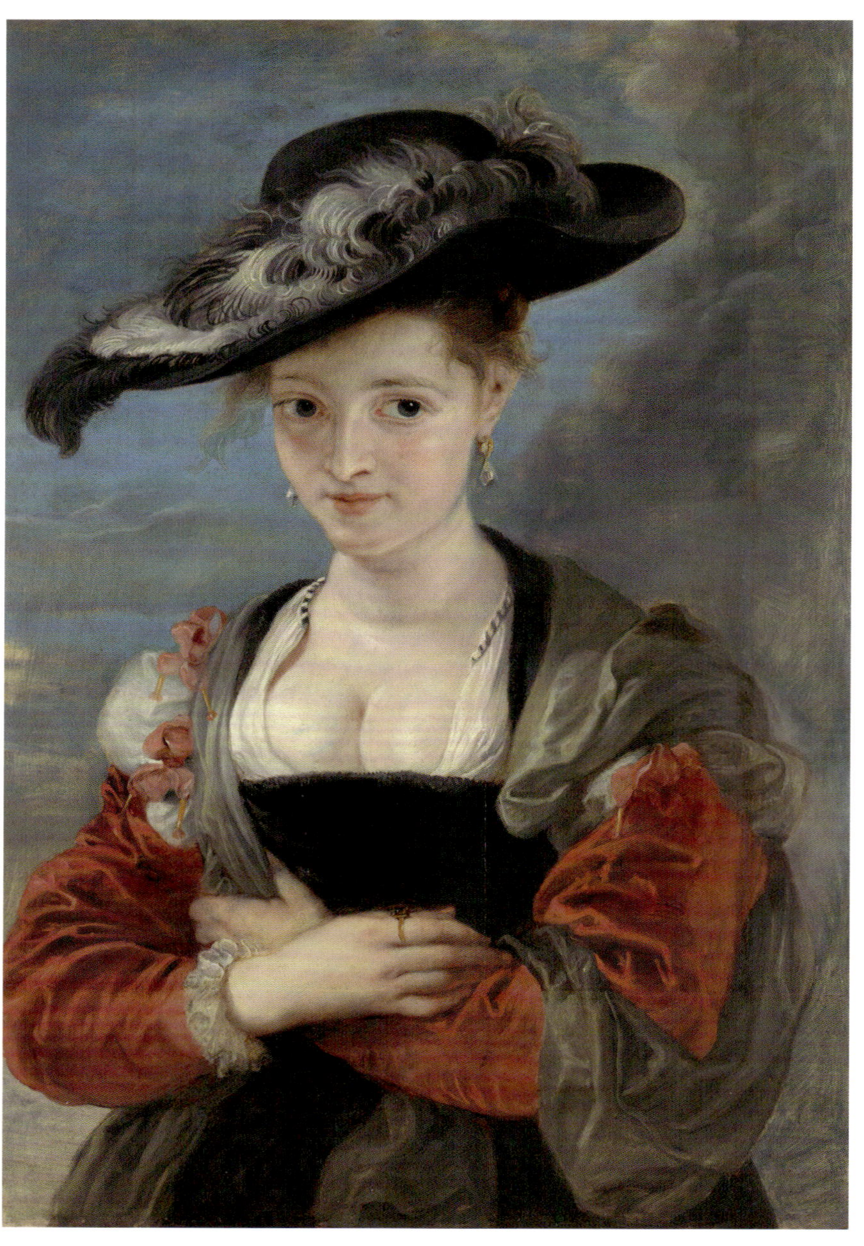

Peter Paul Rubens, *Portrait of Susanna Lunden 'Le Chapeau de Paille'*, 1622–25.

ÉLISABETH VIGÉE LE BRUN

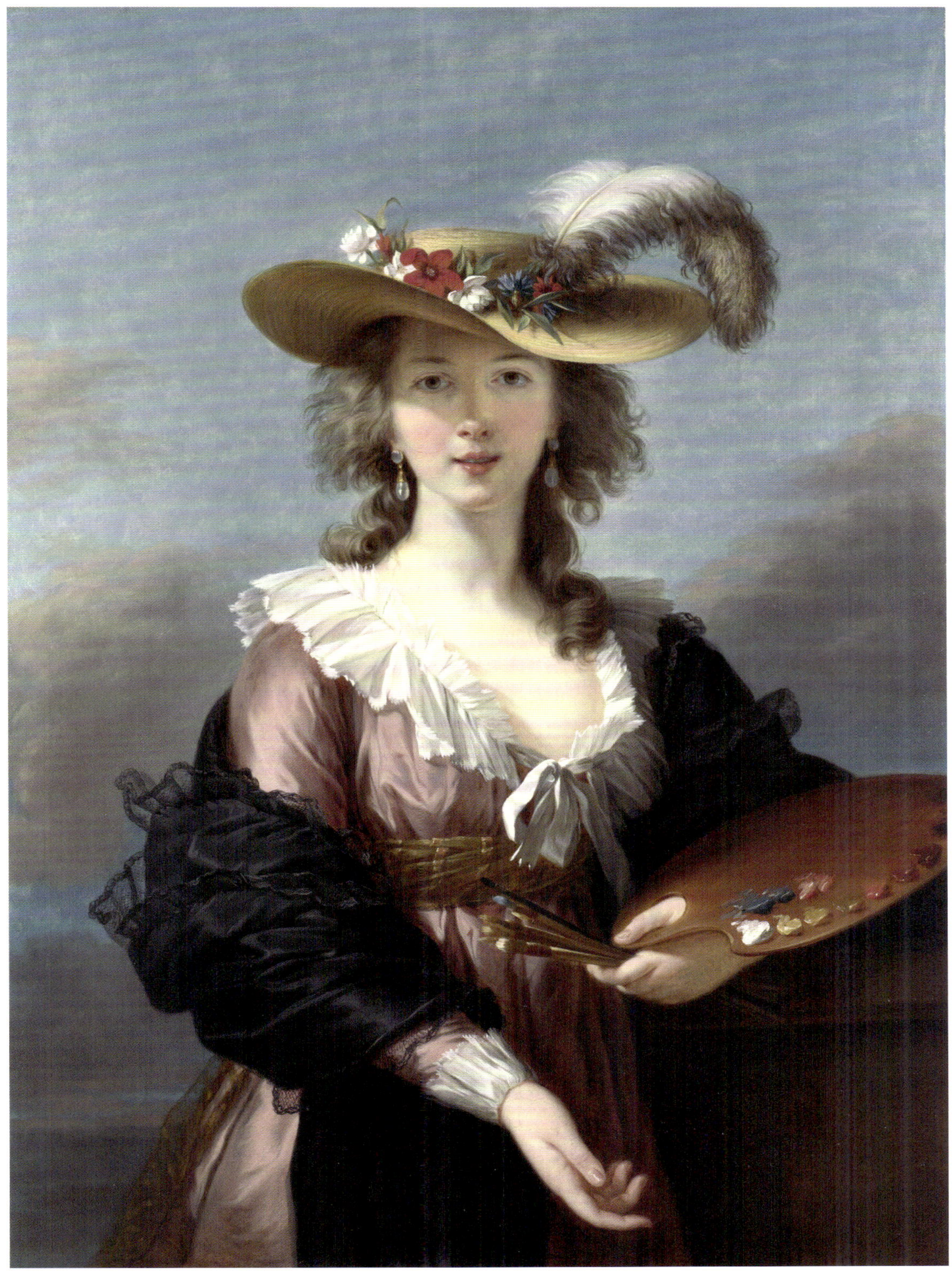

MARIE ANTOINETTE IN A CHEMISE DRESS

*In a country like France
with a lucrative fashion
industry, clothes mattered,
as Marie Antoinette
discovered on arrival
at the French court*

society were used to. This would prove to be the beginning of less stuffy royal portraits – much to the chagrin of the French court.

Her rise to royal portraitist was swift and phenomenal, as Marie Antoinette felt more comfortable around her than the court-appointed painters. As she would later write in her memoirs: 'Before the revolution, women ruled. The revolution dethroned them.'[2]

THE QUEEN AND THE PAINTER

There was said to be an instant connection between Marie Antoinette and Vigée Le Brun. They were of the same age, and both were in unhappy marriages; they had children, and each had lost a child. They were also both considered 'outsiders', Marie Antoinette as an Austrian reigning over a hostile Versailles, and Vigée Le Brun as a rare female painter in a field dominated by men.

In her memoirs, Vigée Le Brun wrote: 'It was in the year 1779 that I painted the Queen for the first time; she was then in the heyday of her youth and beauty.'[3] The artist was especially in awe of the queen's complexion: 'I had no colours to paint such freshness, such delicate tints, which were hers alone, and which I had never seen in any other woman.'[4]

In a country like France with a lucrative fashion industry, clothes mattered, as Marie Antoinette discovered on arrival at the French court. Her Austrian clothes were discarded

and she was publicly re-dressed in French fashions, a humiliating but symbolic transformation of the archduchess of Austria into the dauphine of France.

In Austria she had been afforded more freedom, less formality, but the French court was extremely strict and didn't take kindly to change.

One of her main problems was her dull, shy husband, the future Louis XVI, who for eight years was incapable of consummating their marriage and had little interest in schooling her in French diplomacy. By the time he ascended the throne in 1774, they were leading separate lives, and Marie Antoinette had her own circle of advisors and favourites, chosen by her.

That same year Louis XVI gave her the Petit Trianon, a château on the grounds of Versailles, and Marie-Antoinette declared it her private quarters, reserved only for her and her closest friends: the aristocracy was banned, and even the king had to ask for permission to visit.

Her first big mistake was to abolish the morning *toilette*, where the aristocracy could watch the queen as she was dressed by her maidservants. Then she forbade the heavy cosmetics worn by women attending court, and she stopped wearing the popular wide-hooped panniers, which were cumbersome and uncomfortable, opting for more simple dresses like the *robe de gaulle*, the layered muslin dress she would (unfortunately) wear for her portrait of 1783.

Despite giving birth to three children, including Louis XVI's son and heir, she was rarely out of the scandal sheets (known as *libelles*), where she was accused of every sin possible: promiscuity, profligacy and, worst of all, sympathizing with France's enemies (which included Austria at the time). She became known as 'Madame Déficit' during

Élisabeth Vigée Le Brun, *Marie Antoinette with a Rose*, 1783.

  ÉLISABETH VIGÉE LE BRUN

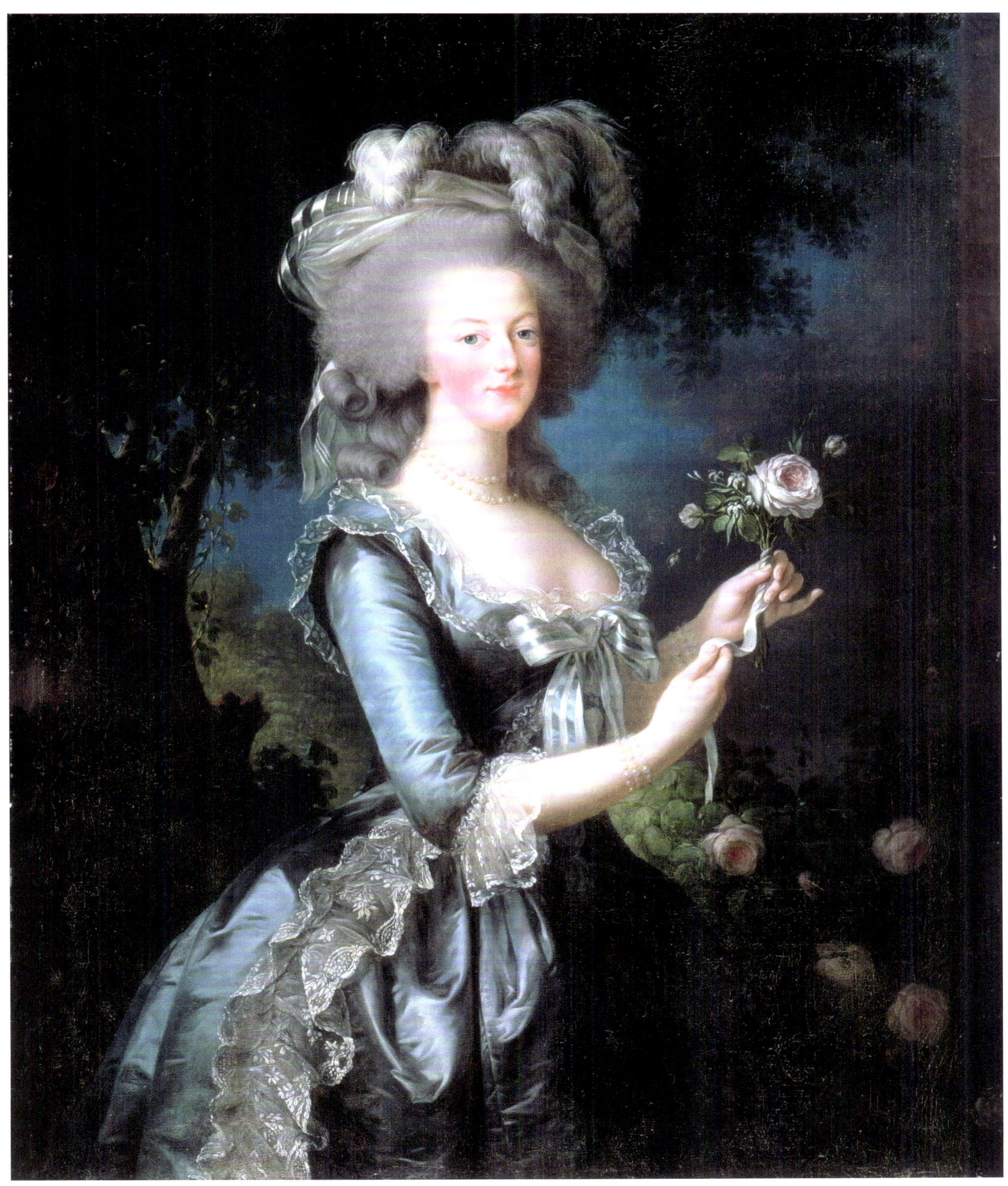

MARIE ANTOINETTE IN A CHEMISE DRESS

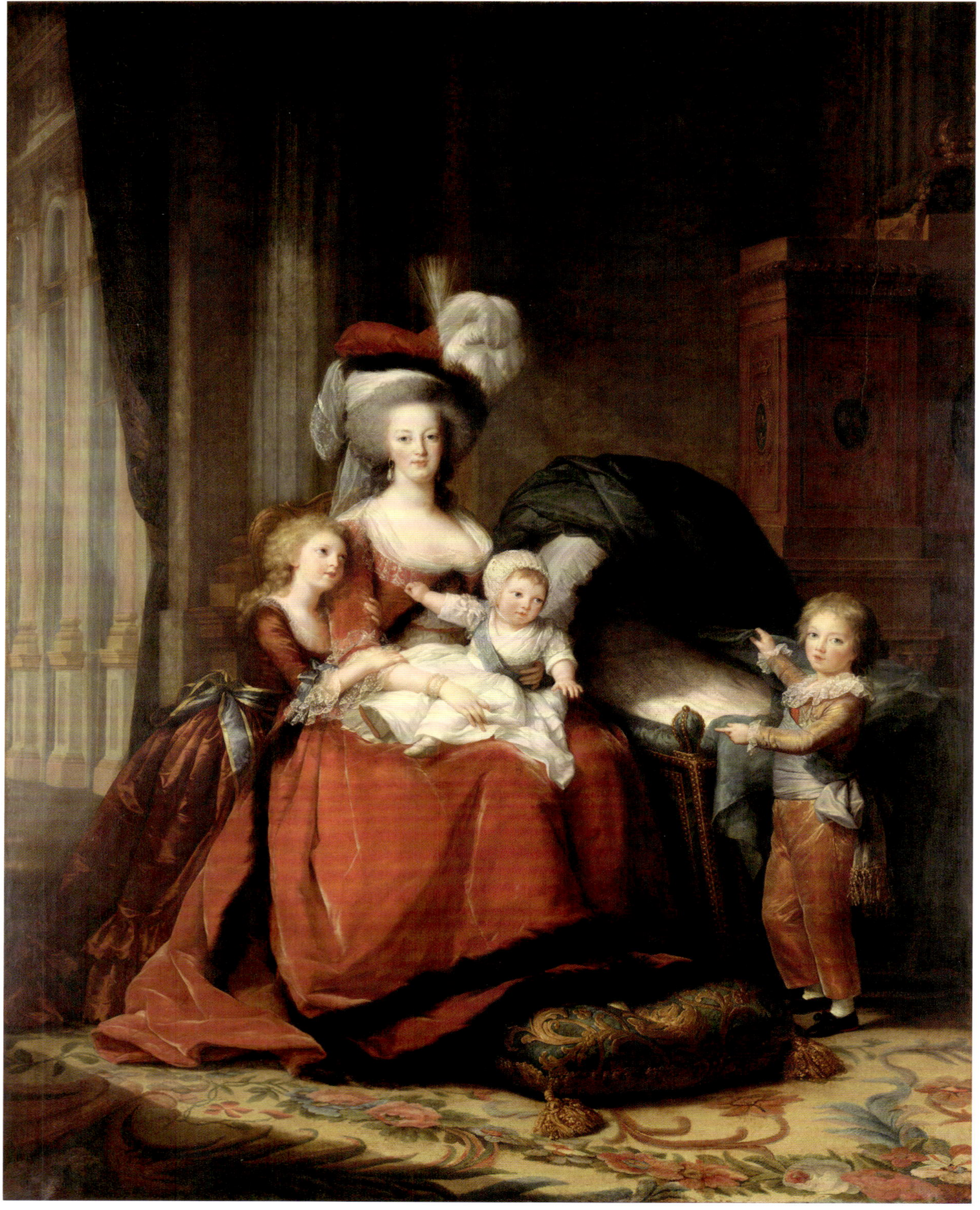

ÉLISABETH VIGÉE LE BRUN

France's financial crisis, and the criticism extended to both what she wore and how she wore it.

Royal portraits are not just about creating a likeness, they are also a form of propaganda; they underline the subject's right to rule and are fiercely nationalistic. Today *Marie Antoinette in a Chemise* seems innocuous, but to 18th-century pre-revolutionary France, it was a gross insult to the establishment and to the country at large.

Since the reign of Louis XIV, luxury fashion had been viewed as a symbol of French power and taste, and during his reign about one-third of Parisian wage earners were employed in the clothing and textile trades.[5] Fashion was extremely lucrative, both domestically and as an export commodity.

The queen was openly attacked in the press for her immodesty and for being unpatriotic by promoting fashions that used imported English cotton rather than French Lyonnaise silk, which would have a negative impact on the already failing economy.

She had an important role to play in promoting the luxury goods market in France, and in this, she failed miserably. The dress she wore in the portrait was not only made from material imported from England, France's eternal enemy, but also worn without stays or corseting, and without the French panniers worn by the ladies of the court. All were products supported by a mass workforce, meaning that she was not just snubbing the arbiters of taste, and by extension, those in power, she was also snubbing the French workforce.

To add insult to injury, the portrait also shows the queen performing 'manual labour', arranging flowers in her *robe de gaulle*. She isn't wearing any fancy jewellery (another luxury France was known for), nor is she wearing a wig or powdered hair. The casual

feel of the painting extends to her relaxed curls, which sit underneath a simple straw hat with relatively modest plumes, tied with a grey satin ribbon.

Vigée Le Brun and Marie Antoinette's vision of making her more accessible backfired spectacularly, and the queen was accused of mocking the dignity of the throne of France by appearing in what many saw as underwear.

Despite the furore from the court, the painting was put on display at the Paris Salon of 1783 but was deemed inappropriate and offensive by the organizers. The subsequent scandal resulted in Vigée Le Brun being asked to remove it from the exhibition.[6]

She hastily painted another portrait, *Marie Antoinette with a Rose* (p. 93), as a replacement, but despite the same pose and the same expression, this is a strictly formal work. The queen is wearing a blue-grey silk *robe à la française* with a French lace trim, a string of pearls and powdered, styled hair adorned with lavish ostrich plumes. She is also wearing the appropriate corset and a bonnet, but it was too little too late: the damage was done, and the gossip rags had a field day. Before long, pornographic pamphlets appeared that portrayed the queen as a sexual deviant, and for the first time, the issue of incest was hinted at, something she would be falsely charged with at her later trial.[7]

EXILE

The French Monarchy was overthrown on 10 August 1792, and Marie Antoinette and her children would spend the remainder of their lives in prison, until their eventual execution.

Vigée Le Brun left Paris shortly after the king and queen were arrested at Versailles. She was a loyalist to the *ancien régime*, the French tradition of absolute monarchy, and because of her close association with royalty she was considered an enemy of the people.

Her exile, which she imagined would last only six months, lasted twelve years. However, as a friend of the rich and powerful, she was welcomed by the royal courts and art academies of Europe in Italy, Austria and Germany, as well as in Russia.

She returned to France in 1805 and would die in Paris in 1842, at the age of eighty-six.

CHEMISE À LA REINE

Marie Antoinette may have been reviled by the popular press and the French court, but ironically she remained highly influential when it came to fashion. The *robe de gaulle* became known as the *chemise à la reine* (dress of the queen), and the troublesome garment never quite went out of style – not only in France but also in England, which decimated the French silk industry.

Cotton and muslin almost totally replaced silk as the fashionable fabric, and by the end of the 18th century the demand for raw cotton skyrocketed. New textile manufacturing technology would make cotton even cheaper for the masses, but the craze for cotton would have tragic consequences. At the time of the painting, cotton production was in its infancy in America, at about 3,000 bales per year. Within twenty years that figure had increased more than twentyfold, and the enslaved population in the American South also increased from 650,000 to over a million.[8]

For some, the young queen's choice of a simple muslin chemise in the portrait was to blame for the radical change in the textile industry, and some would even argue that the rise of slavery was a direct consequence of that choice – that Marie Antoinette herself was to blame.

But they would say that, wouldn't they?

     ÉLISABETH VIGÉE LE BRUN

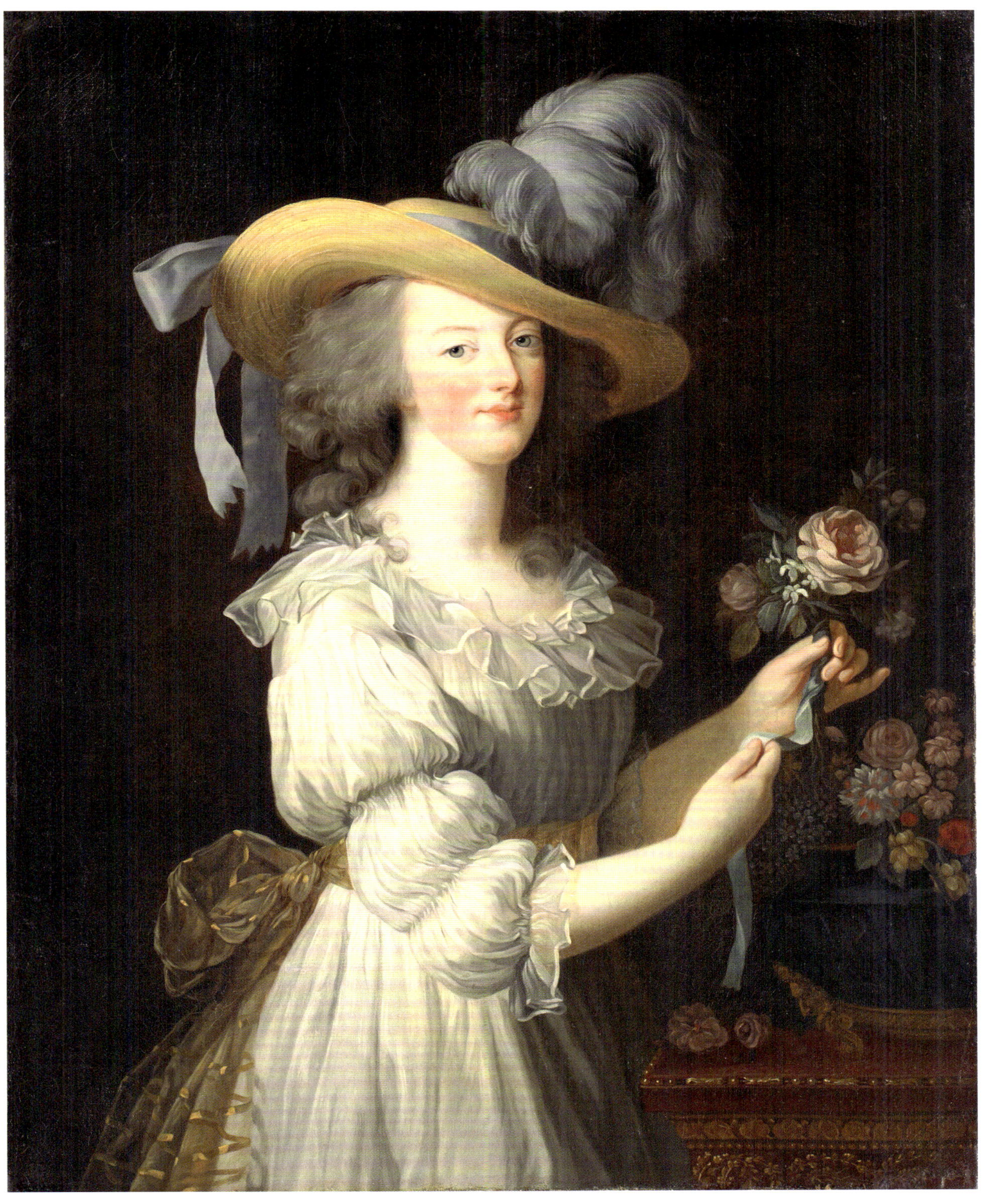

MARIE ANTOINETTE IN A CHEMISE DRESS

10

FRANCISCO DE GOYA

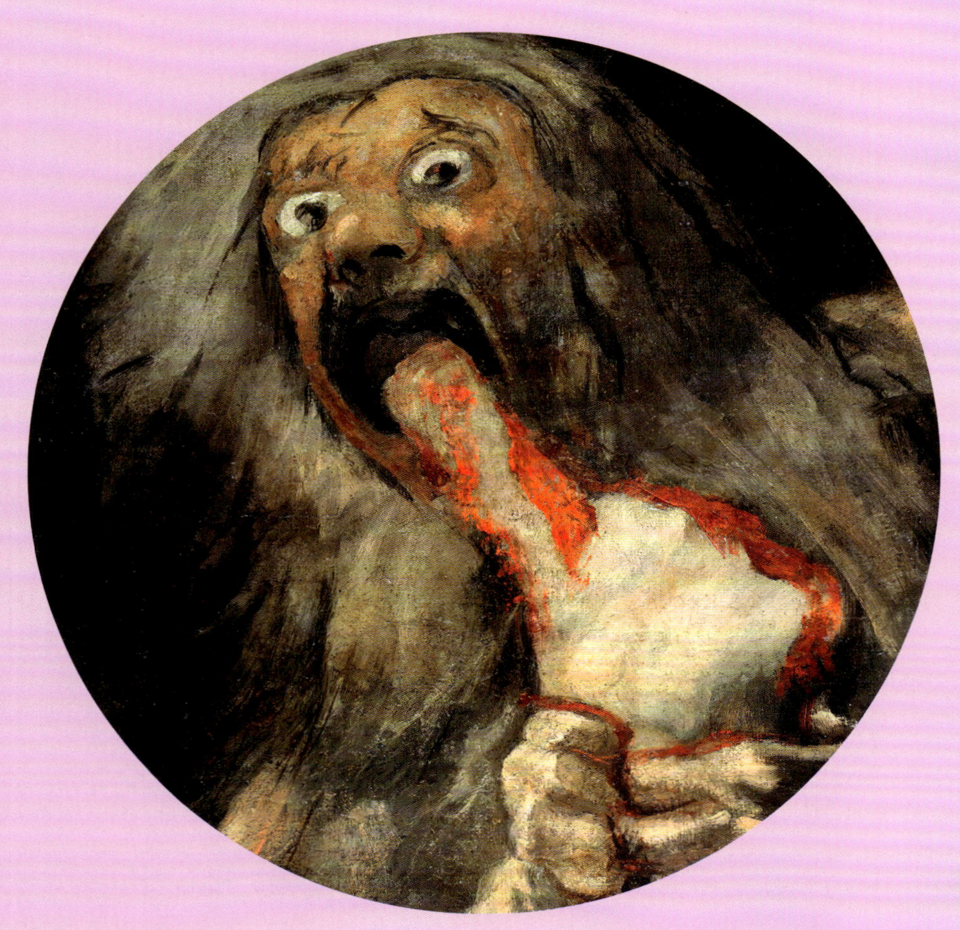

SATURN DEVOURING HIS SON

c. 1819–23

UNCOMFORTABLE TRUTHS

In 1819 the official Spanish court painter Francisco de Goya suddenly withdrew from public life. He left Madrid and the court behind and moved into a house just outside southern Madrid, then the countryside. His wife and most of his friends were dead; he was seventy-three years old, sick, completely deaf and isolated from the Spanish court.

He had produced some of the greatest works of the 18th and early 19th centuries, but he wasn't finished yet. The man who had once painted crucifixions, miracles, saints and priests started a new series of raw and brutal paintings, many of them without even a hint of God.

The series of fourteen works, which would later be known as the *Black Paintings*, was painted directly onto the bare plaster walls of his secluded country house and clearly never intended for public viewing. They were created during his later years in Spain, from around 1819 to 1823, and they convey his deeply pessimistic view of humanity, the most horrific of them being *Saturn Devouring his Son*, a disturbing work that is both profoundly modern and uniquely representative of the 19th century, both human and monstrous.

Their dark and melancholic subject matter would cause them to be regarded as a prefiguration of modern art, but how did Goya get here from painting royal commissions?

FROM THE LIGHT TO THE DARK

Goya was a man from a middle-class background who rose through the ranks to reach the highest level of high society. In 1774 he arrived in Madrid from Zaragoza, where he was painting beautiful works in provincial churches. At first he worked on cartoons for the royal residencies, creating designs to be woven into tapestries for the royal palaces. This would initiate his first contact with the Spanish royal family.

In 1789, the year of the French Revolution, he would be appointed court painter and eventually work for three Spanish kings – first, Charles III, the great reformer, then his son, the inept Charles IV, and then *his* son, the tyrant Ferdinand VII. When Spain was occupied by Napoleon from 1808 to 1814, Goya remained in Madrid and even worked for the French occupying forces. Goya saw himself principally as a painter of portraits, which make up about a third of his painted oeuvre, and around 160 authentic portraits by his hand survive.[1]

Two events would shape Goya's later works. The first was in 1792, when Goya was forty-six. He developed a mysterious illness, possibly an autoimmune disorder, which nearly killed him and caused him to go completely deaf. The isolation and challenges caused by his hearing loss shaped his worldview, driving him towards deeper introspection and influencing his creative output in remarkable

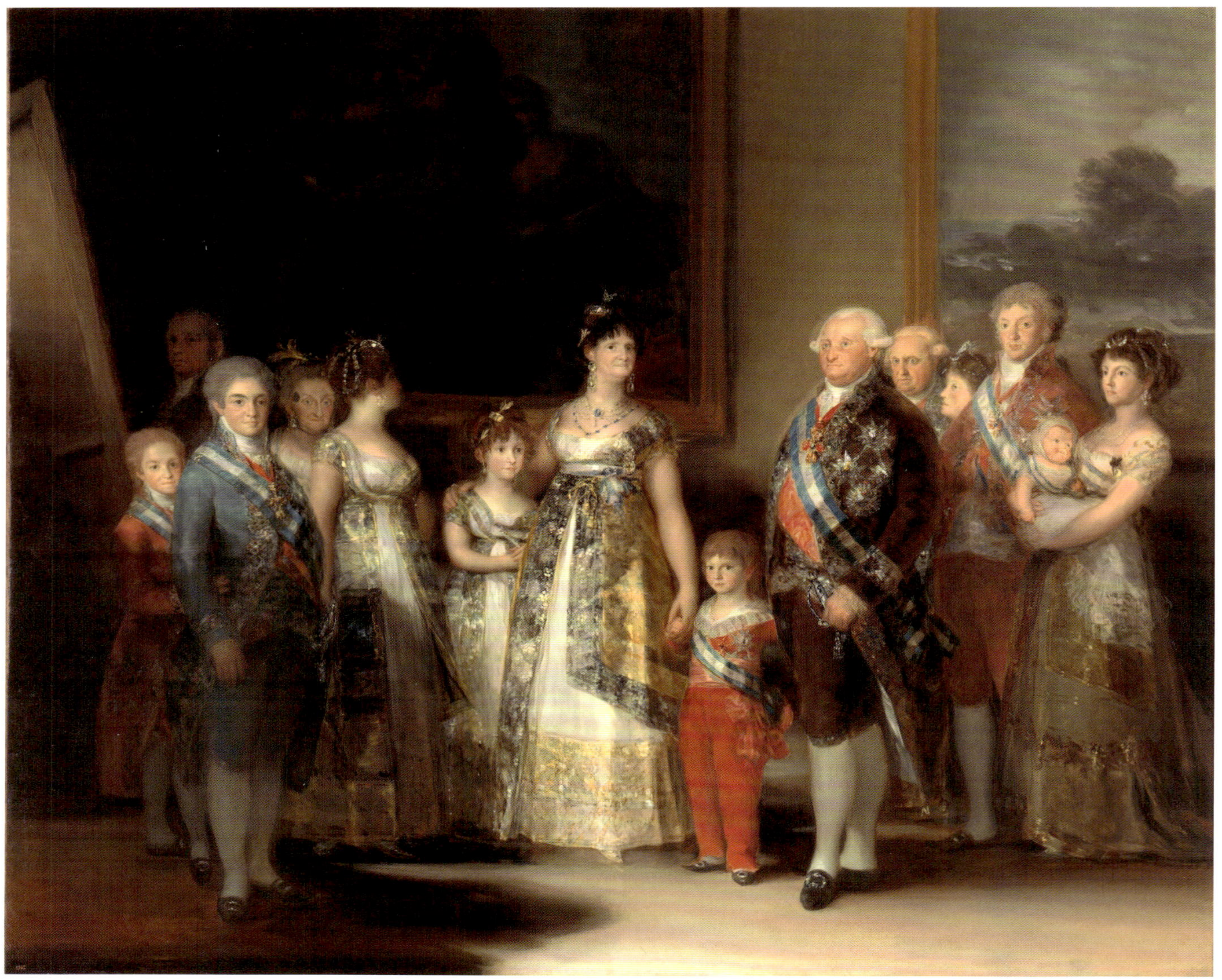

ways. His work became darker and more contemplative as he started to explore his personal visions, reflecting themes of seclusion, mortality and the grotesque.

The second event that shaped his work happened in 1808, when Spain's former ally Napoleon invaded first Portugal then Spain, triggering the Peninsular War (1808–14) and ushering in years of fighting.

THE RETURN OF FERDINAND

Up until the loss of his hearing, Goya had lived a charmed existence, but by the time of the Peninsular War his worsening health, combined with the war and its ensuing atrocities (many of which he personally witnessed), was affecting him deeply. From this point we start to see even darker and more emotional subject matter,

Francisco de Goya, *Charles IV of Spain and his Family*, 1800–1.

FRANCISCO DE GOYA

culminating in his extraordinary series of prints *The Disasters of War* (1810–20), which to this day can be seen as a profound critique of human suffering, violence and the moral degradation that war brings.

After a long and protracted war, Napoleon was forced out of Spain in 1814, and King Ferdinand VII, who had been living in exile, was reinstated. Ferdinand declared himself absolute monarch and set about reversing any democratic changes made by Napoleon. He reinstated the Spanish Inquisition – a draconian judicial institution established to combat heresy, which Napoleon had abolished – annulled the constitution, suppressed the free press and clamped down on dissent with an iron fist. In many people's eyes, he was just another dictator who would do anything to hang on to power.

THE ROAD TO THE BLACK PAINTINGS

Most of Goya's darker works were produced in secret, while he was still an employee of the court. *The Disasters of War* was a revolutionary set of images, a political illustration of how in times of war, ordinary men do extraordinary things. The graphic works show that anyone is capable of evil, and that the Spanish could be

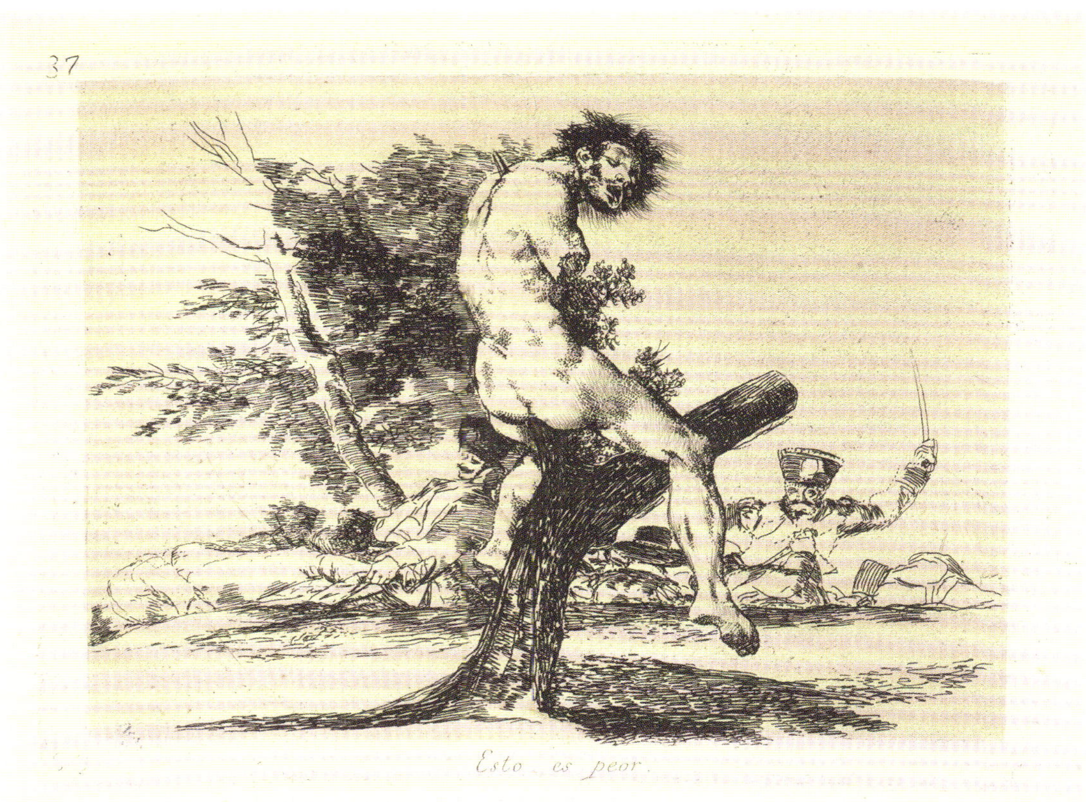

Francisco de Goya,
This Is Worse,
c. 1810–20.

just as cruel and sadistic as the French
– an even-handed approach that was
unprecedented in art concerning conflict.[2]

The restoration of Ferdinand to the
throne turned out to be the beginning of
the end for Goya's career as a court painter
– his liberal sympathies did not sit well
with the king's absolutist and reactionary
monarchy. Even though he painted several
portraits of Ferdinand after the Peninsular
War, none were direct commissions from
the Spanish monarch, but rather for minor
provincial institutions.[3]

Goya, fearful that he too would be
swept up in the unstable political climate,[4]
moved to the outskirts of Madrid in 1819.
This country house would become the setting
for one of the most intriguing chapters of
his life. It was here that he set about creating
a remarkable cycle of fourteen works
painted directly onto the wallpaper of the
two floors of his house. We don't even know
what Goya called them – he never mentioned
them, and nobody else saw them – but
after his death, they were titled the *Pinturas
Negras*, or *Black Paintings*, because of the
dark colours used, their deep pessimism
and their diabolical subject matter.

The *Disasters of War* prints are bleak
enough, but his *Black Paintings* are the work
of an artist who had not only witnessed
animalistic, extreme behaviour during the
Peninsular War and seen his friends exiled
or imprisoned, but one who had become
totally disillusioned with his fellow man
and desperately needed to express it in
the only way he knew how – in paint.

The paintings are filled with grotesque
imagery, sombre tones and disturbing
narratives, and are a stark contrast to his
earlier works. They are the visual diary of
a man confronting his deepest fears and
anxieties in the twilight of his life.

SATURN

Saturn Devouring his Son is the most famous
of the *Black Paintings*, and the most horrific,
but it is worth noting that it is probably more
shocking to us than it would have been to the
19th-century Spanish. We must see the work
in the context of Romanticism, a cultural
obsession with the supernatural and the rise
of the Gothic novel.

Horrific and macabre images were
commonplace at this time and seen as popular
entertainment. 'Phantasmagoria', theatres
where images of monsters and ghoulish subject
matter were projected using lanterns, were
hugely popular at the time in Madrid.

Saturn was originally painted on the
walls of Goya's dining room, a gruesome image
to look at as he ate his supper. Its title was
assigned by later historians, but the subject
does seem to be that of Saturn devouring
his offspring.

In the Roman myth, Saturn overthrew
his father to become the ruler of all the gods,
but he was afraid that history would repeat
itself with one of his own children. So, he
ate – or rather swallowed whole – five out of
his six children. The sixth was Jupiter, hidden
by Saturn's wife, Ops, as soon as he was born,
who then did indeed grow up to overthrow
his father.

The scene has been tackled before by
artists, most notably by Peter Paul Rubens,
whose own painting *Saturn Devouring
his Son* (1636) was in the Spanish Royal
Collection in the 18th century, and likely
inspired this painting.

In Goya's version, Saturn is a crazed
psychopath whose terror-filled eyes show us
he is acutely aware of the deed he is carrying
out against his own flesh and blood but unable
to control his actions. He is a figure in the
grip of hysterical madness, in literal blackness,
but holding on to power at any cost.

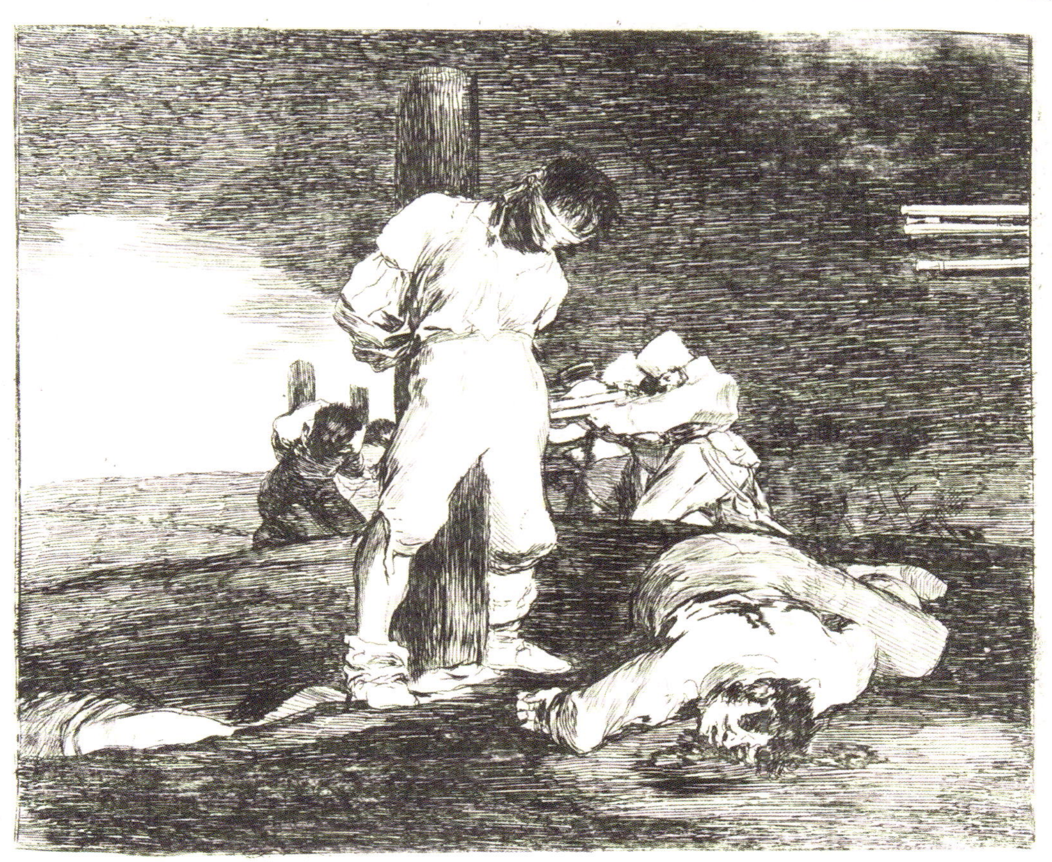

*The graphic works show
that anyone is capable of evil*

 SATURN DEVOURING HIS SON

It is the meatiness of Goya's painting
that makes it horrific; Saturn grips the child's
body so tightly that his knuckles are white
and blood oozes from the crushed corpse.
He has already bitten off the head and devoured
it, along with parts of the infant's arms, but
now Saturn is really chowing down. It is a
deviation from the original story, in which the
child is swallowed whole – only a small detail,
but one that really amplifies the horror.

It is a painting of raw flesh. The flesh
that Goya personally witnessed as innocent
citizens were cut down by armed soldiers
during the Peninsular War, as piles of corpses
were left on the street, and poverty and
hunger left a mass of starving bodies in
Madrid. Goya had witnessed Hell on Earth,
and he transcribed what he saw for future
generations using brushstrokes that are rough
and chaotic, ramping up the primal brutality
and raw emotion.

Many have interpreted the work as a
representation of just how far those in power
will go to retain control, even to the point
of committing murder.[5] It is a stark allegory
for the means by which authority is often
maintained – that is, through violence and
oppression – but it can also be seen as a
warning, illustrating the psychological toll
of holding on to that authority at any cost.

It is quite possible that Goya was using
the myth as a metaphor for his beloved
Spain, a nation driven by fear, paranoia
and a destructive devotion to autocratic

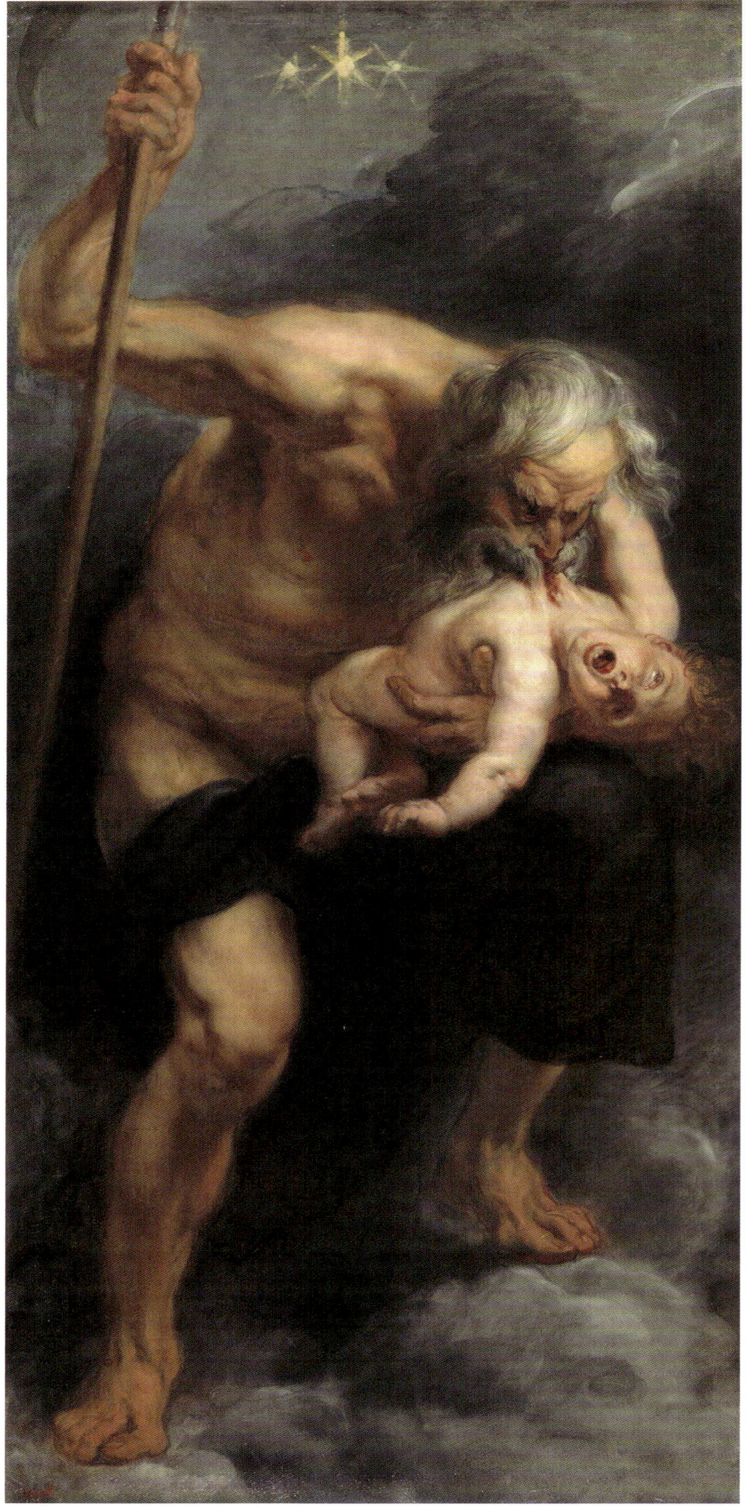

FRANCISCO DE GOYA

opposite
Peter Paul Rubens,
*Saturn Devouring
his Son*, 1636.

Francisco de Goya,
*Saturn Devouring
his Sons* (or *Time
Devouring Men*),
c. 1797.

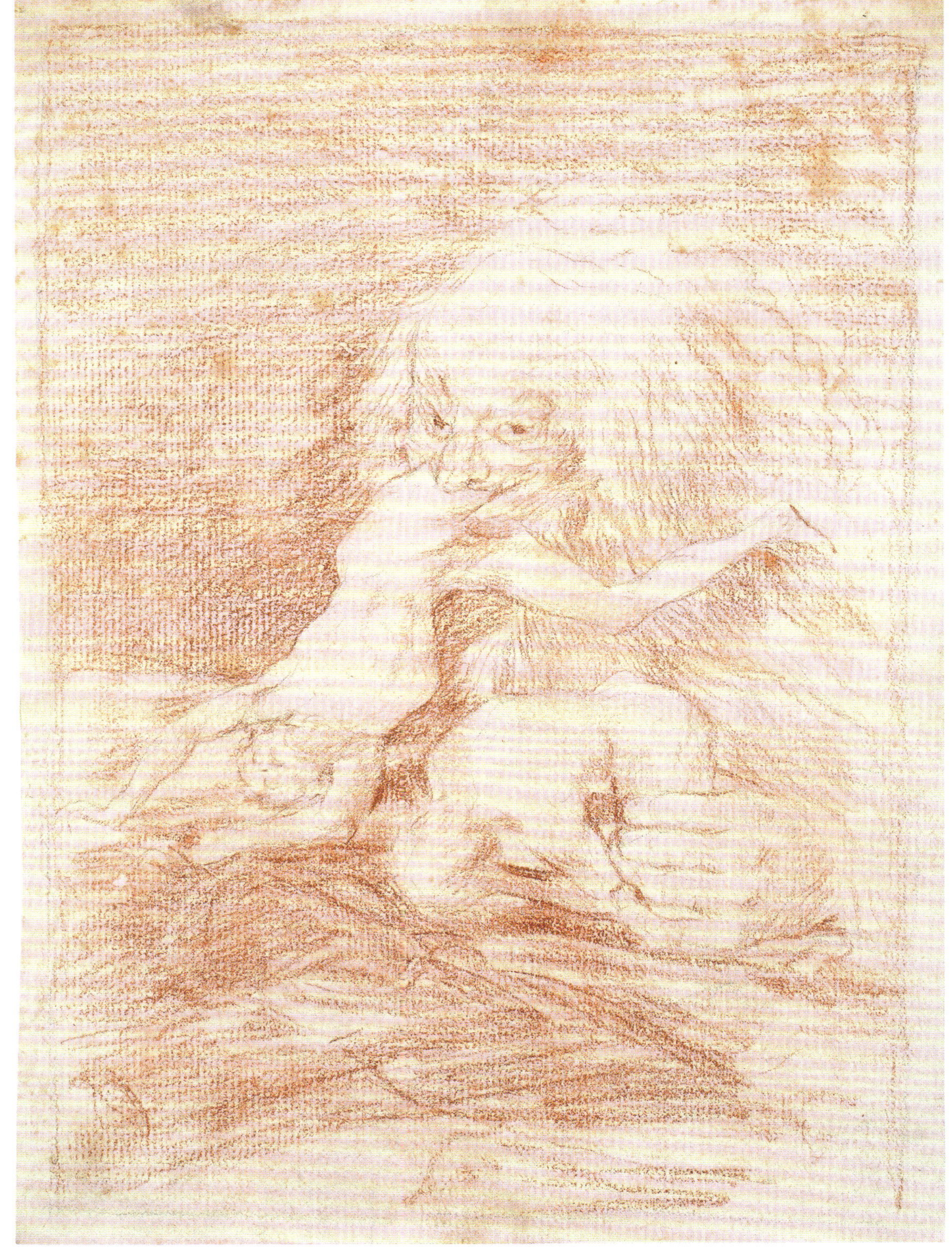

control. Spain as a self-devouring entity, with an uncontrollable addiction to flesh/power.

But there is more than one way to look at *Saturn* and the *Black Paintings*.

In mythology, Saturn is often associated with time (Chronos in Greek mythology), and his devouring of his children can be seen to symbolize time 'consuming' all things, including life itself. The work was painted at a point in Goya's life when he was grappling with the inevitability of death, and with that in mind, it's easy to see *Saturn* from the viewpoint of a tired old man, disappointed and angry with his home country, contemplating his own mortality and the fleeting nature of existence, success and status.

REMOVING THE WORKS

In 1873, thirty-five years after Goya's death, the artist's house was bought by Baron Émile d'Erlanger, a Parisian banker, who shortly after had the paintings along with the wallpaper taken off the walls and transferred to canvas. If you've ever tried to strip wallpaper, you know how impossible that task would have been. Many of the details were lost and repainted by the restorers – and some were purposely altered for aesthetic reasons. *Saturn Devouring his Son* escaped relatively untouched.

The removed works were then shown in Paris in 1878, and there seems to have been little to no reaction, except for one British critic, who called them immoral.[6] In 1881 the baron donated the works to the Spanish state.

FINAL STATEMENT

As the political situation in Spain worsened and Ferdinand's persecutions of liberals increased,[7] Goya moved to Bordeaux in France, where he died in 1828 at the age of eighty-two, perhaps knowing that the *Black Paintings* were to be his final set of masterpieces.

Over the course of his extremely long career, Goya moved from portraiture of the wealthy elite to deeply haunting and enigmatic works. As his subject matter became more challenging, his palette darkened, and his brushstrokes became looser, almost impressionistic, a confrontation both stylistically and politically.

The devastating *Saturn Devouring his Son* still challenges – if not haunts – us today. Goya's critique of authoritarianism remains profoundly relevant 200 years after it was created. It still speaks to us of the continuing dangers of oppressive regimes and political violence, alongside the persistence of human suffering.

FRANCISCO DE GOYA

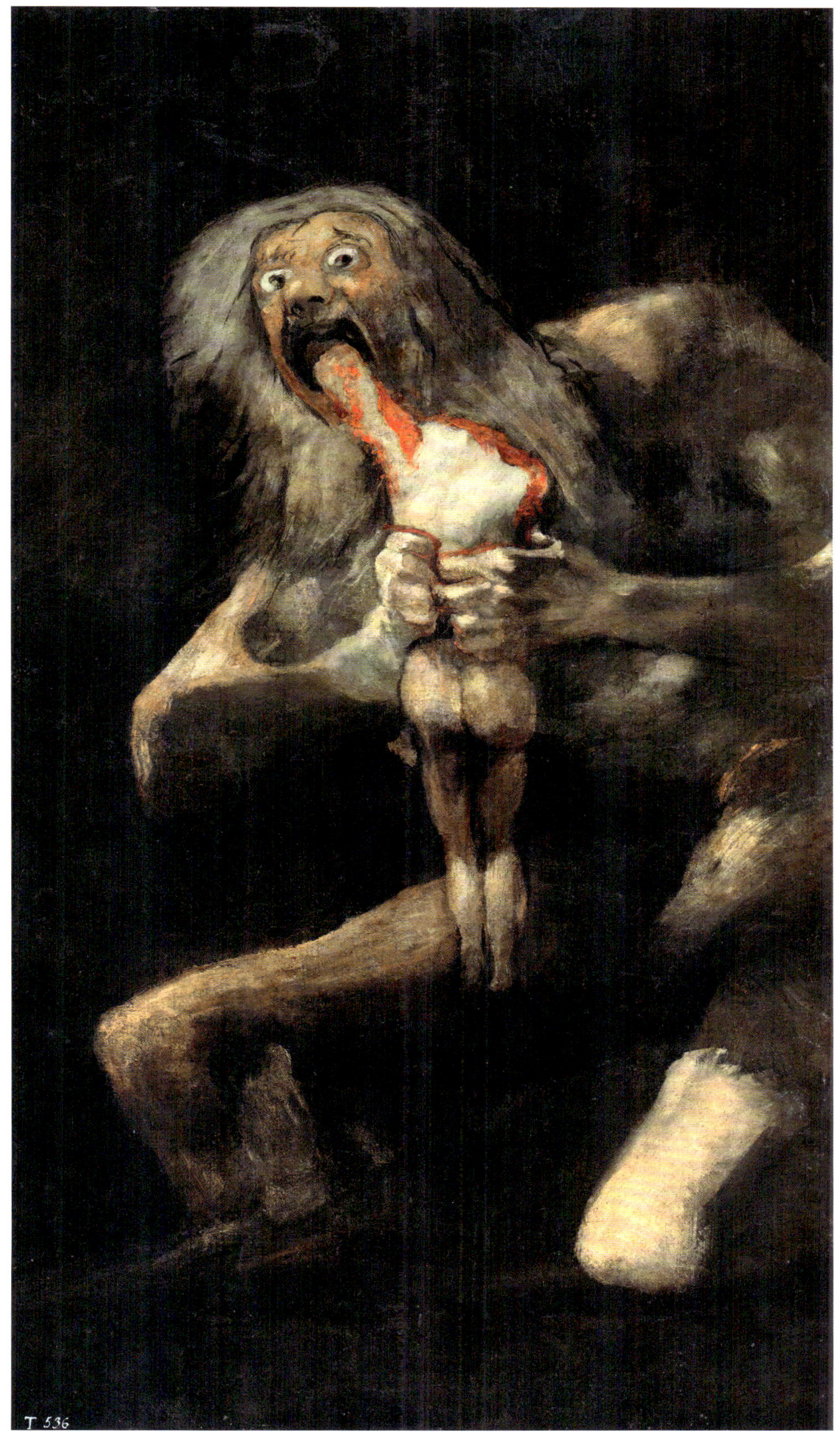

KATSUSHIKA HOKUSAI

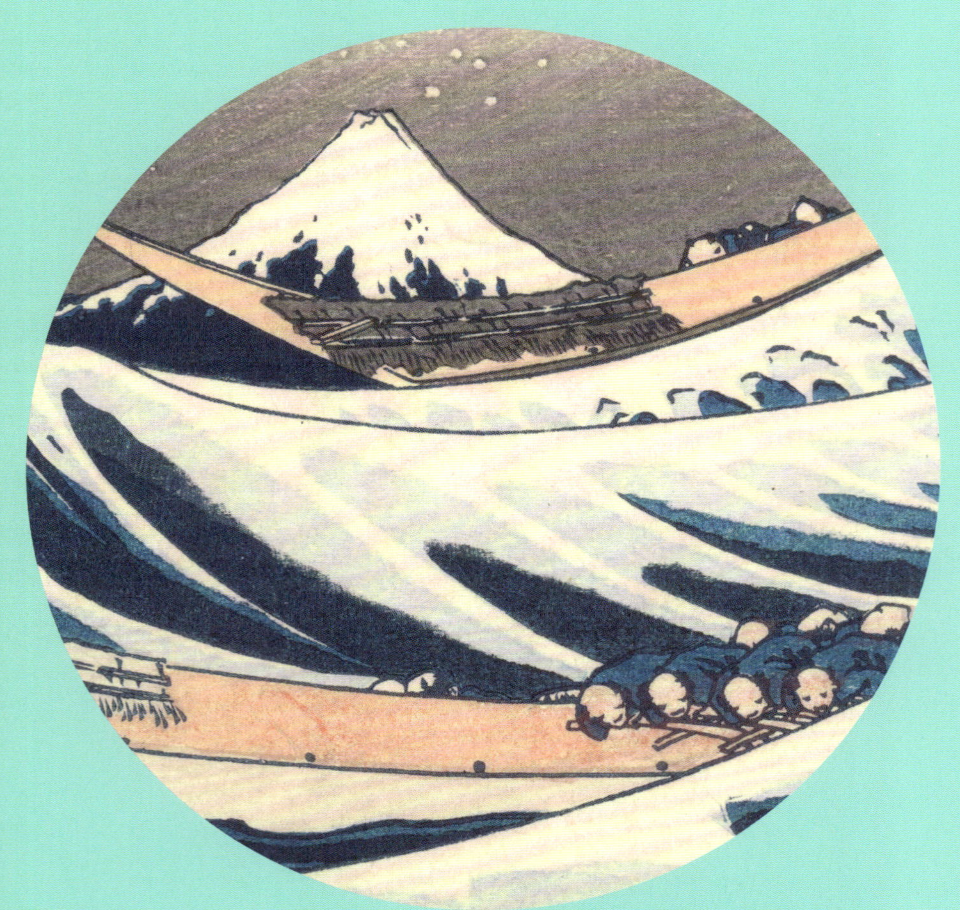

UNDER THE WAVE OFF KANAGAWA

1830–32

ART FOR THE MASSES

In 1639 Japan closed its borders and cut itself off from the outside world for more than 200 years. Foreigners were expelled, Western culture was forbidden and entering or leaving Japan was punishable by death. It was under these circumstances that quintessentially Japanese art developed: art for the people, consumed on an unprecedented scale.

JAPAN CLOSES OFF

Under the Wave off Kanagawa, or *The Great Wave*, by Katsushika Hokusai was created around 1830 during the Edo period, which refers both to the city of Edo – now Tokyo – and to a specific timeframe from 1603 to 1867, during which, after centuries of civil war and unrest, the Tokugawa shogunate took over Japan. It was a time when much of the rest of the world was becoming industrialized, and the Japanese were becoming increasingly concerned about foreign invasions as ships from the West started appearing more frequently on its coastline. There was a rumoured threat of a Russian invasion in 1804, and by 1825 the shogun rulers, or their feudal overlords, ordered all overseas vessels circling the island to be fired upon.

Although Japan only fully opened its waters to trade thirty years after *The Great Wave* was published, the artists of the island nation already had a fascination with the sea. On the one hand, it provided a rich bounty of food, but on the other, it could bring terrible destruction. Japan was not a seagoing nation, as the shogunate had banned the construction of large ships, and the sea, which had protected its peaceful isolation for so long, also threatened to bring foreign invasions – invasions that would eventually lead to the downfall of shogun rule.

Under the Tokugawa shogunate, strict social order was imposed in line with philosophical neo-Confucian thought. At the top of the hierarchy was the aristocracy: the emperor, court nobles and the shoguns. The rest of the population was split into four classes: samurai (侍 shi), followed by farmers (農 nō), then artisans (工 kō) and finally merchants (商 shō). Interaction between the classes was restricted to commerce, and there were strict codes of public behaviour.

Essential trade was permitted only with Korea, the Netherlands and China. In the case of the last two, contact was limited to the tiny artificial island of Dejima in Nagasaki. Overall, the system operated efficiently, and by the mid-18th century Edo was one of the biggest cities in the world, with a population of one million.[1]

Thanks to improved farming techniques, there was significant growth within the agricultural industries, leading to an economic boom in Japan. The people of Edo could afford to relax and had money to spend. Merchants, once considered lower class tradesmen in

The artists of the island nation already had a fascination with the sea

feudal Japan, enjoyed a rise in social and economic status, and could now afford luxuries like education, travel, theatre, books and art.

THE FLOATING WORLD

The merchants' search for sensual pleasures became known as *ukiyo*, 'the floating world', a culture that developed in the Yoshiwara red-light district of Edo. It was here that you could find kabuki theatres, puppet shows and poetry readings, as well as brothels.

Woodblock prints like *The Great Wave* were known as *ukiyo-e*, or 'pictures of the floating world', and were sold in their thousands. Pictures of kabuki actors, beautiful courtesans and geisha were avidly collected.

At about 20 mon (文) – roughly the price of a double portion of noodles – *ukiyo-e* were art for the masses. They were sold much like posters, to be displayed in people's homes, and there was a constant demand for new prints and images of celebrities to collect. Although printed by hand, mass production made them highly profitable for publishers.

Katsushika Hokusai was one of the most successful and prolific commercial artists in the *ukiyo-e* market. Alongside illustrating over 200 books, creating 1,000 paintings and numerous drawings, he had also designed at least 3,000 colour prints before he came round to creating what is now his most recognizable image, *The Great Wave*, when he was in his final years (1820–49).[2]

He once modestly said of himself: 'All I have done before the age of 70 is not worth bothering with.'[3] It was at the age of seventy that the elderly artist embarked on his most ambitious project yet, *Thirty-Six Views of Mount Fuji*, one of which was *The Great Wave*.

THE THIRTY-SIX VIEWS

By the late 18th century, there was a steady flow of Japanese merchants, peddlers, pilgrims and pleasure-seekers heading to Mount Fuji. The mountain was considered sacred and had over 800 shrines dedicated to it, with religious confraternities known as Fuji-kō, or 'Fuji cults'. Buying one of these prints was the equivalent of picking up a souvenir postcard, and *The Great Wave* was probably printed around 8,000 times in this period.[4]

In the prints, Hokusai used Mount Fuji as a backdrop to the everyday activities of ordinary people. The mountain is shown from different viewpoints and distances, and we see farmers and fishermen, wives and servants, going about their business in different seasons and weather conditions, all perfectly captured in hues of mostly blue.

The creation of the views coincided with the new availability of Prussian blue, a synthetic colour that had previously been very expensive. The first five prints in the series were printed almost entirely in this shade – even the outlines, which are usually printed in black. Compared to other blues, Prussian blue was more vivid, had a greater tonal range and, most importantly, didn't fade. It also made the prints 'exotic', and therefore desirable to the public. They would be marketed as *aizuri-e*, 'blue printed pictures'.

In these images, Hokusai used different saturations of the same colour to give us the impression of the hours before dawn or after dusk,[5] when our eyes can't make out distinct shades because of the soft light. The *Thirty-Six Views* were classic Hokusai: condensing images to their purest form and prioritizing line and colour. They feature ordinary working-class

Katsushika Hokusai, *Self-Portrait as a Fisherman*, 1835.

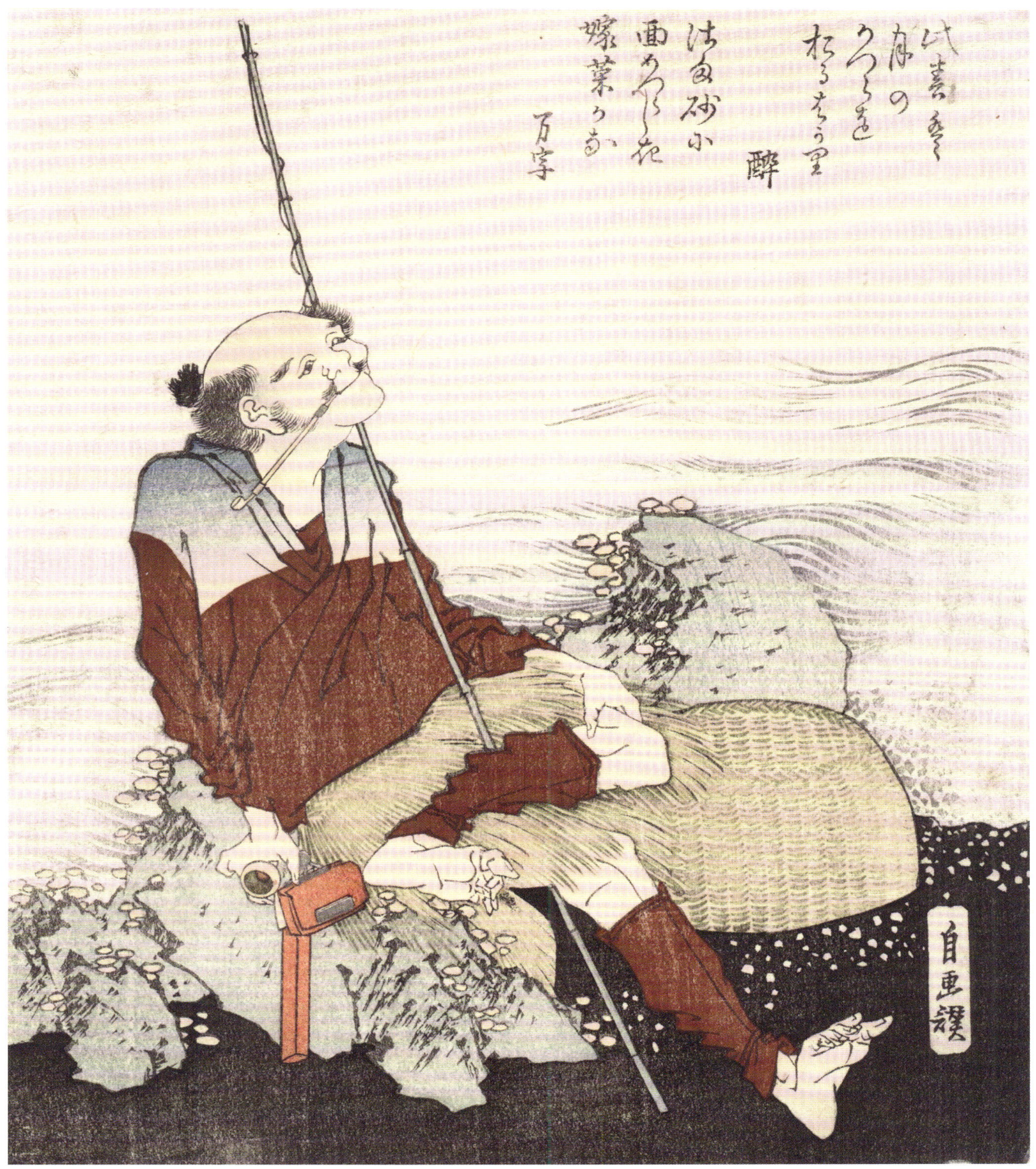

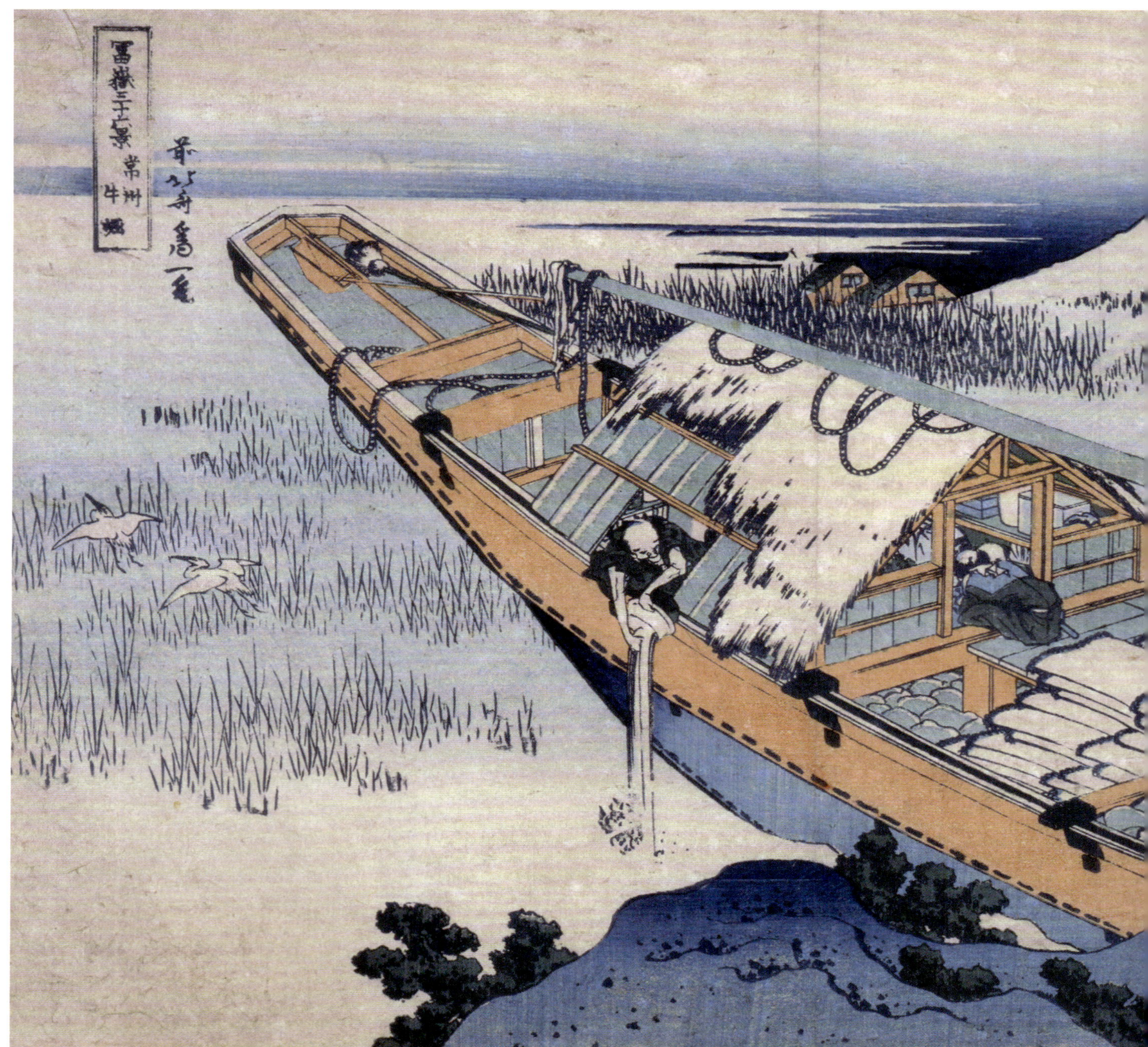

冨嶽三十六景　常州牛堀
前北斎為一筆

men and women along with the sacred
landscape, mostly in the distance, a perfect
blend of the physical and the metaphysical.

In his *Thirty-Six Views of Mount Fuji*,
Hokusai showed Mount Fuji as seen from a
forest, a village, a lake, a river and a beach, but
it was the sea view known as *The Great Wave*
that would create international interest in
Japanese art. At first glance, *The Great Wave*
is simply a seascape, but on closer inspection,
you see that this beautiful, stylized wave is about
to engulf three boats of terrified fishermen, as
Mount Fuji recedes into the distance.

A HYBRID ART FORM

Japan effectively closed its borders in 1603,
with Japanese people banned from leaving and
very few foreigners allowed in.

The Dutch were allowed two trading ships
per year, and this was just about the only direct
connection between Japan and Europe at the
time. When Dutch merchants brought fragile
goods into Japan, they were often wrapped
in cheap Dutch etchings, and in this way
Hokusai and other artists were able to access
Dutch landscape and seascape prints. Later,
in an accidental cultural exchange, Japanese
exporters used cheap Japanese prints to wrap
their goods, and that was how, in the 1860s,
they came to be seen in Europe and to inspire
the Impressionists. In fact, Claude Monet first
came across Japanese prints used as wrapping
paper at a spice shop in the Netherlands.[6]

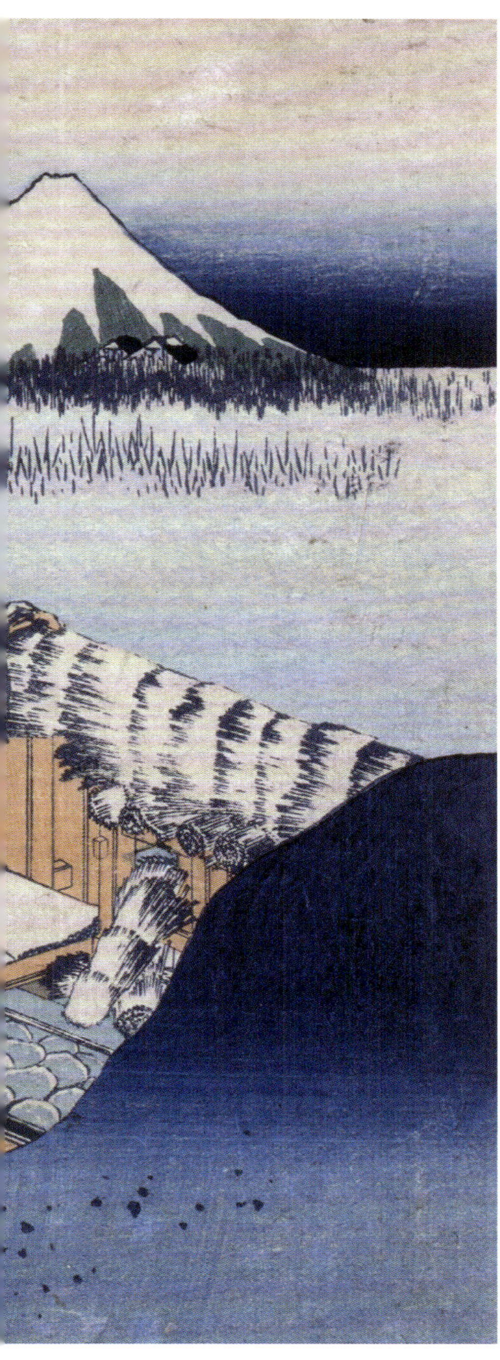

Katsushika Hokusai,
*Ushibori in the
Hitachi Province
(Jōshu Ushibori)*,
from *The Thirty-Six
Views of Mount Fuji*,
c. 1830–33.

UNDER THE WAVE OFF KANAGAWA

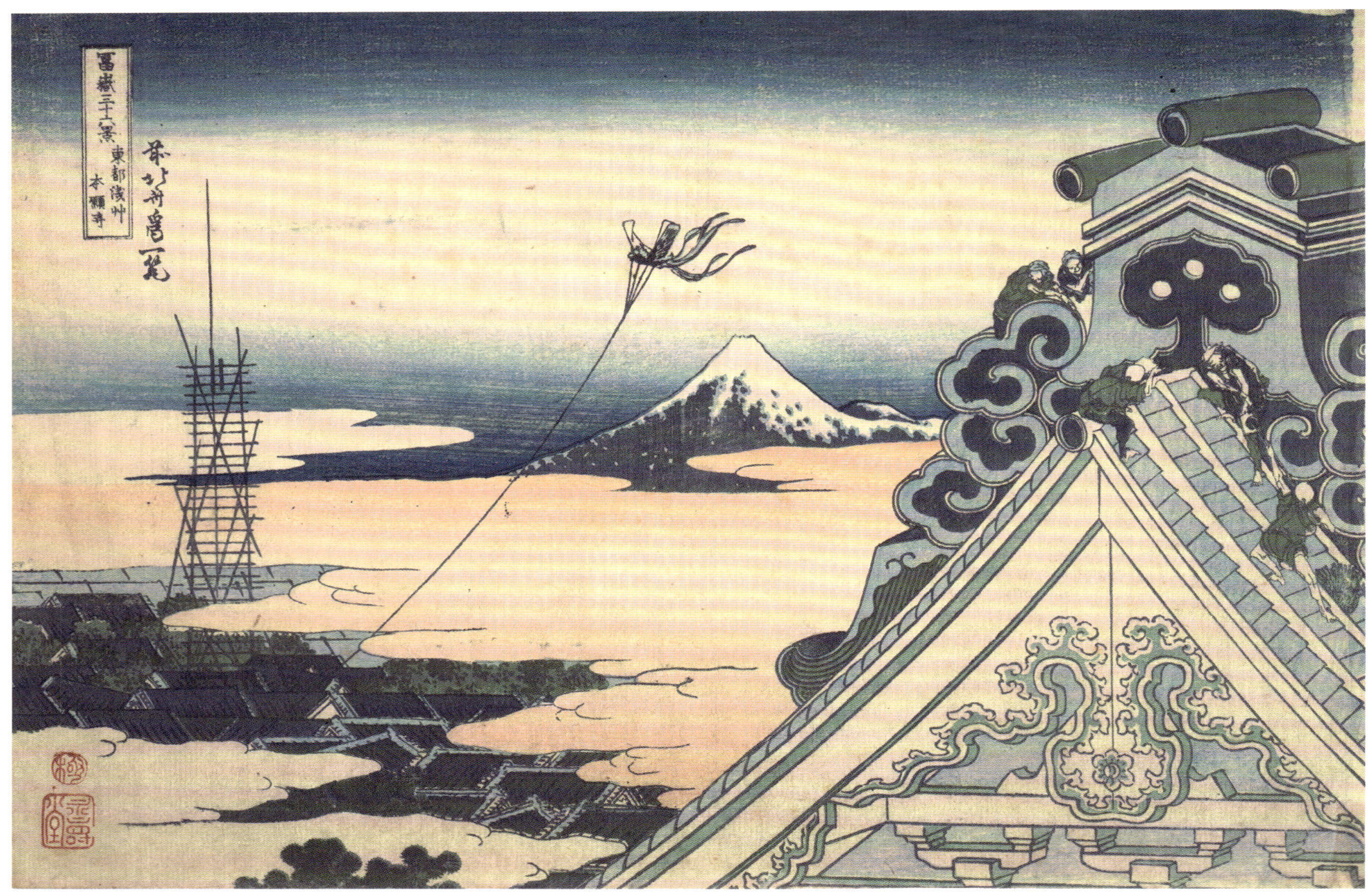

In European artworks of the time, artists used linear perspective to replicate the fixed physical position of the viewer, but in Japanese (and Chinese) landscape painting, there is no distinct point to guide us. The Japanese were inclined to depict a panoramic view of the scene – more like a floating view, or a scattered perspective, as we find in *The Qingming Scroll* (see Chapter One). The floating view was the preferred choice for 'high art' bought by the elite in Japan, such as paintings, but 'low art' prints like *ukiyo-e* used European perspective as a sort of novelty. It even had its own sub-genre: *uki-e*, or 'perspective pictures'.

All of these influences would come together in Hokusai's *Thirty-Six Views*, where the artist used Japanese settings and storytelling but European perspectives and framing mechanisms, and a specific focal point to create depth in his images.

THE GREAT WAVE

Likewise – and ironically for a work that is seen as a characteristically Japanese image – *The Great Wave* is in fact a hybrid of Japanese and European ideas. The choice of a low horizon, typical of Dutch landscapes, adds an element of dynamism through the movement of the wave, which takes up two-thirds of the image.

Katsushika Hokusai,
*Hongan-Ji Temple
at Asakusa in Edo*,
1830–32.

Japanese viewers who were used to a bird's-eye view or floating view in Japanese seascapes would be enraptured by the dramatic and unfamiliar perspective that Hokusai portrayed.

The Great Wave corresponds to an actual geographical location at the mouth of Edo Bay (now Tokyo Bay) where you can see Mount Fuji. The water is notoriously dangerous, and boats still have trouble sailing there today.

The dark shade of the slopes of Mount Fuji and the brightness of the snow-covered cap suggest it is early morning, with the sun rising behind the viewer, lighting the mountain's peak, and the snow line on Mount Fuji indicates that it is spring. Springtime is one of two bonito seasons in Japan, a fish that was considered a very special delicacy in the city of Edo. It was hugely valuable and worth risking the treacherous waters for, as receiving the first catch was a status symbol for which wealthy merchants would pay a fortune.

The boats are pointed away from the shores of Edo, so the boatsmen can't be on their way to the market in the city, so they must be on their way home. However, Hokusai has taken some artistic liberties with the boats' positions, and if we flip the image, the boats would be travelling *towards* the market.

So, the flipped image is 'correct', but it is less dramatic if you read it as Japanese readers did, from right to left. Japanese viewers see an oncoming wave in Hokusai's final version, but an outgoing wave in the flipped version.

With *The Great Wave*, Hokusai would take deep perspective to its ultimate conclusion, with Mount Fuji, the 'star' of the series, dwarfed (and framed) by a huge wave that's started to crest. As the spray breaks, it creates ominous and almost animalistic, claw-like fingers that reach out as if to capture the boatsmen, as its spume then becomes the 'snow' falling on Mount Fuji. It is a masterpiece of design that perfectly evokes a sense of impending danger, perhaps even Japan's very real fear of foreign incursions into their territory.

This is an image of instability and uncertainty.

THE BIRTH OF JAPONISME

The *Thirty-Six Views* prints were hugely successful, and in response to rapid sales of the initial set, Hokusai expanded the popular collection to comprise forty-six woodblock prints. He might not have been rich, but healthy sales of his commercial work meant that he would at least have been financially stable in his final years.

Hokusai didn't live to see Japan's self-imposed isolation come to an end. In July of 1853 a flotilla of fully armed ships sailed uninvited into Edo Bay on behalf of the US government and demanded that the Japanese begin to trade with the United States. Japan agreed to, slowly but surely, reopen its borders, which had been closed for over 200 years.[7] Japanese art was finally revealed to an astonished world, and in France, where there was a craze for all things Japanese, a new term was invented: Japonisme. Bold designs, intense hues, simple lines and areas of flat colour would influence a whole generation of artists and precipitate modern art.

One artist in particular would produce a painting that was directly inspired by *The Great Wave*: Vincent van Gogh's *Starry Night* (see Chapter 14).

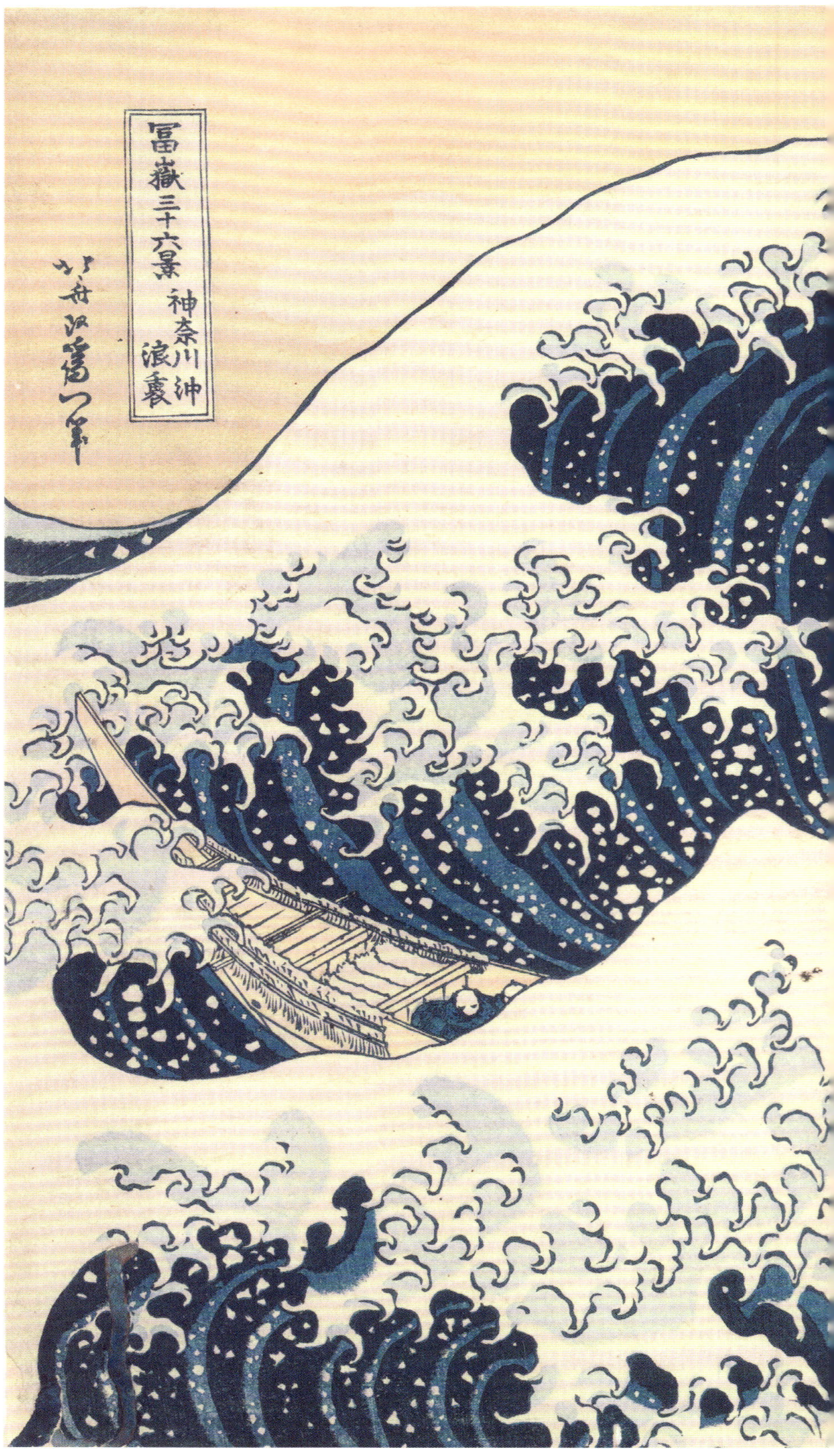

Katsushika Hokusai, *Under the Wave off Kanagawa*, from *The Thirty-Six Views of Mount Fuji*, c. 1830–33.

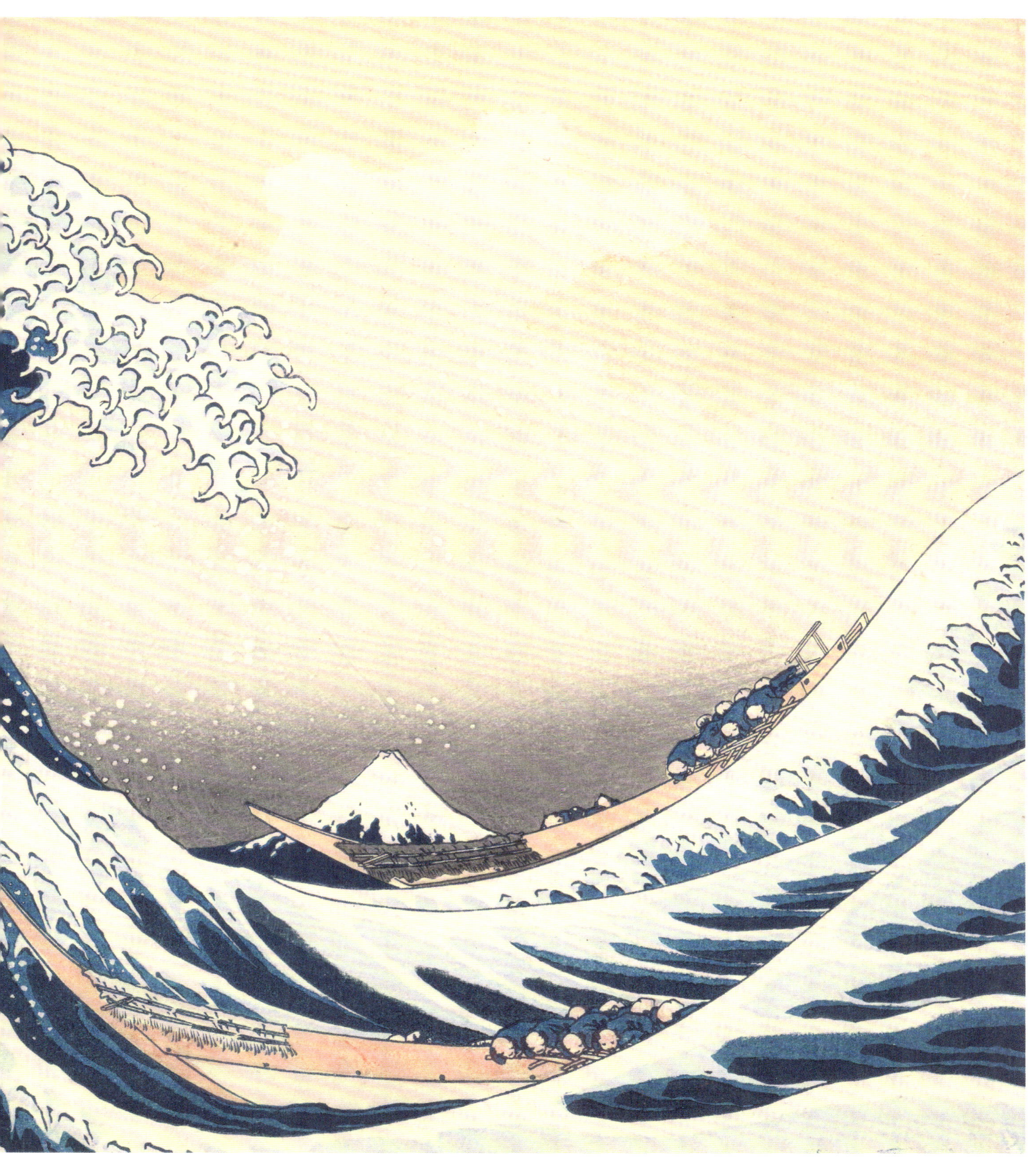

J. M. W. TURNER

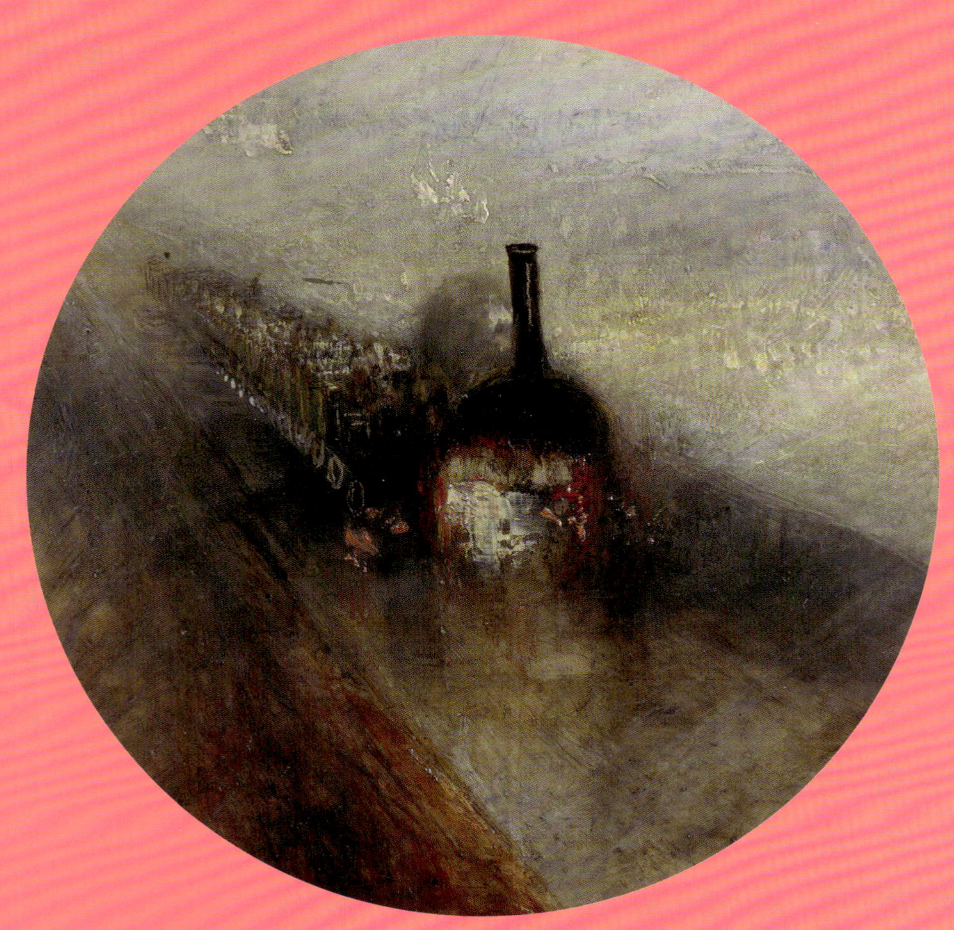

RAIN, STEAM AND SPEED – THE GREAT WESTERN RAILWAY

1844

A PAINTER OF OUR TIMES

The Industrial Revolution was in full swing by the time Joseph Mallord William Turner painted one of his last great oil paintings, *Rain, Steam and Speed – The Great Western Railway*, in 1844.

When we think of a painter like Turner, we think of glorious sunsets, dramatic skies, rocky outcrops and stormy seas; we think of nature, and we think of the sublime. But there is another side to Turner. By the time he painted *Rain, Steam and Speed*, he had already transformed landscapes, and now he was attempting to do the same with a radical kind of art that embraced the modern world with enthusiasm, the world of science, machines, technology and industry.

From 1775, the year Turner was born, until his death in 1851, Britain experienced a monumental and unprecedented leap in technological innovation, from the harnessing of electricity and the invention of the steam railway locomotive to the discovery of new elements, and even plans for the world's first computer. Advances that would change the world forever.

A WORKING-CLASS MAN

Turner was an artist who defied convention: he was out of step with the culture of his time,[1] and engaged in themes rarely explored by his contemporaries. His private life too was equally unconventional. He was notoriously antisocial, never married (but had two daughters) and was variously described as odd, rude and secretive, with some critics even questioning his sanity.[2]

Unlike his rival John Constable, who was born to a wealthy family, Turner was an outsider who never lost his strong cockney accent (for which he was mocked by the establishment).[3] He was the son of a barber and began to draw as soon as he could walk. His father encouraged his talent, and even displayed his drawings in his barbershop.[4]

All his life, Turner had an incredible work ethic, to the exclusion of everything else, and by his twenties he was a wealthy man. He would be criticized for being pushy, money-grabbing and ambitious, but he really had to work hard to build connections, while other more well-heeled artists like Constable and Sir Thomas Lawrence benefitted from a network of family and neighbours who helped them meet influential patrons.[5]

The critics loved Turner initially, but that started to change late in his career as his mature style became less and less realistic.[6] Works like *The Fighting Temeraire Tugged to Her Last Berth to Be Broken Up, 1838* (1839) focused less on specific details and more on atmospheric conditions; they became much more fluid and abstract, more like studies of colour and light.

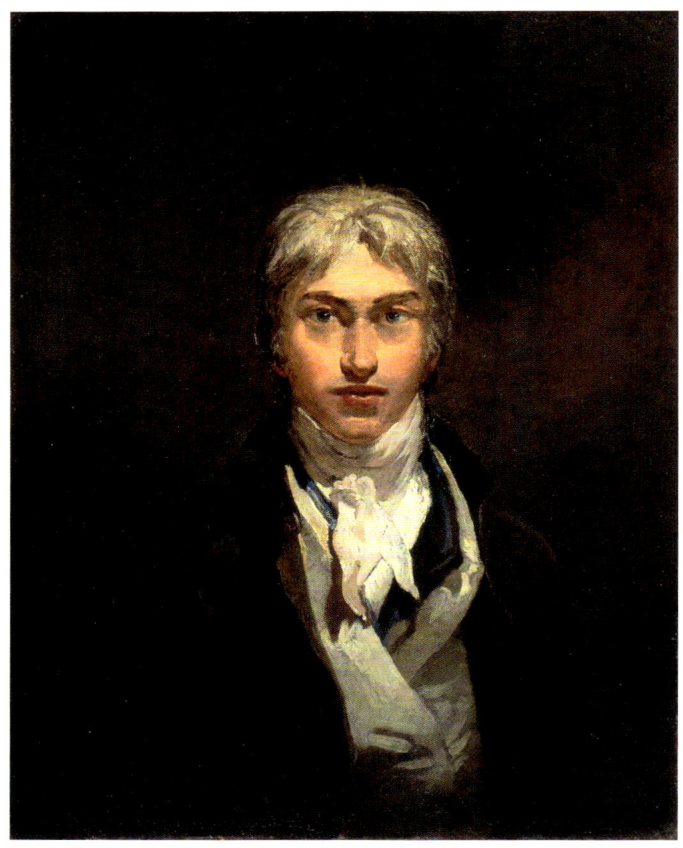

ROMANTICS AND THE SUBLIME

Turner would become a leading light in the Romantic movement, a period roughly from 1760 to 1870 when there was much debate about the meaning of the 'sublime'.

It was a theory that developed in the 18th century to explain the extreme emotion one can experience when seeing art, an overwhelming feeling of awe that is both terrifying and pleasurable, which served as a basis for Romanticism.

Turner's sea storms and mountain scenes exemplified the sublime, and later his more industrial works like *Snow Storm – Steam-Boat off a Harbour's Mouth* (1842) and *Rain, Steam and Speed* evoked the kind of strong emotional reactions that transcend ordinary experience, another aspect of the sublime.

In the mid-19th century Britain was still in the early days of train travel; the first railway line had opened in 1825 and transformed the nation. The Victorians were experiencing a railway frenzy, travelling across the country at unimaginable speeds (on average 33 mph, or 53 kph!). At the time of this painting, millions of passengers were using the railways.

And yet, considering the dramatic potential of trains, they hardly featured in academic art, confined instead to more popular art forms like engravings and cartoons.

TOWARDS THE FUTURE

The train in the painting passes over Maidenhead Railway Bridge, crossing the River Thames on the route from Paddington to Bristol, still a vital part of Britain's railway infrastructure. It was the largest elliptical arch bridge of its time, built using flat brick arches and spanning a particularly broad stretch of the Thames, designed to allow boats to pass easily through its arches. It was built five years before *Rain, Steam and Speed* was painted and was seen as a triumph of engineering.[7]

Several features in the painting might seem strange to a modern viewer. The train's proportions don't look right, but that's because it is a broad-gauge train, much wider than the ones we use today. There are just three small puffs of steam coming out of the engine's funnel – strange, as we associate huge,

The critics loved Turner initially, but that started to change late in his career as his mature style became less and less realistic

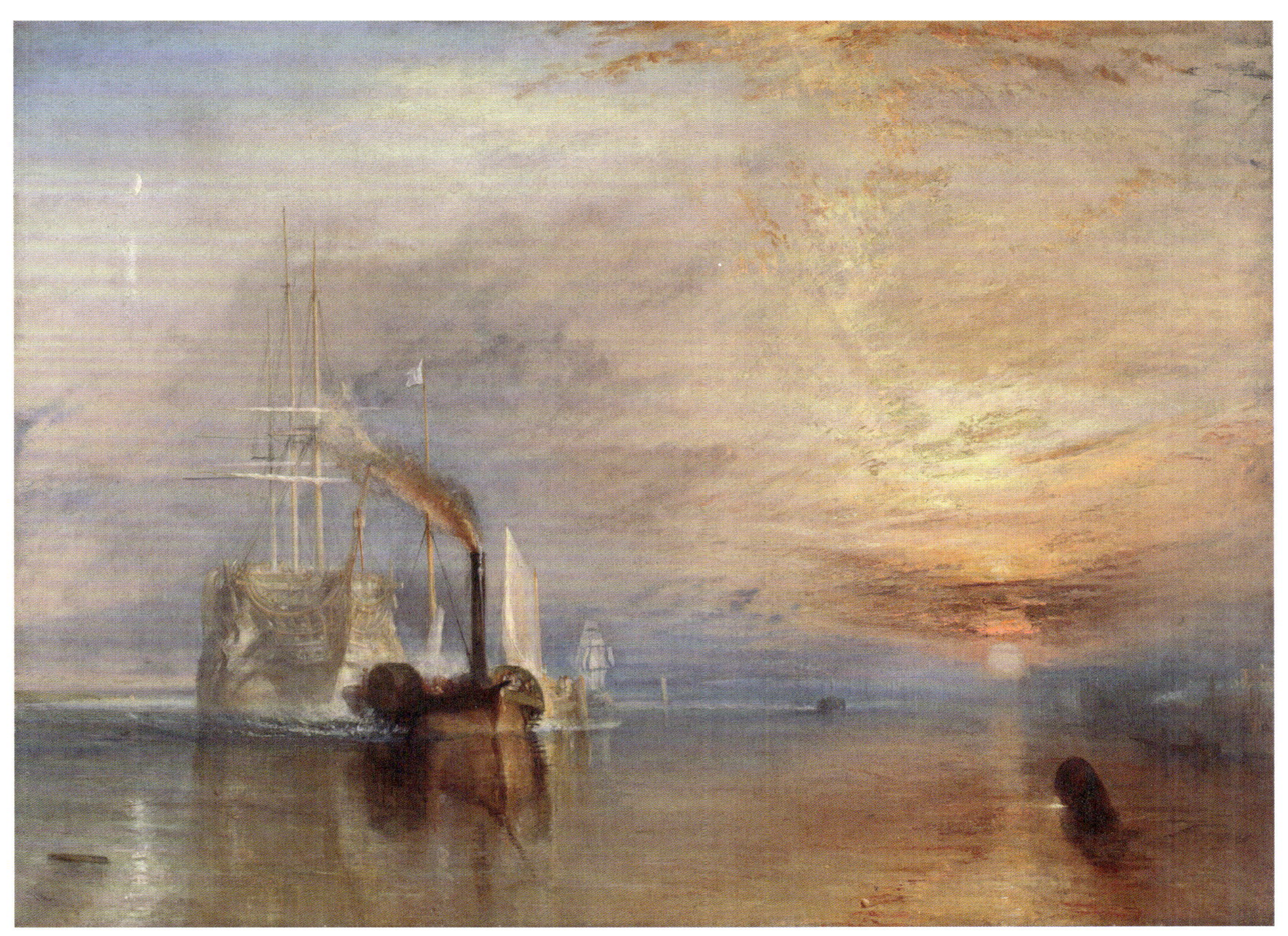

billowing plumes with steam locomotives, but engines of this period did not produce these great clouds.

We can see the top hats of figures exposed to the elements, and that's because it is not the luxurious carriages ridden by the upper classes but an open-topped goods wagon, on which passengers could travel for a small fee. The Railway Regulation Act of 1844 meant that all carriages would eventually be roofed.

Nobody had painted trains like this before. Victorian paintings had shown the occasional train choo-chooing away in the distance, but Turner depicted a train hurtling out of the canvas, towards the future. It is above all a painting by someone who had a keen interest in the fast new technology of steam ships and trains, and the overwhelming feel of the painting *is* that of motion.

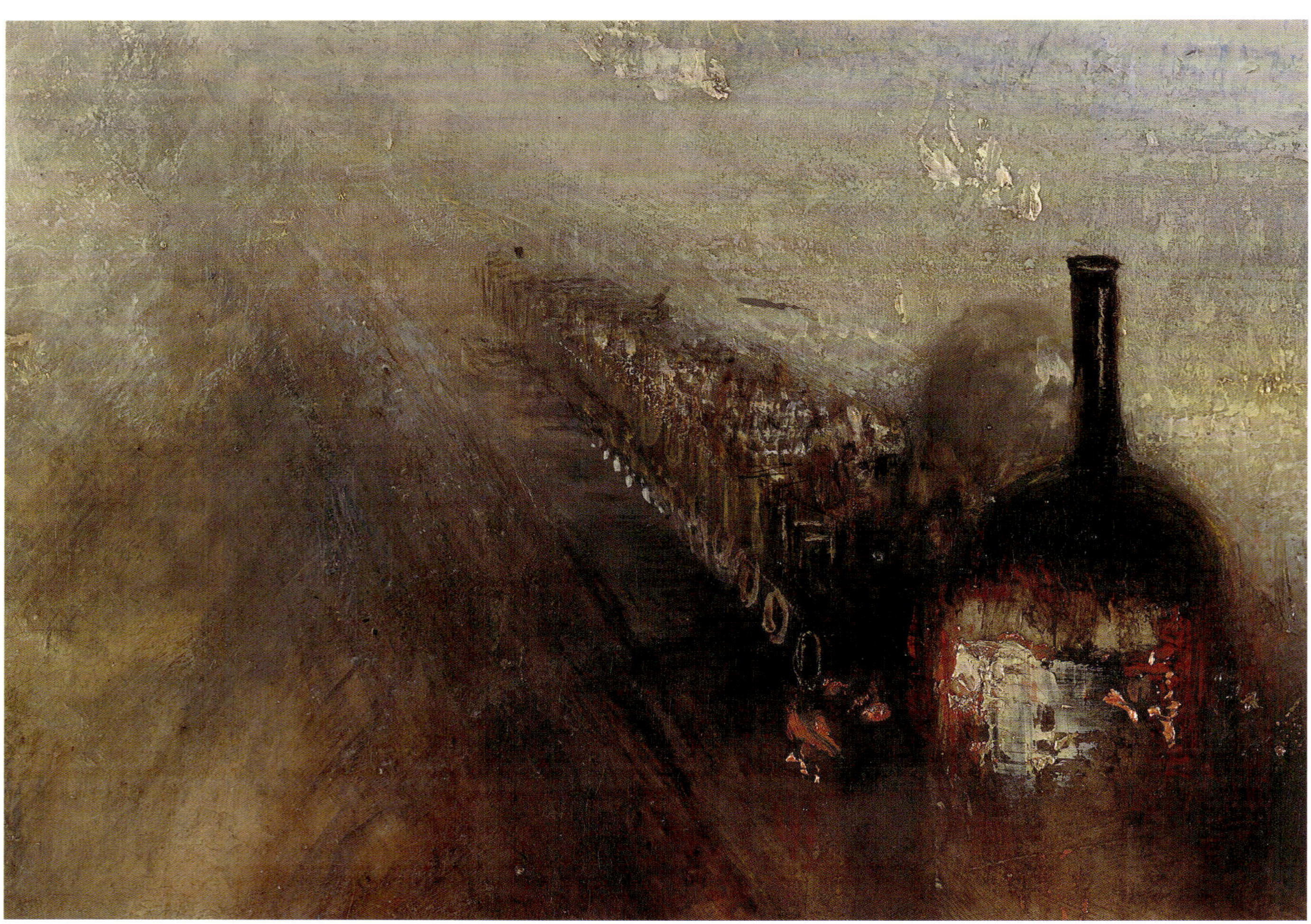

J. M. W. TURNER

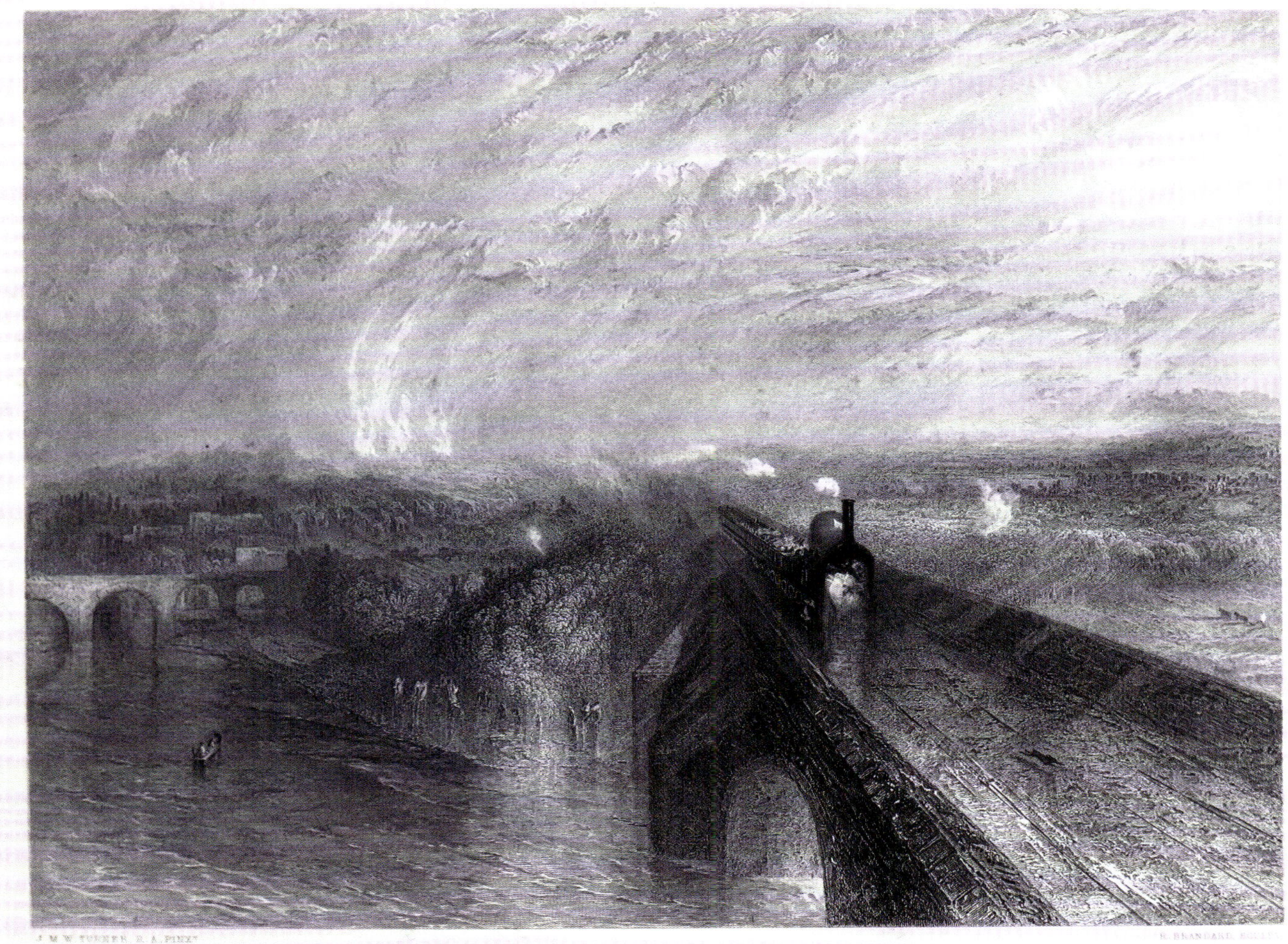

THE PAINTING

Turner was sixty-nine when he painted *Rain, Steam and Speed*. While his contemporaries were churning out romanticized idyllic landscapes, he embraced the fairly risky modern subject of the Industrial Revolution, becoming the chronicler of new technology as it developed.

The painting manages to perfectly capture the essence of the industrial age while retaining Turner's Romantic fascination with light, atmosphere and the sublime. Many viewers at the time hadn't experienced a train journey yet, but Turner made sure they really could imagine the heat and the speed, the rain lashing against their faces and the wind rushing past as soot flies around.

He would start a painting like *Rain, Steam and Speed* by making wide brushstrokes

opposite
Rain, Steam and Speed
(carriage detail).

Robert Brandard
(after J. M. W. Turner),
Rain, Steam and Speed,
1859.

across the canvas with a paint-loaded, hard-bristled brush that would often leave brush hairs behind. He would swirl and merge colours together: the sky in *Rain, Steam and Speed* fuses with the horizon and details get lost in the mists. The train itself appears as a dark, almost ghostly shape emerging from the fog, with its locomotive only partially visible, and speed is suggested by the perspective, rather than mechanical detail.

Turner rarely used underdrawings, instead painting directly onto the blank canvas. He used a palette knife to apply thick impasto to the centre of *Rain, Steam and Speed*,

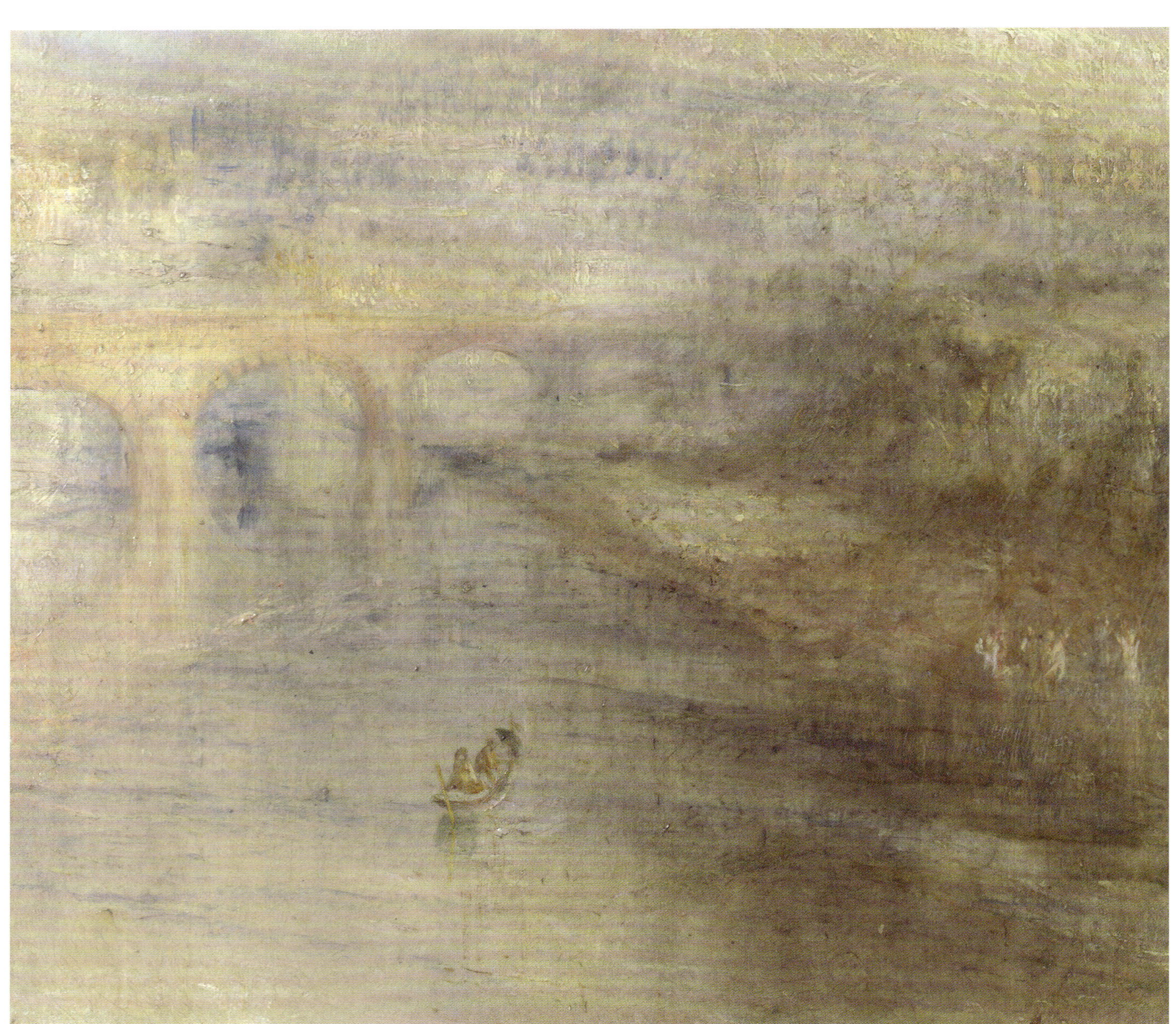

J. M. W. TURNER

harnessing its depth and texture to achieve the swirling rain. He would use any technique to achieve his desired aesthetic; brush, palette knife, rags, sticks or fingers, anything would do to get thick layers of paint on the canvas.

The firebox of the train looks as if it has eaten through the casing of the engine chassis, exposing the sharp red of the furnace. It was a classic Turner trick to use a splash of bright red to pull focus where he wants us to look – in this painting towards the red-hot centre of that swirling vortex he has created – and he knew the Victorians equated train travel with speed, steam *and* fire.

He would constantly revise his paintings; even after the paint dried, he would come back and add fresh paint, which would cause problems for later conservators as the paint would sometimes flake off.

One casualty of this is a hare which appears in front of the train, as if trying to outrun it. Barely visible now, we know the hare is there because of a later engraving that Turner approved (p. 123).

The hare, traditionally associated with speed and agility, is a contrast to the modern machine's power and relentless motion. It may be there to symbolize the relationship between humanity, nature and the unstoppable force of technological advancement.

There was always the possibility of a last-minute change during 'varnishing days', a tradition at the Royal Academy where artists were allowed to touch up their paintings on the walls, or 'varnish' them, after paintings had been installed for exhibiting. Turner was notorious for adding elaborate finishing touches in front of other artists, and the hare was one such late addition.[8]

PAST, PRESENT AND FUTURE

As we would expect of someone who taught perspective at the Royal Academy, Turner's

The sky in Rain, Steam and Speed fuses with the horizon and details get lost in the mists

use of vanishing perspective really does make the train race towards us out of the haze. The strong diagonals of the railway line cut straight through the composition and disrupt the existing countryside, which suggests that while the painting *is* an homage to the beauty of the railways, their growth and progress was also seen as destructive – a popular sentiment at the time.

Elements of Britain's past disappear behind the train, like the maidens dancing on the banks of the Thames and the tiny boat in the river below, headed in the opposite direction – scenes highlighting the shift from older, slower ways of life to the fast-paced, industrialized world.

A farmer with a horse-drawn plough can be seen in a practice that is not long off being mechanized, and like the figures in the boat, the farmer too is moving towards the background in the opposite direction of the train.

Time is important in this painting, both in the immediate sense of motion and the broader sense of historical change. By placing the viewer in the train's path, Turner suggests that time, an unstoppable force, is rushing towards us, while the past, is receding to the back of the painting, a vanishing way of life.

THE FATHER OF IMPRESSIONISM

Many of Turner's contemporaries resisted the spread of industrialism that was changing the landscape of Britain; Turner, however, not only faced up to these challenges but celebrated them, producing a Romantic vision of the modern world.

When *Rain, Steam and Speed* was shown
at the Royal Academy in 1844, it caused a
sensation, and huge crowds queued around
the block just to see it. Nobody else was
producing work like it; nobody else was even
remotely thinking like Turner in his final
years. The critics however had reservations,
and the reviews were mixed, with the *Morning
Chronicle* describing it as 'probably the most
insane and the most magnificent of all these
prodigious compositions'.[9]

It is of course anachronistic to use terms
like 'Impressionism' when talking about Turner,
but just under twenty years after his death
in 1851, Claude Monet and Camille Pissarro
moved to London to avoid conscription for the
Franco-Prussian war and stayed for several
months. In that time, they visited the National
Gallery several times and discovered Turner's
radical explorations into the effects of light
and colour.[10]

His themes and concerns made their way
back to Paris in 1871, and a year later, Monet
produced *Impression Sunrise*, the painting that
would give Impressionism its name, before
producing a series of works depicting Gare
Saint-Lazare railway station in 1877.

J. M. W. Turner may have been Britain's
greatest Romantic painter, but we can safely
say he was also the father of Impressionism.

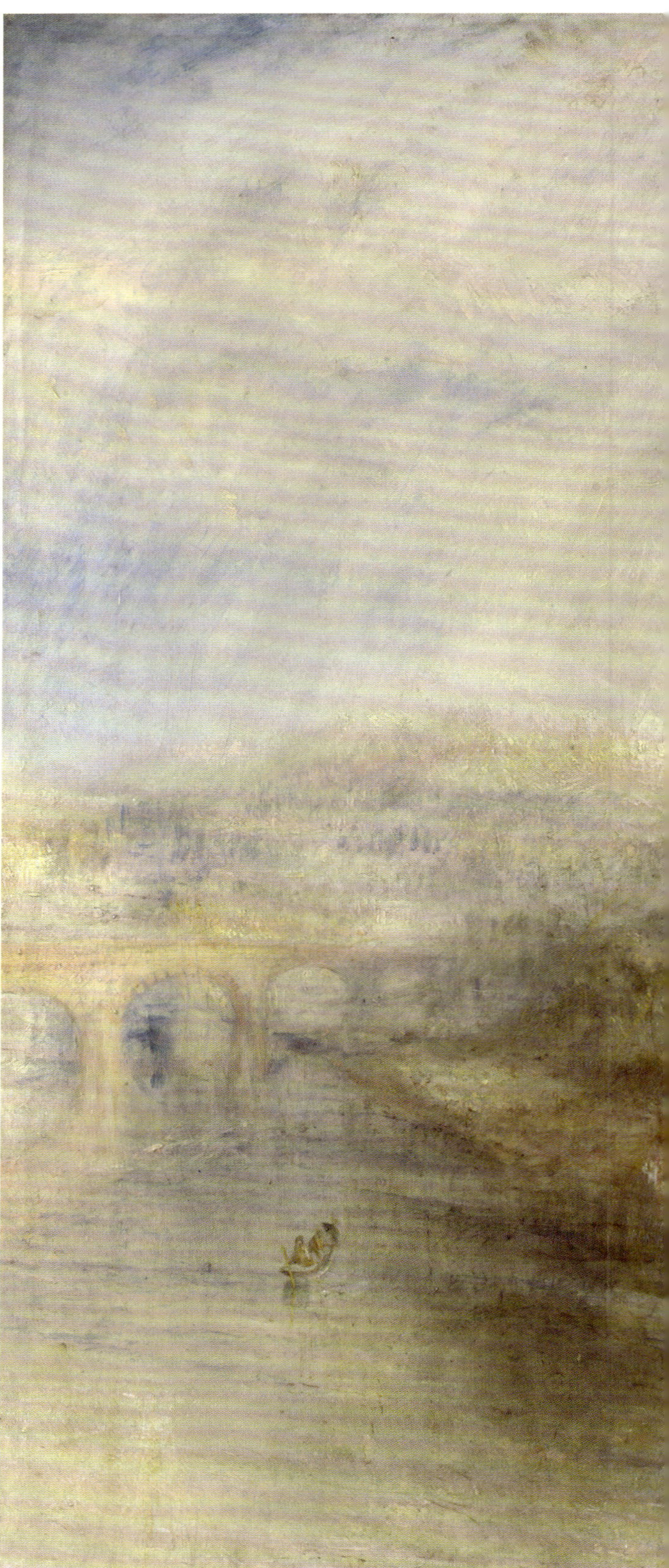

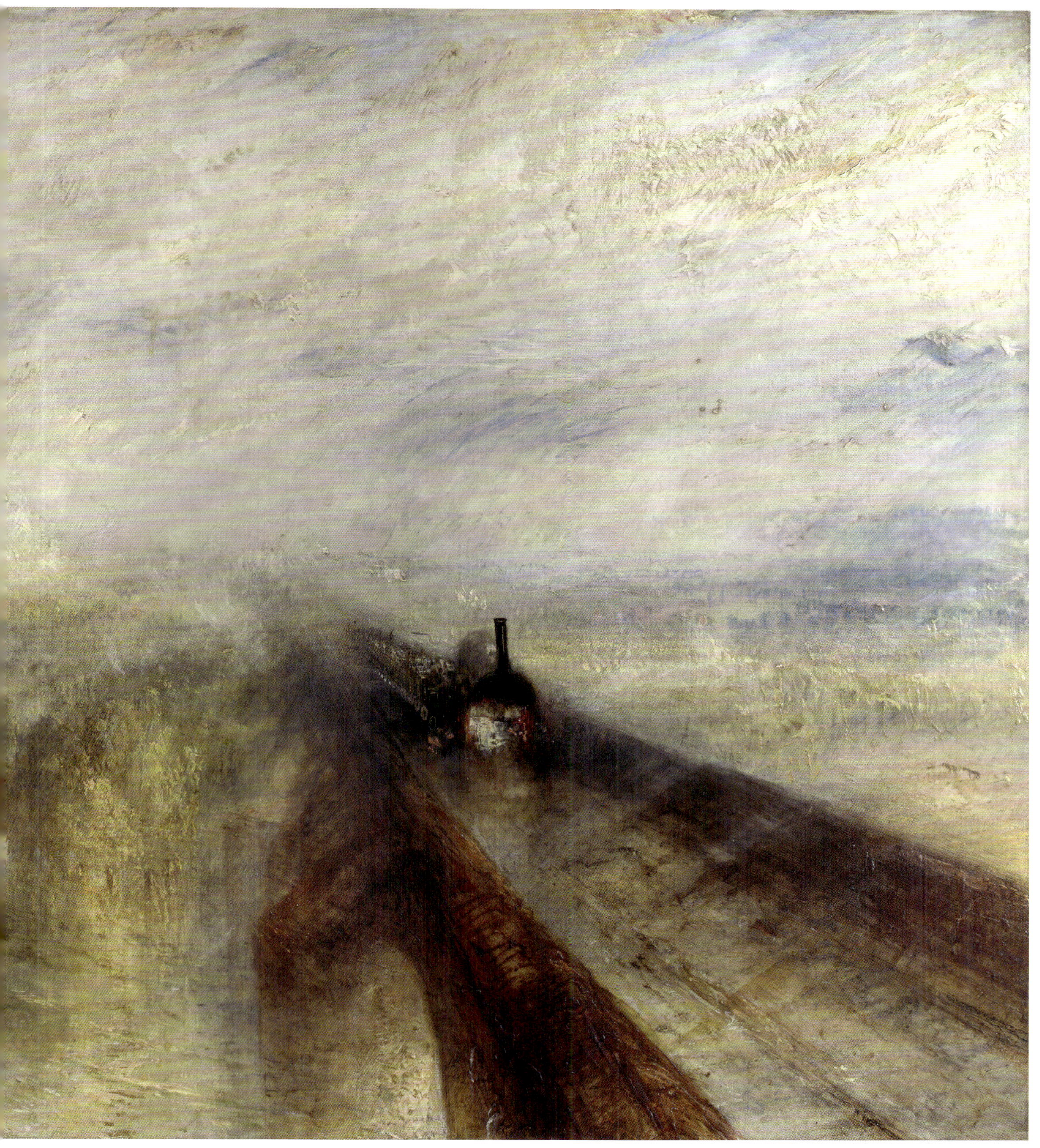

AUGUSTE RODIN

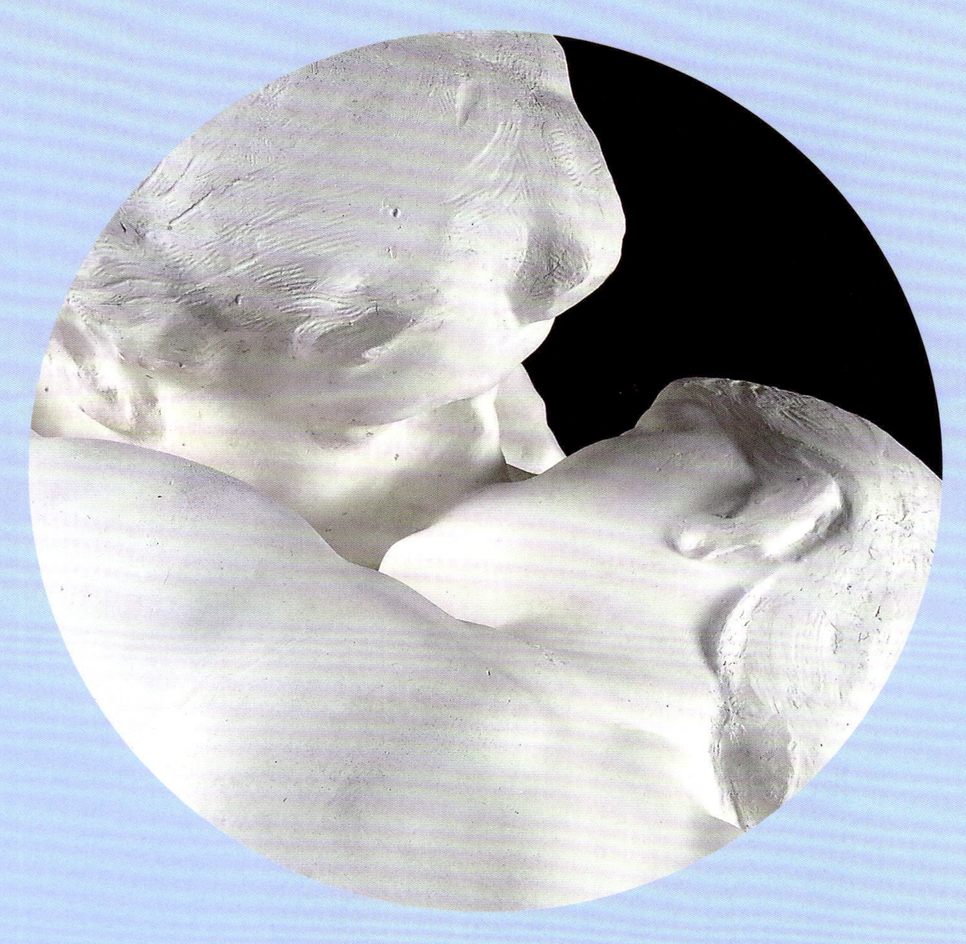

THE KISS

1882

THE 'NEW' MICHELANGELO

The Kiss by Auguste Rodin is a sculpture that has come to be seen as a perfect image of idealized romantic love, though this was not the artist's original intent. The sculpture was conceived from the outset as a depiction of the real-life adulterous lovers Paolo Malatesta and Francesca da Rimini, who are condemned to the second circle of Hell in Dante Alighieri's *Divine Comedy* (*c*. 1321) as punishment for their lust.

While *The Kiss* is now considered one of the greatest erotic sculptures of all time, Rodin himself regarded it as overly conventional, describing it as nothing more than 'a large sculpted knick-knack following the usual formula'.[1]

A JOBBING CRAFTSMAN

Rodin's is an old-fashioned rags-to-riches story. He was born into poverty in 1840, and despite having an extraordinary gift as an artist, he was dismissed repeatedly by the art establishment, coming to see himself as a lifelong 'outsider'. Rejected by the Académie des Beaux-Arts in Paris three times, which devastated him,[2] he instead served a long and difficult apprenticeship as a jobbing craftsman in dozens of studios – including that of the highly successful and prolific sculptor Albert Carrier-Belleuse – learning numerous skills that would serve his own practice later.

At the age of thirty-five, after more than two decades working outside of academic sculpture, Rodin was struggling. He was going through a period of intense re-evaluation: his training up to that point gave him unparalleled technical virtuosity, but the work he produced was conventional and essentially decorative.

MICHELANGELO

In February of 1876 he risked a stable job and steady income and set off on a trip to Italy to study the works of Michelangelo, a trip that has been described as 'one of the seminal events in modern art'.[3] Michelangelo worship was at a peak in the 1860s and 1870s,[4] and the work of the Italian master would have a decisive influence on Rodin's career, pushing him to explore new, complex ideas.

He was profoundly impacted by Michelangelo's portrayal of the human body, particularly his ability to express a wide array of emotions and psychological depth through the nude form, from raw strength to deep vulnerability. This approach resonated deeply with Rodin, who wanted to capture these elements in his own sculptures. He would later acknowledge that 'My liberation from academicism was via Michelangelo.'[5]

Like his hero, Rodin made stone breathe, and he too would push materials in new directions, advancing the development of modern sculpture. By drawing on lessons from Michelangelo, as well as classical traditions, Rodin would create radical, innovative forms,

Auguste Rodin,
The Kiss (detail),
1882.

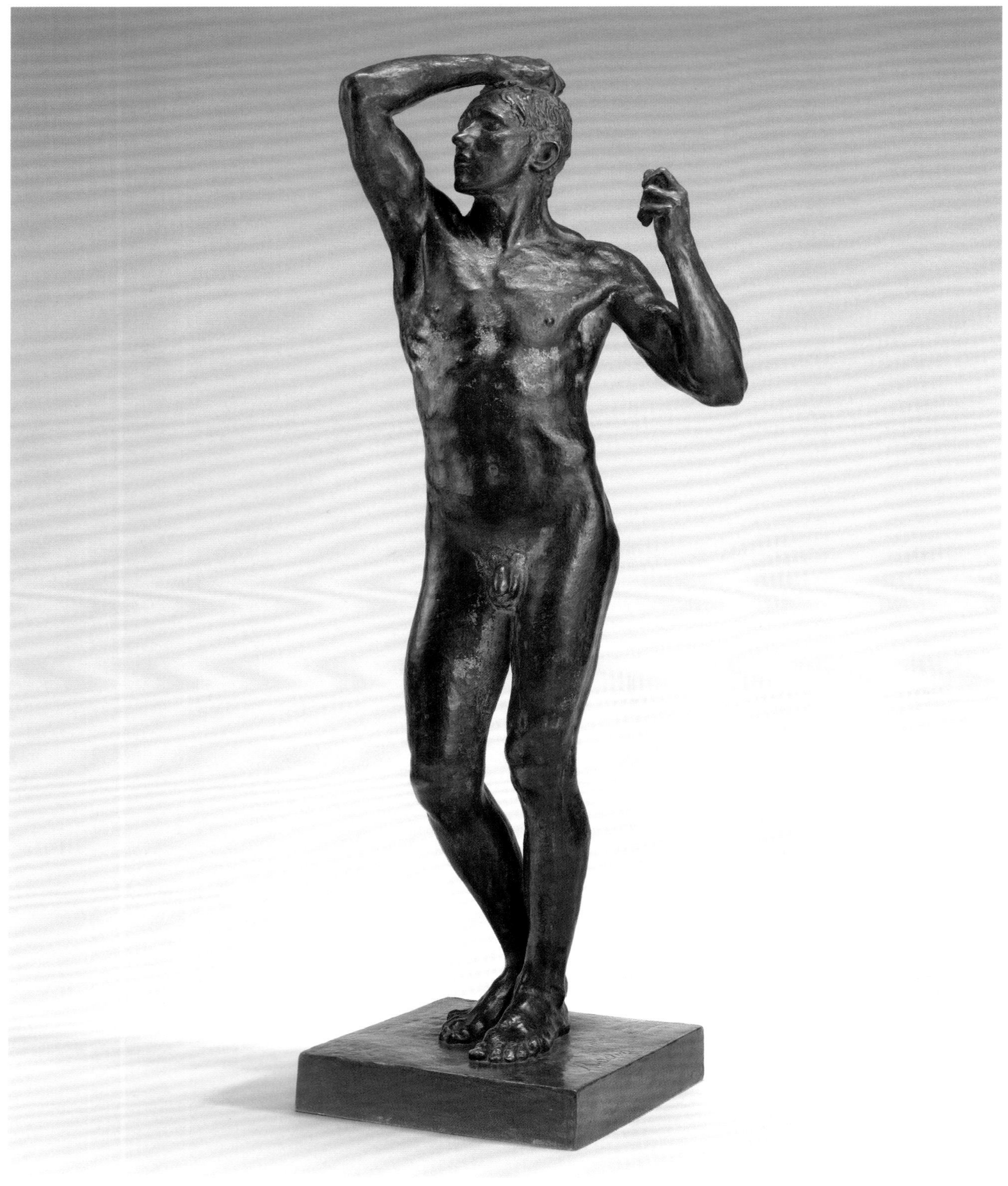

AUGUSTE RODIN

but he would infuse them with a sensuality that had never before been seen in Western art.

ART FOR ART'S SAKE

Immediately after his return from Italy, he resumed working on his first important sculpture, *The Age of Bronze* (1877), which he would show at the Paris Salon that same year. He was thirty-seven years old, and in a career often overshadowed by scandals, such as his numerous extramarital affairs, this would be his first, but not for the reasons you'd think.[6]

The Age of Bronze was exactly life-size and extremely realistic, and for that reason, it was initially rejected by the selectors of the Paris Salon, who accused him of cheating by casting it from a live model rather than carving it. He was found innocent following

He was profoundly impacted by Michelangelo's portrayal of the human body, particularly his ability to express a wide array of emotions and psychological depth

an investigation, and although critics came to appreciate and praise the work in later years, Rodin swore never to make an exact life-size sculpture again.

The media frenzy surrounding the accusation and acquittal made the artist a household name, but despite this, the first

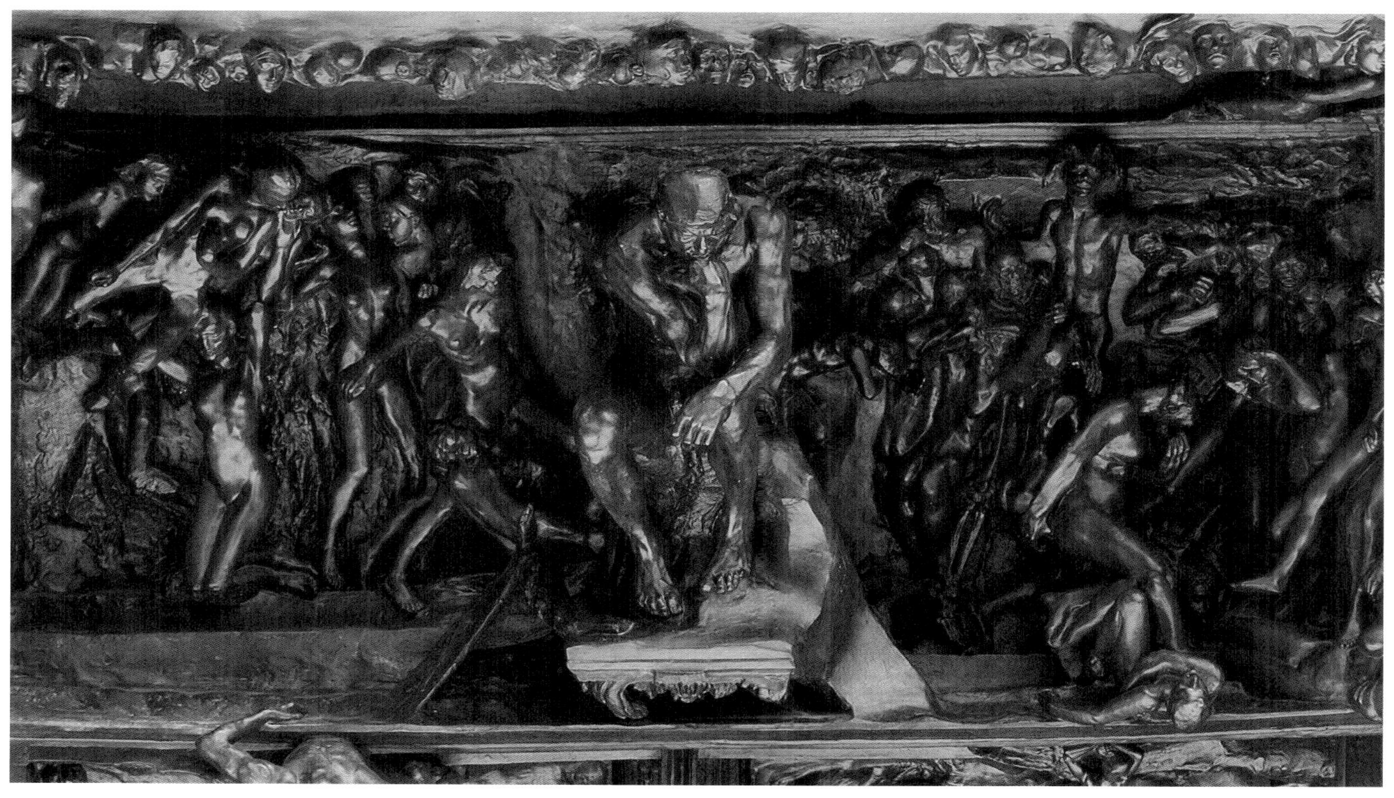

THE KISS

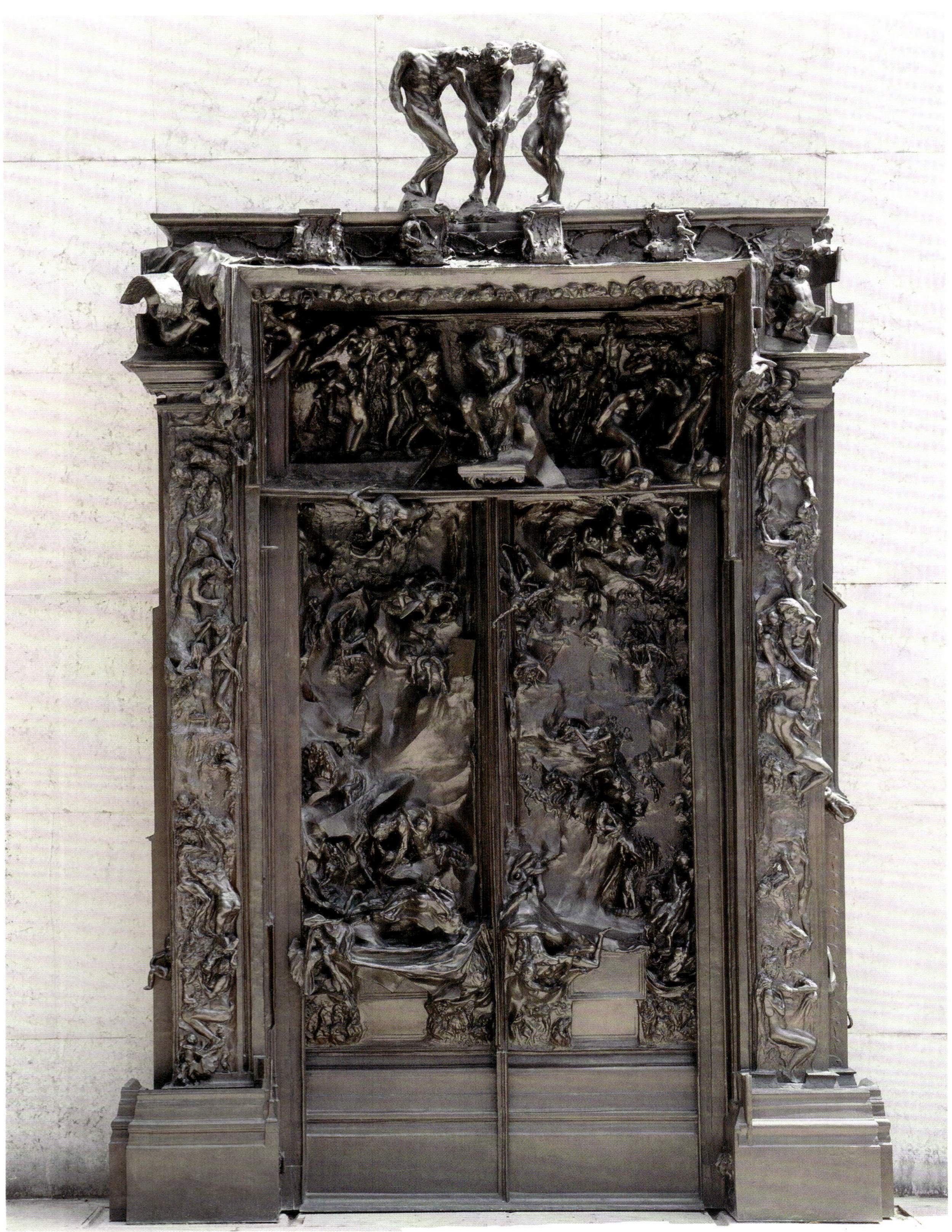

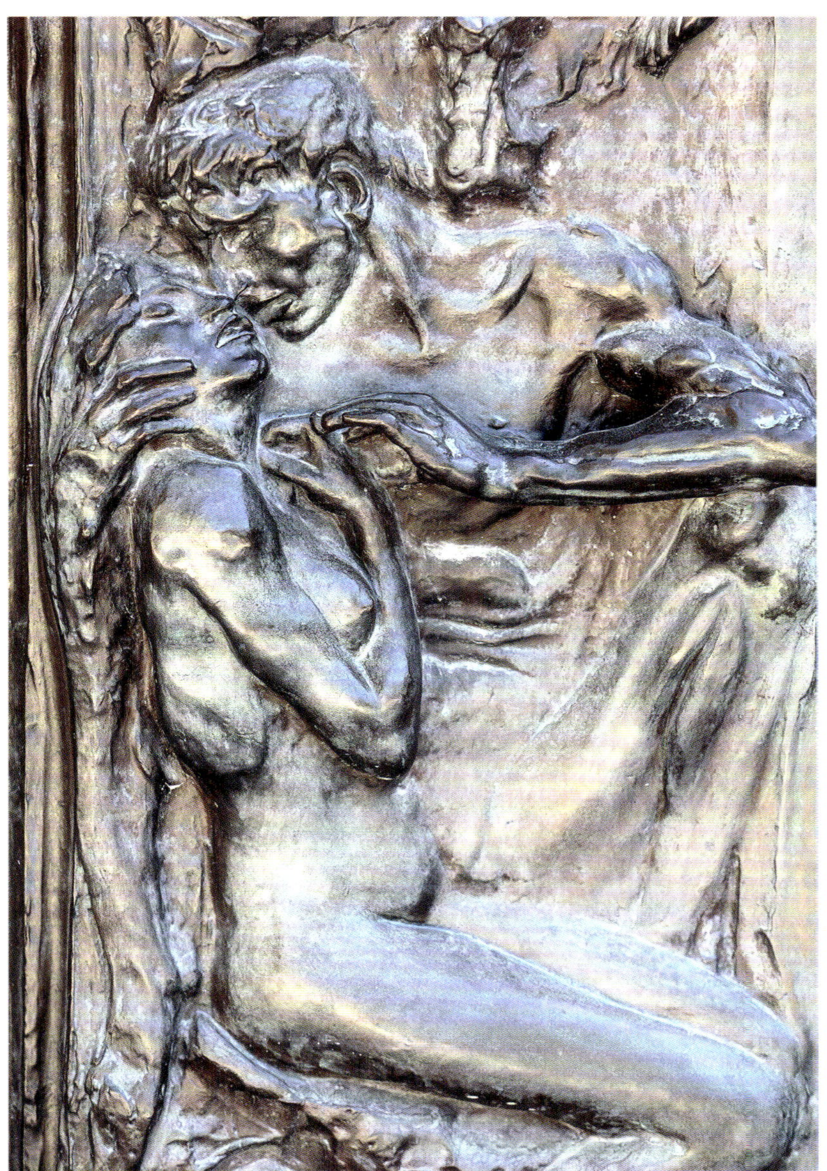

The sensual connection ultimately led Rodin to separate them from the more tortured figures surrounding them

casting of it didn't sell for another three years.[7] *The Age of Bronze* would eventually be cast in bronze more than fifty times (twenty-six in Rodin's lifetime),[8] and it became one of Rodin's biggest commercial successes. It would also lead to his first major commission, *The Gates of Hell* (1880–1917), from which we get *The Kiss*.

THE GATES OF HELL

In 1880 Rodin was commissioned to make the monumental entrance doors to the Musée des Arts Décoratifs in Paris, to be built on the site of what is now the Musée d'Orsay. These doors, titled *The Gates of Hell*, were conceived to be over 6 metres (20 ft) tall and feature more than 200 individual sculptures.

Rodin envisioned the doors as an homage to *The Gates of Paradise* (1425–52) by Lorenzo Ghiberti,[9] which he had seen during a visit to Florence. We can also see the influence of *The Last Judgement* (1535–41) by Michelangelo in the writhing, tortured figures,[10] as well as William Blake's visionary illustrations (1824–27) for Dante's *Divine Comedy*, which he almost certainly saw on one of his many visits to the British Museum in London.[11]

The museum never opened, and the gates were never finished. He stopped working on them in 1890 but exhibited them in 1900 in uncast plaster fragments. Then in 1917, Léonce Bénédite, the Musée Rodin's first curator, persuaded Rodin to allow him to reconstruct the doors so he could have them cast in bronze.

The question of what is 'original' is something to be addressed when it comes to Rodin

Unfortunately, Rodin died before he could see the work completed,[12] but many of the clay models he created for it would have an altogether different existence.

Seated on the tympanum of the gates is the figure that would become *The Thinker* (p. 131), but in 1880 was still known as 'The Poet'. It represented Dante himself, surrounded by just over 180 of his creations from his epic poem.

The Kiss was initially positioned within the chaotic mass of figures on the gates' left side, but the sensual connection ultimately led Rodin to separate them from the more tortured figures surrounding them, and like *The Thinker*, give them a new lease of life.

THE FACTORY

Rodin's unique and incredibly diverse body of work required him to master a whole range of techniques, which he developed over the two decades he spent working in commercial art studios, outside the constraints of academic sculpture. These skills were not only important to his art, but also to the running of a busy sculptural practice.

Despite existing film footage of Rodin chipping away at a large block of marble in 1915, he rarely, if ever, made the large-scale works we think of today as his, such as *The Kiss*. His training included carving, but it was impossible to work on every multiple (during his lifetime Rodin authorized hundreds of bronze casts of *The Kiss*), and in his workshop he would have simply supervised.

One of his greatest skills, in some way, was employing the best, most highly trained plaster casters, carvers and founders, who would turn his small clay models into enormous works. In essence, the sculptor was running a small 'factory', no different to the modes of art production that Andy Warhol, Damien Hirst or Jeff Koons would later be criticized for.

Rodin was not precious about the finished product and often allowed his workers to improvise, to leave the casting seam, an uneven finish or even fingerprints, which were then visible when cast in bronze. He encouraged what is known as the *non-finito* (unfinished) look, something he applied from about 1890 onwards with his marble works.[13]

'ORIGINALS'

In the 19th century there was a huge demand for public statuary, and artists couldn't keep up. Rodin had started his artistic career as a commercial artist, part of a team, and he would maintain those business ethics as a respected sculptor in his own right. His workers were highly skilled, and he treated them with the kind of respect he felt he didn't get as an artist in the commercial world, insisting his clients and journalists call them 'collaborators' rather than 'assistants'.[14]

The question of what is 'original' is something to be addressed when it comes to Rodin, as at least 319 bronze versions of *The Kiss* were cast in the foundry in four different sizes between 1898 and 1918,[15] all of them considered to be a 'Rodin' regardless of whether he personally worked on them, or even supervised their production.

Nowadays, the number of bronzes that may be cast from an original work is limited to twelve by the French government, and traditionally, the Musée Rodin in Paris keeps one of the twelve new castings as part of the French national collections.

Rodin in his studio in Meudon, c. 1902.

AUGUSTE RODIN

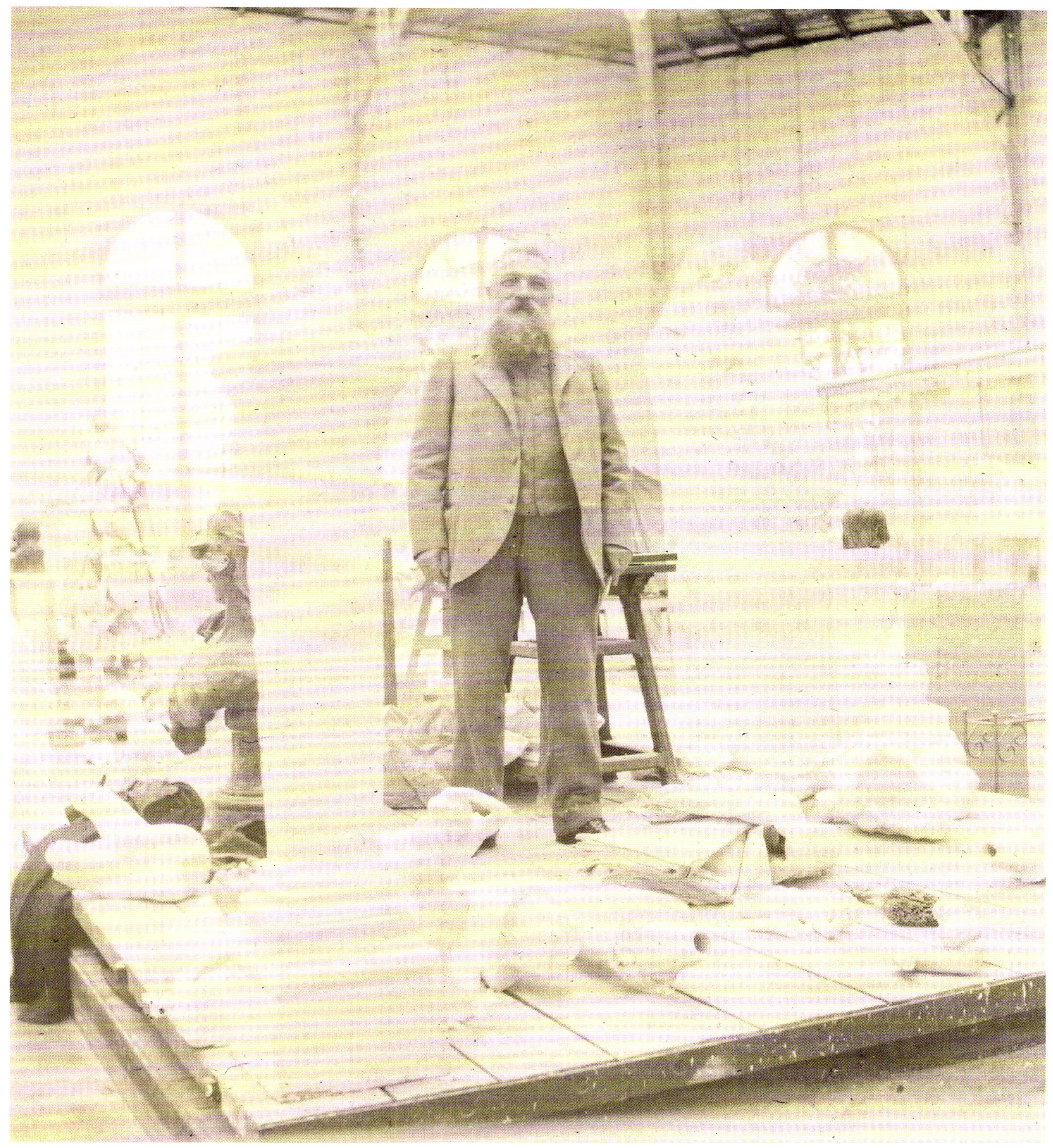

THE KISS

THE SCULPTURE

In 1887 the French state commissioned Rodin to create a larger-than-life marble version of *The Kiss*. The work was initially entitled *Francesca da Rimini*, after the female figure in the sculpture, a contemporary of Dante who was murdered by her husband, along with her lover Paolo. Almost immediately, however, the public saw it as an allegory, or as a universal symbol of love, and it was renamed simply *The Kiss*.[16]

This is partly because Rodin's sculpture focuses on the beauty of their love, offering an almost redemptive interpretation, unlike the couple's punishment in Dante's tale. Their passion is elevated to something timeless and transcendent.

The figures in the sculpture *are* caught in a suspended moment of passion, unable to fully consummate their love, which reflects Dante's interpretation. This is evident in the delicate touch of the man's hand on the woman's thigh and the fact that their lips never meet, highlighting the moment of anticipation before tragedy strikes.

The polished surfaces of the figures enhance their sensuality, and Rodin deliberately contrasted this with the rough, unfinished texture of its plinth, showing his interest in the *non-finito*. The choice of the contrasting textures really highlights the duality of his piece: the smoothness of the lovers' bodies enhances their sensuality and emotional intimacy, their idealized, almost otherworldly passion, while the raw, unrefined plinth reflects the earthy, primal nature of the material and the grounding reality of the sculptural process.

This juxtaposition is a hallmark of Rodin's approach, a stylistic choice that reflects the sculptor's interest in blending classical traditions with modern, experimental techniques, creating a tension between form and material.

SUCCESS

Rodin was quite dismissive of *The Kiss*, but it would become a hugely influential work of art and would serve as a bridge between classical traditions and the avant-garde movements that defined 20th-century sculpture, prioritizing experimentation over formal conventions.

The sculptor who cut his teeth in a lacklustre career producing decorative objects became a hugely successful artist, and on the way, he challenged conventions of beauty by suggesting that beauty lies in truth and emotional resonance rather than physical perfection. By embracing asymmetry, rough textures and incomplete forms, Rodin highlighted the process of creation and the authenticity of his subjects.

By the time of his death from influenza in 1917, 300 casts of *The Kiss* had been made,[17] and Rodin would be known as the new Michelangelo. For a working-class, self-educated man, this was surely a title he would have felt honoured to receive.

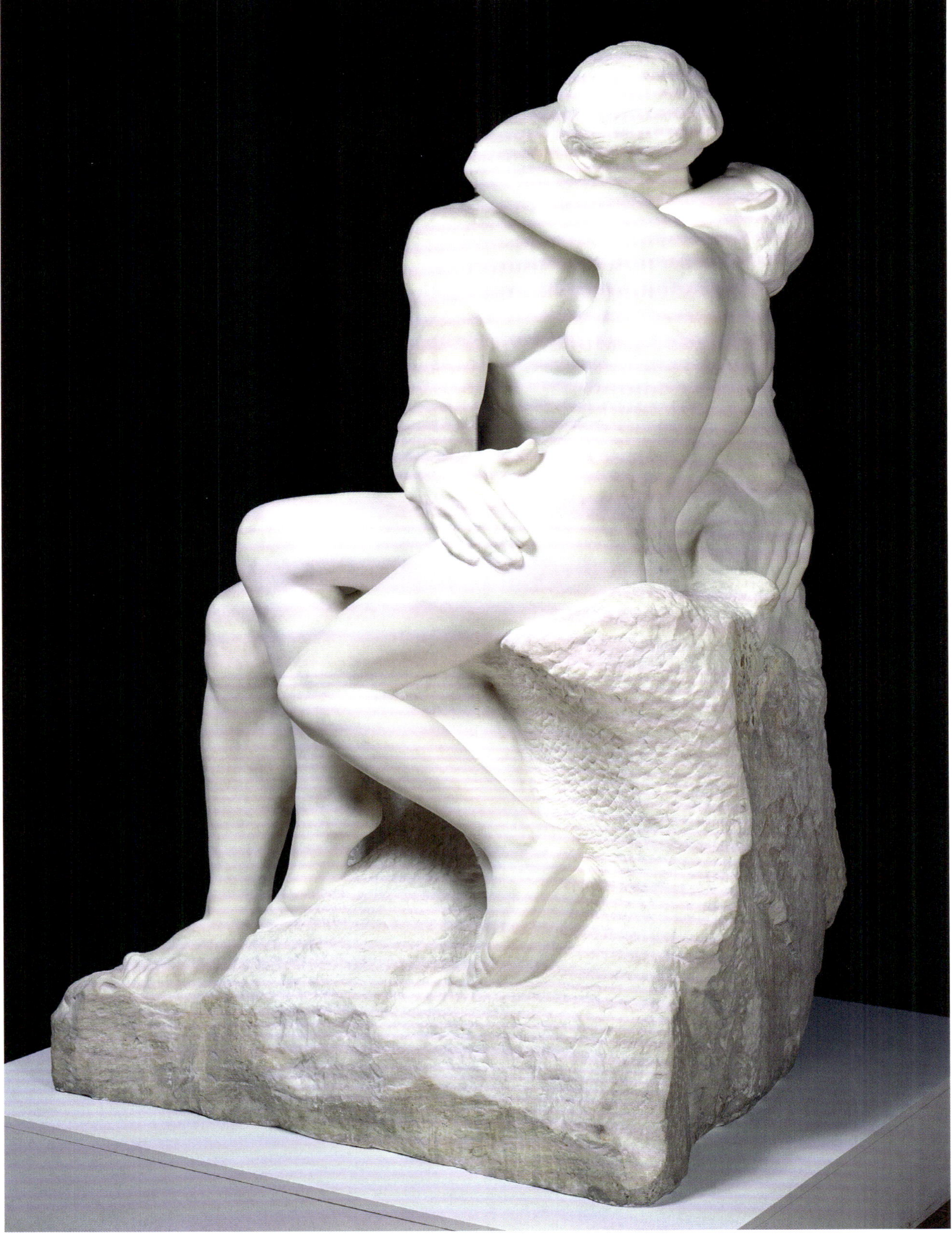

VINCENT VAN GOGH

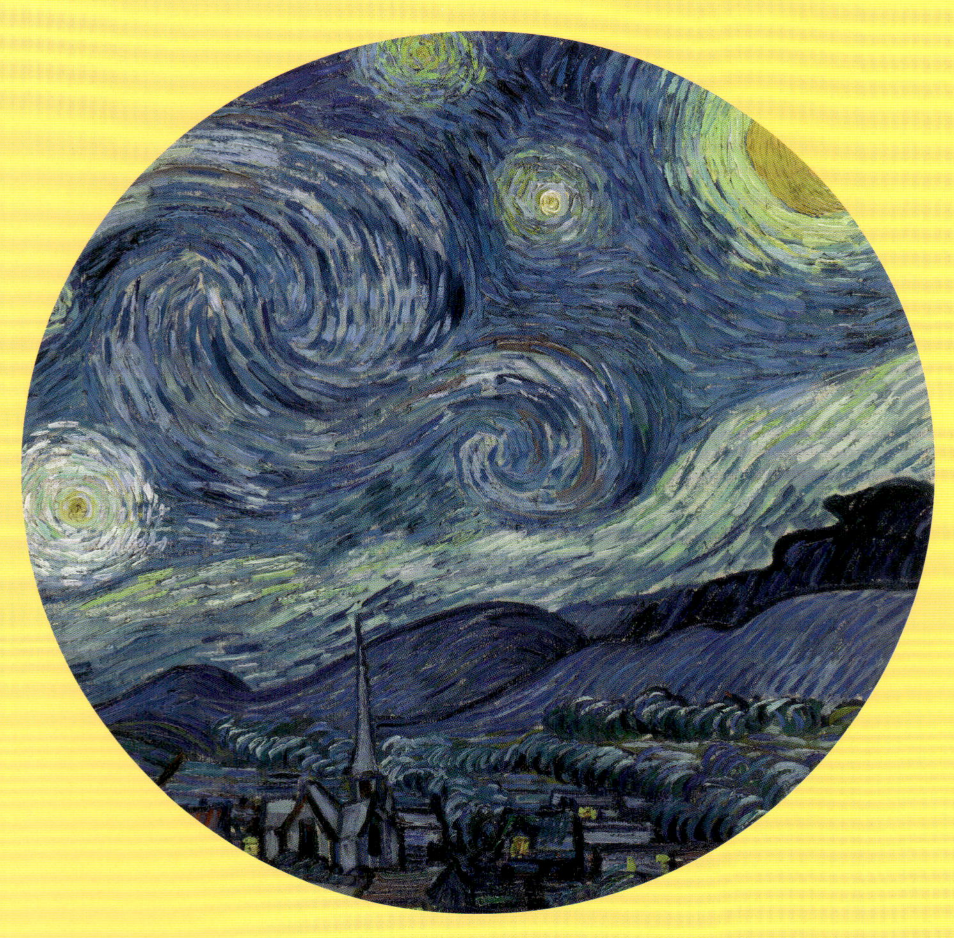

THE STARRY NIGHT

1889

A FAILURE OF A PAINTING

Vincent van Gogh was plagued by chronic mental health issues, but it is a myth that he was unwell for his entire adult life. As far as we know, he didn't have his first major episode until Christmas of 1888, when he was thirty-five. He did however spend twelve of his last eighteen months in an asylum, and his illness would eventually claim his life, shortly after his thirty-seventh birthday.

SAINT-RÉMY

Van Gogh was admitted to a psychiatric hospital outside Saint-Rémy in Provence on 8 May 1889. He had originally planned to recuperate in a large public institution right in the heart of Marseille, with over a thousand patients. If this had been the case, there is no chance that he would have produced the extraordinary work he did.

In the hospital at Saint-Rémy, home to only forty-one patients, Van Gogh would be treated with kindness and understanding. The doctors quickly realized that for him to survive, he needed the space and the freedom to paint and create. Art would keep him alive.

During this period, the artist's creativity and work ethic were stronger than ever. He worked extremely quickly, often finishing a painting in just a few hours, and incredibly, considering his circumstances, he finished at least 150 paintings during his stay – about one painting every other day. It was on or around 18 June 1889 that he painted *The Starry Night*.

SOME FORM OF SOLACE

When we think of 19th-century psychiatric hospitals, we tend to imagine horrific, torturous places, but the founder of the Saint-Rémy institution, Dr Théophile Peyron, was a progressive. He planted extensive gardens on the hospital grounds and encouraged the healing power of art and music, believing that being surrounded by nature and creativity was good for troubled minds.

In the hospital, Van Gogh's destructive lifestyle was much improved: no absinthe, no complicated romances and a regular routine with three meals a day. Isolation turned out to be good for him, and with no outside distractions, he would channel all his energy into his work.

Recent discoveries show us that Van Gogh was probably the sanest patient at Saint-Rémy,[1] and that overall, the institution had a positive effect on his mental health. But it was not easy for him, of course, and he suffered attacks of mania when he was unable to paint. Towards the end of his stay, he began to feel that he was 'more catching the illness of the others than curing [his] own',[2] but it could have been a lot worse.

On his arrival, Van Gogh was led to a modest room with bars on the windows, but

a spectacular view beyond, which gave him
some form of solace. Golden wheatfields and
olive groves spread out as far as he could see,
reaching to the distant foothills of the Alpilles,
a low mountain range that would feature
in *Starry Night*. Initially the artist just painted
the view he saw from his window, or within
the grounds of the hospital, but within
weeks he could wander around the dramatic
countryside alone – within reason.

The morning after his arrival at the
institution, Van Gogh went into the walled
garden and set up his easel, and by lunchtime
he had painted *Irises*, one of his first asylum
masterpieces. He was pleasantly surprised
to find that the other patients mainly left
him alone to work, and within two weeks
he had used up all the paints he had brought
with him, requiring fresh supplies to be
sent from Paris.[3]

THE ROAD TO THE STARRY NIGHT

Van Gogh was a largely self-taught artist who
didn't actually pick up a paintbrush until he
was around twenty-seven years old. His two
years in Paris from 1886 to 1888 are widely
thought to have laid the foundation for his
unique later style, exposing him to the influence
of Impressionists, such as Claude Monet
and Camille Pissarro, but also to a younger
generation of artists, including Paul Signac
and Henri de Toulouse-Lautrec, who would
remain his friends up until his death.

The Impressionists in Paris gave him
looser, lighter brushstrokes, and the pointillist
Georges Seurat introduced him to optical
mixing – the illusion of a third colour when two
shades are placed next to each other. Colour,
above all, was Van Gogh's visual vocabulary,
and he had an innate, even avant-garde
tendency towards shades that were expressive
and intense. His interest in colour was piqued
after seeing paintings by artists like Peter Paul

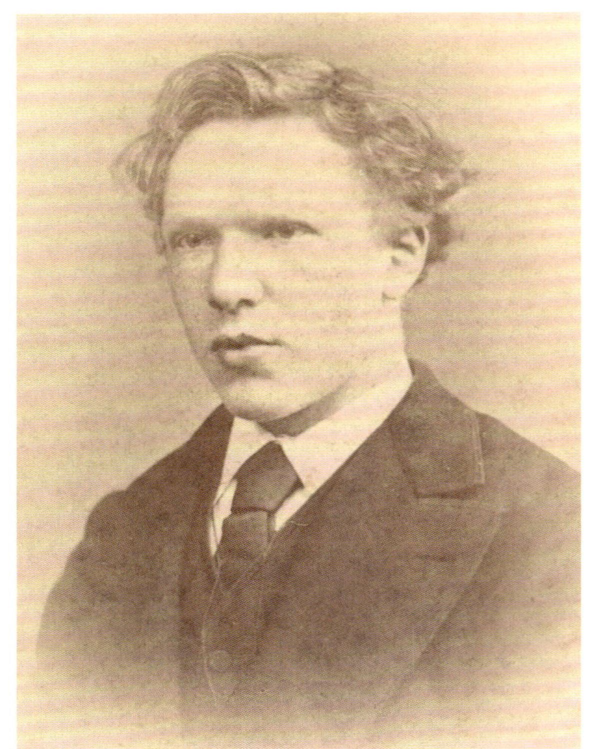

Rubens and, in particular, Eugène Delacroix
in Paris. Van Gogh read everything he could
on Delacroix's colour theories, which prioritized
the use of complementary colours – that is,
colours on opposite sides of the colour wheel
– for maximum contrast and high impact.

It was in the final five years of his career
that the style for which he became known
really developed. The dark muted colours he
had used in the Netherlands were superseded
by a bright new palette, coinciding with the
invention of many new synthetic pigments.

As well as his Parisian influences,
Japanese art had a major effect on his later
works; as he once wrote: 'all my work is based
to some extent on Japanese art'.[4]

Like many of his generation, Van Gogh
was particularly influenced by Japanese *ukiyo-e*
prints, distinguishable by their use of blocks
of pure colour, dark outlines, unusual cropping

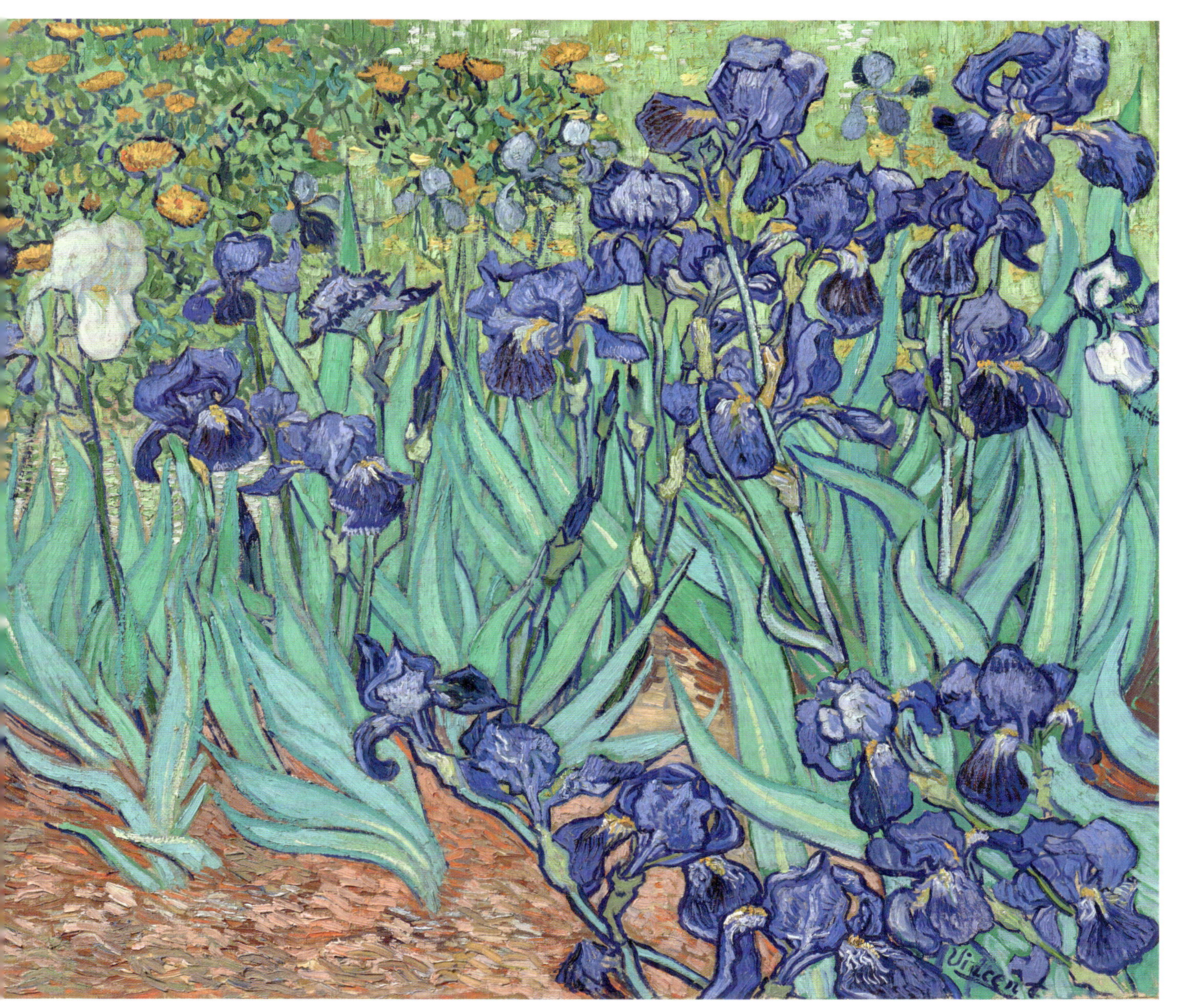

THE STARRY NIGHT

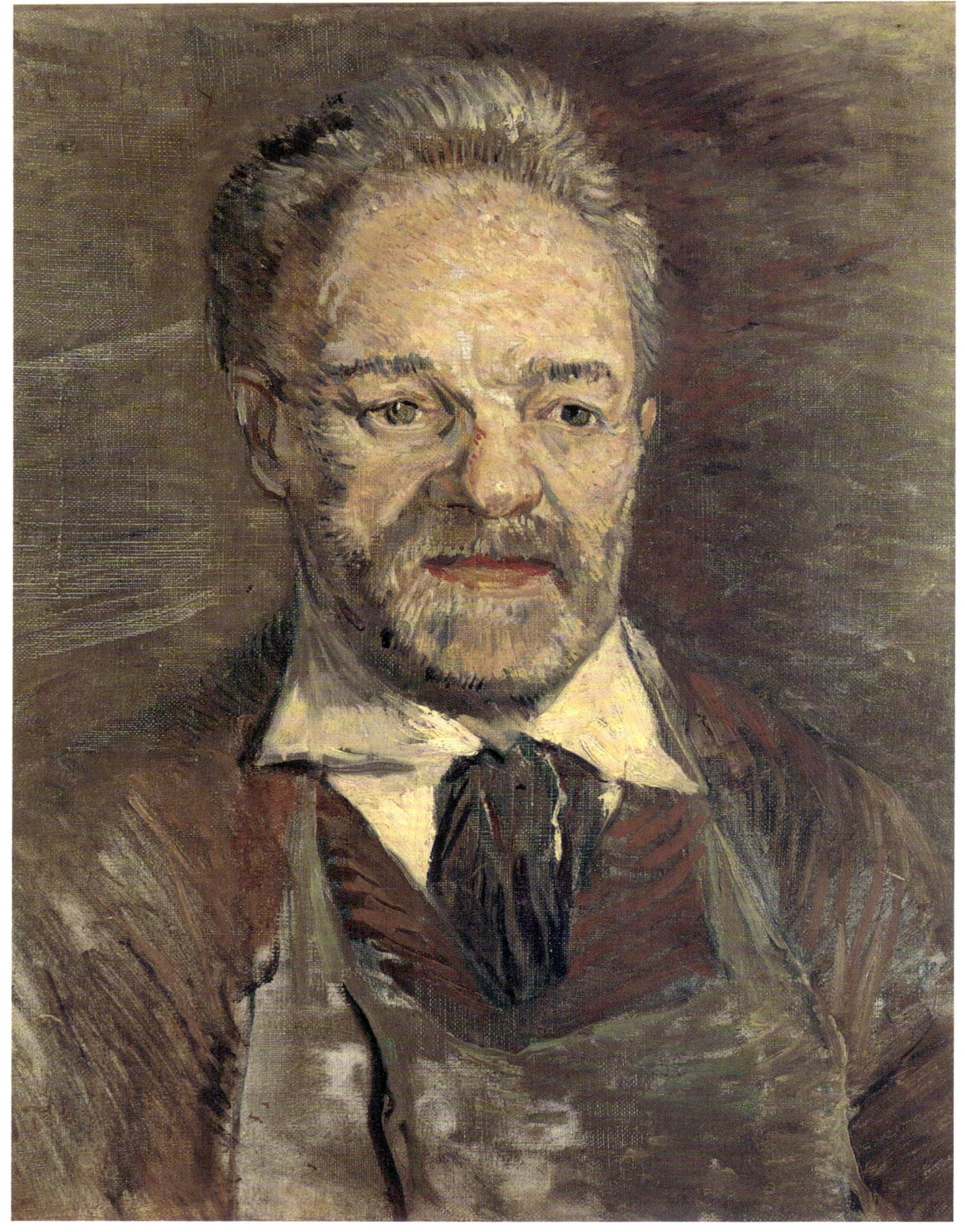

VINCENT VAN GOGH

His two years in Paris from 1886 to 1888 are widely thought to have laid the foundation for his unique later style

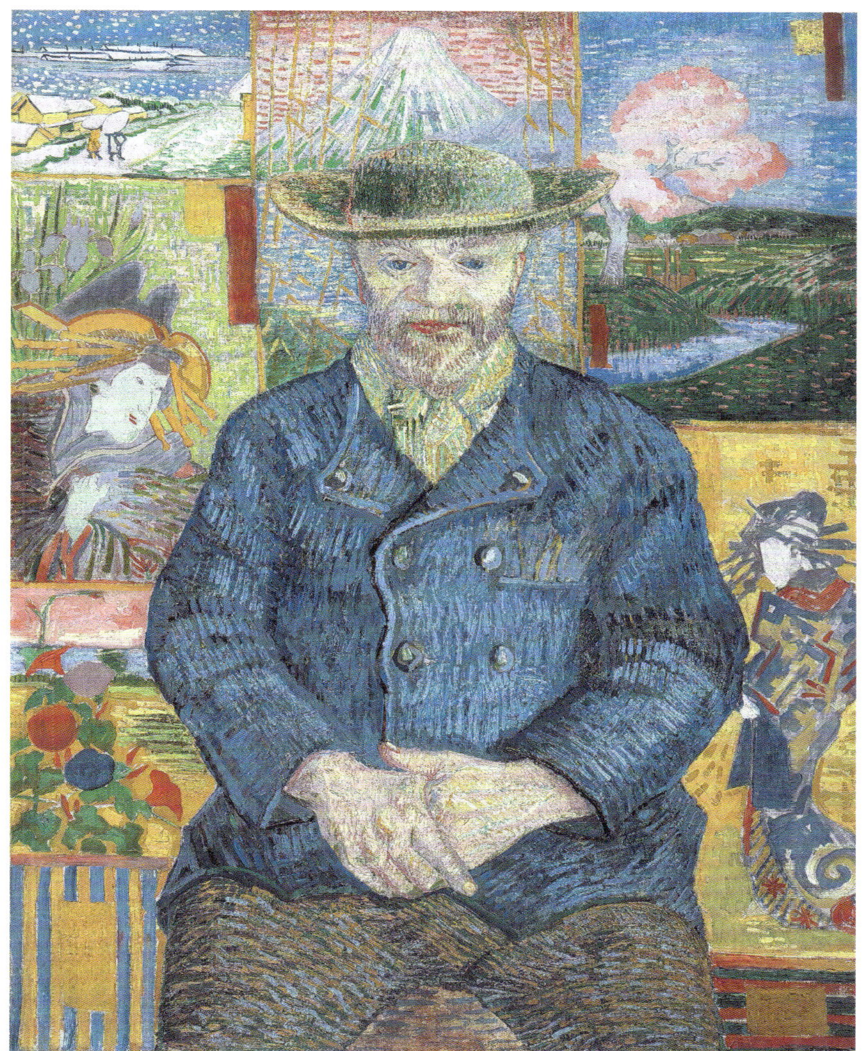

and distorted perspective. We know for a fact that the artist was an admirer of Hokusai's *The Great Wave* (see Chapter Eleven),[5] and we can make direct comparisons between not only the highly stylized composition, but also the rich blue tones of Hokusai's tempestuous seas and the turbulent skies of *The Starry Night*. Both images are energetic and daring interpretations of the power of nature.

THE STARRY NIGHT

At the beginning of June 1888, Van Gogh wrote to his brother, Theo: 'This morning I saw the countryside from my window a long time before sunrise, with nothing but the morning star, which looked very big.'[6]

This was just one of many letters the artist wrote that mentioned a 'starry sky'. Not long after his arrival at the hospital he described seeing Venus before sunrise,[7] and it is thought he painted *The Starry Night* sometime over the weekend of 15–16 June.

Like the Impressionists, Van Gogh had always insisted on working directly from nature, but a few months earlier, Paul Gauguin had tried to persuade him to paint from his imagination. Van Gogh had resisted, but in the institution, with limited freedom, it was a necessity.

The Starry Night depicts the view from his hospital window on the upper floor. He had already painted the view dozens of times, but this time it was a nightscape, which, as he couldn't paint in the dark, means it was created from memory during the day in his ground-floor studio. It is in fact an amalgamation of night-time and dawn views, as well as an exaggerated aesthetic interpretation.

In reality, the cypress trees were much smaller and beyond the far wall enclosing the wheat field, but in the painting Van Gogh brings the tree much closer to the foreground of the picture plane, mirroring the tight cropping of Japanese prints.

The cypress tree, known as a symbol of death and immortality in Mediterranean culture, was a newly discovered motif for Van Gogh, and he uses it to link the town of Saint-Rémy with the heavens above.

It was fairly large town, but he depicts it as just a cluster of scattered houses with impossibly bright interior lighting, to counter-balance the stars of the night sky. Likewise, in reality, the church of Saint Martin has a domed roof, but he paints it with a pitched roof more reminiscent of Dutch churches. Both of these stylistic choices give the setting a much more domestic scale, creating a pronounced contrast with the vast skies. Even the backdrop to the town, the hills of the Alpilles (which he had painted so often from his bedroom window), are another invention, as they are in fact in the opposite direction.

Astronomers have worked out that on the night Van Gogh painted *The Starry Night*, the moon was almost full, rather than the crescent we see in the painting, and Venus, 'the evening star' – but actually a planet – was only visible just before dawn, by which time the moon would not have been visible from the artist's room.

If we were to look at a modern image of the whirlpool galaxy, it bears a striking resemblance to Van Gogh's stars. This seems like it should be an impossibility, but a drawing of nebulae made by the Irish astronomer William Parsons, 3rd Earl of Rosse, *was* published in 1850, and Van Gogh, who was passionate about astronomy, had even met him in Paris.

Reality is not important in this highly charged picture. It is a painting of something we cannot see or touch, something immaterial, electric. It is an image of how we imagine the night sky to be.

Van Gogh had just received fresh paint supplies sent by Theo, including a more than adequate supply of ultramarine, which he uses liberally in the painting in his signature short brushstrokes of thick impasto, applied thickly – sometimes straight from the tube – and spread like butter with a palette knife.

Like all great paintings, *The Starry Night* has been interpreted in many ways, notably concerning his religious beliefs. Van Gogh was an evangelical preacher in his twenties, but he later rejected Christianity; he spoke of art as a new kind of religion, a way to console people, and *The Starry Night* in particular reflected these beliefs. Nature for him was deeply emotional, almost mystical, and it profoundly shaped his artistic vision. As he once wrote to Theo, 'If you truly love nature, you will find beauty everywhere.'[8]

Despite this, he and Theo would dismiss this work – what would become his most famous painting – as a 'failure', and it's possible that, had he have lived longer, he might have painted over it, as he did with so many others.

CURED

When Van Gogh was released from the hospital, Peyron's report noted that he had suffered several attacks while in treatment,

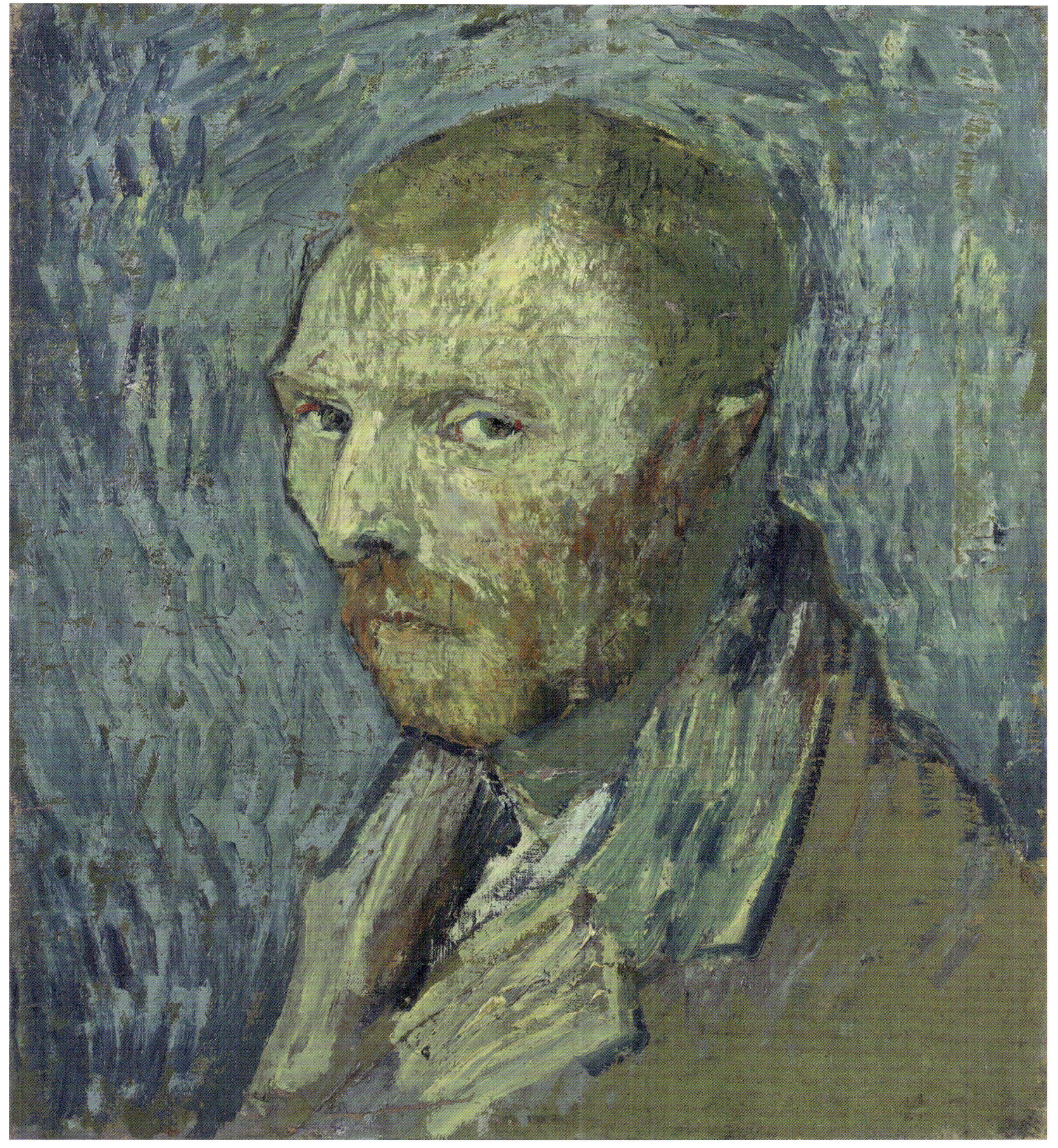

          THE STARRY NIGHT

but in between he was lucid, calm and
passionately devoted to painting. The
understanding of mental health at this period
was fairly basic, and at the bottom of the
report the doctor optimistically wrote 'cured'.[9]

On 6 July 1890, Van Gogh went to Paris
to visit Theo, whose wife Jo remarked on
how healthy the artist looked. However, he
cut his visit short because he'd had enough of
the busy city, and just wanted to paint again.[10]

He then moved to the village of Auvers-
sur-Oise, 20 kilometres (12⅖ mi.) north of
Paris, where he spent his last seventy days on
Earth frantically creating another seventy-four
paintings. On 27 July, Van Gogh went to the
outskirts of the village, to a peaceful wheatfield
as the sun was setting (possibly one he had
painted), and shot himself in the chest. The
wound wasn't immediately fatal, however, and
he staggered back to his lodgings, succumbing
to his injuries two days later, which meant that
Theo, the brother who supported him both
financially and emotionally, was able to be
by his side.

Vincent's body was laid out in the room
that he used as a studio in Auvers, surrounded
by his last canvases and masses of yellow
flowers – including, of course, his beloved
sunflowers.

Vincent van Gogh,
The Starry Night, 1889.

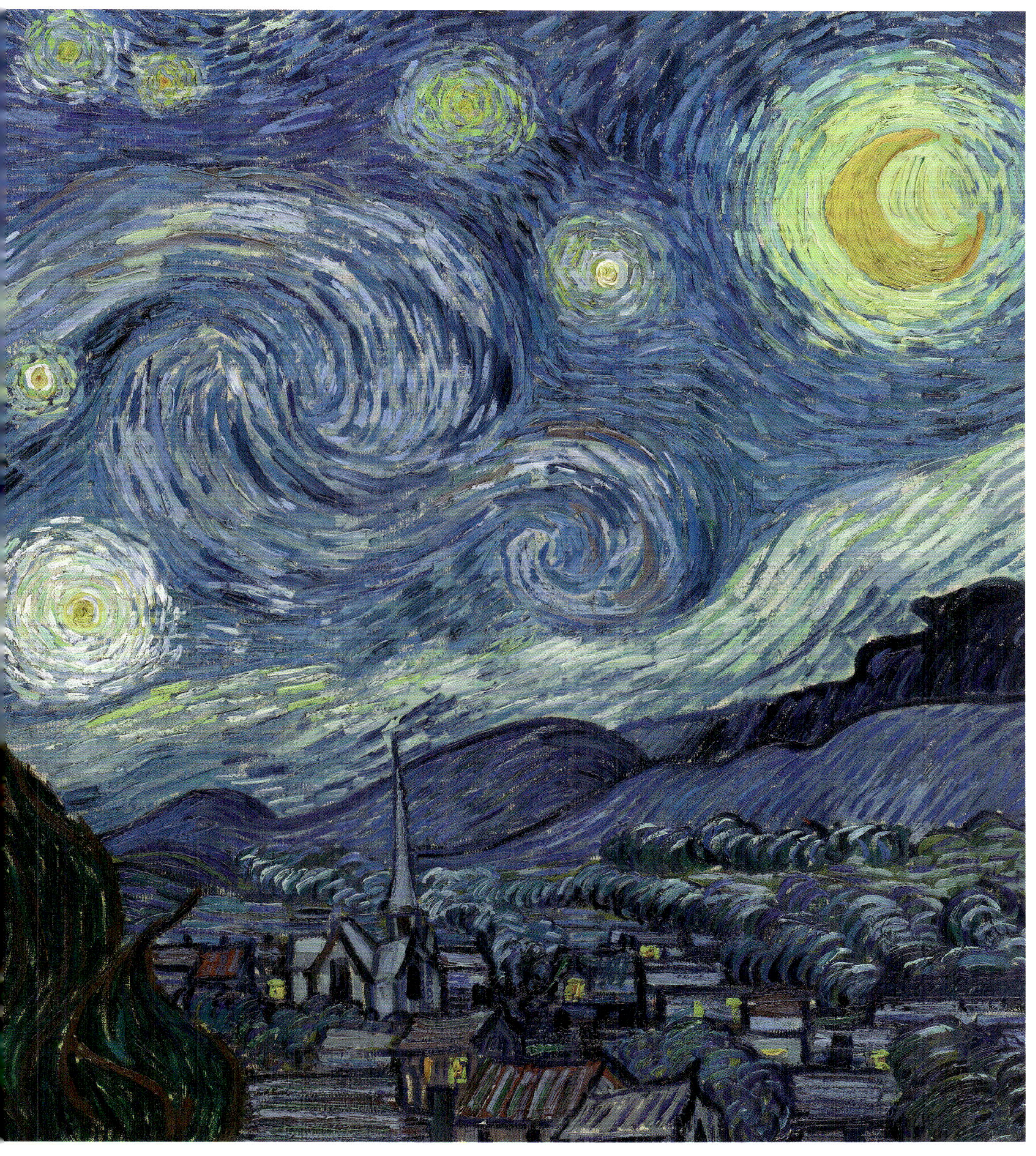

EDVARD MUNCH

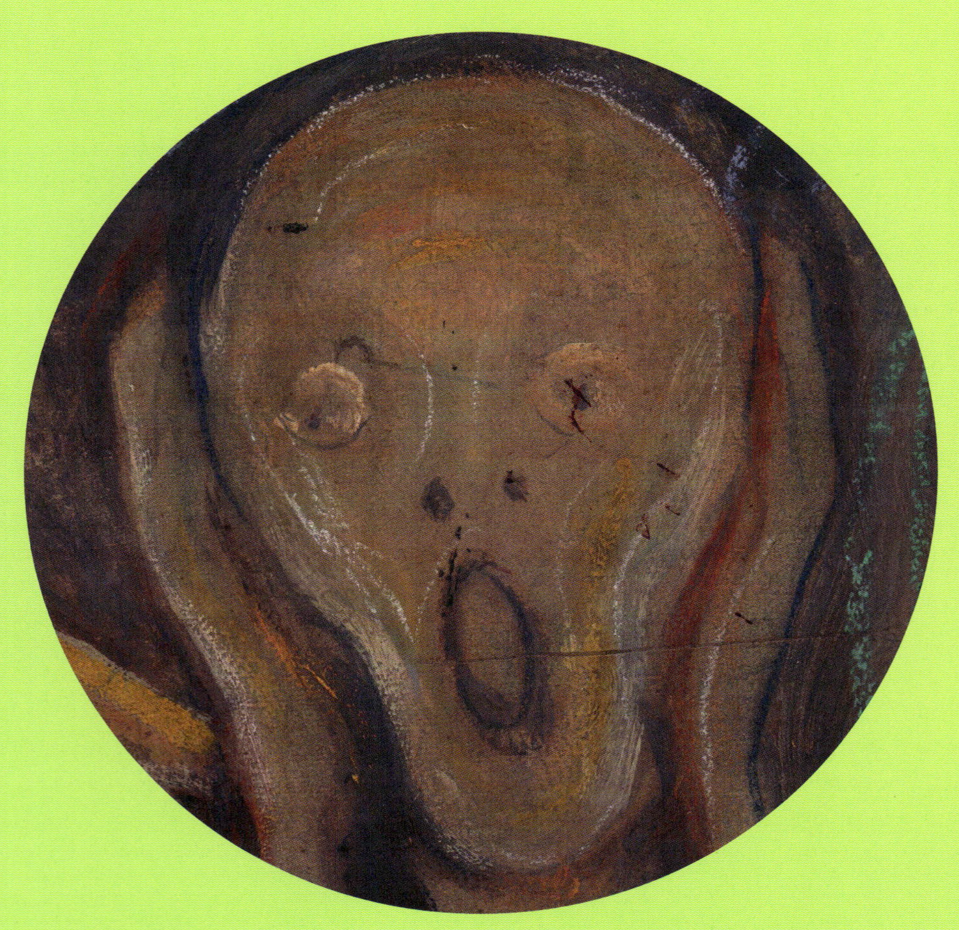

THE SCREAM

1893

PAINTED BY A MADMAN

While J. M. W. Turner saw industrialization as a positive thing (see Chapter 12), by the time of the Norwegian painter Edvard Munch and the Second Industrial Revolution (around the late 19th century), the side effects of rapid growth were being more keenly felt.

In the industrial age, just as many people got left behind as benefitted. People's lives changed quickly, and anxiety was on the increase. Edvard Munch, who had a great interest in the link between art and sanity, was making work that reflected society's fears.

Anxiety was something Munch understood very well. He would endure a life ravaged by mental illness, sickness and death. His father and grandfather suffered from depression and his younger sister, Laura, from schizophrenia. His mother and older sister both died of tuberculosis, in 1868 and 1877, respectively, and his only brother would later die of pneumonia in 1895. Edvard, who spent much of his childhood unwell and dominated by his religious father, would turn to art to keep himself occupied.

Munch's masterpiece of 1893, *The Scream*, shows a haunting figure with a skull-like face that appears to be screaming in anguish. It is an image that has become a universal symbol of angst and anxiety. Yet strangely, the figure we often think of as screaming is in fact not screaming at all.

In a passage from Munch's diary a year before he created *The Scream*, he writes: 'I was walking along the road with two friends – the sun went down – I felt a gust of melancholy – suddenly the sky turned a bloody red.' The blood red sky we see in the painting. He continues: 'My friends went on – I stood there trembling with anxiety – and I felt a vast infinite scream passing through nature.'[1] In the painting we see Munch's friends walking off into the distance, and with his diary in mind it becomes clear that the figure, mouth agape, is holding its hands over its ears to block out nature's screams.

THE NOISE GROWS

During the 19th century, the Norwegian capital Kristiania (previously Christiania, now Oslo), where Munch would spend most of his life, became a major shipbuilding port. The sounds of industry were relentless, and people were flooding into the city in the hope of a factory job, the prospect of a steady income attracting those who once made a living off the land.

By 1854, the first railway lines had opened, followed by the introduction of steamboat services in 1893 and the construction of canals. In 1894 Kristiania launched its first electric tram routes, and by the turn of the century, underground railways were in use for the masses, as factories rapidly appeared across the city.

Like other European cities of the time, Kristiania was a hive of construction activity, with new concert halls, opera houses, theatres, art galleries and restaurants transforming the urban landscape. Entertainment and art had become more accessible than ever, leading to a cultural boom.

With all that noise, it's no wonder Munch's figure is blocking its ears.

PARIS

Munch first saw the revolutionary work of the Impressionists in Paris when he was twenty-two years old. He would be deeply influenced by them, particularly their use of form and colour, but their view of 'reality' never really sat well with his practice. Munch was already interested in turning his gaze inward rather than outward; in 1885 he painted *The Sick Child*, based on his sister's death from tuberculosis at fifteen, and he would come to see this work as a personal breakthrough in his practice, calling it 'the foundation stone for everything that followed'.[2] It is now considered a precursor to Expressionism, owing to its focus on emotional impact over realistic representation, not just in its subject matter but also in its colours and brushstrokes. The critics hated it, however, due to its 'scratchy', unfinished appearance; one compared it to 'a fish stew in lobster sauce', and another called Munch a 'poisoner of art'.[3]

He would eventually move to Paris in 1889, where a new generation of artists, including Vincent van Gogh, Henri de Toulouse-Lautrec and Paul Gauguin, was making its mark. We know that Munch visited several exhibitions in which Van Gogh's work was being shown. The Dutch artist may not have been a huge public success, but his paintings were well known among artists.

In a rare admission of another artist's influence, in his diaries, Munch wrote about Van Gogh: 'I have thought, and wished – in the long term, with more money at my disposal than he had – to follow in his footsteps.'[4]

But it was the Symbolist Paul Gauguin with whom he really connected in Paris. Symbolism began as a literary movement that was then taken up by visual artists as a reaction to realism. They were drawn to the intangible, the mysterious and the transcendent, often representing ideas of death, love, desire and the subconscious. Munch, who never fitted in with the Norwegian Social Realists – a group who used realism to critique society – had found his tribe.

THE MOST FAMOUS MAN IN THE WHOLE OF THE GERMAN EMPIRE

In 1892 Munch, now in his late twenties and still a struggling artist, was invited to Berlin to show fifty-five of his works.

The Berliners loved paintings of the Norwegian fjords, and that's what they were expecting. But instead, they got unconventional works like *The Sick Child* and *Melancholy* (1891) that used garish colours and sketchy brushstrokes.

The uproar reached such a level that the Berlin Artists' Association held an emergency meeting and voted to close the exhibition just one week after it opened. This abrupt closure was unprecedented and led to intense media coverage, turning the controversy into a public spectacle and catapulting him into stardom. Munch saw the power of publicity in the scandal and was pleased to be described as 'the most famous man in the whole of the German empire'.[5]

Around this time, he would begin a series of twenty-two works that would be his life's major work. He called them *The Frieze of Life*, and one of them would be *The Scream*.

He would endure a life
ravaged by mental illness,
sickness and death

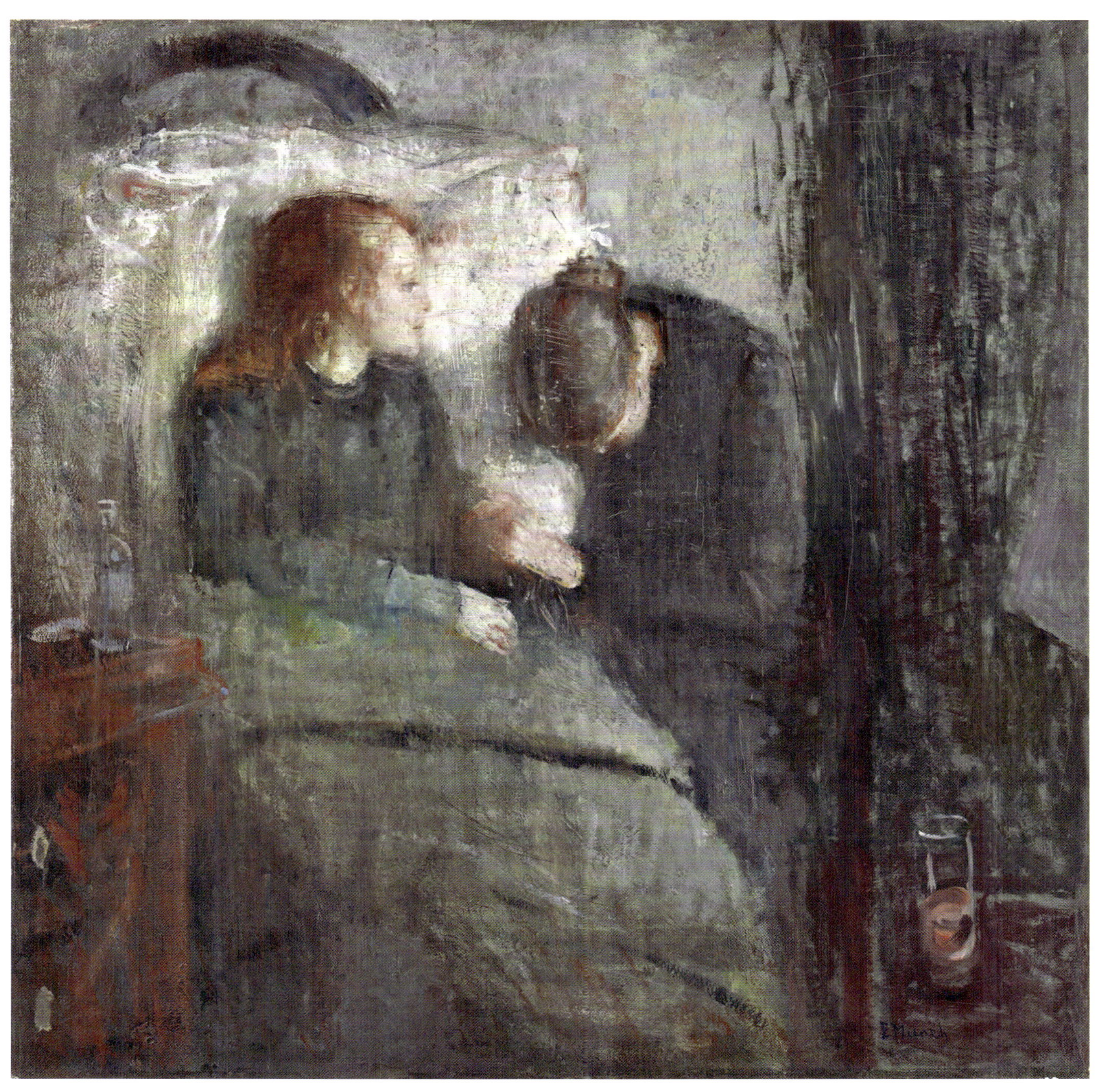

THE FRIEZE OF LIFE

Munch intended *The Frieze of Life* to be seen as a 'poem of life, love and death'. It included the call of love (*Summer Night's Dream – The Voice*, 1893), physical love (*Vampire*, 1893), *Jealousy* (1895) and at its end, despair, in the form of *The Scream*.

He once said that when his works were placed together in groups 'they became quite different from when they were separate: they became a symphony'.[6]

Munch was already producing multiple versions of many of his paintings, sometimes over decades, which allowed him to explore

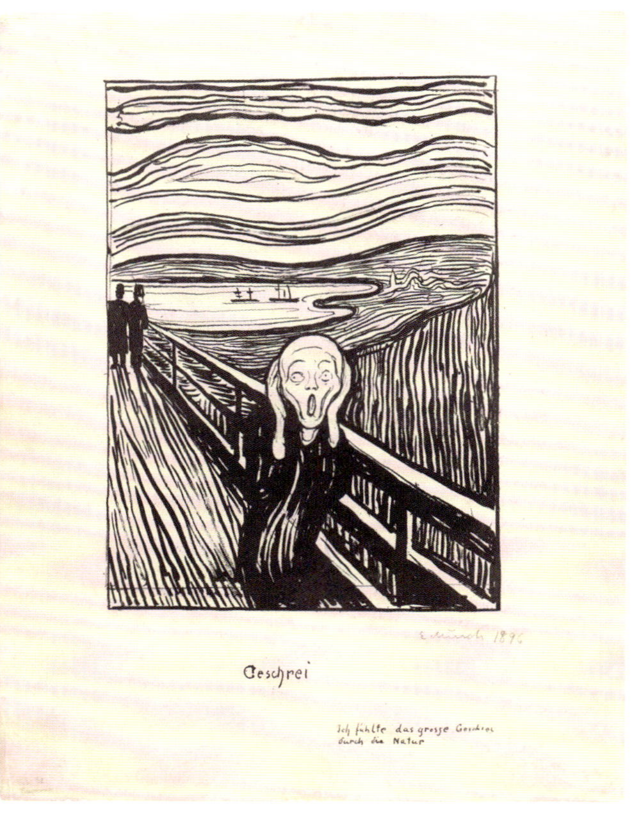

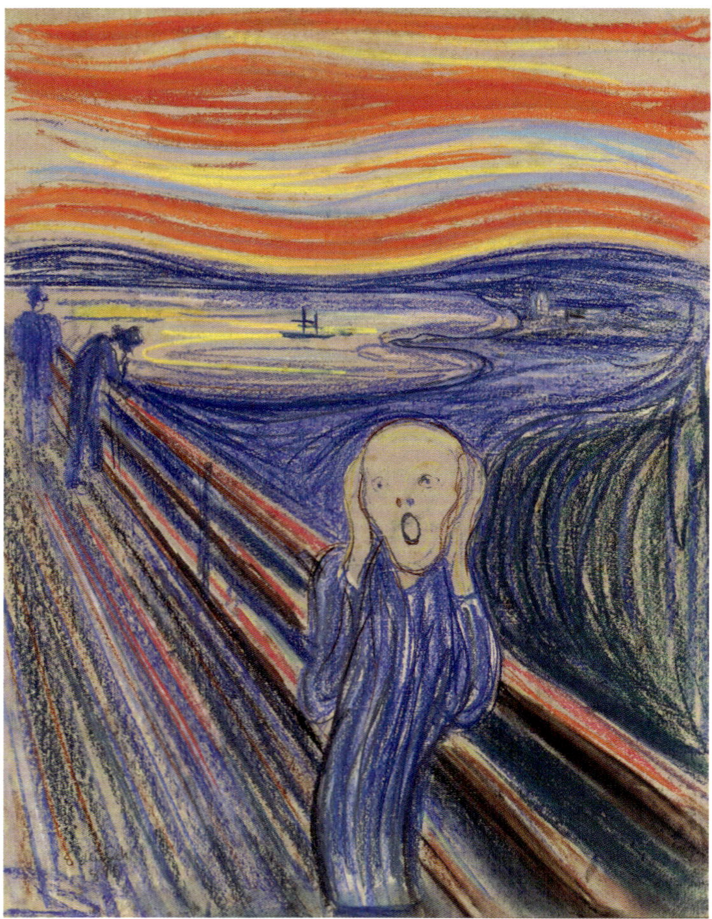

Edvard Munch,
The Scream, 1895.

Edvard Munch,
The Scream, 1910.

EDVARD MUNCH

new techniques, deepen their emotional resonance and refine the ideas they represented. His plan was to keep *The Frieze of Life* together as a set, and eventually – already with an eye on posterity – donate them to a museum in Kristiania when he died. So, when he sold a painting, he produced a copy to replace it, and that way avoided breaking up the group. The more popular the painting, the more copies there are in existence.

THE DRAMA OF LONELINESS

There are four versions of *The Scream*: two are paintings with tempera (1893 and 1910),

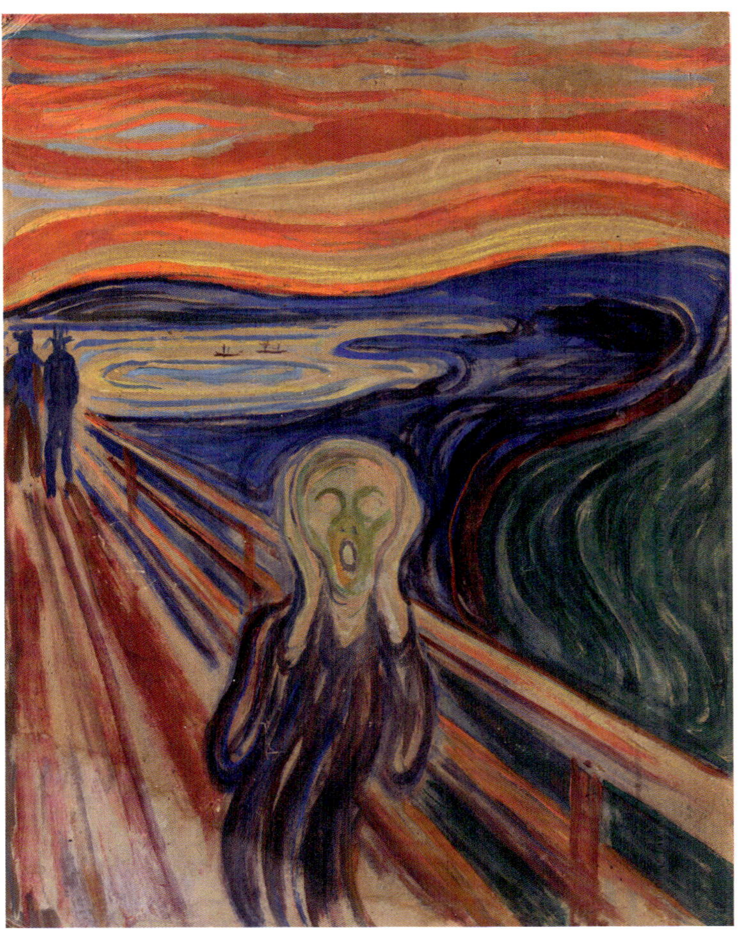

and two are drawings with pastel and crayon (1893 and 1895). Then, in 1894, he took up printmaking, reproducing his best-selling artworks in even greater quantities. He printed at least thirty lithographs of *The Scream*, some of which he hand-painted.

The idea of the figure in the landscape is something that Munch draws on from the Romantic tradition of the earlier 19th century such as Caspar David Friedrich's *Wanderer above the Sea of Fog* (1818). But with *The Scream*, Munch focuses not on nature itself, but on the inner psychology of man in *relation* to nature. Unlike the Romantic and Realist emphasis on depth and grandeur, Munch often flattened perspectives, making landscapes feel more symbolic than real, and he adopted unnatural, vibrant tones to heighten psychological intensity.

Evening on Karl Johan Street (1892) is a work that shares that atmosphere of isolation we find in *The Scream* (which he painted a year later) but uses an urban setting for its drama of loneliness. Munch's crowd have faceless, hollow expressions and symbolize the loss of individuality in modern society,[7] and the abstract, almost dreamlike quality of both works connects them to the Symbolist movement's interest in inner experiences and universal fears.

Despair is considered a precursor to *The Scream*:[8] it has the same red and yellow sky, mountains and fjords in the background, but instead of the skeletal figure staring out at us, there is a self-portrait of Munch. While *Despair* reflects a subdued and internalized hopelessness, *The Scream* externalizes this into

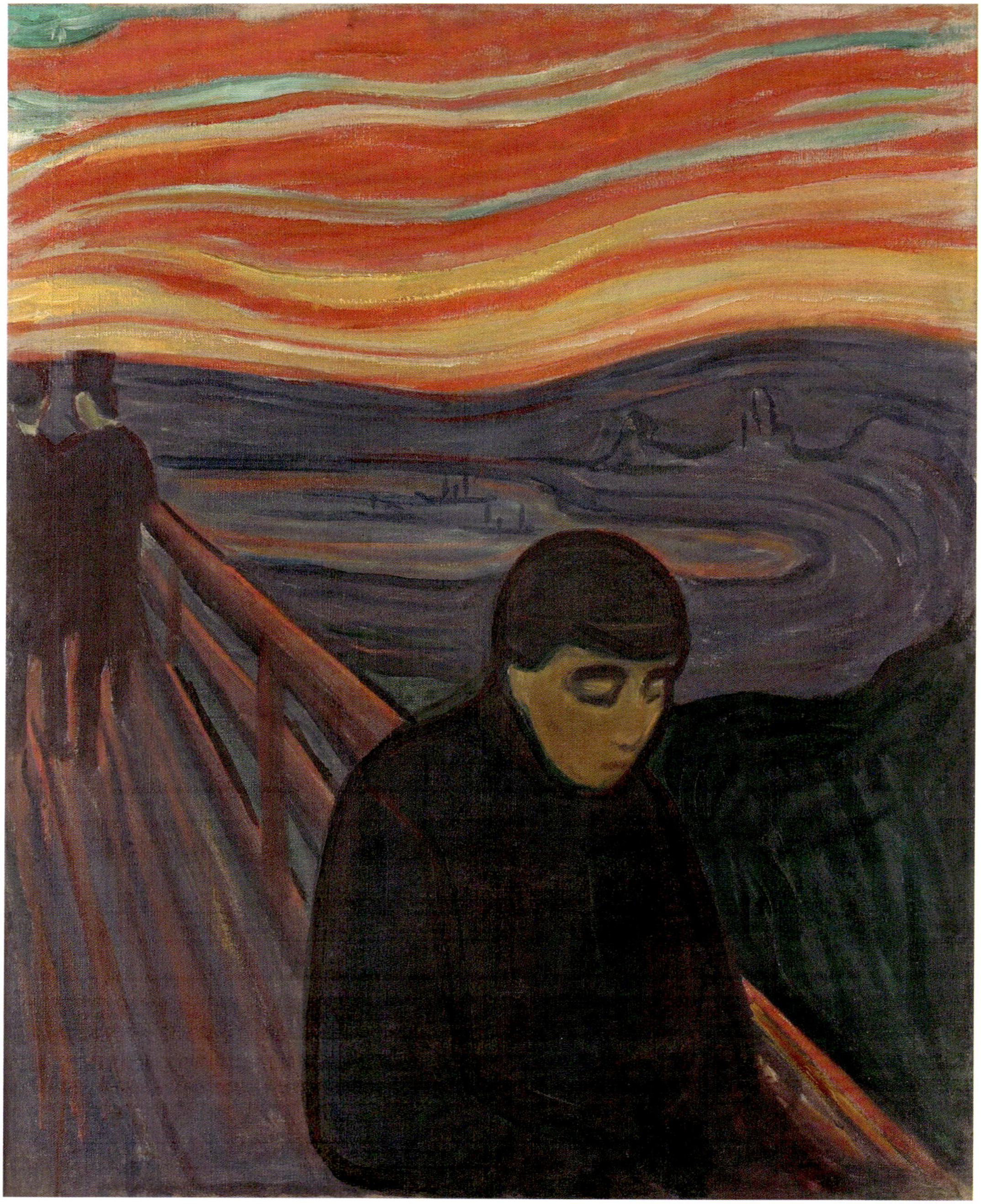

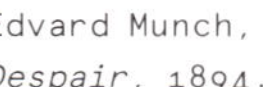

Edvard Munch,
Despair, 1894.

EDVARD MUNCH

a universal, visceral cry of anguish. Together they form a complementary exploration of the human condition, with *Despair* acting as the calm before the storm of *The Scream*.

THE SCREAM

The composition of *The Scream* is simple: we can divide the painting into the bridge, the fjords and the sky. The main figure is androgynous, skeletal, abstract – more of a symbol of anxiety than an actual person. It is created with sweeping, wavy lines that appear to be merging with the background, whereas the two figures (his friends in the diary entry) are solid and vertical, as if designed to anchor us to the real world. The overall sensation is one of motion and emotional intensity.

The two figures are deep in conversation, oblivious to the chaos around them. Munch underlines their emotional distance from the protagonist by placing them at a physical distance, walking away down a straight road. If we take them away completely, however, the scene is not so impactful; it changes the atmosphere.

The painting may look as if it was done quickly, but Munch underwent meticulous preparation. Earlier sketches for both *Despair* (which is on the same diary page as the entry that inspired *The Scream*) and *The Scream* itself show the development of the lone figure as it goes from the far distance to the foreground, and we can see the violent red sky developing. Every element was planned, and changes were made even after it had been exhibited.

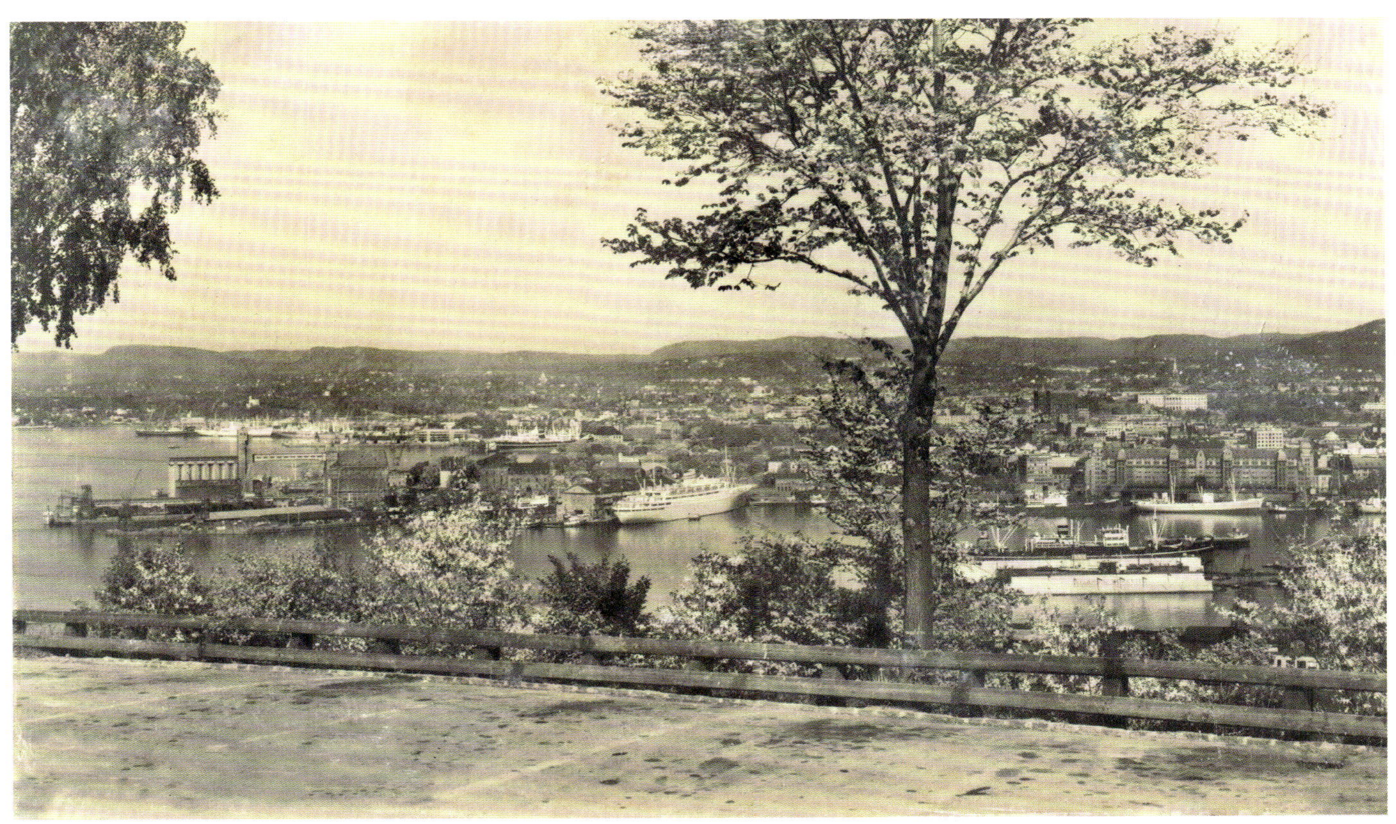

The main figure is androgynous, skeletal, abstract – more of a symbol of anxiety than an actual person

The Scream is painted on unprimed cardboard, a cheap material Munch used often, initially because he couldn't afford canvas and later because the texture suited his aesthetic. It's a surprise that these works have survived at all, as they were often glued straight onto wooden boards.

He used diluted paint, a technique he picked up from Henri de Toulouse-Lautrec in Paris. The mixture flowed more easily across the cardboard, like a wash, enabling rapid application and allowing for spontaneous, gestural brushstrokes, and he left the background visible through the thinned paint, to allow the process to show. He tended to deliberately leave paintings unfinished, as a sort of 'anti-art statement', and at times he violently stabbed on paint with his brush handle for the same effect.

Then there is what he called 'the horse cure', basically leaving his paintings outside in the garden in all weathers (including Norwegian winters!) to fend for themselves. He thought his paintings should have an 'organic life' and he also wanted them to look aged. Many of them are covered in coffee stains and wax drippings, and he rarely varnished his work, which meant the works were less protected. 'It does them good', he once said, 'to fend for themselves.'[9] We can safely say that for someone who was so attached to his paintings, he treated them terribly.

Barely visible on the painting is a pencil inscription that states: 'Could only have been painted by a madman!' Infrared images show that it was Munch's handwriting, and that it was written *after* the painting was first exhibited in 1895. It was probably a reaction to the fact that several critics, after seeing *The Scream*, had questioned Munch's mental health, which hurt him deeply.[10]

BACK TO REALITY

The setting of *The Scream* came about after the artist took the scenic walk he described in his diary, dated 22 January 1892. The actual place is called Ekeberg, a high point that overlooks Oslo Fjord (p. 155), with a view towards the setting sun during the winter months. He was not here for the scenery, however, but to visit his younger sister, who had recently been confined to an asylum nearby.[11]

Both of his parents were dead, and he was supporting his three surviving siblings. After a lifetime of abandonment through death and disease, it is not too difficult to imagine how he must have been feeling as he left his beloved sister behind in a brutal 19th-century asylum. Adding to the distress was a nearby slaughterhouse, and Munch no doubt could hear the screams of both animals and humans as he walked away.

In a world of extreme and rapid change, chaos and endless noise, combined with a life of desperate anxiety and alienation, Munch, who would have a nervous breakdown in 1908, must have felt as if his life was unravelling.

All of us can, in some way, understand the desperate feeling Munch must have had, of wanting to block out all this noise.

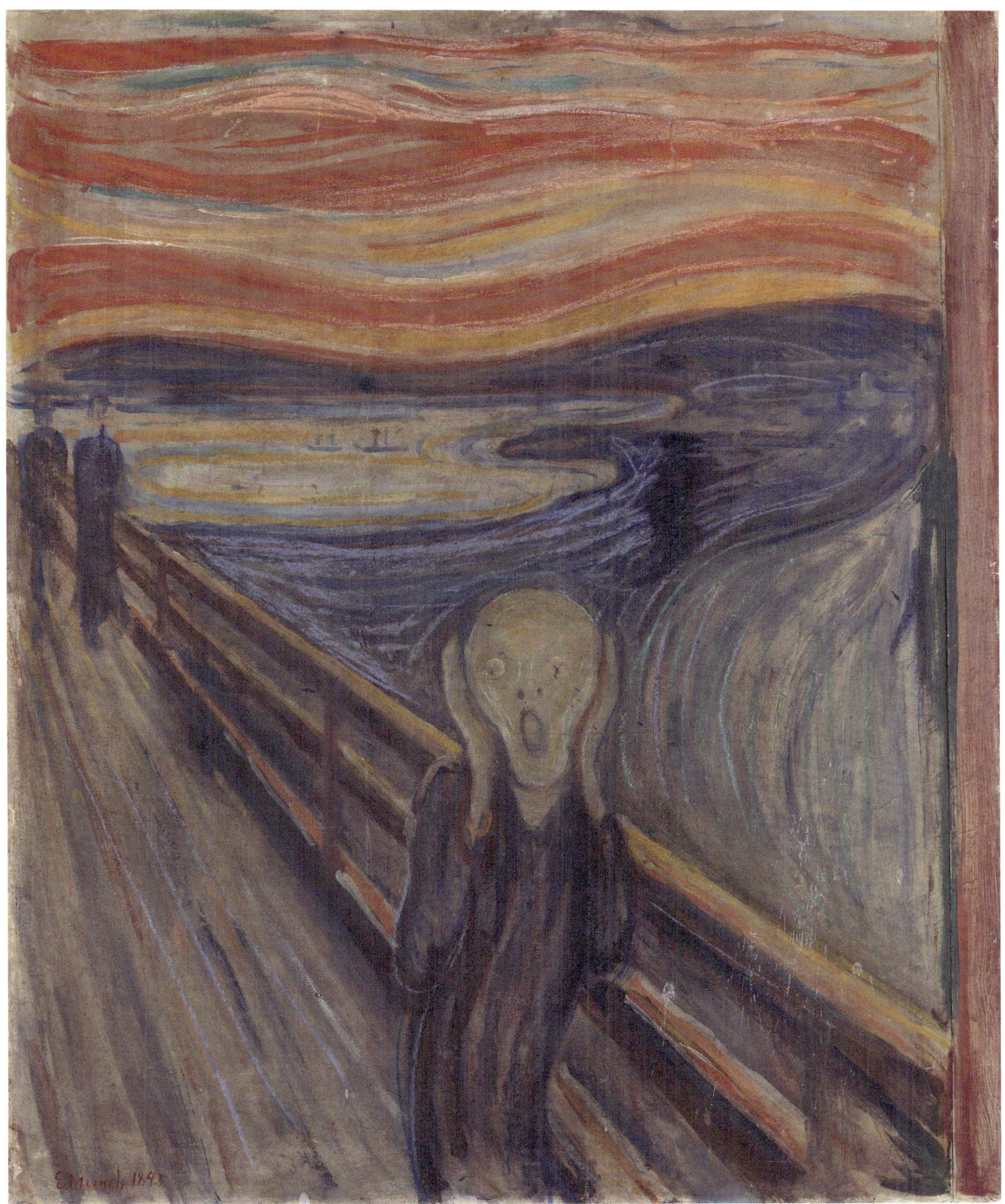

PABLO PICASSO

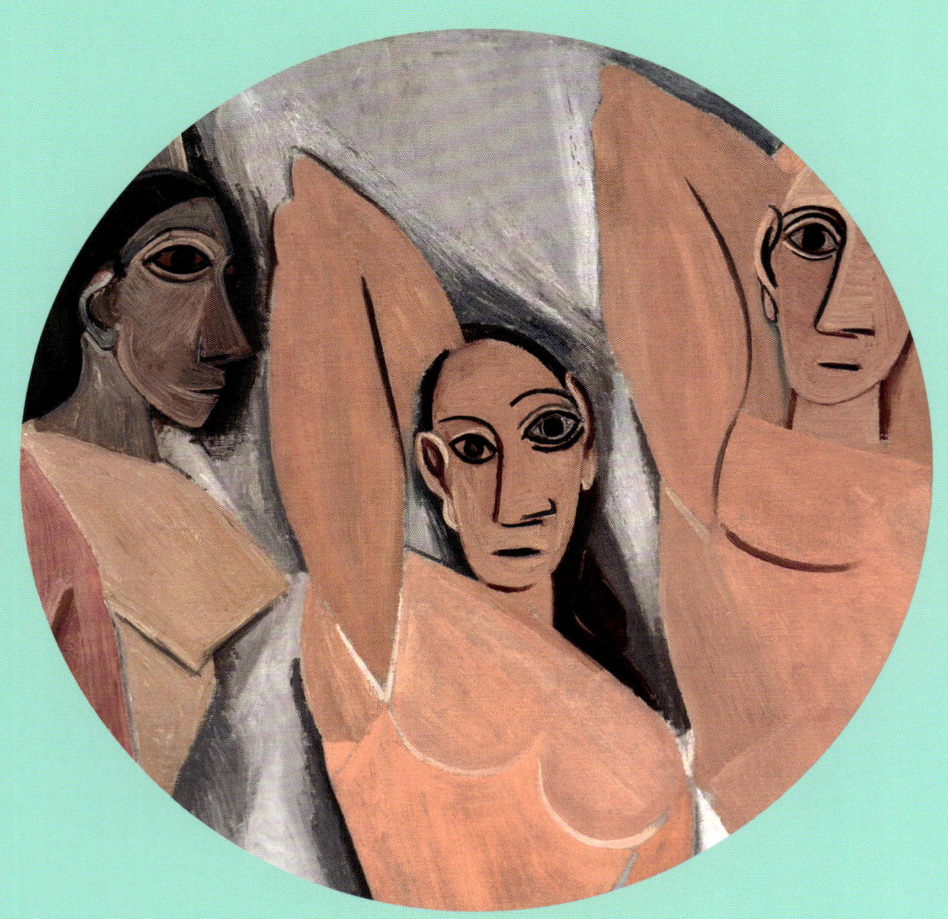

LES DEMOISELLES D'AVIGNON

1907

GREAT ARTISTS STEAL

Pablo Picasso was born in 1881 in Malaga, Spain, where at the end of the 19th century, and well into the 20th, there was an accepted brothel culture. Pablo's father and his friends would make regular trips to such establishments; they discussed it openly and would introduce their sons to the practice when they reached puberty.

In 1907 Picasso created a work that he called *Le Bordel d'Avignon* (*The Avignon Brothel*), later renamed *Les Demoiselles d'Avignon*, and when it was finally shown in 1916, it would shock the world.

This was not a traditional depiction of sex workers in art: erotically enticing figures, rendered with soft, idealized forms to emphasize their sensuality. These women are raw, primal figures, distorted and angular. They are brazenly sexual, confrontational and even unsettling, staring out defiantly at the viewer, and painted in a style that can only be described as revolutionary.

BORN IN MALAGA, CREATED IN PARIS

Picasso left Spain permanently in 1904 and spent most of his adult life in France, first settling in Paris in the Bateau-Lavoir, a seedy tenement building in Montmartre. Paris provided him the freedom, inspiration and intellectual stimulation he needed to develop into a groundbreaking artist, and he thrived in the experimental atmosphere of a city teeming with poets, writers, dancers and artists. He may have been born in Malaga, but he was created in Paris.

From a poverty-stricken young artist in Paris, he would become one of the most famous artists in the world, and a very wealthy man. A prolific innovator of art forms, he would pioneer Cubism and collage and make major contributions to Symbolism and Surrealism.

In a career spanning eighty-seven years, it has been said that he produced nearly 150,000 pieces: 13,500 paintings, 100,000 prints and engravings, 700 sculptures, 4,000 ceramics and 34,000 illustrations.[1]

PICASSO AND MATISSE

Picasso's greatest skill was reinvention: taking traditional academic ideas and reworking them. In *Les Demoiselles d'Avignon*, he plays with idealized female beauty, and later, in his great work of 1937, *Guernica*, he would reinvigorate the genre of historical painting. He is widely quoted as having said that good artists borrow, great artists steal. Who knows if he actually said it, but it's true that he was the magpie of the art world, with an encyclopaedic knowledge of art history and a deep understanding of how visual references such as African and Iberian art could be used to underpin his radical ideas.

Picasso met the artist Henri Matisse in 1905, and as the great writer and salonist

Pablo Picasso, *Les Demoiselles d'Avignon* (detail), 1917.

He was the magpie of the art world, with an encyclopaedic knowledge of art history

Gertrude Stein said, they 'became friends but were enemies'.[2] Picasso was notoriously competitive, and Matisse became well known shortly after they met, thanks to a painting called *Le Bonheur de Vivre* (*The Joy of Life*), which he revealed to the public in 1906. It created an instant scandal and shocked academics, who openly criticized it, not for its subject matter – a mass of prancing nudes – but for its style, its garish colours and its distorted scale and perspective.

On October 1906, Picasso spent the evening at Matisse's studying a Teke figure from Congo that the artist owned, and later that night Picasso created his first studies for *Les Demoiselles*.[3]

He saw the opportunity to out-do Matisse with an even more radical painting, and began working on *Les Demoiselles* immediately.[4] But whereas Matisse had looked to more traditional forms of art, his interest lying mainly in European art history, Picasso would look to what was called 'primitive' art.

'PRIMITIVE' ART

Picasso lived at a time when thousands of African 'objects', such as ceremonial masks, sculptures and carvings, were on display in museums and galleries – a direct result of European imperialism. But he flat out denied that his work related to 'primitive' or ethnographic art.

This seems unlikely, however, as we know that he visited the Musée d'Ethnographie du Trocadéro in Paris in the spring of 1907 and began actively collecting African artefacts. Three of the five women in *Les Desmoiselles* seem to be wearing 'African' masks, their features characterized by geometrical shapes and an overall flattening of facial planes.

One explanation for his denial is that by the 1920s he was very much involved in his own mythmaking, and notoriously competitive about being not only the most *important* artist, but also the *first* to use a particular reference. Admitting that African art played a significant role in his creative process might have detracted from the perception of him as the sole inventor of these radical new ideas. African masks had become a common point of reference; they were so ubiquitous –

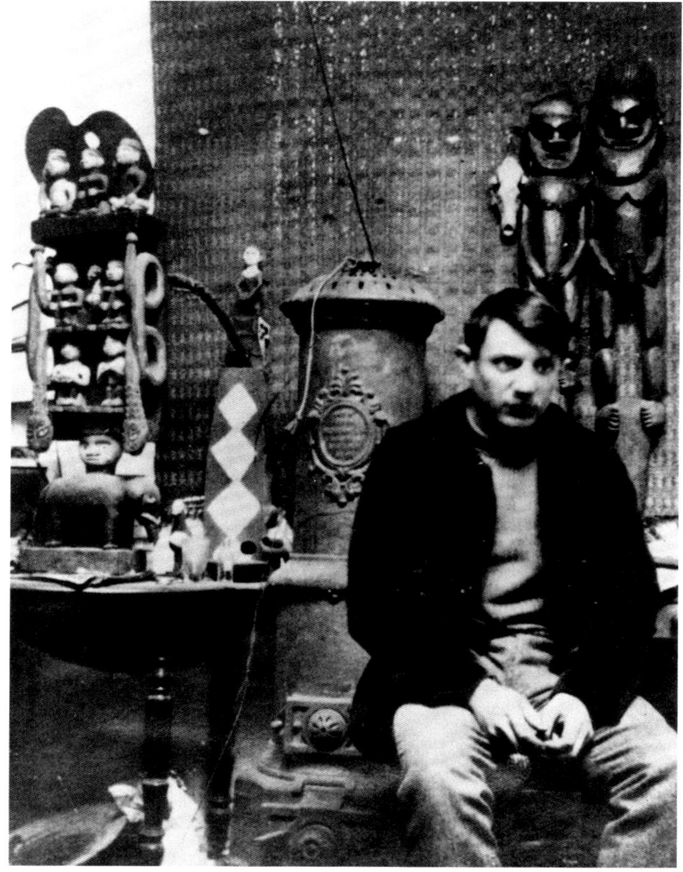

PABLO PICASSO

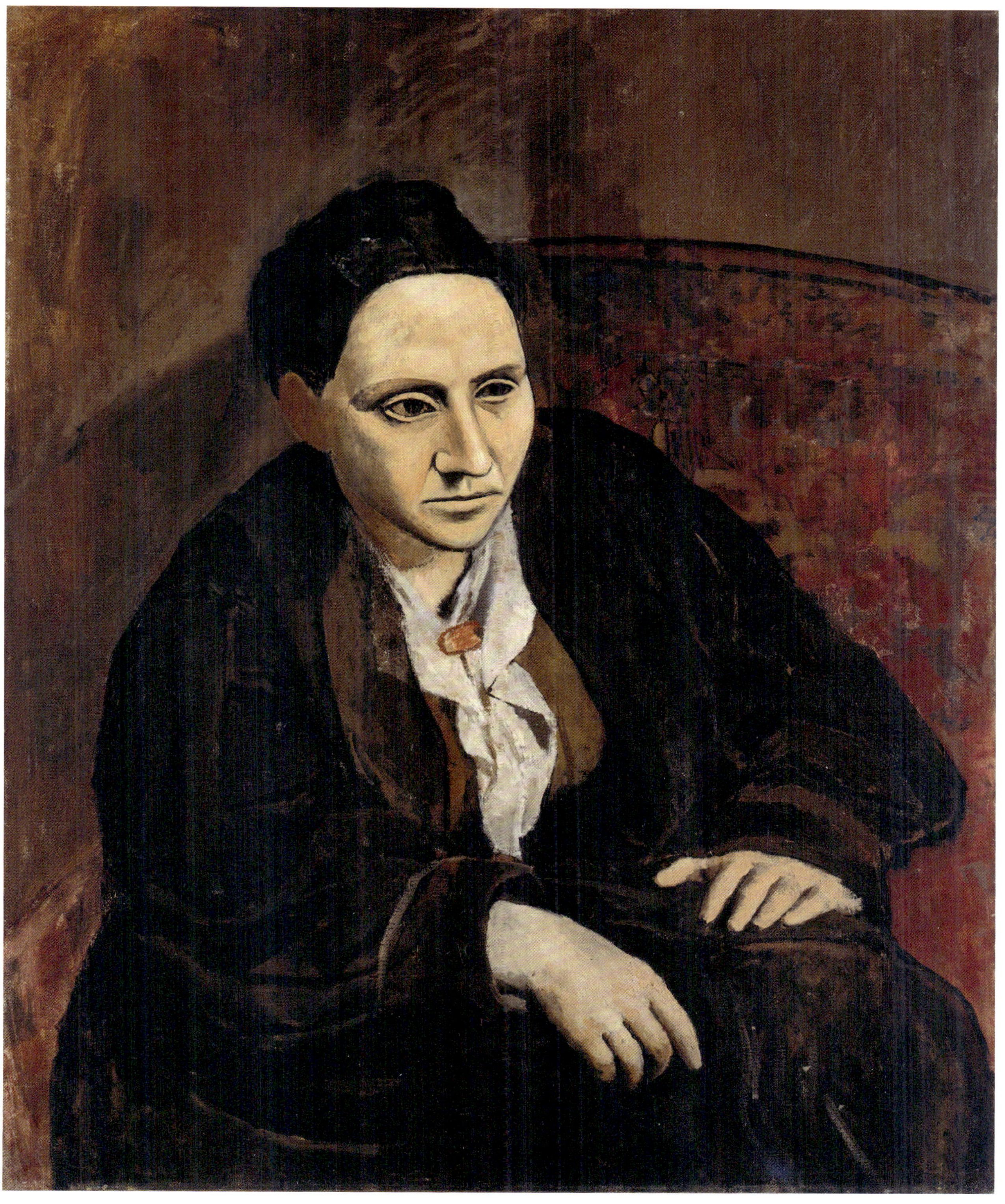

LES DEMOISELLES D'AVIGNON

Picasso explores a more complex relationship between sex, power, desire, the male gaze and artistic representation

and even clichéd – in artistic circles that he wanted to distance himself from their influence.

Picasso first encountered Iberian sculptures, another important influence on him, at the Louvre in 1906. The Iberian heads, especially stone funerary statues and busts of Iberian warriors and nobles, captivated Picasso with their almond-shaped eyes, rigid features and blocky forms.

It was around this time that he painted his friend, Gertrude Stein, with a mask-like face and heavy eyelids clearly influenced by his recent discovery of Iberian sculpture. It is a work that, like *Les Desmoiselles*, has been called a proto-Cubist image – referring to a transitional experimental period from 1906 to 1910 that would give birth to Cubism in 1911.

CÉZANNE AND OTHERS

Les Demoiselles is often mistakenly referred to as the first Cubist painting, but although it has elements of the future art movement, developed by Picasso and his friend Georges Braque, it is not there yet. It is, however, a turning point.

There are numerous reference points to be found in *Les Demoiselles*, but it is perhaps the revolutionary visual language of Paul Cézanne, sometimes called the 'Father of Cubism', that we need to look at first and foremost, in particular his painting *Les Grandes Baigneuses* (*The Bathers*).

Picasso once described Cézanne as 'my one and only master'.[5] *Les Grandes Baigneuses* was an important work for many avant-garde artists in Paris, but particularly for Picasso and Braque, who began to experiment with Cézanne's techniques of flattening space and deconstructing images, ultimately reducing the world into fractured, simplified forms.

But the Spanish Renaissance artist El Greco and his work *The Vision of St John* (1608–14) were just as important to the development of *Les Demoiselles d'Avignon* as Cézanne.[6] Picasso knew the El Greco painting well, and the scale, square-ish format and stylistic similarities, as well as the elongated distorted angularity of El Greco's figures and expressionistic qualities, are all clearly reflected in Picasso's work.

LES DEMOISELLES

By the end of 1904 Picasso's paintings had begun to be dominated by pink and flesh tints, in a phase that came to be labelled as his 'Rose Period'. This period ended in 1906, and within a year he would create *Les Demoiselles d'Avignon*, beginning preparatory work that October and painting the canvas in June and July of 1907.

He made hundreds of sketches and paintings, spending much more time on it than he did any other work. In one of the original sketches (p. 165), of which nearly a hundred survive, we see there are two male figures – clients, perhaps – and five female sex workers. We know the male figure on the left is a medical student, clutching a skull (which some see as a *memento mori*, a reminder of death, possibly referencing sexual diseases in an era before antibiotics), and the one in the centre is a sailor.[7] They were later cut from the composition, and Picasso shifted the women's gaze towards the viewer.

By eradicating the men and focusing exclusively on female figures, Picasso explores a more complex relationship between sex,

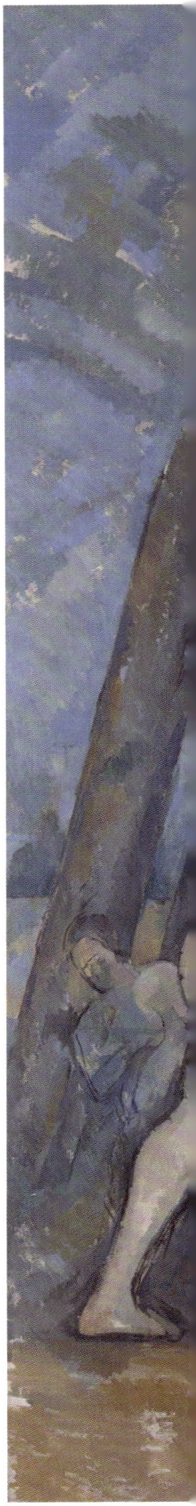

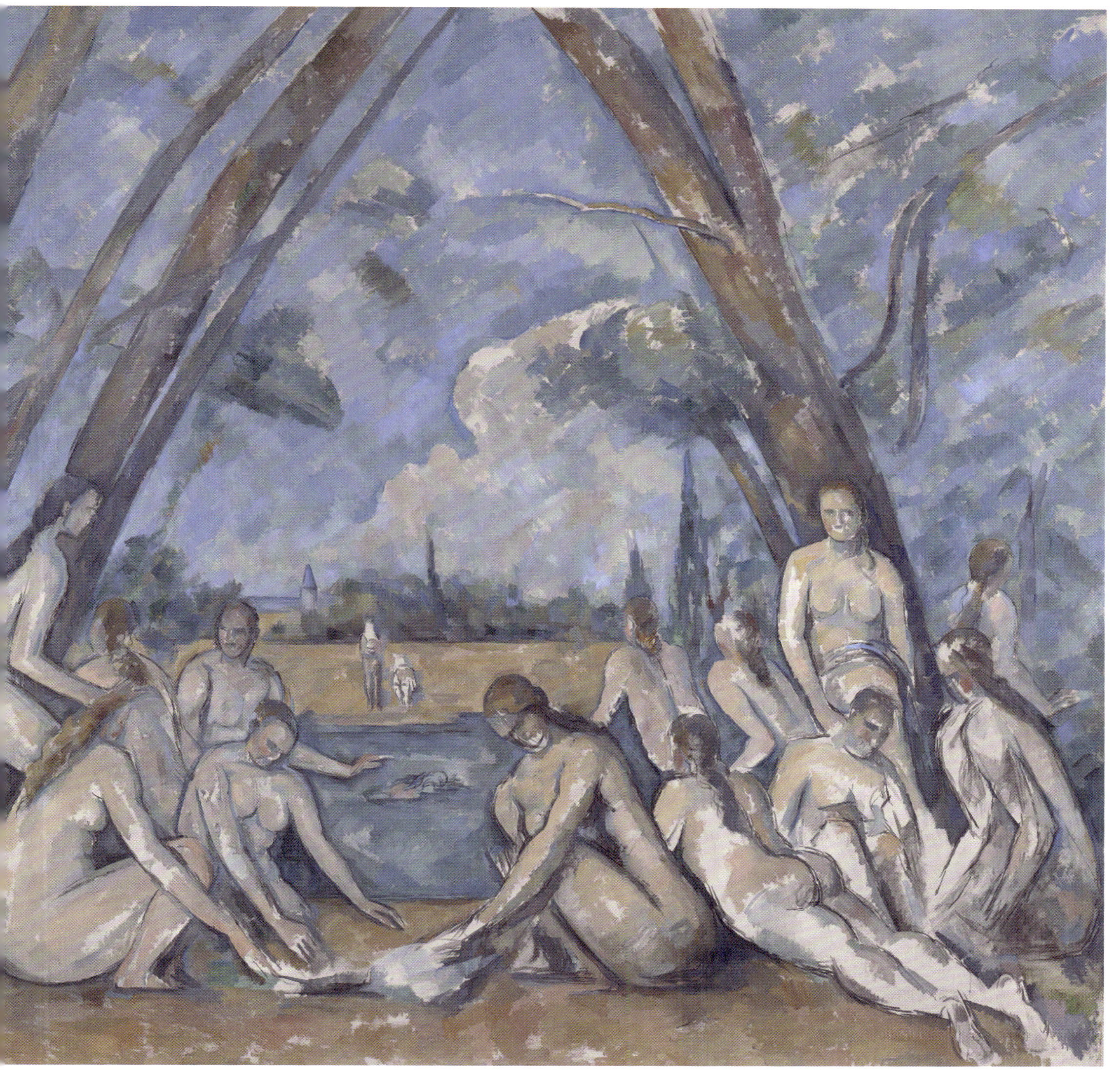

Paul Cézanne,
Les Grandes Baigneuses, 1906.

     LES DEMOISELLES D'AVIGNON

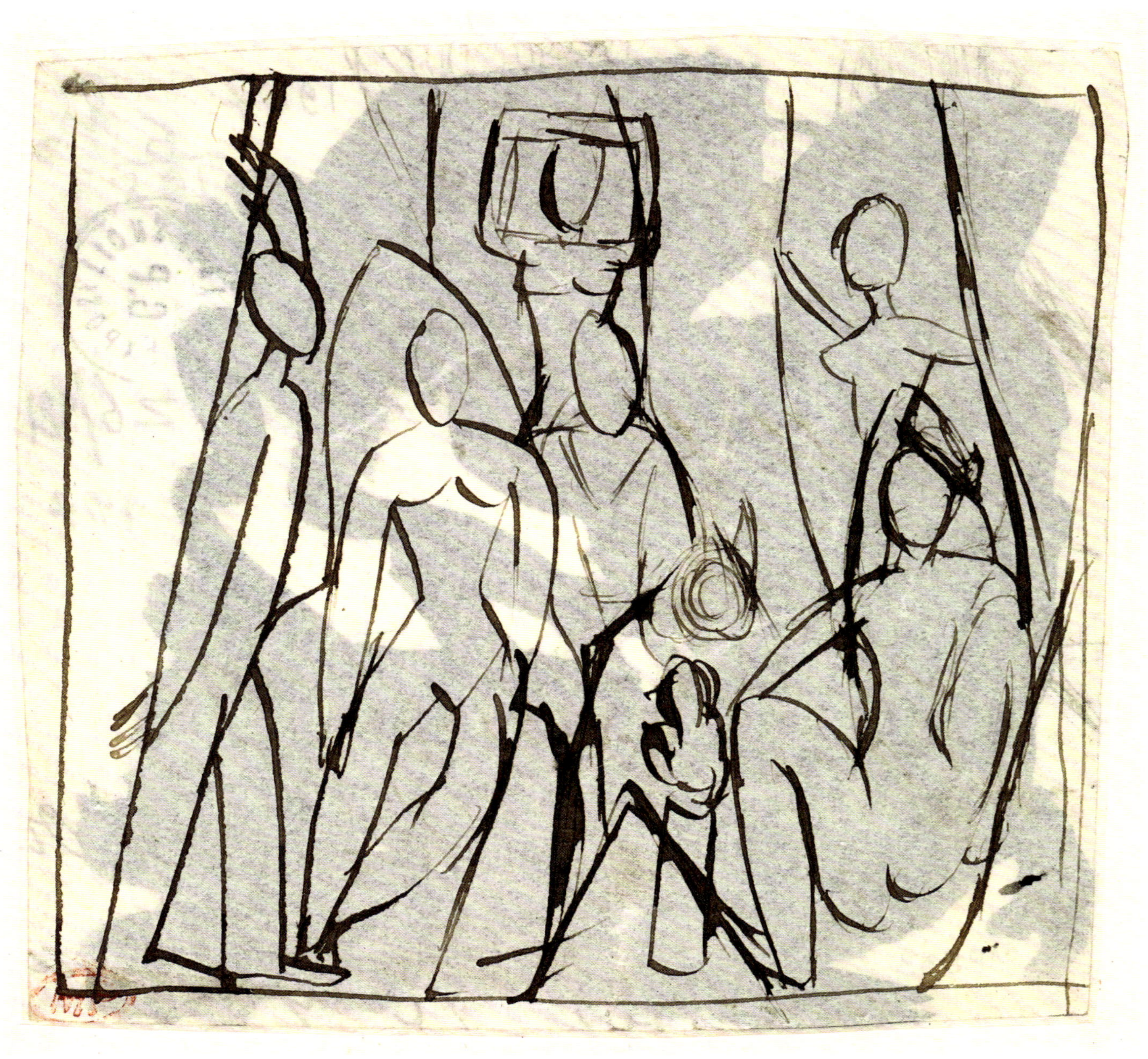

The women are tightly
packed in geometric,
disconnected shapes

Pablo Picasso,
study for *Les Demoiselles
d'Avignon* (on recto
of study for two nudes),
winter 1906-7.

PABLO PICASSO

power, desire, the male gaze and artistic representation. With the female figures' attention directed away from the clients and towards us, the viewer, we are implicitly cast in the role of a potential client, transforming our viewing experience into an uncomfortable encounter with the act of looking and consuming the female body.

Picasso wasn't the first artist to portray a brothel with naked, confrontational women, but it was how he did it, emphasizing form over content, that was groundbreaking.

The women are tightly packed in geometric, disconnected shapes. Despite the curtains pressing against them, filling every inch of space, they seem isolated or detached from each other. There is no depth to the work, no interplay of light and shadow, and the flatness forces the figures awkwardly into the viewer's space, their direct gaze intense and disturbing.

A curious detail is the 'still life' in front of them, a bowl of fruit. The slice of melon and grapes have been interpreted as a phallic

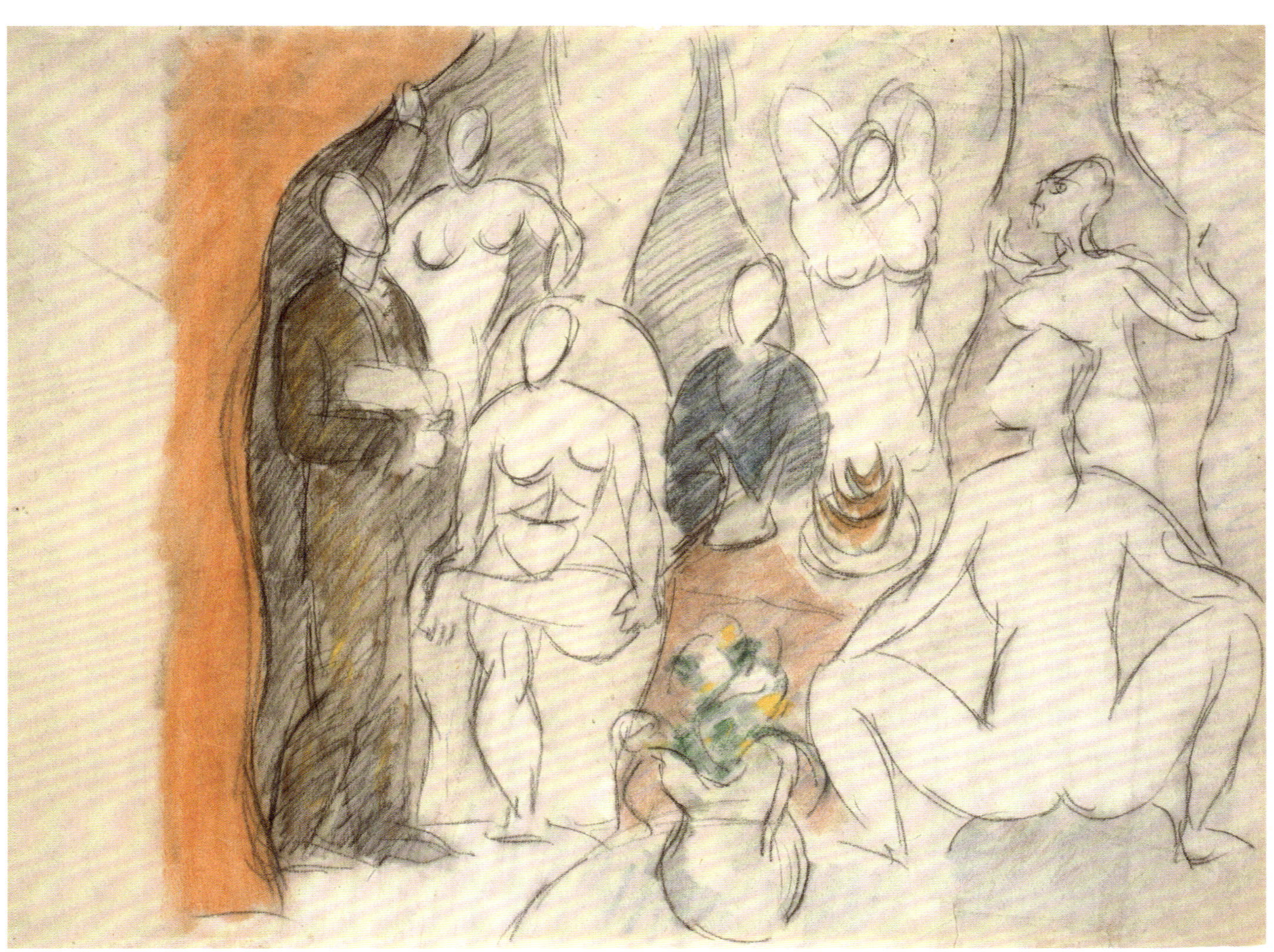

LES DEMOISELLES D'AVIGNON

reference,[8] but they also work as a (possibly phallic) divider to separate our space from the sex workers'. Still lifes, particularly those featuring fruit, have a long tradition in Western art, and often signify fertility, abundance, sexuality and temptation.

When the painting was finally shown in July 1916, the name was changed (against Picasso's will[9]) from *The Brothel of Avignon* (a street in Barcelona, not the French city) to *The Young Ladies of Avignon*, in the hopes that it might make the painting more palatable to the public. It didn't work – but the name stuck.

PROBLEMS WITH PICASSO

It is impossible to separate Picasso's obsession with sex from his obsessive creativity, and his insatiable sex life from his limitless creative life; likewise, it is hard to discuss this painting without acknowledging Picasso's misogyny. The artist's deplorable treatment of women left behind a trail of destruction. But as we know, great art is often made by problematic artists, and issues connected with artists like Picasso, Gauguin or Caravaggio are something we should address. Can art be separated from the artist? After all, Picasso himself said that his canvases were like the pages of his diary.

On the one hand, the sex workers in this painting follow the well-worn trope of goddess/whore, or femme fatale, but on the other hand, they are totally stripped of the sentimentality we often see in representations of the female nude in the arts.

Their masks and angular bodies act as a form of armour, one that repels yet dares you to touch. This is not the female nude as decoration or object of titillation, but rather a matter-of-fact representation of the intense alienation involved in the institution of exchanging sex for money, and it makes us uncomfortable. Still.

YOU CANNOT BE INDIFFERENT

No work of art has left its mark in quite the same way that *Les Demoiselles d'Avignon* has. With a painting of five naked women and a bowl of fruit, Picasso broke away from 500 years of representational European painting that began with the Renaissance, creating the first definitive 20th-century masterpiece. His radical experimentation with space and form, his challenge to how we view a painting and his innovative approach to depicting multiple perspectives helped redefine the possibilities of art.

Les Demoiselles is a work that has been called everything from groundbreaking to contemptuous, incendiary to revolutionary and angry to confrontational. You can say what you like about this painting, but even more than a century after it was created, you cannot be indifferent.

PABLO PICASSO

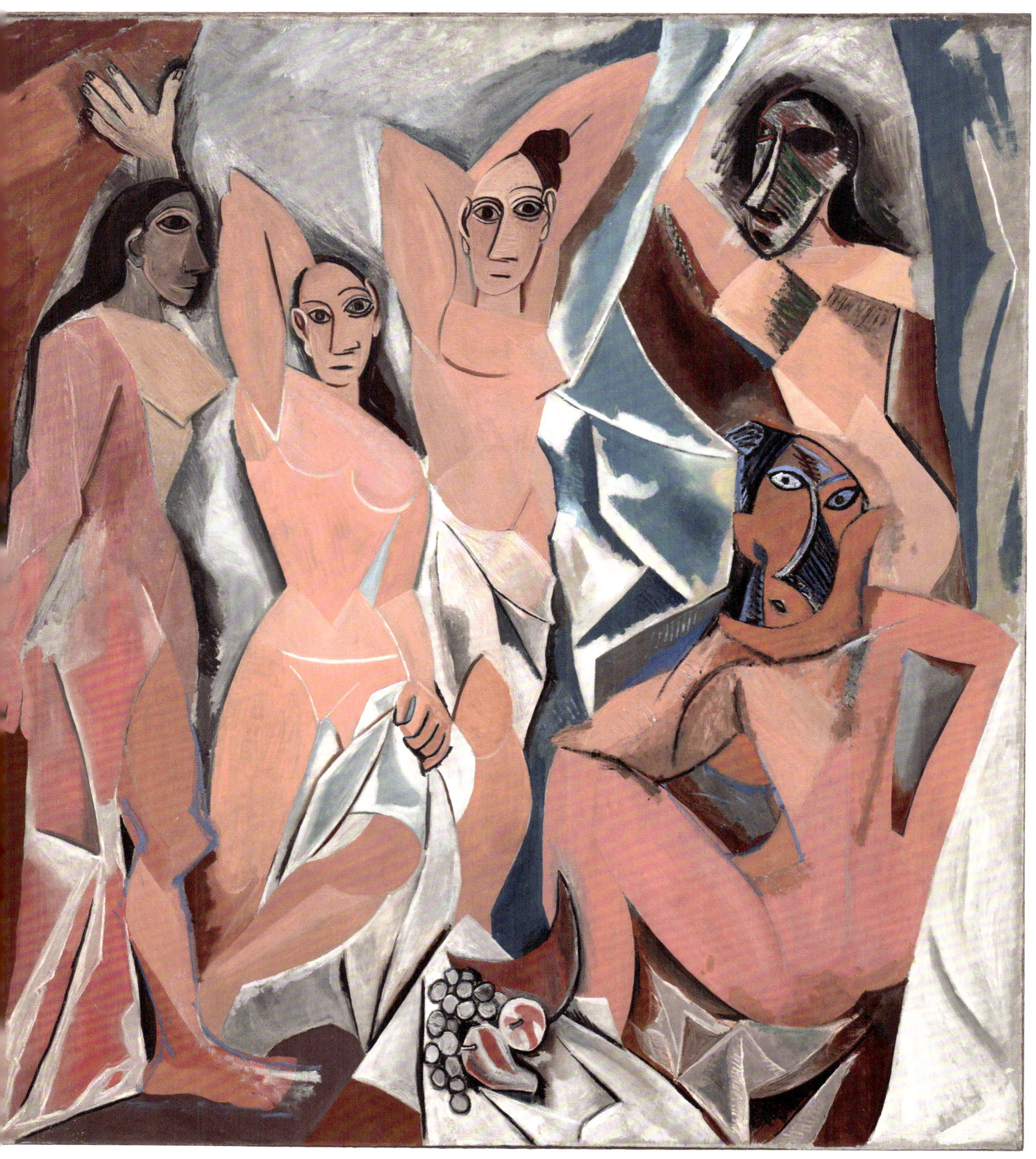

GUSTAV KLIMT

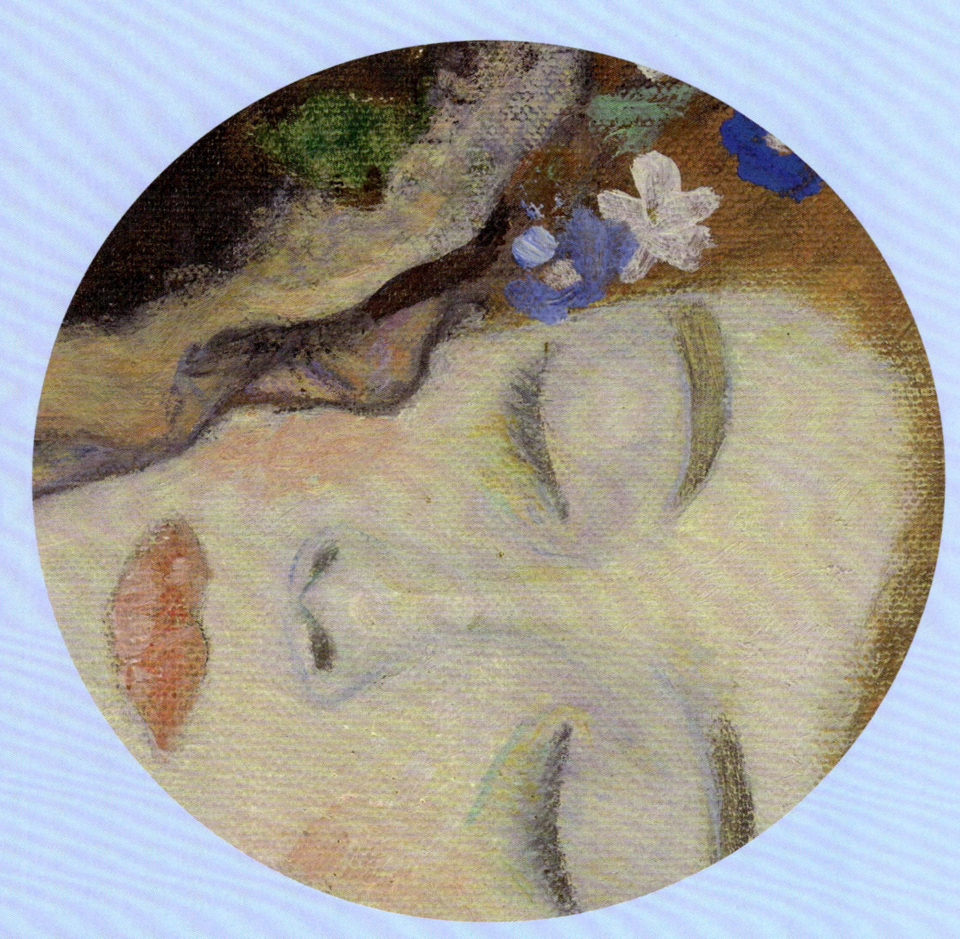

THE KISS

1907–8

KLIMT AND
THE GOLDEN AGE

By the end of the 19th century, Vienna, an uptight, stuffy and conservative city, was changing. Artists, architects, musicians and social scientists were experimenting in ways that would transform their individual fields. On the one hand, Vienna was a traditional city, home to academic art, the composer Johann Strauss II and the Habsburg Empire, but on the other, it produced radical artists such as Gustav Klimt and Egon Schiele, who were shocking audiences with their explorations of sexual themes. Vienna was at the forefront of modernity, fostering a new golden age that would shape the 20th century.

EARLY LIFE

Gustav Klimt, born in 1862, grew up in poverty in a small suburb of Vienna. The second of seven children, in 1876 Gustav and his younger brother Ernst won scholarships to the Vienna School of Arts and Crafts. They honed their skills in the hope that they would be able to earn a living as teachers,[1] but within three years both were supporting themselves through their art.

In 1883, when Klimt was twenty-one, he and Ernst established a business focused on producing allegorical murals for new public buildings in Vienna. Their venture was very lucrative, with murals reflecting the traditional, mythological themes typical of 19th-century academic art. Klimt's experience as a decorative artist during this period laid the foundation for the more avant-garde direction his work would later take.

As Klimt's style evolved in the 1890s, he began to challenge the artistic norms of the time, becoming more aligned with modernist movements. And as he began to reject artistic conventions, so he began to reject societal norms, too, taking a more bohemian approach to his personal life.

Klimt never married, but he and Emilie Flöge, a Viennese fashion designer and businesswoman, shared a complex and close relationship that spanned over decades. Their bond was both professional and personal, and they influenced each other's work significantly.

He was a prodigious lover, allegedly leaving behind fourteen children by as many women (and a plethora of paternity claims),[2] but he went home each night to the mother he adored and his two unmarried sisters.

THE GREAT SCANDAL

In 1894 Klimt's company was commissioned to decorate the University of Vienna with a series of allegorical paintings representing the four faculties. By this time, he was breaking away from his previous classicist style, and in 1897 was one of the founders of the Vienna Secession, a society of young artists and architects fighting against the rigid academic style, declaring a 'war on sterile routine, on rigid Byzantinism, on all forms of bad taste'.[3]

Gustav Klimt,
The Kiss (detail),
1907-8.

The university was expecting works that represented 'the triumph of light over darkness', but when the first three paintings, *Philosophy*, *Medicine* and *Jurisprudence*, were presented to the public in 1900 it caused a huge outcry, with Klimt accused of creating 'pornography'. The paintings featured nudity and sexually provocative themes, and the university refused to display them. In 1945 all three were destroyed by retreating SS forces.

The idea behind the Vienna Secession group was to bring art, craft, architecture and design together in one great movement. They embraced decorative and ornamental elements, as well as symbolism and abstraction, in their practice, and Klimt's *The Kiss* would come to be seen as an emblem of the Secession movement.

THE PAINTING

The painting is square and practically life-size, making it an intimate and immersive experience that alters our emotional and physical engagement with the piece. It is as if we are witnessing a deeply personal and private moment; as if we are standing in the same space as them.

It is a deceptively simple painting on the surface, yet there are several things that make it complex. Visually, there is the deliberate contrast between the realistically rendered flesh and the flat, uniform gold background, further emphasizing the abstract, otherworldly

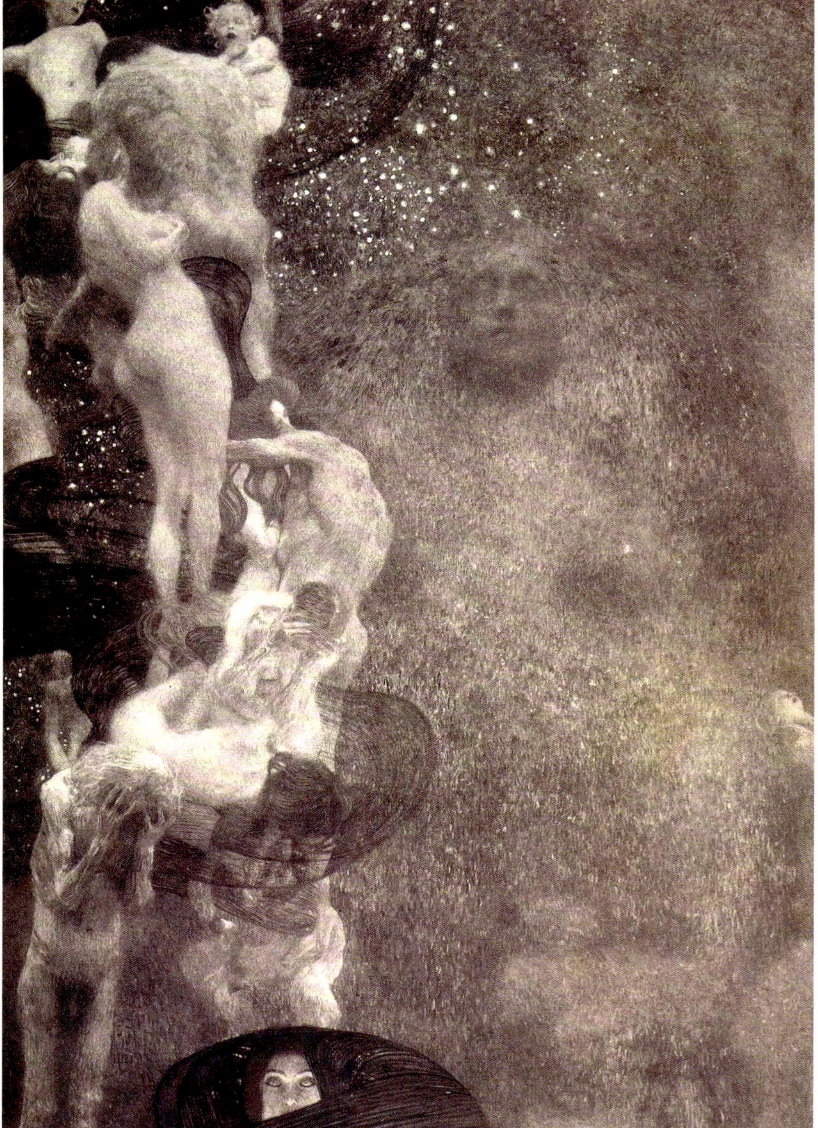

nature of their embrace. This deliberate lack of context keeps the focus entirely on the figures and their interaction, isolating the moment of their embrace from any broader narrative or external world.

It is a painting you need to approach as a physical object. Texture plays a crucial role in *The Kiss*; it guides the viewer's eye around the painting, adding dynamism to the otherwise still and serene embrace, making the painting feel alive and engaging. For example, if we look at where the background meets the meadow, we can see how the artist was playing with different textures in relief. He used eight different types of gold and other precious metals in the painting, building up texture underneath gold leaf to give it a three-dimensional aspect that catches the light.

THE GOLDEN ARTIST

Klimt's 'Golden Phase' refers to a specific time in his artistic career, typically dated from around 1899 to 1910, when he extensively used gold leaf and gold paint in his works. Klimt's father was a gold engraver, and the artist had a long-held fascination with the precious metal.

His use of gold in *The Kiss* evokes a sense of otherworldliness and sacredness and is suggestive of altarpieces, with the halo-like shape around the couple's heads subtly hinting

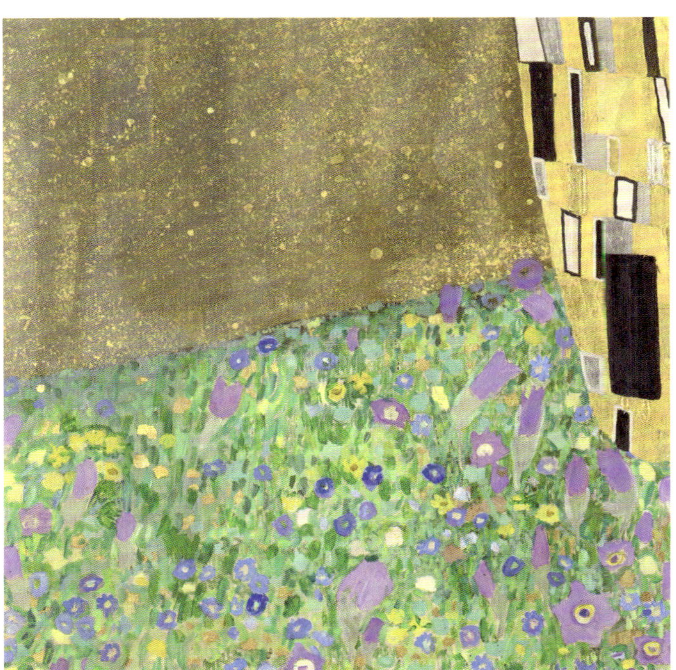

Texture plays a crucial role in The Kiss; it guides the viewer's eye around the painting

at spiritual associations. These qualities have turned the artwork into a symbol of the post-religious era in which Klimt lived.

Gold leaf is fragile and comes in gossamer-thin sheets. To create the relief sections, Klimt would use gesso, which is a mixture of animal glue and chalk dust used to prime canvases, painting the thick mixture on and then applying the gold leaf, which was sometimes silver and, less often, platinum.

The background was achieved by covering the entire canvas with sheets of gold leaf before painting over it with a dark wash, which he then flicked with flakes of gold.

Gold was not used for 'realism' but rather as an indicator of wealth. Klimt often used it to confer status on the nouveau-riche women of Vienna, to elevate his subjects, making them appear iconic, monumental and timeless, like religious figures in Byzantine art, while also emphasizing the sensuality and ornamentation that defined much of his work.

THEMES AND INFLUENCES

The theme of two lovers kissing was not new, but the overt eroticism was. Klimt knew Edvard Munch's painting *The Kiss* from over ten years before, and both artists were aware of Rodin's even earlier sculpture of the same name (discussed in Chapter 13).

Figures kissing or embracing were a common motif for Klimt from the first time he painted *Love* in 1895, thirteen years before *The Kiss*.

*The theme of two lovers
kissing was not new,
but the overt eroticism was*

Likewise, Klimt's *Beethoven Frieze* features an embracing couple similar in both composition and aesthetics to *The Kiss*. The frieze was part of a successful group show of the Secessionists inspired by Beethoven's 9th Symphony, a watershed in both Vienna's and Klimt's artistic evolution.

The Kiss owes much to a 1903 trip to Ravenna, of which Klimt wrote, 'Lots of miserable things in Ravenna – [but] the mosaics are unbelievably wonderful.'[4] He was talking about the mosaics of San Vitale, which employ gold accents with an emphasis on flattened forms, intricate patterns and the integration of symbolism.

The figures in *The Kiss* are wearing loose, flowing robes decorated with elaborate geometrical patterns, another textural contrast to their lifelike skin. This style mirrors his companion Emilie Flöge's designs (pp. 174–75), which emphasized unstructured, comfortable garments that promoted natural movement, a stark contrast to the rigid clothing of the era.

The intricate patterns on the robes in *The Kiss* are created with a variety of shapes and textures – rectilinear motifs on the man's cloak and circular, organic forms on the woman's, symbolizing the complementary nature of male and female energies. The patterns might also be a visual metaphor of erotic love, his said to symbolize masculinity and hers the ova.[5]

METAMORPHOSIS

Klimt's complicated feelings towards love come out in *The Kiss*. The figures are pictured on a patch of flowery meadow, but they are teetering at the edge of a cliff. Despite the aesthetic comparisons with religious icons, with garlands in their hair, the lovers have a distinctly pagan look. The man wears a crown of vines, which is possibly a laurel wreath, a symbol of triumph, and could suggest that he has won his conquest. The woman wears a crown of flowers, suggesting that the image is the consummation of some kind of ritual.

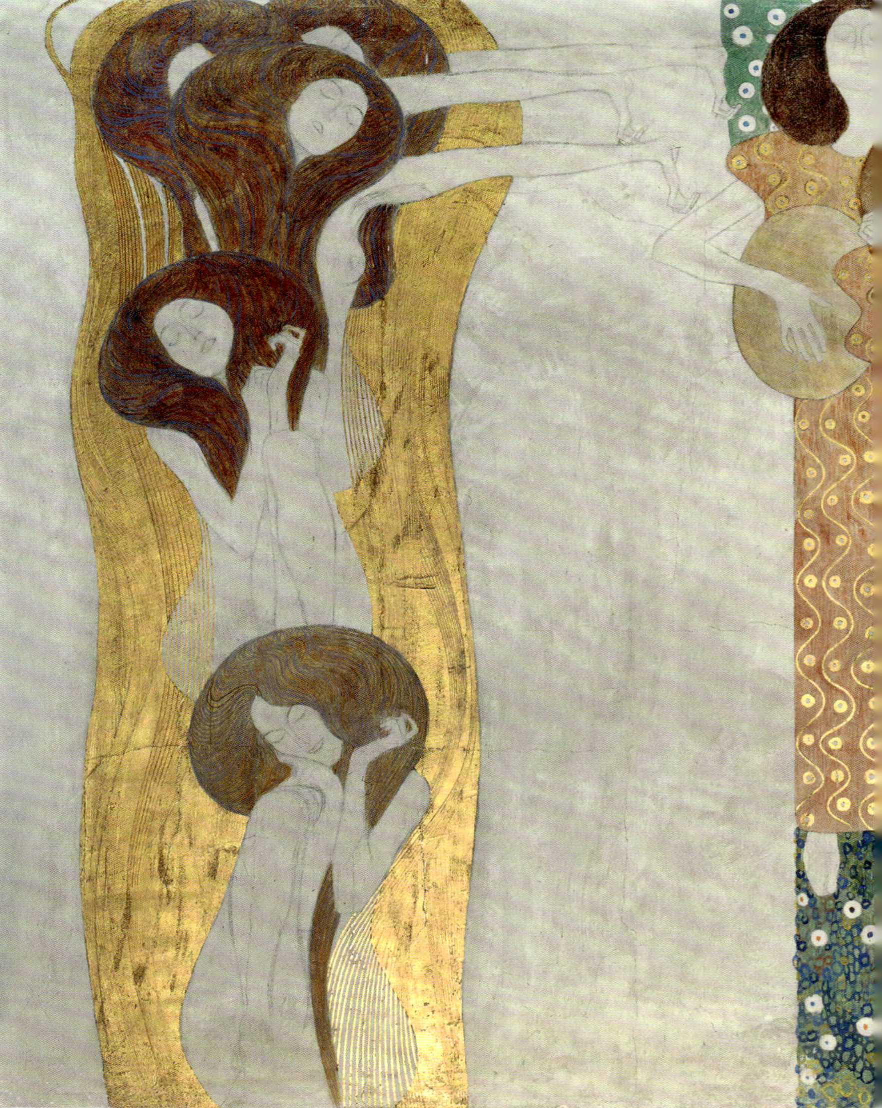

Gustav Klimt,
Beethoven Frieze,
1901–2.

GUSTAV KLIMT

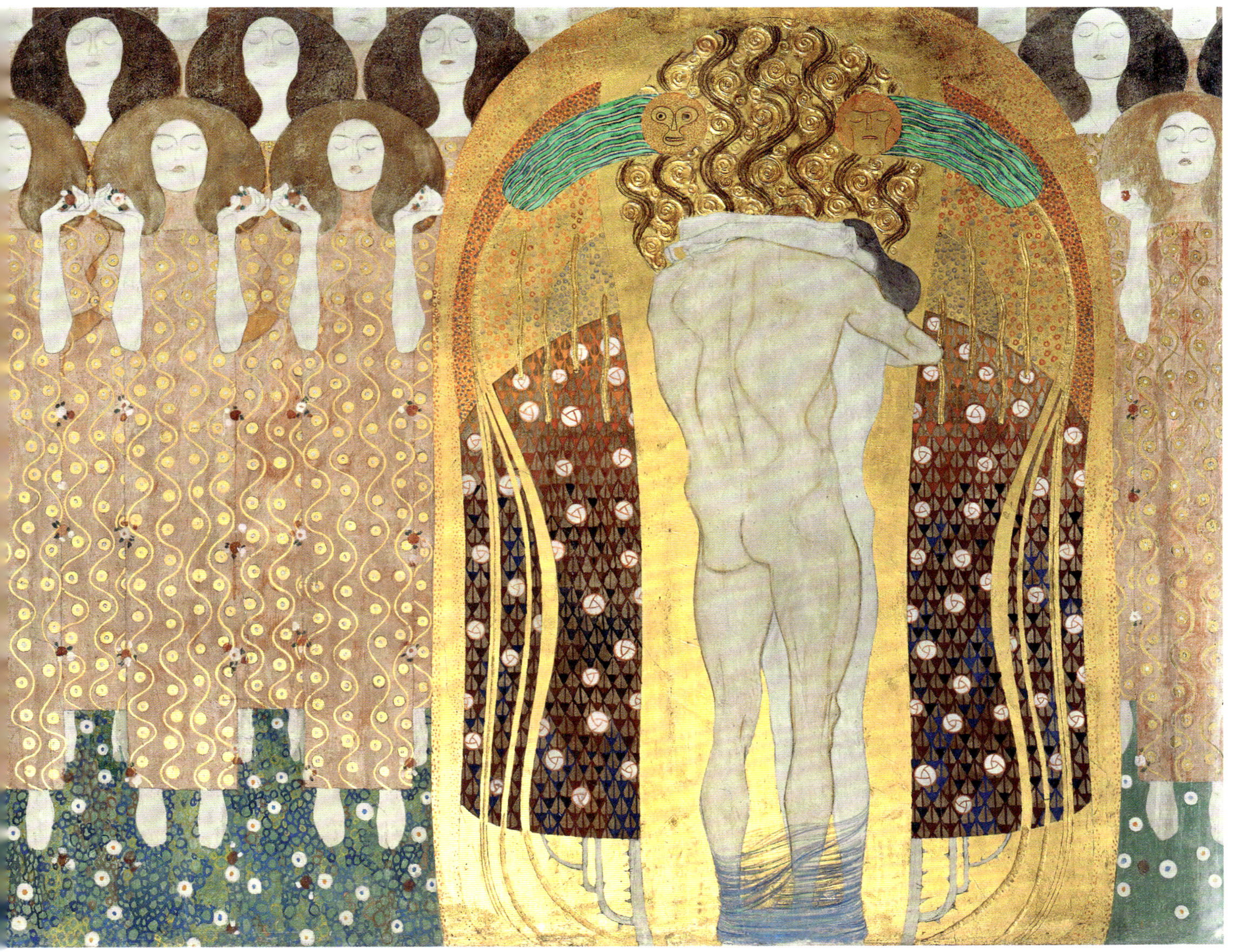

Mythological themes and symbolism frequently appeared in Klimt's artwork, particularly during his 'Golden Phase'. One theory is that in this picture the artist was representing the myth of Apollo and Daphne, from Ovid's *Metamorphoses*.

There are thematic parallels between the painting and Ovid's themes of love, transformation and sensuality. According to the myth, Apollo fell deeply in love with Daphne, who did not share his feelings. As Apollo pursued her, Daphne pleaded with her father, the river god Peneus, to help her escape, and in response, Peneus transformed Daphne into a laurel tree.

In *The Kiss*, the legs of the woman seem to be sinking into the ground, as tendrils of golden laurel leaves, which emanate only from her body, root themselves into the meadow, suggesting Daphne's transformation or transcendence.

LOVE, SEX OR FRIENDSHIP?

There has been endless debate about what exactly the relationship between the couple in the painting is, and it has even been suggested that there is a certain distance between the couple, '[a]s if there were in fact no relationship between them'.[6]

It is difficult to pin down the exact nature of the relationship, which is something that drives its enduring appeal. But it is possible that with the ornate gold background, the timelessness of the piece, the abstract ornamentation and the divine aura around the figures could hint at a symbolic connection beyond physical love, and more towards an idealized, universal concept of love, desire and surrender rather than a physical, earthly one.

THE MODELS

Another great mystery of *The Kiss* is: who are the models?

It is suggested that it is a portrait of Klimt and Flöge, whose innovative clothing was often worn by Klimt's models, and who became integral to the visual aesthetic of his paintings. *The Kiss* is also one of the few works of his where a male figure takes a central role, so many believe that Klimt may have projected his own identity onto the figure.

Like the couple in the painting, Klimt and Flöge's relationship was ambiguous. The man tries to kiss her, but she turns her head away. There is a tenderness there, an acceptance of affection, but without compliance. Her eyes

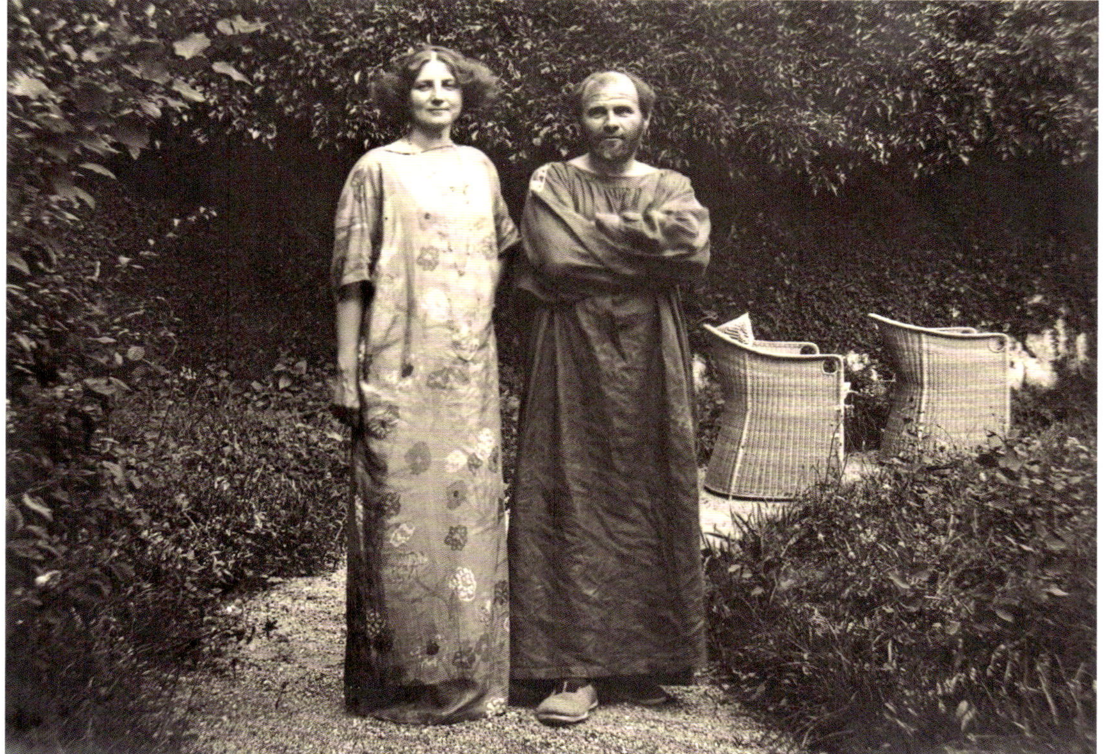

GUSTAV KLIMT

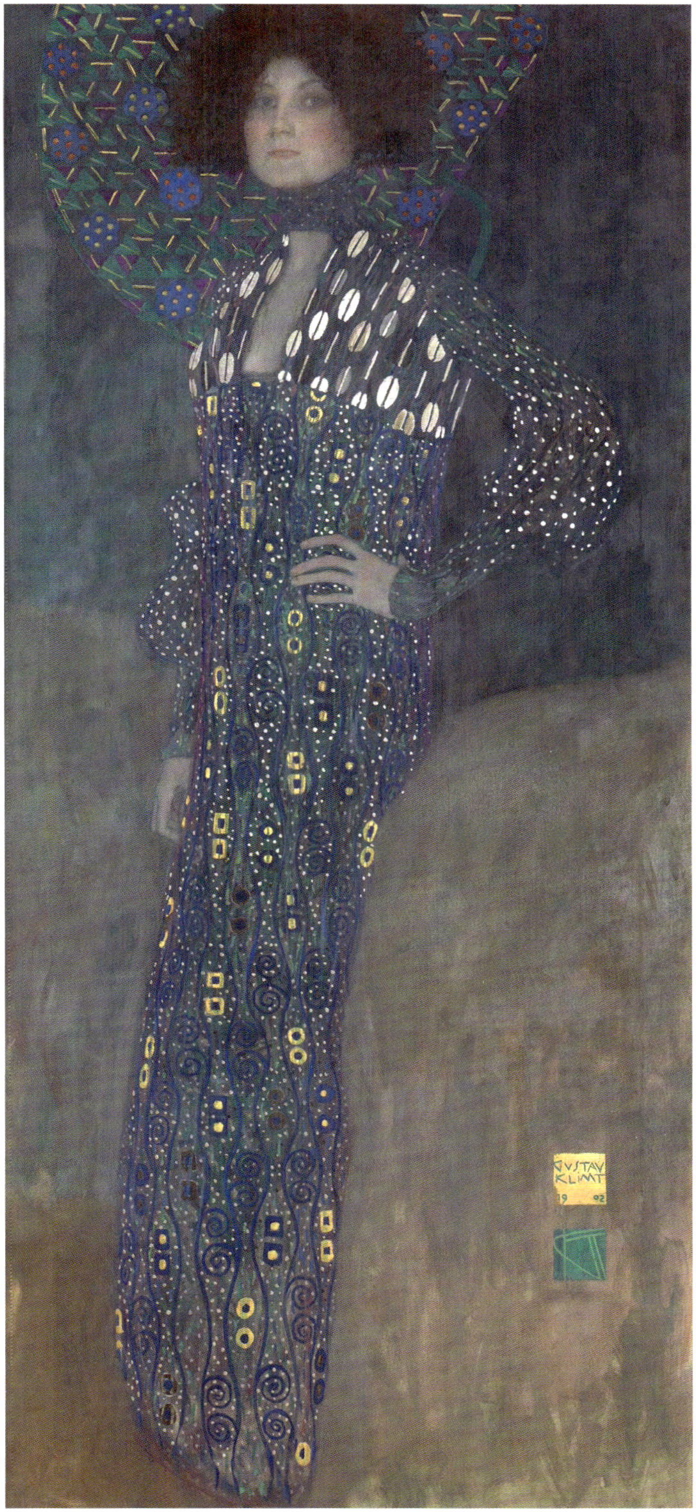

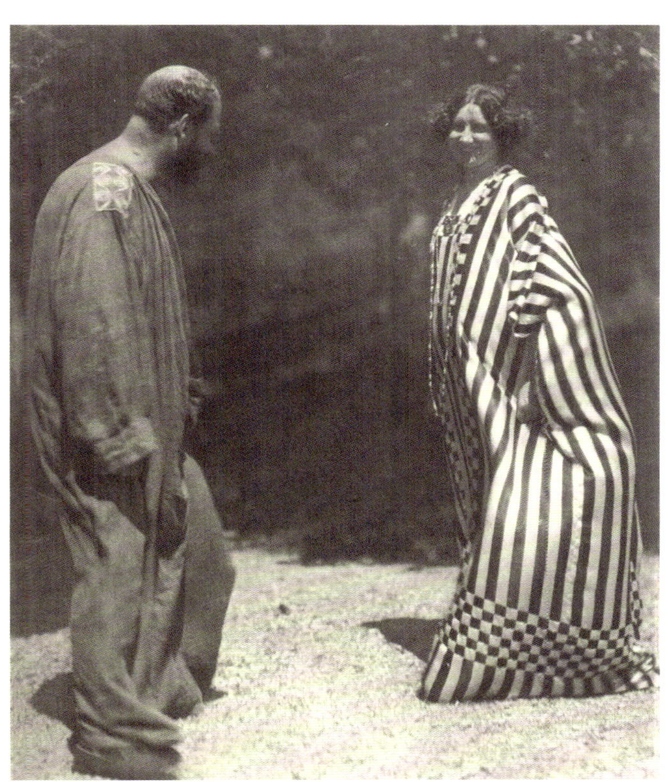

Like the couple in the painting, Klimt and Flöge's relationship was ambiguous

THE KISS

There is a tenderness there, an acceptance of affection, but without compliance

Gustav Klimt,
The Kiss, 1907–8.

and mouth are also firmly closed – unusual for Klimt's paintings, in which women's mouths tend to be open and erotically charged.

Klimt and Flöge had a deep, life-long bond, both personally and professionally, but whether their relationship was romantic or not has never been confirmed. The vast amount of surviving correspondence between them is strictly platonic.

Could *The Kiss*, once thought to be the most romantic painting in history, be a depiction of a friendship?[7]

That, like Klimt and Flöge's relationship, is open to interpretation.

WHAT I AM AND WHAT I WANT

Gustav Klimt was part of the last cultural explosion before the demise of the Austro-Hungarian empire, a political entity that was to die in the same year that Klimt did – 1918.

His work is significant for bridging the gap between academic realism and the emerging realm of abstraction, and for pushing the boundaries of artistry and decency as far as he could, portraying human figures in sensual ways never before seen in Austrian polite society.

We don't really know about Klimt's thoughts on *The Kiss* – but maybe we don't need to. As he once said: 'Anybody who wants to find out about me – as an artist – should look attentively at my pictures and try to learn from them what I am and what I want.'[8]

GUSTAV KLIMT

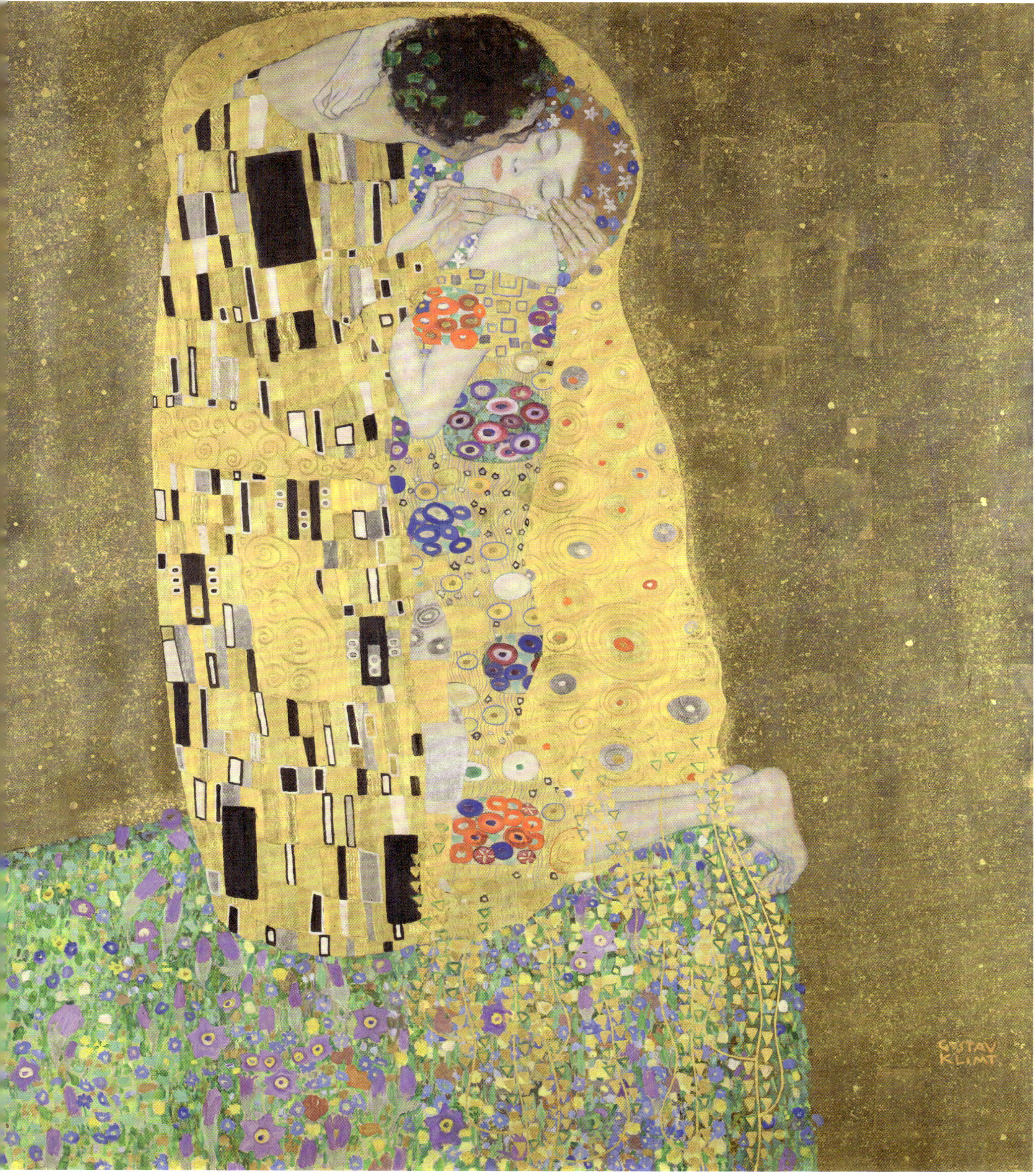

CLAUDE MONET

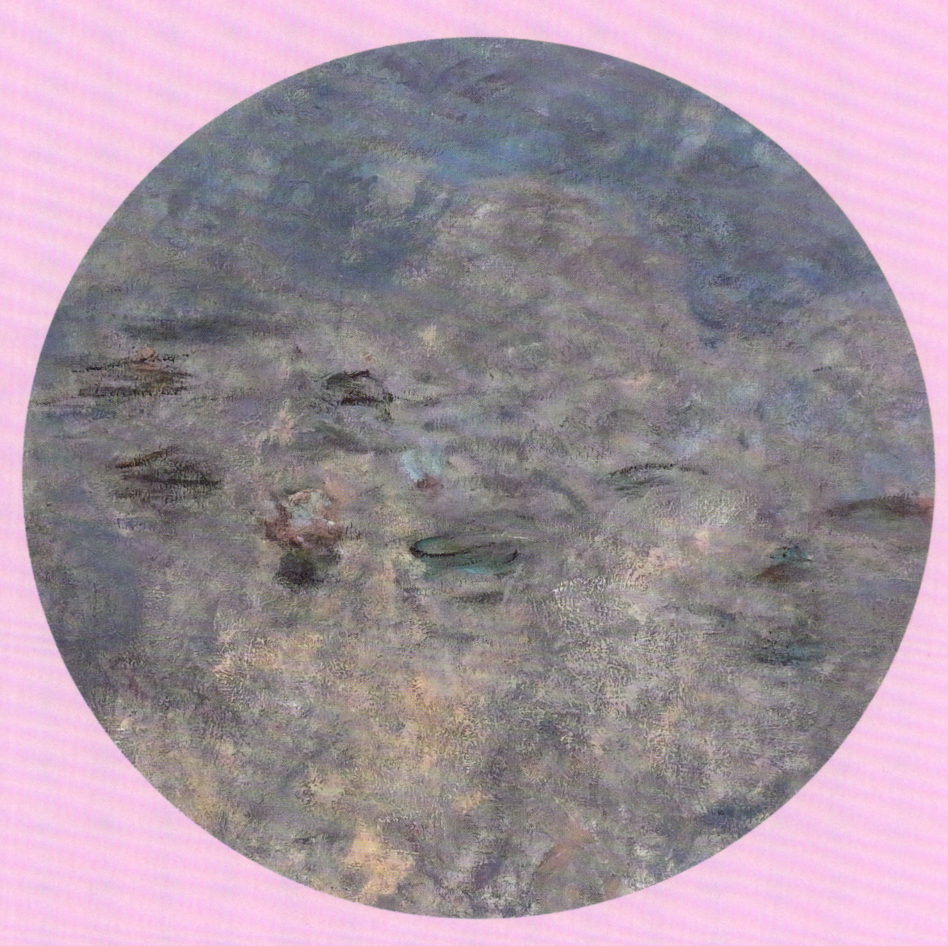

WATER LILIES

1914–26

THE SISTINE CHAPEL OF IMPRESSIONISM

Among the last works by Claude Monet are his enormous water-lily canvases, now on display in the Musée de L'Orangerie, or the Orangery, in Paris. These paintings are so overwhelmingly beautiful that the story of their complicated creation is usually overlooked; they have come to be viewed simply as an aesthetic interpretation of the garden that obsessed him. But that couldn't be further from the truth.

The works may have started as what Monet himself called 'grande décoration' for a dining room, but by the time of their completion, they had metamorphosed into a direct response to the most savage and apocalyptic period of modern history.

AN UNLIKELY FRIENDSHIP

In 1883 Monet and his partner Alice Hoschedé moved permanently to Giverny, a small village located in the Normandy region of northern France, along with her six children from her previous marriage and Monet's two children from his own. Ten years later he bought some land with a pond and created a water-lily garden, which would be the focus of his art for the rest of his life. He created in total almost 300 paintings of his garden, over forty of which were large format.[1]

Visitors came to Giverny regularly to pay homage to the old man of Impressionism: Claude Renoir and Paul Cézanne, journalists and biographers, American collectors and Japanese fans all came on one of the daily trains from Paris.[2] Georges Clemenceau, a newspaper editor and a prominent figure in French politics, was a regular visitor; he and Monet had been friends since they were young men in the 1860s.[3]

It was an unlikely friendship, as Monet only cared about art, his garden and gourmet food. He had no interest in politics, in fact he had never even voted, whereas Clemenceau had been a political animal his whole life.[4] They both shared two passions, however: one was the new-fangled motorcar (Monet had a Rolls Royce Silver Ghost), and the other was art.

A SHORT-LIVED RETIREMENT

Monet had been suffered problems with his eyesight since the early 1910s, and was diagnosed with cataracts in 1912, which worsened steadily over the years. Age-related cataracts manifest as yellowing and clouding of the lens and have a major effect on colour perception as well as visual sharpness.

The septuagenarian had accomplished everything he wanted to and now claimed to find painting 'unremitting torture'. He was ready to retire and spend his old age gardening and speeding around Giverny in his motorcar. But luckily for us, Clemenceau visited him in Giverny in late April 1914.

The politician and his circle had been discussing the idea of a cycle of Monet's

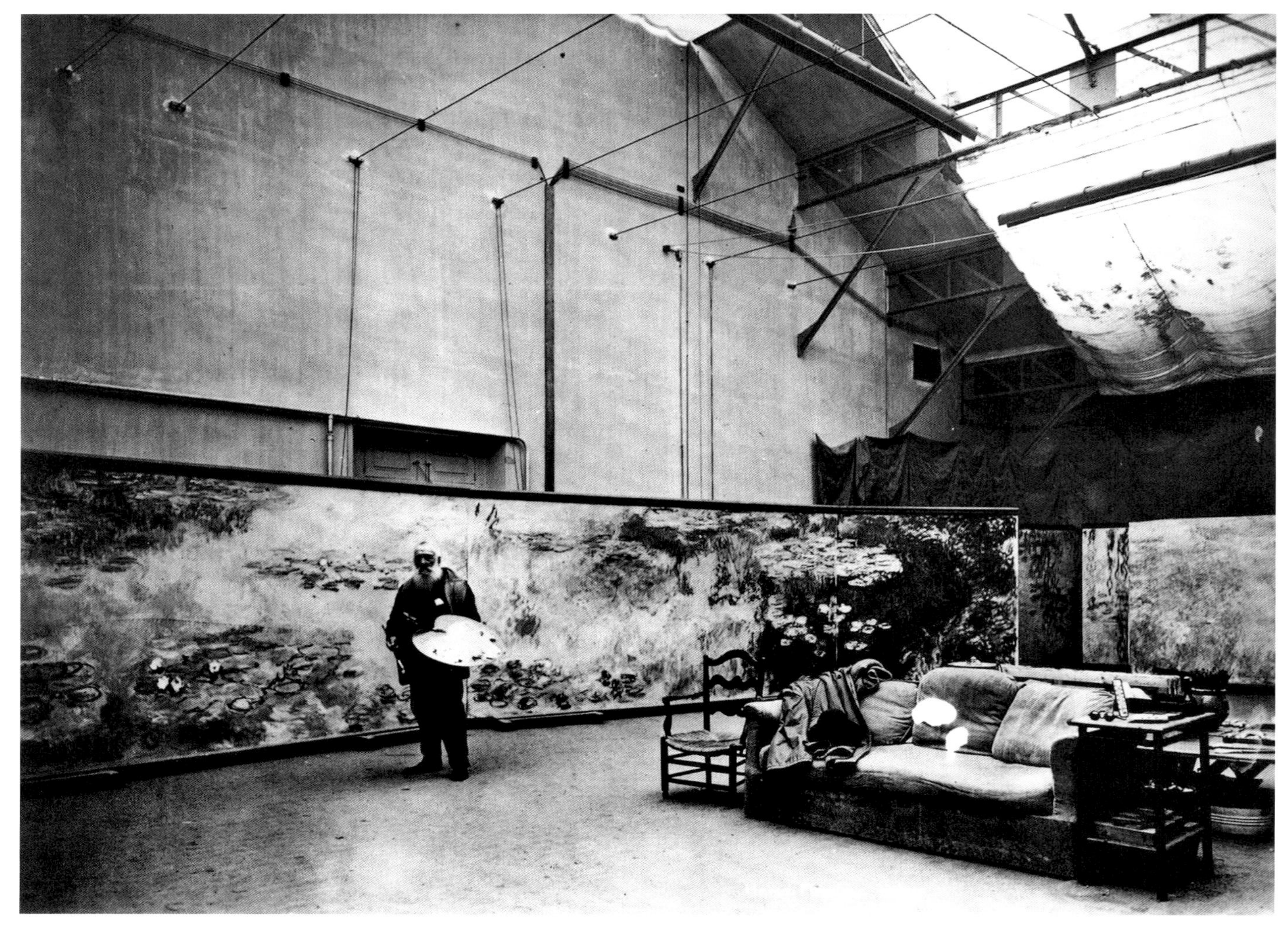

*These paintings are so
overwhelmingly beautiful
that the story of their
complicated creation
is usually overlooked*

The artist knew exactly how their arrangement, rhythm and spacing would interact within the future gallery

paintings serving as a national monument since 1895.[5] In that 1914 visit the politician would flatter and sweet-talk the depressed Monet, coaxing him out of retirement to create a project more ambitious than any he had attempted in the last seventy-four years, and one which he would work on right up until his death in 1926.[6]

PATRIOTIC DUTY

In the 1890s Monet oversaw the creation of his water garden in Giverny, complete with the water lilies that would be his main subject matter for the next thirty years.[7]

In his initial water-lily series (1897–99), he painted the pond's surroundings with its plants, bridge and trees, all structured by a clearly defined horizon. As his work progressed, Monet became increasingly unconcerned with traditional notions of pictorial space, and by the time he created his final *Water Lilies*, part of his third series, the horizon line had disappeared entirely.[8]

The artist had been discussing a circular room with paintings since he first set up his easel by his pond in 1897, but over the years he lost interest in the project. Clemenceau's visit in 1914 would inspire Monet not only to pick up his brush again but also to 'serve his country', initially by donating two works in 1918 as a way to 'take part in the victory'.[9] These works would form the collection we know today in the Orangery.

For Clemenceau, who would lead France as prime minister during the First World War, art in general and Monet's paintings in particular were the highest expression of French civilization, standing up to the threat of German barbarism. In that sense, Clemenceau explained to the artist in 1914, to keep painting was Monet's patriotic duty.

PROTO-INSTALLATION ART

Unlike his previous smaller water-lily paintings, these works were enormous. All eight curved panels would be the same height but differ in length. Together they would span a total length of nearly 100 metres (328 ft), and cover a staggering 200 square metres (239 sq. yd) of canvas.[10] They were designed to hang across the curved walls of two egg-shaped rooms (forming the symbol for infinity), purpose-built and designed to Monet's own specifications, and would show the full span of his pond in Giverny, including the sky and clouds reflected in the water. The results would be complete immersion for the viewer, exacerbated by the oval design of the galleries. In that sense, they could be considered 'proto-installation' art.

Monet worked on up to twelve canvases at the same time, placing them on easels fitted with castor wheels and rotating them according to the light that fell through the skylights in his studio. While painting the canvases, the artist knew exactly how their arrangement, rhythm and spacing would interact within the future gallery. At the Orangery, as in his studio, natural light streaming from above would illuminate the works. Panels with sunrise tones were intended for east-facing walls, while sunset scenes were designed for the west-facing walls. The changing weather and shifting sunlight would transform the character of his works, allowing them to evolve dynamically throughout the day.

The water lilies were created with simple abstract strokes, accented by pale yellows, greens, occasional flecks of red, and touches of lilac and blue to suggest shadows. Rather than mixing colours on his palette, Monet applied short, deliberate brushstrokes of colour side

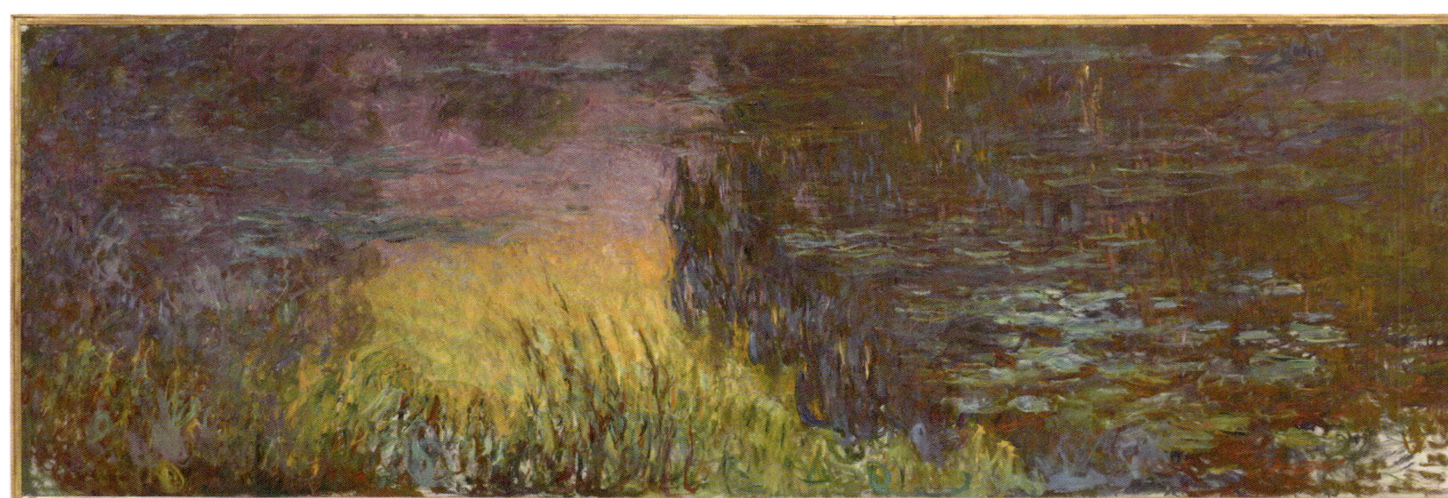

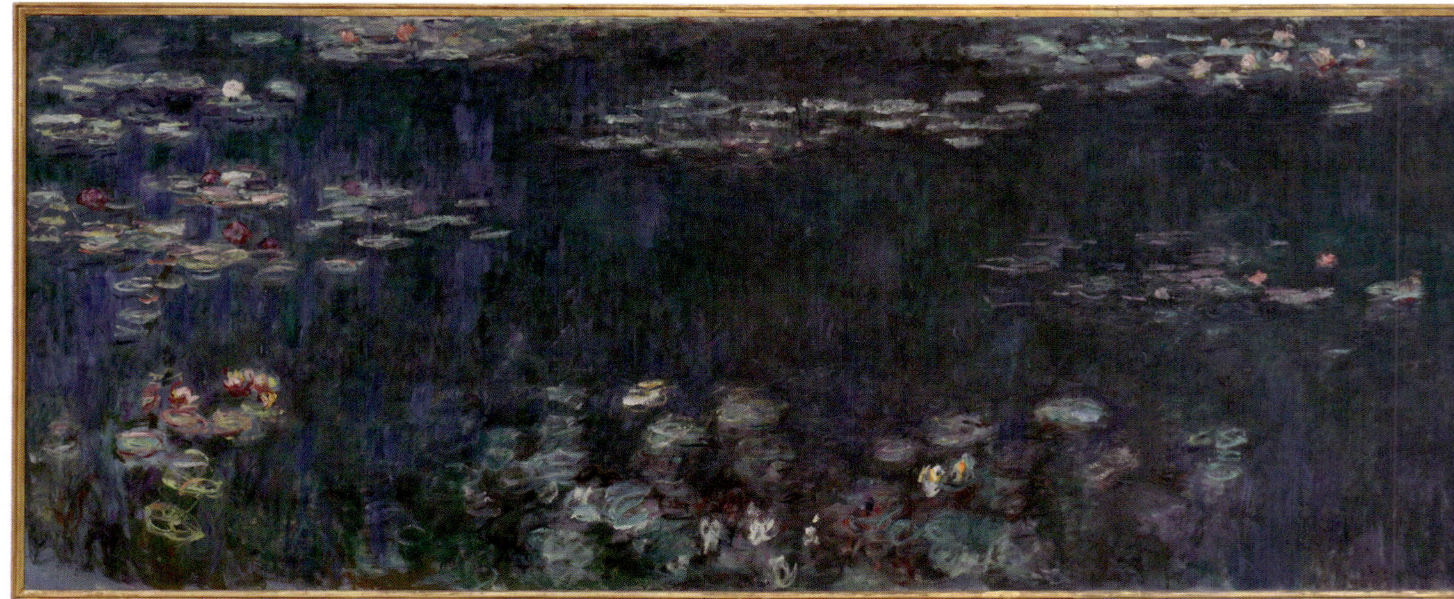

by side, allowing the viewer's eye to blend them from a distance. His brushstrokes changed as the project continued over the years, however, and the dabs of the earlier works were replaced by more fluid brushstrokes, broadly applied.[11]

Cataracts blurred the artist's vision, which explains the more abstract application of paint in these later water lilies. This visual limitation may also have influenced his decision to work on such a huge scale.[12]

REFLECTED LANDSCAPES

A key feature absent from Monet's *Water Lilies* is the horizon, a cornerstone of Western painting since the Renaissance.

In traditional landscape art, the horizon establishes spatial orientation, creating a sense of distance and perspective. It acts as the dividing line between the Earth and sky, helping us understand the scale and layout of the scene. Without a horizon to anchor us, it is hard to work out what we are seeing on the shifting canvases. Monet blurs distinctions between sky, water and reflection,

The changing weather and shifting sunlight would transform the character of his works

and in so doing he transcends traditional landscape art, emphasizing colour, light and texture over form.

By leaning towards abstraction and allowing the water to dominate the canvases entirely, stretching from edge to edge, Monet created what are essentially reflected landscapes.

The perspective, or lack thereof, creates a sense of disorientation, as there's no clear distinction between what is above, below or reflected. What we are left with is a vast field of unfathomable nothingness, of light, air and water. We have no sense of scale, and so we are truly immersed in this strange, abstract, bewildering vision.

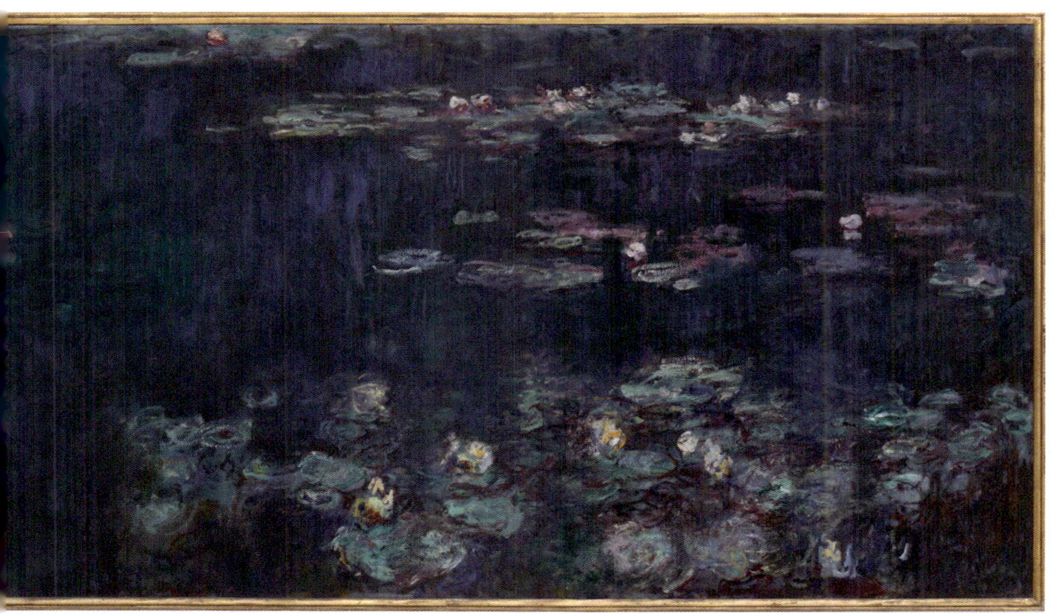

MEMORIAL

Monet was deeply affected by the grim realities of war: his stepson engaged in frontline combat, and his own son Michel enlisted in 1915. The paintings recall the haunting imagery of the landscape of the Western Front, battlegrounds that seemed to stretch endlessly, with no beginning or end, and with no discernible horizon. Soldiers found themselves submerged in a vast sea of mud, surrounded by surreal, waterlogged vistas that obliterated any sense of time or space.

There is a clear sense of mourning in the paintings, with Monet's use of foreshortened weeping willow trees that seem to sweep us up in their embrace. Since ancient Greece, the willow tree has been used as a symbol of mourning and grief in art, due to its drooping branches, and it was often planted in French cemeteries as a symbol of memorialization.

The 'Great War' is infused in every inch of these canvases,[13] and they are, as Monet intended, not only symbolic of the human loss in the First World War, but perhaps all those that Monet had lost, too.

THE LAST WATER LILIES

Persuading Monet to make the paintings was light work; persuading him to part with them was the difficult bit.

The rooms at the Orangery were completed and ready for installation, but Monet still hadn't delivered the paintings. He was transfixed on reworking them, seemingly incapable of finishing, as if painting was keeping him alive. In 1926, in his final letter to Clemenceau, two months before he died, he wrote that they were ready to be transferred to the Orangery,[14] a full twelve years after the project had started.

Monet died on 5 December 1926 at the age of eighty-six, with Georges Clemenceau at his bedside, holding his hand.[15] The odd couple had been friends for over six decades, and it was one of the most profound friendships of both their lives.

A few months after Monet's death, the public saw the *Water Lilies* for the first time; sadly they weren't particularly dazzled. Impressionism was already considered passé, and the paintings were attacked by critics

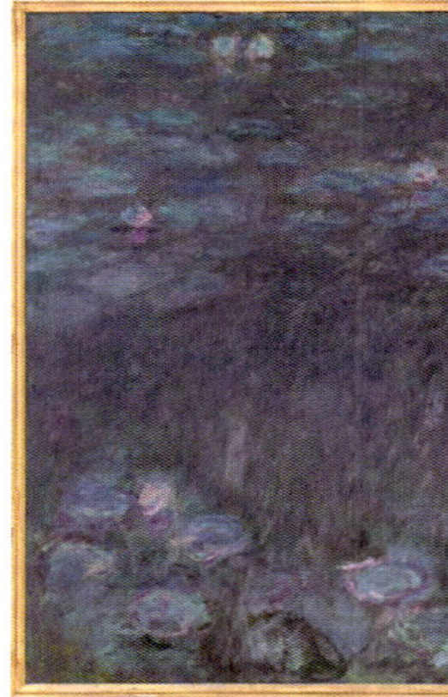

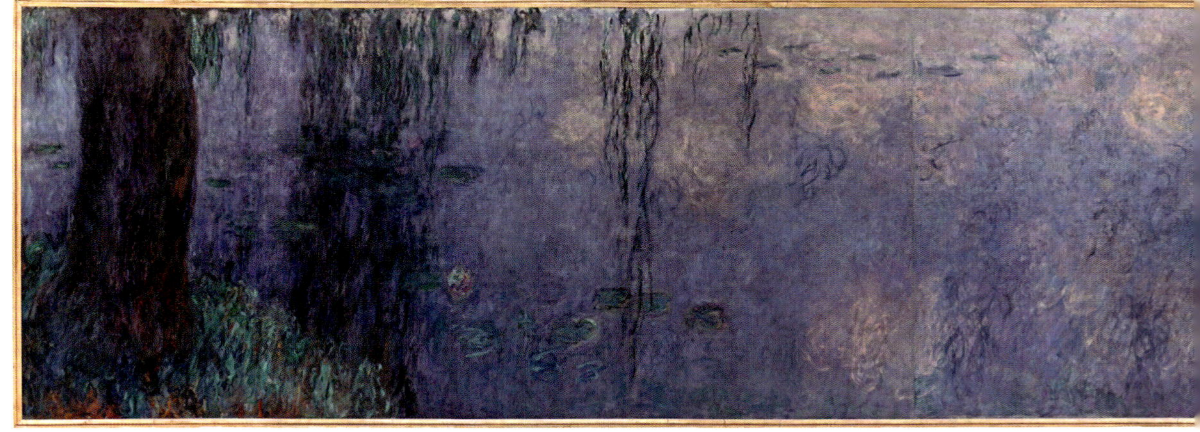

as 'the work of an old man' and 'devastatingly dull'.[16] The artist who had been rejected by critics in the 19th century for being too radical was now being criticized in the 20th century for not being radical enough.

Then, in the 1950s, a new generation of American artists rediscovered Monet's last *Water Lilies*. The Abstract Expressionists, such as Mark Rothko and Jackson Pollock, were inspired by the paintings' epic scale, powerful energy, emotional connection and of course, their audacious use of colour.[17] For them, Monet's love of the painting process was thrilling.

Nowadays the genius of Monet is indisputable, and the Orangery a shrine to his talent. But although the artist painted what is now called the Sistine Chapel of Impressionism, he would never have done it without the vision of a politician, Georges Clemenceau.

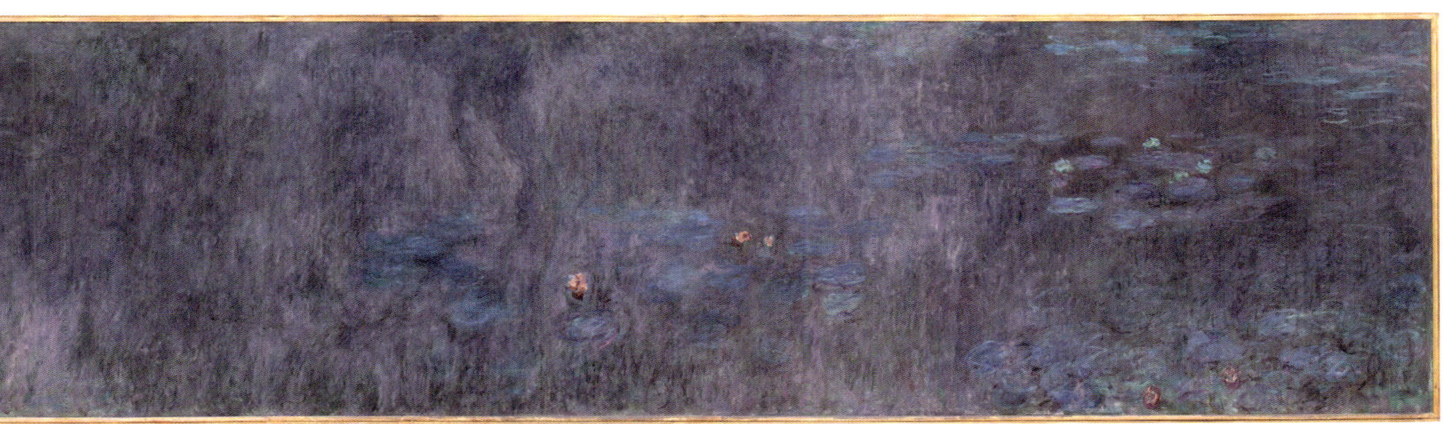

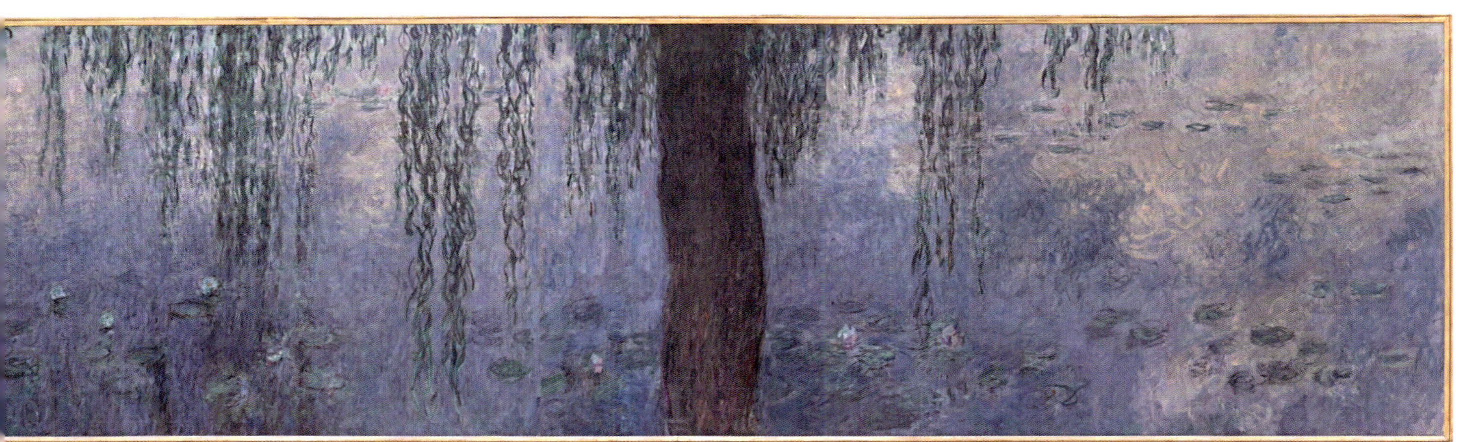

WATER LILIES

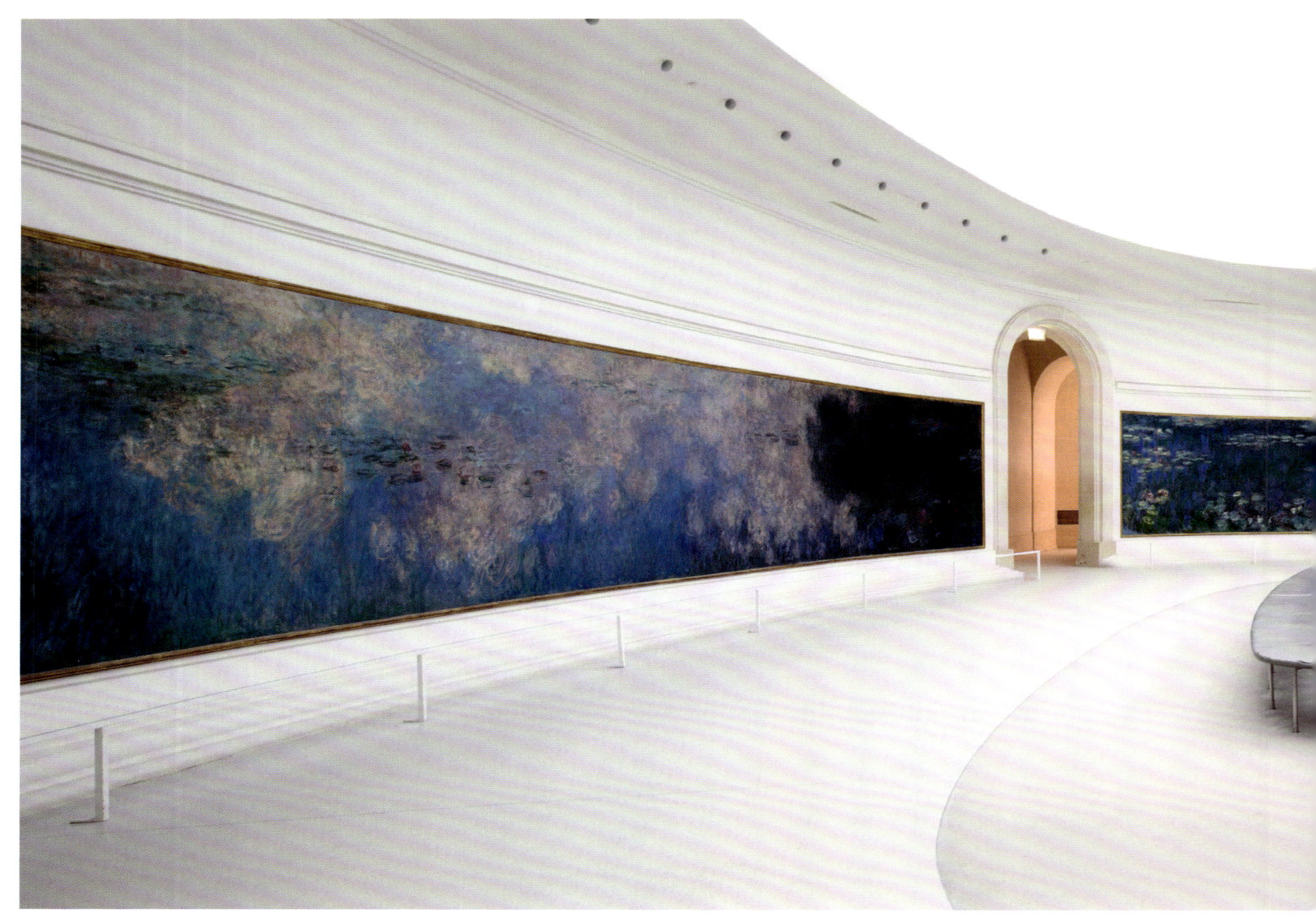

View of *Water Lilies –
Clouds; Green Reflections;
Morning*, Musêe de l'Orangerie.

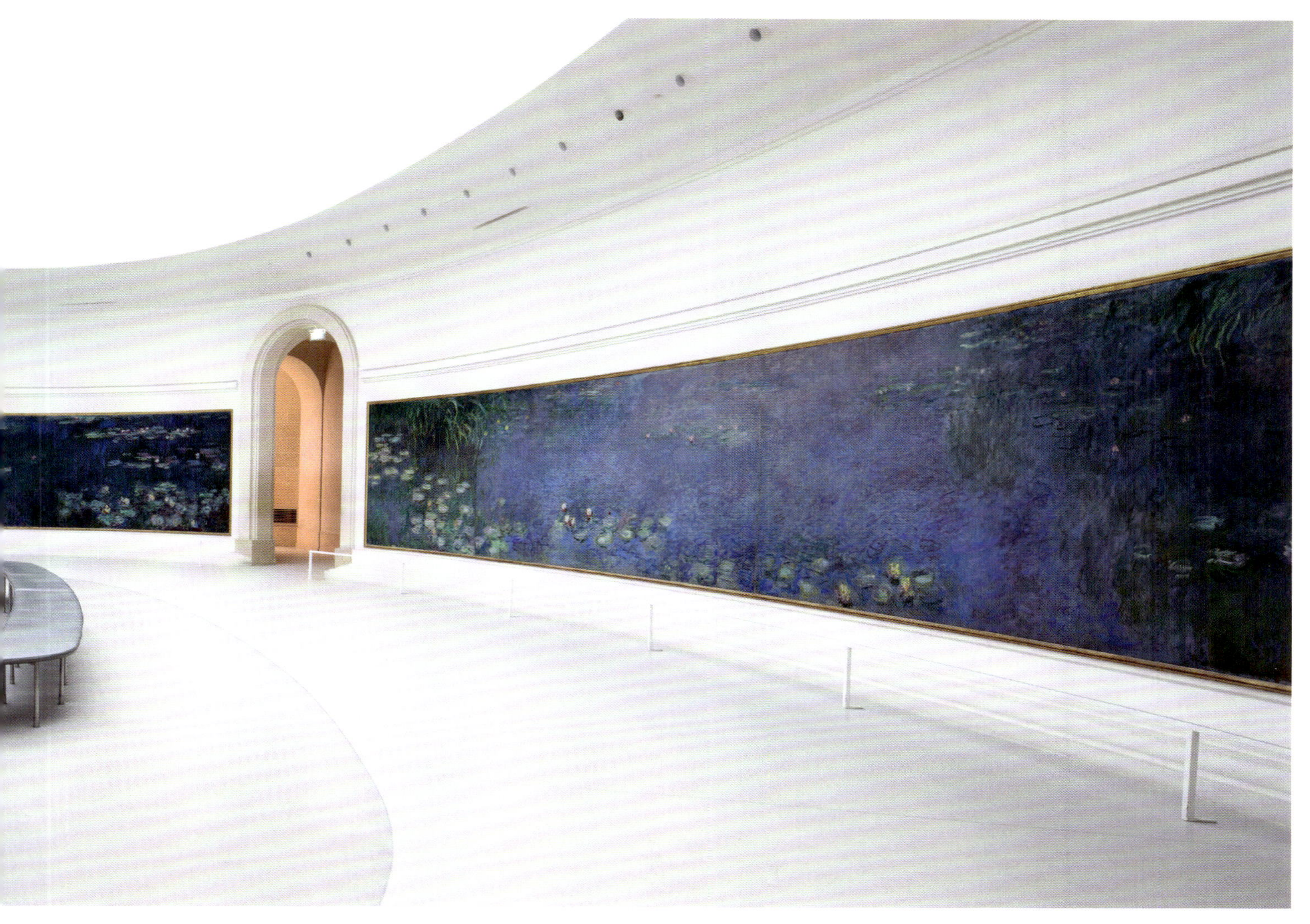

WATER LILIES

HILMA
AF KLINT

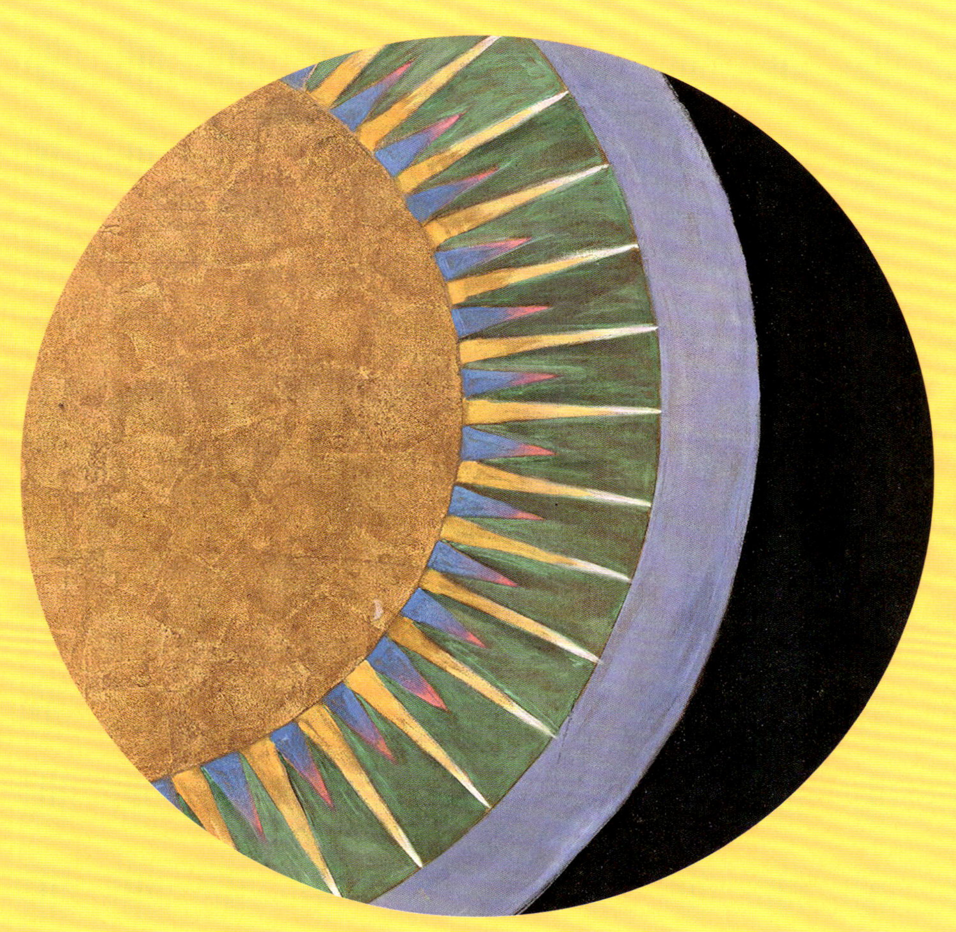

GROUP X,
ALTARPIECE NO. 1

1915

MAKING THE INVISIBLE VISIBLE

When Hilma af Klint died in 1944, at the age of eighty-one, she had lived the life of a moderately successful portrait and landscape artist. Her nephew Erik af Klint inherited her possessions, which he put into storage. When he opened them in the late 1960s, he was astonished to discover his quiet, unassuming aunt had lived another life entirely, creating strange abstract works that took their inspiration directly from the spirit world. His aunt was in fact a clairvoyant and mystic who, in conjunction with her spirit guides, had produced over a thousand extraordinary abstract paintings, hundreds of sketches and 26,000 pages of notes in 124 notebooks.

As may be expected of an artist who was discovered by art historians relatively recently, a few myths have grown up around af Klint. One of the great myths is that she worked on her abstract paintings in secret and never wanted them to be exhibited. This is not true. Evidence in her notebooks shows that she struggled to exhibit them for twenty years before the 'spiritual' paintings were eventually included in a 1913 group show in Stockholm. She also showed *The Paintings for the Temple* (1906–15) in an exhibition in 1928 in London, but the reception to her work there was hostile.[1] It would be seven decades after her death before she received a major solo show.

CHARTING THE UNSEEN

Born in 1862, just outside Stockholm, af Klint grew up in a naval family of cartographers, navigators and mathematicians. This background in precision and mapping informed her groundbreaking art, which can be seen as an attempt to chart the invisible realms of existence and the mysteries of the spiritual world.

The death of her younger sister in 1880 had a profound impact on af Klint, deepening her attachment to the spiritual realm and sparking her interest in séances. She began to feel that there was something more to the world than that which could be seen and touched.

She was admitted to the Royal Academy of Fine Arts in Stockholm at the age of twenty, one of few women to study on equal terms with the male students. Although the sexes studied separately, the art school was progressive in that women students took life drawing classes with nude males. She excelled there, studying drawing, portraiture and landscape painting for five years before going on to a commercial art career in Stockholm, producing unremarkable but skilful works.

Her interest in spiritualism grew as she studied, but it wasn't until the 1890s that she began to incorporate it into her work.[2]

SPIRITUALISM

At the age of forty-four, she broke away from her academic training and started a process

The group meditated daily, followed a strict vegetarian diet and dressed mainly in black

of unlearning, ready to begin what she called her 'life's work': creating abstract paintings through spirit guides.

The vibrant intellectual and cultural scene in Stockholm during the 1890s profoundly influenced af Klint. Great radical thinkers like August Strindberg, Henrik Ibsen, Selma Lagerlöf and Edvard Munch were shaking up traditional arts by blending realism and mysticism; Ellen Kay was advocating for women's rights in Sweden; while engineers like Alfred Nobel and Lars Magnus Ericsson pushed applied sciences forward, making Sweden and its surroundings a flourishing cultural and intellectual climate.

In common with other intellectuals in Stockholm and beyond, she was intrigued by how we might interweave scientific discoveries with spiritual beliefs, and her later work often contained biological, botanical and chemical symbolism alongside occultist symbols.

Swedish spiritualism was born in the 1870s when the director of the Hamburg mail service, Johan Carl Hellberg, travelled around Sweden and lectured on the subject.[3] After this, spiritualist organizations flourished in the country. By the end of the 19th and beginning of the 20th century, traditional religion was losing its grip on society, and people were looking for new ways to connect with the unseen. Breakthroughs in fields like physics, biology and chemistry challenged literal interpretations of religious texts, and a growing emphasis on individualism and personal autonomy encouraged people to

seek personal spiritual paths rather than stick to traditional religious practices.

At its peak, near the end of the 19th century, spiritualism had about eight million followers in the US and Europe. It was intellectually respectable, akin to a science, with enthusiasts such as W. B. Yeats, Gustav Mahler, Piet Mondrian and Wassily Kandinsky in its ranks.

THE FIVE

In 1896 af Klint became part of a group of Swedish artists called De Fem (The Five), with four other women: Anna Cassel, Cornelia Cederberg, Sigrid Hedman and Mathilda Nilsson.

The group meditated daily, followed a strict vegetarian diet and dressed mainly in black. They lived a simple ascetic life devoted to art and studied both Rosicrucianism, the followers of which believe they possess secret wisdom passed down from the ancients, and theosophy, a philosophical system that combines mysticism and spiritualism with metaphysics, and encourages followers to transcend human consciousness through meditation and connection with the spirit world.

They would start their meetings with prayers, followed by meditation, a Christian sermon with a reading from the Bible and finally a séance, where they communicated with spirits who gave them artistic instructions. In one of her notebooks, af Klint wrote that she didn't make preliminary drawings when the spirits spoke through her, instead working quickly, 'without changing a single brush stroke'.[4]

We can trace af Klint's abstract work back to the theosophical goal of a universal language of symbols, using signs, charts and numbers. Even her use of colour was theosophical: yellow meant masculinity, blue, femininity, and green, a unity of the two.

Hilma af Klint in her studio, 1885.

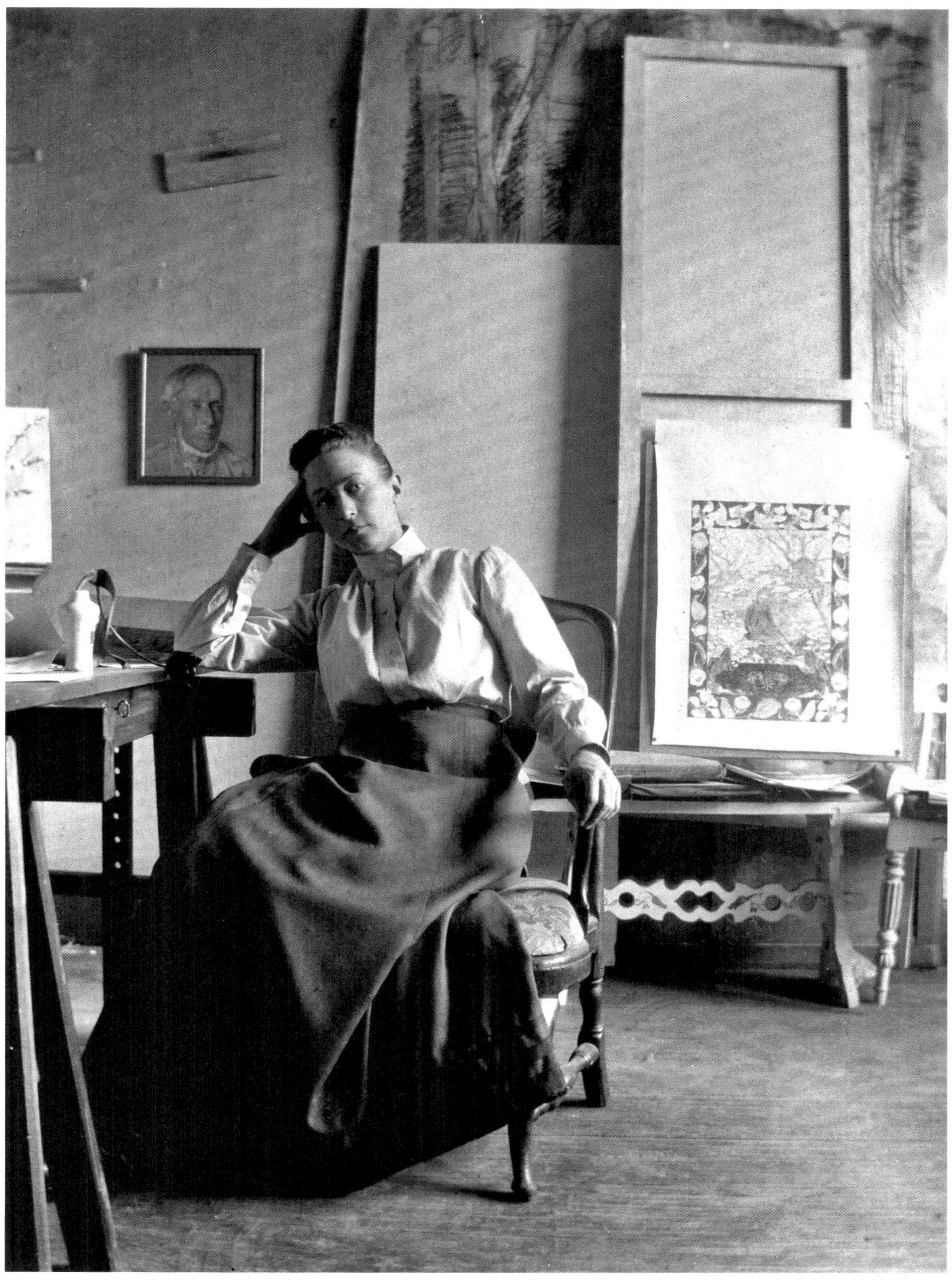

          GROUP X, ALTARPIECE NO. 1

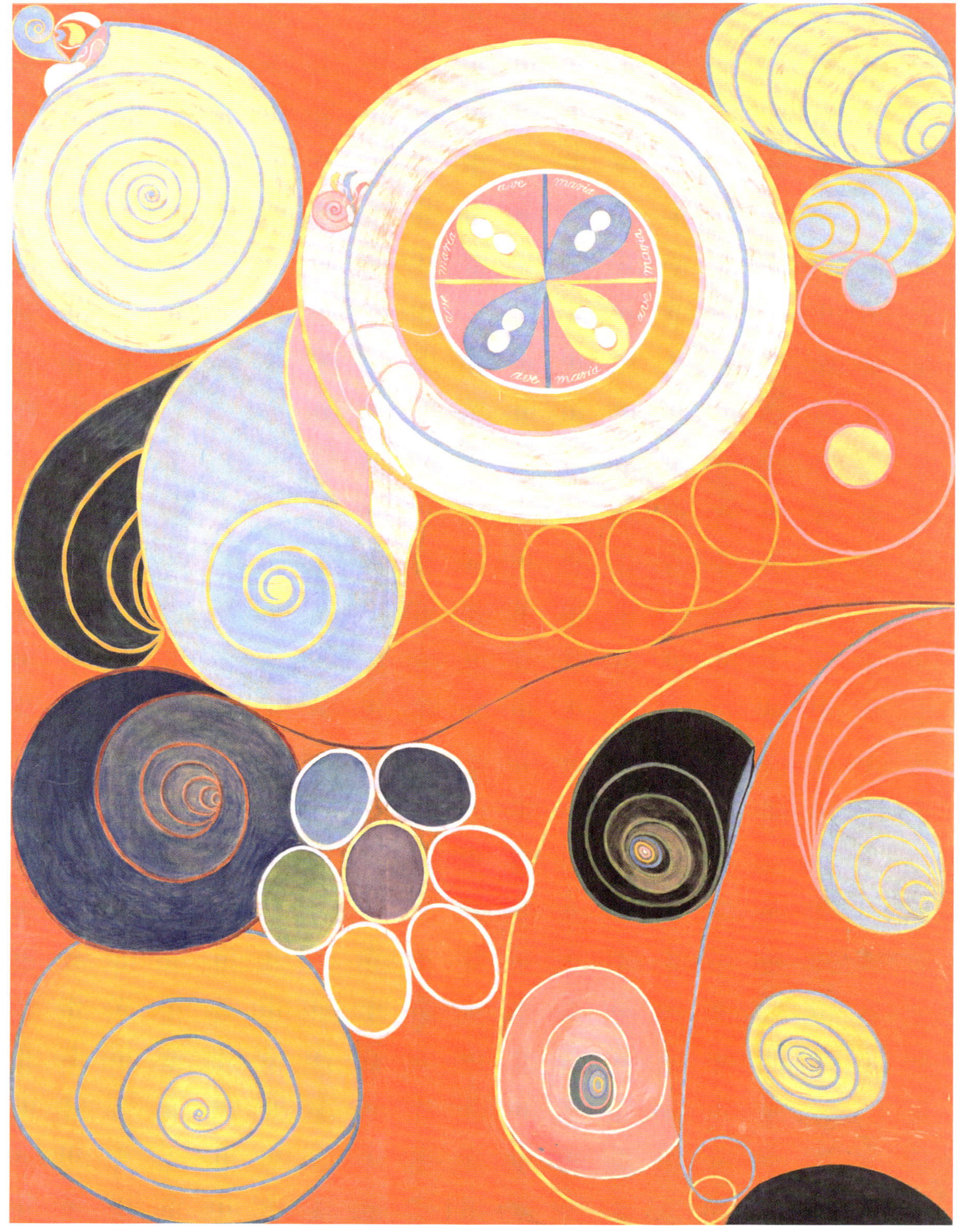

HILMA AF KLINT

The Five also developed a unique way of writing, called 'psychic writing', which then developed into 'automatic drawing' decades before the Surrealists came up with the same concept in the 1920s.

THE PAINTINGS FOR THE TEMPLE

At one of these séances af Klint received a 'commission' from her spirit guide to create *The Paintings for the Temple*: 193 works to decorate a yet unnamed place of worship. Between 1906 and 1908 she produced 111 paintings, then stopped for four years to care for her blind mother before her death, returning to produce eighty-two more between 1912 and 1915.

People were looking for new ways to connect with the unseen

They are organized into ten groups with some measuring over 3.1 metres long and 2.3 metres wide (even the dimensions were dictated by the spirits). They are linked together through the repetition of abstract shapes and forms and the common goal of revealing an unseen world. She was told by the spirits that these images would have important messages for future generations.

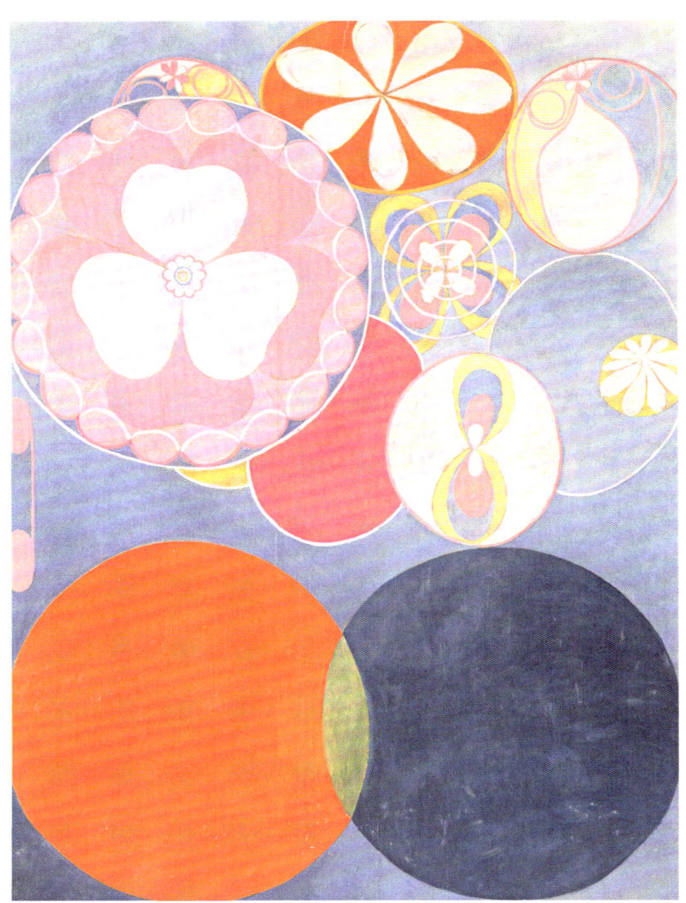

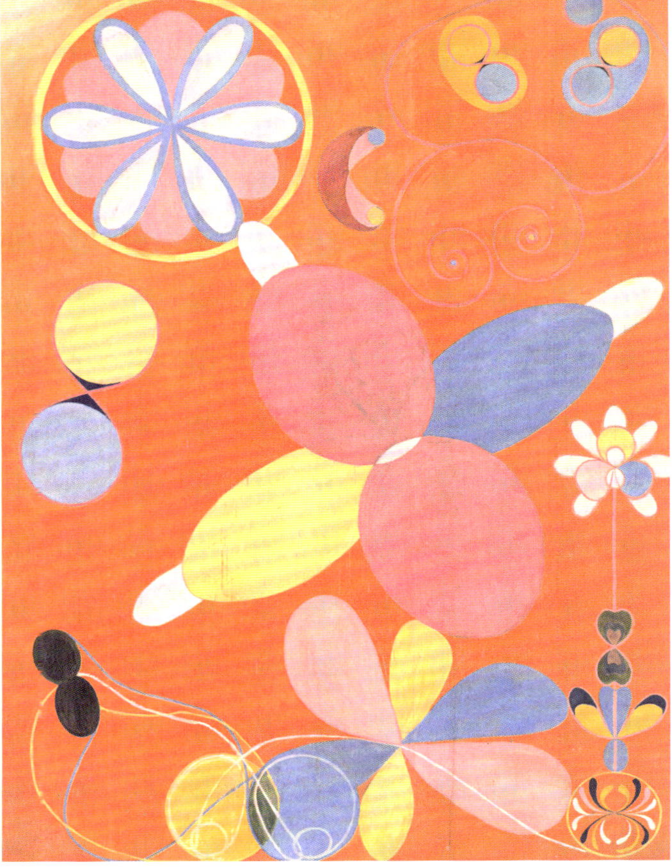

GROUP X, ALTARPIECE NO. 1

These beliefs in a higher power through the occult and spiritualism are the key to af Klint's work and the language used to create it. She employed a complex geometrical language, an abstract series of symbols dictated by the spirits: the rose (and rose cross), snake, snail, lilies, and chemical and botanical imagery.

The final series of works from *The Paintings for the Temple*, completed in 1915, includes three large canvases that af Klint referred to as the *Altarpieces*, intended to occupy the highest point within the temple structure.

Af Klint saw the *Altarpieces* as the climax of the *Temple* series, an illustration of the theosophist belief that the universe is a single entity, with the steps in her paintings representing sixteen reincarnations before enlightenment.[5] The theosophists believe humans evolved in two ways: we ascended from the physical to the spiritual and we

descended from the divine to the material world. We see those two 'paths' or stairways often in her works.

Altarpiece No.1 shows the ascent into enlightenment via sixteen multicoloured 'rainbow steps' leading the eye up to a radiant gold-leaf sun. In *Altarpiece No. 2*, a dark, inverted triangle symbolizes the channelling of celestial forces towards the Earth, while *Altarpiece No. 3* features a luminous circle radiating energy. Used throughout af Klint's

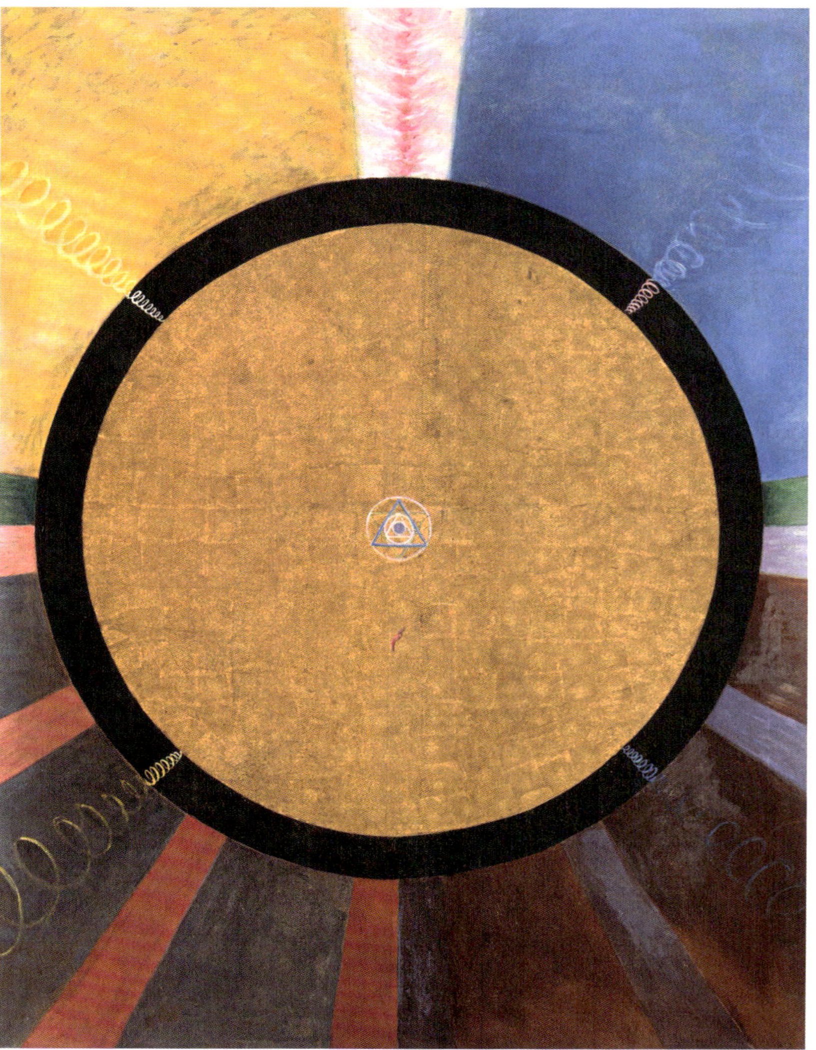

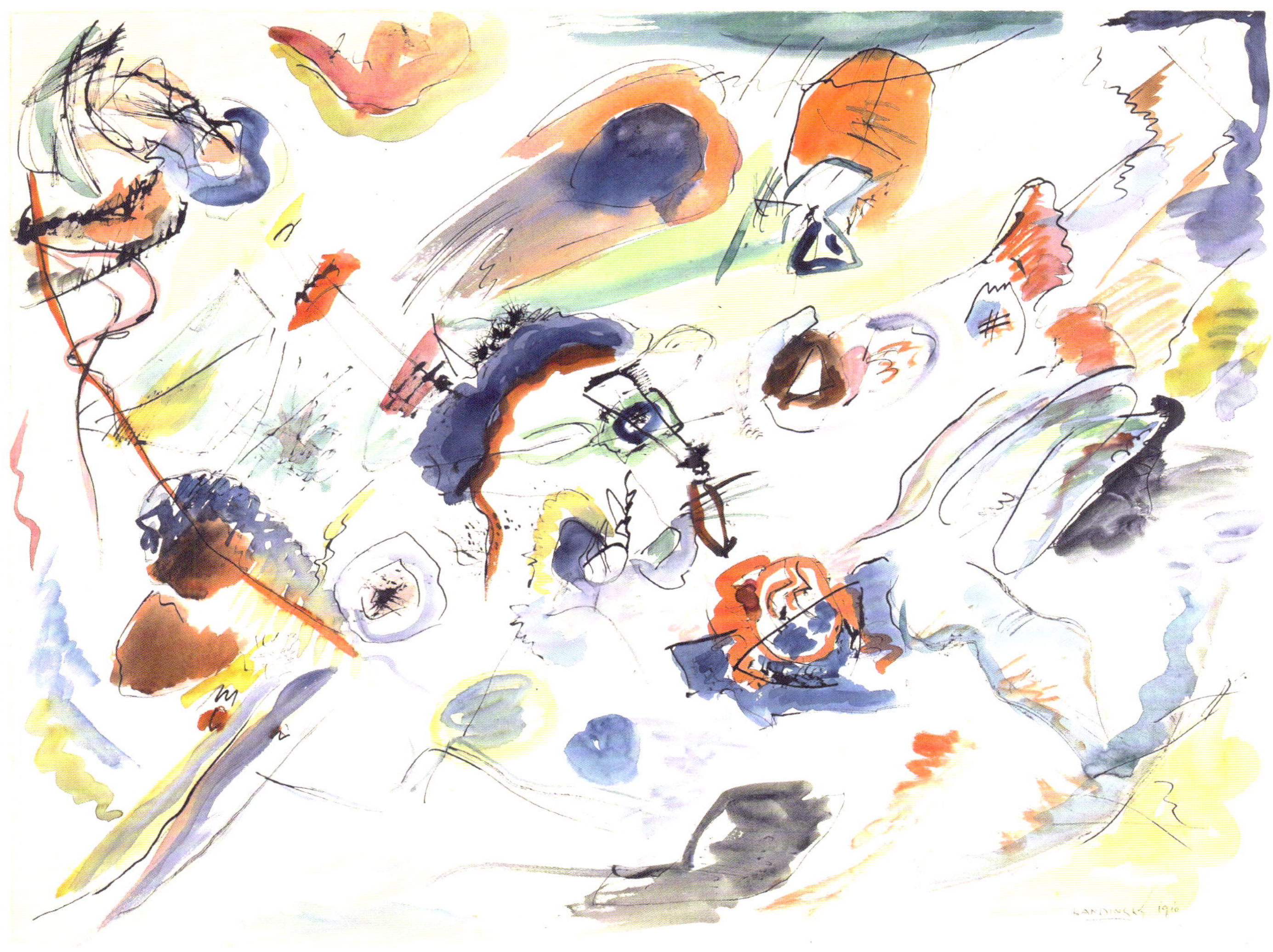

opposite left
Hilma af Klint,
*Group X, Altarpiece
No. 2*, 1915.

opposite right
Hilma af Klint,
*Group X, Altarpiece
No. 3*, 1915.

Wassily Kandinsky,
*Untitled (First
Abstract Watercolour)*,
1910.

oeuvre and once described by the founder of theosophy, Madame Blavatsky, as 'divine Unity, from which all proceeds, whither all returns',[6] the meaning of the circle is not dissimilar to the Christian idea of eternity.

In 1931, fifteen years after the works' completion, af Klint was instructed by the spirits to design a more comprehensive plan of a temple to house the paintings. These drawings were precise and detailed,[7] and according to the spirits' instructions, the temple was to be built on the Swedish island of Ven. She made several loose sketches of a circular temple with spiral paths leading to the summit, symbolizing spiritual evolution and humanity's journey towards enlightenment.

THE WORLD'S FIRST ABSTRACT PICTURE

Untitled (First Abstract Watercolour) by Wassily Kandinsky (p. 195) is dated 1910 and is generally agreed to be the first abstract work in Western art. But af Klint began painting abstract artworks in 1906, several years before Kandinsky, Kazimir Malevich or Piet Mondrian would begin to make non-representational paintings. Unlike these artists, however, af Klint was a woman, living in Sweden, and was not one for self-promotion.

Along with Blavatsky, the philosopher Rudolf Steiner, whose work was based on the premise that human intellect has the ability to contact spiritual worlds, was a major influence on af Klint and many other artists and intellectuals. Mondrian and Kandinsky attended a number of his lectures, and later, Joseph Beuys likewise embraced his teachings. Steiner was a theosophical star with almost daily lectures, and first appears in af Klint's notes in 1908.[8]

That same year, Steiner visited af Klint's studio to see if he could interpret the symbols that the spirits had dictated for her in her works. She was devastated when he disapproved of not only her practice but also her methods. He thought her reliance on spirits was too passive and that she should develop her own spiritual ideas through meditation, taking a more inwardly active and intellectually independent role in her artistic choices. He did however concede that her paintings 'belonged to the astral world'.[9]

It is said that Steiner advised her not to show her work for at least fifty years, but that is another myth connected with af Klint for which there is no evidence.[10] We do know, however, that after Steiner met af Klint he also met Kandinsky, who at the time was not yet an abstract painter.[11] Some art historians insist that Kandinsky may have been in influenced by af Klint via Steiner,[12] but that is just yet another theory. We'll never know for sure.

In December 1935 Wassily Kandinsky wrote to his New York gallerist, expressing his eagerness to reaffirm that he, and only he, had created the first abstract painting in 1911. He emphasized, 'It is the world's first ever abstract picture, because back then not one single painter was painting in an abstract style.'[13] It is something that has been accepted ever since within art history, but with the discovery of Hilma af Klint's work, we know that back then, there *was* a painter working in an abstract style before 1911.

So, can we now say that Kandinsky being the first abstract painter is also a myth?

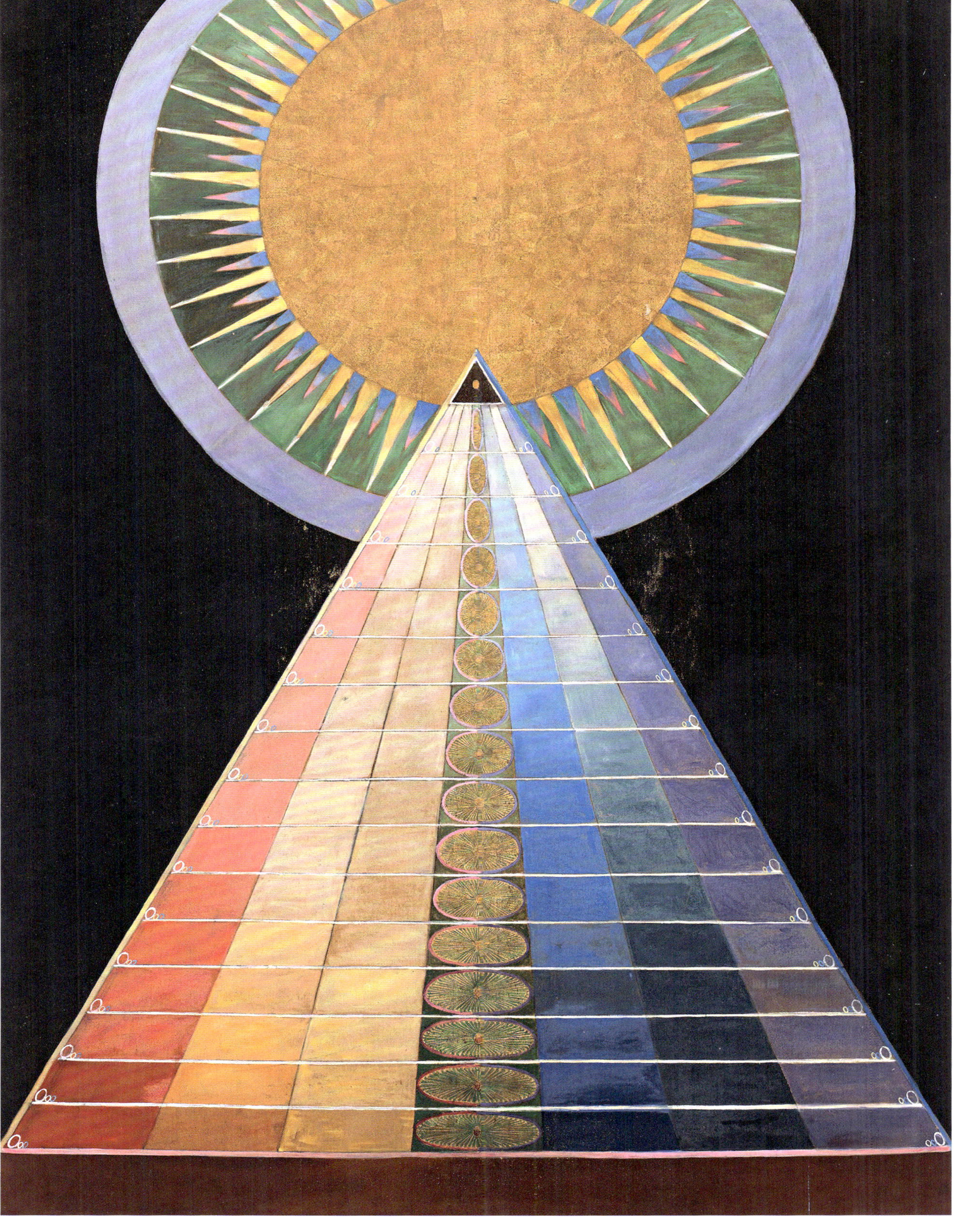

SUZANNE VALADON

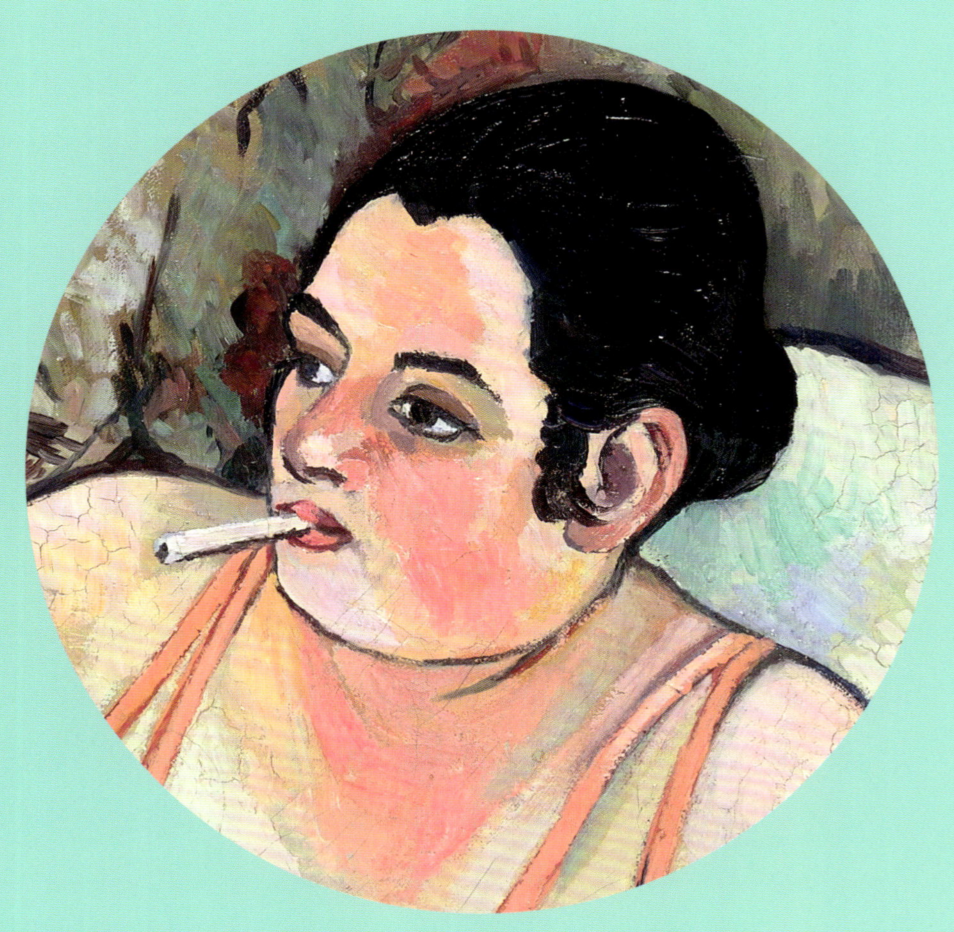

THE BLUE ROOM

1923

MODEL, PAINTER, RADICAL

Suzanne Valadon went from a poverty-stricken childhood to circus acrobat, a popular artist's model to an artist herself, championed by Henri de Toulouse-Lautrec, Edgar Degas and Pierre-Auguste Renoir. She lived a life so extraordinary that it reads like fiction.

In art, as in life, she was a rule-breaker, and in her painting *The Blue Room* (1923) she radically subverted traditional representations of women in art. The model in the work is Valadon herself, a woman in her late fifties who is no passive Venus, but a modern, unembellished woman, celebrating her individuality. She is full-figured, lounging on a daybed in loose striped pyjamas and a pink camisole. A cigarette dangles from her mouth and books are close at hand. She smokes, she reads, and she couldn't care less.

Valadon's own life experience as a model, self-taught artist and single mother informs the painting and reflects a deep understanding of both being observed and of controlling the narrative of one's own representation.

A LIFE APART

Marie-Clémentine Valadon was born in 1865 to an unmarried laundress in Montmartre. She was later given the nickname 'Suzanne' by Toulouse-Lautrec, who suggested she was like the biblical Susanna, spied on by older men.[1]

Although she had sketched from the age of nine,[2] traditional artistic training was beyond her financial means, so her education came from living on the streets and observing artists from the studio divans she modelled on. Her earliest surviving drawings, from the 1880s, show she was already a gifted draughtsperson by her teenage years.

Unlike her middle-class precedents, Berthe Morisot and Mary Cassatt, the working-class Valadon had to define her own identity outside of prevailing social norms.

Valadon started working at the age of eleven in a milliner's workshop and then became a waitress. When she was still a teenager she got a job as an acrobat in a circus, which she continued until she injured herself falling from a trapeze. It is said that Berthe Morisot's pastel drawing *Tightrope Walker* (1886) features the teenage Valadon.[3]

She was fifteen when she debuted as a model for painter Pierre Puvis de Chavannes, and over the next ten years she became one of the most sought-after models in Paris. Valadon was said to be excellent at holding her pose for long periods without breaks, and never complained when she was expected to pose for eight hours a day.

The most famous paintings featuring Valadon are by Renoir. In *Dance at Bougival* (1883) she was pregnant with her son, the future painter Maurice Utrillo, who, although of uncertain parentage, was rumoured to have been fathered by Renoir or Puvis, both of whom Valadon had posed for. Renoir painted her features once again the same year in *Dance in the Country*, which Aline Chariot, Renoir's companion, later had replaced by her own.[4]

YOU ARE ONE OF US

While Renoir and other Impressionists respected Valadon as a model, they saw her mainly as a muse; it was Edgar Degas who recognized her raw artistic talent and encouraged her to pursue painting.

The two met and became friends in the early 1890s when she modelled for him. Degas, whose nickname for her was 'the illustrious Valadon', was impressed by her bold line drawings and paintings, and he taught her engraving as well as how to work with pastels. His mentorship was a turning point for her, and he encouraged her to quit modelling and take up fine art full-time, unfortunately an impossibility for a single mother of little means.

Then in 1896 she married the wealthy stockbroker Paul Mousis and moved her family – that is, her mother and son – to his house in Montagny, north of Paris. They would remain married for thirteen years, giving her the financial means, and the time, to establish her career.

Degas bought her first professional paintings and hung them on his walls beside works by Jean-Auguste-Dominique Ingres, Eugène Delacroix, Édouard Manet and Paul Gauguin, stating, 'you are one of us'. He then introduced her to Paul Durand-Ruel, the most important art dealer of the 19th century, and later she would be championed by the only female art dealer of the age, Berthe Weill.[5]

Degas would remain one of her closest friends and supporters until his death in 1917, but although he had played an important role in her early career, Valadon soon developed her own distinct style, characterized by bold colours, realistic portrayals and emotionally complex subjects. She was driven, ambitious and confident, and she approached nudity and sensuality very differently to other artists. Her entrée into the artistic milieu was as an object of the male gaze as a life model, which was a notoriously short career, but eventually she would take up the tools of her former

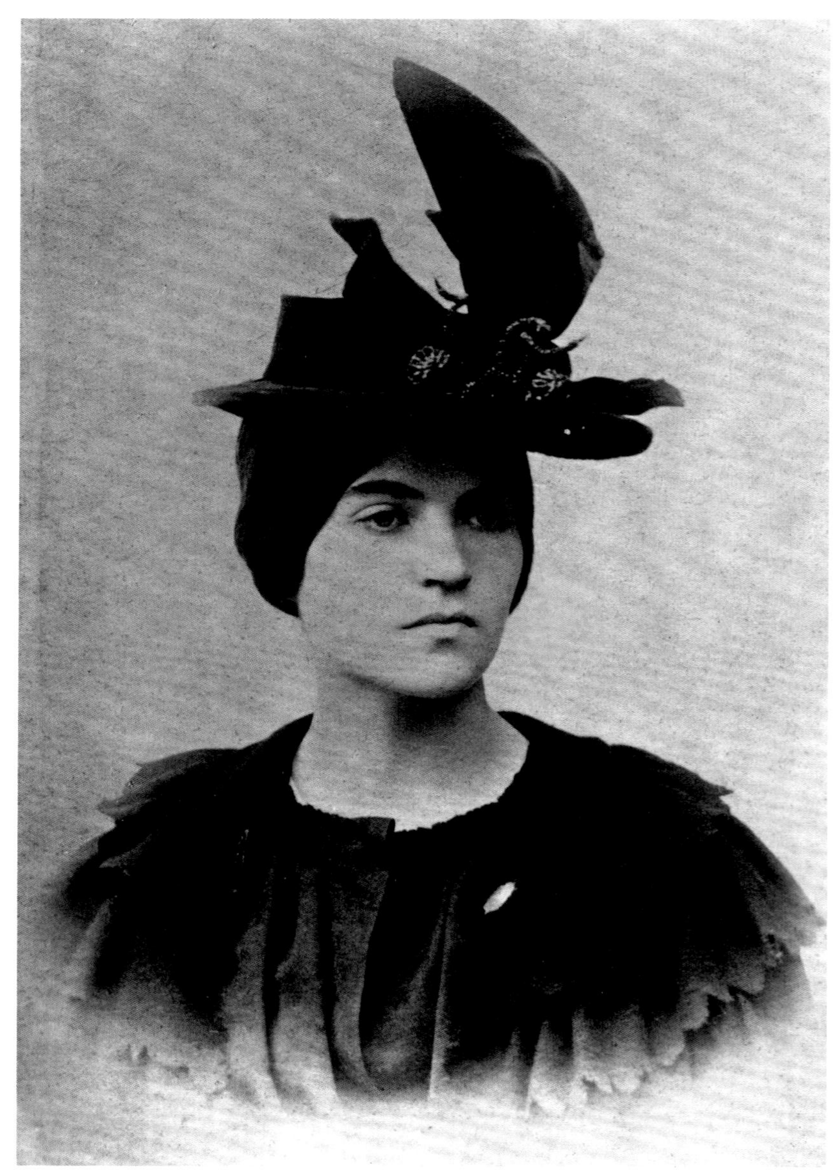

SUZANNE VALADON

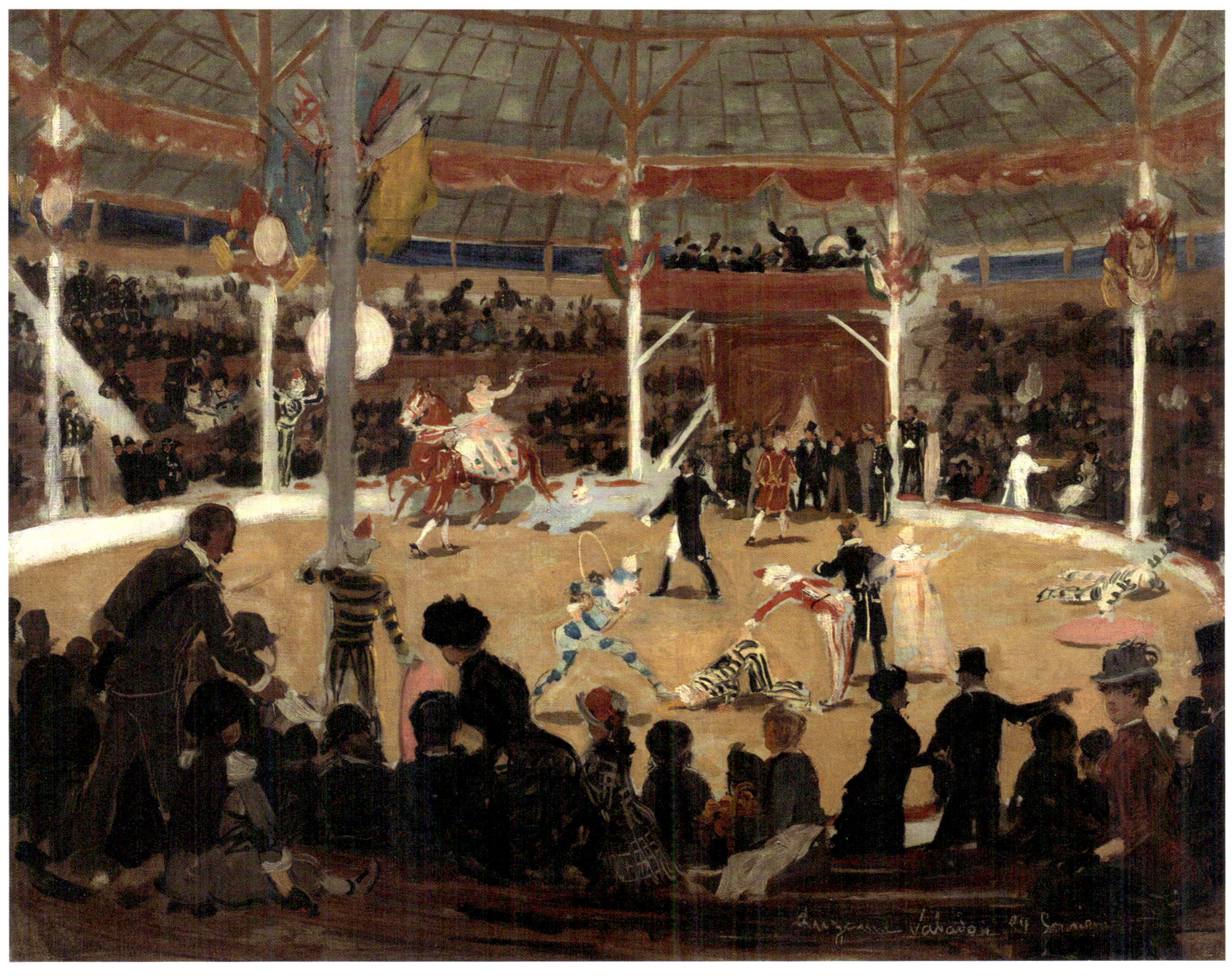

*It was Edgar Degas
who recognized her raw
artistic talent*

THE BLUE ROOM

*As a model, she had
direct experience of the
objectification of women*

employers and show them just how to paint women. As she later said: 'I had great masters. I took the best of them, of their teachings, of their examples. I found myself, I made myself, and I said what I had to say.'[6]

Paris was a city that attracted not only avant-garde painters but those coming from the fringes of society, and it opened its arms to Valadon, who became the first self-taught woman artist to exhibit at the Société Nationale des Beaux-Arts in 1894.[7] She was painting female nudes at this time, but she was also creating nude self-portraits, which was unheard of for a woman artist.

As a model, she had direct experience of the objectification of women, which gave her an insight most artists didn't have, and added new depths to her paintings. Her nudes are less idealized than those of the male post-Impressionist generation: they are imperfect, honest depictions of the human body.

THE MALE NUDE

Auguste Rodin (see Chapter 13) had already shocked Paris with his exploration of female sexuality, but these were from male point of view. Valadon painted *Adam and Eve* in 1909, a time in which the expression of female sexuality by a woman was extremely rare.

Apart from casting herself as the so-called temptress Eve, this is considered the first work by a woman in the history of modern art to feature a male nude.[8] Valadon cast fellow artist André Utter, her lover (and future second husband) who was twenty-one years her junior, as Adam for the painting.

Neither one of the figures in the painting is idealized, and Valadon's version of the biblical story has no serpent. Instead, the man and woman reach for the apple together. Originally Adam was completely nude, but Valadon was forced to cover his genitals so she could exhibit the work at the Paris Salon.

Valadon, her son Utrillo and Utter lived together in Montmartre and were described by the locals as 'the unholy trio', thanks to their blazing rows. She would use Utter as the model for several large-scale nude paintings, which were equally provocative and scandalous.

Valadon's outsider status gave her an edge. As if tackling taboos on female nudity with her self-portraits wasn't enough, she also explored the last taboo for a female artist: depicting the male nude. These were some of the first examples in modern art of the male body as an object of desire, given the same treatment as idealized female nudes created by men.

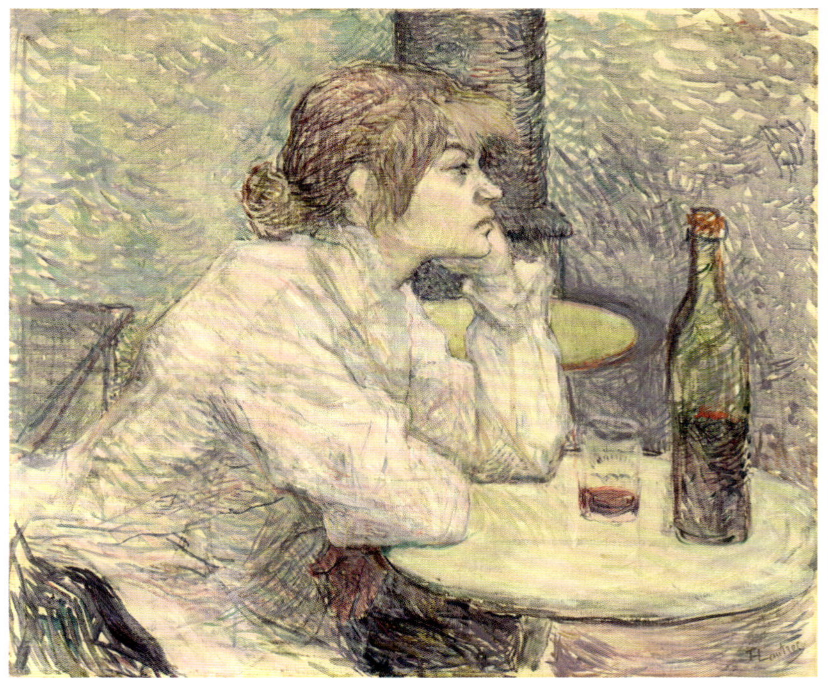

SUZANNE VALADON

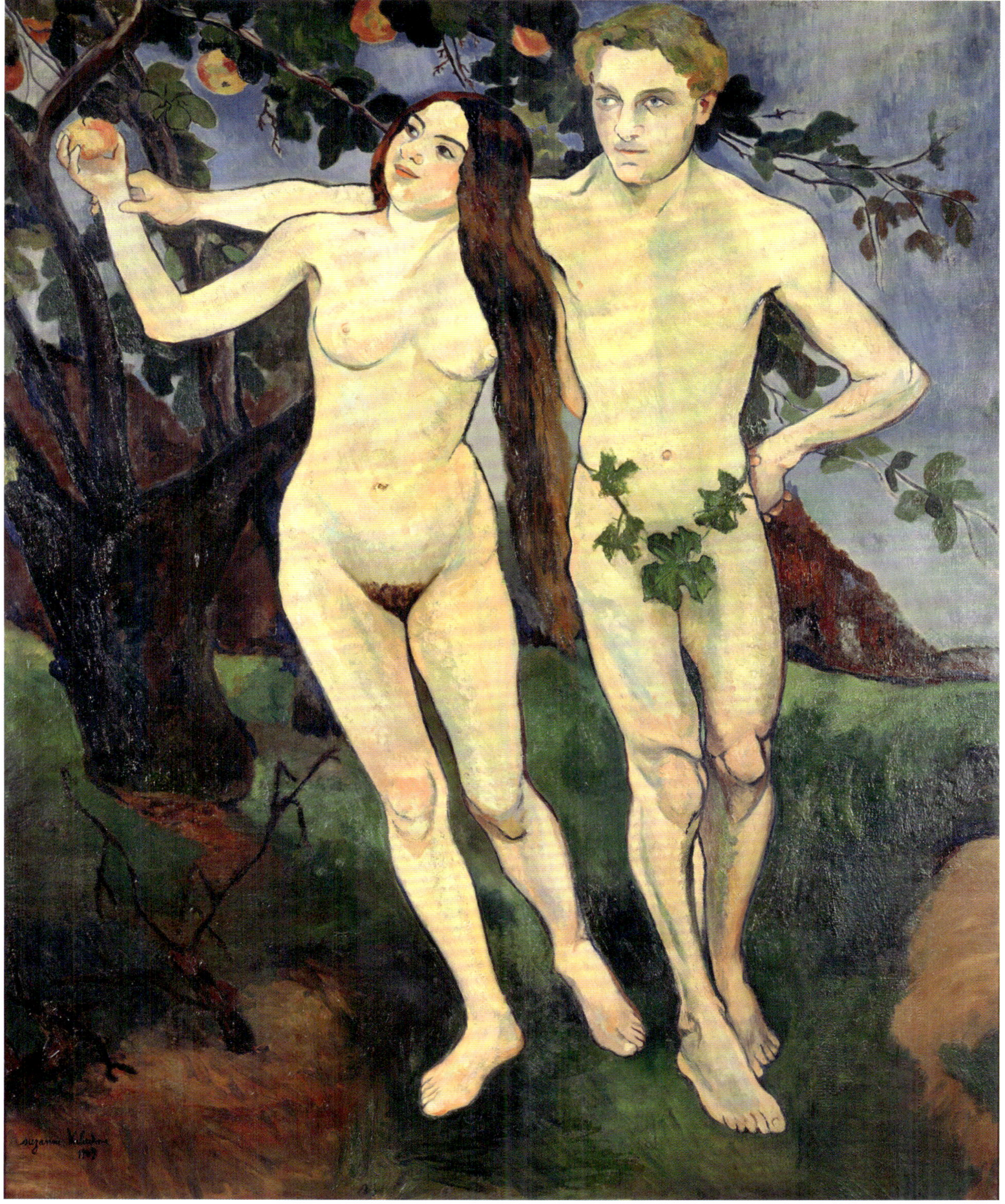

                    THE BLUE ROOM

THE BLUE ROOM

Valadon plays a familiar role in *The Blue Room* (*La Chambre Bleue*) as the artist's model, totally at ease with her body, as well as the artist, confident in her skills. The composition takes up the traditional scheme of the voluptuous nude framed by curtains and set against a backdrop of a bohemian studio, giving the quiet scene a theatrical air.

Valadon once said: 'Don't bring me a woman who is looking for kindness or beauty – I will find her out straight away,'[9] and here she is, unapologetic, lounging on a messy daybed covered in blue-and-white floral sheets. She is a mature woman with sturdy hands and, by the standards of the day, a fuller-figured body that didn't conform to the delicate femininity expected of women at the time.

The Blue Room clearly references Édouard Manet's *Olympia* (1863–65), itself modelled after Titian's *Venus of Urbino* (1534). Both paintings feature a reclining woman as the focal point, a pose long associated with the tradition of the odalisque in Western art.

Édouard Manet, *Olympia*, 1863–65.

opposite
Suzanne Valadon, *Self-Portrait*, 1927.

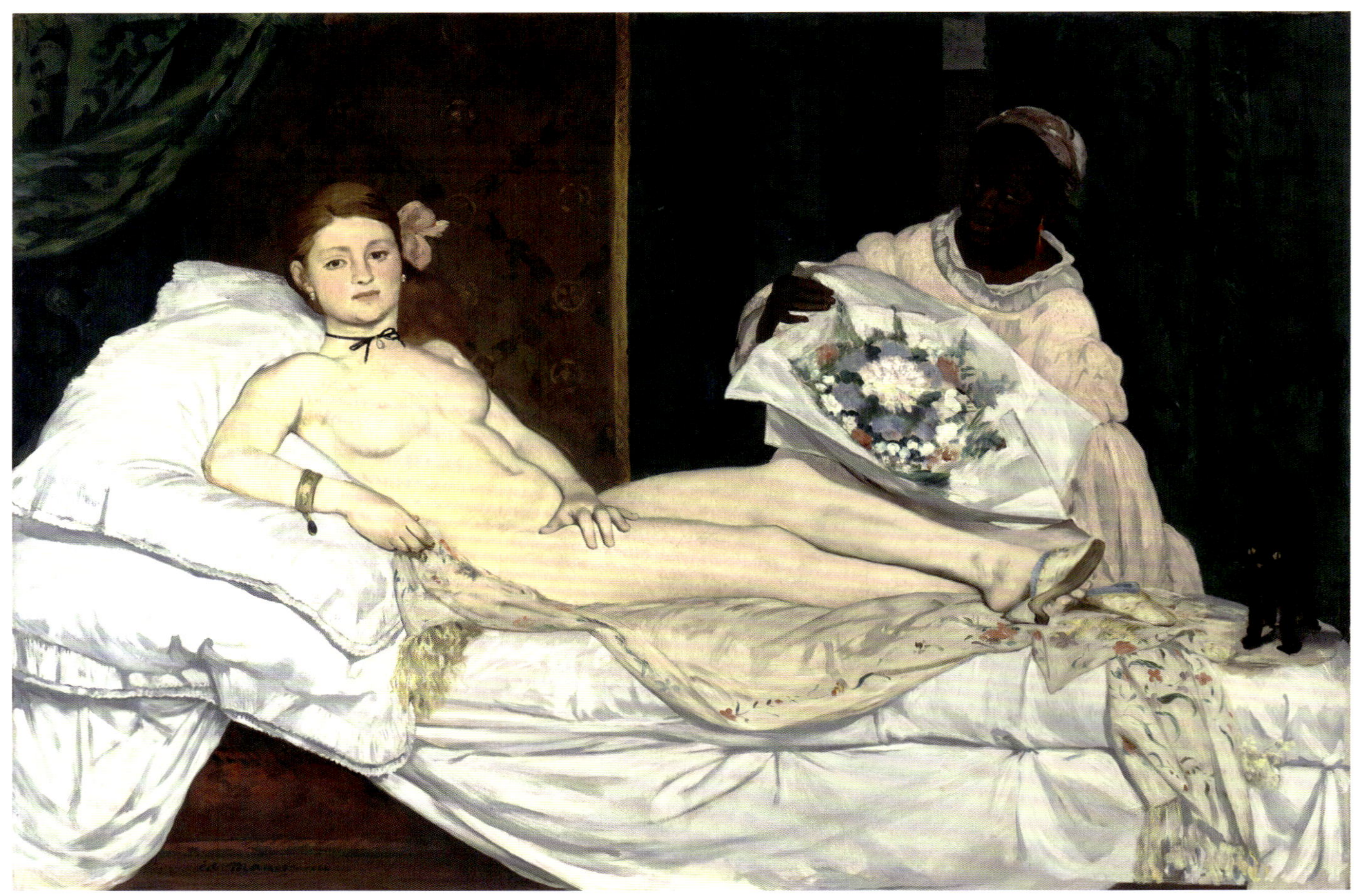

Unlike Olympia, who looks provocatively
at the viewer, Valadon has a more casual
(if not disinterested), self-assured demeanour.
And while Manet broke with conventions by
portraying a nude woman with stark realism,
rather than presenting her as a mythological
or idealized figure, Valadon takes this further
by depicting a clothed woman in a similar
pose but challenging the expectation of nudity
for female subjects in such compositions.
Her body is unidealized, emphasizing
naturalism and individuality over perfection
and sexuality.

The background plays a crucial role
in shaping the atmosphere of the painting.
The textiles and patterns seem to envelop the
subject, blurring the line between foreground
and background. This is a stark contrast
to the sparse, neutral spaces seen in Manet's
Olympia or Titian's *Venus of Urbino*. By filling
the space with patterns, textures and colours,
Valadon rejects the traditional emphasis on,
and illumination of, the female figure as the
sole focus, instead embedding her subject in
a setting that reinforces the idea that she is at
home in her own space and in her own identity.

She gazes off to the right, avoiding the
viewer as if caught in reverie or in a state
of boredom, no doubt reflecting her own
experience of posing for long hours. As we've
noted, it was as a former model that she had
first-hand experience with the objectification
of women in art, and it's quite possible to
view *The Blue Room* as her reclamation of
control both through her art and through
her subject.

A CONTEMPORARY TALE

In 1937 the Musée du Luxembourg purchased
three of her major paintings, as well as many
of her drawings. A year later, on 7 April 1938,
Valadon was painting at her easel when
she unexpectedly suffered a stroke. She died

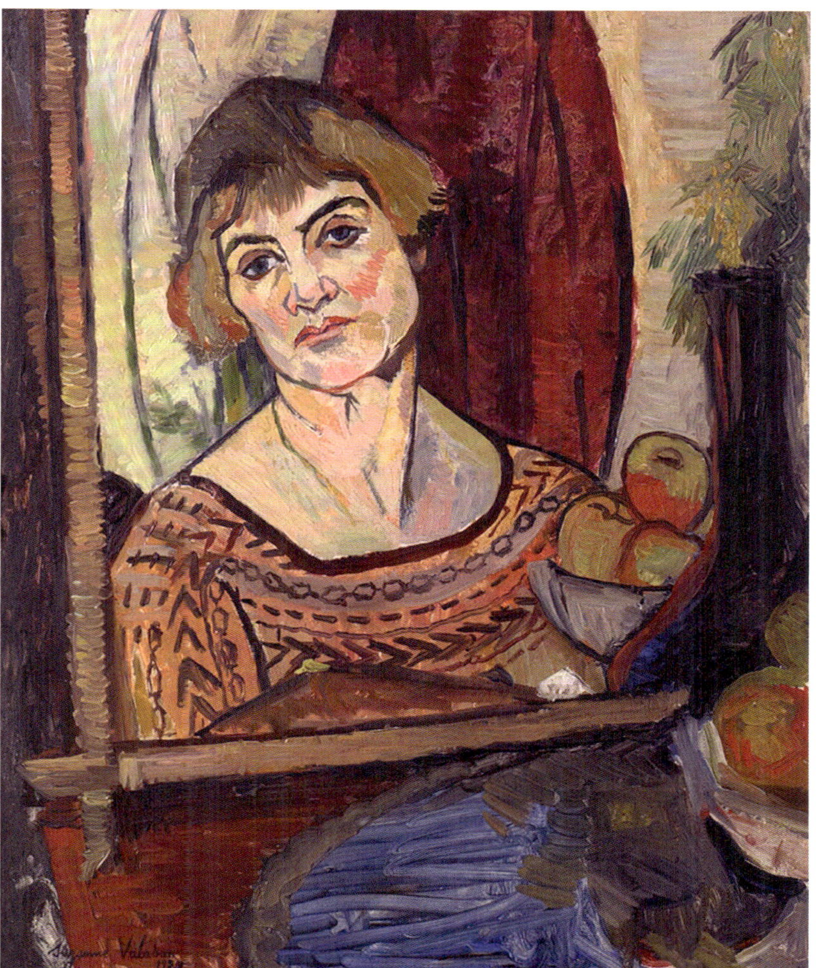

at the hospital just hours later at the age
of seventy-two.

It is a complete myth that Valadon was
unknown in her lifetime: she received much
critical acclaim and was even mentioned on the
front page of the French newspaper *Le Gaulois*,
which described her work as 'truthful'. Yet,
like many women artists of the 20th century,
she was overshadowed by male counterparts,
including her own son, and ignored by later
critics and art historians.

In 1967 the Musée National d'Art Moderne
in Paris held a Suzanne Valadon retrospective,
but apart from inclusion in a few group shows,

her work was rarely seen. In recent years,
however, her reputation has grown, first with
several important solo shows and finally in 2023
she had her first major retrospective in nearly
sixty years at the Georges Pompidou Metz,
which then travelled to Barcelona.

We can directly connect Suzanne Valadon
with artists like Frida Kahlo, Alice Neel,
Cindy Sherman and Jenny Saville, who share
a focus on subverting traditional depictions
of femininity. While they belong to different
artistic and historical contexts, they all engage
across time in conversations about identity,
realism and the autonomy of the subject.

Suzanne Valadon was a pioneer who
managed to overcome the class and gender
expectations that others imposed on her and
improbably rose from a working-class model
to a celebrated artist, breaking new ground
without conforming or compromising. Hers
is a contemporary tale.

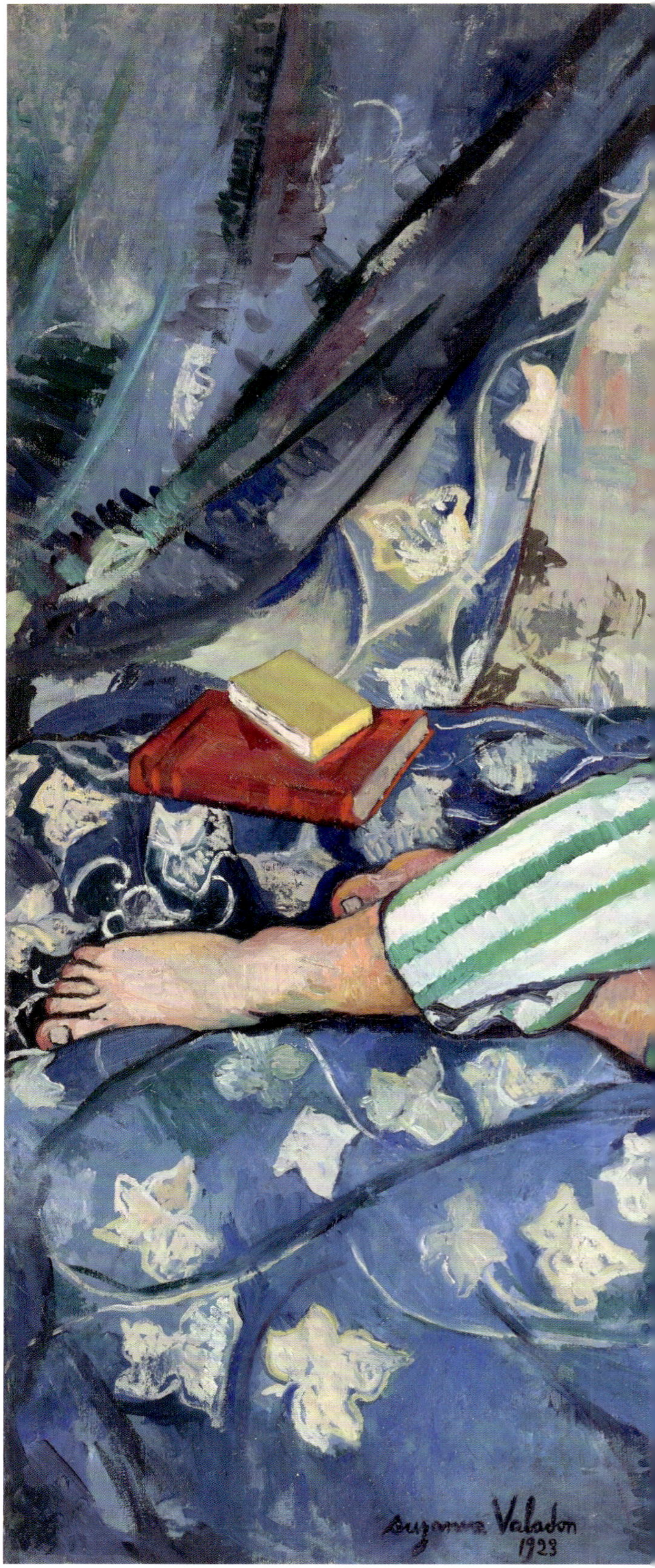

Suzanne Valadon,
The Blue Room, 1923.

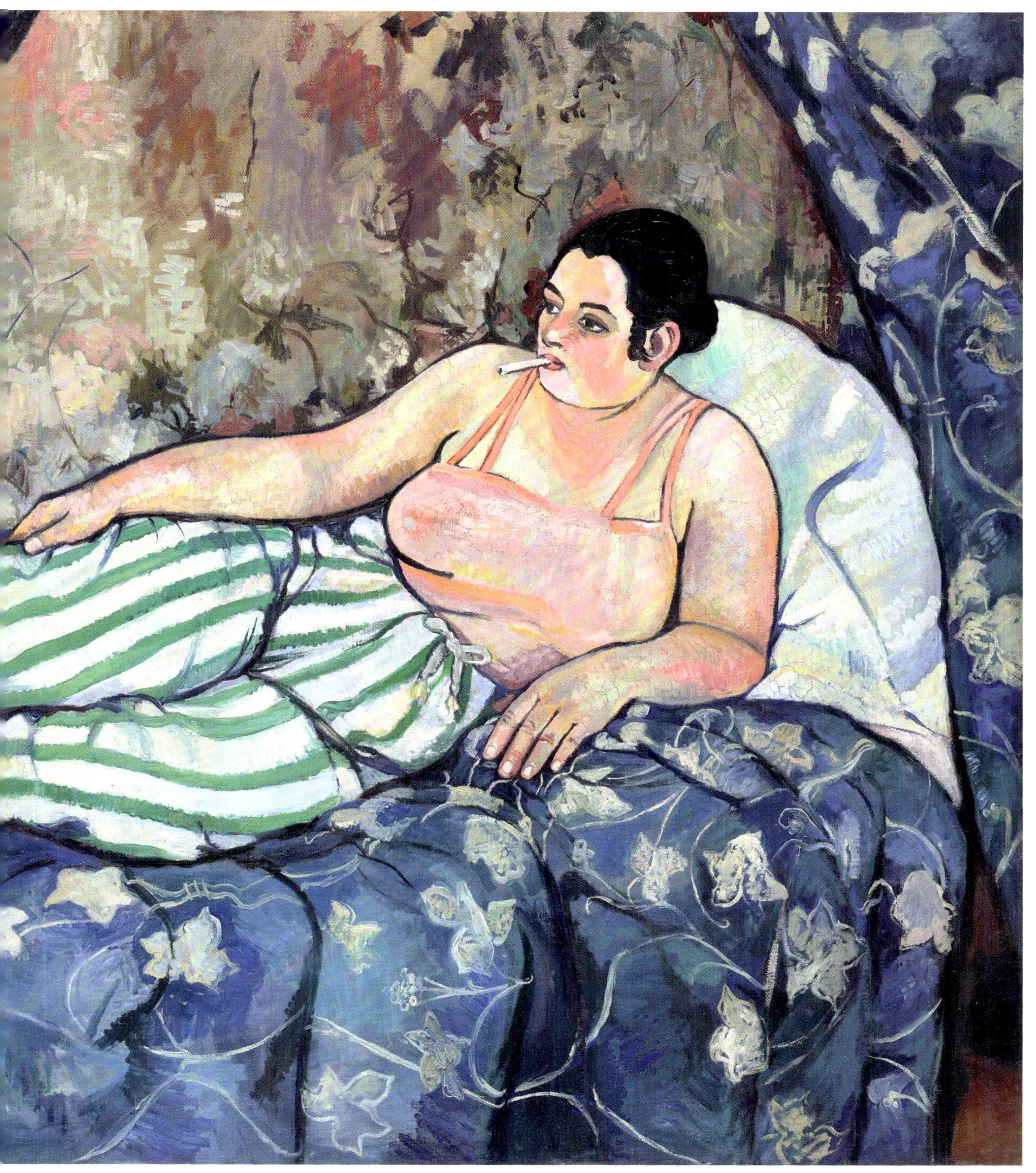

21

GEORGIA O'KEEFFE

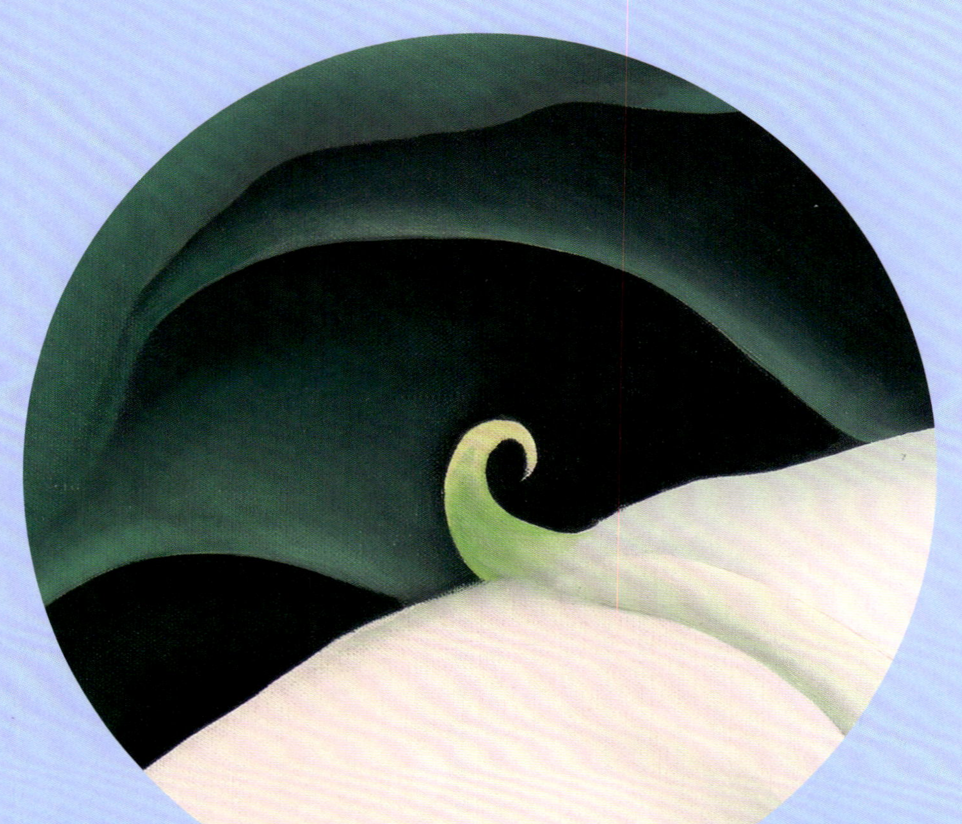

JIMSON WEED/WHITE FLOWER NO. 1

1932

THE SEXUALIZATION OF GEORGIA O'KEEFFE

During the Great Depression of the late 1920s and early 1930s a sense of unease and disillusion seeped into art. It was an era when people were searching for symbols of strength and stability.

Artists who sought to define modern America appeared on the art scene, like Georgia O'Keeffe and Edward Hopper, both uniquely American painters. Hopper's work took a more realistic, theatrical tone, while O'Keeffe's was more abstract and infused with a magical surrealism. Works like *Jimson Weed/White Flower No. 1* (1932) forced viewers to engage with forms and shapes at a level of intimacy that had never been done before. Her work straddled the line between abstraction and realism in an open and fearless way. She was an uncompromising artist whose work was inseparable from the way she lived her life: simple, essential, yet achingly expressive.

ROOTED IN NATURE, DRAWN TO ART

It is said that even as a child, O'Keeffe was a non-conformist and had an acute awareness of her image and style. She wore her hair pulled back austerely, and she dressed simply – the start of a lifetime habit.

She was born in 1887 on a dairy farm in Wisconsin to second-generation Americans. O'Keeffe had a profound connection to nature throughout her life, and this is vividly reflected in her work. It was those endless prairie horizons that fired her visual imagination and gave her a sense that wide-open spaces were *her* territory, a feeling that would later reverberate throughout her work.[1]

O'Keeffe wanted to be a painter from a young age, but her family were not wealthy, and at the turn of the century, women without funds had little to no access to a college arts education. But she was determined, and in 1905 she applied successfully to the School of the Art Institute of Chicago, the alumni of which include Grant Wood, Jeff Koons and Joan Mitchell. Most of her studies here, and later at the Art Students League in New York, were concerned with traditional academic painting.

FROM THE PRAIRIES TO FIFTH AVENUE

When O'Keeffe was twenty-eight and working as a high school art teacher, her friend took some of her charcoal drawings to Alfred Stieglitz, a renowned photographer, the owner of 291 gallery in New York and a visionary in the burgeoning modern art scene.

Stieglitz, who had previously shown Cézanne, Matisse and Picasso at his gallery, included ten of her charcoal drawings in a 1916 group show without her permission, and it would change her life.

The drawings were a radical departure from the representational work she had produced up until this point. They were deeply

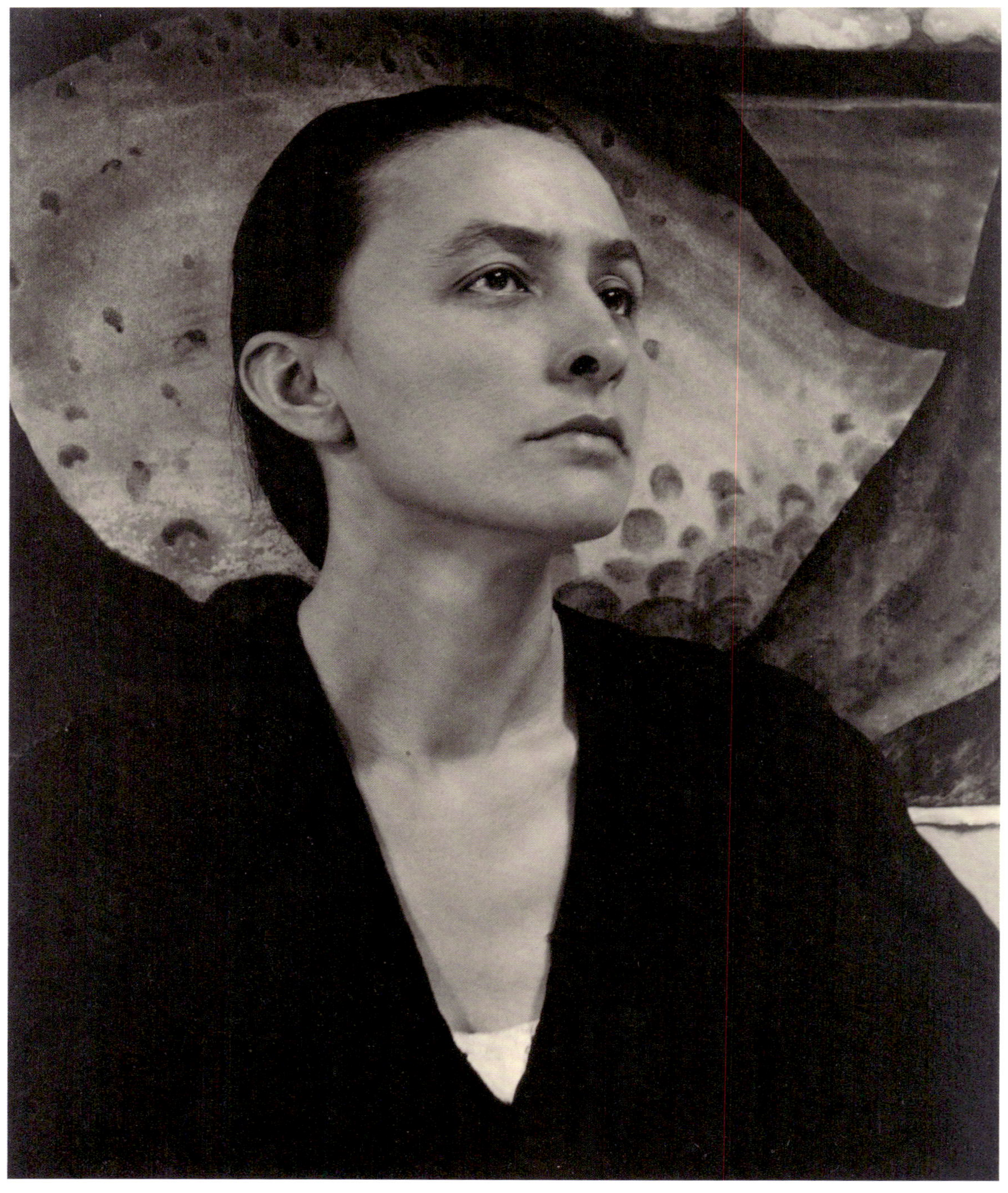

Alfred Stieglitz,
Georgia O'Keeffe,
1918.

     GEORGIA O'KEEFFE

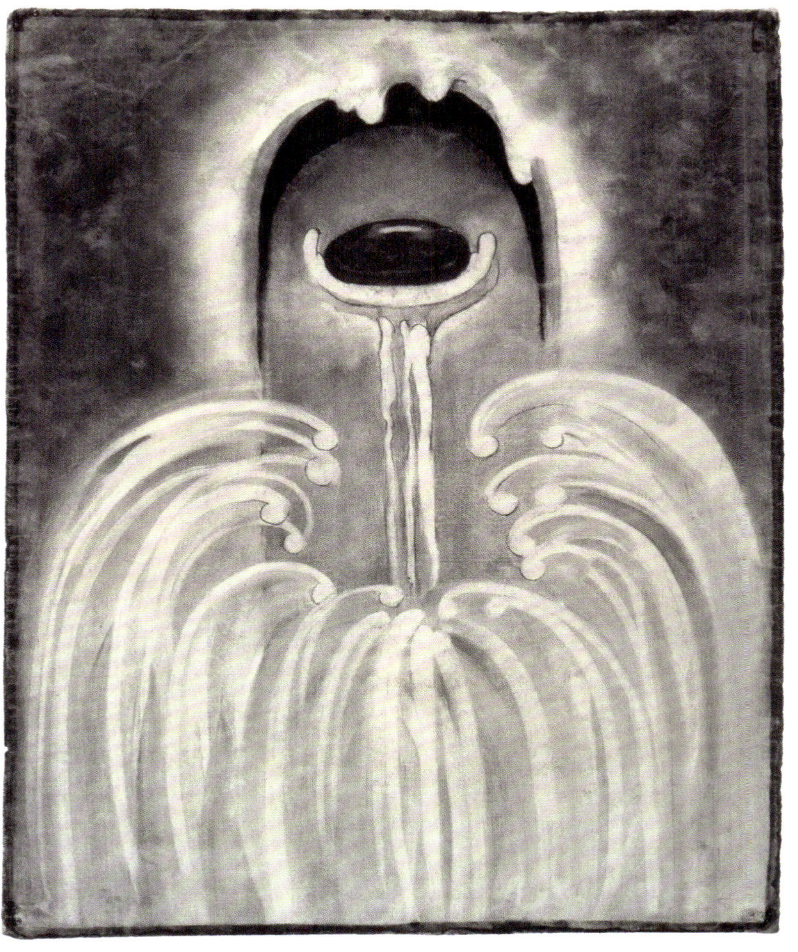

personal works, exploring her emotions and inner experiences through bold, abstract forms and minimalistic lines. They revealed a raw, emotional quality, suggesting landscapes, natural forms or even the human body, without explicitly depicting them.

Critics and artists were immediately drawn to her work, and the show helped to lay the groundwork for her future success as a leading figure in the emerging modern art movement.

Stieglitz may have given O'Keeffe her first exhibition, but he was also responsible for creating the misinterpretation of her work that has persisted to the present day, by suggesting a sensual interpretation of her work, particularly in her abstract flower paintings.[2] This thinking would dominate critical theory around her practice for the rest of her career. In 1929 she wrote to a friend on the subject: 'I think I would never have minded Stieglitz being anything he happened to be if he hadn't kept me so persistently off my track.'[3]

One critic described her flower paintings as 'sexual', and 'metaphors for the female body', which O'Keeffe was deeply offended by: 'I almost wept,' she later said, 'I thought I could never face the world again.'[4] These critics were missing the more obvious fact that flowers naturally share similarities with human reproductive organs due to their role in plant reproduction.[5]

After she moved to New York in 1918, Stieglitz and O'Keeffe became involved in a complex and intense love affair. They were married in 1924, but their entire relationship would be strained by his infidelity and controlling behaviour.

PHOTOGRAPHY

Stieglitz was the first dealer to exhibit photographs alongside modern paintings, including those by Paul Strand.

JIMSON WEED/WHITE FLOWER NO. 1

O'Keeffe met the photographer and filmmaker in 1917, and his work became a huge influence on her. 'Did you meet Paul Strand?' she once wrote to her friend, '[his] photographs… are as queer in shapes as Picasso's drawings'.[6] She had a deep affinity with photographers, and like them was investigating new, radical ways of seeing. She drew inspiration from photographers' compositions, lighting and focus, as well as their tendency towards minimalism and manipulation of scale.

O'Keeffe's sense of composition was strongly influenced by photographic principles. She used close-ups, zooming in on particular elements of landscapes or flowers, making it seem larger than life and more abstract; she cropped and positioned to emphasize form and pattern, using deep, contrasting lighting.

She also often focused on a single subject or motif across multiple paintings. O'Keeffe would return to the same flower, bone or landscape again and again, each time exploring it from different angles, with different lighting, or emphasizing different aspects. This repetitive exploration is similar to a photographer's series, where the same subject is reinterpreted through different shots, exposures or variations.

MAKING THE MINIMALIST MAXIMALIST

Nobody in America was doing work like O'Keeffe, paintings that took a radical look at how we perceive and imagine the natural world through a modernist lens. By reducing subjects to their essential, often abstract, forms, she made them as much about design and composition or visual language as they were about nature. By using fluid lines, soft gradients and bold colours, she emphasized shape and structure over literal representation.

Jimson Weed/White Flower No. 1 (1932) was painted in a period when O'Keeffe was focused on large-scale flowers, a subject she had explored since her first iconic flower painting in 1924, *Petunia No. 2*.

Jimson is one of O'Keeffe's most famous and largest floral paintings, featuring a close-up, magnified view of a Jimson weed (or datura) blossom. The spiralling, trumpet-shaped petals and luminous whiteness against a darker background give the flower a surreal, ethereal quality.

Large-scale works like this evoke a powerful emotional response because they

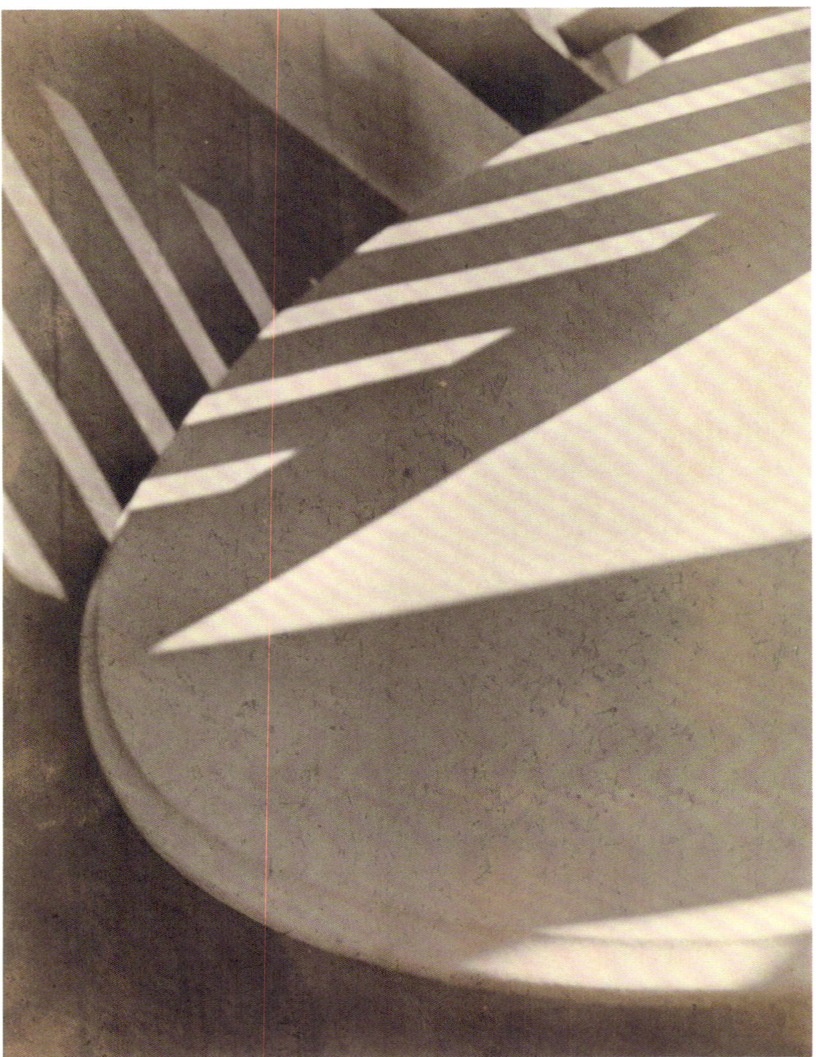

Paul Strand, *Abstraction, Twin Lakes, Connecticut*, 1916.

opposite
Georgia O'Keeffe, *Music, Pink and Blue No. 2*, 1918.

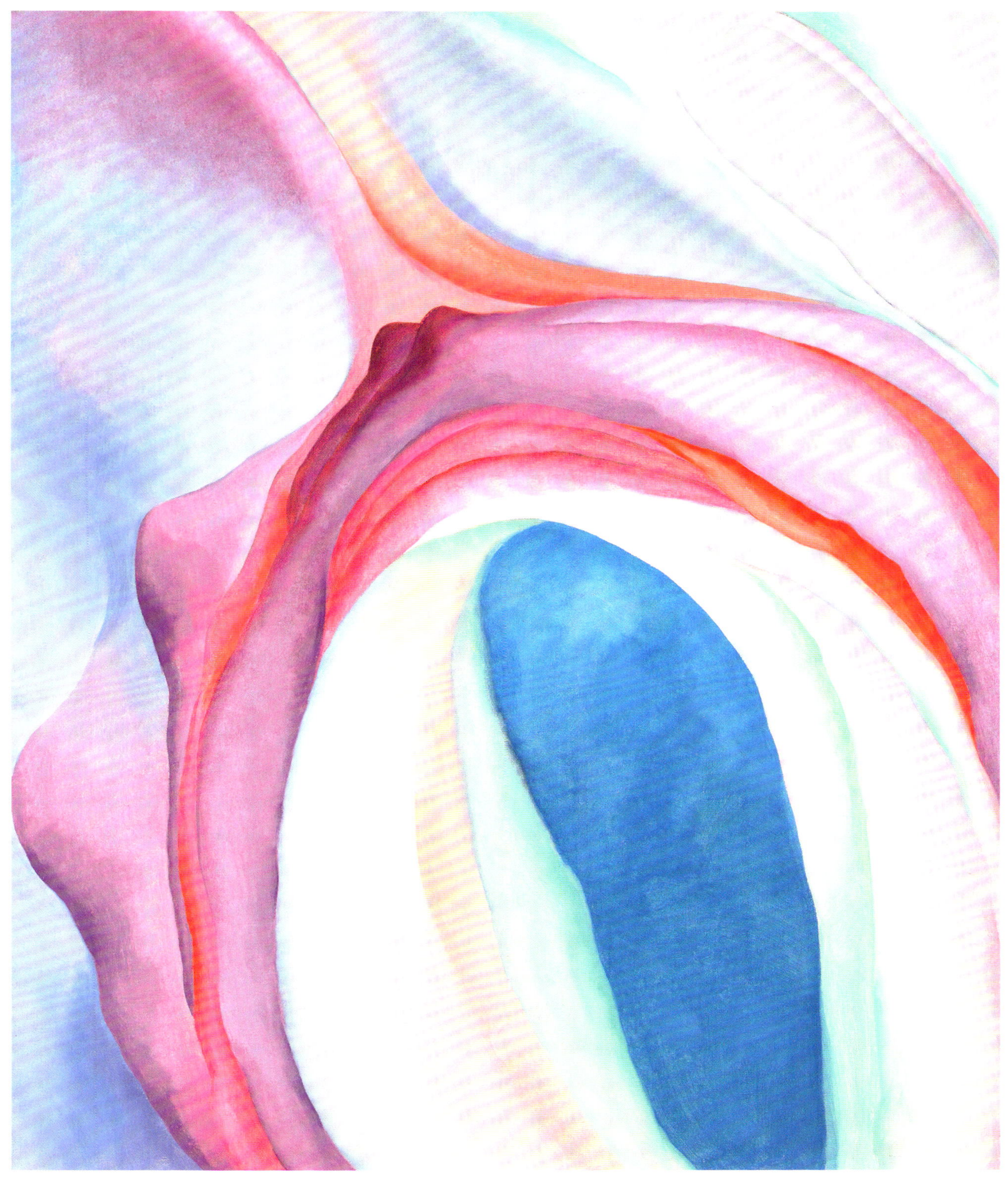

JIMSON WEED/WHITE FLOWER NO. 1

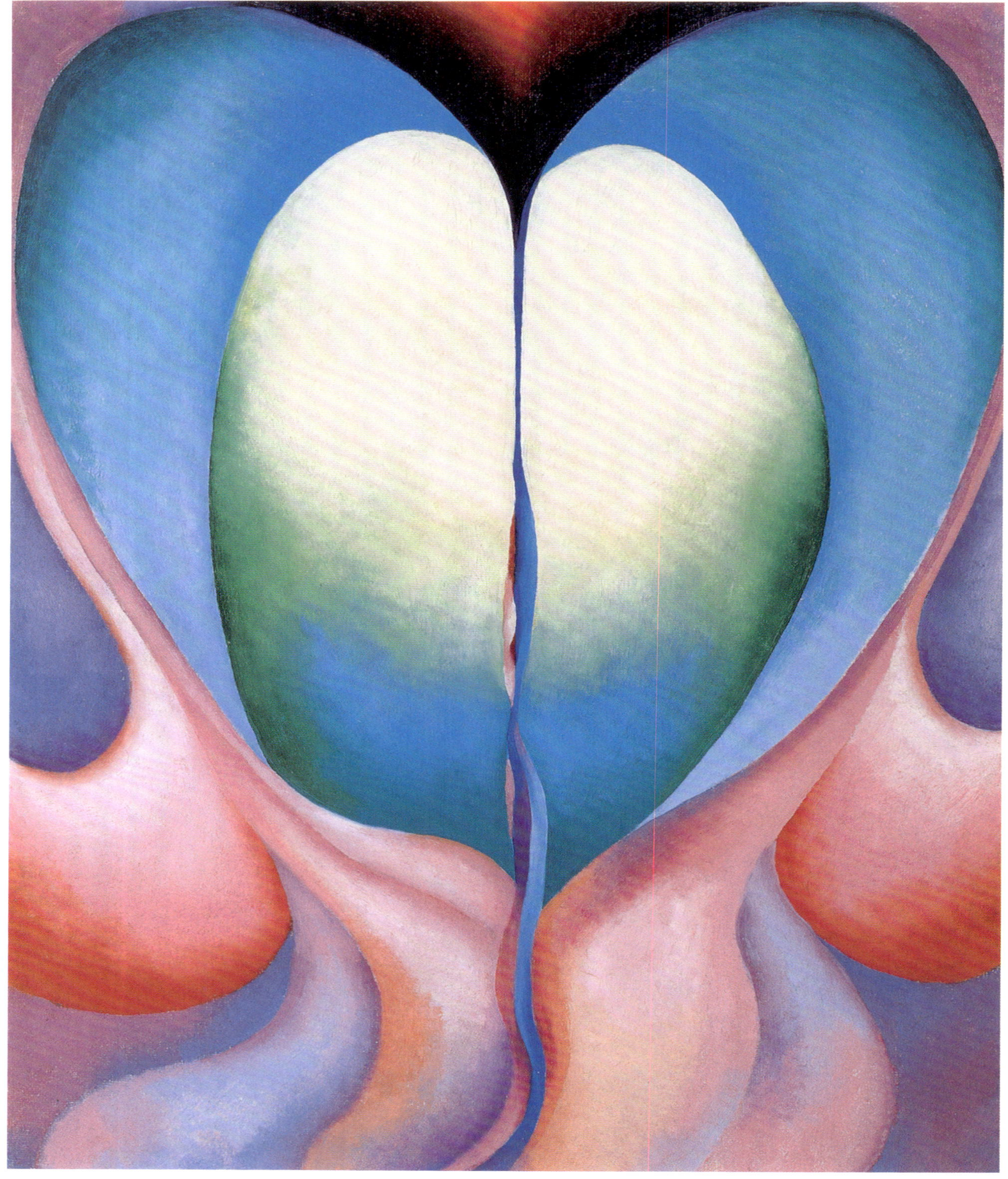

GEORGIA O'KEEFFE

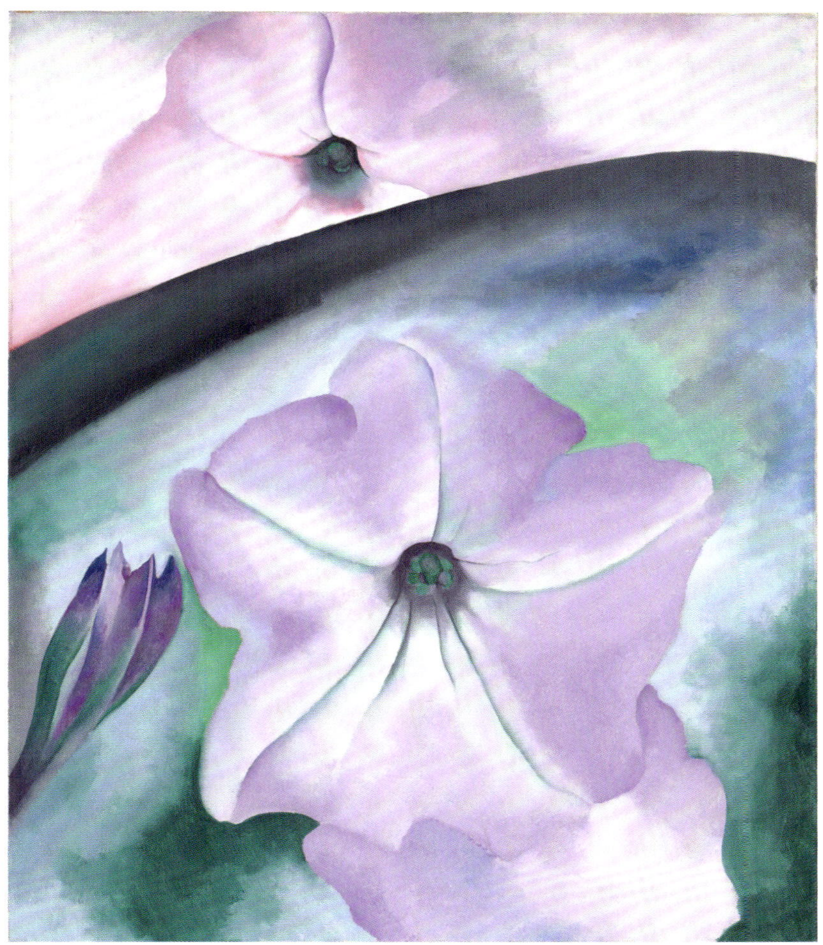

of perception, magnification and spatial awareness. It shows the viewer that abstract beauty and surrealism can be found in the everyday by making the minimalist maximalist.

By enlarging the Jimson weed so significantly, and through her ability to combine realism with abstraction, O'Keeffe encouraged viewers to see her works as powerful, almost sculptural forms, rather than simply decorative objects.

Jimson transcends its subject matter, and represents a high point in Georgia O'Keeffe's exploration of magnified flower paintings. In 2014, the painting gained worldwide fame when it was sold for $44.4 million at auction, setting a record at the time for the highest price paid for a painting by a female artist.

FINANCIAL SUCCESS AND NEW MEXICO

When Stieglitz first saw her new large-scale floral paintings, he showed little enthusiasm, as was often the case when she ventured into new artistic directions not dictated by him. However, when these paintings were exhibited for the first time in 1925, it was to instant success and acclaim.

Despite her critics, O'Keeffe found a way to explore the beauty of nature and express her own emotional responses to the world around her. Floral paintings had marked a new and risky direction for the artist at the time, but were a financial success and remained a

dominate the viewer's visual field. By making her flowers enormous, O'Keeffe gave them a presence that could overwhelm or draw the viewer in, and the exaggerated size added an emotional weight to otherwise delicate subjects, making them feel monumental.

As a child, O'Keeffe painted delicate watercolours of flowers from the prairies, but now she painted them enlarged from unfamiliar angles, magnifying them and isolating small sections, removing the subject from its context. *Jimson* is deceptively simple, but it is in fact a continuation of her engagement with complicated theories

opposite
Georgia O'Keeffe,
Series I, No. 8, 1919.

Georgia O'Keeffe,
Petunia No. 2, 1924.

frequent theme throughout the 1930s, during which time she created more than sixty finished paintings and pastels.[7] They were deeply personal paintings, as she saw in them her beloved Southwest, where she now spent a significant portion of her life.

In 1929, shortly after her husband openly began an affair, O'Keeffe took her first extended trip to New Mexico. She spent most of her summers there, alone, from this time onwards and would eventually move there permanently in 1949.

It was to that otherworldly landscape that she formed a deep spiritual connection. The bright yellow and red terrain, white cliffs and fierce sun influenced her colour palette, as did the scale of the desert and its surroundings.

The public perception of Georgia O'Keeffe, which persists to this day, was created in the New Mexico desert. In article after article, most notably *Life Magazine*'s 1968 cover story, she would be portrayed as a loner, a hermit and an artistic puritan hiding out in the 'New Mexico Badlands'. Except she wasn't. She had friends who stayed often and she had a team of servants. It was another myth, as central to her mystique as it is untrue.[8]

What the New Mexico desert gave her was new and stimulating subject matter, such as bleached animal bones and skulls, and desert flora. These objects became recurring symbols in her work, and she was fascinated by the juxtaposition of life and death that bones encapsulated, as well as their stark beauty.

A TRUE AMERICAN ICON

When it came to modernism, Georgia O'Keeffe was a pioneer who left an indelible mark on the art world for an impressive seven decades, while staying true to her unique vision.

Her decision to move to New Mexico in 1949 and make it her permanent home helped her remain physically and creatively separate from the dominant art scenes in New York and Europe. In the isolation of the Southwest, she was free from the pressures of contemporary art trends. The expansive, timeless desert landscape became her muse.

Her New Mexico paintings and her earlier flower series, though inspired by different subjects, are deeply interconnected through their thematic exploration of scale, abstraction, form and the natural world. We could say she even employed the same technique with both genres, but reversed the focus. Rather than zooming in, as with her flowers, in her later works she often pulled back, portraying sweeping, expansive views of the desert. However, in both genres, the sense of immensity and grandeur is the same.

O'Keeffe died on 6 March 1986, at the age of ninety-eight. Today, her paintings have an iconic status in the collective imagination, particularly her flower paintings, but it is crucial to remember the revolutionary nature of her work. Her boldness and innovation were truly ahead of her time, making her a radical force in the world of art.

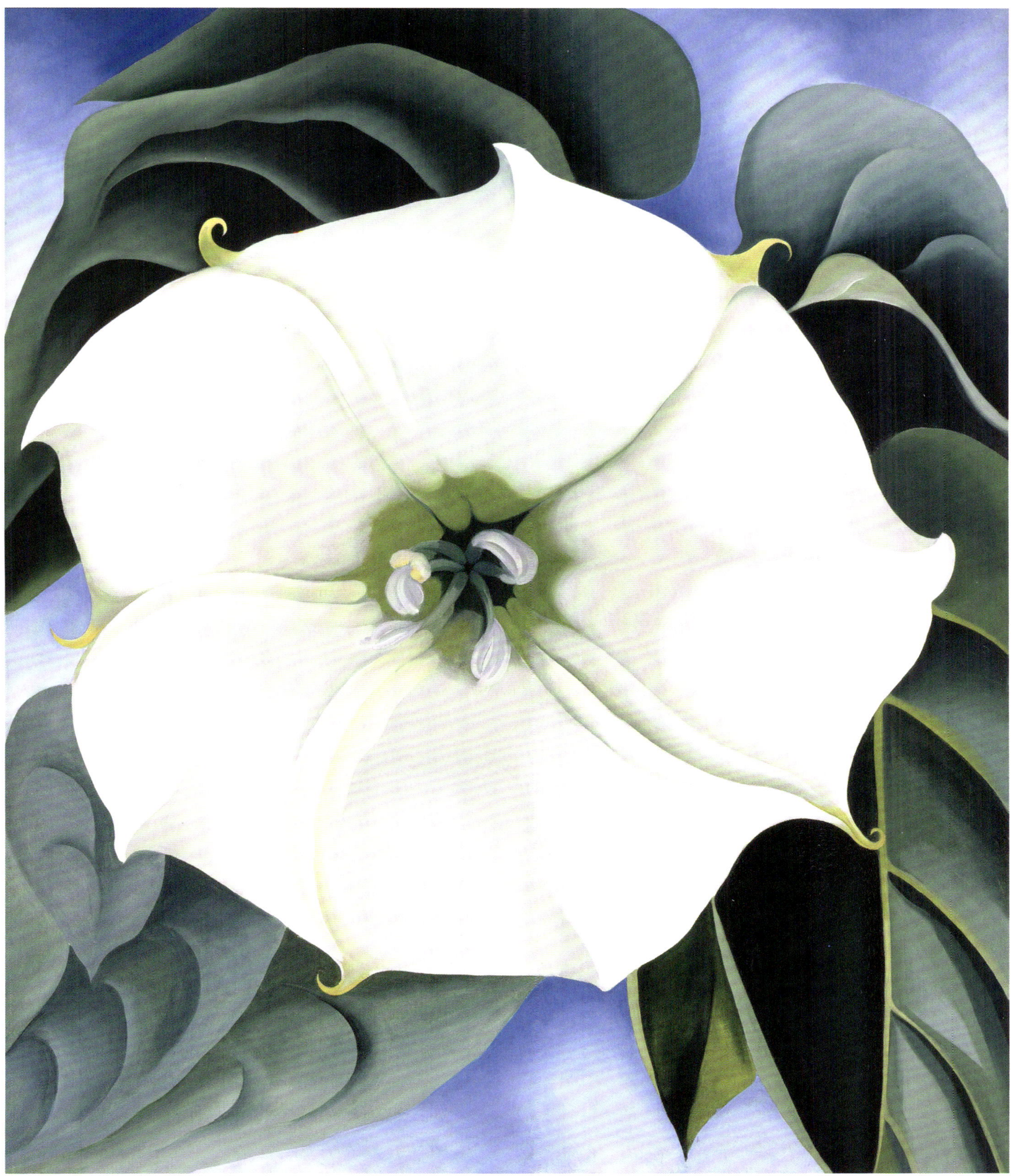

22

FRIDA KAHLO

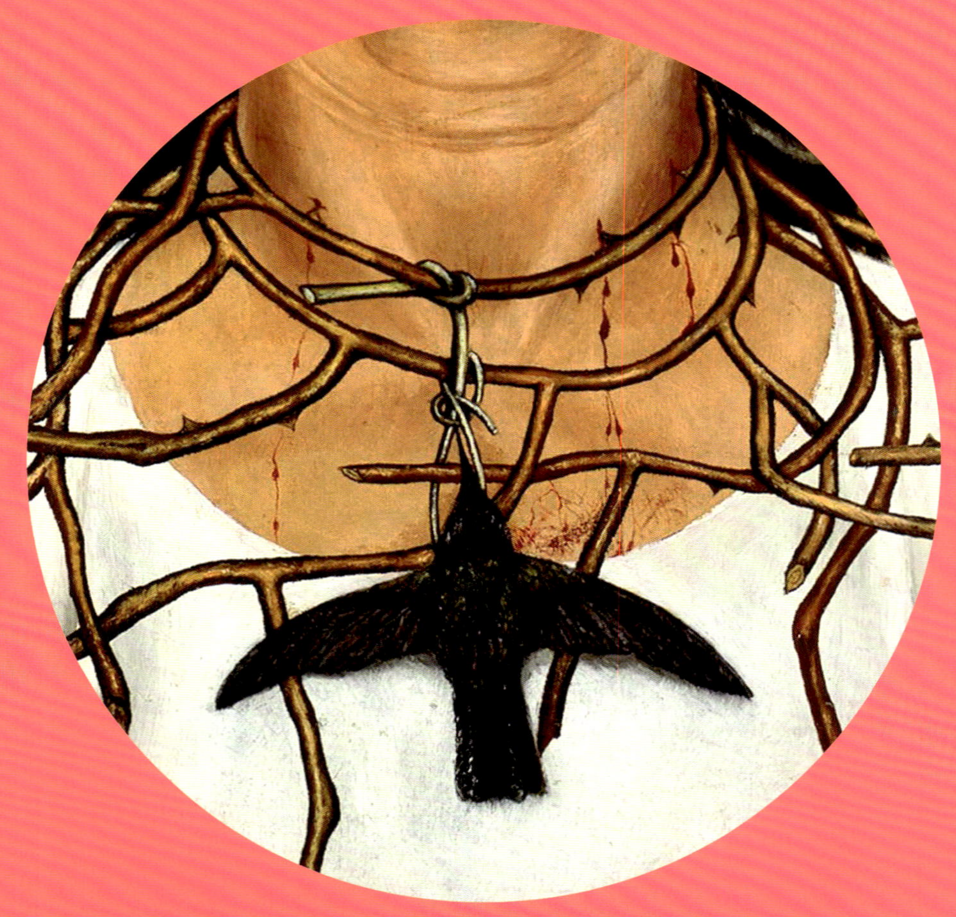

SELF-PORTRAIT WITH THORN NECKLACE AND HUMMINGBIRD

1940

A VISIONARY ICON

A large proportion of Frida Kahlo's paintings – fifty-five of them, to be exact – are self-portraits. She used them to explore her identity and portray her relationship with her culture, her friends, family and lovers, her body and her gender, as shown in *Self-Portrait with Thorn Necklace and Hummingbird*.

Frida Kahlo is one of the most famous artists in the world, her image as instantly recognizable as that of Andy Warhol or Salvador Dalí. She may have died more than seventy years ago, but her influence can still be seen from the high street to Hollywood to social media, and if anything, her legacy seems to be stronger than ever. She has transcended art history to become one of those artists considered a 'brand'.

Kahlo and her artworks are often sanitized and 'de-revolutionized' for commercial gain, when in fact, she was a trailblazing painter who shattered societal norms. A disabled female artist in male-dominated post-revolutionary Mexico, whose challenges to established conventions would reshape 20th-century discourse surrounding gender roles and artistic expression in ways that still resonate today.

A visionary icon, she embraced unorthodox depictions of womanhood, laying bare raw and candid experiences on the canvas – experiences that don't always translate onto a T-shirt, a mug or a key chain.

A LIFE-CHANGING ACCIDENT

On 17 September 1925, eighteen-year-old Kahlo was in a terrible bus accident that would change her life. She was impaled by a metal handrail which punctured her abdomen and uterus. Her spinal column, collar bone and pelvis were broken, as well as suffering dozens of fractures.

It took three months recovering in a full body cast to regain her mobility, but although she was able to walk again, her health was seriously affected for the rest of her life. She often had to wear a metal corset as support to keep her spine from collapsing, and she underwent over thirty major operations in her lifetime.

After the initial operation, she had to spend a year in bed recuperating. To keep her occupied her father gave her paints, and her mother had a special easel made and placed a mirror above her so she could paint herself. For the rest of her life, she would spend long periods recuperating in bed, often with a restraining back brace, and these working conditions explain why most of her works are small, as large canvases were not practical under the circumstances.

The confinement also contributed to her adopting the self-portrait as her primary genre. Kahlo's depiction of her own suffering, constant pain and disability would be groundbreaking, and her body would become a focal point of her art.

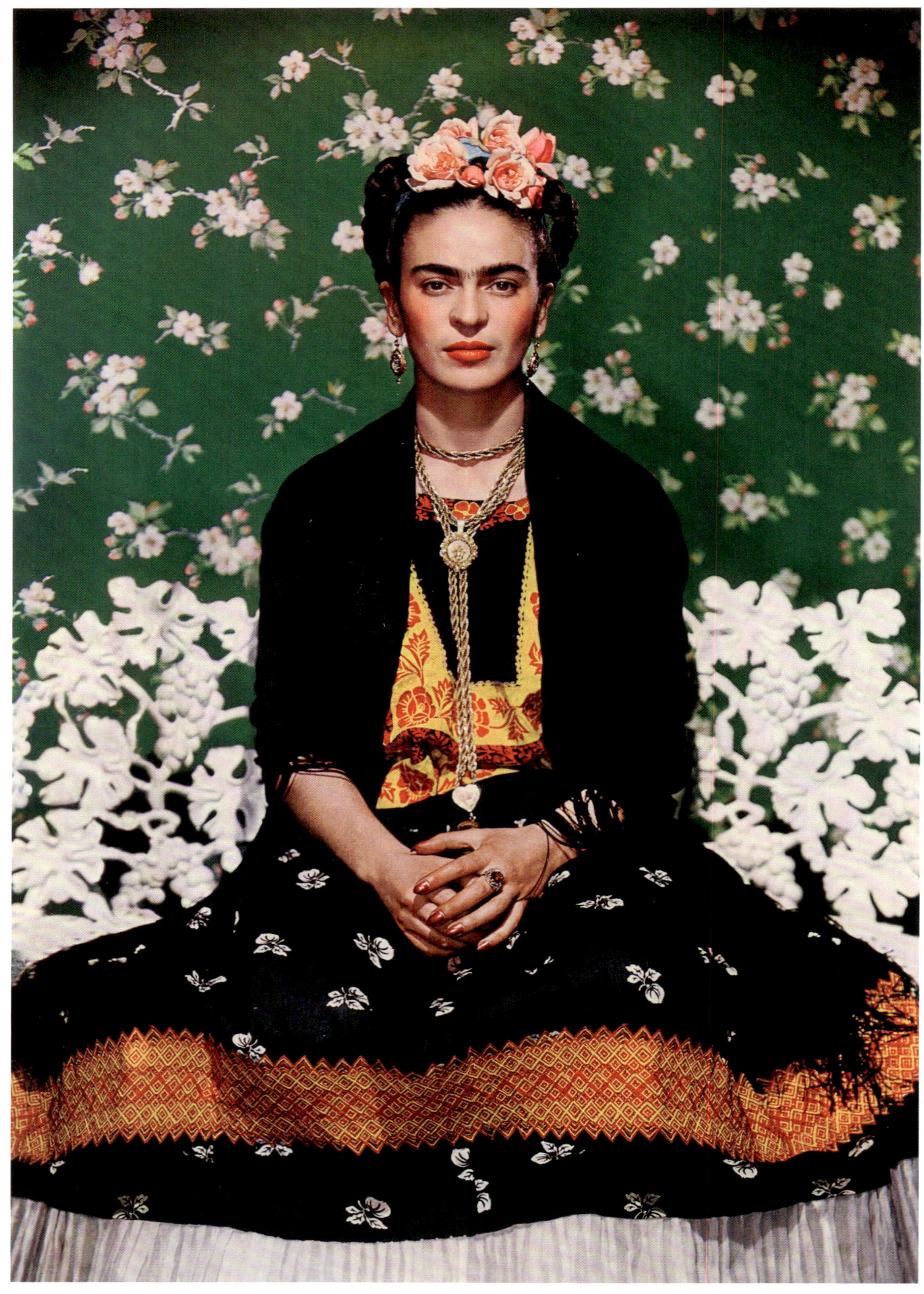

Nickolas Muray,
*Frida Kahlo on White
Bench, New York*, 1939.

opposite
Frida Kahlo, *Frida
and Diego Rivera*, 1931.

FRIDA KAHLO

DIEGO AND FRIDA

By 1940, Frida Kahlo's career had taken off, but her personal life was falling apart. It was under these circumstances that she produced one of her greatest paintings: *Self-Portrait with Thorn Necklace and Hummingbird*.

Eleven years before, she had married Diego Rivera, a world-renowned Mexican muralist and painter who was twenty-one years her senior. Referred to as simply 'Diego and Frida',[1] the couple were under intense media scrutiny from the start of their marriage.

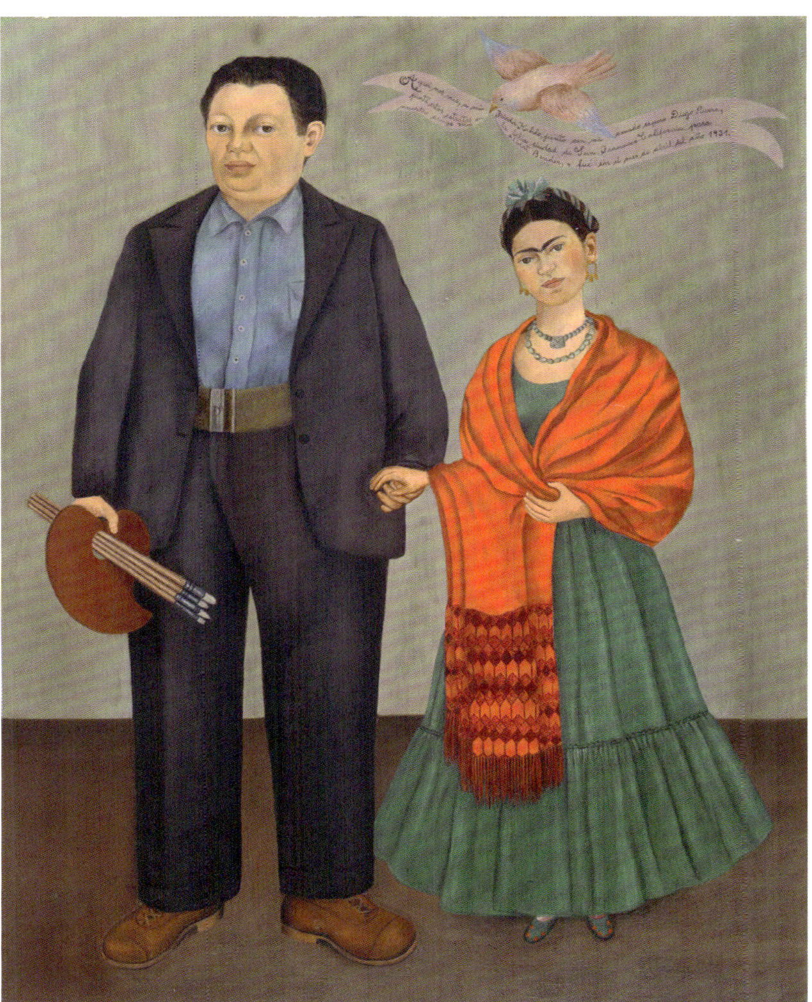

Their physical difference was constantly referenced, and this is made evident in Kahlo's wedding portrait of 1931 (actually painted two years after their nuptials in 1929), where Rivera is gigantic next to his tiny wife.

The disparity in size could also refer to their career status. Kahlo, an unknown artist, nods deferentially to Rivera, while he confidently stares out at us, the tools of his trade in his hand and his feet firmly planted on the ground, seemingly anchoring his wife with his bulk.

MEXICANIDAD

The Mexican Revolution (November 1910– December 1920) ended the dictatorship of Porfirio Díaz and established a constitutional republic. It was in this new climate that artists began to experiment with themes of Mexican identity.

Kahlo, like other contemporary Mexican artists, was deeply influenced by *Mexicanidad*, a form of romantic nationalism that emerged after the revolution, which emphasized indigenous cultures and moved away from colonialist aesthetics.

She chose to wear traditional Mexican peasant clothing to highlight her heritage: long colourful skirts, huipils (a sort of slipover blouse), rebozos (scarves), intricate headdresses and a wide range of indigenous jewellery.[2] Her appearance was a political statement in and of itself, and she constructed her identity to show allegiance with Mexican nationalists,[3] but also to reflect her own mixed-race heritage (she was of Mexican and German descent).

LIKE A RIBBON AROUND A BOMB

Rivera encouraged her to explore her own Mexican identity and heritage in her art, and she had an influence on him in return, who began to incorporate more personal and emotional elements into his practice.

Frida and Diego's relationship has to be one of the most obsessive and tumultuous in art history

Their marriage was an open one: they both took lovers, in Frida's case, both men and women, and most famously, perhaps, Leon Trotsky. In Diego's case, his lovers were young artists infatuated with his fame. Frida and Diego's relationship has to be one of the most obsessive and tumultuous in art history, their infatuation, passion and devotion matched by jealousy, anger and betrayal. Emotions which would be channelled directly (and honestly) into Frida's work.

In 1938, following a period of intense relationship problems, Frida had a life-changing trip when she spent three months in New York, away from Mexico, Rivera and the endless drama that came with him. It was there that she had her first solo show, arranged by the Surrealist André Breton, which was a huge success.

She had another solo show in Paris in January 1939, which was also a critical triumph. The Louvre bought one of her pieces (the first 20th-century Mexican work in their collection), and the Surrealists 'adopted' her, with Breton describing her painting as 'a ribbon around a bomb'.[4] The affection was not mutual, however, and she wrote in a letter to a friend: 'this bunch of coocoo lunatics and very stupid surrealists, who are so crazy "intellectual" and rotten that I can't even stand them anymore'.[5]

DIVORCE

During Frida's absence in Europe, Diego had also enjoyed his 'independence' and conducted numerous affairs. This was part and parcel

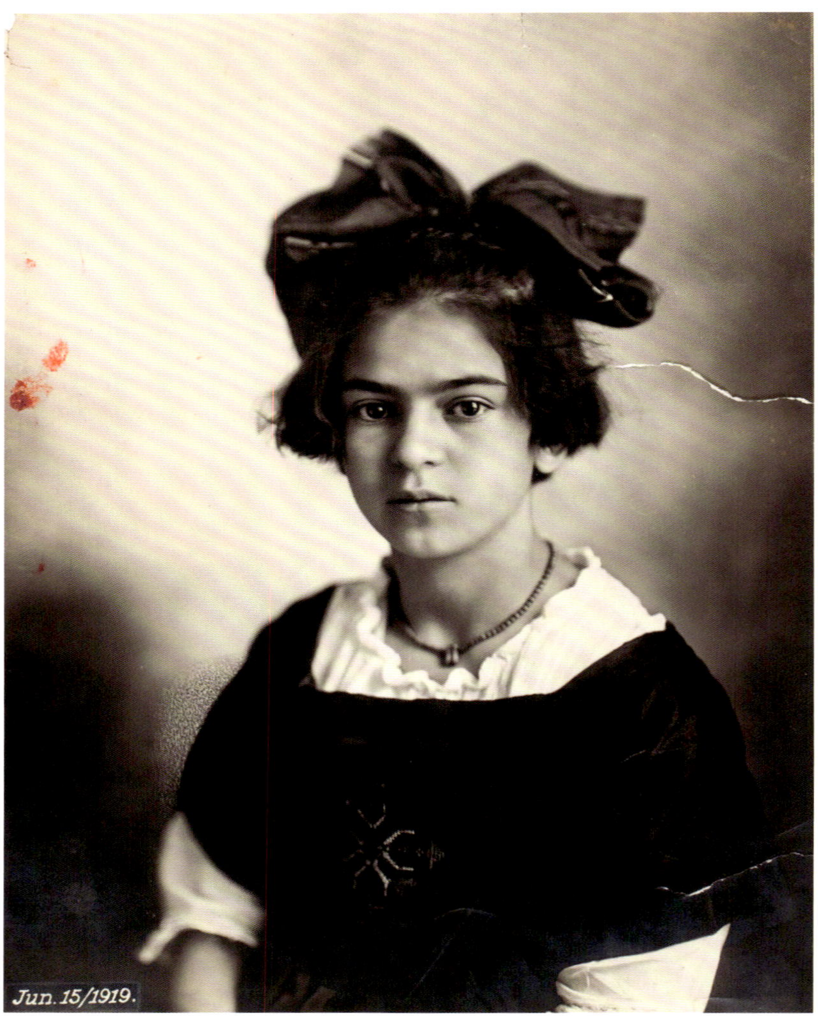

of their non-monogamous marriage, but this time he had crossed the line by having an affair with Kahlo's sister, an unforgivable act.

Their relationship, already fragile, started to implode, and in November 1939 Rivera initiated divorce proceedings.[6]

Kahlo was distraught after their separation, and as was often the case for her in times of anguish, there followed a period of intense creativity. She began to produce quarter-length self-portraits, as her agent advised her they were easier to sell,[7] which proved to be the case.

Frida Kahlo aged twelve. Photo by her father, Guillermo Kahlo.

INFLUENCES

Her interest in portraiture can be traced back to her father, a brilliant photographer who would take pictures of Frida, looking straight at the camera with characteristic defiance, from a very young age. It is a direct gaze that would be replicated throughout her career.

Her mother was a devout Catholic, and although Frida rejected religion, Catholic imagery filtered down into her self-portraits. Often, she would use thorns as a metaphor for martyrdom, and like the Catholic saints her mother kept on her wall, Kahlo would depict herself expressionless.

A further major influence was ex-votos, inexpensive paintings by self-taught artists on small panels, often made of tin. Frida had a huge collection of them, and her works would emulate this style of folk art in their pared-down aesthetics, their lack of realism or perspective and their use of allegory and personal narrative.

Ex-votos are deeply personal images that are offered to saints as a thank you for

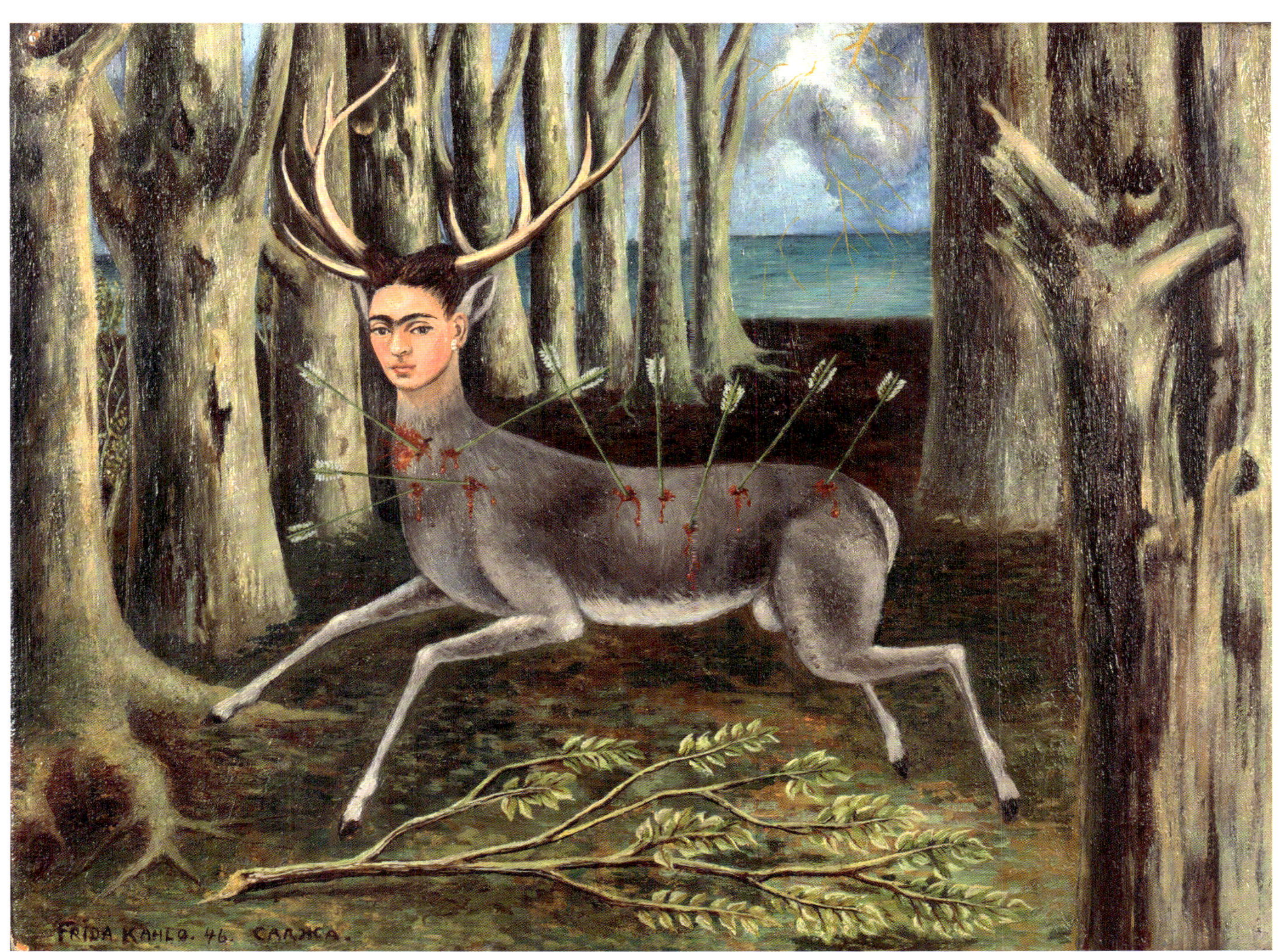

   SELF-PORTRAIT WITH THORN NECKLACE AND HUMMINGBIRD

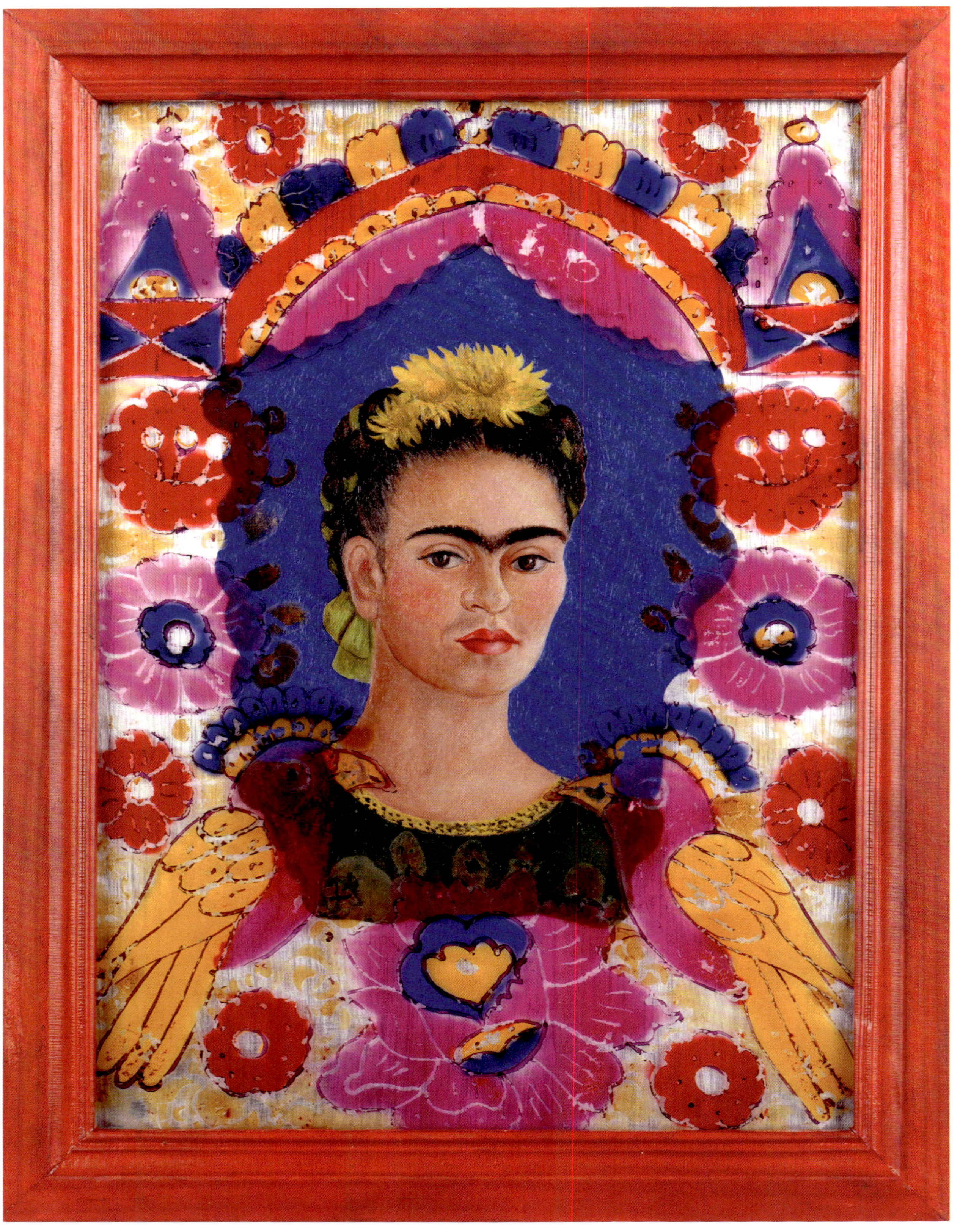

answered prayers. Almost any subject is possible for gratitude, from finding a missing pet to surviving an operation, and there is often an unexpected surreal quality: saints float above the dying, donkeys fly through the air and limbs appear out of nowhere.

THE PAINTING

Self-Portrait with Thorn Necklace and Hummingbird is a small painting that shows Kahlo wearing the traditional outfit worn by indigenous Tehuantepec women. As in the earlier marriage portrait, she – alongside many other post-revolutionary Mexican artists and intellectuals at that time – was celebrating the indigenous heritage and imagery that had for so long been marginalized in Mexican culture and art.

In most of her self-portraits, she presents herself holding a strong, challenging gaze, and in this painting, at first glance, it would seem so too. Kahlo appears to look straight at us, which in her other paintings creates a sense of engagement, but here her gaze is slightly downcast, looking past us to the distance, which creates not only a barrier but also a more introspective portrait. There is a sense of inner turmoil, and we

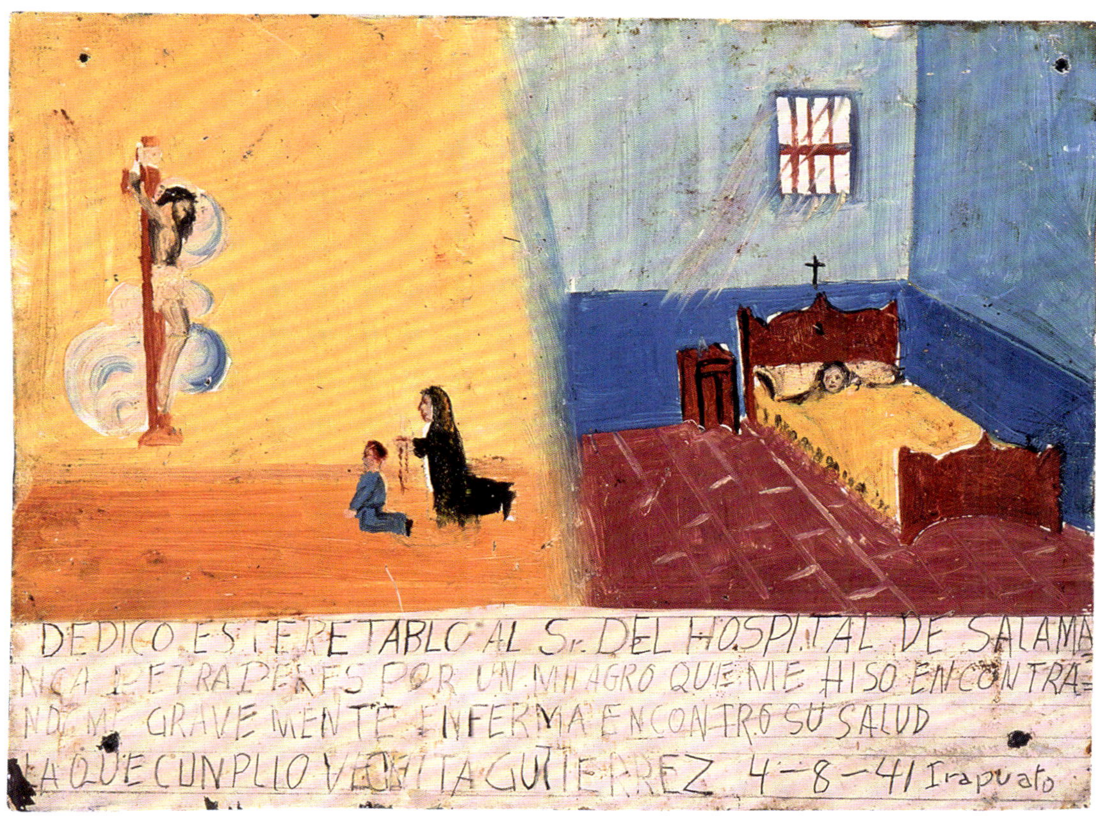

opposite
Frida Kahlo,
The Frame, 1938.

Unknown artist, Exvoto
Devocionario Señor
del Hospital, n.d.

are encouraged to consider her private thoughts as she patiently endures the pain of her thorn necklace.

The painting is loaded with symbols, but the dominant and titular symbol is the thorn necklace, an allusion to Christ's crown of thorns that places Kahlo, rather dramatically, in the role of a martyr.[8] Much like most depictions of Christ, she appears unfazed by the thorns that pierce her neck as they spread out their roots, strangling her and cutting into her skin.

Hanging from the necklace is a dead hummingbird, its wings echoing the shape of her eyebrows. The hummingbird is often seen in Latin culture as a symbol of strength through life's struggles, and even today, there is a thriving illegal market in dead hummingbirds as love charms.[9]

There is no room to breathe in the image; it oozes claustrophobia, as plants and animals crowd around an indifferent Kahlo. A black cat emerges over her shoulder, a standard symbol of bad luck in European folklore. On her other shoulder, a monkey plays with the thorn necklace, making her bleed further, but she doesn't flinch. In real life, Kahlo was always surrounded by a menagerie of exotic animals, and Rivera had given her a spider monkey as a gift. By showing the monkey inflicting pain, was she using it as a stand-in for Rivera?

The overall feeling of the painting is deeply pessimistic, but perhaps an element of hope is the two butterfly hair clips, and the two hovering dragonflies above them. In Christian art, butterflies were used to symbolize the resurrection of Jesus, and dragonflies were more broadly seen as a form of metamorphosis or change.[10] It could be read here as Kahlo's resurrection or rebirth from the confines of her chaotic and tempestuous marriage. That rebirth, however, was not to last.

REMARRIAGE

Rivera, like Kahlo, did not get over the divorce, and bombarded her daily with marriage proposals, until finally she acquiesced. Frida and Diego were remarried in 1940, less than a year after their divorce. Frida insisted on two conditions: that she should be financially independent and that the couple 'would have no sexual intercourse'.[11] Despite this, their second marriage was just as tumultuous as the first, but they stayed together until her death in 1954.

Frida Kahlo's life, including her marriage, is often seen as a distraction from her art, but the thing about Kahlo is that, despite Rivera, she drove her own narrative. She constructed her identity around her politics, ethnicity and disability, her pain, emotions and experiences, in a profound and powerful way that we can all understand.

FRIDA KAHLO

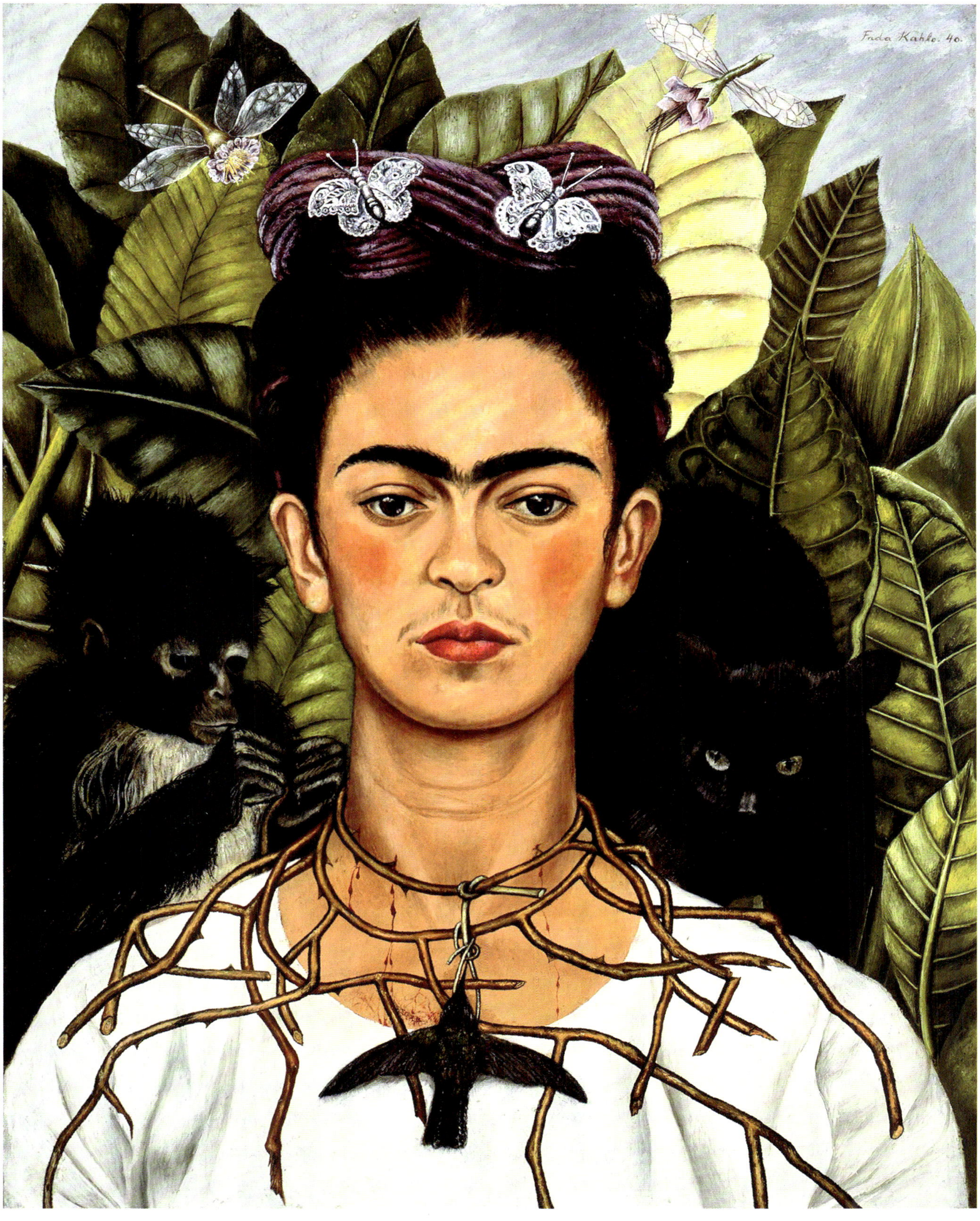

EDWARD HOPPER

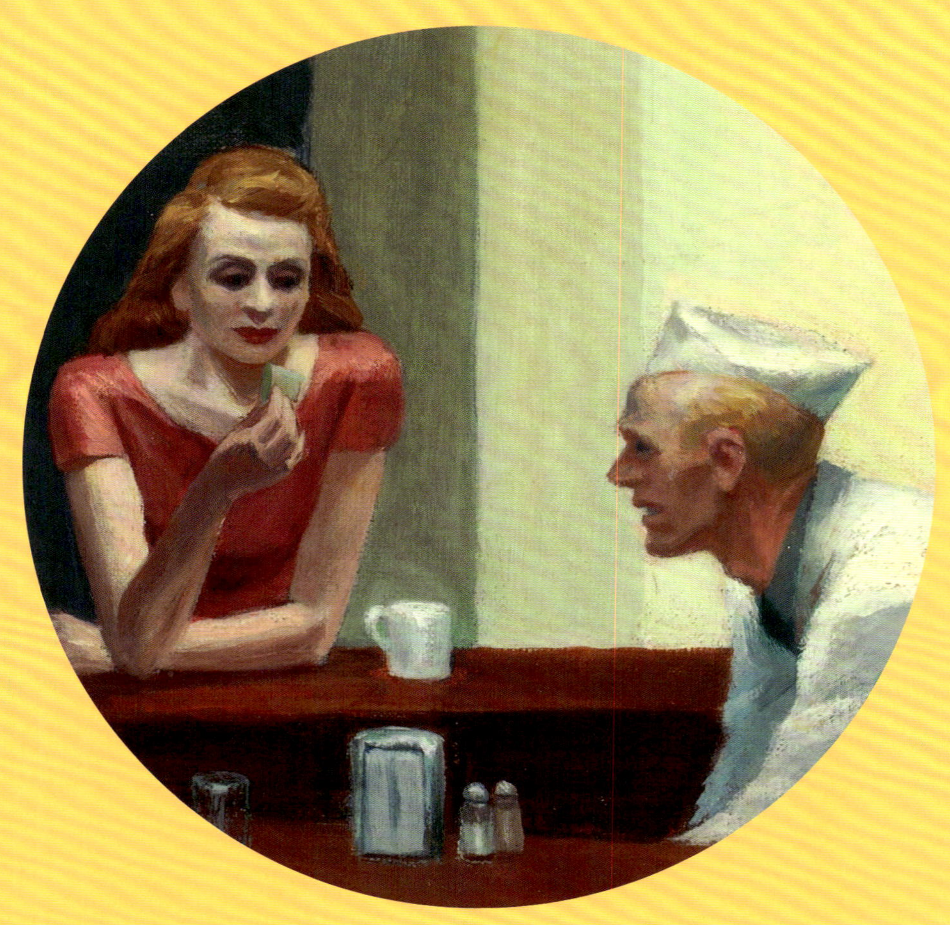

NIGHTHAWKS

1942

NEW YORK STORIES

Edward Hopper's world was New York, one of the most populous cities on Earth, and *Nighthawks* suggests the isolation that he felt to be part of the fabric of urban life.

He began working on the painting in December 1941, shortly after the Japanese air force launched the attack on the American naval base in Pearl Harbor, Hawaii. This ensured America's involvement in the Second World War on the side of the Allies. Hopper's wife Josephine wrote in her diary at the time: 'Ed refused to take any interest in our very likely prospect of being bombed … He's doing a new canvas and simply can't be interrupted!'[1]

The painting was completed on 21 January 1942, by which time America had declared war on Germany. While *Nighthawks* does not make overt references to it, the themes of loneliness, introspection and urban alienation resonate with the emotional and psychological impact of knowing that your country is at war.

To prepare for air raid attacks (which in fact never happened), New York had already initiated blackout drills before Hopper started on the painting, and lights were often dimmed in public spaces. Streets emptied out due to widespread fear, meaning Hopper's city was often ominously dark, and silent. The feeling of dread affecting many Americans surely infused the painting.

DIFFERENT WORLDS

Edward Hopper was born in 1882 in Nyack, a suburb of New York about an hour's drive from Manhattan, into a solidly middle-class Baptist family who were supportive of his artistic side.

At the age of twelve, Hopper was already 6 feet tall (he would reach 6 ft 5 in. post-adolescence), but he was painfully shy, with loner tendencies,[2] and this sense of isolation continued into his adulthood. He spent most of his adult life in New York City, in a small walk-up apartment in Greenwich Village, sharing it with Josephine (Jo) after their marriage in 1924.

Jo Nivison was herself an accomplished artist and had a profound influence on Hopper's career, but they couldn't have been more different. Jo was sociable and loved entertaining; Edward was morose and introspective. It was not a happy marriage; they argued a lot, in some cases violently, and would often not talk to each other for days, so that much of their marriage was spent in silence. Despite this, they remained married for forty-three years, until Hopper's death in 1967.

Hopper's paintings were for a long time ignored by critics, while his fellow artists found fame. It was thanks to Jo that Hopper became a success: she introduced him to curators at the Brooklyn Museum, who eventually bought his painting *Mansard Roof* (1923), and launched

He was painfully shy, with loner tendencies

his career – for which, she said, he never thanked her.[3]

Their unhappy marriage almost certainly contributed to Hopper's signature depiction of figures who seem emotionally unresolved, couples who do not communicate, touch or display any affection, relationships which are ambiguous and characters who do not interact with each other in any way. Characters who may share the same space but inhabit different worlds.

CINEMA ON CANVAS

Compared with many artists I've looked at, it seems to me that Hopper was primarily influenced by the cinema, which from childhood on he went to several times a week. 'When I don't feel like painting,' he once said, 'I go to the movies for a week or more. I go on a regular movie binge.'[4] His paintings often have the feeling of a movie still, capturing singular emotionally charged moments that suggest a larger narrative outside the frame.

Hopper was taught by Robert Henri, a prominent figure in the realist 'Ashcan School', between 1900 and 1906. He urged Hopper to visit theatres and cinemas to observe people enjoying communal activities. However, Hopper chose to focus on the solitude of individuals, capturing moments of quiet anticipation as they waited for the performance to begin or the lights to dim.[5]

We see this in an early etching, *The Balcony* (1928), depicting two isolated figures looking down on an unseen screen, as well as, of course, his 1939 masterpiece, *New York Movie*.

He often went to the cinema alone, at night, in search of inspiration, and it was the films noir shot in Hollywood in the 1930s and 1940s that Hopper really loved – films whose aesthetic was itself derived from German Expressionist cinema and its use of stark lighting.

Films like Fritz Lang's *Scarlet Street* (1945), or Billy Wilder's *Double Indemnity* (1944), feature the kind of lonely characters navigating morally ambiguous situations that we see in Hopper's work. Aesthetically, the diner in *Scarlet Street* mirrors the isolation and stark lighting of Hopper's diner.

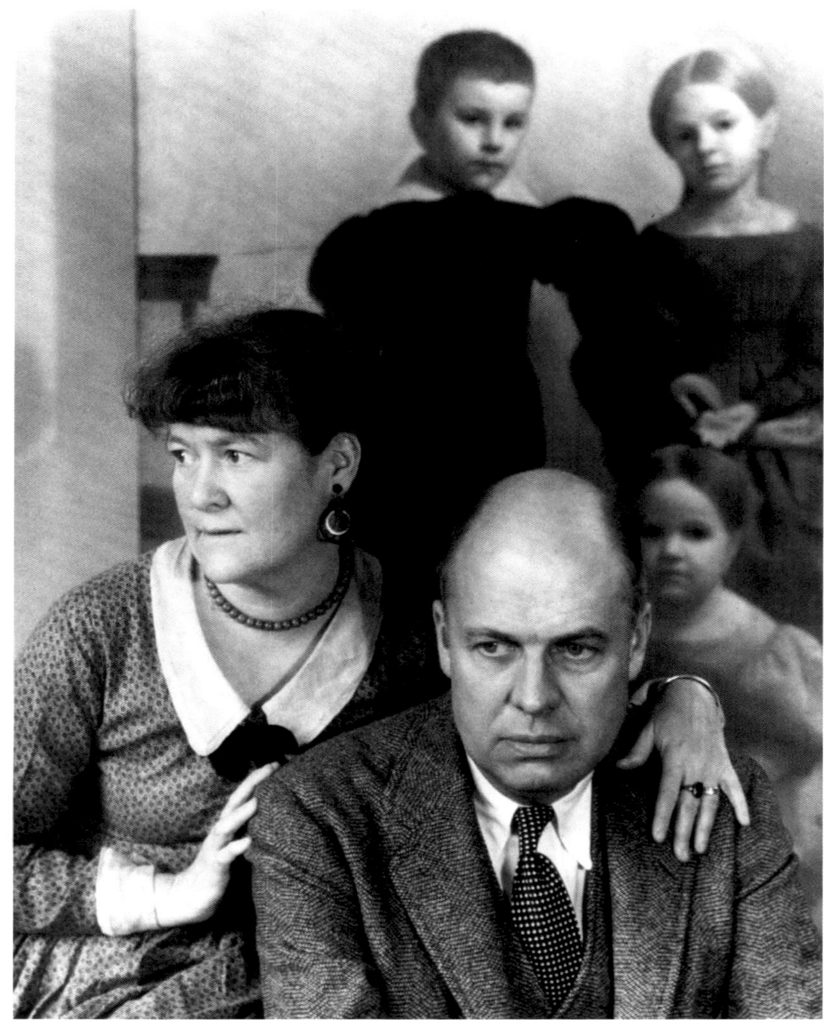

EDWARD HOPPER

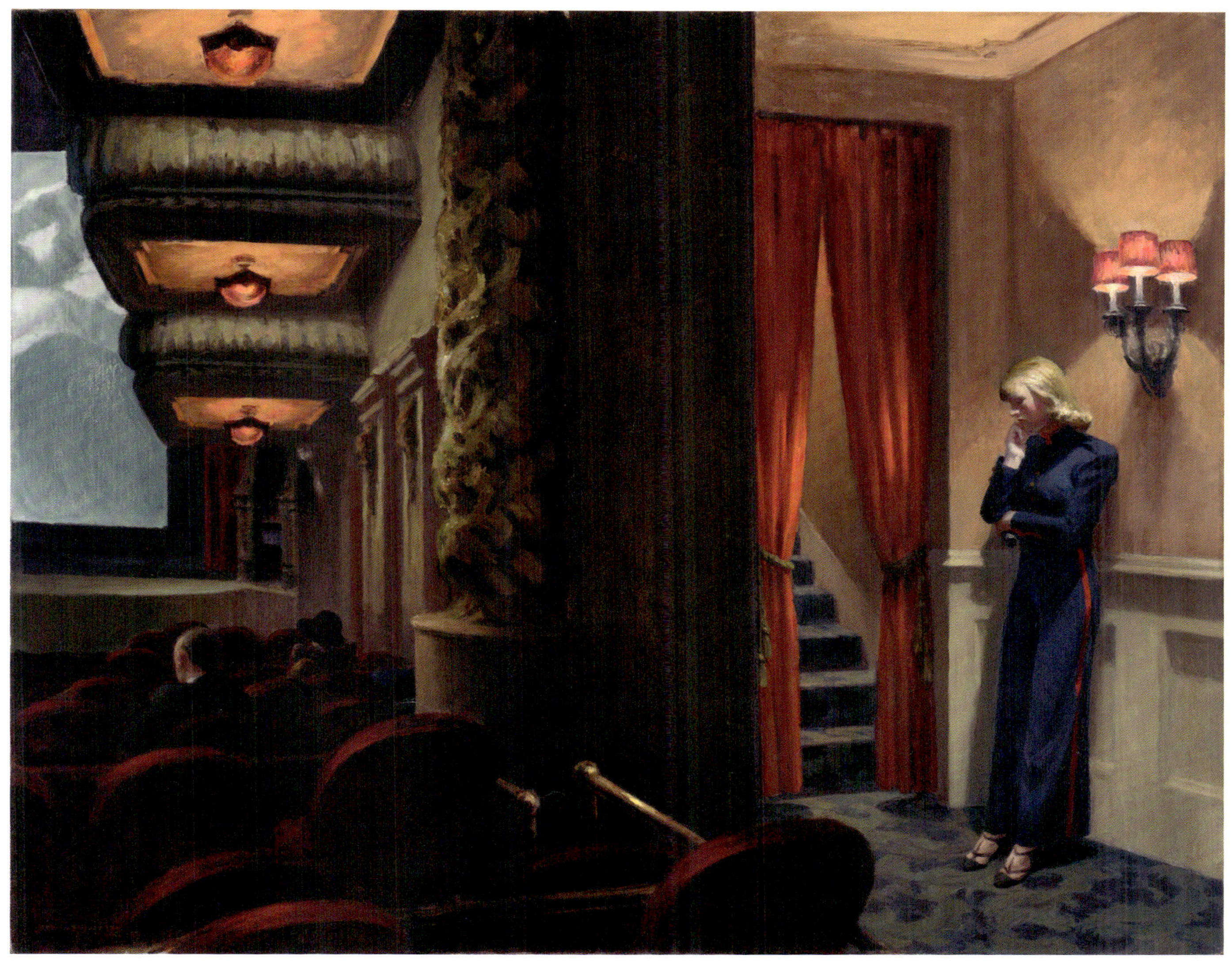

*His paintings often
have the feeling of
a movie still*

With classic film noir, it is all about the tone, as it is with Hopper's paintings. There is a voyeuristic streak in both the films and his paintings, the characters in both are often emotionally or physically isolated, and they take a familiar narrative element, moody visuals, existential themes and psychological complexities and apply layer after layer of possible meaning, leaving the viewer guessing about the backstory or outcome, engaging them in an implied story without resolution.

SYMBIOSIS

Ernest Hemingway's short story *The Killers* (1927) is considered the main inspiration for *Nighthawks*. The story opens with two thugs entering a diner in search of their next victim. In a curious symbiotic relationship between Hopper and cinema, the classic 1946 movie version of the book was inspired by the aesthetics of Hopper's *Nighthawks*.

The primary influence of film noir can be seen in what many consider a classic of the genre, John Huston's *The Maltese Falcon* (1941), released the year before Hopper completed *Nighthawks*. In it, Humphrey Bogart bears a striking resemblance in attitude and dress to the man with his back to us at the bar in *Nighthawks*.

Alfred Hitchcock also cited Edward Hopper as an influence, with films such as *Rear Window* (1954) having the same voyeuristic quality we find in Hopper. Likewise, the aesthetic and imagery of *Psycho* (1960) was directly influenced by Hopper's 1925 painting

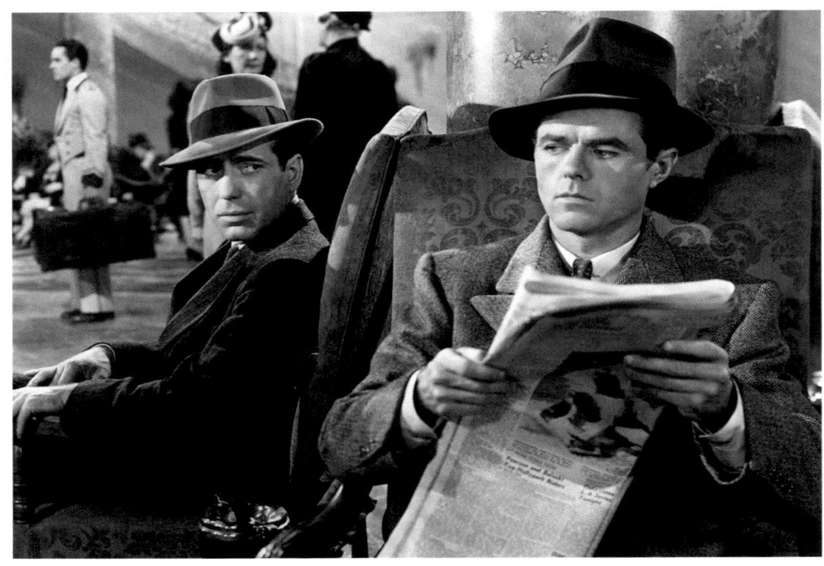

House by the Railroad, as was Terrence Malick's *Days of Heaven* (1978).

Modern directors such as Wim Wenders, Todd Haynes and Steve McQueen have taken inspiration from Edward Hopper, whose ability to suggest a narrative extending far beyond a single frame reveals a cinematic sensibility so profound that in another life, he might have been a film director himself.

A WORLD SHUT DOWN

Nighthawks reminds us of a scene on an illuminated stage, as if we are watching in a darkened theatre. The composition is directly influenced by set design, stage lighting and the kind of cropping and angles we often see in film noir.

There are nineteen surviving sketches for *Nighthawks*, but Hopper would have probably done many more. He planned *Nighthawks* as a film director would, with storyboards. He would use life drawings to plot out the painting, and we know from Jo's notes that she posed for the woman and Edward posed for the three men. (The title of the painting also came from

Humphrey Bogart (left)
in *The Maltese Falcon*
(dir. John Huston, 1941).

opposite
Edward Hopper,
Study for Nighthawks,
1941/42.

EDWARD HOPPER

Nighthawks reminds us of a scene on an illuminated stage

Jo, who described the male character as having a hawk-beaked nose[6]).

The artist uses strong diagonal lines that extend offscreen to imply a world beyond the painting, and colour to guide us into to the centre of the image, and the four figures in the painting. The deeper red and green tones outside the diner contrast sharply with the vibrant yellow interior, prompting our eyes to move from the external surroundings to the inner space.

There is no life outside the diner and the few details are minimal. We can see a cash register in the deserted store across the way, and an ad above the diner, but the buildings around are empty. This is a world shut down.

Hopper's use of windows in his paintings serve both as a compositional device and a symbolic tool to explore themes of isolation,

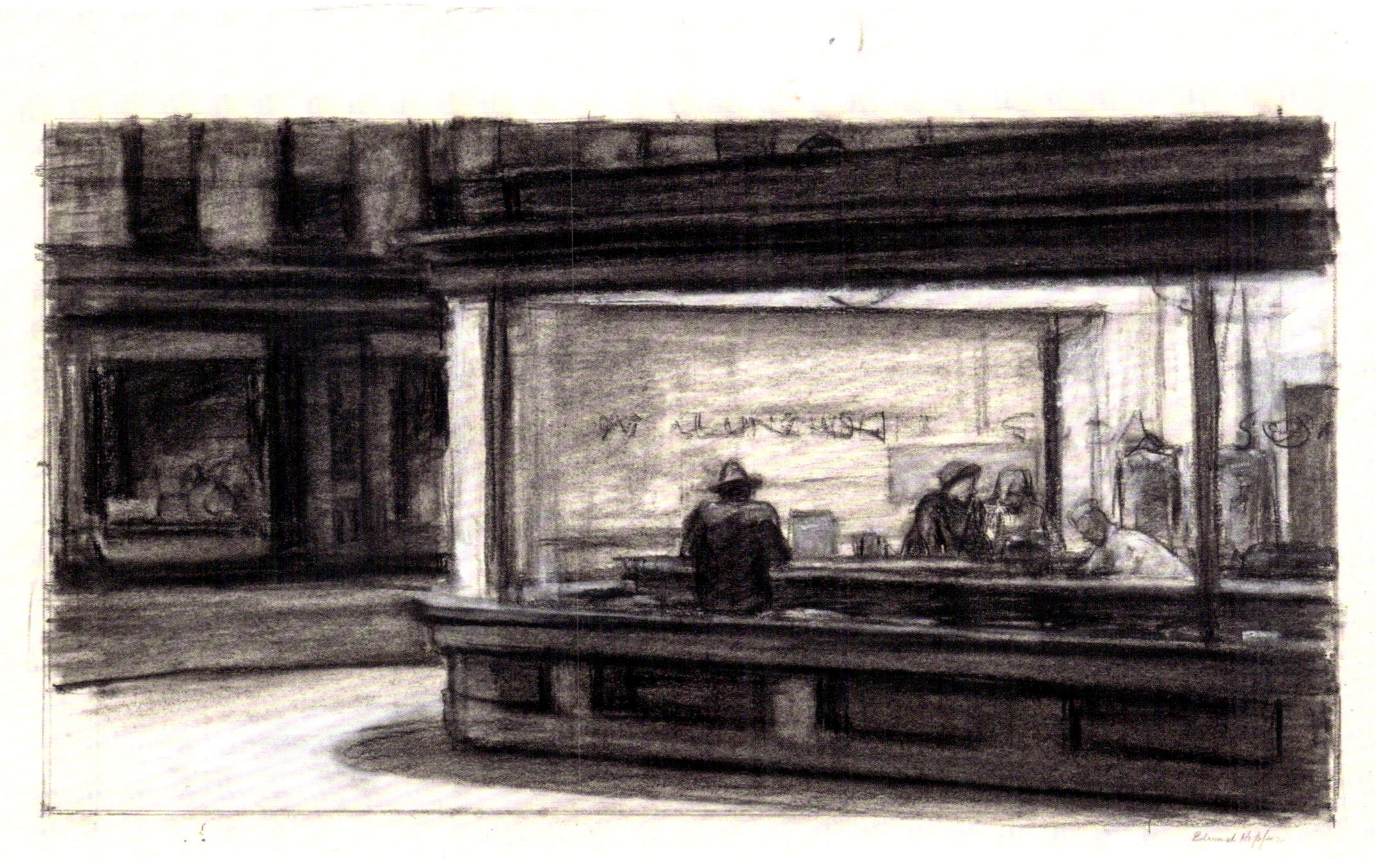

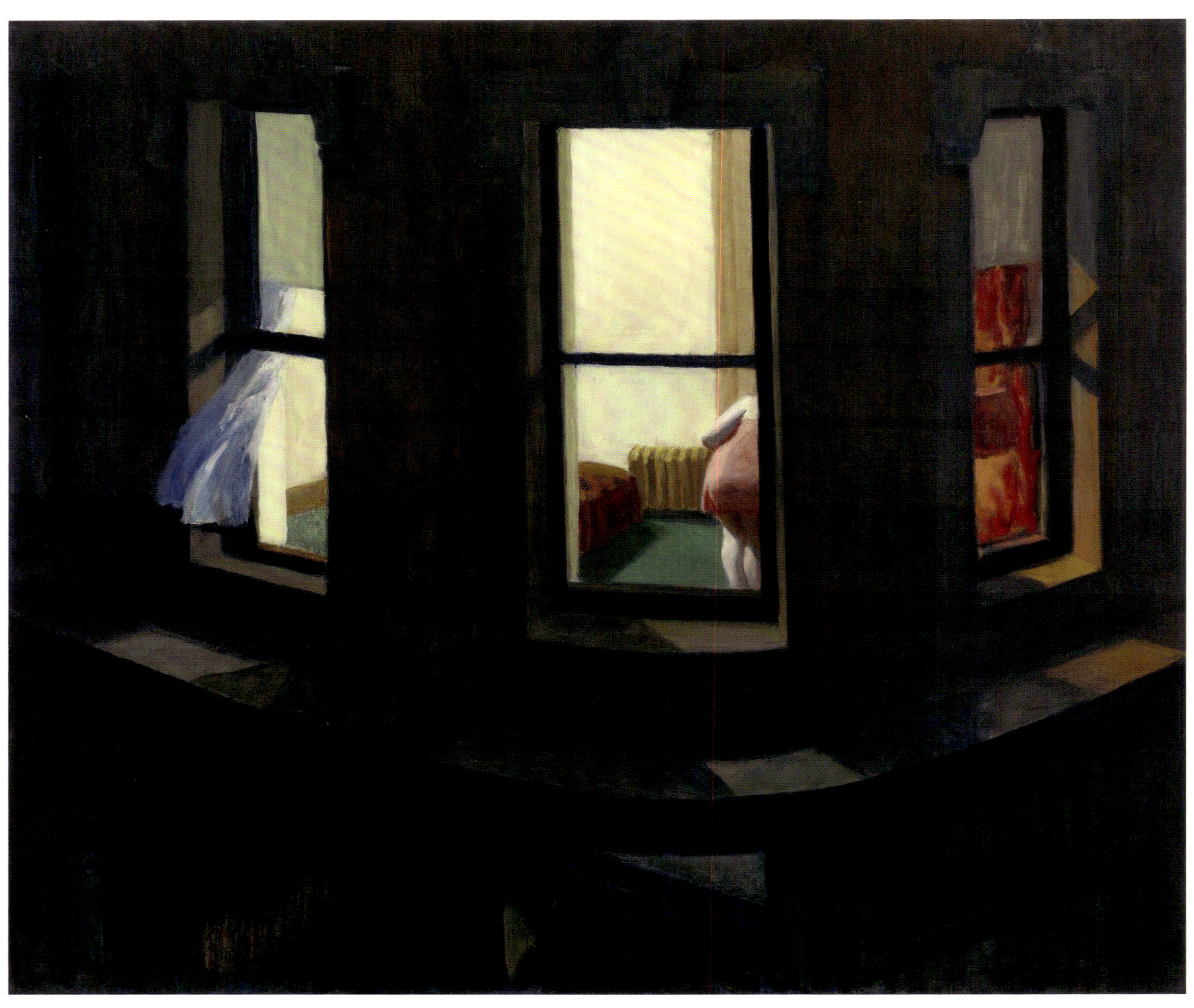

EDWARD HOPPER

voyeurism and the interplay between public and private spaces. In a painting like *Night Windows* (1928), they suggest a longing for escape or connection, but in *Nighthawks* they serve as a framing device, reinforcing the confinement of Hopper's figures.

Hopper's paintings represent specific times of day and are often titled with a time (*Eleven A.M.* (1926), *Morning Sun* (1952)). Night was a particular favourite, however (*Summer Evening* (1947), *Night Windows*), and is often equated with sex or anxiety in his work – or sometimes both.[7]

In Hopper's diner, the only light source is artificial, although there are no visible light fixtures within the painting. The lighting is exceptionally bright and intense, which contrasts strongly with the shadows of the surrounding streets; it gives an eerie glow and contributes to the painting's overall surreal atmosphere.

If you are looking for a door to welcome us in – or let the figures out – there isn't one. The diner is hermetically sealed, effectively keeping the viewer at bay.

The characters are in their own worlds, and as is usual with Hopper, none of the figures in the painting appear to be engaged in conversation or interacting with one another. They seem lost in their own thoughts, isolated despite their physical proximity. This absence of interaction heightens the feeling of loneliness and disconnect, emphasizing the theme of urban alienation. Tension somehow radiates from them.

The couple in the painting are physically close yet psychologically miles apart – in fact, who's to say they are even together? We think that their hands are touching but they are not. It could be that the woman has just arrived, as only her coffee cup is steaming. Her companion holds an unlit cigarette, as she fingers a matchbook as if deciding whether or not to light it.

The isolation of the solitary man with his back to us is accentuated by the couple. A closer look shows that he is holding a glass with his right hand, and he has a newspaper folded flat underneath his left. The front page, no doubt full of news of the war.

And for whom is the random glass to the left of the waiter? Maybe it's for us.

The sense of alienation and longing depicted in the painting is easy to understand, but the power of the work, and the reason it resonates with so many of us, lies in the ambiguity of the characters' action – or lack thereof.

WE ARE NOT ALONE

The painting was bought by the prestigious Art Institute of Chicago for $3,000 in 1942, and it is still there today. It is seen as an image of loneliness, isolation and quiet anguish by some, but others find in it a sense of comfort. Every visitor to the museum will have a different idea; the artist himself was cagey about the meaning, once saying, 'It's probably a reflection of my own loneliness, I don't know.'[8]

Edward Hopper was the quiet everyman of American painting, but he was also complicated and troubled, an intellectual who struggled to find inspiration, and grappled with meaning.

He met Jo in his forties, and she was his first significant relationship. It must have seemed that his years of loneliness were over when they married, but as many people discover, you can be with someone and still feel utterly alone.

In fact, ironically, this painting, which is seen to depict loneliness so well, shows us that when it comes to loneliness, we are not alone.

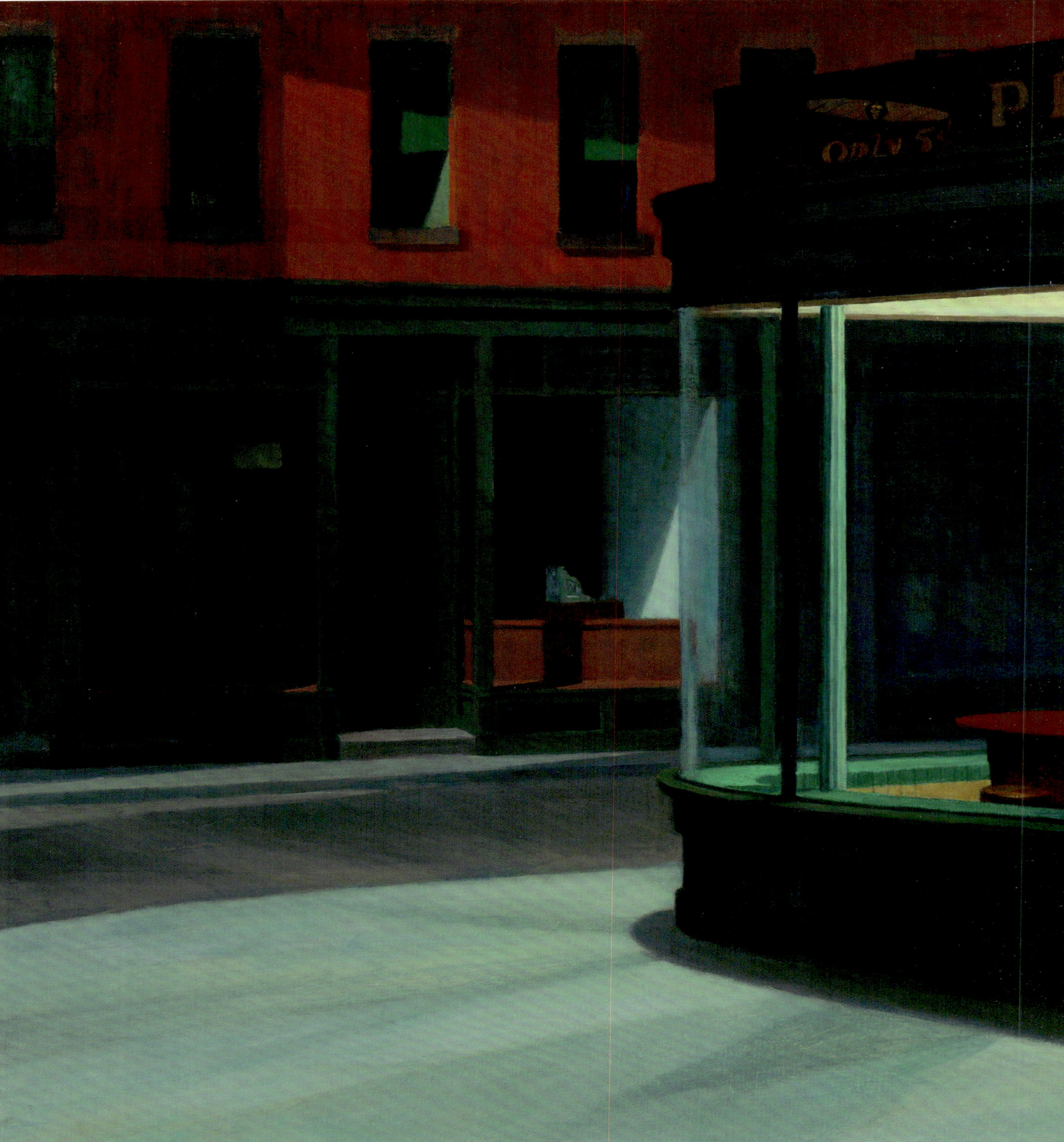

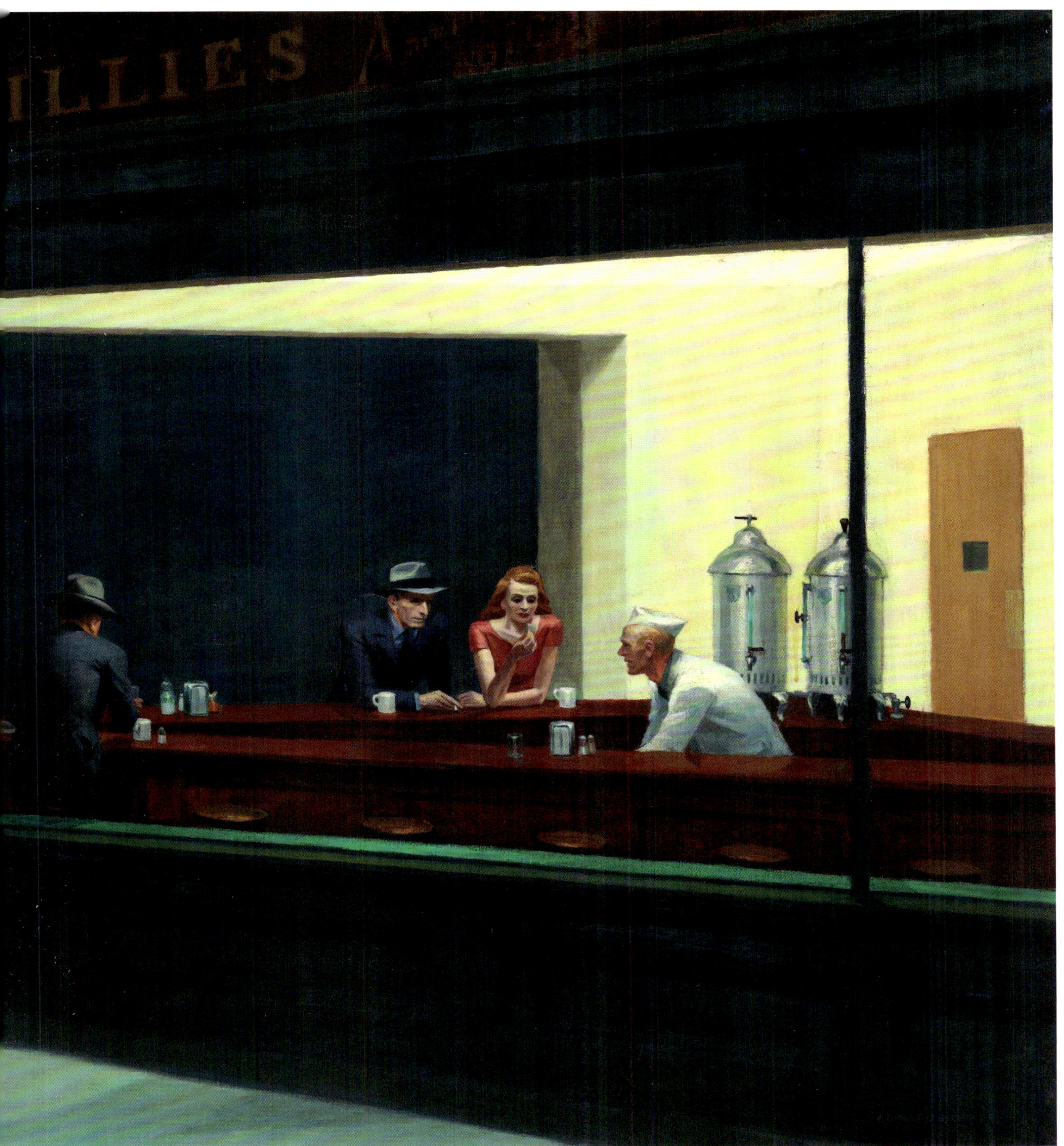

ILLIES

FRANCIS BACON

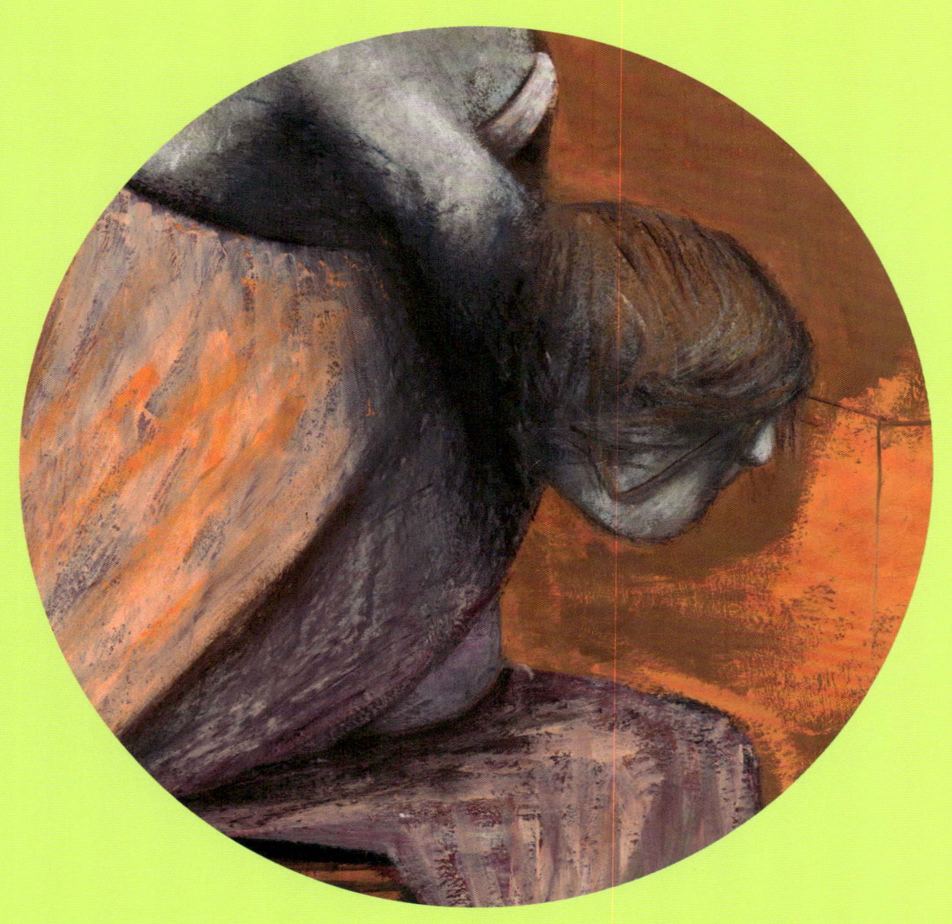

THREE STUDIES FOR FIGURES
AT THE BASE OF A CRUCIFIXION

1944

THE ARTIST AS MYTH-MAKER

When Francis Bacon first showed *Three Studies* in London in April 1945, it was the final months of the Second World War and the city was a bombsite. London had experienced human suffering on an unimaginable scale and was still in the grip of intense anxiety. Auschwitz had been liberated in January of that year, and the horrific images of the concentration camps were being seen for the first time. With these three figures, Bacon managed to convey the terror and horror that had penetrated the lives of Europeans for six years.

But the roots of *Three Studies*' frenzied and violent aesthetic were not just attributable to the Second World War. Bacon was thirty-five years old when he debuted the triptych, and the seeds of violence existed within him already. His tendency to lean into the darker side of human nature can be traced back further to a torturous and abusive childhood, to a risky love life and to an addiction to alcoholism, gambling and sadomasochism. 'When you paint,' he once said, 'you are painting not only the subject… you are painting yourself as well.'[1]

Three Studies caused a sensation when it went on display, and from that point on, Bacon rarely discussed his previous work, or indeed life. The artist preferred the myth that Francis Bacon the wit, the raconteur, the flaneur, arrived on the art scene fully formed in April 1945 with *Three Studies*, which wasn't true at all.

DUBLIN TO BERLIN TO LONDON

Most of the myths surrounding Bacon can be traced back to the artist himself. It was common, in an era when homosexuality was a criminal offence, for gay people to hide much of their lives. But Bacon was a master at controlling his own narrative through a combination of revelation and mystification (and by destroying almost all his pre-1945 works). As much planning went into the creation of Bacon the man as it did into his creative process.

He was born in Dublin, Ireland, in 1909 to wealthy English parents whose business was horse breeding. Bacon was incapacitated by shyness as a child, and to his bullying father's disgust, he was noticeably effeminate. He knew he wasn't 'normal' from an early age and grew up lonely and isolated.[2] He also suffered from debilitating asthma, which would affect him his whole life.

Bacon later recalled how his father tried to 'make a man of him' by arranging for his small son to be regularly horsewhipped by the grooms and stable boys. He got his revenge when he seduced the same grooms, and so began his fixation on working-class men, alongside a well-documented equating of love and pleasure with violence.

After being thrown out of the family home as a teenager, Bacon took himself off to Berlin and Paris, where he was introduced

Francis Bacon,
*Three Studies
for Figures at the
Base of a Crucifixion*
(detail), 1944.

to the avant-garde art scene as well as the
seedy and decadent nightclub scene. His art
would be fuelled by extremes: he was an
alcoholic and a compulsive gambler, and his
partners were often violent petty criminals,
two of whom later committed suicide.

During the Second World War, Bacon
was pronounced unfit for service because
of his asthma, but as a volunteer in the Civil
Defence Service his duties included the
recovery of the dead. As he sifted through the
rubble in the gruesome search for dead and
dismembered bodies, the copious dust would
set off violent asthma attacks.

Likewise, at the outset of his career,
during the damp, wet winter months in
London, Bacon would struggle to breathe as
he painted in his cold, cramped studio. In so
many of his images, including *Three Studies*,
we see figures that are traditionally interpreted
as screaming, but they could also be interpreted
as gasping desperately for air, or suffocating.

Bacon's first ambition was to be an actor,[3]
but during the 1920s and '30s he became an
interior designer. He retained a sense of
drama and theatricality his whole adult life,
both with the staging and design of his work
and with the 'staging' of his personality.

Although he later refused to acknowledge
it, his experience with interior design
certainly honed his sensitivity to space and
structure, and to how objects relate to their
environment, as well as giving him an aesthetic
understanding of texture, colour and light.

'A' CRUCIFIXION

Three Studies was first shown at the Lefevre
Gallery in London, where it featured in a group
exhibition alongside works by prominent artists
such as Henry Moore, Graham Sutherland and
other well-known figures in the British art
scene (Bacon was a last-minute stand-in when
Ben Nicholson dropped out).

The work is painted on fibreboard, as
canvas was hard to get hold of during the war,
and Bacon completed it in less than two weeks
in his ground-floor flat in west London, which
was a studio by day and an illegal casino run
by Bacon and his former nanny, Jessie Lightfoot,
at night, attracting the low-life of London.

The most important word in the title *Three
Studies for Figures at the Base of a Crucifixion*
is also the shortest: 'a'. It is *a* crucifixion, not
the Crucifixion. While *Three Studies* may have

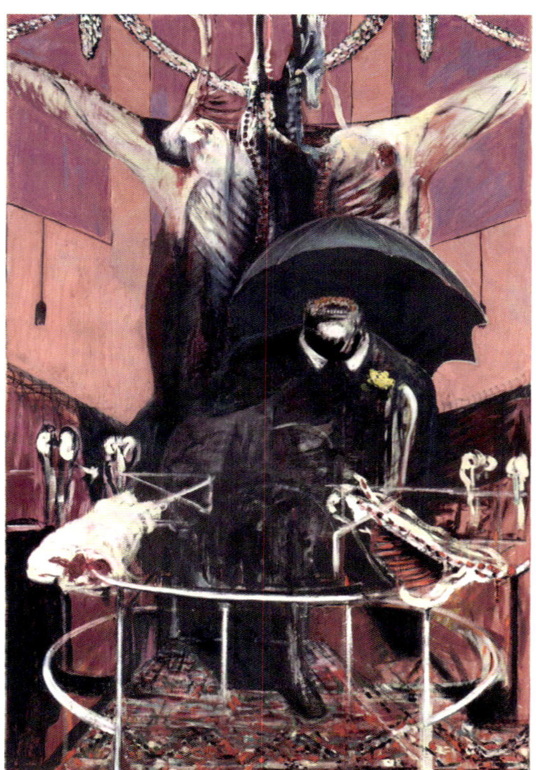

Francis Bacon,
Painting, 1946.

FRANCIS BACON

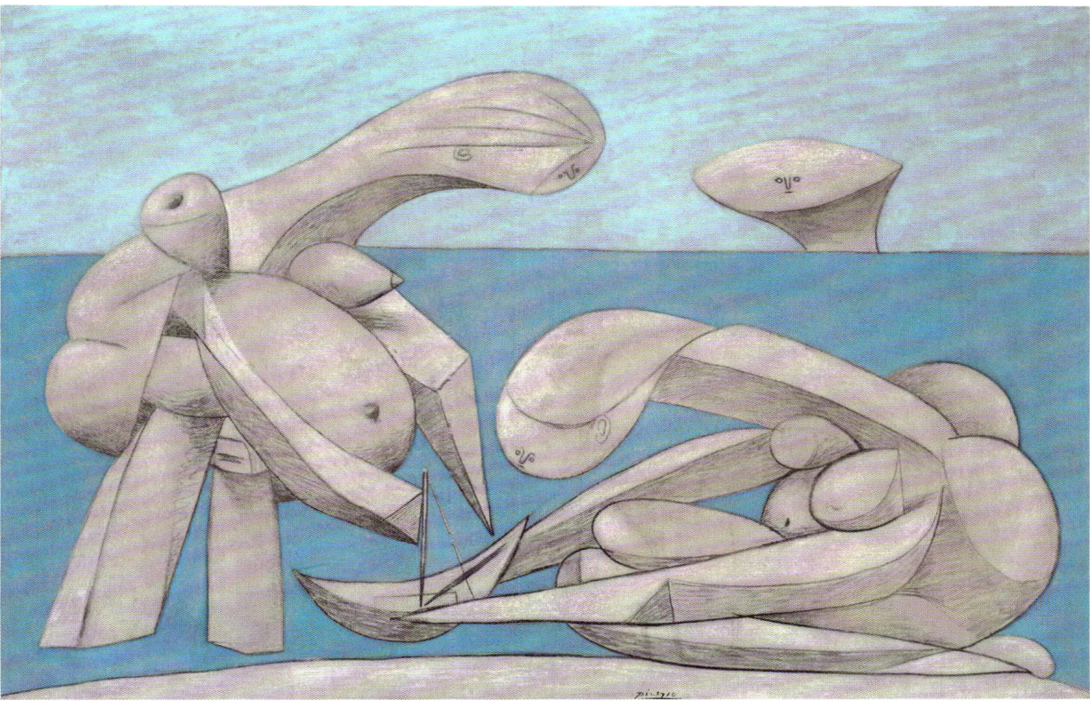

begun life as a representation of the Crucifixion scene, it soon turned into something completely different;[4] the concept of the Crucifixion became simply a framework for exploring complex human emotions.

By distorting the human figure, and employing abstract, emotionally intense imagery to strip back the narrative, Bacon focuses on the horror of human existence without redemption or salvation. The contorted image becomes less about a specific event than it is a universal depiction of anguish, horror, alienation and suffering.

VELÁZQUEZ AND OTHERS

It is really thanks to Pablo Picasso that Bacon even considered becoming an artist. He saw an exhibition of Picasso's work in Paris in 1927, and borrowed heavily from the Spanish artist's 'biomorphs' – abstract images or forms that reference living things, such as plants and the human body – for *Three Studies*, among other paintings.

It is common knowledge that Bacon was a Picasso and Velázquez obsessive, but less well known is the influence of Sutherland, one of the great 20th-century British painters and the first of a group of figurative artists that would include Bacon, Frank Auerbach and Lucian Freud.

At the time of the Lefevre Gallery group show, Sutherland was an established artist, but Bacon was just another unknown painter. They both understood the power of surrealistic imagery, however, and how to utilize abstraction to dramatic effect; we can certainly see parallels to *Three Studies* in Sutherland's earlier paintings of twisted organic shapes isolated against strong coloured backgrounds.

Where Sutherland was a practising Catholic, Bacon was a militant atheist. Historians assume that the format of a triptych

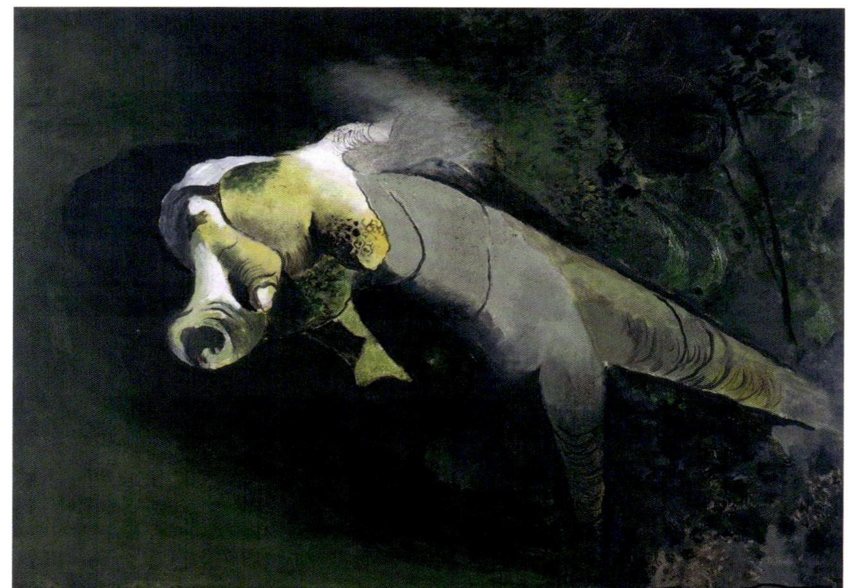

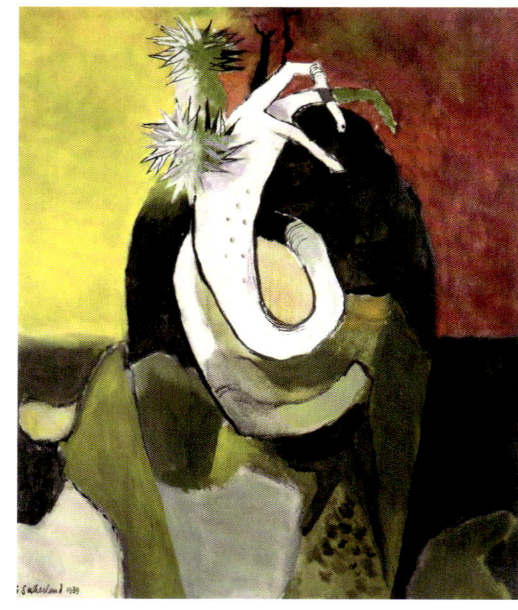

They both understood the power of surrealistic imagery

(which Bacon often used) is related to religious art, but in 1985 it was said that the triptych formula came from Abel Gance's film *Napoléon* (1927), the final scene of which is split across three screens.[5] Both Gance and Sergei Eisenstein were early cineastes Bacon revered, and their use of montage and superimposition informed his work. In 1993 Bacon made a rare admission: he had been inspired by Gance's film, and said he would have been a filmmaker if he hadn't been a painter.[6]

THE REEK OF HUMAN BLOOD

Many of Bacon's paintings were influenced by writers such as T. S. Eliot and W. B. Yeats, but it was the Greek tragedy *Oresteia* that he later cited as the major influence on *Three Studies*.[7] In the tragedy, Orestes is pursued by the Furies, three female deities of vengeance who punish human wrongdoing, and it is these three characters that are represented in the triptych. Although the work is no more an illustration of *Oresteia* than it is of a crucifixion, Bacon's stated aim was to represent how the book made him *feel* when he read it.[8]

Everything about *Three Studies* defies logic. We don't know if these hideous, animalistic creatures with phallic necks are victims of violence or perpetrators. Their distorted and dismembered bodies (a sight Bacon often saw as a volunteer wartime warden) evoke primal fears as they squirm and convulse in their abstract setting, where normal rules of logic, space and time do not apply.

The left figure, perched on a table-like structure, is the most human-like, and with its bowed head it could be a mourner. The central figure, where we would normally see Christ, has its mouth on its neck and is blindfolded. It is often traced back to

FRANCIS BACON

Matthias Grünewald's *Mocking of Christ* (1503–5),[9] a work that Bacon had a battered postcard of in his studio. This idea makes sense, but *Three Studies* likely referenced the walking wounded of London, too.

Though the figures are not in literal rooms, the way they are positioned and constrained within their frames suggests a sense of confinement. The creatures appear trapped or restricted, as if in some form of mental or emotional 'room' or cage. Bacon would later use this kind of spatial confinement more explicitly, employing cage-like structures in his paintings to heighten the feeling of entrapment.

Bacon stated that he wanted to paint a mouth the way Monet painted a sunset,[10] and his treatment of the mouth in *Three Studies* and subsequent paintings can be traced back to a phrase from *Oresteia* that haunted Bacon: 'the reek of human blood smiles out at me'.

PHOTOGRAPHY AND FILM

As a teenager in Berlin, he saw the film *Battleship Potemkin* (1925) by Sergei Eisenstein, in which a pivotal scene with a screaming woman takes place on the Odessa steps. Bacon kept a picture of this still in his studio and referenced it obsessively. It is probably the open mouth in the middle panel of *Three Studies*, and it would appear later in his iconic painting of 1949, *Head VI*, as well as *Study for a Head* (1952).

Bacon's studio was filled with wildlife books, alongside Eadweard Muybridge's nineteenth-century photographs of humans and animals in motion, and the strange hybrid images in the triptych blur the lines between animals and humans, revealing primal characteristics.[11]

Bacon also kept a large collection of Nazi propaganda photos ripped from Britain's *Picture Post*, and one showed a shouting Joseph Goebbels in his studio, which is likely the inspiration for the screeching right-hand figure of *Three Studies*.

STUDIO LIFE

Only a select few were invited to see Bacon's chaotic studio (as much of a mess as his private life) and observe his working methods, and although he appeared often on TV, he never allowed them to film him working. After his

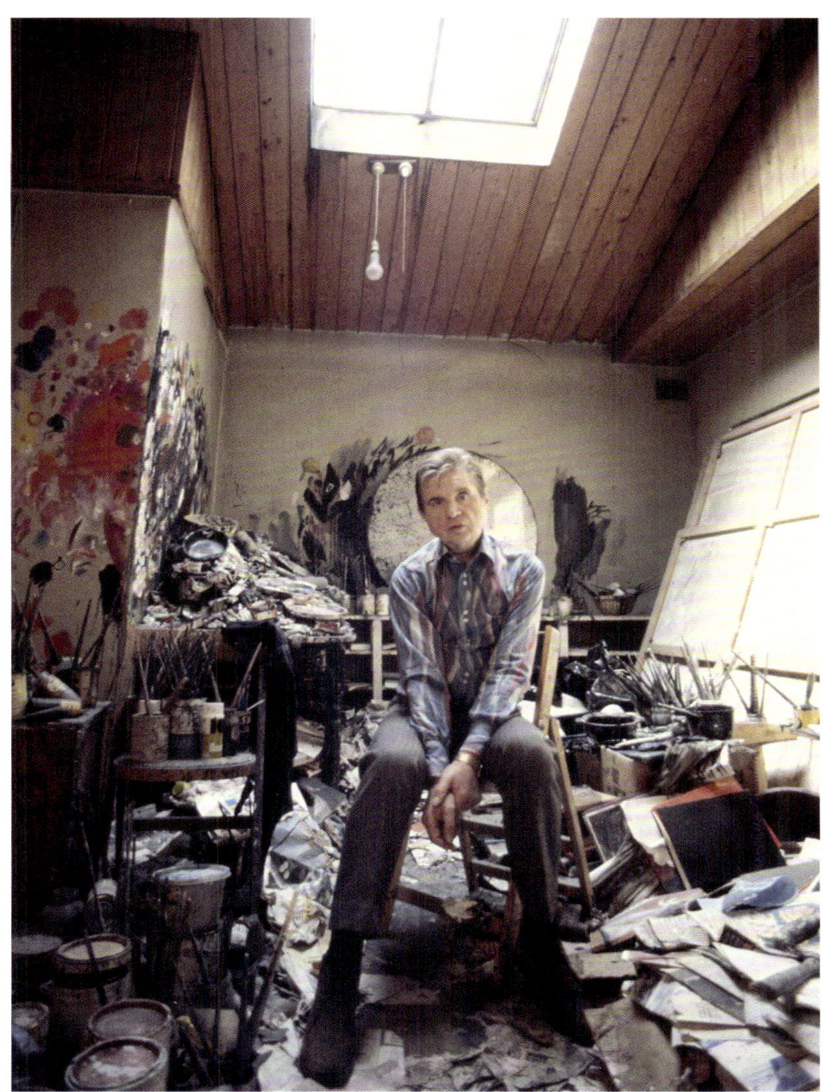

THREE STUDIES FOR FIGURES AT THE BASE OF A CRUCIFIXION

Bacon used photographs not as an aide-mémoire but to envisage distortions

death in 1992, thousands of images ripped from medical books, wrestling magazines, the beefcake magazine *Physique Pictorial* and news clippings were discovered in every corner of his studio, putting paid to the self-created myth that he didn't use outside references or photographs, or create preparatory work. Unfinished work left in his studio also revealed that he sketched his compositions in advance, albeit directly onto the canvas.[12]

Bacon used photographs not as an aide-mémoire but to envisage distortions in the final paintings; he would fold, tear and smear them, pulling them apart and reconstructing them until he created a new image that he could use as source material. These deconstructed images are works of art in themselves, and really *were* his sketches.

His wariness about discussing his working methods and his 'embellishing' of the truth was partly to play with interviewers and partly an insecurity about his lack of formal training. He kept his previous job as an interior designer

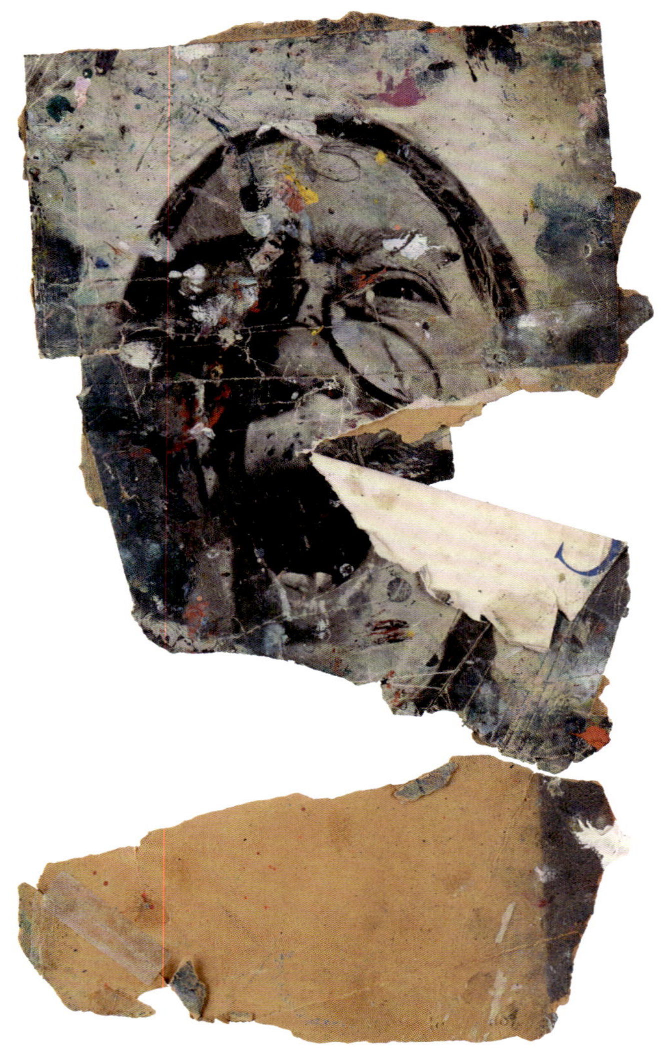

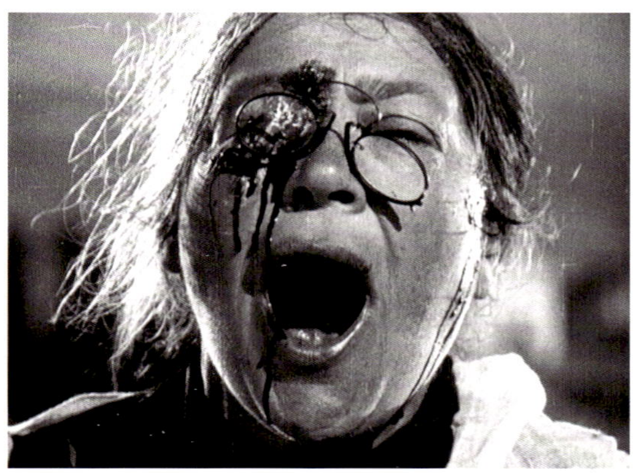

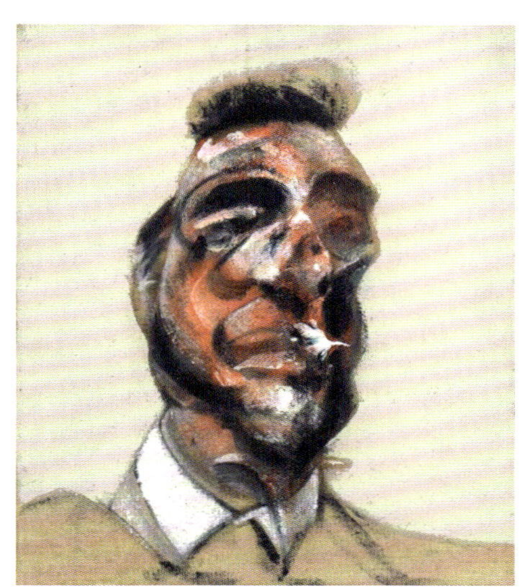
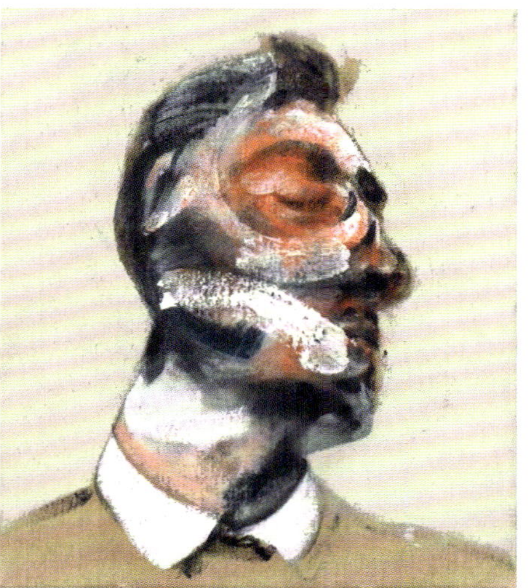
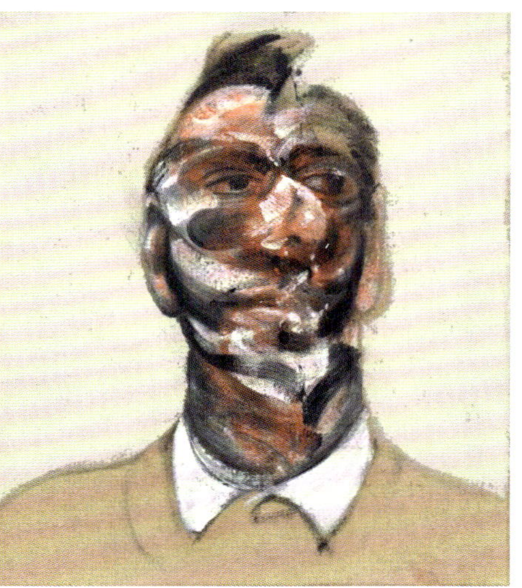

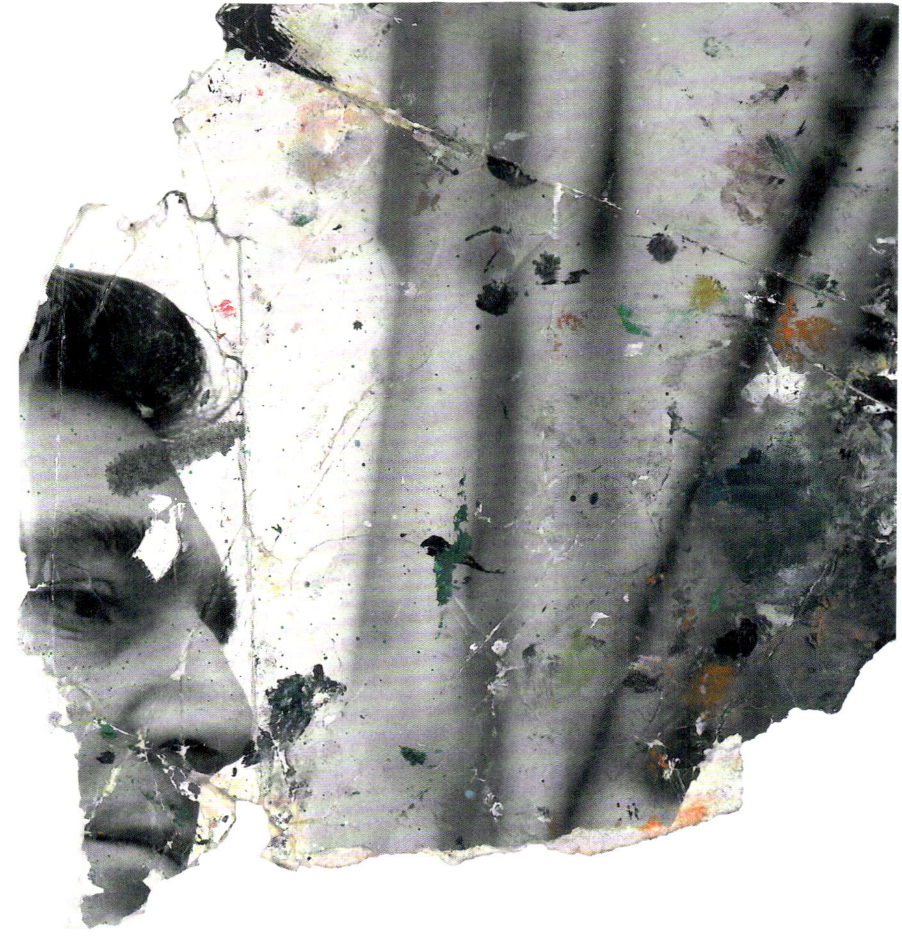

a secret from the press and most of his friends because he was fearful his paintings would be seen as merely 'decorative' or 'beautiful'.

PROFOUNDLY MODERN

Three Studies launched Bacon's career overnight with a painting that wasn't abstract, and most certainly wasn't 'decorative'. While the work references the Crucifixion, a deeply traditional theme in Western art, Bacon strips away any sense of spiritual redemption or salvation, making it a subversive piece that embodies the dehumanizing violence and the brutal reality of human suffering during war.

But it's more than an exploration of personal and collective trauma: Bacon's investigations into pain and suffering remain strikingly relevant today. The painting's universal themes of suffering and psychological depth transcend historical context, speaking to us as we continue to grapple with alienation, identity, trauma, conflict and the fragility of life.

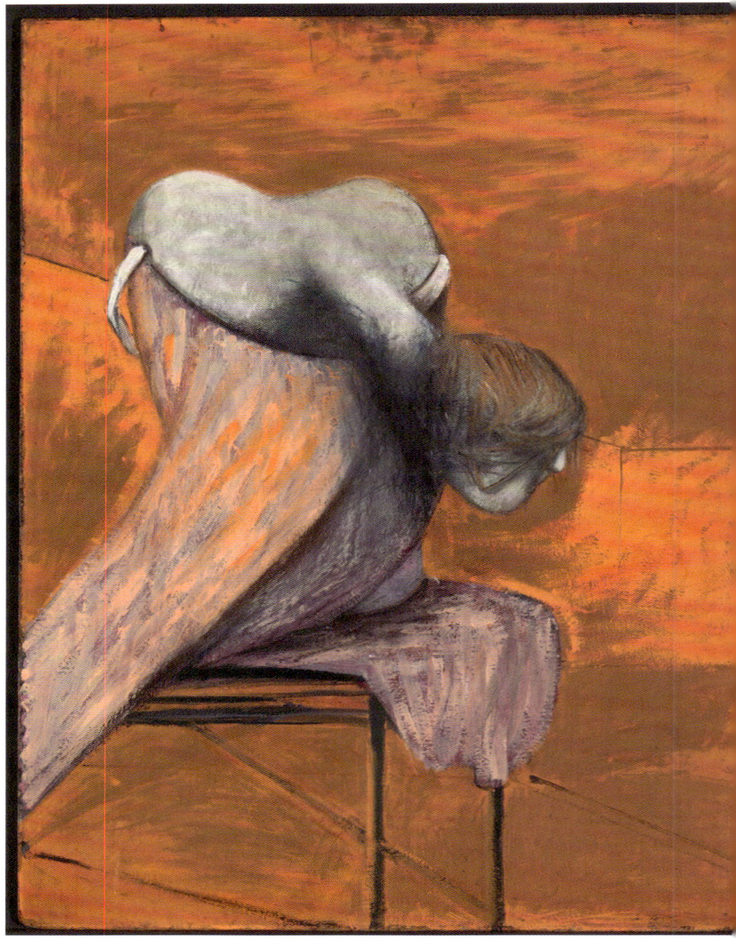

FRANCIS BACON

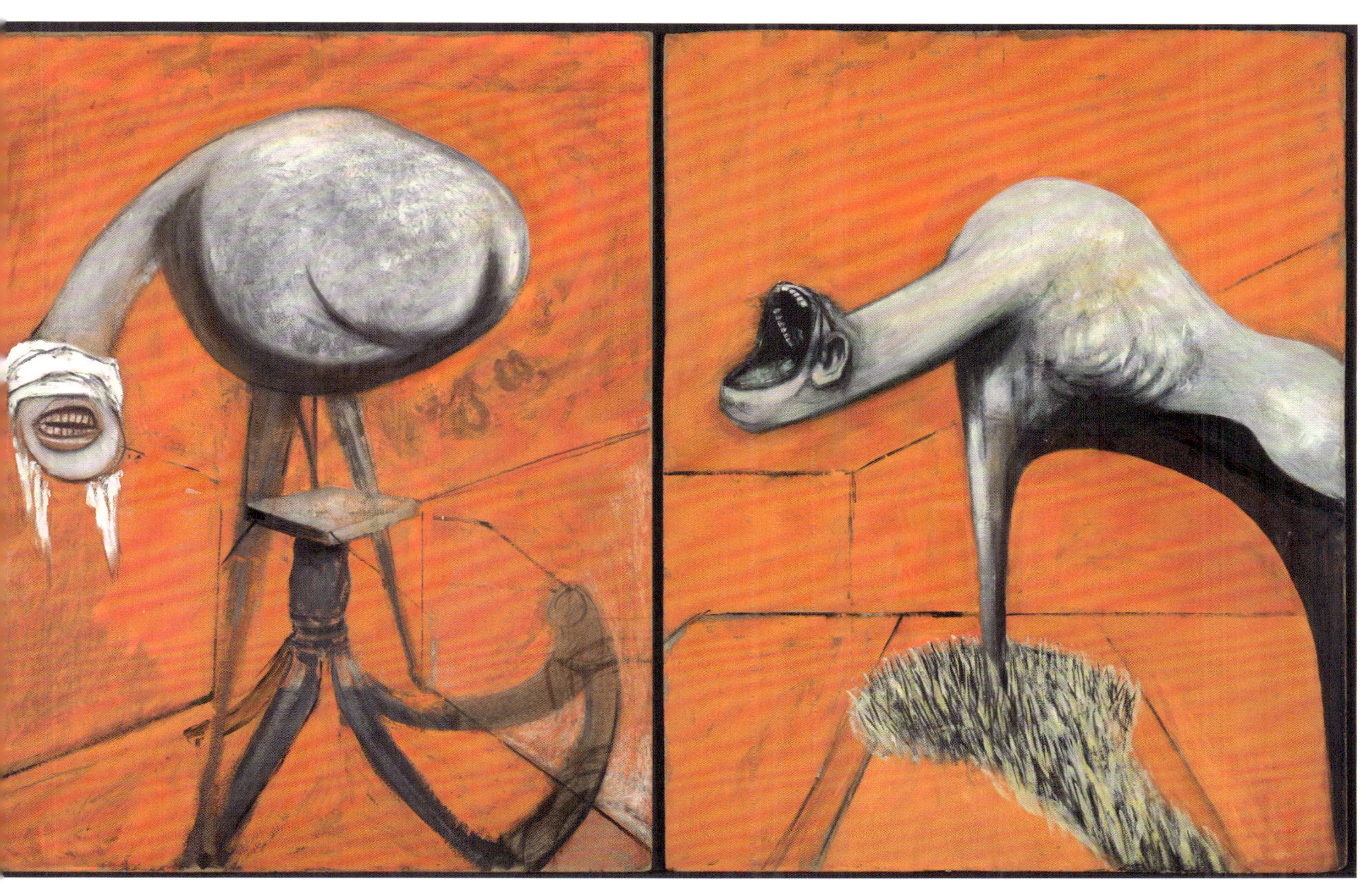

THREE STUDIES FOR FIGURES AT THE BASE OF A CRUCIFIXION

25

SALVADOR DALÍ

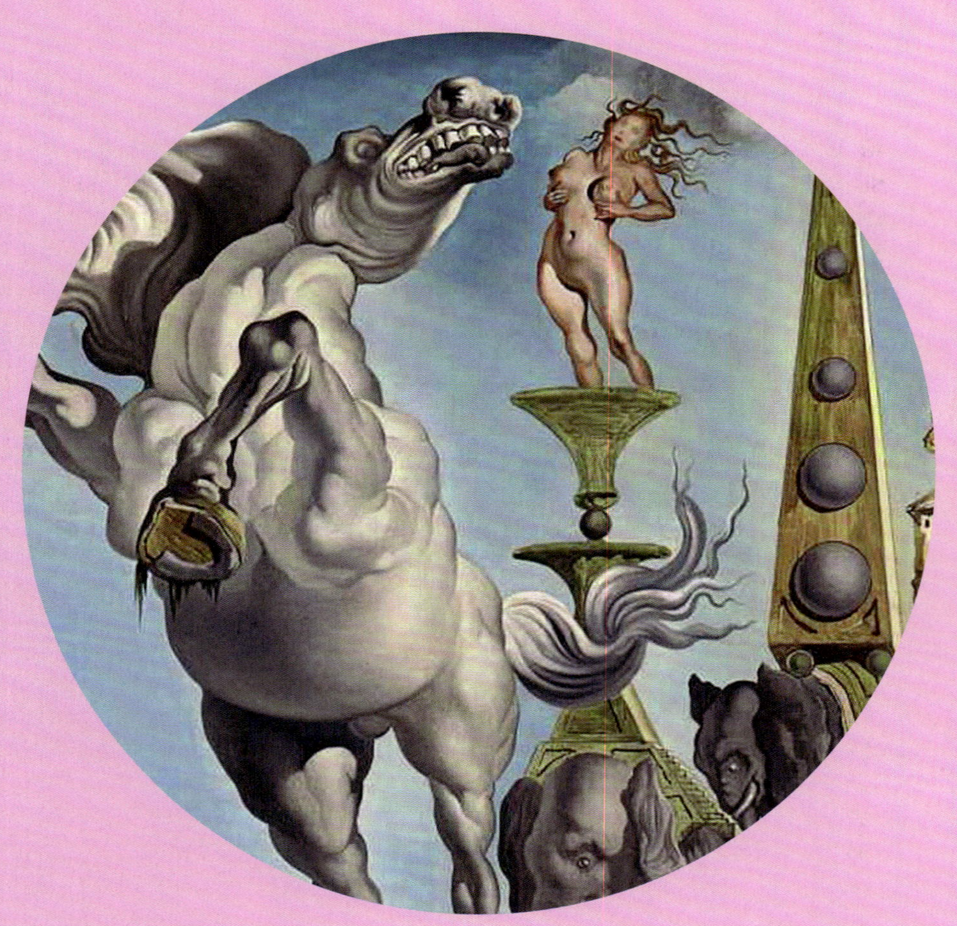

THE TEMPTATION
OF ST ANTHONY

1946

HOLLYWOOD CALLING

In 1946, in an effort to drum up publicity, the film director Albert Lewin held an art competition for a painting on the theme of St Anthony's Temptation, with the winning entry to feature in his next movie, *The Private Affairs of Bel Ami*. Eleven artists were invited by the film company to submit paintings, and the contest was won by the German Surrealist Max Ernst, whose work was then featured in the film. However, the most well-known of these paintings is by a failed contestant, Salvador Dalí, whose interpretation would go on to enjoy far greater acclaim than the winning entry.

Strange, confusing and often disturbing dreamscapes had made Dalí a household name by the time he came to paint this deeply religious subject. The competition was a publicity stunt for the movie, but it wasn't the Spanish artist's first foray into Hollywood; he was already working on a film project with Walt Disney, *Destino* (which would finally be completed in 2003, long after his death), and in 1945 he had worked on Alfred Hitchcock's *Spellbound*.

INTERPRETATION OF DREAMS

Early in his career, Salvador Dalí was obsessed with Sigmund Freud – and you could say his beginnings were more than a little Freudian! His mother gave birth to her first son in 1901, a child she named Salvador, who died shortly before his second birthday. Nine months later, the Salvador we know was born, and he was given his dead brother's name.

Just a few years before Dalí was born, Freud published his *Interpretation of Dreams* (1899), in which he put forward the theory that dreams are the key to unlocking the secrets of the unconscious mind. The book became almost a bible for the Surrealists and was a major influence on André Breton's Surrealist Manifesto of 1924. Dalí said that '[the] book presented itself to me as one of the capital discoveries in my life'.[1]

Freud's essays on human sexuality were translated into Spanish in 1922, and these theories would permeate Dalí's art.[2] In fact, one of the most important themes explored in *The Temptation of St Anthony* is the temptation of human sexuality.

THE PUBLIC FACE OF SURREALISM

Conflict often generates great art, and Dadaism and Surrealism were two movements that developed as a direct result of the horrors of the First World War, a war so brutal and incomprehensible that it created a fertile ground for the exploration of the irrational, the subconscious and the dreamlike.

Growing up in Spain, a country that remained neutral during the war, Dalí was not directly affected by the violence, but the broader political and cultural upheaval had an indirect impact on his formative years.

Salvador Dalí,
*The Temptation
of Saint Anthony*
(detail), 1946.

Strange, confusing and often disturbing dreamscapes had made Dalí a household name

As a student in Madrid, the young Dalí had experimented with lots of styles, including Fauvism, Naturalism and Cubism. Then, in 1926, he visited Paris for the first time – the cultural centre of the world – and began interacting with artists such as Picasso, which led to Dalí's first Surrealist works.

There is no dominant painting style in Surrealism, but the public face of it would become Dalí – the moustachioed self-promoter who was as instantly recognizable as his landscapes of melting watches.

CATHOLICISM AND THE BOMB

Today the art world is near unshockable, but in the early 20th century, Dalí's uncensored imagination, his images of sex, blood and excrement, even under the guise of the subconscious, were subversive and scandalous, and at times were considered irreligious if not anti-clerical. One of the greatest shocks, though, was to his fellow Surrealists, when at the height of his fame, Dalí announced that he had become a Catholic. In 1949 he attended a private audience with Pope Pius XII, and soon after announced himself a Catholic, or what he called a 'Catholic without faith'.[3]

Salvador Dalí's relationship with religion was complicated. His mother held strong Catholic beliefs but his father was a staunch atheist, and the young Dalí adopted his father's distaste for religion. In 1929 Dalí collaborated with filmmaker Luis Buñuel on films like

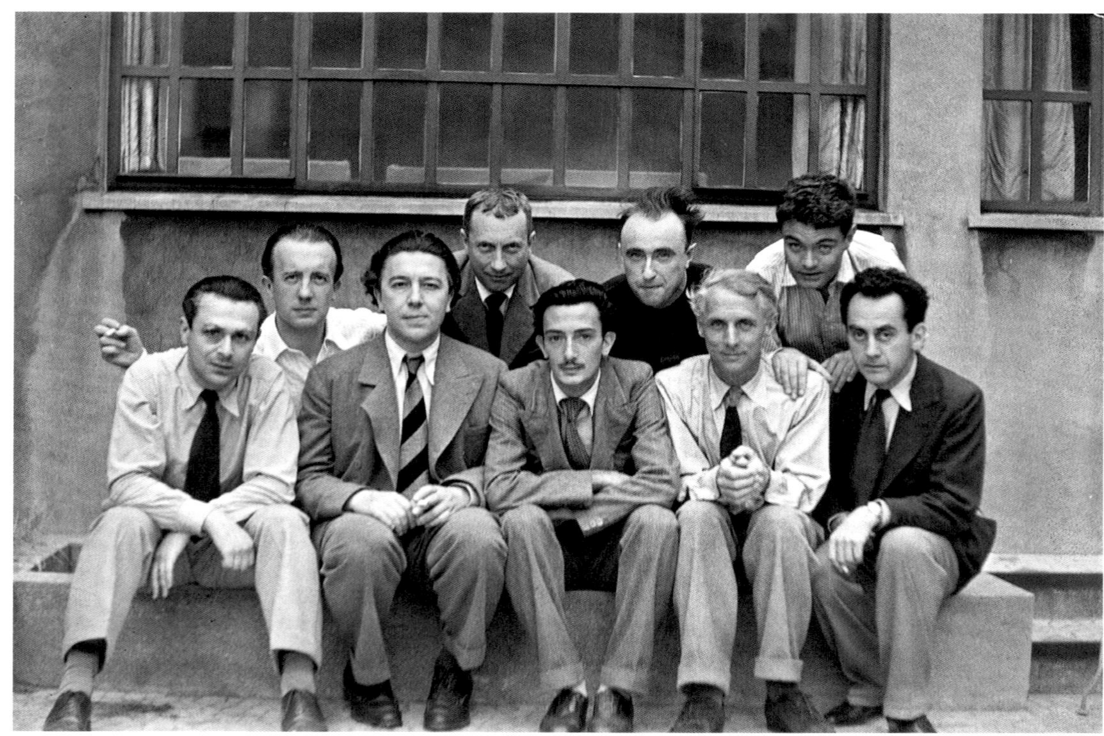

SALVADOR DALÍ

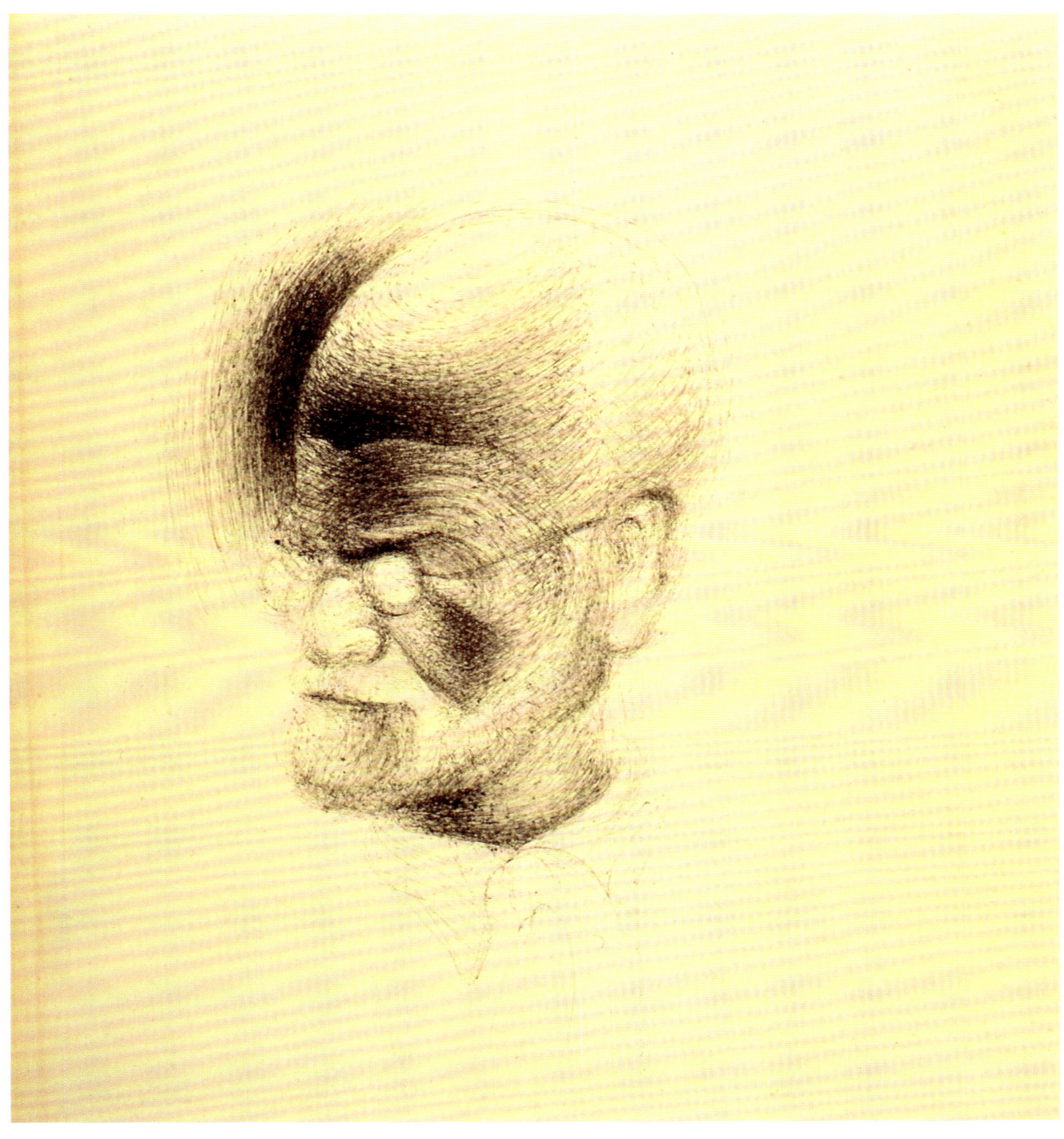

Salvador Dalí, *Sketch of Sigmund Freud*, 1938.

THE TEMPTATION OF ST ANTHONY

Un Chien Andalou and *L'Age d'or*, which depict the clergy as corrupt, ignorant and hypocritical, causing huge scandals worldwide.

While Dalí blamed his intense guilt about matters of sexuality on Catholicism, his perspective began to change after the explosion of the atom bomb in 1945. The event marked a turning point for the artist, who saw it as a symbol of both destruction and of the immense power of science. He became increasingly interested in the intersection of science, religion and art, which led to a new phase in his work known as 'Nuclear Mysticism', a hybrid of nuclear science and Catholic doctrine,[4] during which *The Temptation of St Anthony* was produced.

THE SUBJECT

The Temptation of St Anthony refers to the legend of St Anthony the Great, an influential Christian monk and hermit who lived during the 3rd and 4th centuries CE. The story revolves around his trials and temptations in the desert, where he struggles against demonic temptations and faced various forms of spiritual, sexual and psychological challenges that tested his faith.

Artists prior to Dalí had used the story of St Anthony's temptation as a vehicle to explore complex themes of spirituality. Hieronymus Bosch painted an equally surreal and fantastical version of it in 1501, showing grotesque creatures attempting to lead St Anthony astray from his devotion to God during his time of solitude and meditation in the desert.

In 1556 Pieter Bruegel the Elder used St Anthony allegorically to represent Everyman caught up in a world gone mad, and Joos van Craesbeeck's extraordinary version from 1650 features the screaming head of a giant spewing out devils, as St Anthony clings desperately to the scriptures. All fine demonstrations of how the subject matter lends itself quite easily to Surrealism.

THE PAINTING

The Temptation of St Anthony marked the beginning of merging ideas of the metaphysical and the earthbound in Dalí's paintings. His consummate skill was painting the unreal world, the world of mysticism, using the language of classicism, such as perspective and the depiction of anatomically correct figures, with such skill that no matter how irrational the vision, it is still believable.

Following the familiar story, Dalí's portrayal of St Anthony places him in the desert. St Anthony is in the bottom left corner, naked and holding up a cross to the parade heading his way. A human skull rests by his right foot, and he uses his left hand to supports himself on a rock, which almost certainly represents St Peter ('petros' meaning 'rock'), the 'rock' upon which Jesus would build his church.[5] By portraying St Anthony naked, Dalí emphasizes his vulnerability, and his fragile positioning suggests a struggle with temptation.

The temptations take the form of gigantic, elongated animals – most notably elephants – that carry classical nude figures, temples and other luxurious symbols on their backs. The elephants have impossibly long spindly legs and are led by a horse with reversed forehooves. In art of the Middle Ages – a period by which Dalí was often influenced – distorted and unsettling imagery such as the reversed hooves was often a symbol of the deceptive and disorientating influence of the Devil. To further identify the horse as Satan, Dalí has it rearing up and turning away in panic from St Anthony's primitive wooden cross.

Metamorphosis was a key concept in the Surrealist movement, exemplified by the paradox of Dalí's rendering of the hardest, most mechanical of objects, watches, into a soft, flaccid form in *The Persistence of Memory* (1931). And here he does the same with elephants, large and heavy animals who in Dalí's world,

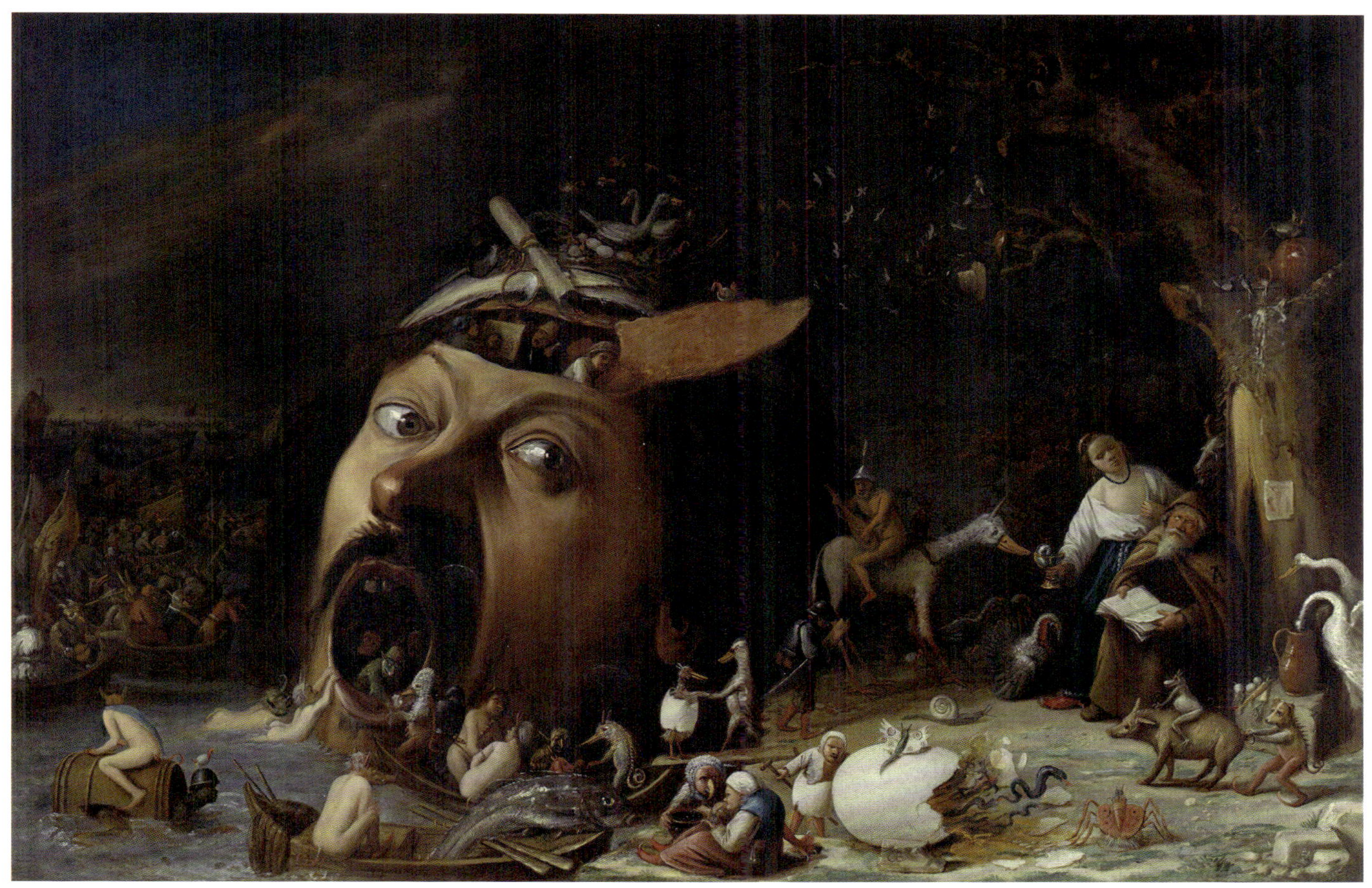

leave behind the laws of physics as they balance precariously on legs which could never support their weight, and symbolize the transcendence of physical limitations and the precarious nature of temptation and desire.

The elephants are all carrying symbols of the temptations St Anthony faced. The first has a nude woman presenting her breasts to St Anthony as she stands on a teetering golden cup of lust, embodying the temptation of carnal desire that St Anthony must overcome. In Christian tradition, St Anthony is often tested by visions of beautiful women, which are seen as distractions from his spiritual devotion. Dalí uses her nudity to emphasize the power of lust and its seductive pull on the human psyche.

The second carries an obelisk and is similar to Gian Lorenzo Bernini's sculpture

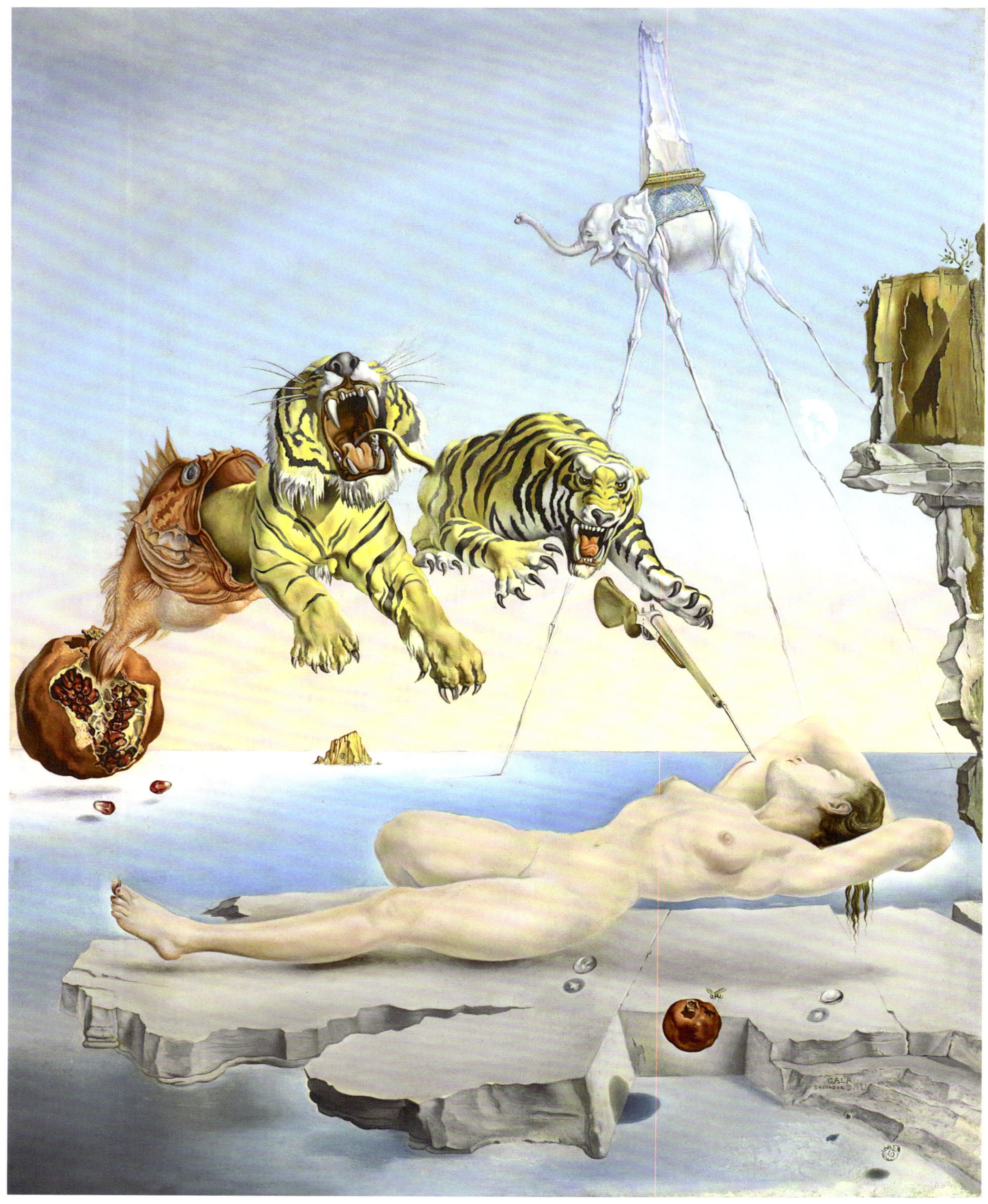

SALVADOR DALÍ

Elephant and Obelisk. Bernini's sculpture was designed to represent the solid harmony between strength and wisdom, and Dalí's depiction, so precariously balanced, symbolizes the worldly temptations of power, ambition and knowledge.

Dalí often used architecture as a symbol for the complexity of the human mind, and the third and fourth elephants are heavily weighed down with Venetian buildings in the style of the Renaissance architect Andrea Palladio, symbols of the burdens and temptations that distracted St Anthony from his spiritual pursuits.

The architect Palladio was known for his neoclassical designs that were associated with wealth and social status due to their use in grand villas and palaces. In Dalí's painting, the depiction of these grand architectural forms atop the spindly elephants symbolizes the allure of material success and worldly power.

Within the building on the back of the third elephant is a disembodied nude torso. Dalí was famously repulsed by sex; he openly discussed his voyeuristic tendencies and extremely unconventional attitudes towards sexuality, and the peep-show aspect of this image is evident.

Behind them, the fifth elephant carries a tall tower that has obvious phallic overtones, to further emphasize the sexual theme of the temptations. Beyond it, in the clouds, we can see a real building, the El Escorial in Madrid, which stands as a symbol of spiritual authority that has been intertwined with power and wealth, further complicating St Anthony's internal struggle as a hermit and ascetic, between humility and temptation.

AVIDA DOLLARS

The painting was completed in New York. Dalí had moved to the United States in 1940 to escape the war in Europe and started a quest for fame and fortune that was so open that he

Dalí often used architecture as a symbol for the complexity of the human mind

was given the anagrammatic nickname 'Avida Dollars' by the founder of the Surrealist movement, André Breton. He reached dizzying heights of fame in America, but his critical reception during these years cooled. He was increasingly viewed as a commercial artist, and his work was often greeted with tepid enthusiasm at best, outright suspicion at worst. His 'religious works' were not always well received either, and in 1956 *Time Magazine* famously described them as 'junk'.

Many of Dalí's later works have been described as 'religious kitsch',[6] and it is sometimes easy to see why, but *The Temptation of St Anthony* is one of those flashes of Dalí's genius, which, for good reason, is one of the most celebrated Surrealist canvases ever painted. A work that combines his complex philosophical ideas and the ravings of his subconscious mind with the techniques of the old masters, using powerful imagery to tap into our fantasies, our dreams, our imagination, fears and hallucinations.

Dalí's last years were dogged by bad health and financial scandals, and he began to slowly retreat from public life. He had a fear of mortality that he traced back to the death of his brother, and he spoke often of 'avoiding' death, but even for Dalí, this proved impossible. He passed away at the age of eighty-four, shortly after receiving the last rites…

from a Catholic priest.

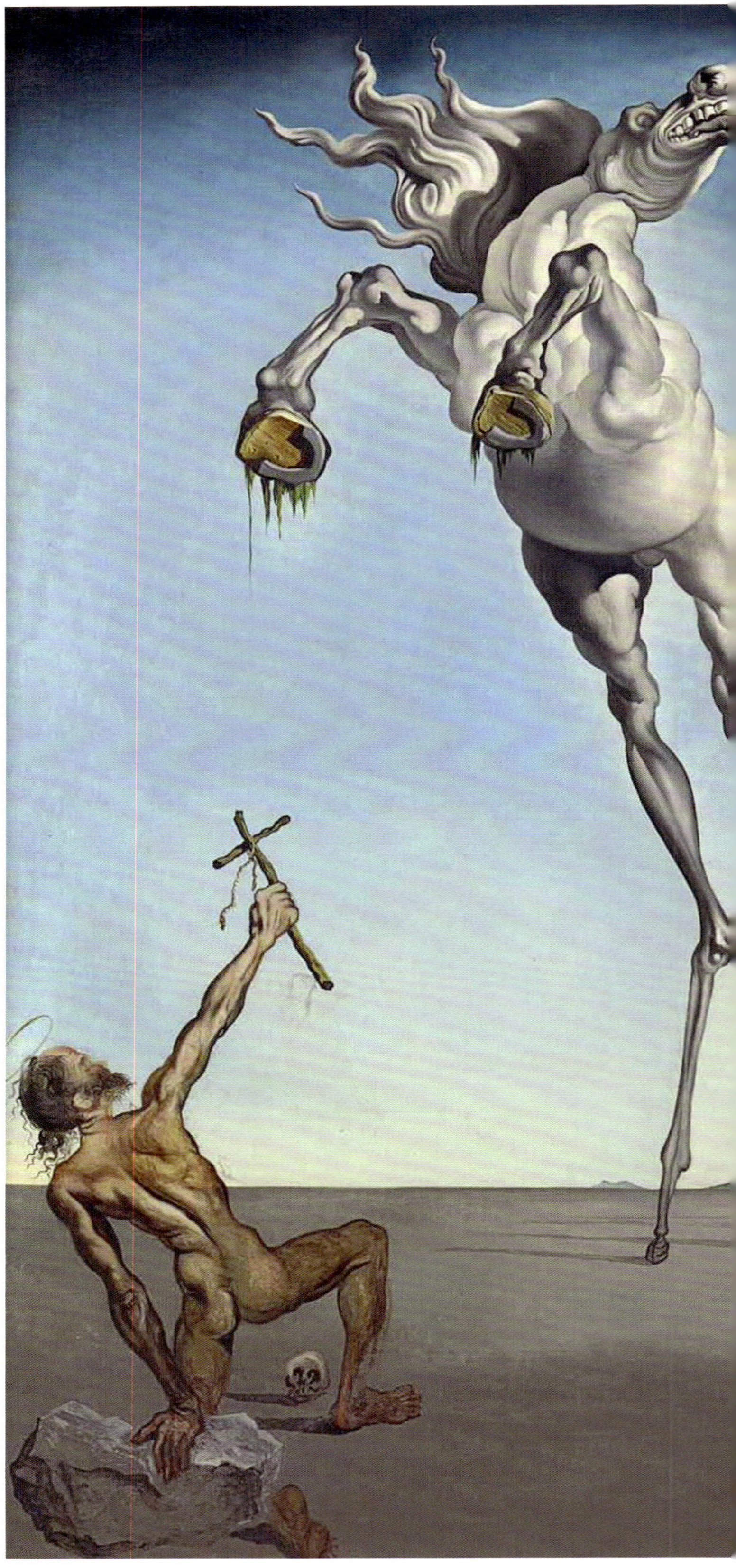

Salvador Dali, *The Temptation of St Anthony*, 1946.

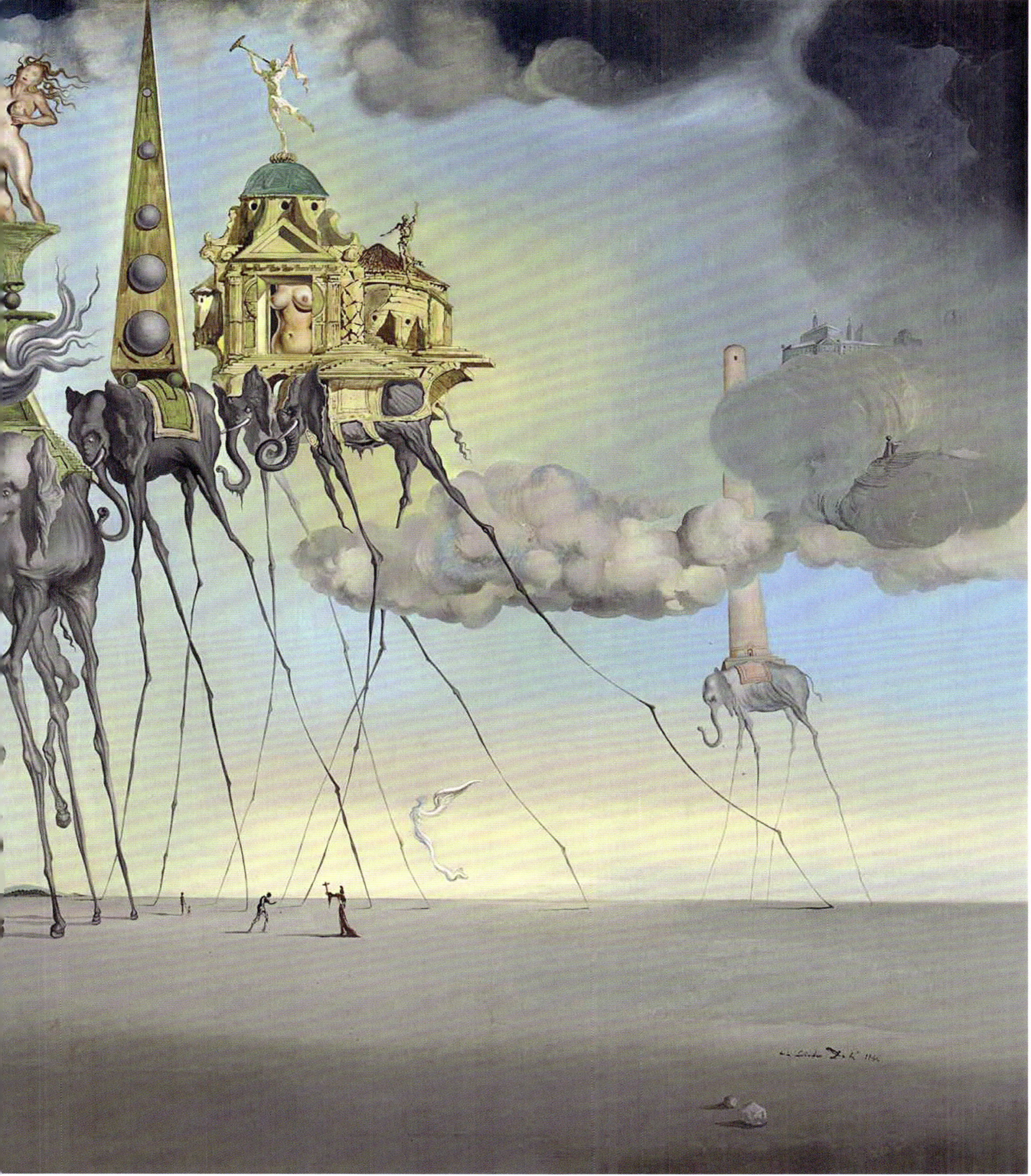

26

JEAN-MICHEL BASQUIAT

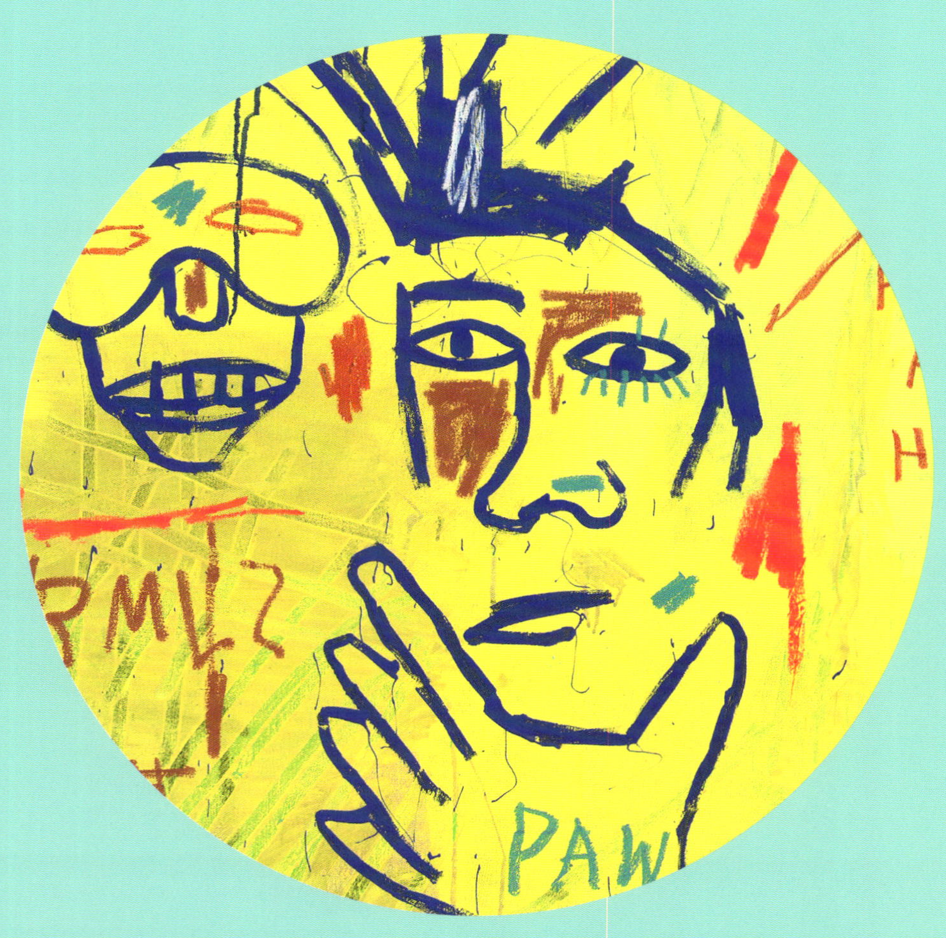

HOLLYWOOD AFRICANS

1983

A BRIEF AND SPECTACULAR CAREER

Before his untimely death, Jean-Michel Basquiat experienced a meteoric rise in his popularity, from teenage 'street artist' to globally recognized and acclaimed painter in under five years. At one point he was considered a divisive figure in the art world, and his talent was often questioned by the public, as well as art critics who accused dealers of promoting him unjustly.[1]

But now his work is widely exhibited in prestigious museums across the Western world. He attracts an enthusiastic crowd, *and* critical acclaim.

His painting *Hollywood Africans* gives us an insight into themes central to his practice: socio-political concepts such as race, class and identity; the stark realities of institutional racism, police brutality and inequality; and a combination of autobiographical elements, raw, uncensored emotion and the written word, reflecting his early days as a street poet in New York.

YOUNG, GIFTED AND BLACK

Basquiat's rapid ascent in the early 1980s and the prices his works commanded sent shockwaves through the downtown Manhattan art scene. That scene at the time consisted of mostly white artists, and even with the arrival of Basquiat, Fab 5 Freddy and Futura 2000, the imbalance between ethnicities was painfully noticeable.

This was an era when Black artists rarely received critical attention,[2] and Basquiat's

work, on show in the blue-chip galleries, would give a voice and a name to subjects that had been disregarded in these spaces.

A GIFTED CHILD

But Basquiat also wanted to break down those assumptions and move away from the way Black people were being portrayed in the media at the time. Far from the 'raw' street artist he was made out to be, he was in fact an intensely ambitious, middle-class young man who knew his art history, particularly when it related to the presence and absence of Blackness in Western art.

Basquiat was born in 1960 to a Haitian father and a Puerto Rican mother, in a solidly middle-class household in Brooklyn. He was a gifted child who could read and write by the age of four and spoke three languages fluently. He was very close to his mother, who encouraged his artistic side, taking him to museums and art galleries regularly and enrolling him as a junior member of the Brooklyn Museum.[3] The young Basquiat would spend every second drawing.

He left home for good at the age of seventeen, first living rough on the streets of Manhattan and in fleabag hotels before graduating to friends' and lovers' sofas and beds. Then, in 1977, he teamed up with an old school friend, Al Díaz, to form the street art duo SAMO© (a derivative of SAME OLD SHIT).

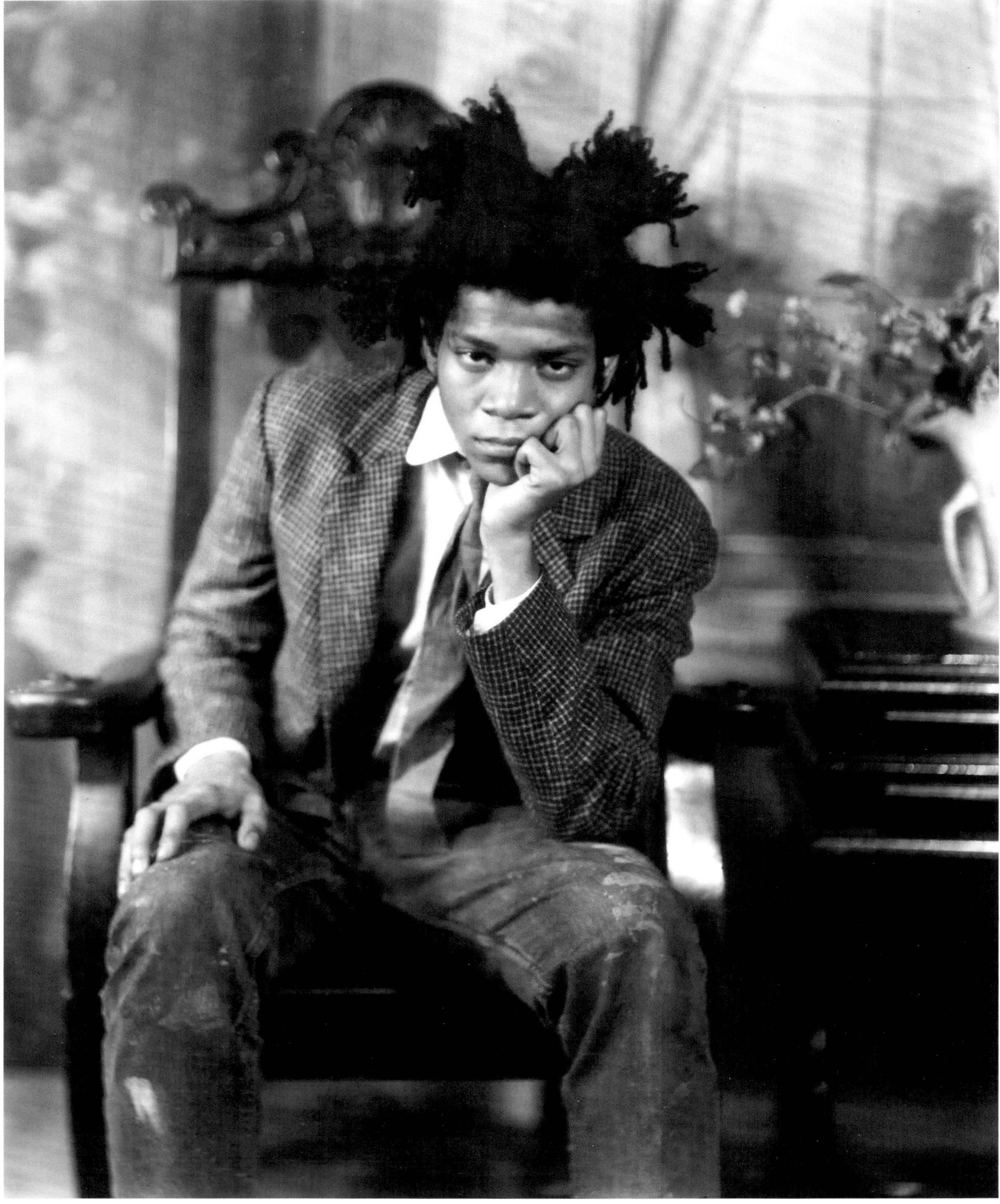

JEAN-MICHEL BASQUIAT

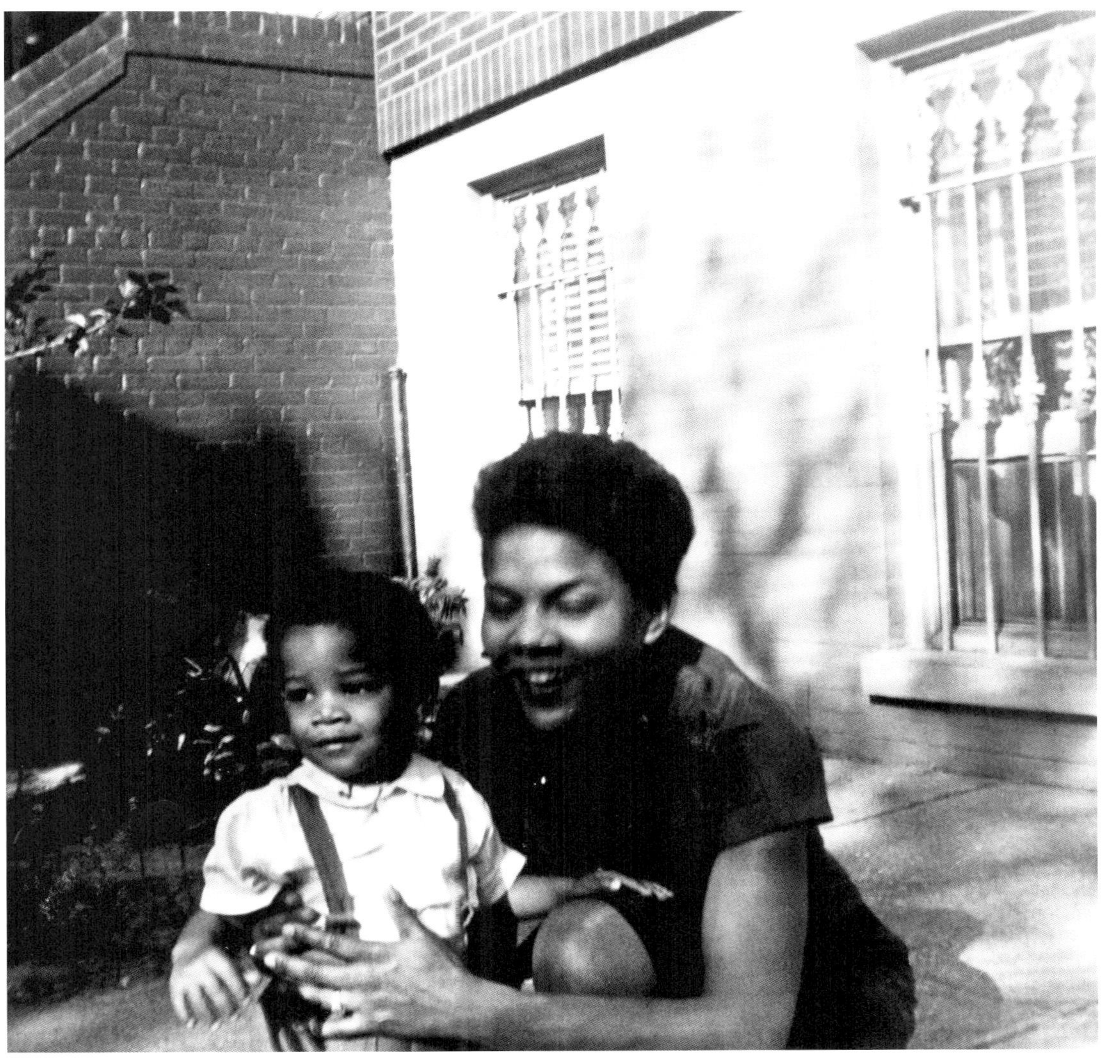

SAME OLD SHIT

In early 1978, SAMO© began spray-painting and mark-making on buildings on the Lower East Side, creating surrealistic texts like 'SAMO© AS AN ALTERNATIVE TO GOD'. The expressions were designed to provoke thought around social issues by mirroring the enigmatic and sometimes nonsensical sayings that the advertising industry used.

If this was graffiti, it was quite different. Basquiat and Díaz were political poets and provocateurs, writing witty cryptic messages about consumer culture, religion and even the art market on walls right next to the major art galleries. It got people's attention, and within weeks of being hailed as new and exciting graffiti artists, they were interviewed by the *Village Voice*, where Basquiat said SAMO© was 'a tool for mocking bogusness'.[4]

Fame drove a wedge between Díaz and Basquiat, however, and they began to argue.[5] Then, in 1980, at the height of the duo's press

　　　　　HOLLYWOOD AFRICANS

attention, Basquiat called it quits and decided to pursue painting full-time as a solo artist.

It is essential to our understanding of Basquiat that he never considered SAMO© to be graffiti, yet even when he was a hugely successful artist showing in major galleries, Basquiat, despite his protestations, would be described as a 'graffiti artist' or an 'ex-graffiti artist', a term he found simplistic and racist.

But fighting the designation was a losing, and exhausting, battle, for while Basquiat was trying his best to challenge stereotypes, critics and dealers were pushing the racialized idea that Basquiat was an 'exotic' or 'primitive' artist. It was clear that those selling his work liked the story of the down-and-out prodigy or the street artist who sprang from nowhere, and it was a useful trope for marketing his work.

In 1979, Basquiat and his friend Jennifer Stein began making postcards, which they sold on the streets for a dollar. One day, while touting them in SoHo, Basquiat spotted Andy Warhol at a restaurant. He was a big fan of the Pop artist and was thrilled when he sold him a postcard titled *Stupid Games, Bad Ideas*, featuring the noughts-and-crosses graphics he would incorporate into many of his later paintings. Years later, Basquiat and Warhol would become good friends.

SAMPLING AND SUCCESS

Basquiat's reference points were fine artists like Cy Twombly, Jean Dubuffet, Robert Rauschenberg and Pablo Picasso. Writers like Jack Kerouac, Brion Gysin, William Burroughs and Robert Farris Thompson. Musicians like David Bowie and Miles Davies.

It was a form of sampling that hip-hop music had been exploring since the 1970s, a multi-referential approach drawing on a myriad of sources from both the Western canon and African symbolism and traditions.

Basquiat's sources were many and eclectic: the medical 'dictionary' *Gray's Anatomy*, poetry, jazz, trash TV, typography and art history. He used his art to explore the African diaspora and the slave trade, and to reference his own Haitian and Puerto Rican heritage. They enabled him to create visual collages that were profoundly original, and at the same time rooted in a rich linguistic history. He would fuse words and images together instinctively, and like a musician uses samples, he would mix visual signs on the canvas to make astonishing new sense out of them.

Basquiat worked hard at his craft and painted nonstop. Madonna, his one-time girlfriend, spoke about him working through the night on his canvases.[6] He went from being pretty much unknown in 1981 to being very rich in 1982. 'I watched him sell his first

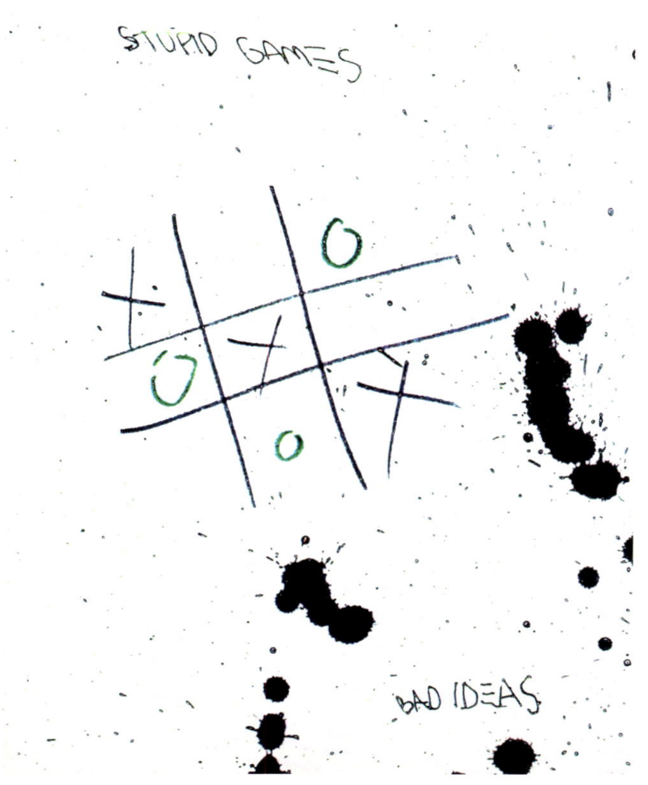

JEAN-MICHEL BASQUIAT

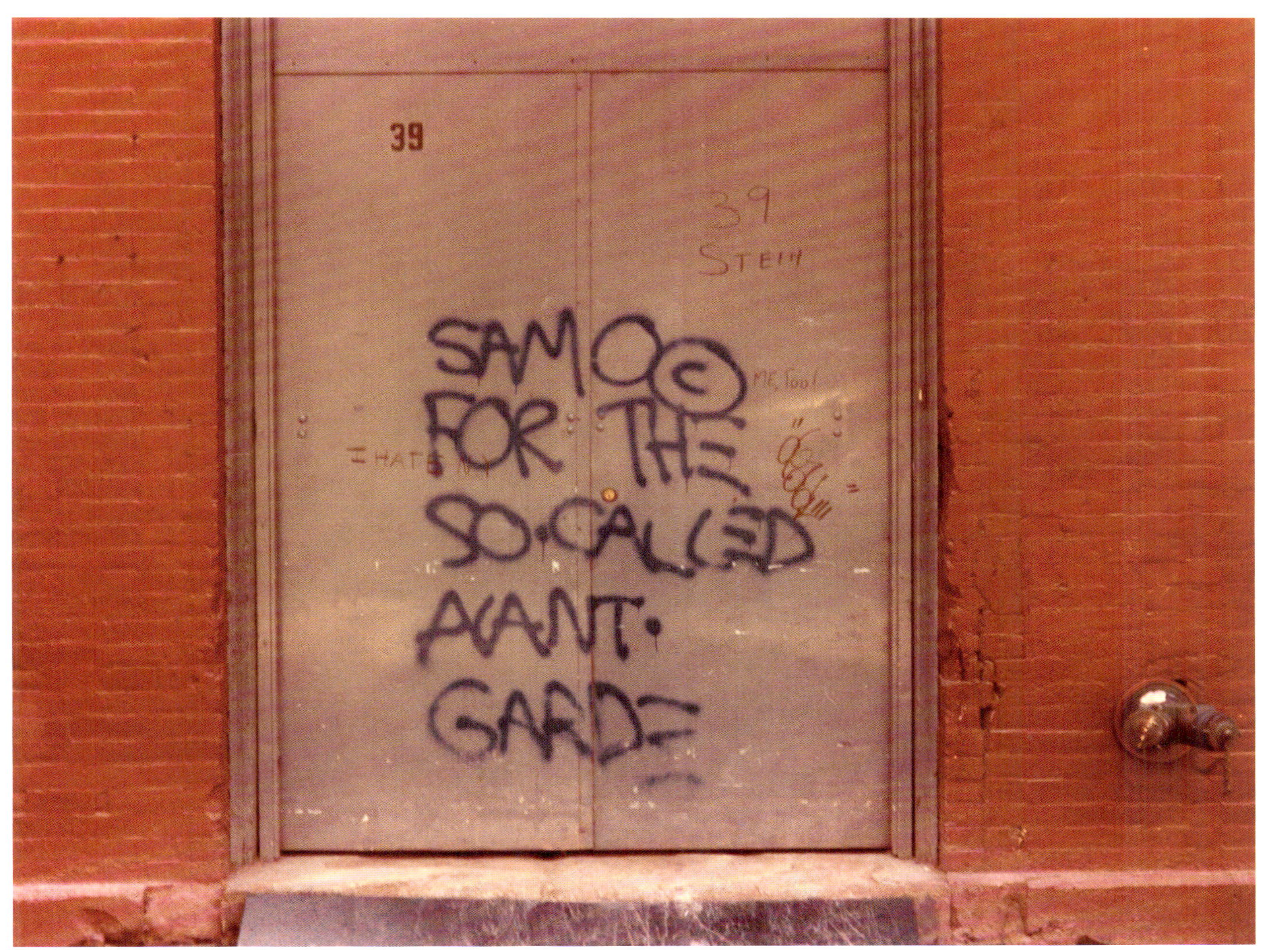

opposite
Jean-Michel Basquiat
and Jennifer Stein,
*Stupid Games,
Bad Ideas*, 1979.

Henry Flynt, Photo
from the SAMO© Graffiti
Portfolio, 1979–91.

It is essential to our understanding of Basquiat that he never considered SAMO© to be graffiti

HOLLYWOOD AFRICANS

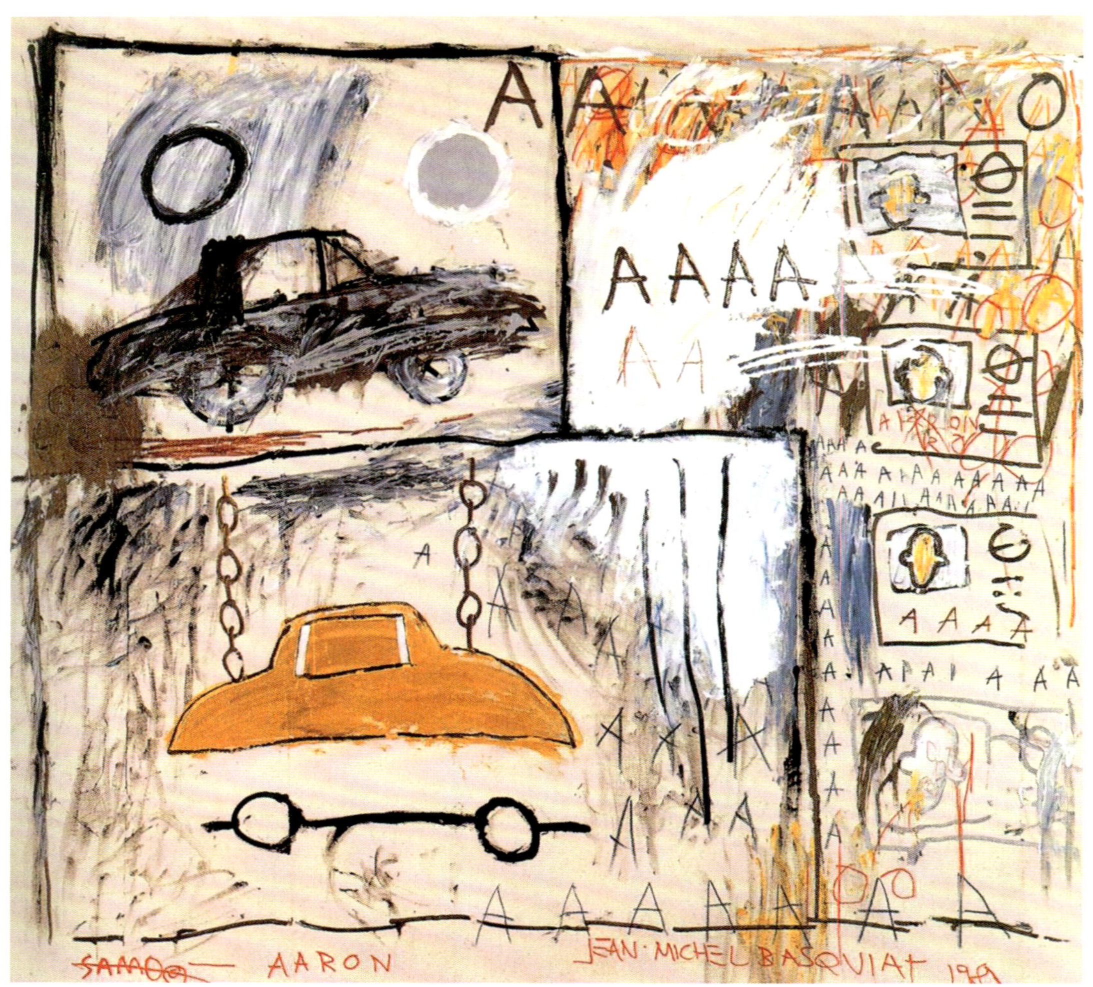

painting to Deborah Harry for $200,' his friend Suzanne Mallouk explained, 'and then a few months later he was selling paintings for $20,000 each, selling them faster than he could paint them.'[7] He was only twenty-two years old.

HOLLYWOOD AFRICANS

Hollywood Africans belongs to a series of paintings by Basquiat exploring the experiences of African Americans in the entertainment industry.

In 1983, Basquiat, who was once in a band, produced the hip-hop single by graffiti artists Rammellzee and K-Rob, as well as designing the record sleeve. Basquiat was a music obsessive, and hip-hop in New York emerged from the same creative cultural scene of the late 1970s and early 1980s that he did. That same year, Basquiat brought Rammellzee over to LA, along with another friend, the street artist Toxic, to attend the opening of his exhibition at the Gagosian Gallery in West Hollywood.

Larry Gagosian, then a small gallerist, had given Basquiat his first West Coast show in spring 1982. Basquiat would eventually

spend eighteen months there and produce
about 100 paintings between 1982 and 1984,[8]
including some of his most iconic pieces, such
as *Hollywood Africans*.

Basquiat was a leading figure in the
short lived Neo-Expressionist movement,
with Keith Haring and Kenny Scharf, among
others. It was free, raw and expressive, both
stylistically and emotionally. The paintwork
in *Hollywood Africans* is block colour (mostly
yellow), roughly applied straight from the tube
with no thinners. He uses bold lines, bright
colours and his familiar pictograms, words,
symbols and diagrams, scratched or drawn into
the canvas spontaneously and energetically.

Basquiat and his friends feature in the
painting – from left to right, Toxic, Rammellzee
and then Basquiat[9] – and at the top of the work,
the words 'Hollywood Africans' are struck
through. This method of exclusion or erasure
was often used by Basquiat as a way of
directing our attention towards the words
and encouraging us to decipher them: 'I cross
out words so you will see them more,' he once
said, 'the fact that they are obscured makes
you want to read them.'[10]

The copyright symbol he incorporates
here is ironic or tongue-in-cheek, a direct
descendant of that which was used in SAMO©.
It is of course a traditional sign of authorship,

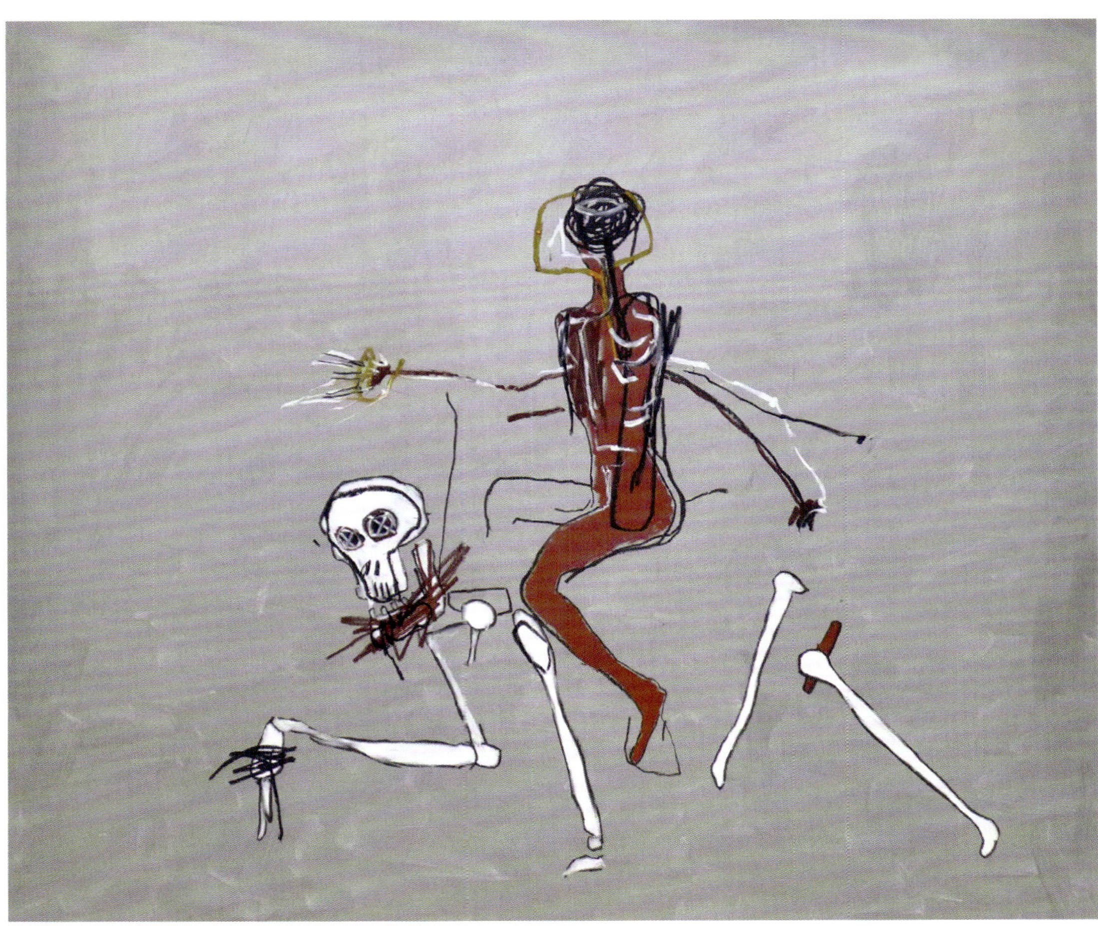

Jean-Michel Basquiat,
Riding with Death, 1988
– one of his final works.

As 'street artists' and
rappers, he and his friends
were often given a culturally
reductive role

and Basquiat uses it to stamp his authority
on his intellectual property – a right that is
so often stripped from Black artists. At the
same time, his accompanying text points
out consumer culture, commercialization
and the sale and resale of artists/actors.

Bottom left is one of his most used
pictograms, the crown. It is a symbol that
graffiti artists often use as a sign of respect
for other artists' work,[11] but in Western art, it
comes loaded with historical baggage. Basquiat,
who had an obsession with fame,[12] was not
averse to mocking that same desire, using the
crown to challenge notions of race and power.
He used it often in his works to ridicule the
whole Western colonial obsession with
crowning a ruler or leader as the 'winner'.

He created paintings filled with explicit
text references to European colonization,
the slave trade and the industries and
commodities that both relied on. In *Hollywood
Africans*, we see the words 'TOBACCO' and
'SUGAR CANE' writ large, referencing a
film industry where enslaved people were
traditionally depicted through demeaning
stereotypes, such as 'the mammy'.

This is cross-referenced with the text
'MOVIE STAR FOOT PRINTS©' over a pair
of footprints, referencing the Hollywood
walk of fame. Above that is an Oscar statuette,
and 'HOLLYWOOD AFRICANS FROM THE
NINETEEN FORTIES', which refers to the
year that Hattie McDaniel became the first
African American to win an Oscar for her role
of an enslaved maid in *Gone with the Wind*

– an Oscar that was presented to her in front
of a segregated audience.

Underneath the word 'HERO.ISM' are
the numbers 22 60 12, a numerical anagram
of Basquiat's date of birth (22 December 1960),
which he often used as a signature for his work.

On another level, by including himself
and his two friends in the picture, Basquiat can
be seen to be placing himself alongside these
stereotyped Black figures of Hollywood. As
'street artists' and rappers, he and his friends
were often given a culturally reductive role.

With this single artwork, Basquiat
expressed profound insights not just about
Hollywood but also about America, the world
of art and his experience of being Black in
both realms.

MAKING IT

In 1985 Basquiat was on the cover of the
New York Times Magazine, but he would still
leave gallery parties and find it impossible
to get a cab,[13] or be turned away from fancy
restaurants.[14] For him, 'making it' didn't mean
getting a show or a dealer, or even having a
fortune; he wanted recognition from the art
establishment, but despite his fame, he only
had two museum shows in his lifetime.[15]

When Jean-Michel Basquiat died at the
age of twenty-seven of a heroin overdose,
he was the most financially successful Black
visual artist in history.[16] His was a brief and
spectacular career; he raised questions of race,
power and representation, and he can certainly
be described as a pioneer and a trailblazer
whose visceral work continues to capture
the popular imagination.

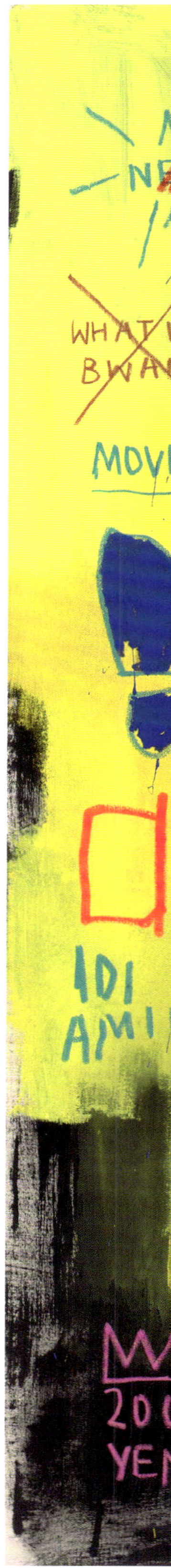

Jean-Michel Basquiat,
Hollywood Africans, 1983.

JEAN-MICHEL BASQUIAT

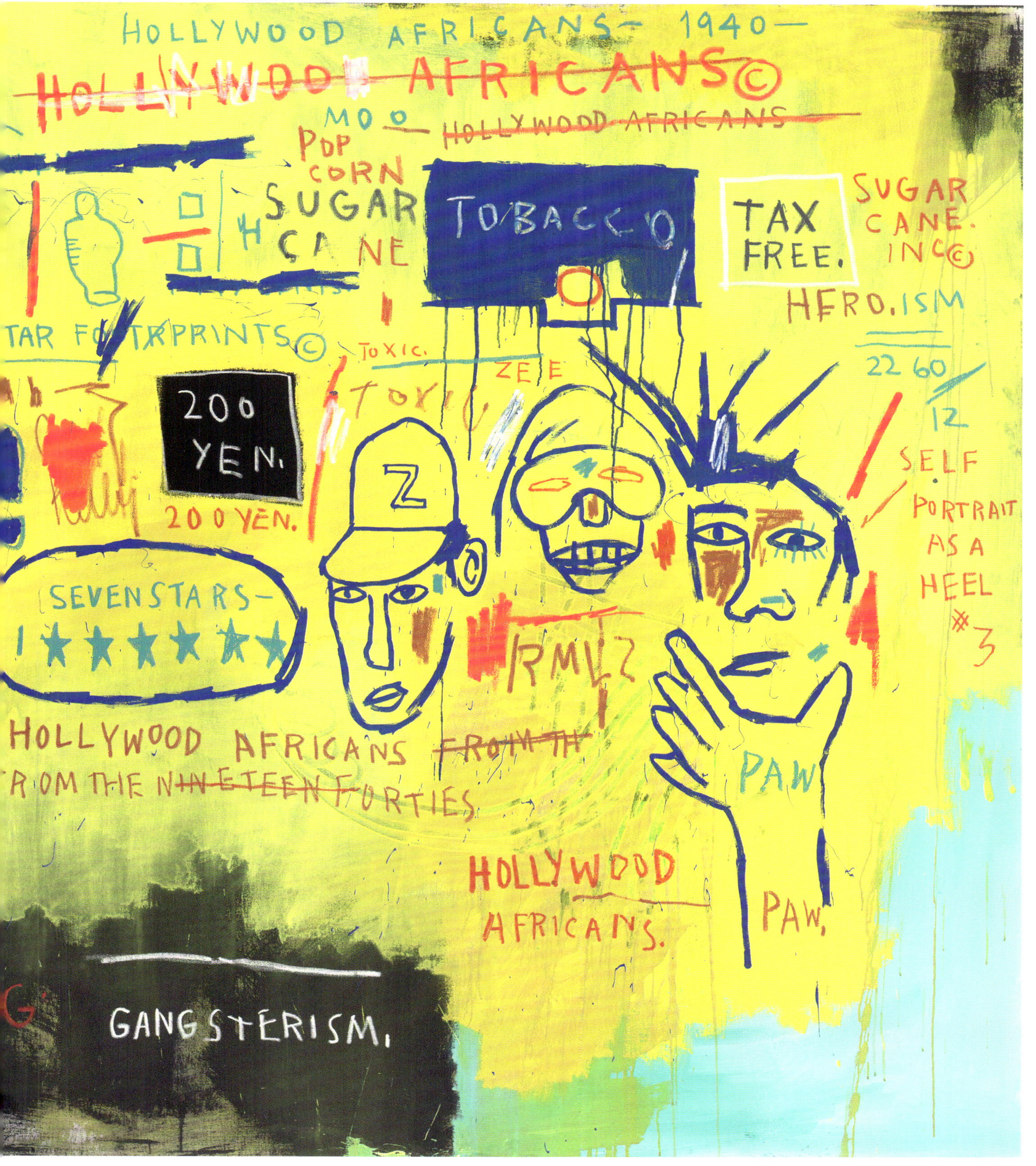

HOLLYWOOD AFRICANS - 1940 -
HOLLYWOOD AFRICANS©
HOLLYWOOD AFRICANS
MOO
POP CORN
SUGAR CANE
TOBACCO
TAX FREE.
SUGAR CANE. INC©
STAR FOOTPRINTS©
TOXIC.
ZEE
HERO.ISM
22 60
12
SELF PORTRAIT AS A HEEL #3
TOXIC
200 YEN.
200 YEN.
Z
SEVENSTARS-
RMLZ
HOLLYWOOD AFRICANS FROM TH
FROM THE NINETEEN FORTIES
PAW
HOLLYWOOD AFRICANS.
PAW,
G
GANGSTERISM.

FAITH RINGGOLD

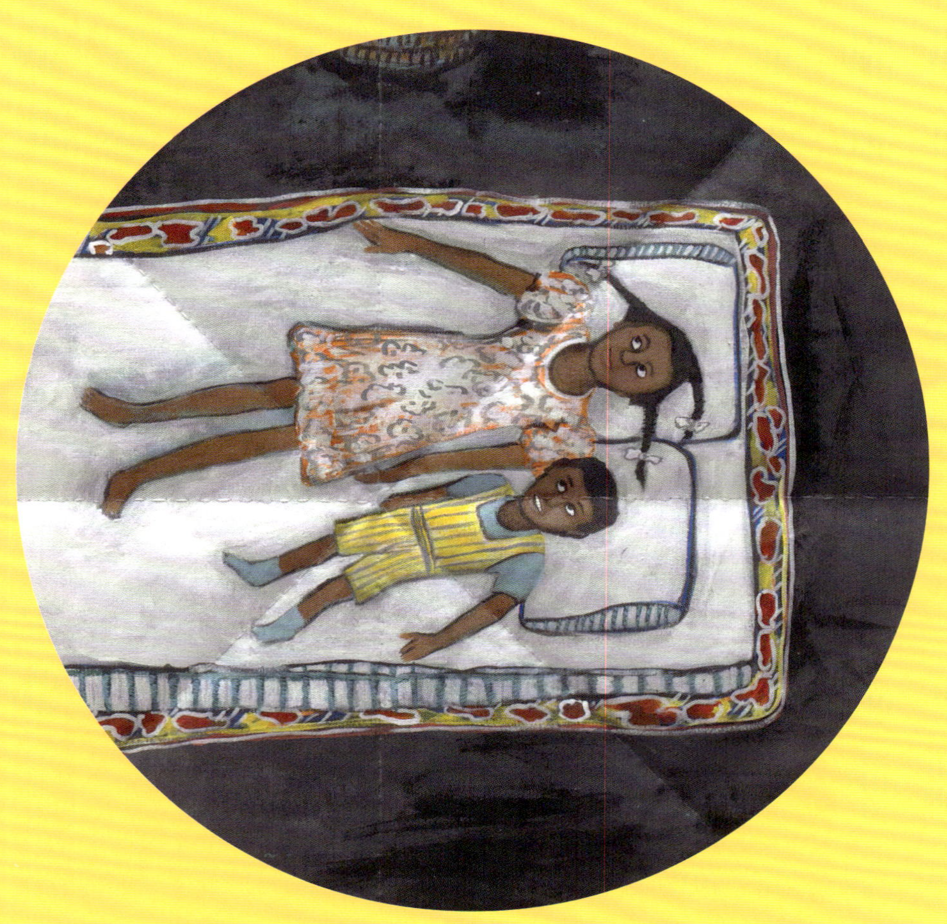

WOMAN ON A BRIDGE #1 OF 5: TAR BEACH

1988

THE WORLD STARTS TO CATCH UP

Over a career spanning seventy years, Faith Ringgold created a body of work that includes prints, paintings, sculpture, performance art, public murals and subway mosaics, but she is perhaps best known for her narrative quilts like *Woman on a Bridge #1 of 5: Tar Beach*.

As a younger artist, she had tried in vain to get her autobiography published, but no one was interested in her story the way she wanted to tell it. Publishers thought Ringgold's happy childhood during the Great Depression didn't ring 'true'; as she said in 2019, her 'experience of being born and raised in Harlem should not have been such a lovely and idyllic story because I am black and therefore all kinds of awful things should have happened to me'.[1]

She decided that the only way she could make her voice heard was to incorporate her story into her art, and for the next fifteen years that's what she did. She began to fill her works with text: biographical details, opinions and stories.

ANYONE CAN FLY

Ringgold was born in 1930 in Depression-era Harlem, New York, and her quilt series *Woman on a Bridge* captures her childhood in the district. As a child, she suffered from severe asthma, and while recuperating would read, write, draw and colour in her books, her creativity actively encouraged by her parents. Her mother, a fashion designer, taught her how to sew and work with fabric. She once said that she couldn't remember a time when she was not doing some form of art.[2]

The *Woman on a Bridge* story-quilts (of which there are five) depict an eight-year-old girl, Cassie Louise Lightfoot, and are inspired by her own happy memories of growing up in Harlem with a loving family.

Cassie is empowered by flying around her neighbourhood, over bridges and above buildings, and Ringgold's work often features flight as a metaphor. Even as a child, she believed that anything is possible; that anyone can fly.

THE HARLEM RENAISSANCE

In the 1920s and 1930s Harlem experienced its own Renaissance, a cultural explosion that saw poets, jazz musicians, artists, dancers, opera singers and authors united by expressing what it means to be Black in the United States. This came about due to factors like the Great Migration, during which Black families from the South moved to the northern states to escape Jim Crow laws. Affordable housing, better opportunities for work and a supportive community made the neighbourhood a cultural hub for Black intellectuals and artists. Proximity to publishers and theatres also allowed creativity to flourish, establishing Harlem as the symbolic 'capital' of Black America.

Faith Ringgold,
*Woman on a Bridge
#1 of 5: Tar Beach*
(detail), 1988.

The musician Duke Ellington lived up the street from Ringgold; Bessie Smith was singing the blues in the Cotton Club; and Augusta Savage was creating sculptures and opening her own art gallery. The prominent jazz musician Sonny Rollins was Ringgold's friend, and her mother regularly took a very young Faith to see celebrated musicians at the Apollo Theater. 'Black people didn't come to America to be free,' the character Lonnie says in Ringgold's 2015 children's book *Harlem Renaissance Party*: 'We fought for our freedom by creating art, music, literature, and dance.'

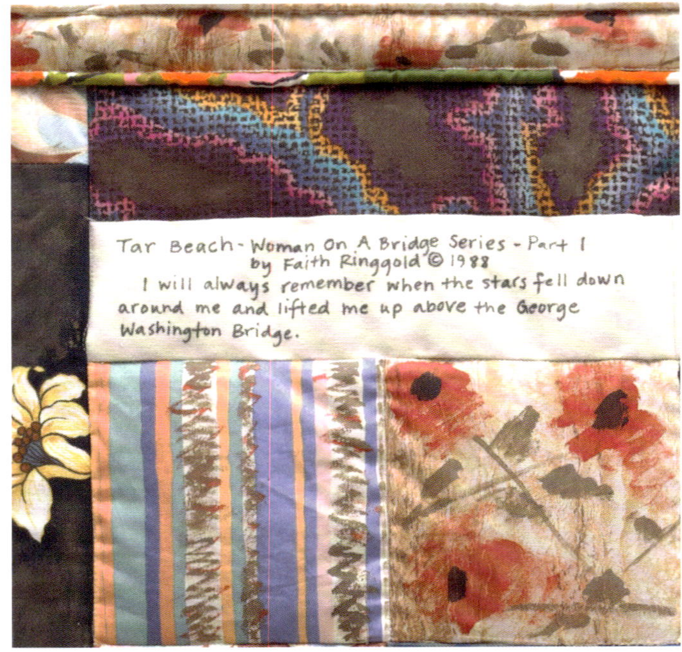

A CALL TO ARMS

Her great grandparents were enslaved, but her grandparents both became teachers, and she grew up in a family that saw education as a way to 'fly'. Ringgold inherited her grandparents' tenacity and determination, and succeeded in getting a place at the City College of New York, from where she received her bachelor's and master's degrees in visual art in 1955 and 1959, respectively.

America was a divided nation. Violence was rife, and protests were breaking out across the country against racial segregation. On 28 August 1963, 250,000 people marched on Washington as part of the rapidly expanding Civil Rights movement. It was here that the world heard Martin Luther King's 'I Have a Dream' speech for the first time.

Meanwhile, Faith Ringgold was thirty-two years old and working without gallery representation. She was painting academic work – landscapes, still lifes and flowers – when the gallerist Ruth White suggested to her that what she was doing was nothing special; these subjects were being painted all over America.[3]

Ringgold took this as a call to arms, and instinctively knew that what she should be doing is painting work that reflected her experience as a Black woman living in America in those times. She needed to tell her story.[4]

Between 1963 and 1967, Ringgold produced her first 'super realism' paintings (as she called them[5]), the *American People* series (p. 272). They were inspired by paintings produced by the artist Jacob Lawrence and the writing of James Baldwin, and would lead to her first and second solo shows. The works addressed issues of racism in America head on. 'Now I knew where my art was going,' she recalled, 'I had so many ideas that I barely had time to execute them.'[6]

Trained as painter, she would next turn to quilt-making, a medium historically tied to African American craft and storytelling, and combine it with painting to create a unique hybrid art form.

Faith Ringgold,
Sonny's Bridge, 1986.

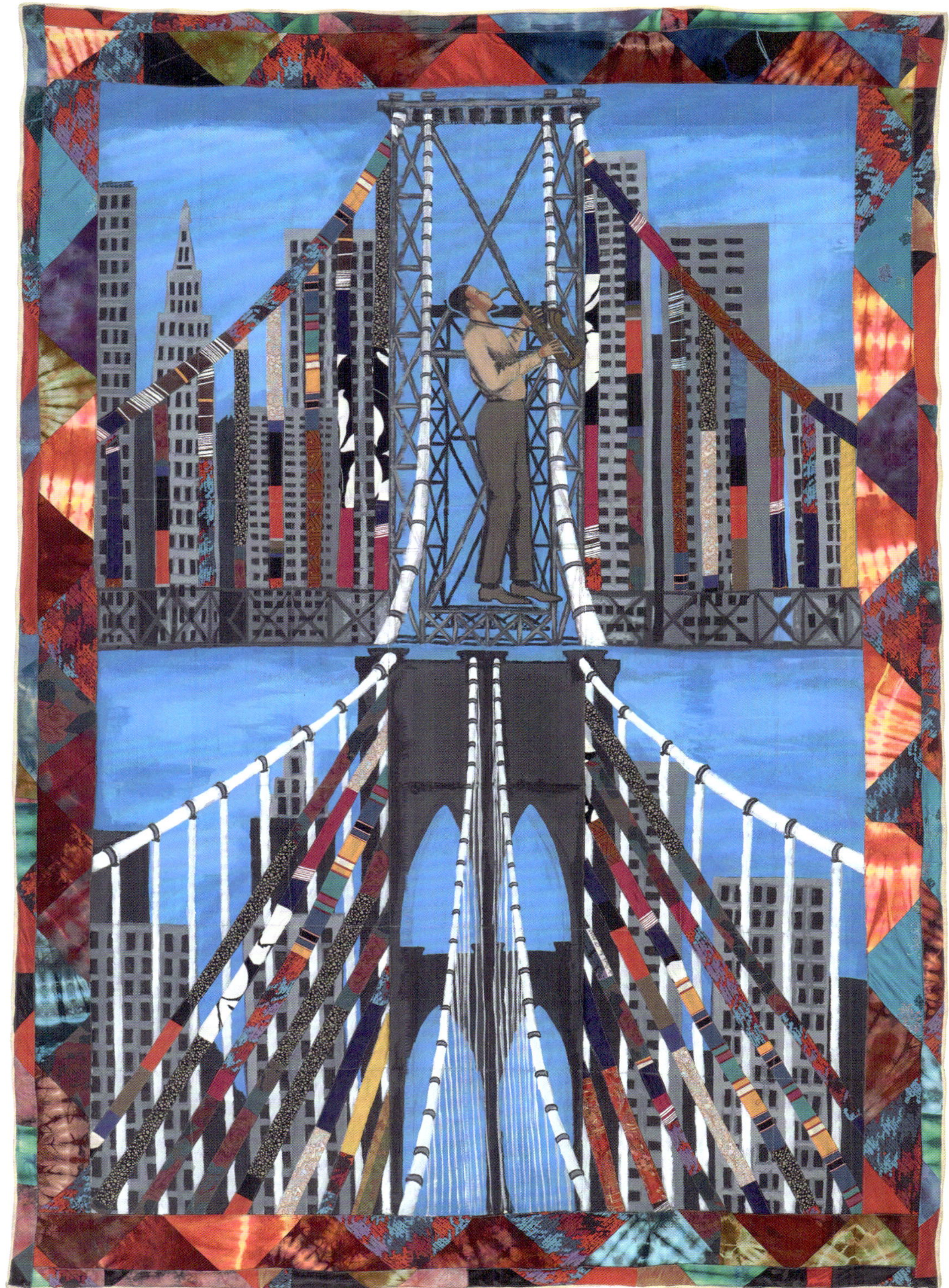

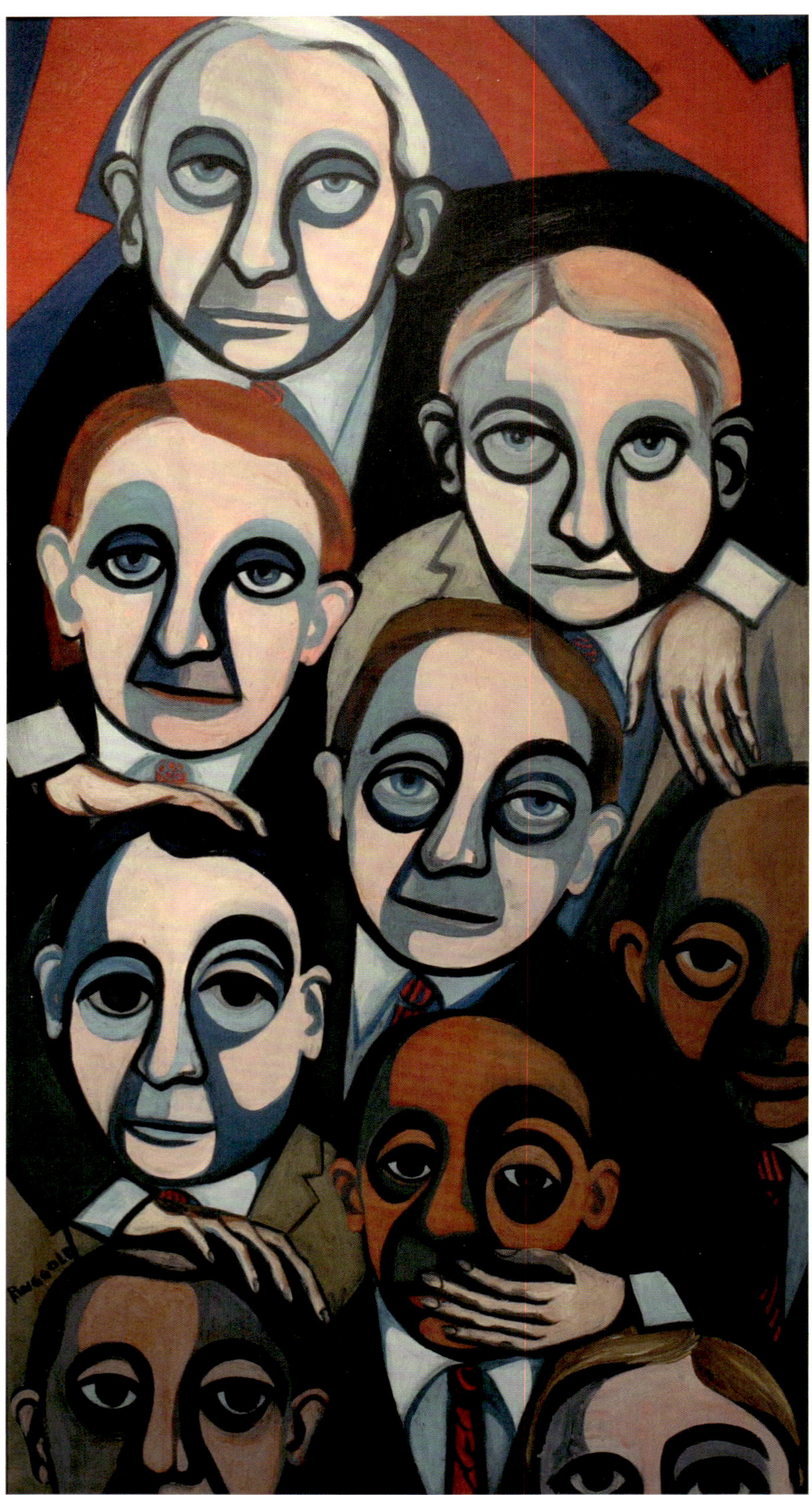

Faith Ringgold,
*American People #8:
The In Crowd*, 1964.

QUILTS IN AMERICA

Quilt-making is a vitally important art form in American history. Early European colonists brought over the quilt-making tradition, and it became a common practice among all communities in America. Initially, quilts were essential household items, often made from fabric scraps and repurposed materials. But over time they became artistic pieces, showcasing intricate patterns and symbolic designs.

Enslaved Africans contributed unique techniques, incorporating bold colours, asymmetry and symbolic motifs, creating quilts that blended African and American aesthetics, often involving storytelling.

Following emancipation in the late 19th century, quilting became a way of preserving African American cultural heritage and family histories across generations. The most well known of these quilts were created on a cotton plantation in Gee's Bend, Alabama. The women of Gee's Bend, descendants of enslaved people on local plantations, developed a unique style of quilt-making characterized by vibrant colours, geometric patterns and improvised designs.

The works addressed issues of racism in America head on

PAINTING THE INSIDE OF HER HEAD

In the 1980s Ringgold turned to quilt-making as a way to express her own experiences as an African American, beyond the traditional boundaries of painting. By combining fabric and painted imagery with handwritten text,

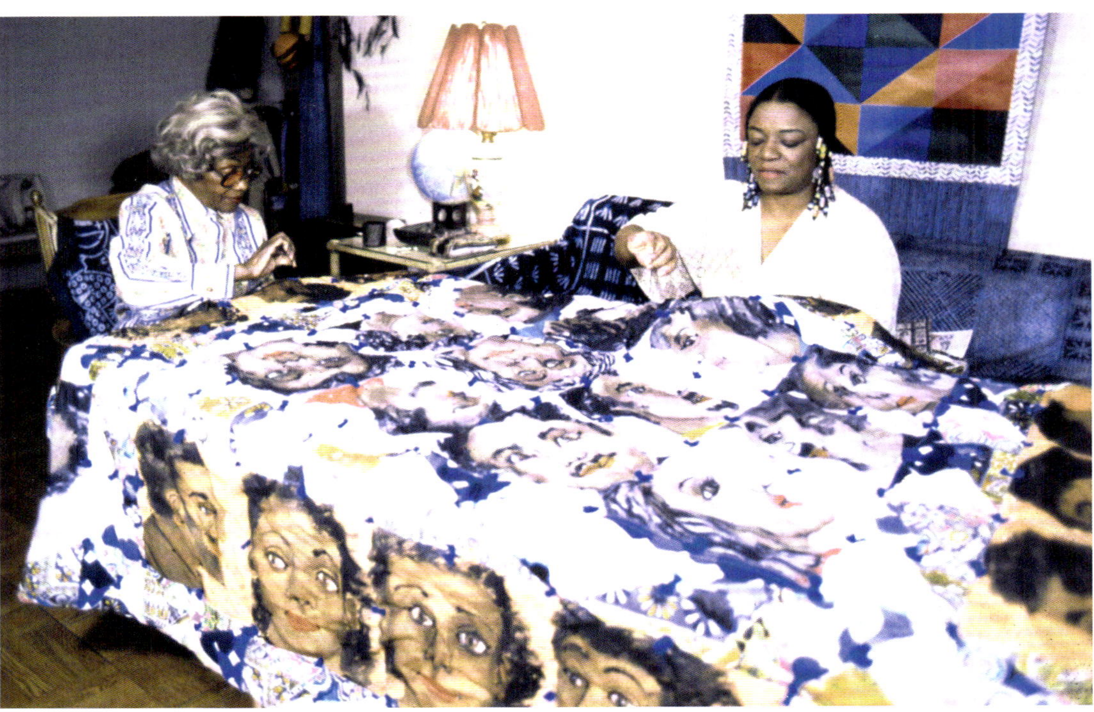

Faith Ringgold with her mother, Madame Willi Posey.

These quilts allowed her to capture not just personal but historical narratives

she created her 'story quilts', merging narrative with visual art. These quilts allowed her to capture not just personal but historical narratives. It was an art form that she could use to address complex issues of race, identity and social justice in a format that also honoured African American women's craft traditions.

Ringgold's mother, Madame Willi Posey, was a fashion designer and seamstress, and it was in collaboration with her that she created her first quilt, *Echoes of Harlem*, in 1980. Sadly, it would be the only quilt they collaborated on, as her beloved mother died soon after in 1981, without seeing Ringgold's success.

Up until her mother's death, her work had been focused on specific issues, but during this mourning period she began painting what she called 'the inside of my head' – more personal, autobiographical works.[7]

She soon started work on the *Baby Faith and Willi* series of quilts, named after her first granddaughter, born in 1982, and her mother. The quilts feature for the first time a flying figure that she later said 'suggests the presence of mother'.[8]

Ringgold's quilts were a critical success, and led to her first major museum show in New York, in 1984, at the age of fifty-four. To make her works, Ringgold would plot out her design and paint the main image directly onto a canvas before taking assorted fabrics, which she got from upholstery stores in New York, and patchworking them all together around the painting. She would then border the piece with hand-lettering to accompany the visuals.

TAR BEACH

Her quilts would go on to tell many kinds of stories, from memories of the Harlem Renaissance to clashes with racist neighbours, but in 1988 she made her most iconic quilt series, *Woman on a Bridge*, with the best known of them being *Tar Beach*.

This is a work that celebrates the art of storytelling. It uses folkloric, almost whimsical visuals to tell powerful tales of race, gender discrimination, liberation and transcendence, using flight as a metaphor for overcoming obstacles that allows Ringgold's characters, particularly Black women and girls, to break free from societal boundaries.

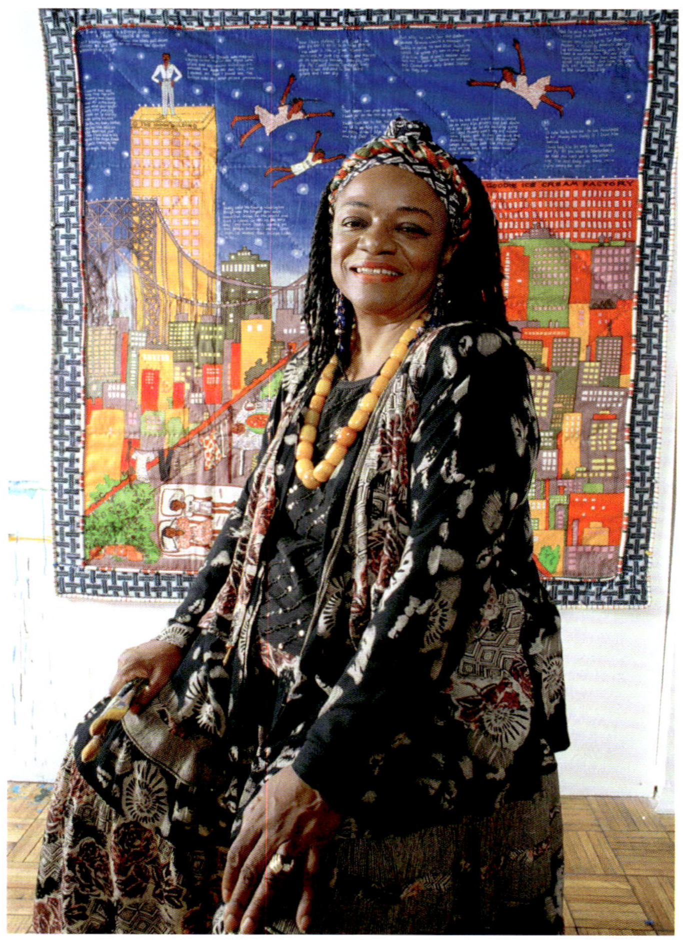

FAITH RINGGOLD

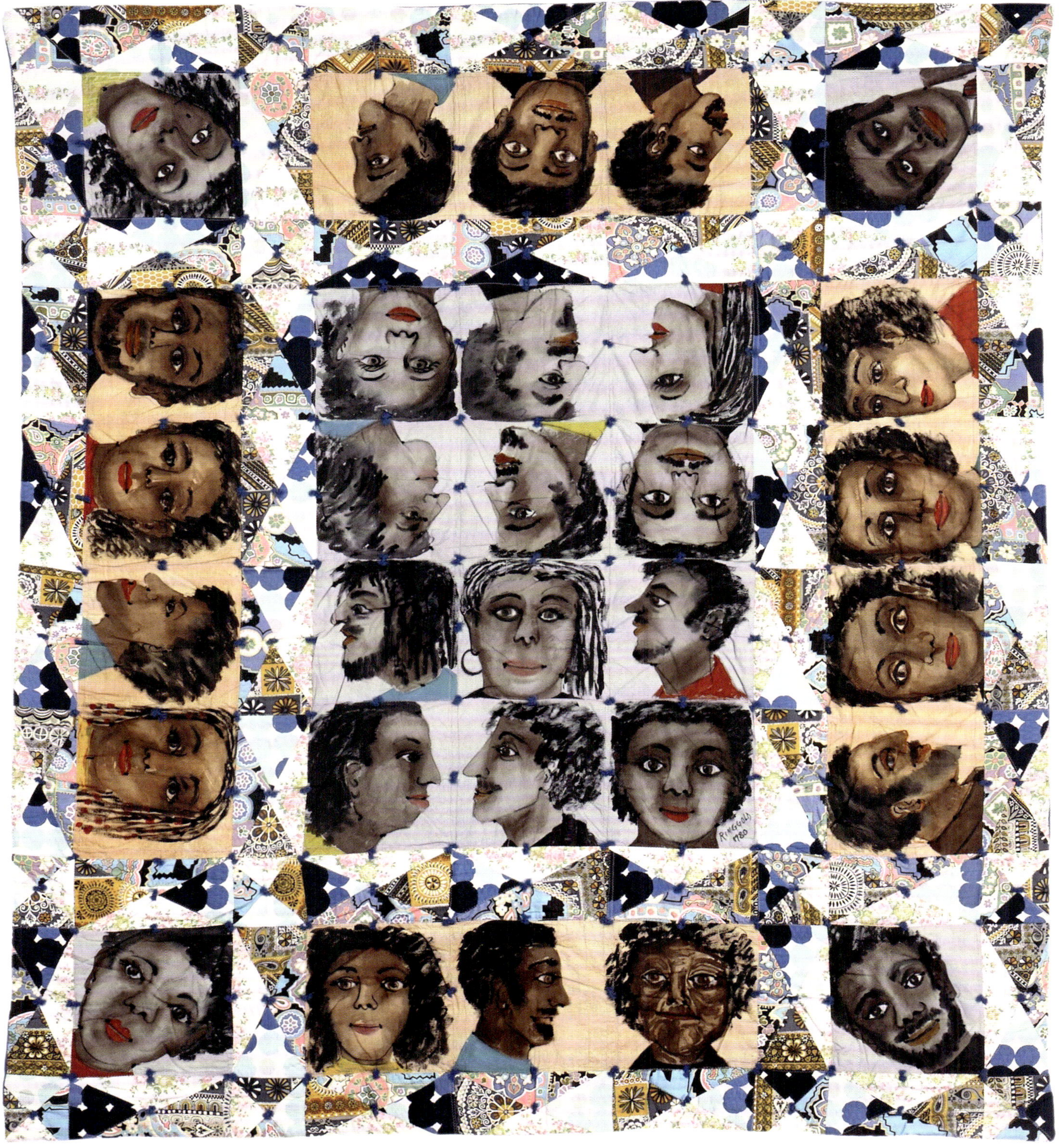

WOMAN ON A BRIDGE #1 OF 5: TAR BEACH

This is a work that celebrates the art of storytelling

'We used to go up on the roof of our building in Harlem, in the summertime when it got hot in the city,' she said in 2019, in conversation with curator Hans Ulrich Obrist. 'My father would bring up a mattress and my brother, sister and I would lie on that. It was gorgeous, and we could see the George Washington Bridge.'[9]

The *Tar Beach* quilt tells the story of one such hot summer night in Harlem, when Ringgold's heroine, eight-year-old Cassie Louise Lightfoot, fantasizes about flying over the same nearby bridge. Cassie's story echoes that of the young Faith, who also dreamt of possibilities beyond her limitations.

The George Washington Bridge comes with its own symbolism for Ringgold: it opened when she was a year old, literally towering over her life and her neighbourhood. It was built during the most severe economic depression in modern history, and was seen as a beacon of hope, a technical wonder. It was a major presence for the young Faith, and a cultural reference point that she returned to many times in other quilts.

Tar Beach shows her mother and father and their neighbours Mr and Mrs Honey playing cards under the night sky, clothes hanging on a washing line next to them. Home-cooked food is laid out on a flowery tablecloth and Cassie and her baby brother 'Bebe' are on a mattress, relaxing on the roof of their apartment block, enjoying what Harlemites called a 'Tar Beach'. As Cassie and Bebe dream under the stars, another version of Cassie flies overhead.

A NEW GENERATION

Ringgold had tried to get her quilts published in a book for years, but was told there was no market for it. Then in 1988 Andrea Cascardi, a children's book editor who had seen a poster for an upcoming exhibition of the artist's work,[10] got in touch with Ringgold to propose that the stories woven into her quilts would make a great children's book. Ringgold had never even thought about writing a children's book, but agreed immediately.[11]

Tar Beach (1991) launched her unexpected career as a published author and illustrator of children's books, winning the prestigious Coretta Scott King Award for illustration in 1992. The same year it was named a Caldecott Honor Book, and it is still in print today.

Her children's books allowed her to extend the messages of her quilts – freedom, empowerment, heritage and resilience – to a new, global audience who may not have encountered her artwork in museums, and in a format accessible to young people. In effect, it democratized her art, enabling her messages of self-worth, cultural pride and social justice to inspire in ways that traditional art exhibits might not.

Ringgold passed away in April 2024, but her legacy lives on through her art practice; as she wrote in her memoirs, there is now 'an audience of children who will grow up knowing that an artist does not have to be white or male...[who] will be our next artists, museum directors, curators, collectors, art critics, and teachers of art'.[12]

Faith Ringgold,
*Woman on a Bridge
#1 of 5: Tar Beach*, 1988.

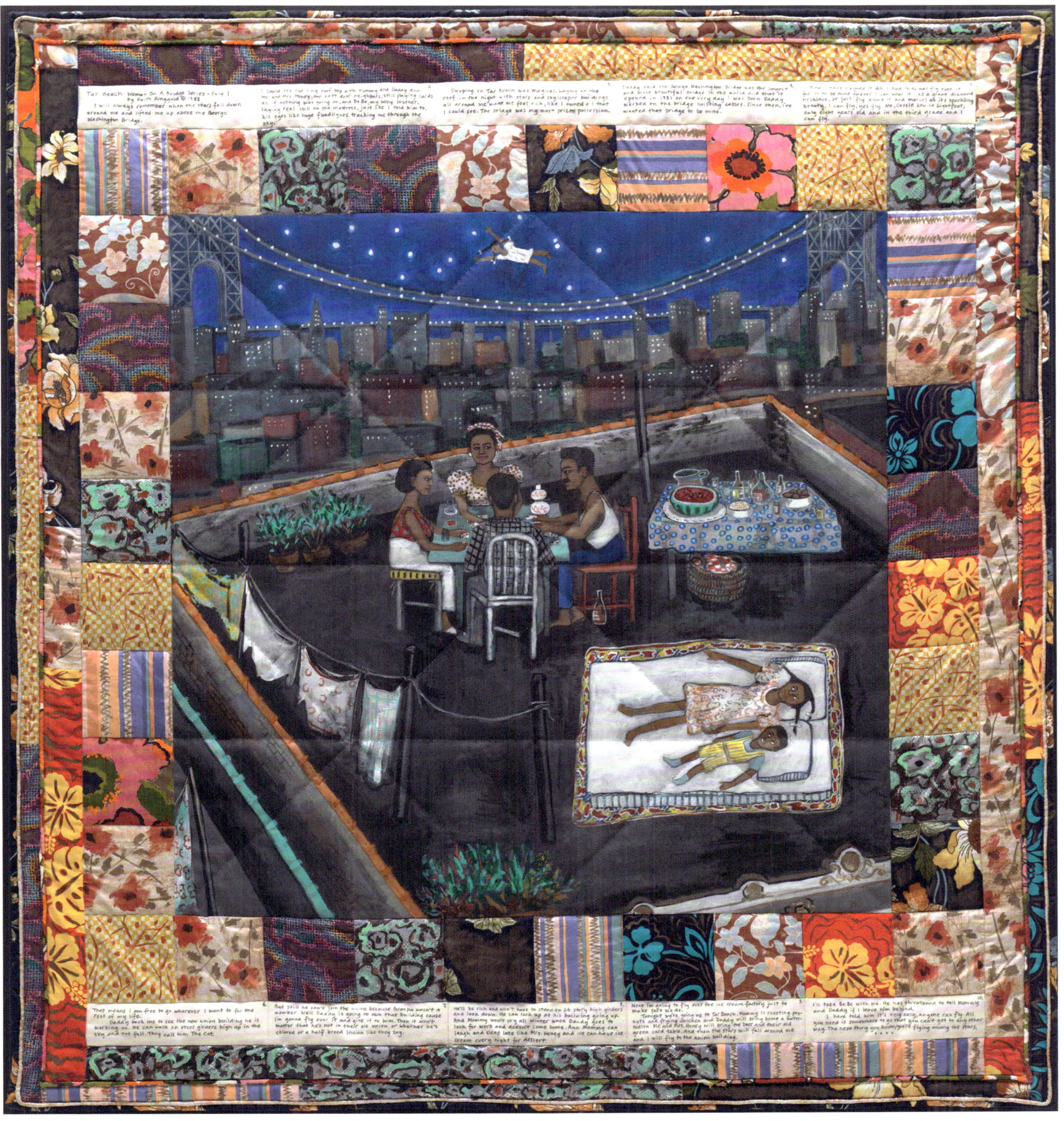

28

EL
ANATSUI

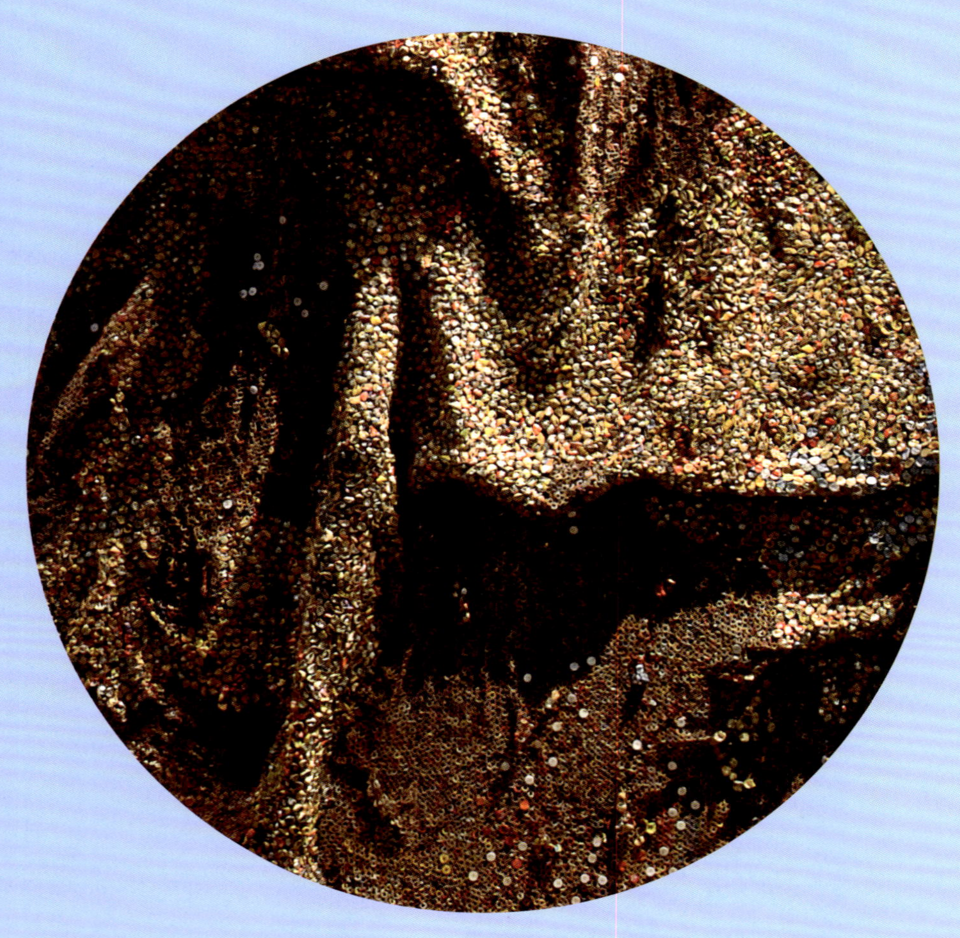

DUSASA II

2007

A COMPLETE PICTURE

In 1984 the Museum of Modern Art in New York opened the exhibition 'Primitivism in 20th Century Art: Affinity of the Tribal and the Modern', which featured approximately 150 works by modern artists like Pablo Picasso and Constantin Brancusi alongside more than 200 objects from the indigenous cultures of Oceania, Africa and North America. The exhibition would be remembered not for the works, however, but rather the ensuing scandal. Critics lambasted the show for its Eurocentric gaze, decrying it as a demonstration of 'Western egotism still as unbridled as in the centuries of colonialism and souvenirism'.

The pieces were displayed with a complete lack of contextualization, only serving to illustrate how they facilitated 'superior' artists from the Global North. The criticism forced the art world to re-evaluate language and codification around art and artists from the Global South.

But apart from a handful of successes, contemporary art created by artists from Africa remained virtually unknown in the West and marginalized in international art markets until the 1990s.[2]

DUSASA II

El Anatsui is a contemporary African artist whose work references traditional African art forms and practices, using modern-day detritus as materials.

The wall hanging *Dusasa II* is an immense interconnected work made from thousands of discarded aluminium bottle caps, which El Anatsui and his team flattened, reshaped and tied together with copper wire. Along with two other installation works, *Awakened* and *Fresh and Fading Memories* (also large-scale metal tapestriews), *Dusasa II* was first presented at the 2007 Venice Biennale, a moment that has been described by some as a 'turning point' in Anatsui's career,[3] and was quickly bought by New York's Metropolitan Museum of Art.

His 'tapestries' are neither paintings nor sculptures, yet they aren't installations either. They are a combination of all those things, defying categorization.

The artist is from Anyako, in the Volta region of Ghana, and is a citizen of the Ewe nation, an ethnic group that extends up to Togo. The title 'Dusasa' comes from the Ewe words *du* and *sasa*, meaning a fusion of disparate elements on a monumental scale, and this translates precisely into his art. Anatsui describes his work as a 'communal patchwork made by a team of townspeople', referencing the artist's team of assistants.[4]

ART SCHOOL

Before he achieved global success, Anatsui had a distinguished forty-year career as a professor of sculpture and departmental head at the

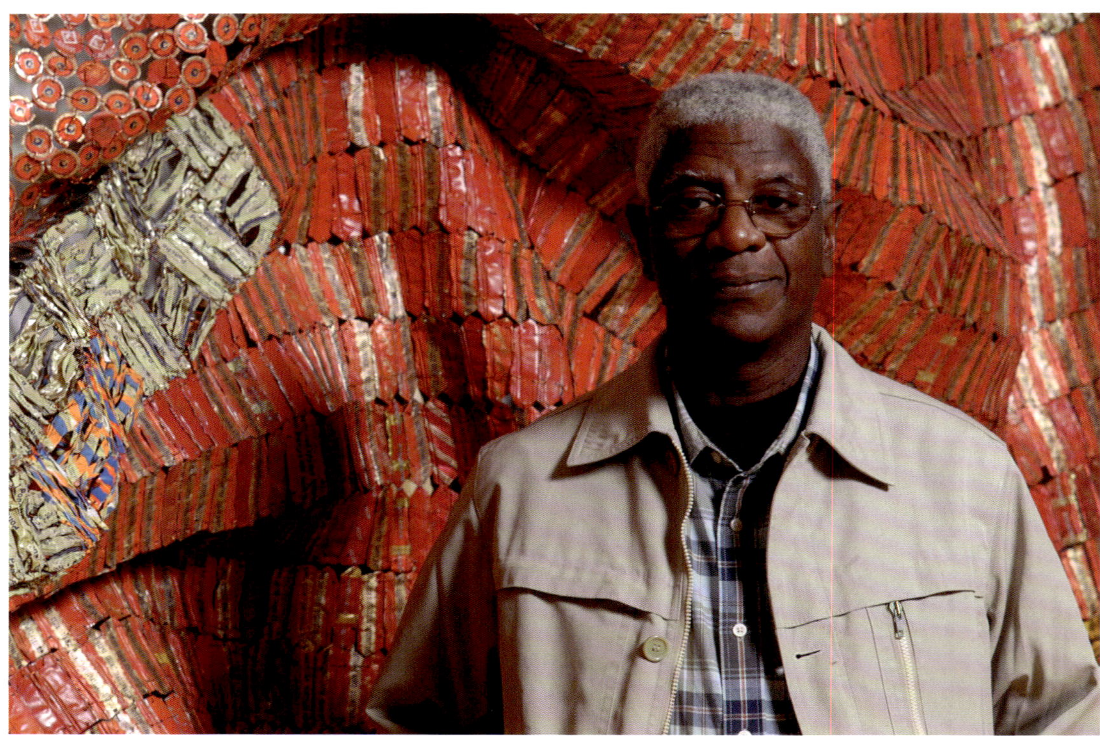

University of Nigeria. By 1990 his works had been shown in group shows in Europe, Japan and the United States and an iconic 1995 solo show in the UK, but he remained little known to the general public in the West until his metal hangings appeared at the Venice Biennale and caused a sensation.

After Ghanaian independence from British colonial rule in 1957, artists, whose education up until now focused entirely on European art history, began to reject foreign influences and cultural references,[5] instead drawing inspiration from African traditions and imagery. It was in this climate of growing creative liberation that Anatsui attended the College of Art at Kwame Nkrumah University of Science and Technology in Kumasi, Ghana, in 1965. Here he gained an increased awareness of indigenous art, but was still receiving 1960s neo-colonialist training, based mainly on Western practices.

During his final year at university, he was exposed to indigenous art forms such as pottery, weaving and wood carving that would lay the groundwork for his exploration of materiality, form and transformation. In particular, his studies of adinkra cloth, which he would draw on for his 'tapestries'.

Adinkra are symbols that can be found hand-printed on Ghanaian dyed fabric, which is often large in scale, and each symbol has

El Anatsui with *Dusasa II*, 2007.

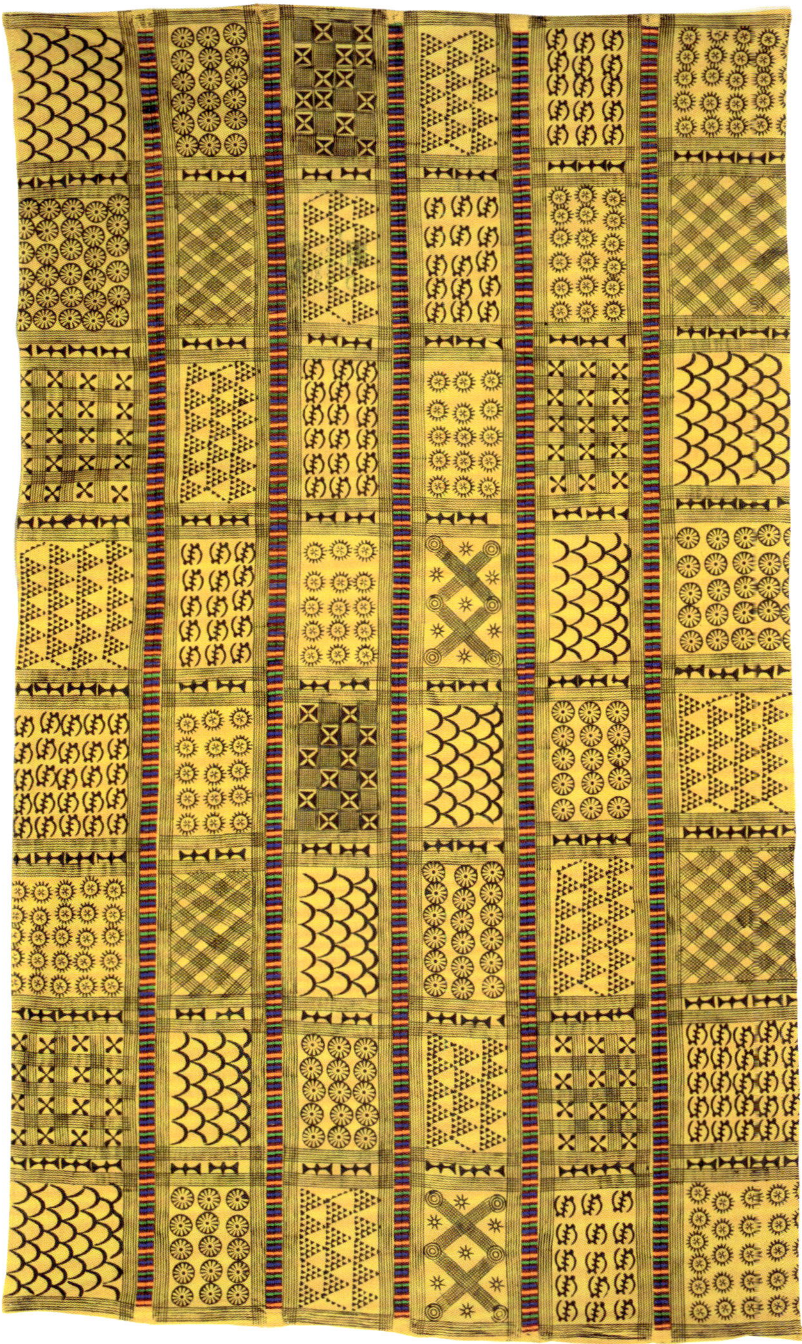

its own meaning. Africa has one of the greatest concentrations of linguistic diversity in the world, with over 500 languages spoken in West Africa alone, and abstract patterns and pictographic symbols were developed as a means of visual communication.

Anatsui was inspired by the abstraction, the colours, the craftsmanship and the symbolism of traditional textiles, and his work would imitate the draping, the fluidity and the textures to blur the lines between textiles and sculpture.

He would take these ideas and historical references – in particular, the way adinkra cloth uses abstract, geometric symbols to convey complex ideas – and inlay them with contemporary meaning.

BOTTLE TOPS AND TIN CANS

In 1998 Anatsui happened upon a bag full of aluminium seals from African liquor bottles. At the time, he didn't see it as any more significant than other found materials; 'I let the material lead me,' he said. 'If it can't say something, then it better not be *made* to say it.'[6]

Anatsui's work uses locally sourced materials that are often readily available. Whether it's used bottle caps, tin cans and clay pottery or the wooden trays used for carrying goods in Ghanaian markets, it is most important to him that the materials have had a previous life. Anatsui says that once they have been used, 'they [acquire] a lot of history and meaning and a lot of maybe spiritual energy, as well'.[7]

Every object is carefully selected and has a resonance, a story to tell. The colourful glinting caps are so beautiful when combined that we are drawn to them aesthetically; it's only afterwards that we realize what they are, and what they might represent.

When European colonizers came to Africa, distilled spirits like rum and gin were introduced, first as gifts and then as currency

Every object is carefully selected and has a resonance, a story to tell

for both goods and the enslaved people who were brought to America and the Caribbean. Anatsui's first bottle top works draw upon these specific connections with the transatlantic slave trade that linked Europe, Africa, and the Americas.

Dusasa II is just one example of how simple materials can raise complex issues and introduce viewers to hidden histories. Anatsui sees the materials as so much more than a simplistic comment on recycling or repurposing; they are a springboard for exploring diverse themes of migration, identity, globalization, colonization and the passage of time. As he once said: 'I think my work has principally been about change,'[8] and this emphasis can be seen as a metaphor for the constant evolution of both the physical and cultural landscape.

One of his early projects was a series of wall-based pieces constructed from wooden display trays used in Ghanaian market stalls. Anatsui used hot iron tools to 'brand' the plates with adinkra symbols.

We can look at early works like these as the formation of ideas and the establishment of working practices that would lead to his later wall hangings; the use of found local materials; the transformation of an ordinary object into art; and the beginning of collaboration with local people that would carry through to today.

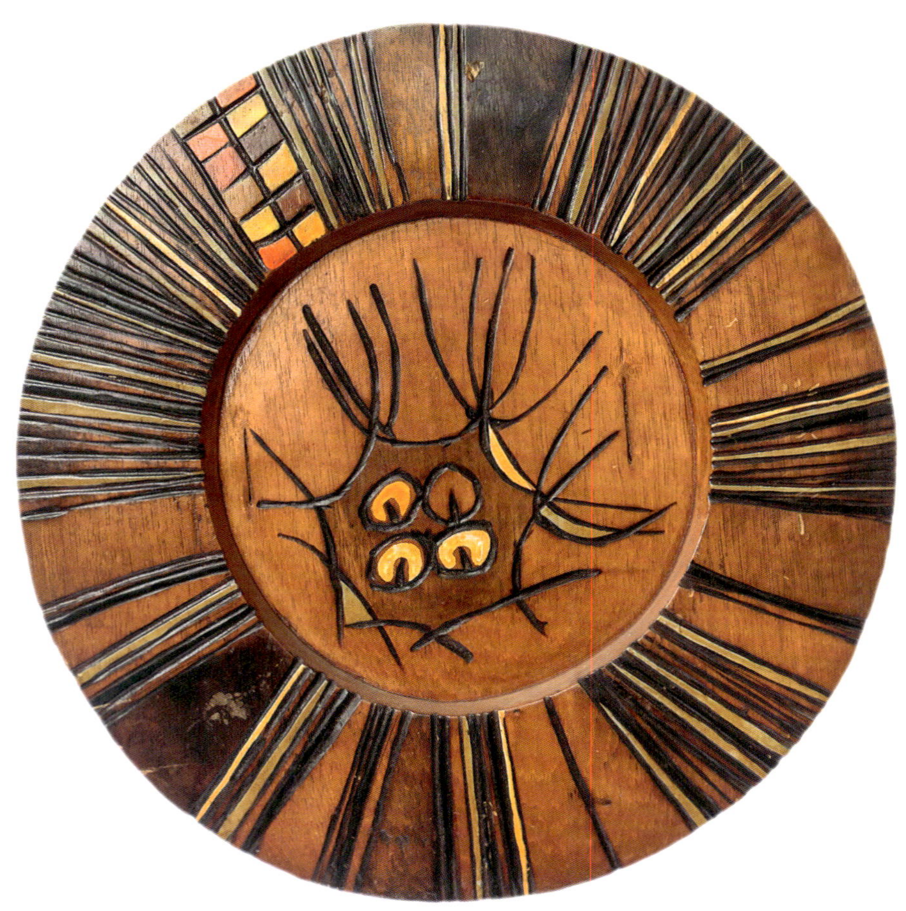

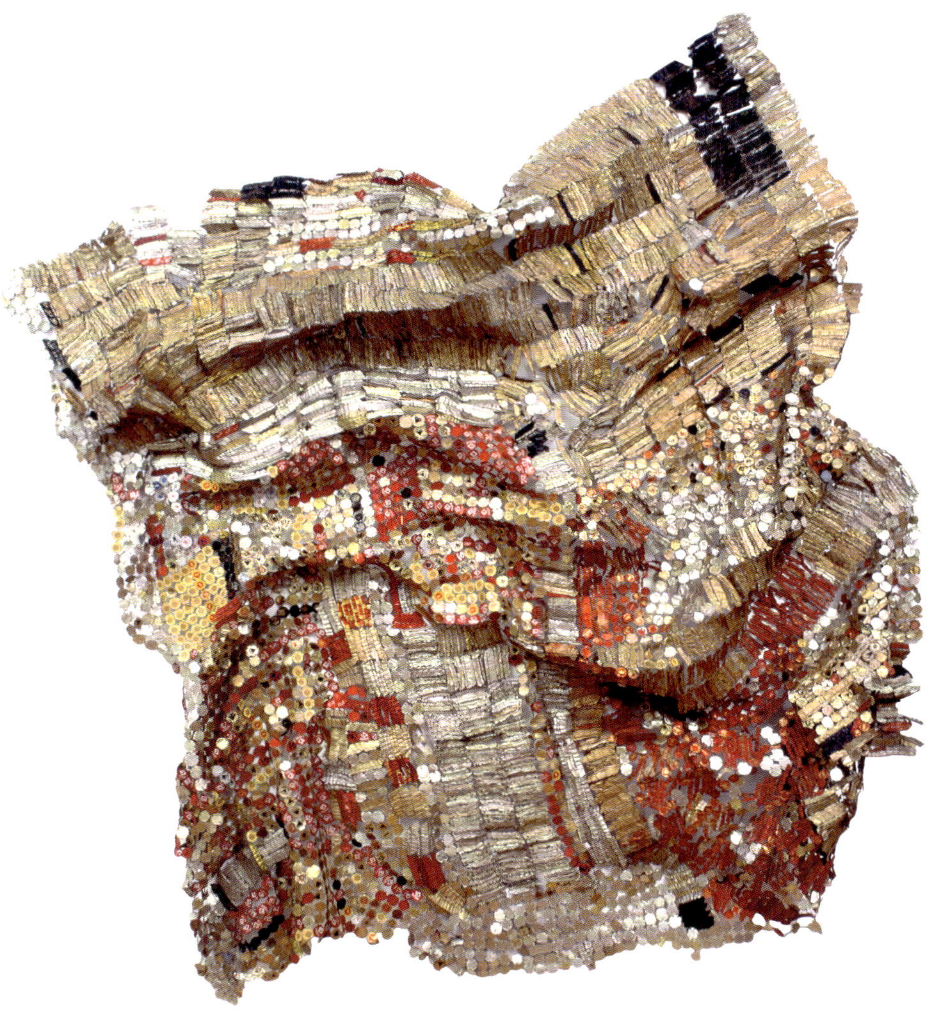

VENICE BIENNALE

Anatsui's work at the 2007 Biennale may have been a turning point, but two of his earlier 'metal cloth' works, *Woman's Cloth* and *Man's Cloth* (2002), were shown in Europe in 2002. Featuring in an exhibition at the October Gallery in London, the pieces got the attention of important collectors and were bought by the British Museum that same year.

Yet although Anatsui was known to some mainstream critics and collectors, the wider art world and press were taken by surprise when they experienced *Dusasa I* and *Dusasa II* at the Venice Biennale, works new to international audiences.[9]

The curator of the 52nd Biennale, Robert Storr, who had invited Anatsui to exhibit his work, said 'this is the recycling of industrial production into something that is completely transcendent and made out of junk'. He continued, 'it has a kind of exaltation I have not seen before'.[10]

As an artist, Anatsui miraculously transforms his materials, as if creating gold from base metal. A teacher for over four decades (he started in 1975), Anatsui encouraged a new

Anatsui's sculptures
are designed to be shaped
in amorphous ways
and altered in appearance
for each installation

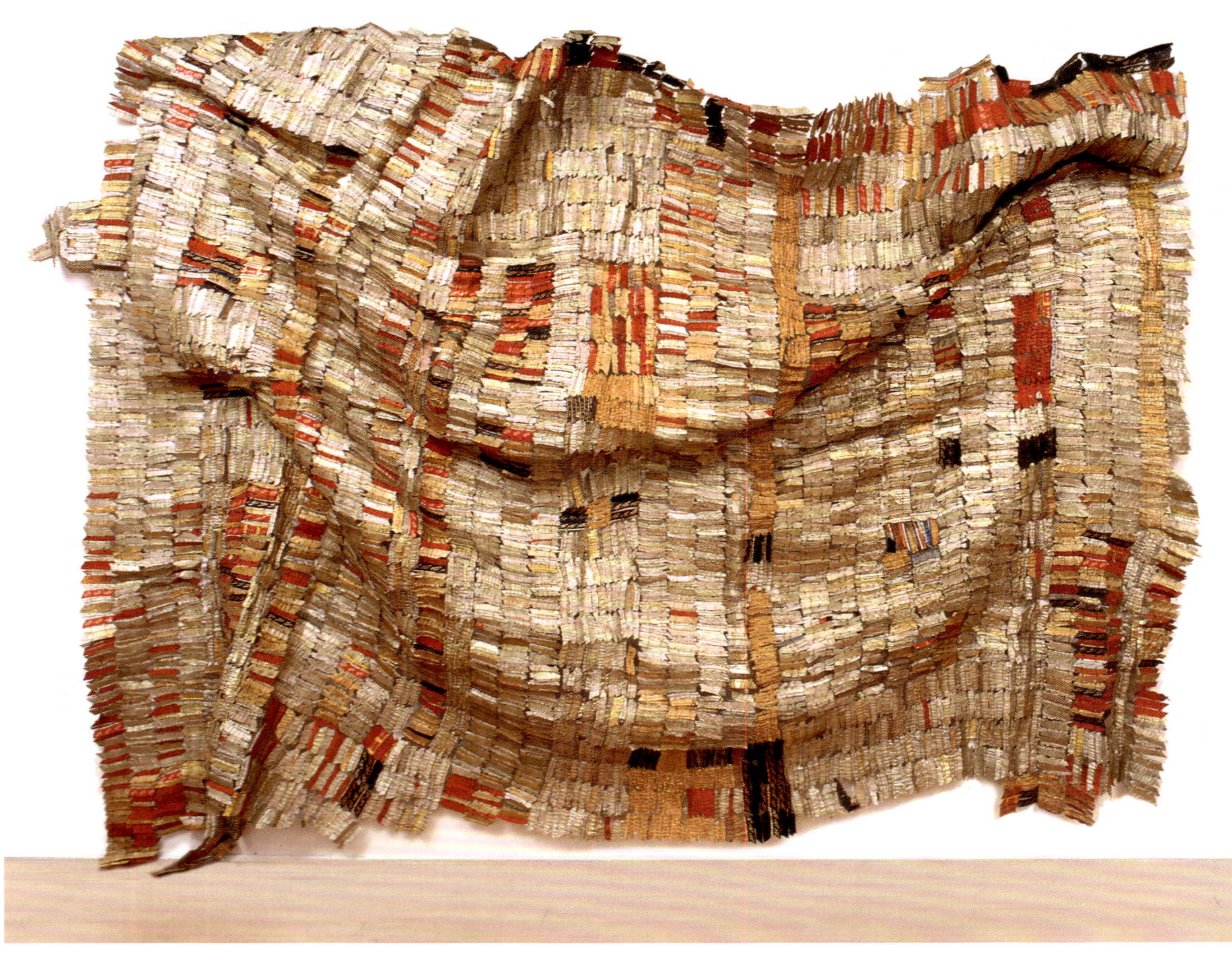

EL ANATSUI

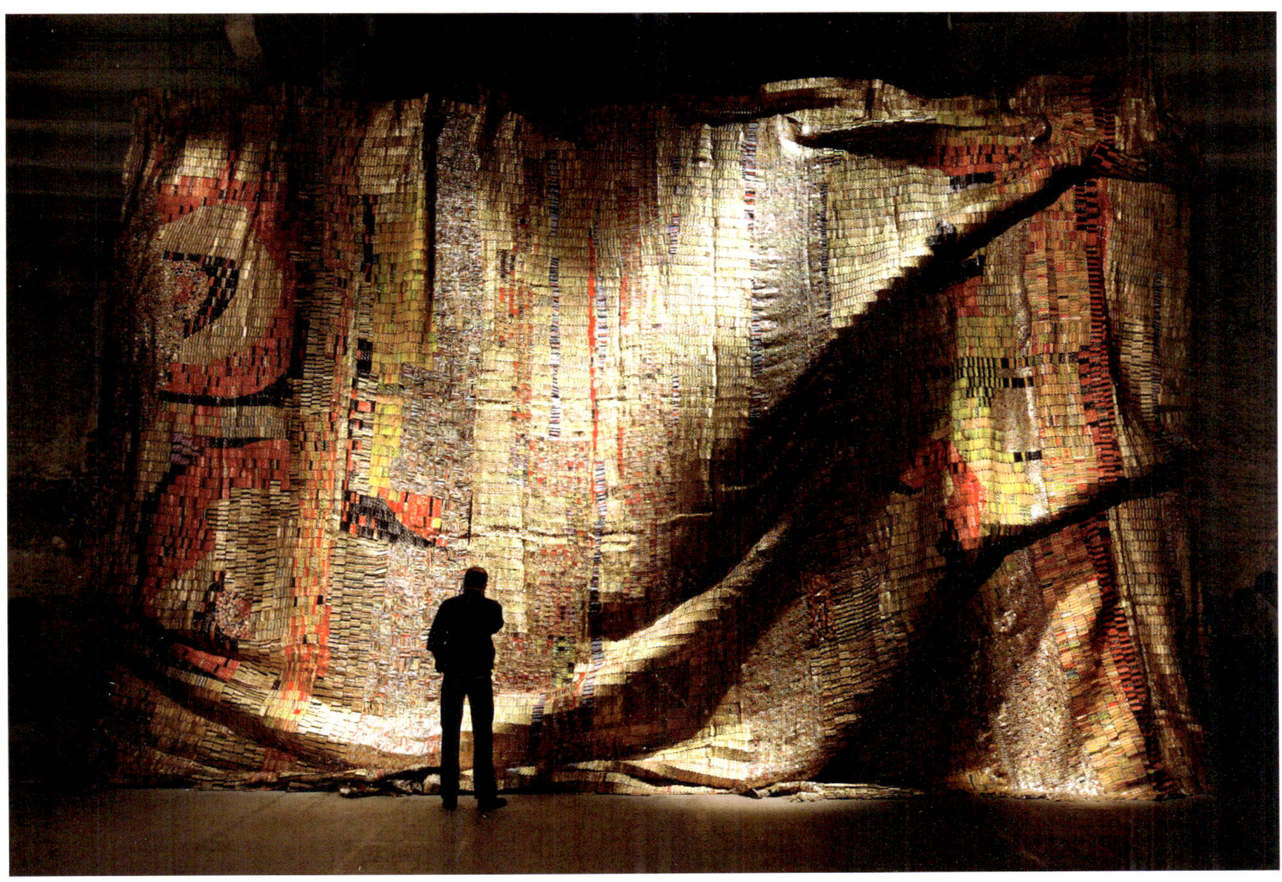

generation of African students to use materials that can be acquired easily from the local environment at little to no cost. His impact as an educator was profound, shaping the contemporary art landscape in West Africa and beyond.

TECHNIQUE

Anatsui's methods are not dissimilar to the use of *andamento* in a mosaic, meaning the visual flow created by the placement of rows of tesserae. *Dusasa II* is made from thousands of discarded aluminium caps from liquor bottles produced in distilleries across Nigeria. The caps are shaped and flattened by a team of assistants who then construct 'blocks' of joined bottle caps on the ground, divided by shade and colour, to be shifted around on the studio floor as Anatsui decides on the composition of the piece.

The metallic wall hangings, which one might presume to be solid and stiff, are in fact flexible and relatively light, so they can easily be moved around. The bigger sheets are made of separable sections, which allows the work to be easily transported. 'The process', Anatsui says, 'was subverting the stereotype of metal as a stiff, rigid medium and rather showing it as a soft, pliable, almost sensuous material.'[11] In fact, he delivered the first two metal wall hangings he showed in London in suitcases.

Most of the works in this book are designed to be seen a certain way – they have

opposite
El Anatsui, *Man's Cloth*, 2002.

El Anatsui, *Dusasa I*, 2007.

a fixed viewpoint, usually dictated by the artist. Rodin's *Kiss* in London is no different physically from the one in Paris (see Chapter 13). But *Dusasa II* is different every time it is shown, and it is intentionally 'unfixed'. Anatsui's sculptures are designed to be shaped in amorphous ways and altered in appearance for each installation. When museums or galleries show his work, he doesn't provide installation instructions as a matter of principle. They are the rarest of artworks in that the artist allows the museum, gallery or collector to decide how his work is seen.

AFRICAN ART TAKES CENTRE STAGE

The climate in the art world has changed somewhat since 2007. International auction houses such as Sotheby's and Christie's now have modern and contemporary African art departments, and it is not uncommon for modern and contemporary African art to sell for millions of dollars. As Anatsui says: 'Artworks from hitherto unacknowledged regions of the world, not only Africa, are being collected as artworks rather than curios or ethnological objects.'[12]

Contemporary African art is more widely appreciated in the international art world, and it seems that the rest of the world is finally recognizing what artistic and creative circles across Africa knew all along, that El Anatsui, one of the most remarkable artists working today, is not alone.

While there were influential African artists before him and there are numerous talents emerging today, the rising prominence of African art goes far beyond financial value or fame. It's about offering a fuller, nuanced and more balanced understanding of art, culture and history. It is a step towards creating a more representative global art scene.

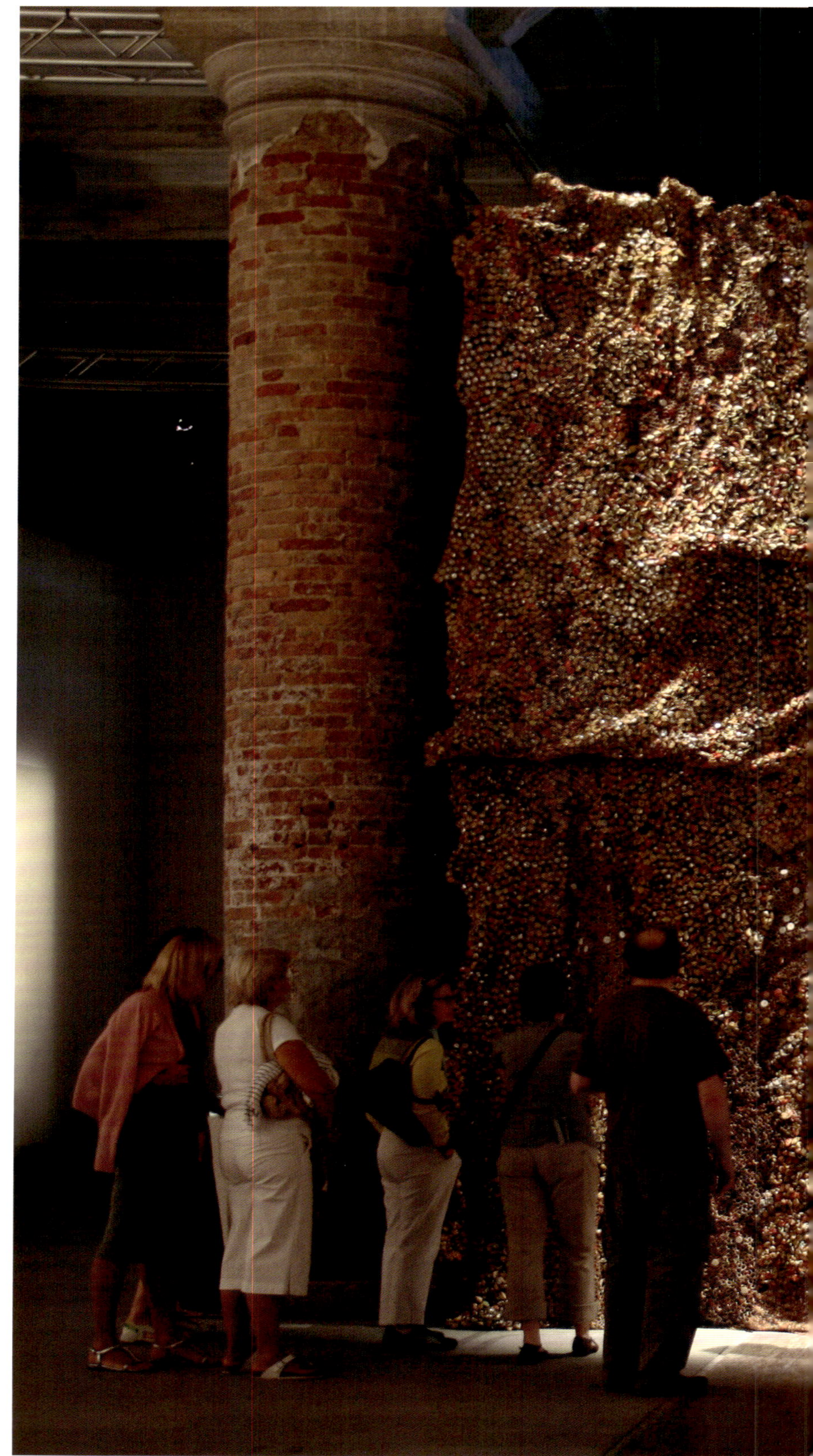

El Anatsui, *Dusasa II*, 2007.

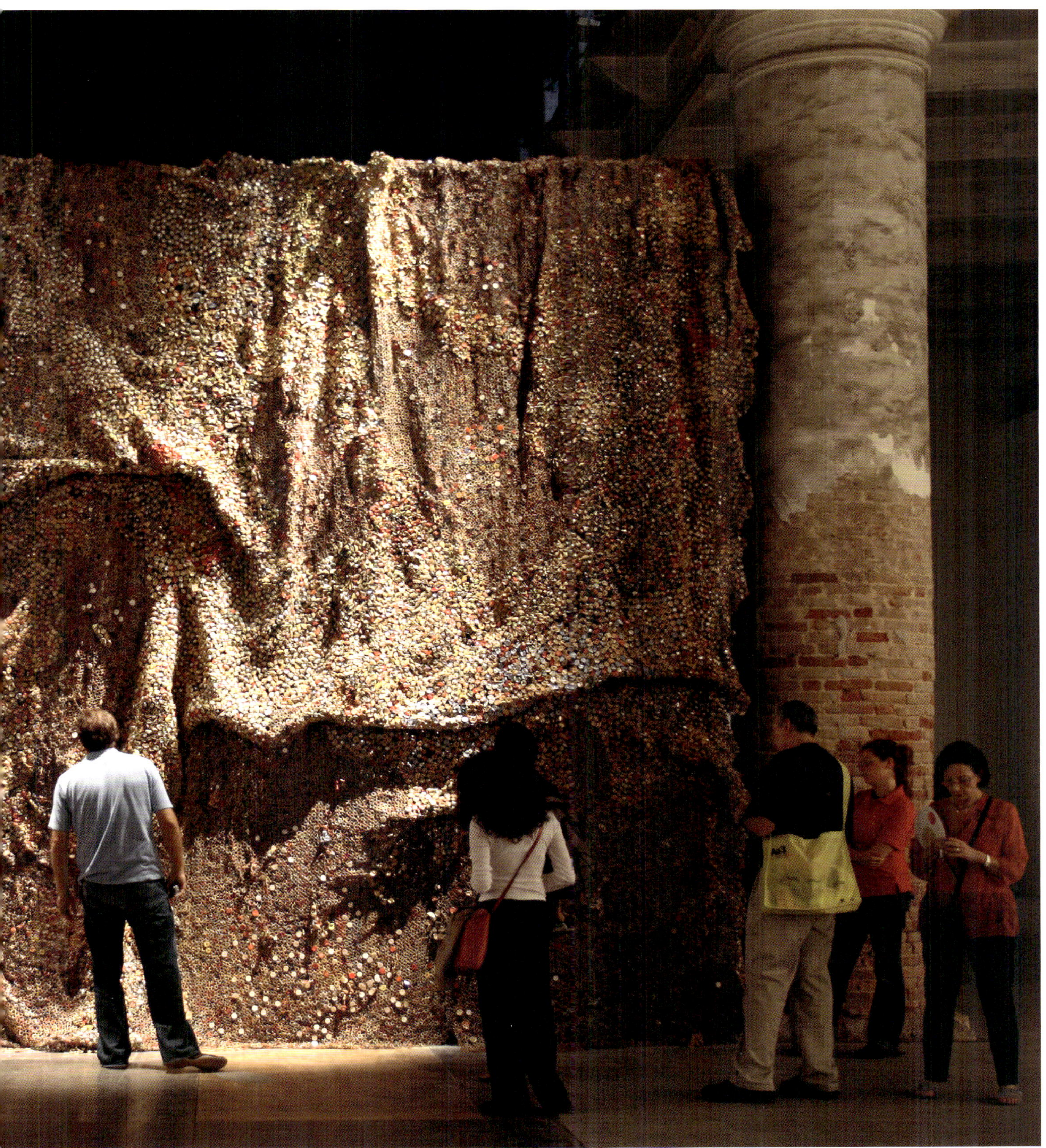

29

YAYOI KUSAMA

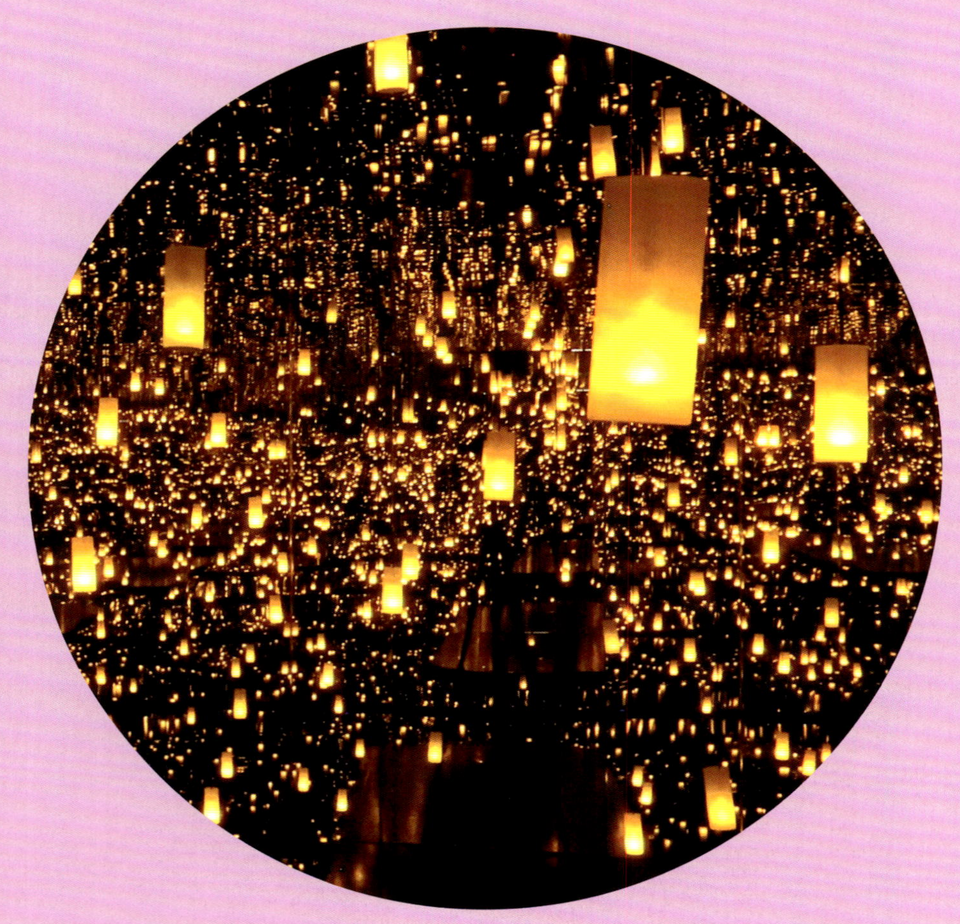

THE AFTERMATH OF OBLITERATION OF ETERNITY

2009

SELF-OBLITERATION

At around the age of ten, Yayoi Kusama had her first hallucination, which she described as 'flashes of light, auras, or dense fields of dots'.[1] Kusama's polka dots became her battle cry and have remained one of her most consistent motifs. 'Bring on Picasso,' she would say. 'Bring on Matisse, bring on anybody! I would stand up to them all with a single polka dot.'[2]

Kusama has struggled with her mental health for her whole life and has openly shared her experiences with hallucinations and obsessive thoughts, which shaped her artistic vision. Creating art became a way for her to process and manage these experiences, turning her visions into tangible ideas.

In 2001 the documentary film-maker Heather Lenz applied for funding to make a documentary film about Kusama but was told that the artist 'had no name recognition'.[3] Although Kusama has exhibited in international institutions throughout her career, her intense global recognition, what some have called the 'Kusama brand', is a relatively new phenomenon. The film *Kusama: Infinity* was finally released in 2018 to great acclaim and commercial success.

So, what happened between 2001 and 2018? Kusama's rise was fuelled by a renewed interest in experiential art and virtual spaces but, in part, the acceleration in her level of fame has been driven by social media, most importantly the image- and video-centred platform Instagram, which like it or not has changed how many people relate to art.

It is clear from Kusama exhibitions around the world that the artist has a very loyal, and very young, audience. People queue up for hours for just a minute or two in one of her *Infinity Room* installations – time enough to take an infinite selfie that will join millions more on the internet, itself infinite.

A MINUTE OR TWO

Kusama's *Infinity Rooms* are immersive installations featuring mirrored walls that create the illusion of infinite space, often filled with repeating objects like polka-dotted forms or suspended lights. Visitors step into these rooms and find themselves surrounded by endless reflections, losing a sense of physical boundaries as their images multiply. By enveloping viewers in an expansive, otherworldly environment, the *Infinity Rooms* invite us to contemplate our place in the universe.

Kusama produced her first *Infinity Room*, *Phalli's Field*, in 1965. Prior to this she had spent two years stuffing fabric phalluses and attaching them to chairs, tables and soft furnishings for a body of work known as *Accumulations*. They were daring, erotic and challenging, but with a humorous edge typical of Kusama. She explained the process as 'making penises in order to heal my feelings of disgust toward sex'.[4]

*Visitors step into these
rooms and find themselves
surrounded by endless
reflections, losing a sense
of physical boundaries*

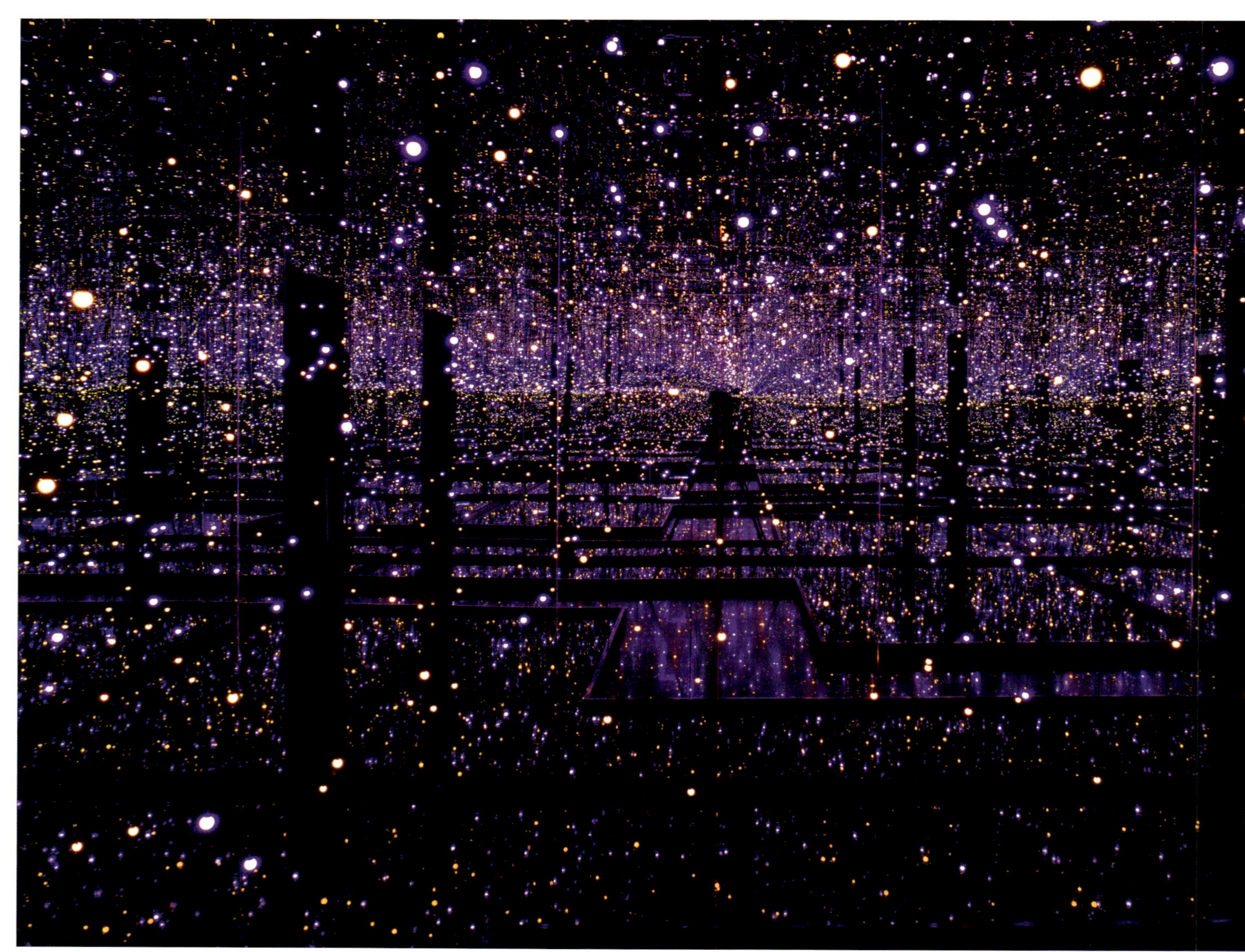

YAYOI KUSAMA

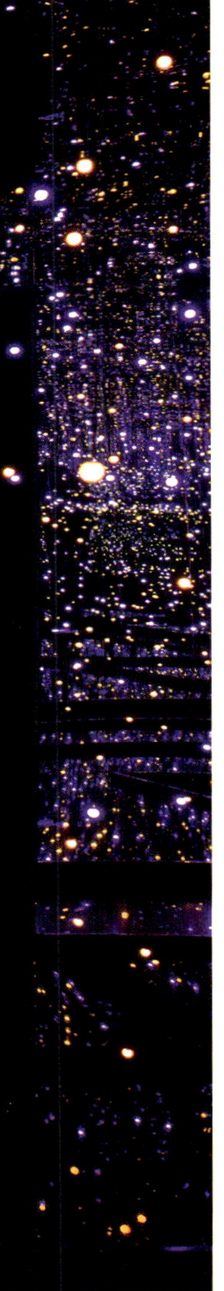

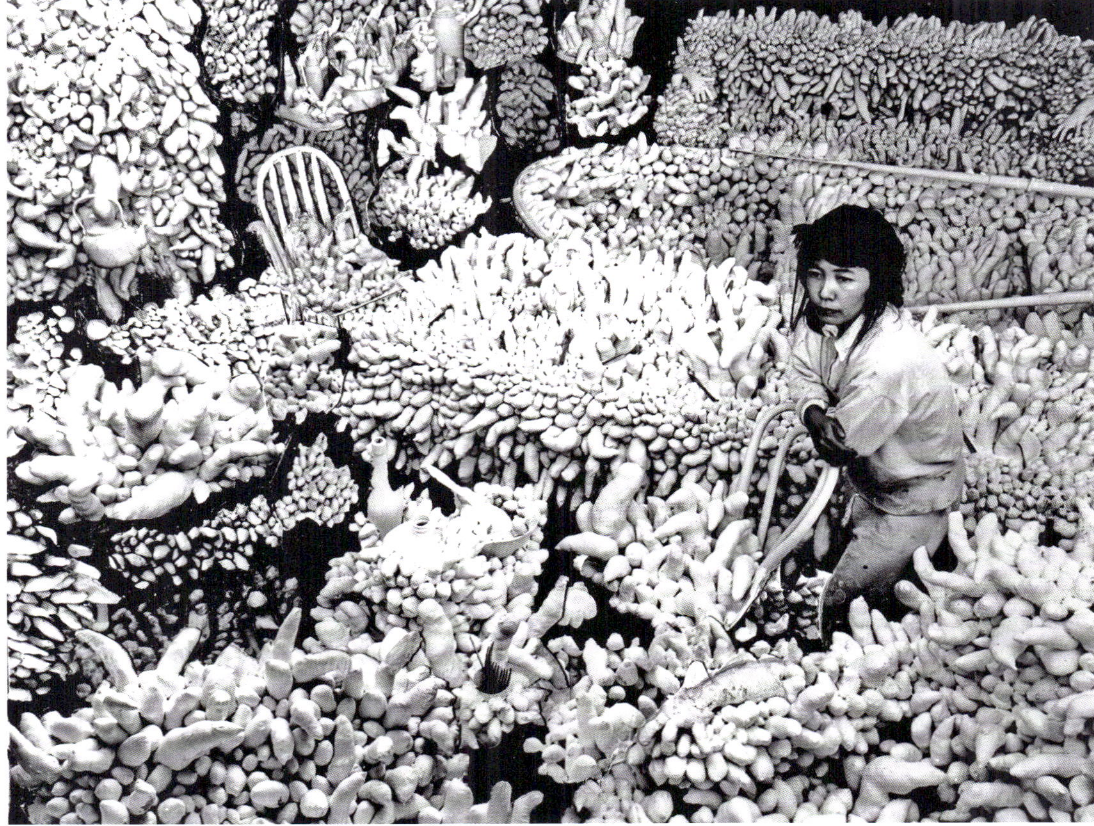

As a child, her mother insisted that the young Kusama spy on her own father, who was having an affair, which was so traumatic that she developed a lifelong aversion to sex. 'All the inner factors that cause me to perceive sexual intercourse as violence', she said, 'find form in the shape of the male sex organ',[5] and art was a way to work through the trauma.[6]

To fill a room with thousands of stuffed phalluses was incredibly labour-intensive, and physically and mentally exhausting, so Kusama came upon the solution of using mirrors to achieve repetition on a far greater scale.[7]

In November 1965, at the Castellane Gallery in New York, she covered the floor of the space with her stuffed phalluses before lining the room with mirrors, which created the illusion of stuffed phalluses recurring infinitely around the viewer.

The installation challenged traditional boundaries in art by transforming space into an experiential, all-encompassing environment that blurred the lines between viewer and artwork. The success of *Phalli's Field* propelled Kusama into further explorations of infinity, self-obliteration and immersive environments, eventually cementing her reputation as a pioneering figure in installation art.

Over the course of her career, she would produce more than twenty distinct *Infinity Rooms*, from peep shows to multimedia installations, and this mesmerizing art form is now the one most commonly associated with the artist.

JOURNEY TO NEW YORK

Kusama was born in 1929 in a rural town in Japan to a wealthy family. That same year the stock markets crashed, and civil unrest in Japan was followed by intense militarism.

Her mother was physically and mentally abusive, and it was expected that Kusama would have an arranged marriage followed by a life as an obedient housewife. Japanese women were generally discouraged from pursuing careers at this time, and Kusama's mother did everything in her power to stop her daughter from becoming an artist, going so far as to destroy her drawings, tearing them up in front of her.[8]

Art was Kusama's escape from an unhappy childhood, and a lifeline that helped relieve her hallucinations, depression and anxiety. She dreamed of moving to America from a very young age, and a chance discovery in a local second-hand bookshop would change her life. The American artist Georgia O'Keeffe (see Chapter 21) had works in every major museum in the US, but she was pretty much unknown in Japan. Yet somehow, miraculously, a book of her paintings found its way into the young Kusama's hands in rural Japan, who then wrote to her and sent her drawings.

In an incredible show of generosity, O'Keeffe wrote back to Kusama, and they started a regular correspondence.[9] In November 1957, with O'Keeffe's encouragement, Kusama set off for America at the age of twenty-eight. Although her work was beginning to gain attention in Japan, escaping the then conservative country was a priority for her. She wouldn't return to her home country permanently until 1973.

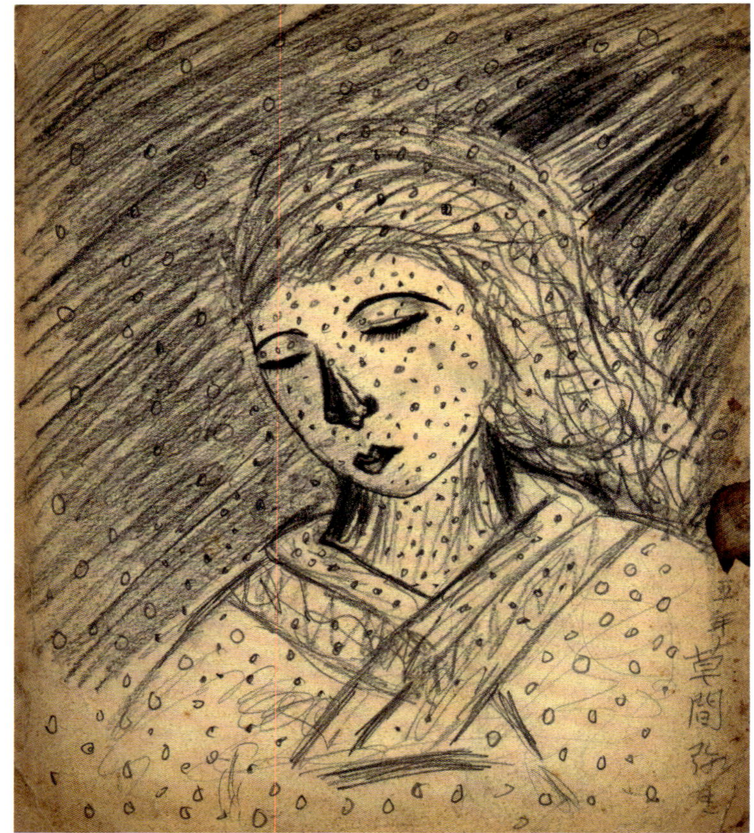

We mustn't underestimate what a difficult task it was for a young Japanese woman from a small town, with no support and little to no English, to up sticks and move to New York in the 1950s. It required monumental determination. She went from a wealthy life in Japan to living in abject poverty in New York. No wonder Kusama often describes how she craved fame and fortune. It is something many artists rarely discuss, but for Kusama it was a driving force.

THE POLKA DOT

Kusama first used the dot that would become her trademark at ten years old, in a drawing possibly depicting her mother. The dots came from within, and the repetition of them was

Yayoi Kusama,
Untitled, 1939.

          YAYOI KUSAMA

a way to overcome her fear and anxiety. They were, as she said, a way to disappear into her artwork.[10] Later, in New York, Kusama began applying the polka dot to animals, paper, canvas, walls and naked bodies.

INFINITY NETS

Her breakthrough came in 1959. New York was under the spell of Abstract Expressionism, but Kusama's first solo show there consisted of five enormous *Infinity Net* paintings: minimalist works using a recurring gesture of tiny loops, like interlocking scales, white-on-pale grey, which started the obsessive, repetitive works that would define her career.

The future Minimalist Donald Judd, who was a critic for *ARTnews* at the time, wrote a rave review of the 1959 show – a great start for Kusama after less than a year in the city.

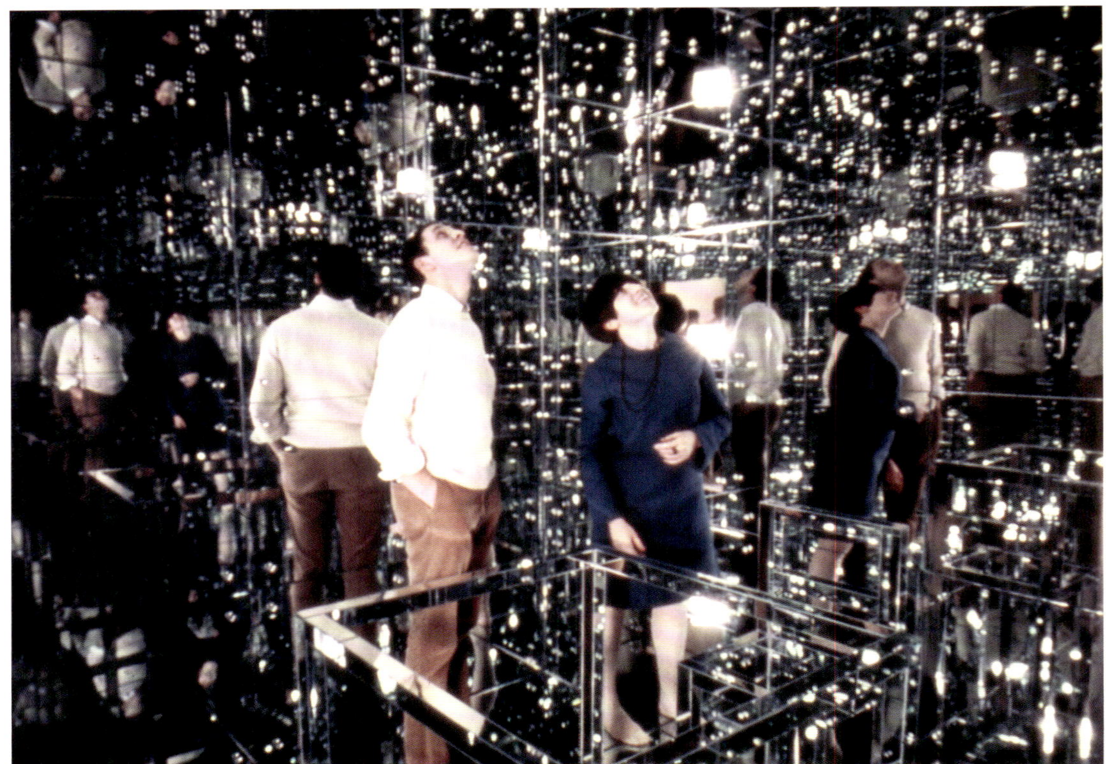

The artist spent every waking hour making *Infinity Net* paintings, which led to extreme hallucinations that caused her to be placed in a psychiatric institution. Her mental health both then and now is not something the artist dismisses, but she came to accept it as part of her working practice, maintaining that 'artwork is an expression of my life, particularly of my mental disease'.[11]

Despite the backing of Judd, Frank Stella and even Andy Warhol, real financial success eluded her, and watching her male peers gain recognition for ideas she felt she had initiated proved painful.

In *Kusama: Infinity*, Kusama specifically addresses how her work was co-opted by male artists who showed their works in more established galleries. Claes Oldenburg was creating objects with hard materials like aluminium, wood and papier-mâché in the early 1960s. But just months after his work was exhibited alongside Kusama's soft sculptures in June 1962, at the Green Gallery in New York, he put on a show filled with his own soft sculptures. According to Kusama, 'when he did a show that September, I was very surprised. If you looked around, it was all soft sculpture.'[12] These works launched Oldenburg's international career, but Kusama's innovation in the art form received little recognition.

In 1965 Kusama showed *Phalli's Field* at the Castellane Gallery, but no more than seven months later artist Lucas Samaras presented a similar mirrored environment at the more established Pace Gallery to rave reviews and a sold-out show. Once more Kusama's pioneering work was overlooked, and she struggled financially as others succeeded.[13]

VENICE BIENNALE

In 1966 Kusama participated in the 33rd Venice Biennale, the most prestigious arts festival in the world. She wasn't officially invited, but she did get permission to install her work *Narcissus Garden*, a lake comprising 1,500 reflective balls – a witty take on the commercialization of the art world. But when she proceeded to sell the balls for $2 each in an early guerrilla performance, the Biennale authorities stopped her, objecting to the sale of art 'like hot dogs or ice-cream cones'.[14]

RETURN TO JAPAN

Kusama was one of the first artists outside of America or Europe to achieve international prominence in the period following the Second World War, but financially and mentally she was still struggling in New York, and so in 1973 she returned to Japan, where she was relatively unknown.

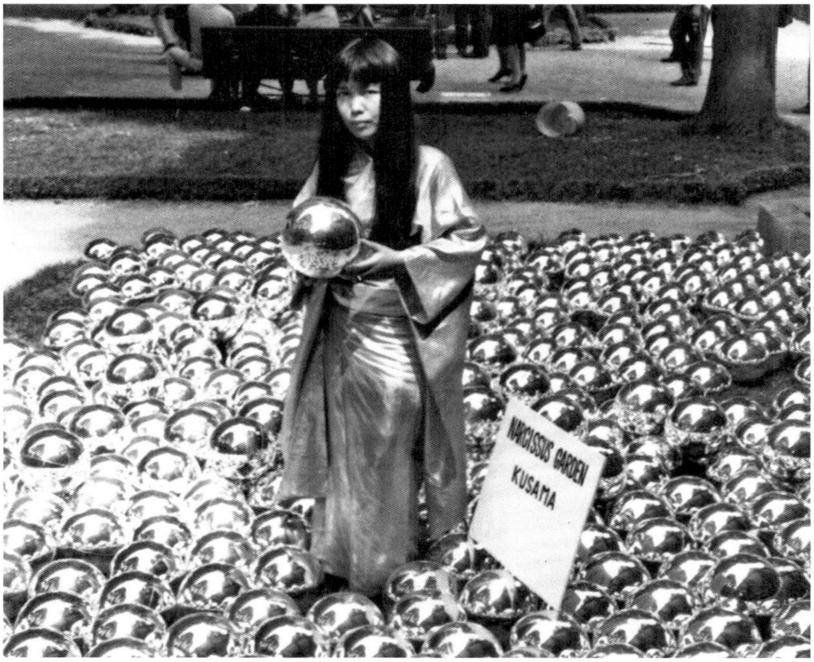

In 1977, after a lifetime of fighting anxiety and hallucinations, she checked herself into a psychiatric hospital in Tokyo – and has lived there ever since. At first Kusama faced difficulty reintegrating, due to her mental health struggles and her reputation as an outsider in the art world. However, over time, her work gained recognition and respect internationally, especially after her 1989 retrospective at the Center for International Contemporary Arts in New York, which was seen as her return to the international stage.[15]

Now in her nineties, she still works every day. When asked what the advantage of living in a psychiatric hospital was, and how it had informed her practice, she replied: 'It made it possible for me to continue to make art every day, and this has saved my life.'[16]

A RADICAL ARTIST

Today Kusama is as productive as ever.

Often dismissed as quirky or populist, she is in fact a radical artist who made some of the most important artworks of the 20th century. A crucial figure in Conceptual art, an innovator and rule breaker, she created works that look at how women's bodies are commodified, addressed ecological concerns, condemned racial and gender stereotypes and criticized American war policy.

Like many artists who have famously struggled with their mental health, it is impossible to separate the art of Yayoi Kusama from her diagnoses. But why should we? Mental illness is part of the human condition. For nearly half a century Kusama has worked from within a psychiatric institution, and her life is a glorious testament to perseverance and the healing powers of creative practice.

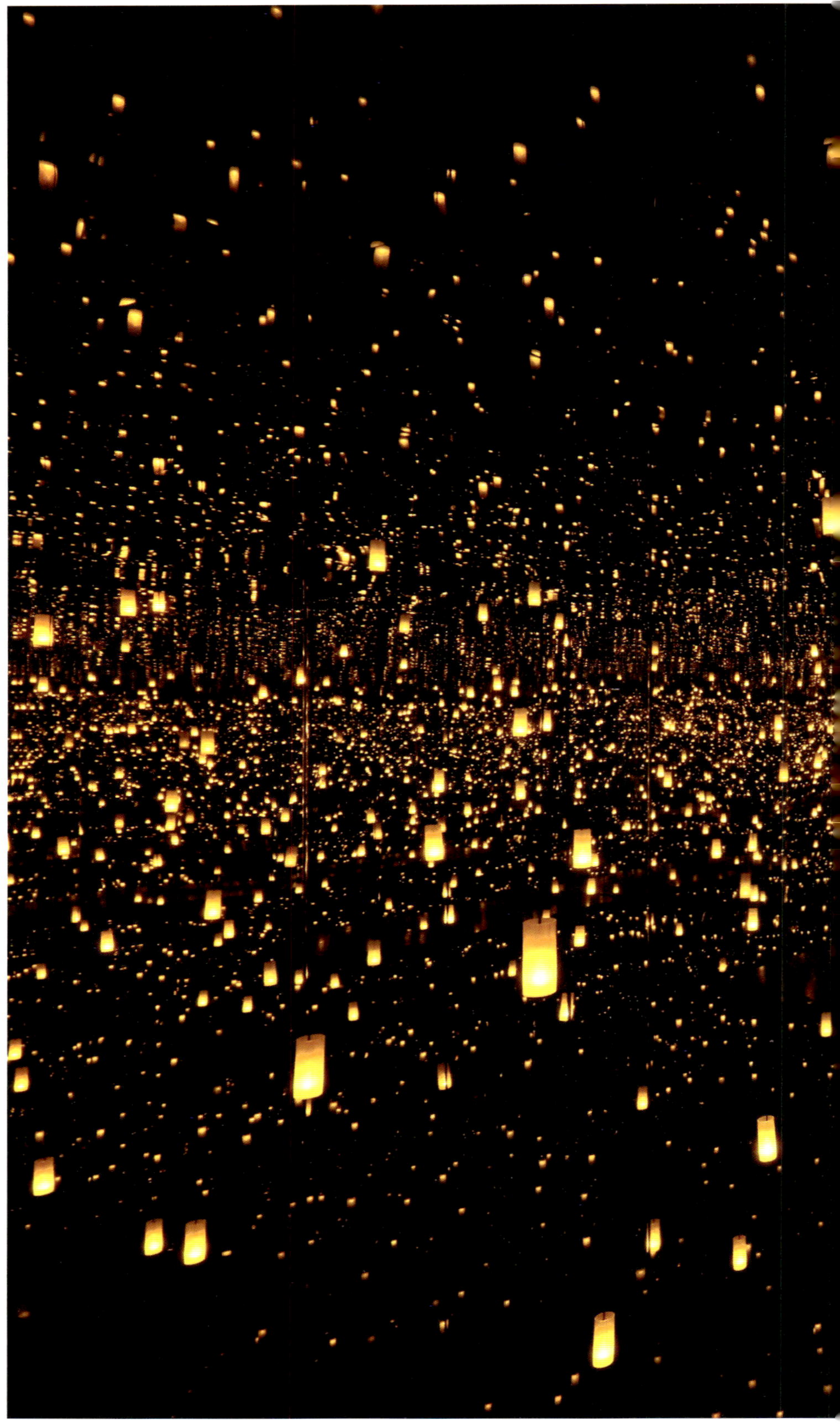

Yayoi Kusama,
*The Aftermath
of Obliteration
of Eternity*, 2009.

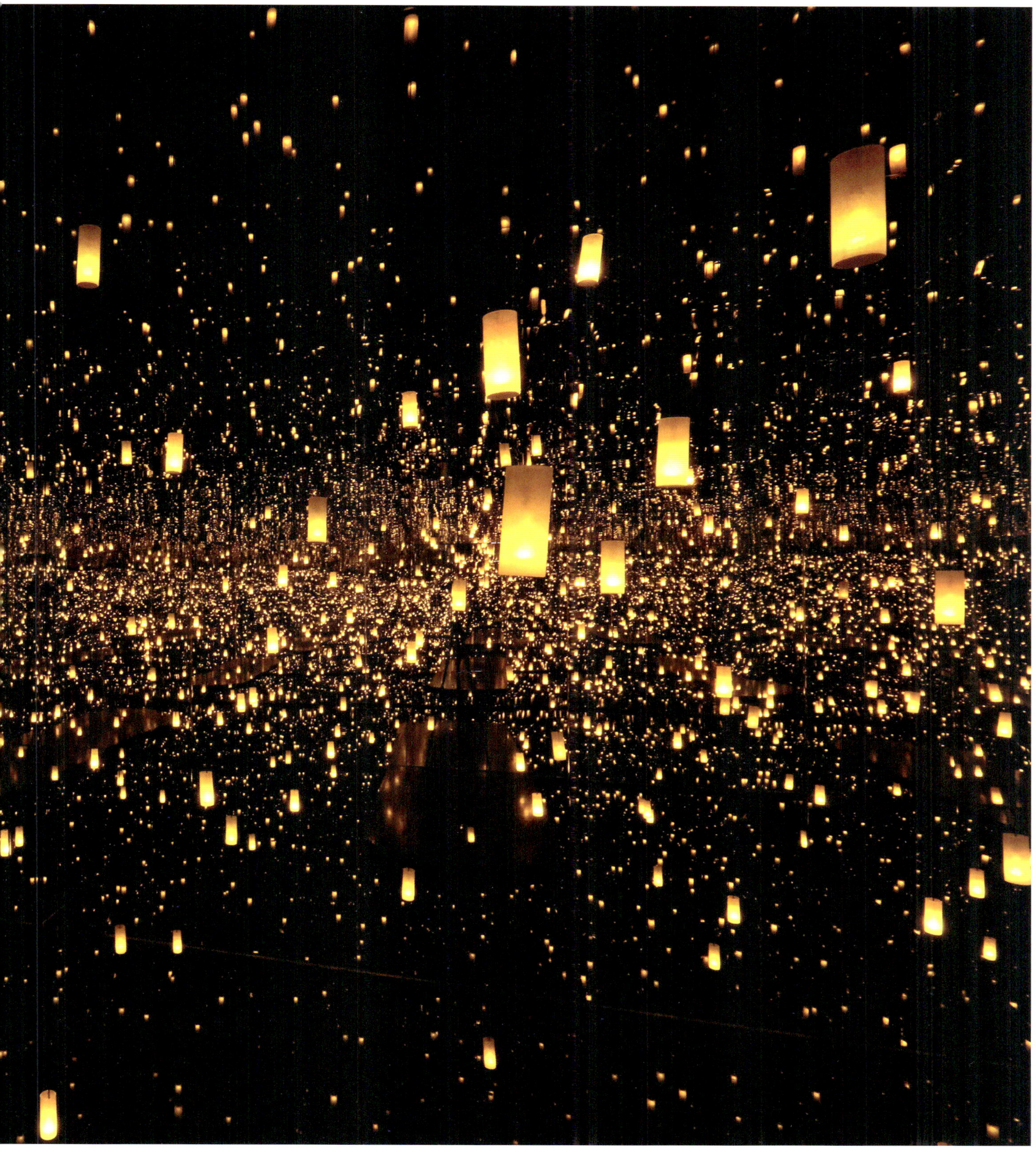

30

ISAAC JULIEN

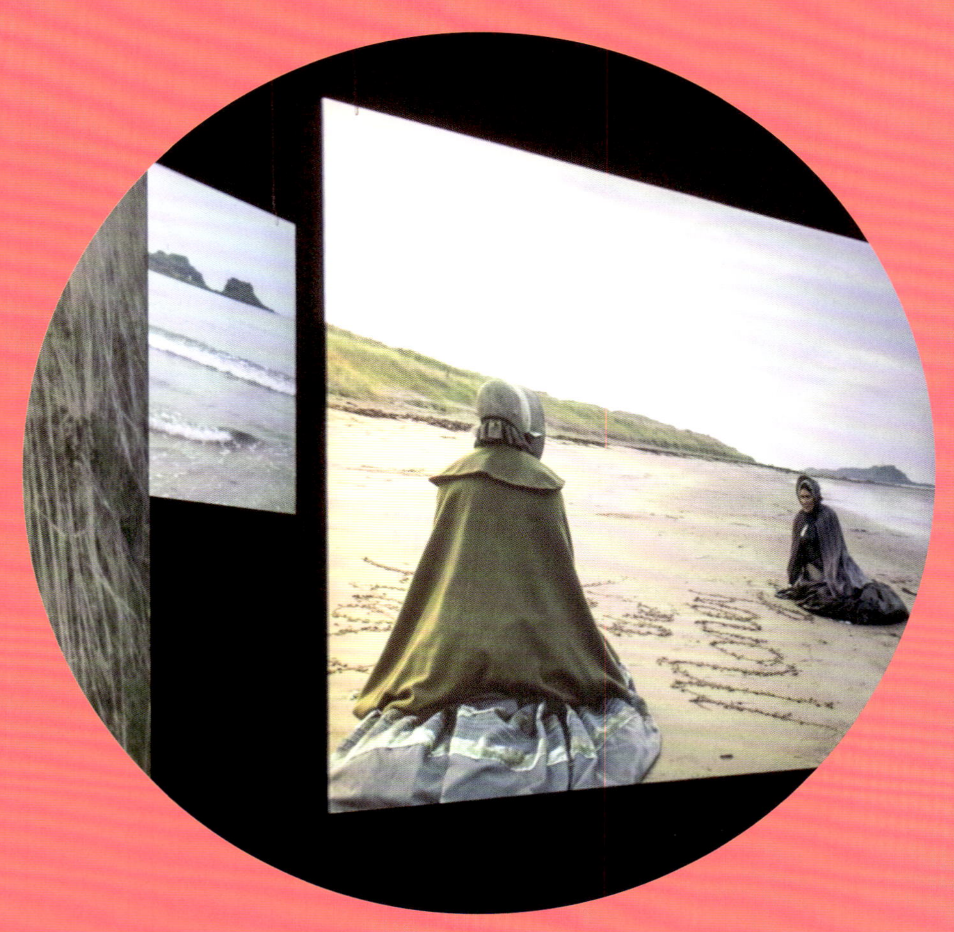

LESSONS OF THE HOUR

2019

A VISIONARY IN MULTIMEDIA ART

'I come from cinema,' Sir Isaac Julien once said. 'It's cinema I'm quoting from and cinema I reappropriate.'[1]

Julien is a British artist and filmmaker known for his powerful aesthetic and his complex explorations of identity, race, sexuality and history. With a career spanning over four decades, he is one of the most influential figures in the contemporary art world, whose work combines elements of film, theatre, photography, sculpture and installation art to create immersive experiences that challenge conventional narrative threads in a fusion of style and rebellion.[2]

The artist's body of work is thought-provoking, deeply intellectual and visually stunning, merging cinema, art, philosophy and music in radical ways. Julien, who once described himself as a poet,[3] first gained significant attention with *Looking for Langston* (1989), a lyrical homage to the Harlem Renaissance and to the poet and activist Langston Hughes.

Like much of Julien's work, *Langston* not only looks at how Black individuals have shaped and reshaped their own narratives in the face of adversity, but also asks us to consider how the stories of these iconic historical figures resonate in contemporary society. It is a film that examines the ambiguously queer identity of the poet, and it established Julien's reputation for creating evocative, layered pieces that bring together documentary realism and rich, often-dreamlike visual elements.

REGGAE, PUNK, SOUL, FUNK

Born in 1960 in London to parents of Caribbean heritage, Julien grew up in a rough, poor part of east London, which he described as a 'political battleground'.[4] It was a time of tremendous cultural upheaval, where issues of race, identity and post-colonialism were being debated through music and the arts but ignored in mainstream culture. He studied at St Martin's School of Art in London and would emerge as part of a group of radical new filmmakers whose 'works were breaking down preconceptions of what "film" should be'.[5] His contemporaries like Cerith Wyn Evans, John Maybury and Derek Jarman used video as a medium for activism and counter-narrative, challenging the fractious political landscape of Margaret Thatcher's Britain.

The Brixton riots of 1981 took place during his second year of college, sparked by longstanding tensions between the Black community and law enforcement in London, driven by issues like police brutality, unemployment and systemic discrimination. It was a seminal moment for artists, activists, musicians and intellectuals across the UK, including Julien. He began to make films in response to these issues as a way of challenging what he called 'a certain fixed ways of looking'.[6]

Isaac Julien,
Lessons of the Hour
(detail), 2019.

Between 1982 and 1992, Julien made works that investigated Black identity and culture as part of Sankofa Film and Video Collective, one of which was *Looking for Langston*.

Music and nightclubs were a huge influence for Julien and his friends, and the scene in London at the time was at its most exciting and rebellious. Funk music, pioneered by artists like James Brown, was big on the alternative scene in London clubs, where Julien spent most of his evenings. Bright, brash and political, it promoted self-expression, freedom and resistance. Rhythm, Julien has said, is essential to the structure of his work, and funk was the music he was really drawn to, because of its perfect melding of politics and aesthetics. Even today, he feels like his own work in film is 'a translation of that same impulse into a different arena'.[7]

PAST AND PRESENT

In his cinematic work, Julien employs a linear – or at least semi-linear – narrative, which allows him to explore storytelling in a more traditional framework. Films like *Looking for Langston* or *Young Soul Rebels* (1991) have structured plots that unfold in a way we expect from conventional cinema. This format helps Julien reach broader audiences while conveying complex themes, the clear, continuous flow helping to engage audiences in a more sustained, time-bound manner.

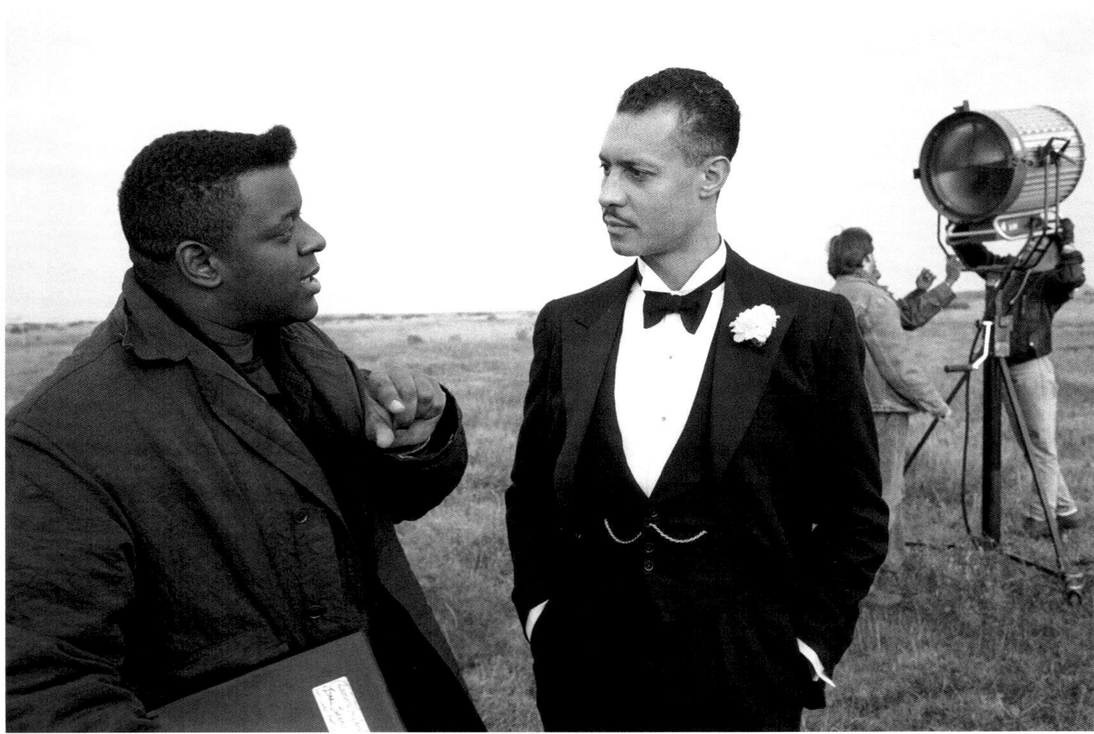

Isaac Julien on the set of *Looking for Langston* (1989): *Mise-en-scene No. 2 (Looking for Langston Vintage Series)*, 1989/2016.

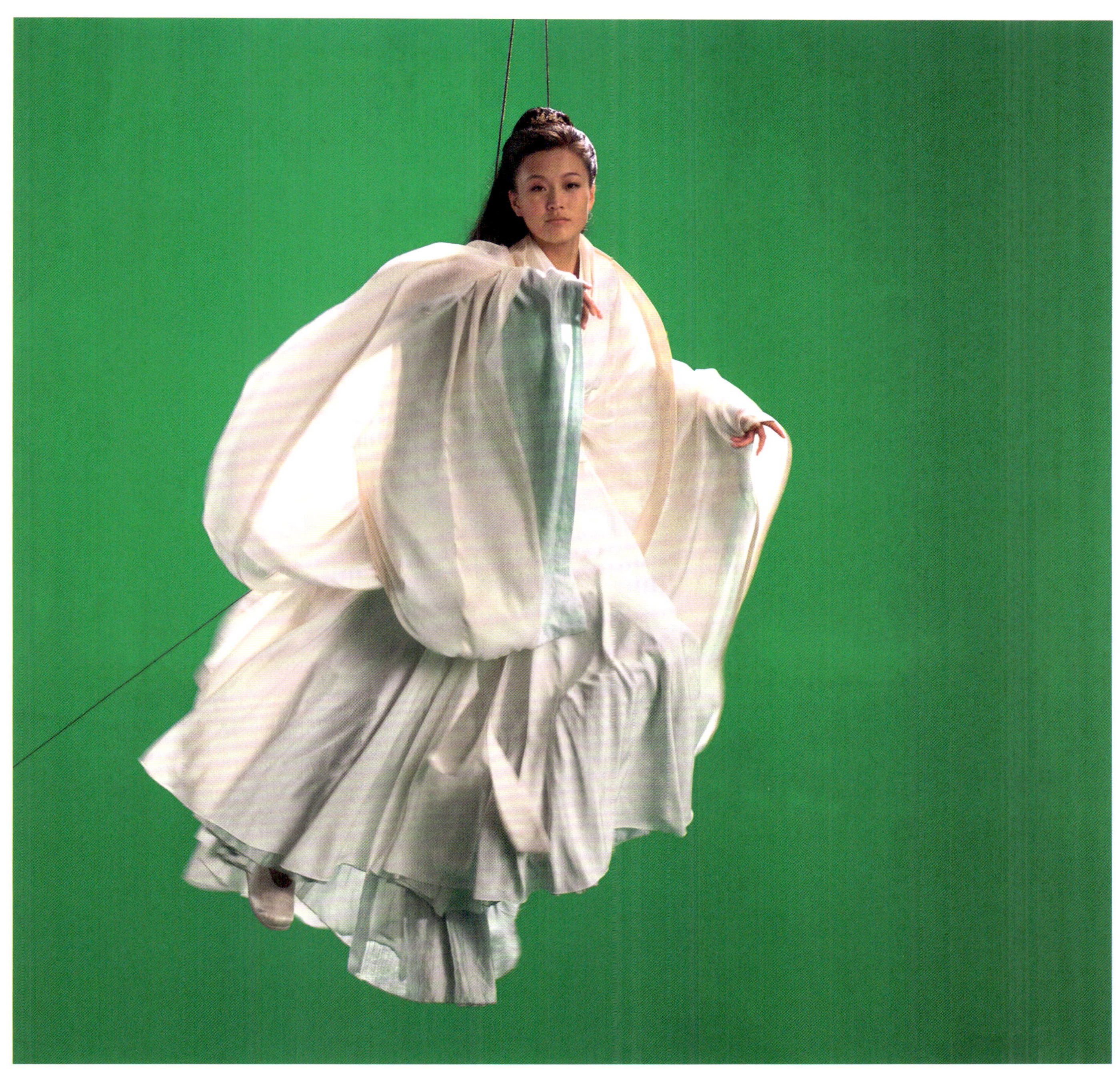

Isaac Julien,
Ten Thousand Waves, 2010.

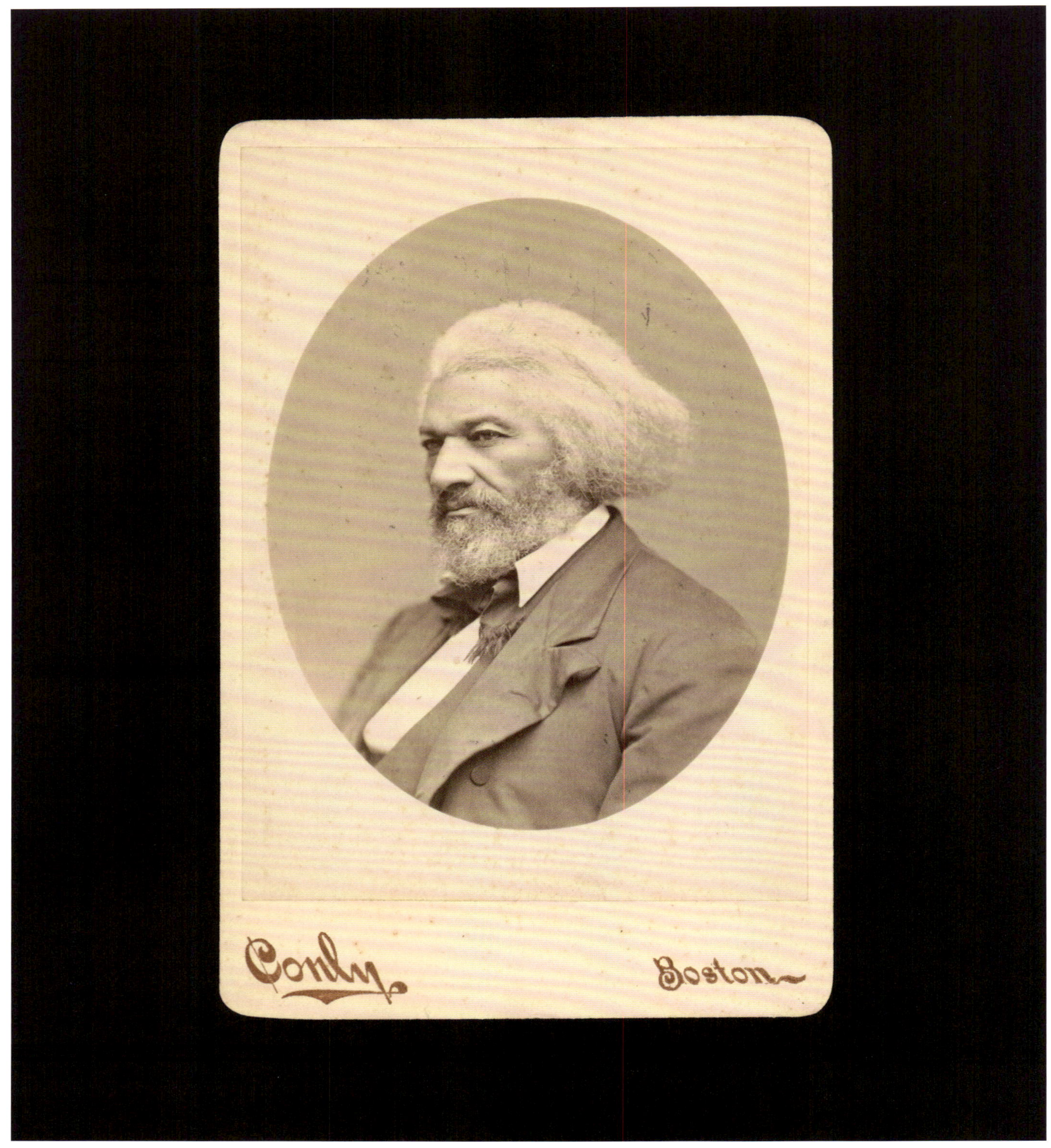

ISAAC JULIEN

But his multiscreen installations, like *Lessons of the Hour* and *Ten Thousand Waves* (2010), break from traditional storytelling and embrace a more fragmented, nonlinear approach, using those multiple screens to present multiple perspectives simultaneously. Viewers aren't directed through a single story; instead they are invited to explore, move around and piece together narratives at their own pace. This set-up reflects a more complex, layered approach to storytelling, but it also highlights Julien's understanding of identity as multifaceted and fluid. To look at his work is to engage with various points of view, both literally and figuratively, between past and present.

LESSONS

A statue of the 19th-century abolitionist and orator Frederick Douglass was installed in Rochester, New York, in 1899, the nation's first statue dedicated to an African American. It was while visiting this statue in 2016 that Julien was inspired to come up with the idea for *Lessons of the Hour*.[8]

Lessons is one of Julien's most ambitious projects, and perfectly illustrates his approach to using multimedia to tell complex stories. The ten-screen video installation is a meditation on the legacy of Douglass, a writer and former slave whose life story resonates deeply with themes of race, freedom and equality. The cast of actors was carefully chosen to convey the historical authenticity and emotional resonance of the narrative, blending dramatic performances with Julien's signature visuals.

The work is centred around three of Douglass's speeches: 'Lessons of the Hour', which addressed lynching in the South, 'What to the Slave Is the Fourth of July?', which criticized the slave trade, and 'A Lecture on Pictures', on the power of photography as a political tool.

Identity, representation and the power of self-image are themes central to Julien's body of work

Douglass was the most photographed man of the 19th century,[9] and his speech on photography detailed the power of the medium as both a social leveller and a means of empowerment. He began to circulate photographs of himself in which he was posed and dressed according to his own preferences, offering a counter-narrative to the racist depictions of African Americans of the day.

Identity, representation and the power of self-image are themes central to Julien's body of work. And in much the same way Douglass once imaged himself in countless photos, we see a reflection in *Lessons*, with the same event playing on multiple screens simultaneously.

The real-life characters that Douglass interacts with in the installation are mostly women, chosen for being representatives of ideals of equality.[10] He was supported by women throughout his life, and some played a crucial role in helping him gain freedom. His first wife, Anna Murray Douglass, was a Black woman who died following a series of strokes at the age of sixty-nine, and his second wife was the white suffragist Helen Pitts, both of whom appear in *Lessons*. Also featured are the English Quakers Anna and Ellen Richardson, who helped raise the money to purchase Douglass's freedom; Susan B. Anthony, a prominent American suffragist; and Ottilie Assing, a German American feminist, free-thinker, friend and romantic partner who was deeply involved in the abolitionist movement.[11]

By highlighting these figures, Julien acknowledges women's often-overlooked

*Lessons is deeply political,
but it is also a masterclass
in filmmaking*

contributions to history and offers a more nuanced portrayal of Douglass and this era. It means we see him in *Lessons* not just as an isolated hero, but as a man deeply influenced by and connected to those around him.

A MEDITATION ON IDEAS

This multi-video installation cleverly weaves episodes from Douglass's life and work with selections from his speeches, writings and personal letters. Each screen offers a different angle, image or moment from Douglass's life, creating a kaleidoscopic view of his experiences and ideas. The immersive set-up invites viewers to engage actively with the piece, moving around the installation to view different scenes from different perspectives, and in so doing, each person experiences it differently, the format echoing both the fragmented nature of memory and history and the multiplicity of Douglass's identity.

Julien's works break up not just the narrative, but the gallery space itself. 'Whenever I make a work,' he says, 'I'm making an intervention into the museum and the gallery, an intervention with the moving image.'[12]

Lessons of the Hour is far more than just a biographical reflection on freedom, photography and identity. It is a cinematic meditation on ideas, a disruption of the viewing experience and a visual poem.

BEAUTY AS A POLITICAL TOOL

Julien spent four years painstakingly researching Douglass, filming at sites in Washington, DC, London and Edinburgh (Douglass made several visits to Edinburgh from 1845 to 1847 while campaigning against slavery across the UK and Ireland). *Lessons* is deeply political, but it is also a masterclass in filmmaking. The visuals are meticulously crafted, with the artist's signature attention to colour, lighting and composition. Every shot is like a carefully composed painting that could be pulled out and framed. It is visually astonishing, but that is also something Julien has been criticized for.[13]

Julien's films are seductively beautiful and sensuous, methodically filmed, edited and soundtracked, with Hollywood production values, and some critics have found the presentation too beautiful for the subject matter, even calling his work 'slick mannerism'.[14] But from the beginning of his career, he resisted the need to stick to a prescribed 'political aesthetic', refusing to differentiate between video art, experimental film and political documentary. Julien has consistently pushed the boundaries of filmmaking as an art form by using beauty as a political tool. Growing up in grim, poverty-stricken east London instilled in him a desire to embrace the aesthetic, and he has spoken unapologetically of his pursuit for beauty within his pieces.[15] His work challenges the idea that political art needs to be gritty and dour; as he once said: 'I like the idea of exploring things poetically, I'm not a newscaster.'[16]

In addition to the visuals, the sound design in *Lessons of the Hour* is integral to the experience – it is, he says, '50 per cent of the work'.[17] The readings from Douglass's speeches and writings are bolstered by ambient sounds that evoke the environments he inhabited. The layering of these sounds across multiple screens creates a complex sonic landscape that mirrors the visual fragmentation of the images. As we walk around the installations the sound moves too; rattling chains, voices, steam trains and music

Still from *Lessons of the Hour*, 2019.

intertwine; stereo and mono blend, fade and disappear. Julien's masterful creation of a multisensory environment immerses us in the emotional and intellectual world of his subjects.

HONEST, TRUTHFUL AND VIRTUOUS

Julien's body of work reminds us that history is not just a series of facts and dates but a living, breathing entity that continues to shape our world. *Lessons of the Hour*, *Looking for Langston* and others are a powerful testament to his ability to blend art and social commentary in a way that is both intellectually engaging and emotionally resonant.

For over forty years, Julien has created spaces where viewers can experience history as a dynamic, multifaceted and even seductive phenomenon. His works are beautiful, engaging and emotional, but perhaps their strongest achievement is encouraging us to think critically about the ways in which history is remembered, represented and reimagined.

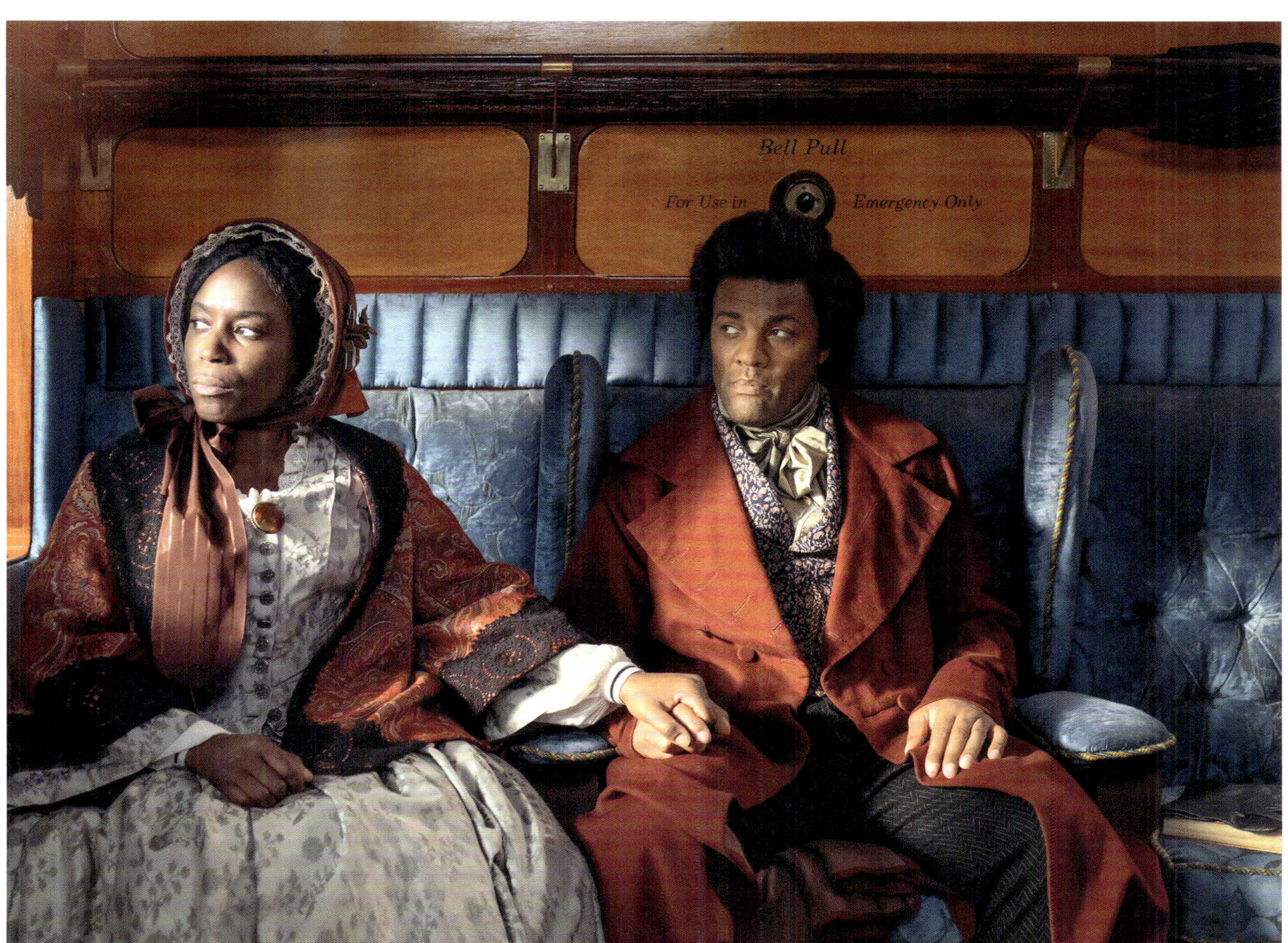

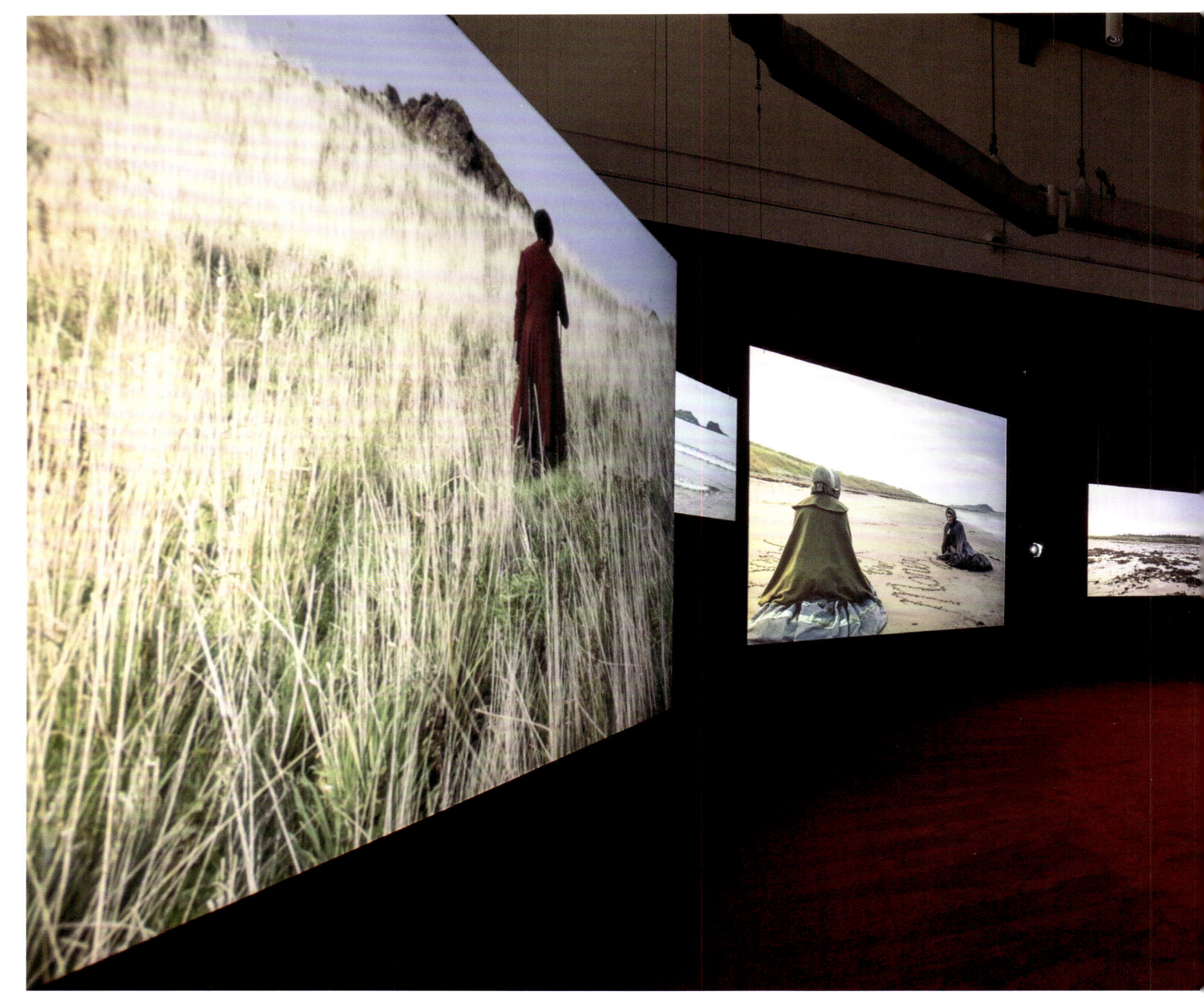

Installation view of
Lessons of the Hour, 2019.

ISAAC JULIEN

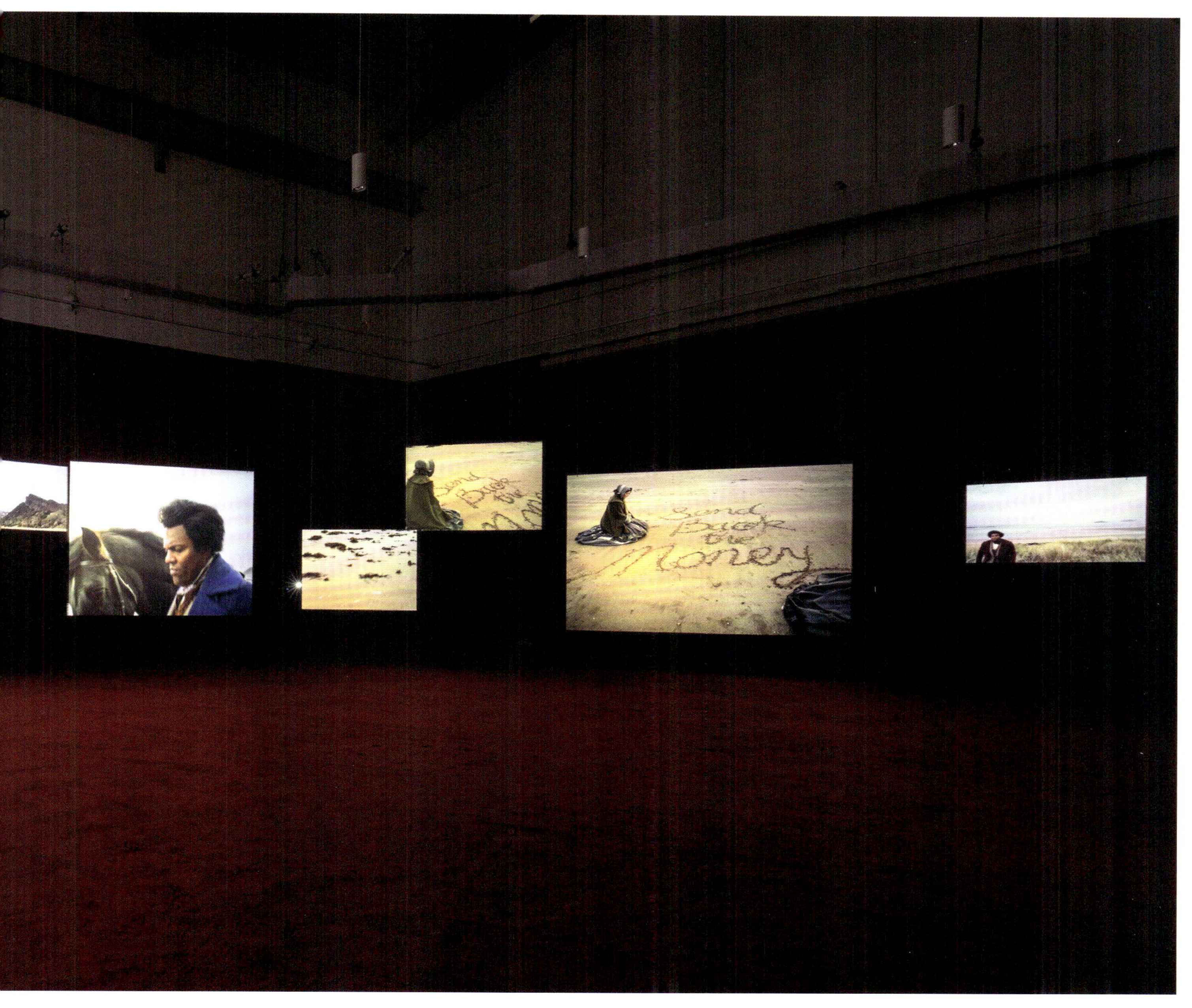

LESSONS OF THE HOUR

NOTES

1 THE QINGMING SCROLL

1 Dawn Delbanco, 'Chinese Handscrolls' (April 2008), www.metmuseum.org/toah/hd/chhs/hd_chhs.htm.

2 'Landscape Painting in Chinese Art', www.metmuseum.org/toah/hd/clpg/hd_clpg.htm, accessed 17 September 2024.

3 Mary Tregear, *Chinese Art* (London: Thames & Hudson, 1997), p. 7.

4 'A Special Exhibition of Paintings on "Up the River During Qingming" in the Museum Collection', www.npm.gov.tw/Exhibition-Content.aspx?sno=04007005&l=2, accessed 17 September 2024.

5 Ronald G. Knapp, 'Rainbows and Centipedes: 20th Century Discoveries of China's "Lost Bridges"', *Orientations Magazine* (April 2008), pp. 30–39.

6 Hansen, 'The Beijing Qingming Scroll', p. 4.

7 See 'Spring Festival Along the River', https://scrolls.uchicago.edu/view-scroll/52, accessed 17 September 2024.

2 JAN VAN EYCK

1 Alfred Acres, *Jan van Eyck within his Art* (London: Reaktion Books, 2023), p. 169.

2 Till-Holger Borchert, *Van Eyck* (London: Taschen, 2022), p. 52.

3 Acres, *Jan van Eyck within his Art* p. 178.

4 Borchert, *Van Eyck*, p. 52.

5 Carola Hicks, *Girl in a Green Gown: The History and Mystery of the Arnolfini Portrait* (New York: Vintage Publishing, 2012), p. 32.

6 'The Arnolfini Portrait: Jan van Eyck', www.nationalgallery.org.uk/paintings/jan-van-eyck-the-arnolfini-portrait, accessed 28 November 2024.

7 Hicks, *Girl in a Green Gown*, p. 23.

8 'The Arnolfini Portrait: Jan van Eyck'.

9 Jonathan Jones, 'The Arnolfini Portrait', *The Guardian*, 15 April 2000, www.theguardian.com/culture/2000/apr/15/art.

3 SANDRO BOTTICELLI

1 Frank Zöllner, *Botticelli* (London: Prestel, 2015), p. 132.

2 Stephen J. Campbell and Michael W. Cole, *A New History of Italian Renaissance Art* (London: Thames & Hudson, 2012), pp. 252–53.

3 Zöllner, *Botticelli*, p. 138.

4 Campbell and Cole, *A New History of Italian Renaissance Art*, p. 253.

5 Barbara Deimling, *Botticelli* (London: Taschen, 2023), p. 59.

6 Campbell and Cole, *A New History of Italian Renaissance Art*, p. 254.

7 Lauro Martines, *Fire in the City* (Oxford: Oxford University Press, 2006), pp. 140–41.

8 Zöllner, *Botticelli*, p. 132.

9 Campbell and Cole, *A New History of Italian Renaissance Art*, p. 300.

10 Zöllner, *Botticelli*, p. 83.

11 'Girolamo Savonarola', www.nationalgallery.org.uk/people/girolamo-savonarola, accessed 29 November 2024.

12 'Reflections of a World in Crisis: Art in Florence circa 1492–1512', www.sothebys.com/en/articles/reflections-of-a-world-in-crisis-art-in-florence-circa-1492-1512, accessed 29 November 2024.

13 Zöllner, *Botticelli*, pp. 86–90.

14 Vasari quoted in 'Reflections of a World in Crisis'.

15 Zöllner, *Botticelli*, p. 180.

4 HIERONYMUS BOSCH

1 Margaret D. Carroll, *Hieronymus Bosch: Time and Transformation in The Garden of Earthly Delights* (New Haven, CT, and London: Yale University Press, 2022), pp. 15–16.

2 J. R. Hale (ed.), *The Travel Journal of Antonion de Beatis – Germany, Switzerland, the Low Countries, France and Italy 1517–1518* (London: Hakluyt Society, 1979), pp 94–95.

3 Reindert Falkenburg, *The Land of Unlikeness* (Zwolle: Waanders BV, Uitgeverij, 2012).

4 'God made the dome and divided the water under the dome from the water above the dome; that is how it was.' Genesis 1:7. 'Dome' here is sometimes translated as 'firmament', from the word 'firm' or 'solid'.

5 'But there rose a fountain out of the earth, and watered the whole face of the earth.' Genesis 2:6–16.

6 'And the rib that the LORD God had taken from the man he made into a woman and brought her to the man.' Genesis 2:22.

7 'These are the birds you are to regard as unclean and not eat because they are unclean:…the horned owl, the screech owl…the little owl.' Leviticus 11:13–17.

8 'And the Lord God made for Adam and his wife, garments of skins, and clothed them.' Genesis 3:21.

9 Carroll, *Hieronymus Bosch*, p. 77.

10 Ibid., p. 131.

11 'And it shall come to pass in that day that there shall be no light, but cold and frost.' Zechariah 14:6.

12 'Babylon the great is fallen, is fallen, and has become a dwelling place of demons, a prison for every foul spirit, and a cage for every unclean and hated bird!' Apocalypse 18:2.

5 MICHELANGELO

1 Patricia Emison, *Creating the 'Divine Artist': From Dante to Michelangelo* (Leiden: Brill, 2004).

2 Martin Gayford, *Michelangelo: His Epic Life* (New York: Fig Tree, 2013), p. 37.

3 Giorgio Vasari, *The Lives of the Artists* (Oxford World's Classics), trans. Julia Conway Bondanella and Peter Bondanella (Oxford: Oxford University Press, 2008).

4 Gayford, *Michelangelo: His Epic Life*, p. 76.

5 'Michelangelo's Prisoners or Slaves', www.accademia.org/explore-museum/artworks/michelangelos-prisoners-slaves, accessed 26 November 2024.

6 Val Tate, 'Michelangelo's Working Process through Rare Original Drawings', 22 November 2019, https://blogs.getty.edu/iris/exhibition-michelangelo-working-process-rare-original-drawings.

7 'Chapel of the Pieta', https://stpetersbasilica.info/Altars/Pieta/Pieta.htm, accessed 26 November 2024.

8 Vasari, *The Lives of the Artists*.

9 John Pope-Hennessy, *Italian High Renaissance and Baroque Sculpture* (London, Phaidon: 1971), p. 304.

10 Gayford, *Michelangelo: His Epic Life*, p. 145.

6 LEONARDO DA VINCI

1 Veit Probst, director of the Heidelberg University Library, 'Manuscript Reveals True Identity of Mona Lisa', quoted in *Der Spiegel*, 15 January 2008.

2 Ibid., p. 102.

3 Walter Isaacson, *Leonardo da Vinci* (New York: Simon and Schuster, 2017), p. 479.

4 Giuseppe Pallanti and Martin Kemp, *Mona Lisa: The People and the Painting* (Oxford: Oxford University Press, 2017), p. 56.

5 'The Mona Lisa', www.museodelprado.es/en/the-collection/art-work/the-mona-lisa/80c9b279-5c80-4d29-b72d-b19cdca6601c, accessed 16 September 2024.

6 Sarah Evans, 'One Mona Lisa Mystery Solved', https://cen.acs.org/articles/88/i30/One-Mona-Lisa-Mystery-Solved.html, accessed 16 September 2024.

7 Isaacson, *Leonardo da Vinci*, p. 483.

8 Ibid., p. 397.

9 Ibid., p. 176.

10 Margaret Livingstone, 'Light Vision', *Harvard Medical Alumni Bulletin* (Autumn 2003). p. 19.

7 ARTEMISIA GENTILESCHI

1 Letizia Treves (ed.), *Artemisia* (London: National Gallery, 2020), pp. 12–13.

2   Elizabeth S. Cohen, 'The Trials of Artemisia Gentileschi: A Rape as History', *The Sixteenth Century Journal*, vol. 31, no. 1 (2000), pp. 47–75.
3   Elizabeth Cropper writing in Treves (ed.), *Artemisia*, p. 13.
4   'Judith and her Maidservant with the Head of Holofernes', www.nasjonalmuseet.no/en/collection/object/NG.M.02073, accessed 24 November 2024.
5   Treves (ed.), *Artemisia*, p. 64.
6   Ibid., p. 125.
7   Catherine McCormack, *Women in the Picture: Women, Art and the Power of Looking* (London: Icon Books, 2021), p. 220.
8   Katy Hessel, *The Story of Art Without Men* (London and New York: Penguin, 2022), p. 18.
9   McCormack, *Women in the Picture*, p. 221.
10 Cohen, 'The Trials of Artemisia Gentileschi'.

8 JOHANNES VERMEER

1   Pieter Roelofs and Gregor J. M. Weber, *Vermeer* (London: Thames & Hudson, 2023), p. 26. Some historians disagree on this number, however.
2   Norbet Schneider, *Vermeer* (London: Taschen, 2023), p. 8.
3   Roelofs and Weber, *Vermeer*, p. 208.
4   Ibid.
5   Mark Brown, 'Dutch researchers coax secrets from Girl with a Pearl Earring', *The Guardian*, 28 April 2020.
6   Abbie Vandivere, Jørgen Wadum and Emilien Leonhardt, 'The Girl in the Spotlight: Vermeer at work, his materials and techniques in Girl with a Pearl Earring', 2 March 2020, https://link.springer.com/article/10.1186/s40494-020-0359-6.
7   Roelofs and Weber, *Vermeer*, p. 212.
8   Ibid., p. 42
9   'Johannes Vermeer', www.rijksmuseum.nl/en/rijksstudio/artists/johannes-vermeer, accessed 16 November 2024.
10 Roelofs and Weber, *Vermeer*, p. 211.
11 'Johannes Vermeer: Girl with a Pearl Earring', www.mauritshuis.nl/en/our-collection/artworks/670-girl-with-a-pearl-earring, accessed 26 November 2024.
12 Ibid.

9 ÉLISABETH VIGÉE LE BRUN

1   Katy Hessel, *The Story of Art Without Men* (London and New York: Penguin, 2022), p. 61.
2   Élisabeth Vigée Le Brun, *Memoirs of Madame Vigee-Lebrun*, trans. Lionel Strachey (New York: Doubleday, 1903), p. 49.
3   Ibid., p. 20.
4   Ibid.
5   Kimberly Chrisman-Campbell, 'The King of Couture', *The Atlantic*, 21 September 2015, www.theatlantic.com/entertainment/archive/2015/09/the-king-of-couture/402952.

6   'Marie Antoinette in a Chemise Dress', www.metmuseum.org/art/collection/search/656930, accessed 22 August 2024.
7   At her trial after the French Revolution, she was falsely charged with incest with her son. See Joseph Toates, 'Marie Antoinette and the Stories We Prefer to Tell', 13 August 2024, www.frontporchrepublic.com/2024/08/marie-antoinette-and-the-stories-we-prefer-to-tell.
8   Peter Kolchin, *American Slavery: 1619–1877* (New York: Hill & Wang, 2003), pp. 93–95.

10 FRANCISCO DE GOYA

1   Xavier Bray et. al, *Goya: The Portraits*, exh. cat. (London: National Gallery, 2015), p. 23.
2   Ibid., p. 273.
3   'Portrait of Ferdinand VII', www.museothyssen.org/en/collection/artists/goya-francisco/portrait-ferdinand-vii, accessed 19 November 2024.
4   Robert Hughes, 'Triumph of the will', *The Guardian*, 12 April 2006.
5   Hughes, *Goya*, p. 383.
6   'Saturn Devouring his Son, 1820–23, by Francisco Goya', www.franciscogoya.com/saturn-devouring-his-son.jsp accessed 19 November 2024.
7   Hughes, *Goya*, p. 388.

11 KATSUSHIKA HOKUSAI

1   'Tokyo's History, Geography, and Population: History', www.metro.tokyo.lg.jp/ENGLISH/ABOUT/HISTORY/history01.htm, accessed 6 September 2024.
2   Timothy Clark (ed.), *Beyond the Great Wave* (London: Thames & Hudson), p. 8.
3   Ibid., p. 21.
4   Ibid., p. 123.
5   Ibid., p. 108.
6   Martin Dean, '7 things you need to know about Japonisme', https://www.sothebys.com/en/articles/7-things-you-need-to-know-about-japonisme, 13 February 2019.
7   Patrick Parr, 'Commodore Perry's black ships deliver a letter to Japan in July 1853', *Japan Today*, 28 January 2021.

12 AUGUSTE RODIN

1   'The Kiss', www.musee-rodin.fr/en/musee/collections/oeuvres/kiss, accessed 27 November 2024.
2   Ruth Butler, *Rodin: The Shape of Genius*, (London and New Haven, CT: Yale University Press, 1996), p. 11.
3   Kirk Varnedoe, 'Rodin's Drawings: 1854–1880', in *Auguste Rodin: Drawings and Watercolors*, ed. Ernst-Gerhard Güse (New York: Rizzoli, 1984), p. 19.
4   Butler, *Rodin: The Shape of Genius*, p. 99.
5   'Rodin and Michelangelo: A Study in Artistic Inspiration', https://philamuseum.org/calendar/

exhibition/rodin-and-michelangelo-a-study-in-artistic-inspiration, accessed 27 November 2024.
6   François Blanchetière, *Rodin* (London: Taschen, 2023), pp. 11–14.
7   Ibid., p. 14.
8   'The Age of Bronze (L'Age d'Airain)', https://collections.vam.ac.uk/item/O102916/the-age-of-bronze-lage-statue-rodin-auguste, accessed 27 November 2024.
9   Blanchetière, *Rodin*, p. 17.
10 'Rodin and Michelangelo: A Study in Artistic Inspiration'.
11 '10 things you might not have known about Rodin', www.britishmuseum.org/blog/10-things-you-might-not-have-known-about-rodin, accessed 27 November 2024.
12 'The Gates of Hell', www.musee-rodin.fr/en/musee/collections/oeuvres/gates-hell, accessed 27 November 2024.
13 Chloé Ariot, 'A Studio Poetics', in *The Making of Rodin*, ed. Nabila Abdel Nabi, Chloé Ariot and Achim Borchardt-Hume (London: Tate Publishing, 2021), pp. 57–61.
14 Butler, *Rodin: The Shape of Genius*, p. 262.
15 Aida Edemariam, 'I think, but I'm not quite sure who I am', *The Guardian*, 2 October 2001, www.theguardian.com/culture/2001/oct/02/artsfeatures.arts.
16 'The Kiss, Large Model', www.musee-rodin.fr/en/musee/collections/oeuvres/kiss-large-model, accessed 27 November 2024.
17 'The shocking story of The Kiss', *BBC Culture*, 19 November 2015, www.bbc.com/culture/article/20151119-the-shocking-story-of-the-kiss.

13 J. M. W. TURNER

1   Sam Smiles, *Late Turner: Painting Set Free* (London: Tate Publishing, 2014), p. 13.
2   Mark Brown, 'Tate Britain explores Turner's later work, aiming to "explode senility myth"', *The Guardian*, 13 March 2014, www.theguardian.com/artanddesign/2014/mar/13/tate-britain-turner-later-work-exhibition-myth-senility.
3   'Joseph Mallord William Turner', www.tate.org.uk/art/artists/joseph-mallord-william-turner-558, accessed 20 November 2024.
4   Andrew Wilton, *Turner in his Time* (London: Thames & Hudson, 2006), p. 14.
5   '"Fire and Water": Turner and Constable in the Royal Academy, 1831', www.tate.org.uk/research/tate-papers/33/fire-water-turner-constable-royal-academy, accessed 20 November 2024.
6   'Joseph Mallord William Turner', www.nationalgallery.org.uk/artists/joseph-mallord-william-turner, accessed 20 November 2024.
7   'The history of Maidenhead Bridge', www.networkrail.co.uk/who-we-are/our-history/iconic-infrastructure/the-history-of-the-maidenhead-bridge, accessed 20 November 2024.

8 Smiles, *Late Turner*, p. 97.

9 Ibid., p. 162.

10 'Turner – Whistler – Monet', www.musee-orsay.fr/en/whats-on/exhibitions/presentation/turner-whistler-monet, accessed 21 November 2024.

14 VINCENT VAN GOGH

1 Martin Bailey, *Starry Night: Van Gogh at the Asylum* (London: Frances Lincoln, 2022), pp. 119–21.

2 Letters 883, to Joseph and Marie Ginoux, Auvers-sur-Oise, Wednesday, 11 June 1890, https://vangoghletters.org/vg/letters/let883/letter.html, accessed 28 November 2024.

3 Letter 772, to Theo van Gogh and Jo van Gogh-Bonger, Saint-Rémy-de-Provence, Thursday, 9 May 1889, https://vangoghletters.org/vg/letters/let772/letter.html, accessed 28 November 2024.

4 Letter 640, to Theo van Gogh, Arles, Sunday, 15 July 1888, https://vangoghletters.org/vg/letters/let640/letter.html, accessed 28 November 2024.

5 Letter 676, to Theo van Gogh, Arles, Saturday, 8 September 1888, https://vangoghletters.org/vg/letters/let676/letter.html, accessed 28 November 2024.

6 Letter 777, to Theo van Gogh, Saint-Rémy-de-Provence, between about Friday, 31 May, and about Thursday, 6 June 1889, https://vangoghletters.org/vg/letters/let777/letter.html, accessed 28 November 2024.

7 Ibid.

8 Letter to Theo van Gogh, London, Thursday, 30 April 1874, https://vangoghletters.org/vg/letters/let022/letter.html, accessed 28 November 2024.

9 Martin Bailey, *Van Gogh's Finale: Auvers and the Artist's Rise to Fame* (London: Quarto, 2021), pp. 17–18.

10 Johanna Bonger quoted ibid., p. 21.

15 EDVARD MUNCH

1 Ragna Stang, *Edvard Munch: The Man and his Art* (New York: Abbeville Press, 1977), p. 90.

2 Munch discussing *The Sick Child* in Sue Prideaux, *Edvard Munch: Behind the Scream* (New Haven, CT, and London: Yale University Press, 2007), p. 90.

3 *Norwegian Intelligencer*, 25 October 1886, quoted in Urich Bischoff, *Munch* (London: Taschen, 2011), p. 12; Prideaux, *Edvard Munch: Behind the Scream*, p. 136.

4 Philippe Dagen, 'Van Gogh + Munch at the Munch Museet, Oslo: shared methods and attitudes', *The Guardian*, 8 August 2015, www.theguardian.com/artanddesign/2015/aug/08/van-gogh-munch-exhibition-oslo.

5 Prideaux, *Edvard Munch: Behind the Scream*, p. 58.

6 Stang, *Edvard Munch: The Man and his Art*, p. 142.

7 Bischoff, *Munch*, p. 53.

8 'I felt a great scream through nature', www.modernamuseet.se/stockholm/en/exhibitions/munch-by-himself/i-felt-the-great-scream-through-nature, accessed 18 November 2024.

9 '10 things you may not know about *The Scream*', www.britishmuseum.org/blog/10-things-you-may-not-know-about-scream, accessed 17 November 2024.

10 'Edvard Munch wrote "madman" graffiti on *Scream* painting, scans show', *BBC News*, 22 February 2021, www.bbc.co.uk/news/entertainment-arts-56127530.

11 Prideaux, *Edvard Munch: Behind the Scream*, p. 151.

16 PABLO PICASSO

1 Sebastian Smee, 'How good, really, was Pablo Picasso?', *Washington Post*, 3 April 2023.

2 John Richardson, *A Life of Picasso: The Painter of Modern Life 1907–1917* (New York: Alfred A. Knopf, 1991), p. 43.

3 Fisun Güner, 'How a small African figurine changed art', *BBC Culture*, 18 August 2017, https://www.bbc.com/culture/article/20170818-how-a-small-african-figurine-changed-art.

4 Yve-Alain Bois, *Matisse and Picasso* (Paris: Flammarion, 1998).

5 Enrique Mallen, 'The Impact of Cezanne in Early Cubism', *International Journal of Culture and History*, vol. 9, no. 1 (2022), p. 41.

6 John Richardson, *Picasso's Apocalyptic Whorehouse* (Milan: A. Mondadori, 1987), pp. 40–47.

7 'Pablo Picasso, Study for Les Demoiselles D'Avignon', www.moma.org/collection/works/79551, accessed 14 October 2024.

8 Lawrence D. Steefel Jr, 'The Neglected Fruit Cluster in Picasso's *Les Demoiselles d'Avignon*', *Artibus et Historiae*, vol. 13, no. 26 (1992), pp. 115–20.

9 Richardson, *A Life of Picasso: The Painter of Modern Life*, p. 19.

17 GUSTAV KLIMT

1 Catherine Dean, *Klimt* (London: Phaidon, 1996), pp. 6–7.

2 Colin B. Bailey (ed.), *Gustav Klimt, Modernism in the Making* (New York: Abrams, 2001), p. 99.

3 Hermann Bahr in the catalogue of the First Secession exhibition in 1898, reproduced in Gilles Néret, *Klimt, 1862–1918* (San Diego, CA: Thunder Bay Press, 1997), p. 17.

4 Bailey (ed.), *Gustav Klimt*, p. 203.

5 Stephanie Auer, curator at the Belvedere Museum, quoted in Eliza Goodpasture, 'Reassessing Gustav Klimt's The Kiss', *The Guardian*, 30 October 2023, https://www.theguardian.com/artanddesign/2023/oct/30/reassessing-gustav-klimt-the-kiss-film.

6 Gilles Néret, *Klimt* (London: Taschen, 2023), p. 61.

7 Goodpasture, 'Reassessing Gustav Klimt's The Kiss'.

8 Laurie Lico Albanese, 'Seeing Like Klimt on an Austrian Lake', *New York Times*, 4 July 2017.

18 CLAUDE MONET

1 'History of the Water Lilies Cycle', www.musee-orangerie.fr/en/node/33, accessed 27 November 2024.

2 Christoph Heinrich, *Monet* (London: Taschen, 2023), p. 76.

3 Ross King, *Mad Enchantment: Claude Monet and the Painting of the Water Lilies* (London: Bloomsbury, 2016) p. 8.

4 Ibid., p. 11.

5 Ibid., p. 15.

6 'Claude Monet, Water Lilies', www.moma.org/collection/works/80220, accessed 27 November 2024.

7 Heinrich, *Monet*, p. 82.

8 'Water Lilies', www.artic.edu/artworks/16568/water-lilies, accessed 27 November 2024.

9 Letter to Clemenceau, 12 November 1918, quoted in Richard Kendall, *Monet by Himself* (Boston, MA: Little, Brown and Co., 2001), p. 252.

10 'History of the Water Lilies Cycle'.

11 Heinrich, *Monet*, p. 84.

12 King, *Mad Enchantment*, pp. 161–63.

13 Ibid., pp. 175–76.

14 Letter to Clemenceau, 18 September 1926, quoted in Kendall, *Monet by Himself*, p. 265.

15 King, *Mad Enchantment*, p. 322.

16 *Le Petit Journal*, 17 May 1926, and *Le Populaire*, 19 May 1926, respectively.

17 Heinrich, *Monet*, p. 84.

19 HILMA AF KLINT

1 Julia Voss and Anne Posten, *Hilma af Klint: A Biography* (Chicago, IL: University of Chicago Press, 2022), p. 6

2 Katy Hessel, *The Story of Art without Men* (London and New York: Penguin, 2022), p. 102.

3 Robert Carleson and Caroline Levander, 'Spiritualism in Sweden', *Western Esotericism in Scandinavia* (2016), p. 522.

4 Quoted in 'Topics and Central Works', www.modernamuseet.se/stockholm/en/exhibitions/hilma-af-klint-2013/topics, accessed 25 October 2024.

5 David Adams, 'Hilma af Klint – A Beginning Anthroposophical Commentary', www.rudolfsteiner.org/fileadmin/user_upload/being_human/bh-articles/adams/DAdams-HilmaafKlint-Commentary.pdf, accessed 4 November 2024.

6   Helena Petrovna Blavatsky, *The Secret Doctrine*, vol. 1 (Wheaton, IL: Theosophical Publishing House, 1993), p. 1.

7   Voss and Posten, *Hilma af Klint: A Biography*, p. 260.

8   Ibid., pp. 154–55.

9   Christine Burgin, Hilma af Klint, *Notes and Methods* (Chicago, IL: University of Chicago Press, 2018), pp. 66 and 74.

10 Voss and Posten, *Hilma af Klint: A Biography*, p. 157.

11 Julia Voss, 'The first abstract artist? (And it's not Kandinsky)', *Tate Etc*, 25 June 2019, www.tate.org.uk/tate-etc/issue-27-spring-2013/first-abstract-artist-and-its-not-kandinsky.

12 Halina Dyrschka (dir.), *Hilma af Klint: Beyond the Visible* (Zeitgeist Films, 2019).

13 Voss, 'The first abstract artist?'.

20 SUZANNE VALADON

1   Hazel Smith, 'Suzanne Valadon: Artist and Muse of Montmartre', https://francetoday.com/culture/suzanne-valadon-artist-and-muse-of-montmartre, accessed 17 November 2024.

2   'Suzanne Valadon', www.moma.org/artists/6055, accessed 17 November 2024.

3   Jeanine Warnod, *Suzanne Valadon* (Norwalk, CT: Easton Press, 1982), p. 13.

4   'Suzanne Valadon: A World of her Own', press release, Centre Pompidou-Metz, p. 14, https://api.centrepompidou-metz.fr/files/891fdc9e/suzanne_valadon_en_web.pdf, accessed 17 November 2024.

5   Katy Hessel, *The Story of Art without Men* (London and New York: Penguin, 2022), p. 134.

6   Thérèse Diamand-Rosinsky, *Suzanne Valadon* (New York: Universe Press, 1994), p. 14.

7   'Susan Valadon', www.christies.com/en/artists/suzanne-valadon?lotavailability=All&sortby=relevance, accessed 17 November 2024.

8   'Suzanne Valadon: A World of her Own', p. 12.

9   Ibid., p. 16.

21 GEORGIA O'KEEFFE

1   Britta Benke, *Georgia O'Keeffe* (London: Taschen, 2022), p. 7.

2   Hannah Ellis-Petersen, 'Tate show to challenge sexual cliches', *The Guardian*, 1 March 2016.

3   In a letter to Mabel Luhan, cited in Roxana Robinson, *Georgia O'Keeffe: A Life* (London: Bloomsbury Press, 1991), p. 341.

4   Benke, *Georgia O'Keeffe* p. 18.

5   Robinson, *Georgia O'Keeffe: A Life*, p. 282.

6   Ibid., p. 182.

7   Ibid., p. 108.

8   Georgia O'Keeffe Museum, 'Hiding in Plain Sight: The O'Keeffe We Never Knew', www.youtube.com/watch?v=WsYMkQLg-Ds, accessed 14 October 2024.

22 FRIDA KAHLO

1   Hayden Herrera, *A Biography of Frida Kahlo* (New York: Perennial, 2002), p. xi.

2   Martha Zamora, *Frida Kahlo: The Brush of Anguish* (San Francisco, CA: Chronicle Books, 2002), pp. 78–80.

3   'Unlocking Frida Kahlo's wardrobe', www.vam.ac.uk/articles/unlocking-frida-kahlos-wardrobe, accessed 8 September 2024.

4   Geoffrey T. Hellman and Harold Ross, 'Ribbon Around Bomb', *New Yorker*, 4 November 1938.

5   Andrea Kettenmann, *Frida Kahlo, 1907–1954: Pain and Passion* (London: Taschen, 2003), p. 51.

6   Margaret A. Lindauer, *Devouring Frida: The Art History and Popular Celebrity of Frida Kahlo* (Middletown, CT: Wesleyan University Press, 2014), pp. 40–41.

7   Herrera, *A Biography of Frida Kahlo*, p. 315.

8   Andrey V., 'The Importance of the Frida Kahlo Self-Portrait with Thorn Necklace and Hummingbird', www.widewalls.ch/magazine/frida-kahlo-self-portrait-with-thorn-necklace-and-hummingbird, accessed 8 September 2024.

9   Rene Ebersole, 'Inside the Black Market Hummingbird Love Charm Trade', *National Geographic*, 18 April 2018.

10 'A creepy crawl through the collection', www.nationalgallery.org.uk/stories/a-creepy-crawl-through-the-collection, accessed 8 September 2024

11 Christina Burrus, *Frida Kahlo: I Paint my Reality* (London: Thames & Hudson, 2008), p. 81.

23 EDWARD HOPPER

1   Diary entry of Josephine Hopper, quoted in Gail Levin, *Edward Hopper: An Intimate Biography* (New York: Rizzoli, 2007), p. 348.

2   Gail Levin, *Edward Hopper: The Art and the Artist* (New York: WW Norton & Co., 1997), p. 16.

3   Ibid.

4   Colton Klein, '21 facts about Edward Hopper', www.sothebys.com/en/articles/21-facts-about-edward-hopper, accessed 16 November 2024.

5   Philip French, 'From *Nighthawks* to the shadows of film noir', *The Guardian*, 25 April 2004.

6   Jo Hopper, Letter to Marion Hopper, 22 January 1942, quoted in Levin, *Edward Hopper: An Intimate Biography*, p. 349.

7   Levin, *Edward Hopper: The Art and the Artist*, pp. 60–63.

8   'Nighthawks', www.artic.edu/artworks/111628/nighthawks, accessed 16 November 2024.

24 FRANCIS BACON

1   The artist in conversation with David Sylvester, *Francis Bacon: Fragments of a Portrait*, first broadcast on BBC1, 18 September 1966.

2   Mark Stevens and Annalyn Swan, *Francis Bacon: Revelations* (Glasgow: William Collins, 2021).

3   'I have made my mind up to go on the stage' – Bacon at fourteen. Ibid., p. 46.

4   Anne Baldassari (ed.), *Bacon – Picasso* (Paris: Flammarion, 2005).

5   Michael Peppiatt, *Francis Bacon: Anatomy of an Enigma* (New York: Skyhorse, 2009).

6   *Francis Bacon: In Conversation with Michel Archimbaud* (London: Phaidon, 1993) p. 16.

7   William Bedell Stanford, *Aeschylus in His Style: A Study in Language and Personality* (Dublin: Dublin University Press, 1942). p. 109.

8   Matthew Gale, *Francis Bacon* (London: Tate Publishing, 2008), p. 216.

9   Peppiatt, *Francis Bacon: Anatomy of an Enigma*, p. 87.

10 David Sylvester, *Looking Back at Francis Bacon* (London: Thames & Hudson, 2000)

11 Exhibition notes from 'Francis Bacon: Man and Beast', Royal Academy of Arts, London, 29 January–17 April 2022.

12 Paul Black and Calvin Winner, 'Francis Bacon: Sketching and the Skeleton in the Cupboard', https://artlyst.com/features/francis-bacon-sketching-and-the-skeleton-in-the-cupboard, accessed 12 October 2024.

25 SALVADOR DALÍ

1   Dawn Ades, *Dali* (London: Thames & Hudson, 1982), p. 107.

2   Stella Rollig and Jaime Brihuega (ed.), *Dali – Freud: An Obsession* (Cologne: Buchhandlung Walther König, 2022).

3   Ian Gibson, *The Shameful Life of Salvador Dali* (New York: WW Norton & Co., 1998), pp. 450–53.

4   Joan R. Kropf, *Salvador Dalí: The Atomic Period, 1945–1960* (Long Beach, CA: California State University, 2000), p. 13.

5   The association of St Peter with the rock in art is rooted in Christian scripture, specifically in the Gospel of Matthew (16:18). In this passage, Jesus says to Peter, 'You are Peter, and on this rock, I will build my church,' where the name Peter (from the Greek 'Petros') translates to 'rock'.

6   Desmond Morris, *The Lives of the Surrealists* (London: Thames & Hudson, 2018), p. 84.

26 JEAN-MICHEL BASQUIAT

1   Richard J. Powell, *Black Art* (London: Thames & Hudson, 2021), p. 184.

2   Jane Alison, 'Foreword', *Basquiat: Boom for Real* (London: Barbican and Prestel, 2017), p. 9.

3   'Basquiat', www.brooklynmuseum.org/exhibitions/basquiat, accessed 9 September 2024.

4   Phillip Faflick, 'SAMO© Graffiti: BOOSH-WAH or CIA?', *Village Voice*, 11 December 1978.

5   Al Díaz in conversation with Ashleigh Kane, 'The story of SAMO©, Basquiat's first art project', *Dazed Magazine*, 6 September 2017.

6   David Blaine, 'Madonna', *Interview Magazine*, 26 November 2014.

7 Suzanne Mallouk in conversation with Miranda Sawyer, 'The Jean-Michel Basquiat I Knew…', *The Guardian*, 3 September 2017.

8 Deborah Vankin, 'A trove of Basquiat's little-seen work arrives in L.A.', *Los Angeles Times*, 29 March 2023.

9 Veronica Esposito, 'How Basquiat found inspiration in California', *The Guardian*, 5 March 2024.

10 Rudy Chiappini (ed.), *Jean-Michel Basquiat*, exh. cat. (Lugano, Switzerland: Museo d'Arte Moderna Cittá di Lugano, 2005), p. 87.

11 Jordana Moore Saggese, *Reading Basquiat: Exploring Ambivalence in American Art* (Berkeley, CA: University of California Press, 2014), pp. 55, 85.

12 Díaz, 'The story of SAMO©'.

13 Marley Marius, 'The Disarming Delights of "Jean-Michel Basquiat: King Pleasure"', *Vogue Magazine*, 9 April 2022.

14 Sawyer, 'The Jean-Michel Basquiat I Knew…'.

15 Ted Stansfield, 'How Basquiat challenged police brutality through his art', *Dazed Magazine*, 18 November 2016.

16 Greg Tate, 'Jean-Michel Basquiat, Flyboy in the Buttermilk', *Village Voice*, 14 November 1989.

27 FAITH RINGGOLD

1 Louisa Buck, 'Faith Ringgold discusses civil rights and children's books in solo London show', *Art Newspaper*, 5 June 2019.

2 Faith Ringgold, *We Flew Over the Bridge: The Memoirs of Faith Ringgold* (Durham, NC: Duke University Press, 2005), p. 9.

3 Andrew Russeth, 'The Storyteller: At 85, Her Star Still Rising, Faith Ringgold Looks Back on Her Life in Art, Activism, and Education', *ArtNews*, 1 March 2016.

4 Ringgold, *We Flew Over the Bridge*, p. 144.

5 Holland Cotter, 'Faith Ringgold's Path of Maximum Resistance', *New York Times*, 8 March 2022.

6 Ringgold, *We Flew Over the Bridge*, p. 145.

7 Ibid., p. 79.

8 Ibid.

9 Faith Ringgold, 'Interview with Hans Ulrich Obrist', *Faith Ringgold*, exh. cat. (London: Serpentine Gallery, 2022).

10 Sally Lodge, 'Knopf Celebrates 25 Years of Faith Ringgold's "Tar Beach"', *Publishers Weekly*, www.publishersweekly.com/pw/by-topic/childrens/childrens-book-news/article/70471-knopf-celebrates-25-years-of-faith-ringgold-s-tar-beach.html, accessed 6 November 2024.

11 Ringgold, *We Flew Over the Bridge*, p. 259.

12 Ibid., p. 269.

28 EL ANATSUI

1 Thomas McEvilly, 'Doctor Lawyer Indian Chief', *Artforum* (November 1984) https://www.artforum.com/features/primitivism-in-20th-century-art-at-the-museum-of-modern-art-in-1984-207620, accessed 12 October 2024.

2 Okwui Enwezor and Chika Okeke-Agulu, *Contemporary African Art Since 1980* (Bologna: Damiani, 2011), p. 5.

3 Susan Vogel quoted in 'El Anatsui, TAGOMIZOR', www.sothebys.com/en/auctions/ecatalogue/2018/modern-contemporary-african-art-l18802/lot.44.html, accessed 27 September 2024.

4 'Dusasa II', www.metmuseum.org/art/collection/search/495553, accessed 27 September 2024.

5 Anatsui quoted in Susan Mullin Vogel, *El Anatsui: Art and Life* (London: Prestel, 2020), p. 33

6 Julian Lucas, 'How El Anatsui Broke the Seal on Contemporary Art', *New Yorker*, 18 January 2021, https://www.newyorker.com/magazine/2021/01/18/how-el-anatsui-broke-the-seal-on-contemporary-art, accessed 12 October 2024.

7 Manuel Toledo, 'Venice Biennale honours Africa's "bottle-top artist" El Anatsui', *BBC News*, 9 May 2015.

8 'El Anatsui in "Change"', https://art21.org/watch/art-in-the-twenty-first-century/s6/el-anatsui-in-change-segment, accessed 12 October 2024.

9 Adrian Searle, 'Venice takes flight', *The Guardian*, 12 June 2007, https://www.theguardian.com/artanddesign/2007/jun/12/art.

10 Quoted in Vogel, *El Anatsui*, p. 82.

11 'El Anatsui (b. 1944), Warrior', www.christies.com/en/lot/lot-6060035, accessed 27 September 2024.

12 Monica Mark, 'Africa's art flourishes as the newly wealthy wake up to its value', *The Guardian*, 10 July 2013, p. 9.

29 YAYOI KUSAMA

1 'Dot on: The rise and rise of Yayoi Kusama', 3 March 2021, https://thamesandhudson.com/news/dot-on-the-rise-and-rise-of-yayoi-kusama.

2 Yayoi Kusama, *Infinity Net: The Autobiography of Yayoi Kusama* (London: Tate Publishing, 2013), p. 30.

3 Tim Adams, 'Yayoi Kusama: the world's favourite artist?', *The Observer*, 23 September 2018, www.theguardian.com/artanddesign/2018/sep/23/yayoi-kusama-infinity-film-victoria-miro-exhibition.

4 Kusama, *Infinity Net*, p. 75.

5 Ibid., p. 42.

6 Heather Lenz (dir.), *Kusama: Infinity* (Magnolia Pictures, 2018).

7 'Infinity Mirror Room – Phalli's Field', https://hirshhorn.si.edu/kusama/infinity-rooms, accessed 6 November 2024.

8 Kusama, *Infinity Net*, p. 23.

9 Katy Hessel, *The Story of Art without Men* (London and New York: Penguin, 2022), p. 285.

10 'Yayoi Kusama: Infinity Mirror Rooms', www.tate.org.uk/whats-on/tate-modern/yayoi-kusama-infinity-mirror-rooms/exhibition-guide, accessed 6 November 2024.

11 Grady T. Turner, 'Yayoi Kusama', *BOMB*, no. 66 (Winter 1999), http://bombmagazine.org/article/2192/yayoi-kusama.

12 Lenz (dir.), *Kusama: Infinity*.

13 Ibid. According to the documentary, that was the final straw. Driven to suicide, Kusama jumped out a window – but landed on a bicycle and survived.

14 Adams, 'Yayoi Kusama: the world's favourite artist?'.

15 Hessel, *The Story of Art without Men*, p. 287.

16 Adams, 'Yayoi Kusama: the world's favourite artist?'.

30 ISAAC JULIEN

1 Isaac Julien, *Isaac Julien: Riot*, exh. cat., Museum of Modern Art, New York, 2013, p. 174.

2 Richard Powell, *Black Art*, revd edn (London: Thames & Hudson, 2002), p. 233.

3 'Isaac Julien – I'm Interested in Poetry | TateShots', www.youtube.com/watch?v=hcQxjcomcK0, accessed 10 November 2024.

4 Julien, *Isaac Julien: Riot*, p. 14.

5 Ibid., p. 26.

6 Ibid., p. 32.

7 Ibid., p. 24.

8 Nadja Sayej, 'Isaac Julien on Frederick Douglass: "It's an extraordinary story"', *The Guardian*, 15 March 2019.

9 Isaac Julien Studio, 'Lessons of the Hour', www.isaacjulien.com/projects/37, accessed 9 November 2024.

10 Ibid.

11 Ibid.

12 'Isaac Julien: What Freedom Is to Me', www.tate.org.uk/whats-on/tate-britain/isaac-julien/exhibition-guide, accessed 9 November 2024.

13 Elizabeth Fullerton, 'Looking for Freedom, Isaac Julien Comes Home', *New York Times*, 28 April 2023.

14 Laura Cumming, 'Isaac Julien: What Freedom Is to Me review', *The Guardian*, 30 April 2023.

15 Julien, *Isaac Julien: Riot*, p. 52.

16 Flor Linckens, 'Isaac Julien: "I like the idea of exploring things poetically"', https://galleryviewer.com/en/article/2310/isaac-julien-i-like-the-idea-of-exploring-things, accessed 10 November 2024.

17 Amah-Rose Abrams, 'Isaac Julien's Tate retrospective: multi-screens, "sonic tapestries" and moments of joy', *Wallpaper*, 13 August 2023.

LIST OF ILLUSTRATIONS

Credits listed by page number; a = above, b = below,
c = centre, l = left, r = right
Dimensions of works are given in centimetres and
inches, height (h) before width (w)

8, 10–11, 12–13a, 12–13b, 14–15, 16–17 Zhang Zeduan,
Along the River During the Qingming Festival,
1085–1145. Ink and colour on silk; handscroll, 25.5 ×
525 (9⅞ × 206¾). Palace Museum, Beijing **18, 20, 21**
Jan van Eyck, *The Arnolfini Portrait*, 1434. Oil on
wood, 82.2 × 60 (32⅜ × 23⅝). The National Gallery,
London **22–23** Jan van Eyck, *Virgin and Child with
Canon van der Paele*, 1434. Oil on Wood, 124.5 × 160
(49 × 62⅞). Groeningemuseum, Bruges **24, 25r, 25b,
27** Jan van Eyck, *The Arnolfini Portrait*, 1434. Oil on
wood, 82.2 × 60 (32⅜ × 23⅝). The National Gallery,
London **28** Sandro Botticelli, *The Birth of Venus, c.*
1485. Tempera on canvas, 172.5 × 278.5 (68 × 109¾).
Gallerie degli Uffizi, Florence **30l** Gentile da
Fabriano, *Madonna and Child, c.* 1405–10. Tempera
on panel, 115 × 64 cm (45⅜ × 25½). Galleria
Nazionale Dell'umbria, Perugia **30r** Massacio,
Virgin and Child with Saint Anne, c. 1424–25.
Tempera on panel, 175 × 103 (69 × 40⅝). Gallerie
degli Uffizi, Florence **31** Unknown artist, *Venus de'
Medici*, late 2nd century BC–early 1st century BC, h.
153 (60). Gallerie degli Uffizi, Florence. Photo Scala,
Florence **32–33** Sandro Botticelli, *Primavera, c.*
1480. Tempera grassa on wood, 207 × 319 (81½ ×
125⅝). Photo Scala, Florence, courtesy of the
Ministero Beni e Att. Culturali e del Turismo.
Gallerie degli Uffizi, Florence. **34** Sandro Botticelli,
St Barnaba Altarpiece, 1490. Tempera on panel, 268
× 280 (105⅝ × 110¼). Photo Scala, Florence. Galleria
degli Uffizi, Florence **36–37** Sandro Botticelli, *The
Birth of Venus, c.* 1485. Tempera on canvas, 172.5 ×
278.5 (68 × 109¾). Gallerie degli Uffizi, Florence **38,
40, 41, 42, 44, 45a, 45b, 46–47** Hieronymus Bosch,
The Garden of Earthly Delights, 1490–1500. Oil on
oak panel, (h): 185.8 (73¼); central panel (w): 172.5
(68); wing (w): 76.5 (30⅛). Museo del Prado, Madrid
48 Michelangelo, *Pietà*, 1499. Carrara marble, 174 ×
195 (68⅝ × 76⅞). Saint Peter's Basilica, Vatican City.
Photo Manuel Cohen/Scala, Florence **50**
Michelangelo, *Battle of the Centaurs*, 1492. Marble,
80.5 × 88 (31¾ × 34¾). Casa Buonarroti, Florence.
Photo Scala, Florence **51** Michelangelo, *The Virgin
and Child with the Infant St John, c.* 1504–5 Marble
relief, h. 106.8 (42⅛). Royal Academy of Arts.
Heritage Image Partnership Ltd/Alamy Stock
Photo **52** Master of the Fogg Pietà, *The Lamentation
over the Dead Christ, c.* 1303. Tempera and gold on
panel, 42.2 × 50 (16⅝ × 19¾). Harvard Art Museums/
Fogg Museum. Photo President and Fellows of
Harvard College **53** Pietro Perugino, *Pietà,
c.* 1493–96. Oil on wood, 168 × 176 (66¼ × 69⅜).

Gallerie degli Uffizi, Florence **54, 55, 56–57**
Michelangelo, *Pietà*, 1499. Carrara marble, 174 × 195
(68⅝ × 76⅞). Saint Peter's Basilica, Vatican City.
Photo Manuel Cohen/Scala, Florence **58** Leonardo
da Vinci, *Mona Lisa*, 1503/1519. Oil on wood, 79.4 ×
53.4 (31⅛ × 21⅛). Musée du Louvre, Paris **60** Digital
composite image of the *Mona Lisa* at Musée du
Louvre and the 'Prado' *Mona Lisa* **61** Workshop of
Leonardo da Vinci, 'Prado' *Mona Lisa*, 1507–16. Oil
on walnut panel, 76.3 × 57 (30⅛ × 22½). Museo del
Prado, Madrid. Photo MNP / Scala, Florence **62, 63,
64, 67** Leonardo da Vinci, *Mona Lisa*, 1503/1519.
Oil on wood, 79.4 × 53.4 (31⅛ × 21⅛). Musée du
Louvre, Paris **68** Artemisia Gentileschi, *Judith
Beheading Holofernes, c.* 1620. Oil on canvas,
146.5 × 108 (57¾ × 42⅝). Gallerie degli Uffizi,
Florence. Photo Scala, Florence, courtesy of
the Ministero Beni e Att. Culturali e del Turismo
70 Artemisia Gentileschi, *Susana and the Elders*,
1610. Oil on canvas, 170 × 119 (67 × 46⅞). Schloss
Weißenstein, Pommersfelden **72** Artemisia
Gentileschi, *Judith and her Maidservant*, 1615.
Oil on canvas, 114 × 93.5 (45 × 36⅞). Palazzo Pitti,
Florence **73** Caravaggio, *Judith Beheading Holofernes,
c.* 1598–99. Oil on canvas, 145 × 195 (57⅛ × 76¾).
Galleria Nazionale d'Arte Antica, Rome **74** Artemisia
Gentileschi, *Self-Portrait as the Allegory of Painting
(La Pittura), c.* 1638–39. Oil on canvas, 98.6 × 75.2
(38⅞ × 29⅝). Royal Collection Trust, UK **75** Artemisia
Gentileschi, *Self-Portrait as Saint Catherine of
Alexandria*, 1615–17. Oil on canvas, 71.4 × 69
(28⅛ × 27¼). National Gallery, London **77** Artemisia
Gentileschi, *Judith Beheading Holofernes, c.* 1620.
Oil on canvas, 146.5 × 108 (57¾ × 42⅝). Gallerie degli
Uffizi, Florence. Photo Scala, Florence, courtesy
of the Ministero Beni e Att. Culturali e del Turismo
78 Johannes Vermeer, *Girl with a Pearl Earring*, 1665.
Oil on canvas, 44.5 × 39 (17⅝ × 15⅜). Mauritshuis,
The Hague, Netherlands **80** Johannes Vermeer,
Girl with a Flute, c. 1669–75. Oil on canvas, 20 × 17.8
(7⅞ × 7). National Gallery of Art, Washington **81**
Johannes Vermeer, *Girl with the Red Hat, c.* 1669.
Oil on panel, 22.8 × 18 (9 × 7⅛). National Gallery
of Art, Washington **82** Johannes Vermeer, *The
Little Street, c.* 1660. Oil on canvas, 54.3 × 44
(21½ × 17⅜). Rijksmuseum, Amsterdam **83** Johannes
Vermeer, *Girl Reading a Letter at an Open Window,
c.* 1657–59. Oil on canvas, 83 × 64.5 (32¾ × 25½).
Gemäldegalerie, Dresden. Carlo Bollo/Alamy Stock
Photo **85** Johannes Vermeer, *The Art of Painting*,
1666–68. Oil on canvas, 120 × 100 (47¼ × 39⅜).
Kunsthistorisches Museum, Vienna **87** Johannes
Vermeer, *Girl with a Pearl Earring*, 1665. Oil on
canvas, 44.5 × 39 (17⅝ × 15⅜). Mauritshuis, The
Hague, Netherlands **88** Élisabeth Vigée Le Brun,
Marie Antoinette in a Chemise Dress, 1783. Oil on

canvas, 93.5 × 79 (36⅞ × 31⅛). Hessian House
Foundation, Museum Schloss Fasanerie. Photo
Hessische Hausstiftung, Kronberg im Taunus,
Germany **90** Peter Paul Rubens, *Portrait of Susanna
Lunden (Le Chapeau de Paille)*, 1622–25. Oil on
canvas, 79 × 54.6 (31 × 21½). National Gallery,
London **91** Élisabeth Vigée Le Brun, *Self-Portrait
in Straw Hat*, 1782. Oil on canvas, 97.8 × 70.5
(38⅝ × 27⅞). National Gallery, London **93** Élisabeth
Vigée Le Brun, *Marie-Antoinette with a Rose*, 1783.
Oil on canvas, 130 × 87 (38⅝ × 27⅞). Musée National
du Chateau, Versailles **94** Élisabeth Vigée Le Brun,
Marie-Antoinette and her Children, 1787. Oil on
canvas, 271 × 195 (38⅝ × 27⅞). Musée National du
Chateau, Versailles **97** Élisabeth Vigée Le Brun,
Marie Antoinette in a Chemise Dress, 1783. Oil on
canvas, 93.5 × 79 (36⅞ × 31⅛). Hessian House
Foundation, Museum Schloss Fasanerie. Photo
Hessische Hausstiftung, Kronberg im Taunus,
Germany **98** Francisco de Goya, *Saturn Devouring
his Son, c.* 1819–23. Mixed media, mural transferred
to canvas, 143.5 × 81.4 (56½ × 32⅛). Museo del
Prado. Photo MNP/Scala, Florence **100** Francisco
de Goya, *Charles IV of Spain and his Family*, 1800.
Oil on canvas, 280 × 336 (110¼ × 132⅜). Museo
del Prado **101** Francisco de Goya, *This is worse
(Esto es peor)*, Plate 37 of *The Disasters of War* series,
c. 1810–20. Etching, lavis and drypoint on paper,
15.5 × 20.5 (6⅛ × 8⅛). National Galleries of Scotland
102–3 Francisco de Goya, *And there is no help
(Y no hai remedio)*, Plate 15 of *The Disasters of War*,
1810. Etching, drypoint, burin, burnisher, 14 × 16.7
(5½ × 6⅝). The Metropolitan Museum of Art, New
York **104** Peter Paul Rubens, *Saturn Devouring a
Son*, 1636–38. Oil on canvas, 182.5 × 87 (71⅞ × 34⅜).
Museo del Prado **105** Francisco de Goya, *Saturn
Devouring his Sons, c.* 1797. Red chalk on paper,
20 × 14.7 (7⅞ × 5⅞). Album/Alamy Stock Photo
107 Francisco de Goya, *Saturn Devouring his Son,
c.* 1819–23. Mixed media, mural transferred to
canvas, 143.5 × 81.4 (56½ × 32⅛). Museo del Prado.
Photo MNP/Scala, Florence **108** Katsushika Hokusai,
The Great Wave at Kanagawa, from the *Thirty-Six
Views of Mount Fuji, c.* 1830–32. Woodblock print;
ink and colour on paper, 25.7 × 37.9 (10⅛ × 15). Photo
The Metropolitan Museum of Art/Art Resource/
Scala, Florence **111** Katsushika Hokusai, *Self-Portrait
as a Fisherman*, 1835. Colour woodblock print with
metallic pigments; surimono shikishiban, 21.3 × 18.5
(8½ × 7⅜). The Art Institute of Chicago **112–13**
Katsushika Hokusai, *Ushibori in Hitachi Province*,
from the *Thirty-Six Views of Mount Fuji, c.* 1830–33.
Woodblock print; ink and colour on paper, 25.2 × 37.2
(10 × 14¾). The British Museum **114** Katsushika
Hokusai, *Honganji at Asakusa in Edo (Tōto Asakusa
Honganji)*, from the series *Thirty-Six Views of Mount*

(Suzanne Valadon), 1887–89. Oil on canvas, 47 × 55.3 (18½ × 21¾). Harvard Art Museums/Fogg Museum **203** Suzanne Valadon, *Adam and Eve*, 1909. Oil on canvas, 162 × 131 (63⅞ × 51⅝). Centre Pompidou, MNAM-CCI. Photo GrandPalaisRmn/Jacqueline Hyde **204** Édouard Manet, *Olympia*, 1863. Oil on canvas, 130 × 190 (51¼ × 74⅞). Musée d'Orsay, Paris **205** Suzanne Valadon, *Self-Portrait*, 1927. Oil on canvas, 34.6 × 28.6 (13⅝ × 11⅛). Private Collection. Art Heritage/Alamy Stock Photo **206–7** Suzanne Valadon, *The Blue Room*, 1923. Oil on canvas, 90 × 116 (35½ × 45¾). Centre Pompidou, MNAM-CCI. Photo GrandPalaisRmn/Bertrand Prévost **208** Georgia O'Keeffe, *Jimson Weed/White Flower No. 1*, 1932. Oil on canvas, 121.9 × 101.6 (48 × 40). Crystal Bridges Museum of American Art, Bentonville, Arkansas, 2014.35. Photo Edward C. Robison III. © Georgia O'Keeffe Museum/DACS 2025 **210** Alfred Stieglitz, *Georgia O'Keeffe*, 1918. Platinum-palladium print, 24.5 × 19.6 (9⅝ × 7¾). The Metropolitan Museum of Art, New York **211** Georgia O'Keeffe, *No. 2 – Special*, 1915. Charcoal on paper, 60.0 × 46.4 (23⅝ × 18¼). The National Gallery of Art, Washington. © Georgia O'Keeffe Museum/DACS 2025 **212** Paul Strand, *Abstraction, Twin Lakes, Connecticut*, 1916. Silver-platinum print, 32.8 × 24.4 (13 × 9⅝). © Paul Strand Archive/Aperture Foundation **213** Georgia O'Keeffe, *Music, Pink and Blue No. 2*, 1918. Oil on canvas, 88.9 × 76 (35 × 29⅞). Digital image Whitney Museum of American Art/Licensed by Scala. © Georgia O'Keeffe Museum/DACS 2025 **214** Georgia O'Keeffe, *Series I, No. 8*, 1919. Oil on canvas, 50.8 × 40.6 (20 × 16). Lenbachhaus, Munich. © Georgia O'Keeffe Museum/DACS 2025 **215** Georgia O'Keeffe, *Petunia No. 2*, 1924. Oil on canvas, 91.8 × 76.5 (36¼ × 30⅛). Georgia O'Keeffe Museum. © Georgia O'Keeffe Museum/DACS 2025 **217** Georgia O'Keeffe, *Jimson Weed/White Flower No. 1*, 1932. Oil on canvas, 121.9 × 101.6 (48 × 40). Crystal Bridges Museum of American Art, Bentonville, Arkansas, 2014.35. Photo Edward C. Robison III. © Georgia O'Keeffe Museum/DACS 2025 **218** Frida Kahlo, *Untitled (Self-Portrait with Thorn Necklace and Hummingbird)*, 1940. Oil on canvas mounted to board, 62.5 × 48 (24⅝ × 19). Nickolas Muray Collection of Mexican Art, Harry Ransom Center at The University of Texas at Austin. **220** Nickolas Muray, *Frida Kahlo on Bench*, 1939. © Nickolas Muray Photo Archives **221** Frida Kahlo, *Frieda and Diego Rivera*, 1931. Oil on canvas, 100.01 × 73.74 (39⅜ × 31). Collection SFMOMA **222** Guillermo Kahlo, *Frida Kahlo*, 15 June 1919. Archivart/Alamy Stock Photo **223** Frida Kahlo, *The Wounded Deer*, 1946. Oil on masonite, 30 × 22 (11⅞ × 8¾). Private Collection. Photo Fine Art Images/Bridgeman Images **224** Frida Kahlo, *The Frame*, 1938. Oil on aluminium, 28.5 × 20.7 (11¼ × 8⅛). Centre Pompidou, MNAM-CCI **225** Anonymous, *Altarpiece to the Lord of the Hospital*, 1941. Oil on sheet. Museo Amparo, Mexico **227** Frida

Kahlo, *Untitled (Self-Portrait with Thorn Necklace and Hummingbird)*, 1940. Oil on canvas mounted to board, 62.5 × 48 (24⅝ × 19). Nickolas Muray Collection of Mexican Art, Harry Ransom Center at The University of Texas at Austin. **228** Edward Hopper, *Nighthawks*, 1942. Oil on canvas, 84.1 × 152.4 (33⅛ × 60). The Art Institute of Chicago **230** Louise Dahl-Wolfe, *Edward Hopper and his Wife, New York*, 1932. © Center for Creative Photography, The University of Arizona Foundation/DACS 2025 **231** Edward Hopper, *New York Movie*, 1939. Oil on canvas, 81.9 × 101.9 (32¼ × 40⅛). The Museum of Modern Art, New York. © Heirs of Josephine Hopper/Licensed by Artists Rights Society (ARS) NY/DACS, London 2025 **232** Still from John Huston's *The Maltese Falcon*, 1941. Photo 12/Alamy Stock Photo **233** Edward Hopper, *Study for Nighthawks*, 1941/42. Fabricated chalk and charcoal on paper, 28.3 × 38.1 (11⅛ × 15). Whitney Museum of American Art, New York. © Heirs of Josephine Hopper/ Licensed by Artists Rights Society (ARS) NY/DACS, London 2025 **234** Edward Hopper, *Night Windows*, 1928. Oil on canvas, 73.7 × 86.4 (29 × 34). The Museum of Modern Art, New York. © Heirs of Josephine Hopper/Licensed by Artists Rights Society (ARS) NY/DACS, London 2025 **236–37** Edward Hopper, *Nighthawks*, 1942. Oil on canvas, 84.1 × 152.4 (33⅛ × 60). The Art Institute of Chicago **238** Francis Bacon, *Three Studies for Figures at the Base of a Crucifixion*, 1944. Oil paint on three boards, support, each: 94 × 73.7 (37⅛ × 29⅛). Tate, London. © The Estate of Francis Bacon. All rights reserved. DACS 2025 **240** Francis Bacon, *Painting*, 1946. Oil and pastel on linen, 197.8 × 132.1 (77⅞ × 52⅛). The Museum of Modern Art, New York **241** Pablo Picasso, *On the Beach*, 1937. Oil, conté crayon, and chalk on canvas, 129.1 × 194 (50⅞ × 76⅜). © Succession Picasso/DACS, London 2025 **242l** Graham Sutherland, *Green Tree Form: Interior of Woods*, 1940. Oil on canvas, 78.7 × 107.9 (31 × 42½). Tate, London. © Estate of Graham Sutherland **242r** Graham Sutherland, *Gorse on a Sea Wall*, 1939. Oil on canvas, 62.2 × 48.3 (24¼ × 19⅛). National Museums NI. © Estate of Graham Sutherland **243** Michael Holtz, *Francis Bacon in his Studio in London*, 1974. Photo 12/Alamy Stock Photo **244l** Still from *The Battleship Potemkin*, 1925. Dir. Sergei Eisenstein, Script Nina Agadzhanova and Sergei Eisenstein, Prod. Jacob Bliokh/Mosfilm **244r** Bacon studio material, 'Screaming Woman' from Sergei Eisenstein, *Battleship Potemkin*, 1925. Leaf from unknown book on film, mounted on brown card. Book, 16 × 17 (6⅜ × 6¾). Collection & image © Hugh Lane Gallery Francis Bacon Archive (Reg. RM98F12:13). © The Estate of Francis Bacon. All rights reserved. DACS 2025 **245a** Francis Bacon, *Three Studies for Portrait of George Dyer (On Light Ground)*, 1963. Oil on canvas, Triptych: Each panel: 35.5 × 30.5 (14 × 12). Private Collection. © The Estate of Francis Bacon. All rights reserved. DACS

2025 **245b** Fragment of Photograph, John Deakin, *George Dyer in a Street in Soho, c.* 1963. B&W photograph, 14.9 × 15.5 (5⅞ × 6⅛). Collection & image © Hugh Lane Gallery Francis Bacon Archive (Reg. RM98F108:3). © The Estate of Francis Bacon. All rights reserved. DACS 2025 **246–47** Francis Bacon, *Three Studies for Figures at the Base of a Crucifixion*, 1944. Oil paint on three boards, support, each: 94 × 73.7 (37⅛ × 29⅛). Tate, London. © The Estate of Francis Bacon. All rights reserved. DACS 2025 **248** Salvador Dalí, *The Temptation of Saint Anthony*, 1946. Oil on canvas, 90 × 119.5 (35½ × 47⅛). Musées Royaux des Beaux-Arts, Brussels. Photo Album/Scala, Florence. © Salvador Dali, Fundació Gala-Salvador Dalí, DACS 2025 **250** Anna Riwkin, *Surrealists in Paris*, 1933. Gelatin silver print, 18 × 24.4 (7⅛ × 9⅝). © Anna Riwkin/ Moderna Museet **251** Salvador Dalí, *Sketch of Sigmund Freud*, 1938. Paper, ink, 34.5 × 28 (13⅝ × 11⅛). Freud Museum, London. © Salvador Dali, Fundació Gala-Salvador Dalí, DACS 2025 **253** Joos van Craesbeeck, *The Temptation of Saint Anthony*, 1650. Oil on canvas, 78 × 116 (30¾ × 45¾). Staatliche Kunsthalle Karlsruhe **254** Salvador Dalí, *Dream Caused by the Flight of a Bee around a Pomegranate a Second before Waking*, 1944. Oil on panel, 51 × 41 (20⅛ × 16¼). Museo Nacional Thyssen-Bornemisza, Madrid. © Salvador Dali, Fundació Gala-Salvador Dalí, DACS 2025 **256–57** Salvador Dalí, *The Temptation of Saint Anthony*, 1946. Oil on canvas, 90 × 119.5 (35½ × 47⅛). Musées Royaux des Beaux-Arts, Brussels, Belgium. Photo Album/Scala, Florence. © Salvador Dali, Fundació Gala-Salvador Dalí, DACS 2025 **258** Jean-Michel Basquiat, *Hollywood Africans*, 1983. Acrylic and oil stick on canvas, 213.5 × 213.4 (84⅛ × 84). Whitney Museum of American Art, New York. © Estate of Jean-Michel Basquiat. Licensed by Artestar, New York **260** James Van Der Zee, *Jean-Michel Basquiat*, 1982. © Estate of Jean-Michel Basquiat. Licensed by Artestar, New York **261** Photographer unknown, *Jean-Michel and his mother, Matilde*. © Estate of Jean-Michel Basquiat. Licensed by Artestar, New York **262** Jean-Michel Basquiat, *Stupid Games Bad Ideas*, 1979. Colour photocopy, 13.3 × 10.6 (5¼ × 4⅛). Collection of Jennifer Von Holstein **263** Henry Flynt, *#18, Jean-Michel Basquiat and Al Diaz, SAMO©*, 1979. Photo Henry A. Flynt Jr. **264** Jean-Michel Basquiat, *Cadillac Moon*, 1981. Acrylic and oilstick on canvas, 162 × 172 (63¾ × 67¾). Private Collection. © Estate of Jean-Michel Basquiat. Licensed by Artestar, New York **265** Jean-Michel Basquiat, *Riding with Death*, 1988. Acrylic and crayon on canvas, 249 × 289.5 (98⅛ × 114). Private Collection. © Estate of Jean-Michel Basquiat. Licensed by Artestar, New York **266–67** Jean-Michel Basquiat, *Hollywood Africans*, 1983. Acrylic and oil stick on canvas, 213.5 × 213.4 (84⅛ × 84). Whitney Museum of American Art, New York **268, 270** Faith Ringgold,

Woman on a Bridge #1 of 5: Tar Beach, 1988. Acrylic paint, canvas, printed fabric, ink and thread, 89.5 × 174 (74⅝ × 68½). The Solomon R. Guggenheim Foundation/Art Resource, NY/Scala, Florence. © 2025 Anyone Can Fly Foundation/DACS **271** Faith Ringgold, *Sonny's Bridge*, 1986. Acrylic on cotton canvas 214.6 × 152.4 (84½ × 60). Photo High Museum of Art/Bridgeman Images **272** Faith Ringgold, *The American People Series #8: The In Crowd*, 1964. Oil on canvas 121.9 × 66.0 (48 × 26). Private Collection. © 2025 Anyone Can Fly Foundation/DACS **273** Faith Ringgold with her mother, Willi Posey Jones. Photo courtesy Faith Ringgold Estate **274** Faith Ringgold in front of her quilt *Tar Beach #2* (1990), 1993. Associated Press/Kathy Willens/Alamy Stock Photo. © 2025 Anyone Can Fly Foundation/DACS **275** Faith Ringgold, *Echoes of Harlem*, 1980. Hand-painted cotton, 204.5 × 227.3 (80½ × 89½). Studio Museum in Harlem, NYC. © 2025 Anyone Can Fly Foundation/DACS **277** Faith Ringgold, *Woman on a Bridge #1 of 5: Tar Beach*, 1988. Acrylic paint, canvas, printed fabric, ink, and thread, 89.5 × 174 (74⅝ × 68½). The Solomon R. Guggenheim Foundation/Art Resource, NY/ Scala, Florence. © 2025 Anyone Can Fly Foundation/DACS **278** El Anatsui, *Dusasa II*, 2007. Found aluminium and copper wire, 546.1 × 655.3 (215 × 258). © El Anatsui. Courtesy of the artist and Jack Shainman Gallery, New York. **280** Portrait of El Anatsui. Courtesy of the artist, October Gallery, London, and Jack Shainman Gallery, New York. **281** Asante, Adinkra cloth. Pigment on cotton, 408.94 × 295.9 (161 × 116½). University of Iowa Stanley Museum of Art, Gift of Alice H. Brown **282** El Anatsui, *Wisdom*, 1974. Tropical hardwood, paint, lacquer, D 40 (15¾). Photo by Adolphus Opara. Courtesy the Artist and October Gallery, London. © El Anatsui **283** El Anatsui, *Woman's Cloth*, 1999–2002, Aluminium and copper wire, 287 × 292 (113 × 115). Collection of the British Museum, London. Courtesy the Artist and October Gallery, London. © El Anatsui **284** El Anatsui, *Man's Cloth*, 1999–2002, Aluminium and copper wire, 297 × 374 (117 × 147¼). Collection of the British Museum. Courtesy the Artist and October Gallery, London and Jack Shainman Gallery, New York. © El Anatsui **285** El Anatsui, *Dusasa I*, installation view at the 52nd Annual Venice Biennale at the Arsenale, 2007. Photo David Levene/Guardian/eyevine. © El Anatsui **286–87** El Anatsui, *Dusasa II*, installation view at the Venice Biennale presented at the Arsenale, 2007. Photo Haupt & Binder. © El Anatsui **288** Yayoi Kusama, *The Aftermath of Obliteration of Eternity*, 2009. Wood, metal, glass mirrors, plastic, acrylic paint and LED, edition 3/3, 415.3 × 415.3 × 287.7 (163½ × 163½ × 113¼). Collection of the artist. Courtesy of Ota Fine Arts, Tokyo/Singapore; Victoria Miro, London; David Zwirner, New York. © YAYOI KUSAMA **290** Yayoi Kusama, *Infinity Mirrored Room – Filled with the Brilliance of Life*, 2011. Room with mirror, LED lights, water pool. 296 × 622.4 × 622.4 (116½ × 245⅛ × 245⅛). Collection SFMOMA. Courtesy of Ota Fine Arts, Tokyo/Singapore; Victoria Miro, London; David Zwirner, New York. © YAYOI KUSAMA **291** Yayoi Kusama, *Compulsion Furniture (Accumulation)*, c. 1964. Silver gelatin photo-collage with paint. 20.32 × 25.08 (8 × 9⅞). Collection of the artist. Courtesy of Ota Fine Arts, Tokyo/Singapore; Victoria Miro, London; David Zwirner, New York. © YAYOI KUSAMA **292** Yayoi Kusama, *Untitled*, 1939. Pencil on paper, 25 × 22 (9⅞ × 8⅝). Collection of the artist. Courtesy of Ota Fine Arts, Tokyo/Singapore; Victoria Miro, London; David Zwirner, New York. © YAYOI KUSAMA **293** Yayoi Kusama, *No. F*, 1959. Oil on canvas, 105.4 × 132.1 (41½ × 52). The Museum of Modern Art, New York. © YAYOI KUSAMA **294** Visitors in Lucas Samaras's *Mirrored Room*, 1966. Mirror on wood, 243.84 × 243.84 × 304.8 (96 × 96 × 120). Buffalo AKG Art Museum/Art Resource, NY/Scala, Florence. © Lucas Samaras Estate, Courtesy Pace Gallery **295** Yayoi Kusama with *Narcissus Garden*, 1966. Installed in Venice Biennale, Italy, 1966. Courtesy David Zwirner, New York; Ota Fine Arts, Tokyo/Singapore/Shanghai; Victoria Miro, London/Venice. © YAYOI KUSAMA. **296–97** Yayoi Kusama, *Aftermath of Obliteration of Eternity*, 2009. Wood, metal, glass mirrors, plastic, acrylic paint and LED, edition 3/3, 415.3 × 415.3 × 287.7 (163½ × 163½ × 113¼). Collection of the artist. Courtesy of Ota Fine Arts, Tokyo/Singapore; Victoria Miro, London; David Zwirner, New York. © YAYOI KUSAMA **298** Isaac Julien, *Lessons of the Hour*, 2019. Installation shot from McEvoy Foundation for the Arts, San Francisco, 2020. Photo Henrik Kam. © Isaac Julien. Courtesy the artist and Victoria Miro Gallery, London **300** Isaac Julien, *Mise-en-scene No.2* (*Looking for Langston* Vintage Series), 1989/2016. Ilford classic silver gelatin fine art paper, mounted on aluminium and framed, 58 × 74.5 (22⅞ × 29⅜). © Isaac Julien. Courtesy the artist and Victoria Miro Gallery, London **301** Isaac Julien, *Green Screen Goddess (Ten Thousand Waves)*, 2010. Endura Ultra photograph, 180 × 239.8 × 7.5 (70⅞ × 94½ × 3). © Isaac Julien. Courtesy the artist and Victoria Miro Gallery, London **302** George Kendall Warren, Frederick Douglass, 1876. Albumen print on card mount, 17 × 11 (6¾ × 4⅜). Liljenquist Family collection, Library of Congress Prints and Photographs Division Washington, DC. **305** Isaac Julien, *The North Star (Lessons of the Hour)*, 2019. Framed photograph on gloss inkjet paper mounted on aluminium, 160 × 213.29 (63 × 84). © Isaac Julien. Courtesy the artist and Victoria Miro Gallery, London **306–7** Isaac Julien, *Lessons of the Hour*, 2019. Installation shot from McEvoy Foundation for the Arts, San Francisco, 2020. Photo Henrik Kam. © Isaac Julien, Courtesy the artist and Victoria Miro Gallery, London

ACKNOWLEDGMENTS

This book was made possible by the work of many contemporary writers, theorists, art historians and artists, as well as the museums and galleries that have welcomed me over the years. I am also deeply grateful to the writers of the past, whose works have been a profound source of inspiration while writing my first book.

I would like to start by thanking Roger Thorp, Editorial Director at Thames & Hudson, who had the initial vision for the project and was instrumental in guiding me to its fruition; likewise editorial manager Mohara Gill, also there from the very beginning, whose counsel has been invaluable. Many thanks to the insightful editorial assistants Anna Bailey and Francesca Anderson, and project editor Phoebe Colley, who orchestrated the final push.

Thanks to the wonderful designer Karolina Prymaka, art director Ramon Pez, production controller Jane Harman and pre-press controller Elisa Merino. I would also like to thank the amazing picture researcher Yasmin Garcha, as well as proofreader Simon Bolitho and indexer Emma Caddy.

Special thanks go to my literary agent, Monica Meehan, who dealt with all the business aspects I have no interest in and who was instrumental during the writing process, and my manager Jacqueline Muehlke and her wonderful team at Helm Talent Group.

Thanks to Joanne Shurvell for her unwavering support, advice, great company on our art trips and calming influence; to Paul Murphy, Jake Phillips, Xiaoying Du, and Valeria Missalina Bembry for their help with research; and Paul Carter Robinson and Sara Faith at Artlyst.com for their support. Thanks to Dr Ben Street, for great advice, and to George Gallagher, Yolanda Zappaterra, Maria Holzamer, Helen Sheehan, Dermot O'Brien, the Cheverall family and the Payne family, everybody at the public library in Framlingham, Suffolk, and so many others. Your encouragement has been so appreciated.

I am beyond lucky to have the support of Greg Cheverall, who has put up with my non-stop talking about art, my ever-expanding book collection, my 6 a.m. starts and late-night finishes, and my annoying desire to tell everyone everything! There is no way this book would exist without him.

Finally, I would also like to thank all the artists in this book, who have been with me my whole life.

First published in the United Kingdom in 2025 by Thames & Hudson Ltd, 6–24 Britannia Street, London WC1X 9JD

First published in the United States of America in 2025 by Thames & Hudson Inc., 500 Fifth Avenue, New York, New York 10110

Great Art Explained: The Stories Behind the World's Greatest Masterpieces © 2025 Thames & Hudson Ltd, London

Text © 2025 James Payne

Interior layout designed by Karolina Prymaka

EU Authorized Representative: Interart S.A.R.L. 19 rue Charles Auray, 93500 Pantin, Paris, France
productsafety@thameshudson.co.uk
interart.fr

A CIP catalogue record for this book is available from the British Library

Library of Congress Control Number 2024944290

ISBN 978-0-500-02595-6
03

Printed and bound in Italy by L.E.G.O. Spa

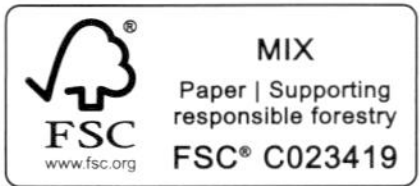